Reading for Rhetoric

CAROLINE SHRODES

CLIFFORD JOSEPHSON

JAMES R. WILSON

San Francisco State College

Reading for
Rhetoric

APPLICATIONS TO WRITING

SECOND EDITION

THE MACMILLAN COMPANY, NEW YORK

FOREWORD

The revised edition of *Reading for Rhetoric*, like the original text, provides a functional approach to rhetoric. It requires close reading, an examination of the anatomy of prose that can lead the student to the discovery of principles of rhetoric applicable to his own writing. It assumes that once the student is led to awareness of the techniques by which successful writers have given shape to their experience, he will use similar methods to control his own work.

The quality of the readings, twenty-four of them new in this edition, has been maintained. The editorial treatment of them is more sharply focused than before. With some temerity we appropriate the words of Fowler and submit that the revision surpasses the first edition, "its prolixities docked, its dullnesses enlivened, its fads eliminated, its truths multiplied."

Reading and writing cannot be separated. In order to improve his writing, the student must first learn to be a critical reader, especially of his own work. Accordingly, we lead him inductively to the study of rhetoric as it has been applied by skillful writers confronted with the practical problems of writing—putting ideas into words. Our approach, incremental as well as inductive, departs from that of the standard rhetoric, which explains rules one at a time in a systematic order. Many editors, faced with the complexity of writing and the simplicity of rules, place rhetoric and reading at opposite ends of a book and illustrate the principles with fragments: a paragraph of sensory description, logical definition, or graphic illustration; a fragment showing precision of diction or irony of statement. We join reading and rhetoric. Our examples are sufficiently complete in their anatomy to encourage the student to note the relationship of the parts to the whole; by studying this relationship, he becomes aware of the inseparability of thought and form.

The exercises serve a variety of functions. Each exercise requires

v

the student to examine the purpose, structure, diction, and tone of the selection; to consider the fusion of thought and form at every level —word, sentence, paragraph, and overall organization. It is not to be assumed that each principle will receive equal attention in every exercise, for the distinctive quality of the essay or narrative has determined the nature of the analysis. It is inevitable, and even desirable, that in ordering and developing complex ideas a writer will draw upon a number of rhetorical modes and devices. Each analysis, however, begins with questions or introductions which focus upon the primary method of development in the hope of sharpening the student's perception of the means the author employs to achieve his purpose. In each exercise the questions enable the student to determine *how* an individual essay is organized and *why* that organization is appropriate. The exercises also explore the various strategies which distinguish the method and make it uniquely the writer's own. The range of rhetorical approach reflected in the exercises encourages the student to select with discrimination those methods most appropriate to his purpose. Each exercise concludes with suggested writing assignments which require the student to apply one or more of the rhetorical principles to his own essay.

The editorial apparatus reflects our pedagogical bias: the most effective way to teach the student is to involve him actively in his own education. A relevant entry from the Glossary, which now introduces each section, suggests to him the primary method of organization and the reason for the placement of each of the selections. The sequence of sections is based upon a sound psychological principle. Since the writer's perception determines his vision of life, it is logical to begin with the method of *identification*, which suggests the diverse ways in which the student may first apprehend his experiences through the senses and then locate them in his world. After he learns to perceive freshly and clearly, he may be guided to organize his perceptions into categories and to recognize that *definition* consists of what is or is not admitted into a category. Since categories have sub-classes, he is inevitably led to *classification* as a method. Once he can classify correctly, the student can attempt *comparison and contrast*, a process limited to members of the same class. *Classification* moves logically to *illustration*, the dramatic presentation of a representative of the entire class. When the student has understood these techniques, he is prepared for their interplay in the subtleties of *analysis* and *argument and persuasion*. *Diction and tone* are relevant throughout, but we devote one section to them because they represent the ultimate refinement of technique and the most demanding test of the writer's power. The exercises are in no way intended to impose a single method of study or to exhaust the possibilities afforded by the richness of the materials. They allow the instructor freedom to select what is useful, to emphasize what is most congenial to him, and thus to design his own course.

The exercises are cumulative. The student's attention is called throughout to the recurring principles of development. At the same time, he is introduced to new techniques, so that by the time he has completed the exercises in any one section, he has become aware of the limitless range of strategies available to him. In the section on *identification* the exercises move from emphasis upon the simple concreteness of Mark Twain's *Memories of a Missouri Farm* to a demonstration, in Anatole Broyard's *Sunday Dinner in Brooklyn*, of the means by which concreteness can express both the alienation and the compassion of the narrator. Under *definition* the exercises begin with the economy and audacity of Thornton Wilder's prose in *Some Thoughts on Playwriting*, in which the classical steps of definition are outlined, and conclude with the highly abstract but lyrical definition of *The Tragic Fallacy* by Joseph Wood Krutch. The student is then introduced to a variety of methods of *classification*: the mechanical and formal approach of Francis Bacon's *Idols of the Mind*; the more sophisticated technique of Virginia Woolf's *The Patron and the Crocus*; and finally, Malcolm Cowley's subtle reclassification in *Nightmare and Ritual in Hemingway*. In the next section, the student first studies the way in which Mencken develops his *comparison and contrast* by abundant use of metaphor, wit, and paradox, and then the means by which Aldous Huxley distinguishes between life worshipers and death worshipers through the use of syllogism, musical form, and literary allusion. Bruno Bettelheim illustrates his indictment of a

mechanistic society by movingly portraying a single individual in
Joey: A "Mechanical Boy." James Thurber employs *illustration* in his
hilarious proliferation of synthetic personalities in <u>What Cocktail
Party?</u> In the following section James Agee's single metaphor illuminates his *analysis* of *Monsieur Verdoux* and prepares the student for
the more complex and satirical analysis of Randall Jarrell's *The
Intellectual in America*. Under *argument and persuasion*, the questions move from a consideration of the sardonic edge of Elizabeth
Hardwick's *tour de force, The Subjection of Women*, to that of
the controlled irony in Swift's *A Modest Proposal*. Finally, under
diction and tone, the exercises examine a wide range of techniques,
from the arresting *diction of* D. H. Lawrence in *Nathaniel Hawthorne
and "The Scarlet Letter"* to the complex tonality of Katherine Anne
Porter's *The Wooden Umbrella*.

The exercises are cumulative in another sense. In their step-by-step
consideration of the writing problems of college students, they provide a basis for the coherent study of rhetoric. They also may be used
to supplement formal and abstract explanations of method. But, rather
than develop the four types of discourse at equal length, *Reading for
Rhetoric* focuses upon *exposition* and *argument*. The student is seldom
called upon to write pure *description* and *narration*; nevertheless,
these forms can teach him how to achieve concreteness and vividness
of expression. Accordingly, we include a short story, Ernest Hemingway's *Big Two-Hearted River*, as well as a number of other selections
that demonstrate how descriptive and narrative elements may enrich
expository writing. Argument and persuasion are joined, for the distinctions between them are frequently blurred in both definition and
practice; polemical argument is often less effective than persuasive
exposition. The last section of the book, prepared for throughout the
text by the inclusion of exercises on diction and tone, is marked by
heightened use of language and striking variation in tone.

We hope that the selections in this book will, on first reading, invite
the student to view the human situation with compassion and understanding; that initially he will be so moved by the ideas and experience
he has shared that he will respond only to them. Once he is involved,

he should be willing to scrutinize the means by which the writer has ordered his experience. Frequently it is a relief to the student to discover that good style, no longer a mysterious abstraction, can be developed through the application of specific techniques to his own essay. In this way the essay returns to its original meaning: an exercise, a considered attempt to impose linguistic order upon ideas.

Reading for Rhetoric is designed to teach the student to write with clarity, vigor, and grace, and to secure his commitment to the discipline of writing, not by the prescription of rules, but through the testimony of eloquent prose.

C. S.

C. J.

J. R. W.

TABLE OF CONTENTS

PART ONE   *Identification*

PART TWO   *Definition*

xi

PART THREE   *Classification*

PART FOUR   *Comparison and Contrast*

PART FIVE   *Illustration*

PART SIX   *Analysis*

PART SEVEN   *Argument and Persuasion*

PART EIGHT   *Diction and Tone*

Part One

IDENTIFICATION

Identification—a process preliminary to definition of a subject. As a method of exposition, it brings the subject into focus by locating it: identification attempts to answer the question, "What is X?", not so much by focusing on X as by describing the physical context in which X appears or the situation which evokes it. In Twain, memories are tied to sensory experiences; in Proust, they are the result of successfully wrestling with inchoate glimmerings; in Melville, philosophical abstractions grow out of the concrete objects of everyday life; in Mencken, the "libido" for the ugly is identified by the objects it creates; in Agee, a description of a summer evening evokes a fragile mood; and in Broyard, ambivalent feelings are brought into focus by the account of a Sunday dinner in Brooklyn.

1

MEMORIES OF A
MISSOURI FARM

MARK TWAIN

My parents removed to Missouri in the early thirties; I do not remember just when, for I was not born then and cared nothing for such things. It was a long journey in those days, and must have been a rough and tiresome one. The home was made in the wee village of Florida, in Monroe County, and I was born there in 1835. The village contained a hundred people and I increased the population by 1 per cent. It is more than many of the best men in history could have done for a town. It may not be modest in me to refer to this, but it is true. There is no record of a person doing as much—not even Shakespeare. But I did it for Florida, and it shows that I could have done it for any place—even London, I suppose. [1]

Recently some one in Missouri has sent me a picture of the house I was born in. Heretofore I have always stated that it was a palace, but I shall be more guarded now. [2]

I used to remember my brother Henry walking into a fire outdoors when he was a week old. It was remarkable in me to remember a thing like that, and it was still more remarkable that I should cling to the delusion, for thirty years, that I *did* remember it—for of course it never happened; he would not have been able to walk at that age. If I had stopped to reflect, I should not have burdened my memory with that impossible rubbish so long. It is believed by many people that an impression deposited in a child's memory within the first two years of its life cannot remain there five years, but that is an error. The incident of Benvenuto Cellini and the salamander must be accepted as authentic and trustworthy; and then that remarkable and indisputable instance in the experience of Helen Keller—However, I will speak of that at another time. For many years I believed that I remembered helping my grandfather drink his whisky toddy when I was six weeks old, but I do not tell about that any more, now; I am grown old and my memory is not as active as it used to be. When I was younger I could remember anything, whether it had happened or not; but my faculties are decaying now, and soon I shall be so I cannot remember any but the things that never happened. It is sad to go to pieces like this, but we all have to do it. [3]

My uncle, John A. Quarles, was a farmer, and his place was in the country four miles from Florida. He had eight children and fifteen or twenty negroes, and was also fortunate in other ways, particularly in his character. I have not come across a better man than he was. I was his guest for two or three months every year, from the fourth year after we removed to Hannibal till I was eleven or twelve years old. I have never consciously used him or his wife in a book, but his farm has come very handy to me in literature once or twice. In *Huck Finn* and in *Tom Sawyer, Detective* I moved it down to Arkansas. It was all of six hundred miles, but it was no trouble; it was not a very large farm—five hundred acres, perhaps—but I could have done it if it had been twice as large. And as for the morality of it, I cared nothing for that; I would move a state if the exigencies of literature required it. [4]

It was a heavenly place for a boy, that farm of my uncle John's. The house was a double log one, with a spacious floor (roofed in) connecting it with the kitchen. In the summer the table was set in the middle of that shady and breezy floor, and the sumptuous meals —well, it makes me cry to think of them. Fried chicken, roast pig;

wild and tame turkeys, ducks, and geese; venison just killed; squirrels, rabbits, pheasants, partridges, prairie-chickens; biscuits, hot batter cakes, hot buckwheat cakes, hot "wheat bread," hot rolls, hot corn pone; fresh corn boiled on the ear, succotash, butterbeans, stringbeans, tomatoes, peas, Irish potatoes, sweet potatoes; buttermilk, sweet milk, "clabber"; watermelons, muskmelons, cantaloupes—all fresh from the garden; apple pie, peach pie, pumpkin pie, apple dumplings, peach cobbler—I can't remember the rest. The way that the things were cooked was perhaps the main splendor—particularly a certain few of the dishes. For instance, the corn bread, the hot biscuits and wheat bread, and the fried chicken. These things have never been properly cooked in the North—in fact, no one there is able to learn the art, so far as my experience goes. The North thinks it knows how to make corn bread, but this is mere superstition. Perhaps no bread in the world is quite so good as Southern corn bread, and perhaps no bread in the world is quite so bad as the Northern imitation of it. The North seldom tries to fry chicken, and this is well; the art cannot be learned north of the line of Mason and Dixon, nor anywhere in Europe. This is not hearsay; it is experience that is speaking. In Europe it is imagined that the custom of serving various kinds of bread blazing hot is "American," but that is too broad a spread; it is custom in the South, but is much less than that in the North. In the North and in Europe hot bread is considered unhealthy. This is probably another fussy superstition, like the European superstition that ice-water is unhealthy. Europe does not need ice-water and does not drink it; and yet, notwithstanding this, its word for it is better than ours, because it describes it, whereas ours doesn't. Europe calls it "iced" water. Our word describes water made from melted ice—a drink which has a characterless taste and which we have but little acquaintance with. [5]

It seems a pity that the world should throw away so many good things merely because they are unwholesome. I doubt if God has given us any refreshment which, taken in moderation, is unwholesome, except microbes. Yet there are people who strictly deprive themselves of each and every eatable, drinkable, and smokable which has in any way acquired a shady reputation. They pay this price for health. And health is all they get for it. How strange it is! It is like paying out your whole fortune for a cow that has gone dry. [6]

The farmhouse stood in the middle of a very large yard, and the yard was fenced on three sides with rails and on the rear side with high palings; against these stood the smoke-house; beyond the palings was the orchard; beyond the orchard were the negro quarters and the tobacco fields. The front yard was entered over a stile made of sawed-off logs of graduated heights; I do not remember any gate. In a corner of the front yard were a dozen lofty hickory trees and a dozen black walnuts, and in the nutting season riches were to be gathered there. [7]

Down a piece, abreast the house, stood a little log cabin against the rail fence; and there the woody hill fell sharply away, past the barns, the corncrib, the stables, and the tobacco-curing house, to a limpid brook which sang along over its gravelly bed and curved and frisked in and out and here and there and yonder in the deep shade of over-hanging foliage and vines—a divine place for wading, and it had swimming pools, too, which were forbidden to us and therefore much frequented by us. For we were little Christian children and had early been taught the value of forbidden fruit. [8]

In the little log cabin lived a bedridden white-headed slave woman whom we visited daily and looked upon with awe, for we believed she was upward of a thousand years old and had talked with Moses. The younger negroes credited these statistics and had furnished them to us in good faith. We accommodated all the details which came to us about her; and so we believed that she had lost her health in the long desert trip coming out of Egypt, and had never been able to get it back again. She had a round bald place on the crown of her head, and we used to creep around and gaze at it in reverent silence, and reflect that it was caused by fright through seeing Pharaoh drowned. We called her "Aunt" Hannah, Southern fashion. She was superstitious, like the other negroes; also, like them, she was deeply religious. Like them, she had great faith in prayer and employed it in all ordinary exigencies, but not in cases where a dead certainty of result was urgent. Whenever witches were around she tied up the remnant of her wool in little tufts, with white thread, and this promptly made the witches impotent. [9]

All the negroes were friends of ours, and with those of our own age we were in effect comrades. I say in effect, using the phrase as a modification. We were comrades, and yet not comrades; color and condition interposed a subtle line which both parties were conscious of and which rendered complete fusion impossible. We had a faithful and affectionate good friend, ally, and adviser in "Uncle Dan'l," a middle-aged slave whose head was the best one in the negro quarter, whose sympathies were wide and warm, and whose heart was honest and simple and knew no guile. He has served me well these many, many years. I have not seen him for more than half a century, and yet spiritually I have had his welcome company a good part of that time, and have staged him in books under his own name and as "Jim," and carted him all around—to Hannibal, down the Mississippi on a raft, and even across the Desert of Sahara in a balloon—and he has endured it all with the patience and friendliness and loyalty which were his birthright. It was on the farm that I got my strong liking for his race and my appreciation of certain of its fine qualities. This feeling and this estimate have stood the test of sixty years and more, and have suffered no impairment. The black face is as welcome to me now as it was then. [10]

In my schoolboy days I had no aversion to slavery. I was not aware that there was anything wrong about it. No one arraigned it in my hearing; the local papers said nothing against it; the local pulpit taught us that God approved it, that it was a holy thing, and that the doubter need only look in the Bible if he wished to settle his mind—and then the texts were read aloud to us to make the matter sure; if the slaves themselves had an aversion to slavery, they were wise and said nothing. In Hannibal we seldom saw a slave misused; on the farm, never. [11]

There was, however, one small incident of my boyhood days which touched this matter, and it must have meant a good deal to me or it would not have stayed in my memory, clear and sharp, vivid and shadowless, all these slow-drifting years. We had a little slave boy whom we had hired from some one, there in Hannibal. He was from the eastern shore of Maryland, and had been brought away from his family and his friends, halfway across the American continent, and sold. He was a cheery spirit, innocent and gentle, and the noisiest creature that ever was, perhaps. All day long he was singing, whistling, yelling, whooping, laughing—it was maddening, devastating, unendurable. At last, one day, I lost all my temper, and went raging to my mother and said Sandy had been singing for an hour without a single break, and I couldn't stand it, and *wouldn't* she please shut him up. The tears came into her eyes and her lip trembled, and she said something like this: [12]

"Poor thing, when he sings it shows that he is not remembering, and that comforts me; but when he is still I am afraid he is thinking, and I cannot bear it. He will never see his mother again; if he can sing, I must not hinder it, but be thankful for it. If you were older, you would understand me; then that friendless child's noise would make you glad." [13]

It was a simple speech and made up of small words, but it went home, and Sandy's noise was not a trouble to me any more. She never used large words, but she had a natural gift for making small ones do effective work. She lived to reach the neighborhood of ninety years and was capable with her tongue to the last—especially when a meanness or an injustice roused her spirit. She has come handy to me several times in my books, where she figures as Tom Sawyer's Aunt Polly. I fitted her out with a dialect and tried to think up other improvements for her, but did not find any. I used Sandy once, also; it was in *Tom Sawyer*. I tried to get him to whitewash the fence, but it did not work. I do not remember what name I called him by in the book. [14]

I can see the farm yet, with perfect clearness. I can see all its belongings, all its details; the family room of the house, with a "trundle" bed in one corner and a spinning-wheel in another—a wheel whose rising and falling wail, heard from a distance, was the mournfulest of all sounds to me, and made me homesick and low spirited, and filled my atmosphere with the wandering spirits of the dead; the vast fireplace, piled high, on winter nights, with flaming hickory logs from whose ends a sugary sap bubbled out, but did not go to waste, for we scraped it off and ate it; the lazy cat spread out on the rough hearthstones; the drowsy dogs braced against the jambs and blinking; my aunt in one chimney corner, knitting; my uncle in the other, smoking his corn-cob pipe; the slick and carpetless oak floor faintly mirroring the dancing flame tongues and freckled with black indentations where fire coals had popped out and died a leisurely death; half a dozen children romping in the background twilight; "split"-bottomed chairs here and there, some with rockers; a cradle —out of service, but waiting, with confidence; in the early cold mornings a snuggle of children, in shirts and chemises, occupying the hearthstone and procrastinating—they could not bear to leave that comfortable place and go out on the wind-swept floor space between the house and kitchen where the general tin basin stood, and wash. [15]

Along outside of the front fence ran the country road, dusty in the summertime, and a good place for snakes—they liked to lie in it and sun themselves; when they were rattlesnakes or puff adders, we killed them; when they were black snakes, or racers, or belonged to the fabled "hoop" breed, we fled, without shame; when they were "house snakes," or "garters," we carried them home and put them in Aunt Patsy's work basket for a surprise; for she was prejudiced against snakes, and always when she took the basket in her lap and they began to climb out of it it disordered her mind. She never could seem to get used to them; her opportunities went for nothing. And she was always cold toward bats, too, and could not bear them; and yet I think a bat is as friendly a bird as there is. My mother was Aunt Patsy's sister and had the same wild superstitions. A bat is beautifully soft and silky; I do not know any creature that is pleasanter to the touch or is more grateful for caressings, if offered in the right spirit. I know all about these coleoptera, because our great cave, three miles below Hannibal, was multitudinously stocked with them, and often I brought them home to amuse my mother with. It was easy to manage if it was a school day, because then I had ostensibly been to school and hadn't any bats. She was not a suspicious person, but full of trust and confidence; and when I said, "There's something in my coat pocket for you," she would put her hand in. But she always took it out again, herself; I didn't have to tell her. It was remarkable, the way she couldn't learn to like private bats. The more experience she had, the more she could not change her views. [16]

I think she was never in the cave in her life; but everybody else went there. Many excursion parties came from considerable distances up and down the river to visit the cave. It was miles in extent and was a tangled wilderness of narrow and lofty clefts and passages. It was an easy place to get lost in; anybody could do it—including the bats. I got lost in it myself, along with a lady, and our last candle burned down to almost nothing before we glimpsed the search party's lights winding about in the distance. [17]

"Injun Joe," the half-breed, got lost in there once, and would have starved to death if the bats had run short. But there was no chance of that; there were myriads of them. He told me all his story. In the book called *Tom Sawyer* I starved him entirely to death in the cave, but that was in the interest of art; it never happened. "General" Gaines, who was our first town drunkard before Jimmy Finn got the place, was lost in there for the space of a week, and finally pushed his handkerchief out of a hole in a hilltop near Saverton, several miles down the river from the cave's mouth, and somebody saw it and dug him out. There is nothing the matter with his statistics except the handkerchief. I knew him for years and he hadn't any. But it could have been his nose. That would attract attention. [18]

The cave was an uncanny place, for it contained a corpse—the corpse of a young girl of fourteen. It was in a glass cylinder inclosed in a copper one which was suspended from a rail which bridged a narrow passage. The body was preserved in alcohol, and it was said that loafers and rowdies used to drag it up by the hair and look at the dead face. The girl was the daughter of a St. Louis surgeon of extraordinary ability and wide celebrity. He was an eccentric man and did many strange things. He put the poor thing in that forlorn place himself. [19]

Beyond the road where the snakes sunned themselves was a dense young thicket, and through it a dim-lighted path led a quarter of a mile; then out of the dimness one emerged abruptly upon a level great prairie which was covered with wild strawberry plants, vividly starred with prairie pinks, and walled in on all sides by forests. The strawberries were fragrant and fine, and in the season we were generally there in the crisp freshness of the early morning, while the dew beads still sparkled upon the grass and the woods were ringing with the first songs of the birds. [20]

Down the forest slopes to the left were the swings. They were made of bark stripped from hickory saplings. When they became dry they were dangerous. They usually broke when a child was forty feet in the air, and this was why so many bones had to be mended every year. I had no ill luck myself, but none of my cousins escaped. There were eight of them, and at one time and another they broke fourteen arms among them. But it cost next to nothing, for the doctor worked by the year—twenty-five dollars for the whole family. I remember two of the Florida doctors, Chowning and Meredith. They not only tended an entire family for twenty-five dollars a year, but furnished the medicines themselves. Good measure, too. Only the largest persons could hold a whole dose. Castor oil was the principal beverage. The dose was half a dipperful, with half a dipperful of New Orleans molasses added to help it down and make it taste good, which it never did. The next standby was calomel; the next rhubarb; and the next, jalap. Then they bled the patient, and put mustard plasters on him. It was a dreadful system, and yet the death rate was not heavy. The calomel was nearly sure to salivate the patient and cost him some of his teeth. There were no dentists. When teeth became touched with decay or were otherwise ailing, the doctor knew of but one thing to do—he fetched his tongs and dragged them out. If the jaw remained, it was not his fault. Doctors were not called in cases of ordinary illness; the family grandmother attended to those. Every old woman was a doctor, and gathered her own medicines in the woods, and knew how to compound doses that would stir the vitals of a cast-iron dog. And then there was the "Indian doctor"; a grave savage, remnant of his tribe, deeply read in the mysteries of nature and the secret properties of herbs; and most backwoodsmen had high faith in his powers and could tell of wonderful cures achieved by him. In Mauritius, away off yonder in the solitudes of the Indian Ocean, there is a person who answers to our Indian doctor of the old times. He is a negro, and has had no teaching as a doctor, yet there is one disease which he is master of and can cure and the doctors can't. They send for him when they have a case. It is a child's disease of a strange and deadly sort, and the negro cures it with a herb medicine which he makes, himself, from a prescription which has come down to him from his father and grandfather. He will not let anyone see it. He keeps the secret of its components to himself, and it is feared that he will die without divulging it; then there will be consternation in Mauritius. I was told these things by the people there, in 1896. [21]

We had the "faith doctor," too, in those early days—a woman. Her specialty was toothache. She was a farmer's old wife and lived five miles from Hannibal. She would lay her hand on the patient's jaw and say, "Believe!" and the cure was prompt. Mrs. Utterback. I remember her very well. Twice I rode out there behind my mother, horseback, and saw the cure performed. My mother was the patient. [22]

Doctor Meredith removed to Hannibal, by and by, and was our family physician there, and saved my life several times. Still, he was a good man and meant well. Let it go. [23]

I was always told that I was a sickly and precarious and tiresome and uncertain child, and lived mainly on allopathic medicines during the first seven years of my life. I asked my mother about this, in her old age—she was in her eighty-eighth year—and said: [24]

"I suppose that during all that time you were uneasy about me?" [25]

"Yes, the whole time." [26]

"Afraid I wouldn't live?" [27]

After a reflective pause—ostensibly to think out the facts—"No—afraid you would." [28]

The country schoolhouse was three miles from my uncle's farm. It stood in a clearing in the woods and would hold about twenty-five boys and girls. We attended the school with more or less regularity once or twice a week, in summer, walking to it in the cool of the morning by the forest paths, and back in the gloaming at the end of the day. All the pupils brought their dinners in baskets—corn dodger, buttermilk, and other good things—and sat in the shade of the trees at noon and ate them. It is the part of my education which I look back upon with the most satisfaction. My first visit to the school was when I was seven. A strapping girl of fifteen, in the customary sunbonnet and calico dress, asked me if I "used tobacco"—meaning did I chew it. I said no. It roused her scorn. She reported me to all the crowd, and said: [29]

"Here is a boy seven years old who can't chew tobacco." [30]

By the looks and comments which this produced I realized that I was a degraded object, and was cruelly ashamed of myself. I determined to reform. But I only made myself sick; I was not able to learn to chew tobacco. I learned to smoke fairly well, but that did not conciliate anybody and I remained a poor thing, and characterless. I longed to be respected, but I never was able to rise. Children have but little charity for one another's defects. [31]

As I have said, I spent some part of every year at the farm until I was twelve or thirteen years old. The life which I led there with my cousins was full of charm, and so is the memory of it yet. I can call back the solemn twilight and mystery of the deep woods, the earthy smells, the faint odors of the wild flowers, the sheen of rain-washed foliage, the rattling clatter of drops when the wind shook the trees, the far-off hammering of woodpeckers and the muffled drumming of wood pheasants in the remoteness of the forest, the snapshot glimpses of disturbed wild creatures scurrying through the grass—I can call it all back and make it as real as it ever was, and as blessed. I can call back the prairie, and its loneliness and peace, and a vast hawk hanging motionless in the sky, with his wings spread wide and the blue of the vault showing through the fringe of their end feathers. I can see the woods in their autumn dress, the oaks purple, the hickories washed with gold, the maples and the sumachs luminous with crimson fires, and I can hear the rustle made by the fallen leaves as we plowed through them. I can see the blue clusters of wild grapes hanging among the foliage of the saplings, and I remember the taste of them and the smell. I know how the wild blackberries looked, and how they tasted, and the same with the pawpaws, the hazelnuts, and the persimmons; and I can feel the thumping rain, upon my head, of hickory nuts and walnuts when we were out in the frosty dawn to scramble for them with the pigs, and the gusts of wind loosed them and sent them down. I know the stain of black-berries, and how pretty it is, and I know the stain of walnut hulls, and how little it minds soap and water, also what grudged experience it had of either of them. I know the taste of maple sap, and when to gather it, and how to arrange the troughs and the delivery tubes, and how to boil down the juice, and how to hook the sugar after it is made, also how much better hooked sugar tastes than any that is honestly come by, let bigots say what they will. I know how a prize watermelon looks when it is sunning its fat rotundity among pumpkin vines and "simblins"; I know how to tell when it is ripe without "plugging" it; I know how inviting it looks when it is cooling itself in a tub of water under the bed, waiting; I know how it looks when it lies on the table in the sheltered great floor space between house and kitchen, and the children gathered for the sacrifice and their mouths watering; I know the crackling sound it makes when the carving knife enters its end, and I can see the split fly along in front of the blade as the knife cleaves its way to the other end; I can see its halves fall apart and display the rich red meat and the black seeds, and the heart standing up, a luxury fit for the elect; I know how a boy looks behind a yard-long slice of that melon, and I know how he feels; for I have been there. I know the taste of the watermelon which has been honestly come by, and I know the taste of the water-melon which has been acquired by art. Both taste good, but the experienced know which tastes best. I know the look of green apples and peaches and pears on the trees, and I know how entertaining they are when they are inside of a person. I know how ripe ones look when they are piled in pyramids under the trees, and how pretty they are and how vivid their colors. I know how a frozen apple looks, in a barrel down cellar in the wintertime, and how hard it is to bite, and how the frost makes the teeth ache, and yet how good it is, notwithstanding. I know the disposition of elderly people to select the specked apples for the children, and I once knew ways to beat the game. I know the look of an apple that is roasting and sizzling on a hearth on a winter's evening, and I know the comfort that comes of eating it hot, along with some sugar and a drench of cream. I know the delicate art and mystery of so cracking hickory nuts and walnuts on a flatiron with a hammer that the kernels will be delivered whole, and I know how the nuts, taken in conjunction with winter apples, cider, and doughnuts, make old people's old tales and old jokes sound fresh and crisp and enchanting, and juggle an evening away before you know what went with the time. I know the look of Uncle Dan'l's kitchen as it was on the privileged nights, when I was a child, and I can see the white and black children grouped on the hearth, with the firelight playing on their faces and the shadows flickering upon the walls, clear back toward the cavernous gloom of the rear, and I can hear Uncle Dan'l telling the immortal tales which Uncle Remus Harris was to gather into his book and charm the world with, by and by; and I can feel again the creepy joy which quivered through me when the time for the ghost story was reached—and the sense of regret, too, which came over me, for it was always the last story of the evening and there was nothing between it and the unwelcome bed. [32]

I can remember the bare wooden stairway in my uncle's house, and the turn to the left above the landing, and the rafters and the slanting roof over my bed, and the squares of moonlight on the floor, and the white cold world of snow outside, seen through the curtainless window. I can remember the howling of the wind and the quaking of the house on stormy nights, and how snug and cozy one felt, under the blankets, listening; and how the powdery snow used to sift in, around the sashes, and lie in little ridges on the floor and make the place look chilly in the morning and curb the wild desire to get up—

in case there was any. I can remember how very dark that room was, in the dark of the moon, and how packed it was with ghostly stillness when one woke up by accident away in the night, and forgotten sins came flocking out of the secret chambers of the memory and wanted a hearing; and how ill chosen the time seemed for this kind of business; and how dismal was the hoohooing of the owl and the wailing of the wolf, sent mourning by on the night wind. [33]

I remember the raging of the rain on that roof, summer nights, and how pleasant it was to lie and listen to it, and enjoy the white splendor of the lightning and the majestic booming and crashing of the thunder. It was a very satisfactory room, and there was a lightning rod which was reachable from the window, an adorable and skittish thing to climb up and down, summer nights, when there were duties on hand of a sort to make privacy desirable. [34]

I remember the 'coon and 'possum hunts, nights, with the negroes, and the long marches through the black gloom of the woods, and the excitement which fired everybody when the distant bay of an experienced dog announced that the game was treed; then the wild scramblings and stumblings through briers and bushes and over roots to get to the spot; then the lighting of a fire and the felling of the tree, the joyful frenzy of the dogs and the negroes, and the weird picture it all made in the red glare—I remember it all well, and the delight that everyone got out of it, except the 'coon. [35]

I remember the pigeon seasons, when the birds would come in millions and cover the trees and by their weight break down the branches. They were clubbed to death with sticks; guns were not necessary and were not used. I remember the squirrel hunts, and prairie-chicken hunts, and wild-turkey hunts, and all that; and how we turned out, mornings, while it was still dark, to go on these expeditions, and how chilly and dismal it was, and how often I regretted that I was well enough to go. A toot on a tin horn brought twice as many dogs as were needed, and in their happiness they raced and scampered about, and knocked small people down, and made no end of unnecessary noise. At the word, they vanished away toward the woods, and we drifted silently after them in the melancholy gloom. But presently the gray dawn stole over the world, the birds piped up, then the sun rose and poured light and comfort all around, everything was fresh and dewy and fragrant, and life was a boon again. After three hours of tramping we arrived back wholesomely tired, overladen with game, very hungry, and just in time for breakfast. [36]

PURPOSE AND STRUCTURE

1. At first glance this seems to be a loosely organized piece, with one thought idly leading to another. A large part of the organization is determined by what Twain apparently wants to write about—the farm itself, but more particularly, the *people*, the *activities*, and the *things* that made the farm memorable. How he integrates all of them will be clear if you write out in order the first sentences of the following paragraphs: 5, 7, 16, 20, 21, 29.

2. What subject matter appears between pars. 7 and 16? between 16 and 20? 21 and 29? 29 and 32?

3. On the basis of your answer to 1 and 2, what can you say about the relationship between places and people? Which do you think Twain is more interested in? How can you tell?

4. If you have difficulty completing a 500-word essay, study this selection with care, especially pars. 5, 15, 32. Account for the difference between, "We had a variety of meats, plenty of vegetables, and delicious desserts," and Twain's description of a meal. See Abstraction in the Glossary.

5. In par. 15, although Twain announces that he can "see all its [the farm's] belongings, all its details," he doesn't describe *all* of them. What does he do? Note that rather than merely listing details, Twain makes each detail function in some way. For example, his aunt *knits*, his uncle *smokes*. How do each of the following "work": spinning wheel, hickory logs, sap, dogs, floor, fire coals, cradle?

6. Students frequently try to make their writing vivid by using many adjectives and adverbs to lend color to pallid abstract nouns and verbs instead of relying on specific concrete nouns and verbs which appeal to the senses. In par. 32, which senses are appealed to in the first half of the paragraph (up to the incident involving the watermelon)?

7. In par. 32 the account of the watermelon is contained in one extraordinarily long sentence. What, if anything, is gained by putting all the independent clauses in one sentence? What does the series of clauses contribute to rhythm and tone? Notice that each clause begins with "I know. . . ." Does this repetition contribute to unity or monotony? Defend your answer.

8. If you are in the habit of thinking of your writing problem as one of language, you have not yet recognized how perception determines what one can write. Remember, it is the experience of small details that makes up a large, general impression. Notice in par. 32 how Twain sees his hawk down to the minutest detail—"with his wings spread wide and the blue of the vault showing through the fringe of their end feathers." Although many may have seen exactly what Twain records, few have the ability to recall it as distinctly and vividly. In the account of the watermelon, what one detail is perfectly familiar to you and yet would have been overlooked if you had been describing a watermelon?

9. How is the topic sentence of par. 32 related to pars. 33, 34, 35, 36?

DICTION AND TONE

1. "It was a simple speech and made up of small words," is Twain's own comment on par. 13. Is any word in par. 12 or 13 not in your active vocabulary or thoroughly familiar to you? On the basis of these two paragraphs what would you say is the relationship between extensive vocabulary and effectiveness? What seems more important than extensive vocabulary?

2. Look at the first sentence in par. 13. It is perfectly balanced. Analyze the sentence so that you can explain what is meant by a balanced sentence.

3. "When I was younger I could remember anything, whether it had happened or not. . . ." What does this remark at the end of par. 3 add to the essay? What does Twain mean by it? Is it in keeping with the rest of the essay?

4. Put in shorter form *It may not be modest in me* (par. 1). Put *impossible rubbish* in more formal and then in less formal language.

APPLICATIONS TO WRITING

Twain teaches us that generalizations are weak unless supported by relevant details—not any details, but *relevant* ones. Your purpose in writing governs the selection of some details and the rejection of others. For example, the details Twain chooses to report produce an over-all effect of coziness in the winter farmhouse. If he had selected such items as drafts, poor lighting, uncomfortable wooden furniture, the general effect would be different.

Before writing your essay, jot down a list of details about your subject. Don't be satisfied with general observation. If your friend was well-dressed, does this mean he wore black calf shoes? or moccasins? with rubber or leather soles? But make your details *work*; do not simply catalogue or inventory.

Here are some suggested topics: Down on the Farm; Summer Camp; A Street Corner; The Neighborhood Store. In making your presentation of people, places, and things vivid and organized, you might adopt Twain's method of organization, using a place as a framework. In accounting for the sights, sounds, tastes, smells, and feel of your experience, report the things that originally stimulated them.

THE LINE

from *Moby Dick*

HERMAN MELVILLE

With reference to the whaling scene shortly to be described, as well as for the better understanding of all similar scenes elsewhere presented, I have here to speak of the magical, sometimes horrible whale-line. [1]

The line originally used in the fishery was of the best hemp, slightly vapored with tar, not impregnated with it, as in the case of ordinary ropes; for while tar, as ordinarily used, makes the hemp more pliable to the rope-maker, and also renders the rope itself more convenient to the sailor for common ship use; yet, not only would the ordinary quantity too much stiffen the whale-line for the close coiling to which it must be subjected; but as most seamen are beginning to learn, tar in general by no means adds to the rope's durability or strength, however much it may give it compactness and gloss. [2]

Of late years the Manilla rope has in the American fishery almost entirely superseded hemp as a material for whale-lines; for, though not so durable as hemp, it is stronger, and far more soft and elastic; and I will add (since there is an æsthetics in all things), is much more handsome and becoming to the boat, than hemp. Hemp is a dusky, dark fellow, a sort of Indian; but Manilla is as a golden-haired Circassian to behold. [3]

20

The whale-line is only two thirds of an inch in thickness. At first sight, you would not think it so strong as it really is. By experiment its one and fifty yarns will each suspend a weight of one hundred and twenty pounds; so that the whole rope will bear a strain nearly equal to three tons. In length, the common sperm whale-line measures something over two hundred fathoms. Towards the stern of the boat it is spirally coiled away in the tub, not like the worm-pipe of a still though, but so as to form one round, cheese-shaped mass of densely bedded "sheaves," or layers of concentric spiralizations, without any hollow but the "heart," or minute vertical tube formed at the axis of the cheese. As the least tangle or kink in the coiling would, in running out, infallibly take somebody's arm, leg, or entire body off, the utmost precaution is used in stowing the line in its tub. Some harpooneers will consume almost an entire morning in this business, carrying the line high aloft and then reeving it downwards through a block towards the tub, so as in the act of coiling to free it from all possible wrinkles and twists. [4]

In the English boats two tubs are used instead of one; the same line being continuously coiled in both tubs. There is some advantage in this; because these twin-tubs being so small they fit more readily into the boat, and do not strain it so much; whereas, the American tub, nearly three feet in diameter and of proportionate depth, makes a rather bulky freight for a craft whose planks are but one-half inch in thickness; for the bottom of the whale-boat is like critical ice, which will bear up a considerable distributed weight, but not very much of a concentrated one. When the painted canvas cover is clapped on the American tub-line, the boat looks as if it were pulling off with a prodigious great wedding-cake to present to the whales. [5]

Both ends of the line are exposed; the lower end terminating in an eye-splice or loop coming up from the bottom against the side of the tub, and hanging over its edge completely disengaged from everything. This arrangement of the lower end is necessary on two accounts. First: In order to facilitate the fastening to it of an additional line from a neighboring boat, in case the stricken whale should sound so deep as to threaten to carry off the entire line originally attached to the harpoon. In these instances the whale of course is shifted like a mug of ale, as it were from the one boat to the other; though the first boat always hovers at hand to assist its consort. Second: This arrangement is indispensable for common safety's sake; for were the lower end of the line in any way attached to the boat, and were the whale then to run the line out to the end almost in a single, smoking minute as he sometimes does, he would not stop there, for the doomed boat would infallibly be dragged down after him into the profundity of the sea; and in that case no town-crier would ever find her again. [6]

Before lowering the boat for the chase, the upper end of the line is taken aft from the tub, and passing round the loggerhead there, is again carried forward the entire length of the boat, resting crosswise upon the loom or handle of every man's oar, so that it jogs against his wrist in rowing; and also passing between the men, as they alternately sit at the opposite gunwales, to the leaded chocks or grooves in the extreme pointed prow of the boat, where a wooden pin or skewer the size of a common squill, prevents it from slipping out. From the chocks it hangs in a slight festoon over the bows, and is then passed inside the boat again; and some ten or twenty fathoms (called box-line) being coiled upon the box in the bows, it continues its way to the gunwale still a little further aft, and is then attached to the short-warp—the rope which is immediately connected with the harpoon; but previous to that connexion, the short-warp goes through sundry mystifications too tedious to detail. [7]

Thus the whale-line folds the whole boat in its complicated coils, twisting and writhing around it in almost every direction. All the oarsmen are involved in its perilous contortions; so that to the timid eye of the landsman, they seem as Indian jugglers, with the deadliest snakes sportively festooning their limbs. Nor can any son of mortal woman, for the first time, seat himself amid those hempen intricacies, and while straining his utmost at the oar, bethink him that at any unknown instant the harpoon may be darted, and all these horrible contortions be put in play like ringed lightnings; he cannot be thus circumstanced without a shudder that makes the very marrow in his bones to quiver in him like a shaken jelly. Yet habit—strange thing! what cannot habit accomplish?—Gayer sallies, more merry mirth, better jokes, and brighter repartees, you never heard over your mahogany, than you will hear over the half-inch white cedar of the whale-boat, when thus hung in hangman's nooses; and, like the six burghers of Calais before King Edward, the six men composing the crew pull into the jaws of death, with a halter around every neck, as you may say. [8]

Perhaps a very little thought will now enable you to account for those repeated whaling disasters—some few of which are casually chronicled—of this man or that man being taken out of the boat by the line, and lost. For, when the line is darting out, to be seated then in the boat, is like being seated in the midst of the manifold whizzings of a steam-engine in full play, when every flying beam, and shaft, and wheel, is grazing you. It is worse; for you cannot sit motionless in the heart of these perils, because the boat is rocking like a cradle, and you are pitched one way and the other, without the slightest warning; and only by a certain self-adjusting buoyancy and simultaneousness of volition and action, can you escape being made a Mazeppa of, and run away with where the all-seeing sun himself could never pierce you out. [9]

Again: as the profound calm which only apparently precedes and prophesies of the storm, is perhaps more awful than the storm itself; for, indeed, the calm is but the wrapper and envelope of the storm; and contains it in itself, as the seemingly harmless rifle holds the fatal powder, and the ball, and the explosion; so the graceful repose of the line, as it silently serpentines about the oarsmen before being brought into actual play—this is a thing which carries more of true terror than any other aspect of this dangerous affair. But why say more? All men live enveloped in whale-lines. All are born with halters round their necks; but it is only when caught in the swift, sudden turn of death, that mortals realize the silent, subtle, everpresent perils of life. And if you be a philosopher, though seated in the whale-boat, you would not at heart feel one whit more of terror, than though seated before your evening fire with a poker, and not a harpoon, by your side. [10]

PURPOSE AND STRUCTURE

1. In contrast to the philosophical ending, Melville begins rather prosaically by considering such things as (a) the composition of the line, and (b) its size. Indicate where Melville describes these items.

2. Once you know *what* the line is, *where* is it? How much space does Melville devote to this question?

3. What does Melville describe after the *what* and *where?*

4. Most of Melville's description is objective—that is, he chooses words to report facts rather than his interpretation of the facts. For example, "Towards the stern of the boat it is spirally coiled away in the tub. . . ." If you had seen the whole line, you could agree that it was spirally coiled and that it was in a tub. Similarly with, "Both ends of the line are exposed. . . ." Any observer could confirm the statement. But when Melville writes *perilous contortions,* he is interpreting how the coils look to him. Another observer might disagree. Thus, the word *perilous* introduces an element of subjective description.

   The first seven paragraphs are generally objectively reported; from the eighth on the description becomes subjective. Support this statement with at least five specific examples from the text.

5. What is gained by reporting the first half objectively?

6. Ordinarily, shifting pronouns from one person to another unnecessarily (from third person to second person, for example) is frowned upon. What is the effect of Melville's shifting persons between pars. 8 and 9? What is gained by using *you* six times in par. 9?

7. Read the second sentence of par. 9 aloud. Notice that the jerky, darting movement of the sentence mimics the action which it describes. Explain how the first sentence of par. 10 operates in this manner.

DICTION AND TONE

1. Melville uses many figures of speech to clarify his explanation: the line is coiled "not like the worm-pipe of a still." Starting with par. 3 identify at least one figure of speech in every paragraph (except par. 7).

2. A subtle change of tone occurs between pars. 9 and 10. This is partly due to the sentence structure (see question 7 above); partly due to the diction, especially to the vowel sounds. The front vowels (a,e,i) are usually light and quick; the back vowels (o,u), dark and heavy. Show how the preponderance of quick, light vowels in the last two sentences of par. 9 contrasts with the dark vowels of par. 10.

APPLICATIONS TO WRITING

In your essay, be as objective as possible in the first part and then, as Melville does, report subjectively on the same subject. For example, a technical description of a house may precede a subjective description of a home. Some suggested subjects: A House and Home; The Fishing Line; The Actual Event and the Newspaper Account; The Party; The Cake—Its Chemistry and Its Taste; An Experiment and Its Significance; The Sailboat and How It Comes Alive.

THE LIBIDO FOR

THE UGLY

H . L . M E N C K E N

On a Winter day some years ago, coming out of Pittsburgh
on one of the expresses of the Pennsylvania Railroad, I rolled eastward for an hour through the coal and steel towns of Westmoreland
county. It was familiar ground; boy and man, I had been through it
often before. But somehow I had never quite sensed its appalling
desolation. Here was the very heart of industrial America, the center
of its most lucrative and characteristic activity, the boast and pride
of the richest and grandest nation ever seen on earth—and here was
a scene so dreadfully hideous, so intolerably bleak and forlorn that
it reduced the whole aspiration of man to a macabre and depressing
joke. Here was wealth beyond computation, almost beyond imagination—and here were human habitations so abominable that they
would have disgraced a race of alley cats. [1]

I am not speaking of mere filth. One expects steel towns to be dirty.
What I allude to is the unbroken and agonizing ugliness, the sheer
revolting monstrousness, of every house in sight. From East Liberty
to Greensburg, a distance of twenty-five miles, there was not one in
sight from the train that did not insult and lacerate the eye. Some

were so bad, and they were among the most pretentious—churches, stores, warehouses, and the like—that they were downright startling; one blinked before them as one blinks before a man with his face shot away. A few linger in memory, horrible even there: a crazy little church just west of Jeannette, set like a dormer-window on the side of a bare, leprous hill; the headquarters of the Veterans of Foreign Wars at another forlorn town, a steel stadium like a huge rat-trap somewhere further down the line. But most of all I recall the general effect—of hideousness without a break. There was not a single decent house within eyerange from the Pittsburgh suburbs to the Greensburg yards. There was not one that was not misshapen, and there was not one that was not shabby. [2]

The country itself is not uncomely, despite the grime of the endless mills. It is, in form, a narrow river valley, with deep gullies running up into the hills. It is thickly settled, but not noticeably overcrowded. There is still plenty of room for building, even in the larger towns, and there are very few solid blocks. Nearly every house, big and little, has space on all four sides. Obviously, if there were architects of any professional sense or dignity in the region, they would have perfected a chalet to hug the hillsides—a chalet with a high-pitched roof, to throw off the heavy Winter snows, but still essentially a low and clinging building, wider than it was tall. But what have they done? They have taken as their model a brick set on end. This they have converted into a thing of dingy clapboards, with a narrow, low-pitched roof. And the whole they have set upon thin, preposterous brick piers. By the hundreds and thousands these abominable houses cover the bare hillsides, like gravestones in some gigantic and decaying cemetery. On their deep sides they are three, four and even five stories high; on their low sides they bury themselves swinishly in the mud. Not a fifth of them are perpendicular. They lean this way and that, hanging on to their bases precariously. And one and all they are streaked in grime, with dead and eczematous patches of paint peeping through the streaks. [3]

Now and then there is a house of brick. But what brick! When it is new it is the color of a fried egg. When it has taken on the patina

of the mills it is the color of an egg long past all hope or caring.
Was it necessary to adopt that shocking color? No more than it was
necessary to set all of the houses on end. Red brick, even in a steel
town, ages with some dignity. Let it become downright black, and it
is still sightly, especially if its trimmings are of white stone, with soot
in the depths and the high spots washed by the rain. But in Westmoreland they prefer that uremic yellow, and so they have the most
loathsome towns and villages ever seen by mortal eye. [4]

I award this championship only after laborious research and incessant prayer. I have seen, I believe, all of the most unlovely towns of
the world; they are all to be found in the United States. I have seen
the mill towns of decomposing New England and the desert towns
of Utah, Arizona and Texas. I am familiar with the back streets of
Newark, Brooklyn and Chicago, and have made scientific explorations
to Camden, N.J. and Newport News, Va. Safe in a Pullman, I have
whirled through the gloomy, God-forsaken villages of Iowa and
Kansas, and the malarious tidewater hamlets of Georgia. I have been
to Bridgeport, Conn., and to Los Angeles. But nowhere on this earth,
at home or abroad, have I seen anything to compare to the villages
that huddle along the line of the Pennsylvania from the Pittsburgh
yards to Greensburg. They are incomparable in color, and they are
incomparable in design. It is as if some titanic and aberrant genius,
uncompromisingly inimical to man, had devoted all the ingenuity of
Hell to the making of them. They show grotesqueries of ugliness that,
in retrospect, become almost diabolical. One cannot imagine mere
human beings concocting such dreadful things, and one can scarcely
imagine human beings bearing life in them. [5]

Are they so frightful because the valley is full of foreigners—dull,
insensate brutes, with no love of beauty in them? Then why didn't
these foreigners set up similar abominations in the countries that they
came from? You will, in fact, find nothing of the sort in Europe—
save perhaps in the more putrid parts of England. There is scarcely an
ugly village on the whole Continent. The peasants, however poor,
somehow manage to make themselves graceful and charming habita-

tions, even in Spain. But in the American village and small town the pull is always toward ugliness, and in that Westmoreland valley it has been yielded to with an eagerness bordering upon passion. It is incredible that mere ignorance should have achieved such masterpieces of horror. [6]

On certain levels of the American race, indeed, there seems to be a positive libido for the ugly, as on other and less Christian levels there is a libido for the beautiful. It is impossible to put down the wallpaper that defaces the average American home of the lower middle class to mere inadvertence, or to the obscene humor of the manufacturers. Such ghastly designs, it must be obvious, give a genuine delight to a certain type of mind. They meet, in some unfathomable way, its obscure and unintelligible demands. They caress it as "The Palms" caresses it, or the art of the movie, or jazz. The taste for them is as enigmatical and yet as common as the taste for dogmatic theology and the poetry of Edgar A. Guest. [7]

Thus I suspect (though confessedly without knowing) that the vast majority of the honest folk of Westmoreland county, and especially the 100% Americans among them, actually admire the houses they live in, and are proud of them. For the same money they could get vastly better ones, but they prefer what they have got. Certainly there was no pressure upon the Veterans of Foreign Wars to choose the dreadful edifice that bears their banner, for there are plenty of vacant buildings along the track-side, and some of them are appreciably better. They might, indeed, have built a better one of their own. But they chose that clapboarded horror with their eyes open, and having chosen it, they let it mellow into its present shocking depravity. They like it as it is: beside it, the Parthenon would no doubt offend them. In precisely the same way the authors of the rat-trap stadium that I have mentioned made a deliberate choice. After painfully designing and erecting it, they made it perfect in their own sight by putting a completely impossible pent-house, painted a staring yellow, on top of it. The effect is that of a fat woman with a black eye. It is that of a Presbyterian grinning. But they like it. [8]

Here is something that the psychologists have so far neglected: the love of ugliness for its own sake, the lust to make the world intolerable. Its habitat is the United States. Out of the melting pot emerges a race which hates beauty as it hates truth. The etiology of this madness deserves a great deal more study than it has got. There must be causes behind it; it arises and flourishes in obedience to biological laws, and not as a mere act of God. What, precisely, are the terms of those laws? And why do they run stronger in America than elsewhere? Let some honest *Privat Dozent* in pathological sociology apply himself to the problem. [9]

PURPOSE AND STRUCTURE

1. In par. 9 Mencken seems to be identifying a scholarly problem: *Here is something that the psychologists have so far neglected: the love of ugliness for its own sake, the lust to make the world intolerable.* Discuss the seriousness of his suggestions for research in psychology and pathological sociology.

2. His essay opens with a description of what he sees from the train as he rolls eastward *for an hour through the coal and steel towns of Westmoreland county* (par. 1). He maintains the unity of the rest of the essay by selecting most of his examples from this same area. What, then, is the purpose of the references to other towns and villages in America (par. 5)? to the villages of Europe (par. 6)? to the Parthenon (par. 8)?

3. The last two sentences of par. 1 repeat a powerful contrast. Notice the use of the dash in each sentence. Why not use a comma or a semicolon instead? Why is this contrast set in the reader's mind early in the essay? What argument could be used against the thesis (par. 7) if Mencken failed to make this point? How does his allusion to *peasants, however poor* (par. 6) and the money of *100% Americans* (par. 8) relate to this point? Why does he exclude *mere filth* (par. 2)?

4. Having developed a thesis—the libido for the ugly—as a result of his examination of Westmoreland, why does Mencken mention wallpaper, *The Palms,* motion pictures, jazz, dogmatic theology, and the poetry of Edgar A. Guest (par. 7)?

DICTION AND TONE

1. Mencken's tone is scathing; he speaks of *appalling desolation* (par. 1), of *sheer revolting monstrousness,* of a *bare, leprous hill* (par. 2). It is important to understand, however, that the satirical power of his attack is not simply a result of his choice of words, of his diction. His tone is also achieved through structure and image.

Examine par. 4, for instance. It begins by stating that the new brick is the color of a fried egg. What happens to this image in the next sentence? Why does Mencken discuss red brick in the next section of the paragraph? Notice that he returns to yellow in the climax of the paragraph, that *the most loathsome towns and villages ever seen by mortal eye* is tied to *uremic yellow.* Is *uremic* an appropriate word at this point in the paragraph?

This careful arrangement of materials is also apparent in par. 3. After describing a possible design, Mencken begins his description of a typical Westmoreland house with a unifying image. What is it? Examine the rest of this paragraph in terms of its structure, its images, its diction. What tone is achieved? How?

Or consider the examples with which Mencken ends his essay (par. 8). Both are planted in par. 2. There is a description of the headquarters of the Veterans of Foreign Wars in par. 2. Why refer to it before par. 8? How is the steel stadium described in par. 2? Would this description be more effective if it were omitted until par. 8? Why is it appropriate to refer to the Parthenon in par. 8? What tone is achieved by comparing the pent-house to *a fat woman with a black eye* (par. 8)? To a *Presbyterian grinning* (par. 8)?

2. Why does Mencken use the uncommon word *libido* in his title?

3. Why does he use the phrase *less Christian levels* (par. 7)?

4. *Macabre and depressing joke* and *race of alley cats* (par. 1) are striking phrases, perhaps too striking. What expectations are set by them? Are the examples of ugliness which follow in the essay anticlimactic? What tone is achieved, for instance, by writing that some buildings were so bad that *one blinked before them as one blinks before a man with his face shot away* (par. 2)?

5. Compare the controlled metaphoric language of Mencken's essay with the literal language in par. 32 of Twain's essay.

APPLICATIONS TO WRITING

1. Mencken compares red and yellow bricks in a simple yet powerful paragraph (par. 5). Write such a paragraph comparing two automobile colors, two paintings, or two TV programs.

2. In par. 3 Mencken compares the typical house of Westmoreland to a *brick set on end*. Write a paragraph using such a concrete image to unify a diverse group of particulars.

3. Drive through an unpleasant section of today's suburban sprawl. Write a *Libido for the Ugly* on what you see. Or write a satirical attack on ugliness, describing what you see on a walk downtown. Look at your particular abominations: advertising billboards, public buildings, or new styles in women's (or men's) clothing in storewindows. Observe carefully, but pay particular attention to your diction, images, and organization.

4. This essay seems to formulate a scientific hypothesis; actually it satirizes the ugliness of American buildings. Write a satirical identification of a scientific or scholarly problem.

5. Call attention to—that is, identify—a situation by inventing a preposterous hypothesis. For example, that people who commute to work belong to a secret religious cult which has a ritual, epiphany, penance, exorcism, etc. Or, that the experience of registering for college classes is precisely the same as the experience of getting a college education.

PROLOGUE

MARCEL PROUST

Every day I set less store on intellect. Every day I see more clearly that if the writer is to repossess himself of some part of his impressions, get to something personal, that is, and to the only material of art, he must put it aside. What intellect restores to us under the name of the past, is not the past. In reality, as soon as each hour of one's life has died, it embodies itself in some material object, as do the souls of the dead in certain folk-stories, and hides there. There it remains captive, captive for ever, unless we should happen on the object, recognise what lies within, call it by its name, and so set it free. Very likely we may never happen on the object (or the sensation, since we apprehend every object as sensation) that it hides in; and thus there are hours of our life that will never be resuscitated: for this object is so tiny, so lost in the world, and there is so little likelihood that we shall come across it. [1]

Several summers of my life were spent in a house in the country. I thought of those summers from time to time, but they were not themselves. They were dead, and in all probability they would always remain so. Their resurrection, like all these resurrections, hung on a mere chance. One snowy evening, not long ago, I came in half frozen, and had sat down in my room to read by lamplight, and as I could not get warm my old cook offered to make me a cup of tea, a thing I never drink. And as chance would have it, she brought me some slices of dry toast. I dipped the toast in the cup of tea and as soon as I put it in my mouth, and felt its softened texture, all flavored with tea, against my palate, something came over me—the smell of geraniums and orange-blossoms, a sensation of extraordinary radiance and happiness; I sat quite still, afraid that the slightest movement might cut short this incomprehensible process which was taking place in me, and concentrated on the bit of sopped toast which seemed responsible for all these marvels; then suddenly the shaken partitions in my memory gave way, and into my conscious mind there rushed the summers I had spent in the aforesaid house in the country, with their early mornings, and the succession, the ceaseless onset, of happy hours in their train. And then I remembered. Every morning, when I was dressed, I went down to my grandfather in his bedroom, where he had just woken up and was drinking his tea. He soaked a rusk in it, and gave me the rusk to eat. And when those summers were past and gone, the taste of a rusk soaked in tea was one of the shelters where the dead hours—dead as far as intellect knew—hid themselves away, and where I should certainly never have found them again if, on that winter's evening when I came in frozen from the snow, my cook had not offered me the potion to which, by virtue of a magic past I knew nothing about, their resurrection was plighted. [2]

But as soon as I had tasted the rusk, a whole garden, up till then vague and dim, mirrored itself, with its forgotten walks and all their urns with all their flowers, in the little cup of tea, like those Japanese flowers which do not re-open as flowers until one drops them into water. In the same way, many days in Venice, which intellect had not been able to give back, were dead for me until last year, when crossing a courtyard I came to a standstill among the glittering uneven paving-stones. The friends I was with feared I might have wrenched my ankle, but I waved to them to go on, and that I would catch up with them. Something of greater importance engaged me, I still did not know what it was, but in the depth of my being I felt the flutter of a past that I did not recognise; it was just as I set foot on a certain paving-stone that this feeling of perplexity came over me. I felt an invading happiness. I knew that I was going to be enriched by that purely personal thing, a past impression, a fragment of life in un-sullied preservation (something we can only know in preservation, for while we live in it, it is not present in the memory, once other sensations accompany and smother it) which asked only that it should be set free, that it should come and augment my wealth of life and poetry. But I did not feel that I had the power to free it. No, intellect could have done nothing for me at such a moment! Trying to put myself back into the same state, I retraced my steps a little so that I might come afresh to those uneven shining paving-stones. It was the same sensation underfoot that I had felt on the smooth, slightly uneven pavement of the baptistry of Saint Mark's. The shadow which had lain that day on the canal where a gondola waited for me, and all the happiness, all the wealth of those hours—this recognised sensation brought them hurrying after it, and that very day came alive for me. [3]

It is not merely that intellect can lend no hand in these resurrec-tions; these past hours will only hide themselves away in objects where intellect has not tried to embody them. The objects which you have consciously tried to connect with certain hours of your life, these they can never take shelter in. What is more, if something else should resuscitate those hours, the objects called back with them will be stripped of their poetry. [4]

I remember how once when I was travelling by train I strove to draw impressions from the passing landscape, I wrote about the little country churchyard while it was still passing before my eyes, I noted down the bright bars of sunlight on the trees, the wayside flowers like those in Le Lys dans la Vallée. Since then, calling to mind those trees streaked with light and that little churchyard, I have often tried to conjure up that day, that day itself, I mean, not its pallid ghost. I could never manage it, and I had lost all hope of doing so, when at lunch, not long ago, I let my spoon fall on my plate. And then it made the same noise as the hammers of the linesmen did that day,

tapping on the wheels when the train halted at stations. The burning
blinded hour when that noise rang out instantly came back to me,
and all that day in its poetry—except for the country churchyard, the
trees streaked with light, and the Balzacian flowers, gained by deliberate observation and lost from the poetic resurrection. [5]

Now and again, alas, we happen on the object, and the lost
sensation thrills in us, but the time is too remote, we cannot give a
name to the sensation, or call on it, and it does not come alive. As I
was walking through a pantry the other day, a piece of green canvas
plugging a broken window-pane made me stop dead and listen inwardly. A gleam of summer crossed my mind. Why? I tried to
remember. I saw wasps in a shaft of sunlight, a smell of cherries came
from the table—I could not remember. For a moment I was like those
sleepers who wake up in the dark and do not know where they are, who
ask their bodies to give them a bearing as to their whereabouts, not
knowing what bed, what house, what part of the world, which year of
their life they are in. For a moment I hesitated like this, groping
round the square of green canvas to discover the time and the place
where my scarcely awakened memory would find itself at home. All the
sensations of my life, confused, or known, or forgotten, I was hesitat-
ing among all of them at once; this only lasted a minute. Soon I saw
nothing more; my memory had fallen asleep again for ever. [6]

How often during our walks have not my friends known me to halt
like this at the turning-off of an avenue, or beside a clump of trees,
and ask them to leave me alone for a minute. Nothing came of it. I
shut my eyes and made my mind a blank to recruit fresh energies for
my pursuit of the past, then suddenly reopened them, all in an attempt to see those same trees as if for the first time, I could not tell
where I had seen them. I could recognise their shapes and their
grouping, their outline seemed to have been traced from some beloved drawing that trembled in my heart. But I could tell no more of
them, and they themselves seemed by their artless passionate attitude
to say how sorry they felt not to be able to make themselves clear, not
to be able to tell me the secret that they well knew I could not
unriddle. Ghosts of a dear past, so dear that my heart beat to burst-

ing, they held out powerless arms to me, like the ghosts that Aeneas met in the underworld. Was it in the walks near the town of my happy childhood, was it only in that imagined country where, later on, I dreamed that Mamma was so ill, close to a lake and in a forest where it was light all night long, a dream country only but almost as real as the country of my childhood which was already no more than a dream? I should never know more of it. And I had to rejoin my friends who were waiting for me at the turn of the road, with the anguish of turning my back for ever on a past I might see no more, of disowning the dead who held out their powerless fond arms to me, and seemed to say, Recall us to life. And before I fell into step and into conversation with my friends, I again turned round for a moment to cast a less and less discerning glance towards the receding crooked line of mutely expressive trees still undulating before my eyes. [7]

Compared with this past, this private essence of ourselves, the truths of intellect seem scarcely real at all. So, and above all from the time when our vitality begins to dwindle, it is to whatever may help us to recover this past that we resort, even though this should entail being very ill-understood by intellectual people who do not know that the artist lives to himself, that the absolute value of what he sees means nothing to him and that his scale of values is wholly subjective. A nauseating musical show put on by a provincial company, or a ball that people of taste would laugh at, may be far more quickening to his memories, far more relevant to the nature of what he dreams of and dwells on, than a brilliant performance at the Opera House or an ultra-elegant evening party in the Faubourg Saint-Germain. A railway time-table with its names of stations where he loves to fancy himself getting out of the train on an autumn evening when the trees are already stripped of their leaves and the bracing air is full of their rough scent, or a book that means nothing to people of discrimination but is full of names he has not heard since he was a child, can be worth incommensurably more to him than admirable philosophical treatises, so that people of discrimination will remark that for a man of talent he has very stupid likings. [8]

Perhaps it will cause surprise that I, who make light of the intellect, should have devoted the following few pages precisely to some of those considerations that intellect, in contradiction to the platitudes that we hear said or read in books, suggests to us. At a time when my days may be numbered (and besides, are we not all in the same case?) it is perhaps very frivolous of me to undertake an intellectual exercise. But if the truths of intellect are less precious than those secrets of feeling that I was talking about just now, yet in one way they too have their interest. A writer is not only a poet; in our imperfect world where masterpieces are no more than the shipwrecked flotsam of great minds, even the greatest writers of our century have cast a net of intellect round jewels of feeling which only here or there show through it. And if one believes that on this important point one hears the best among one's contemporaries making mistakes, there comes a time when one shakes off one's indolence and feels the need to speak out. Sainte-Beuve's[1] method is not, at first sight, such an important affair. But perhaps in the course of these pages we may be led to realise that it touches on very important intellectual problems, and on what is perhaps for an artist the greatest of all; this relative inferiority of the intellect which I spoke of at the beginning. Yet all the same, it is intellect we must call on to establish this inferiority. Because if intellect does not deserve the crown of crowns, only intellect is able to award it. And if intellect only ranks second in the hierarchy of virtues, intellect alone is able to proclaim that the first place must be given to instinct. [9]

PURPOSE AND STRUCTURE

1. If the writer can identify, discover, the objects which will give the reader "the smell of geraniums and orange-blossoms, a sensation of extraordinary radiance and happiness," then he can resurrect the past as Proust does. But it is not easy to evoke such sensations. As T. S. Eliot states, "The only way of expressing emotion in the form of art is by find-

[1] Charles Augustin Sainte-Beuve, 1804–1869, French critic.

ing an 'objective correlative'; in other words, a set of objects, a situation, a chain of events which shall be the formula of that *particular* emotion; such that when the external facts, which must terminate in sensory experience, are given, the emotion is immediately evoked."

Examine an instance of emotional experience in which it is difficult or nearly impossible to find an objective correlative. For example, how does one find a set of objects to express effectively the *inability* to remember? In par. 6 how concretely does Proust present the material object which "contains" the memory?

2. Evaluate the phrase *gleam of summer* (par. 6). Can summer gleam?

3. Do you think that joining sight and smell—*wasps in a shaft of sunlight, a smell of cherries came from the table*—is unwise (par. 6)? If so, attempt to present these memories in separate sentences.

4. This description of a failure of memory illustrates another aspect of effective writing: while intellect, as Proust states, may not be the "crown of crowns, only intellect is able to award it." In other words, only intellect can order and evaluate concrete materials. (See Abstraction.) Notice that par. 6 is *not* simply a string of objects, a chain of memories. The subject of the paragraph is carefully introduced and carefully concluded. The memories are presented as illustrations; they are embedded in a coherent movement of ideas. For instance, why is the image of sleepers waking up to ask their bodies where they are an appropriate one (par. 6)?

5. Why is it suitable to end this paragraph with *my memory had fallen asleep again for ever*?

6. How is the sensation of a failure of memory evoked in par. 6?

7. Why include failures of memory in this essay (pars. 6 and 7)?

8. Par. 8 seems to argue for bad art and *stupid likings*. How does it function in the essay?

9. This essay is an introduction to a book of literary criticism, a work of intellect. Why, then, does Proust challenge intellect's claim in the hierarchy of virtues? How does his attack locate and identify intellect? Why is intellect necessary?

10. Proust contrasts two kinds of memory in par. 1. What are they?

11. Compare the beginning of par. 1 with the last few sentences of the essay. How does the essay join these two statements?

DICTION AND TONE

1. Why does Proust use the word *resurrection* (pars. 2, 4, 5, *etc.*) for a particular kind of memory?

2. What is the tone of par. 1? Is the diction formal or informal? Specify. What metaphor is used for memory? Why? Are the sentences simple or complex? Is the paragraph abstract or concrete? Explain.

3. Proust tasted a piece of toast dipped in tea and "a whole garden, up till then vague and dim, mirrored itself, with its forgotten walks and all their urns with all their flowers, in the little cup of tea, like those Japanese flowers which do not re-open as flowers until one drops them into water" (par. 3). Why is *mirrored itself* appropriate? Why is the simile of *Japanese flowers* appropriate both to its immediate context and to the entire essay?

4. Pars. 1 and 2 make the same point. How do they differ?

5. Rewrite the long last sentence of par. 2 as two or more sentences. Have you improved it? Why use the word *potion? magic past? plighted?*

6. The next to the last sentence in par. 6 (*All the sensations* . . .) seems to be incoherent. Rewrite it or discuss its aptness.

APPLICATIONS TO WRITING

1. Par. 6 (see Purpose and Structure above, 2–10) describes a partial failure of memory. Write a similar paragraph of identification.

2. Par. 7 contains an example of a failure to remember, to recapture the significance of some trees. Identify a clump of trees, a street, a house, or a person who once meant a great deal to you.

3. Often early memories are strongly sensory. Identify in a paragraph your earliest sensory impressions as vividly and as precisely as possible. See Agee's essay, *Knoxville*, for a good example of sensory description.

4. The thesis of *Prologue* is fully and finally stated only in the last sentence. Write an essay in which the full significance is not identified

until the last few sentences. For instance, present a series of seemingly haphazard memories that finally coalesce into one central insight about yourself.

5. Describe a personal identification of a "resurrection," a memory that was released by an odor, a taste, or some other sensation.

KNOXVILLE:

SUMMER 1915

JAMES AGEE

We are talking now of summer evenings in Knoxville, Tennessee in the time that I lived there so successfully disguised to myself as a child. It was a little bit mixed sort of block, fairly solidly lower middle class, with one or two juts apiece on either side of that. The houses corresponded: middle-sized gracefully fretted wood houses built in the late nineties and early nineteen hundreds, with small front and side and more spacious back yards, and trees in the yards, and porches. These were softwooded trees, poplars, tulip trees, cottonwoods. There were fences around one or two of the houses, but mainly the yards ran into each other with only now and then a low hedge that wasn't doing very well. There were few good friends among the grown people, and they were not poor enough for the other sort of intimate acquaintance, but everyone nodded and spoke, and even might talk short times, trivially, and at the two extremes of the general or the particular, and ordinarily nextdoor neighbors talked quite a bit when they happened to run into each other, and never paid calls. The men were mostly small businessmen, one or two very modestly executives, one or two worked with their hands, most of them clerical, and most of them between thirty and forty-five. [1]

But it is of these evenings, I speak. [2]

Supper was at six and was over by half past. There was still daylight, shining softly and with a tarnish, like the lining of a shell; and the carbon lamps lifted at the corners were on in the light, and the locusts were started, and the fire flies were out, and a few frogs were flopping in the dewy grass, by the time the fathers and the children came out. The children ran out first hell bent and yelling those names by which they were known; then the fathers sank out leisurely in crossed suspenders, their collars removed and their necks looking tall and shy. The mothers stayed back in the kitchen washing and drying, putting things away, recrossing their traceless footsteps like the lifetime journeys of bees, measuring out the dry cocoa for breakfast. When they came out they had taken off their aprons and their skirts were dampened and they sat in rockers on their porches quietly. [3]

It is not of the games children played in the evening that I want to speak now, it is of a contemporaneous atmosphere that has little to do with them: that of the fathers of families, each in his space of lawn, his shirt fishlike pale in the unnatural light and his face nearly anonymous, hosing their lawns. The hoses were attached at spigots that stood out of the brick foundations of the houses. The nozzles were variously set but usually so there was a long sweet stream of spray, the nozzle wet in the hand, the water trickling the right forearm and the peeled-back cuff, and the water whishing out a long loose and low-curved cone, and so gentle a sound. First an insane noise of violence in the nozzle, then the still irregular sound of adjustment, then the smoothing into steadiness and a pitch as accurately tuned to the size and style of stream as any violin. So many qualities of sound out of one hose: so many choral differences out of those several hoses that were in earshot. Out of any one hose, the almost dead silence of the release, and the short still arch of the separate big drops, silent as a held breath, and the only noise the flattering noise on leaves and the slapped grass at the fall of each big drop. That, and the intense hiss with the intense stream; that, and that same intensity not growing less but growing more quiet and delicate with the turn of the nozzle, up to that extreme tender whisper when the water was just a wide bell of film. Chiefly, though, the hoses were set much alike, in a compromise between distance and tenderness of spray (and quite surely a sense of art behind this compromise, and a quiet deep joy, too real to recognize itself), and the sounds therefore were pitched much alike; pointed by the snorting start of a new hose; decorated by some man playful with the nozzle; left empty, like God by the sparrow's fall, when any single one of them desists: and all, though near alike, of various pitch; and in this unison. These sweet pale streamings in the light lift out their pallors and their voices all together, mothers hushing their children, the hushing unnaturally prolonged, the men gentle and silent and each snail-like withdrawn into the quietude of what he singly is doing, the urination of huge children stood loosely military against an invisible wall, and gentle happy and peaceful, tasting the mean goodness of their living like the last of their suppers in their mouths; while the locusts carry on this noise of hoses on their much higher and sharper key. The noise of the locust is dry, and it seems not to be rasped or vibrated but urged from him as if through a small orifice by breath that can never give out. Also there is never one locust but an illusion of at least a thousand. The noise of each locust is pitched in some classic locust range out of which none of them varies more than two full tones: and yet you seem to hear each locust discrete from all the rest, and there is a long, slow, pulse in their noise, like the scarcely defined arch of a long and high set bridge. They are all around in every tree, so that the noise seems to come from nowhere and everywhere at once, from the whole shell heaven, shivering in your flesh and teasing your eardrums, the boldest of all the sounds of night. And yet it is habitual to summer nights, and is of the great order of noises, like the noises of the sea and of the blood her precocious grandchild, which you realize you are hearing only when you catch yourself listening. Meantime from low in the dark, just outside the swaying horizons of the hoses, conveying always grass in the damp of dew and its strong green-black smear of smell, the regular yet spaced noises of the crickets, each a sweet cold silver noise threenoted, like the slipping each time of three matched links of a small chain. [4]

But the men by now, one by one, have silenced their hoses and drained and coiled them. Now only two, and now only one, is left, and you see only ghostlike shirt with the sleeve garters, and sober mystery of his mild face like the lifted face of large cattle enquiring of your presence in a pitchdark pool of meadow; and now he too is gone; and it has become that time of evening when people sit on their porches, rocking gently and talking gently and watching the street and the standing up into their sphere of possession of the trees, of birds hung havens, hangars. People go by; things go by. A horse, drawing a buggy, breaking his hollow iron music on the asphalt; a loud auto; a quiet auto; people in pairs, not in a hurry, scuffling, switching their weight of aestival body, talking casually, the taste hovering over them of vanilla, strawberry, pasteboard and starched milk, the image upon them of lovers and horsemen, squared with clowns in hueless amber. A street car raising its iron moan; stopping, belling and starting; stertorous; rousing and raising again its iron increasing moan and swimming its gold windows and straw seats on past and past and past, the bleak spark crackling and cursing above it like a small malignant spirit set to dog its tracks; the iron whine rises on rising speed; still risen, faints; halts; the faint stinging bell; rises again, still fainter; fainting, lifting, lifts, faints forgone: forgotten. Now is the night one blue dew. [5]

Now is the night one blue dew, my father has drained, he has coiled the hose.
Low on the length of lawns, a frailing of fire who breathes.
Content, silver, like peeps of light, each cricket makes his comment over and over in the drowned grass.
A cold toad thumpily flounders.
Within the edges of damp shadows of side yards are hovering children nearly sick with joy of fear, who watch the unguarding of a telephone pole.
Around white carbon corner lamps bugs of all sizes are lifted elliptic,

solar systems. Big hardshells bruise themselves, assailant: he is fallen on his back, legs squiggling.

Parents on porches: rock and rock: From damp strings morning glories: hang their ancient faces.

The dry and exalted noise of the locusts from all the air at once enchants my eardrums. [6]

On the rough wet grass of the back yard my father and mother have spread quilts. We all lie there, my mother, my father, my uncle, my aunt, and I too am lying there. First we were sitting up, then one of us lay down, and then we all lay down, on our stomachs, or on our sides, or on our backs, and they have kept on talking. They are not talking much, and the talk is quiet, of nothing in particular, of nothing at all in particular, of nothing at all. The stars are wide and alive, they seem each like a smile of great sweetness, and they seem very near. All my people are larger bodies than mine, quiet, with voices gentle and meaningless like the voices of sleeping birds. One is an artist, he is living at home. One is a musician, she is living at home. One is my mother who is good to me. One is my father who is good to me. By some chance, here they are, all on this earth; and who shall ever tell the sorrow of being on this earth, lying, on quilts, on the grass, in a summer evening, among the sounds of the night. May God bless my people, my uncle, my aunt, my mother, my good father, oh, remember them kindly in their time of trouble; and in the hour of their taking away. [7]

After a little I am taken in and put to bed. Sleep, soft smiling, draws me unto her: and those receive me, who quietly treat me, as one familiar and well beloved in that home: but will not, oh, will not, not now, not ever; but will not ever tell me who I am. [8]

PURPOSE AND STRUCTURE

1. Unlike *Memories of a Missouri Farm*, this selection gives an initial impression of being carefully organized with transitions between paragraphs clearly stated. Mark each of the transitions.

2. In par. 1 Agee sets the scene in general terms. Notice how he moves outward from the houses: first he mentions the houses, then the trees around them, and finally the fences and yards. This is called spatial order. In describing objects in space, the writer may choose to report the foreground first, move to the middle distance, and finally to the horizon; or he may reverse the procedure and move from horizon to foreground. He may move from top to bottom, bottom to top, from left to right, or from a place in space and radiate outwards. The point is that he moves in an *orderly* and not a haphazard manner. How does the order at the beginning of Agee's first paragraph compare with the pattern of organization in *Memories of a Missouri Farm?*

3. In par. 3 Agee introduces a cast of characters. In what order does he introduce them? This is called time order. Write out the words that indicate sequence in time. Remember that tenses can signal time.

4. In par. 4 Agee introduces action. This action is reported primarily through one sense. Which sense?

5. Agee observes and writes with extraordinary precision and sensitivity. Par. 4 illustrates the dependency of descriptive writing on the writer's ability to perceive and to analyze his perceptions by breaking general impressions into details.

Notice that a number of sentences in par. 4 follow the same pattern: each such sentence starts with a short, relatively general statement, followed by a series of increasingly specific modifiers, each of which develops one detail of the preceding statement or modifier. It is as if Agee has a zoom lens on his eye; he starts his sentence by focusing on an object, then, through his modifiers, he "zooms" in, seeing and reporting smaller and smaller items. For example, in the first sentence he moves from *fathers* (all of them) to *each of them* (fathers singly) to *his shirt* (a detail of father) to *his face* (a smaller detail) and returns at the end to fathers *hosing their lawns*. In the third sentence he starts with *nozzles*, moves to *stream of spray* (a detail issuing from nozzle) to *nozzle wet in hand* (a detail of nozzle) to *water trickling the right forearm* (a detail of wetness) to *peeled-back cuff* (a detail smaller than forearm) before he returns to stream of spray and reports its sound and shape. In one sentence he moves from a stream of water to a single drop! (a) Demonstrate how and to what degree the sentence beginning *These sweet pale streamings in the light* follows the above pattern. (b) Select another sentence from the essay and show how it follows the described pattern. (c) Apply the same method of analysis not to a sentence but to par. 5, beginning with the sentence *People go by; things go by.*

6. What senses in addition to hearing are appealed to in par. 4?

7. What sounds in addition to those of the hoses does Agee report in par. 4?

8. Despite the amount of attention paid to sounds, a quiet rather than a noisy atmosphere results. Account for this seeming paradox.

9. In what way is the reader prepared for the last two paragraphs? Show how the last two paragraphs are or are not an integral part of the composition.

10. What relationship is there between the first and last sentences of the selection?

DICTION AND TONE

1. In par. 5 there is a sentence that begins, "A streetcar raising its iron moan. . . ." Illustrate the poetic devices in the sentence (rhythm, repetition, alliteration, figures of speech). What effect is achieved by its fragmentary character? Contrast it with the sentence that follows.

2. Agee's reporting of details is intimately linked with his diction and figures of speech. When in par. 4 he refers to the water as a *wide bell of film*, he tells us about the shape of the water. But a bell produces sound, and as his paragraph is about sounds, his figure capitalizes on both the shape and function of *bell*. Comment on the nature of the contribution each of the following excerpts from par. 4 makes to the essay (does it contribute to tone? to vividness? to unity or coherence?): *insane noise of violence; tenderness of spray; snorting start of a new hose; the urination of huge children stood loosely military against an invisible wall; green-black smear of smell.*

3. What effect is created by the repetition of sentence structure and ideas in the four sentences that begin *One is . . .* in par. 7? Contrast these sentences with the one that follows.

4. Explain the significance of the following in their contexts: *their necks looking tall and shy* [3]; *lifetime journeys of bees* [3]; *contemporaneous atmosphere* [4]; *the blood her precocious grandchild* [4].

APPLICATIONS TO WRITING

The writer always has to gather information before he writes. Sometimes he goes to the library to obtain information from books; other times he draws upon a lifetime of experience. For this assignment gather information by looking and observing as closely as possible. You may well spend more time observing than you do writing, but this is not at all unusual. A writer can devote years to gathering material and then spend only one year writing a book. The following subjects are no more than suggestions. Sounds of a Summer Evening (try describing the sounds a water sprinkler makes); Street Noises; The Odors of an Old House; A Party; Sounds Outside the Classroom Window.

Although the main point of this exercise is to force you to perceive and then report accurately and in detail, do not forget that Agee's description serves a general purpose. He describes a summer evening in such a manner that a mood of great loneliness and isolation is evoked. Everyone is alone and separated from the others; even at the end when the boy joins the elders on the blanket under the stars, he feels his separateness. It would be wise to make your description serve a similar purpose.

SUNDAY DINNER
IN BROOKLYN

ANATOLE BROYARD

I took a roundabout route to the subway, and because I was going to Brooklyn the Village seemed to have at that moment all the charm of a Utrillo. It was only at times like this, in contrast to something else, that this neighborhood became attractive. Ugly in itself, it was a relief from certain kinds of beauty. To most of those like me who lived there, it was as inviting as a view of a squalid village would seem to a princess imprisoned in an ivory tower. [1]

Since it was summer, the Italians were all outside on stoops and chairs or standing along the curb in their Sunday clothes, the old men in navy blue and the young men in powder blue suits, as though their generation was more washed out than the last. The mothers with their hair pulled back and their hands folded in their laps looked like Neanderthal madonnas, and they were dressed, of course, in black, since it was a miracle if someone in their families had not died within the year. The girls wore long pegged skirts which made their feet move incredibly fast. All of their movements seemed to be geared to this same tempo, and their faces were alert with the necessity of defending the one prize they had against mother and brother alike. [2]

© Partisan Review, 1954. Abridged. Printed in full in the *Avon Book of Modern Writing*, #2.

On the corner squatted their church—a huge casserole, fat, heavy, and plain as the women who prayed in it. Looking through the open doors as I passed, I saw the arches bending downward like a laborer under a heavy load. Even the bells of this church—presumably the voice of their god—were sour, and every Sunday morning I cursed them together with the priest who played some sort of chopsticks tune over and over on them. [3]

On Thompson Street, a block and a half from where I lived, there was a stable, and here a horse's head poked through the window on the second floor. Above him, on the windowsill of the top floor, a geranium grew out of a rusty one-gallon can. Near the corner, a drunk slept in the sun against the wall of the Mills Hotel, and another drunk stood over him, holding out his hand, saying, "Shake, pal. Shake." [4]

The waterless wading pond in the center of Washington Square, the bull's eye of the Village, was overflowing with guitar players, folk singers, folk dancers, conga drummers, communists, anarchists, voyeurs, frotteurs, fairies, dogs, children, Negroes, sightseers, psychotics, anthropology professors, heroin pushers, tea pushers, carriage pushers, lesbians, New York Times readers, people with portable radios, adenoidal girls looking for interesting boys, the uninteresting boys they would eventually wind up with, older girls between affairs, older boys on the lookout for younger girls, and so on. Where they stood, Fifth Avenue dribbled to its conclusion after penetrating Washington Arch. [5]

Looking around, I didn't see any of my crew, so there was nothing else to do but head for the subway. At the entrance on Sixth Avenue and Waverly Place, I took a long breath like a deep-sea diver and went reluctantly underground. [6]

The subway's roaring and screaming in the darkness, the passing under the river with the pressure in my ears—these were such a classical overture to going back home that I was weary of the joke. Riding the wrong way like that, I felt I had left Brooklyn for Manhattan only to discover on arriving that I had forgotten something I needed. Now, retracing my steps, I found the ride an endless torture, as it always inexplicably is under these circumstances, although when I was going in the other direction the distance passed unnoticed. [7]

Of course it was my mother and father I'd forgotten, and I'd do it all over again next time too, but by now I accepted this as in the nature of things. They could hardly forget me though, because they had my picture on the mantle next to the clock. It was ten years old, that picture, but they never asked for a new one, and I was convinced that this was the way they still saw me. Like a criminal, I might alter my appearance, but they were not to be fooled. Each time I arrived, I could see their moist eyes washing away my disguise. [8]

I was holding a book open on my lap—I always carried a book to Brooklyn, as an amulet or charm, a definition of my delicate ego— but for all the reading I did I might just as well have put it into the seat of my pants. My mind kept dropping down the page like a marble in a pinball machine until I finally gave it up, conceding that no book could successfully compete with my favorite fiction, my mother and father. [9]

The train stopped, and a man who had been sitting across from me got out. He had been occupying the seat next to the window at a right angle to the wall. Now a woman placed alone on the seat parallel to the wall and in front of the one he had vacated, quickly changed to his empty seat. Whereupon a man sitting on the outside of the seat corresponding to the one she now occupied but on my side of the train, jumped up to take her former seat, and the man next to me on the seat parallel to the wall shifted to the seat at his left knee just vacated. All of this was done dead-pan, but when I looked again at the woman to see how she was enjoying her new seat, I found her staring at me. She was sour and middle-aged, and her eyes, which were very small, were brooding deeply on me, full of a very personal distaste, as if she were imagining me as her own son. Something about me displeased the hell out of her—the way I was dressed, my haircut, or the expression on my face, which wasn't businesslike enough to spell security for her in her old age. [10]

I didn't feel like answering this look, so I avoided her by staring myself at a man standing a few feet away from me. This man was very visibly chewing gum, and the movements of his bony jaws were so elaborate and so regular that they reminded me of printing presses. I noticed that he was studying himself in the window glass. Arresting his jaws in a position in which all the complications of structure were particularly conspicuous, he observed himself with the close and scientific attention of a Leonardo. Then the machine resumed its hypnotic movements. Now, shifting the gum this way and that, he worked out a wonderful variety of effects. Anyone watching him would have thought he was chewing over a problem. He began by taking it up languidly, indifferently, disarmingly, chewing with his front teeth, his mouth relaxed to the point where it was half open, when suddenly, without warning, he shifted the wad to the left side and began to work it over systematically between his molars. Very businesslike, he gave it an evenly paced pulverizing, and then, just before all the life ebbed out of it, he shifted it again to the center, where his teeth barely dented it, and his tongue turned it over and over in a revivifying massage. [11]

As the train entered another station, without interrupting this ruminating, he stuck his hand through the rubber lip of the door in a Napoleonic attitude, and when the door drew back he flung his hand after it. [12]

I could never chew gum like that, I was thinking, and then I saw the name of my own station through the open door and I jumped up and ran through it barely in time, absolutely confirming the lousy impression I had made on the sour-faced woman. [13]

At the top of the stairs the sun hit me in the eye. It seemed to me that the sun was always shining in Brooklyn, drying clothes, curing rickets, evaporating puddles, inviting children out to play, and encouraging artificial-looking flowers in front yards. Against my will, it warmed over an ineffable melancholy in me. I felt that it was a great democratic source of central heating for this big house in which everyone lived together. [14]

The streets were almost deserted, since everyone ate dinner at the same time in Brooklyn. I knew these streets so well I could have walked them with my eyes shut. There wasn't a tree I passed into which I hadn't thrown my knife, a wall against which I hadn't bounced my ball, a crack I hadn't avoided lest I break my mother's back. Now I saw them in slow motion; everything stood out in a kind of heavy-handed symbolism, as though I were the camera eye in an arty documentary film. When I was a boy, these streets had quickness and life for me, each detail daring me to do something, to match my wits, my strength, my speed, against them. Then I was always running. I saw things on the run and made my running commentary on them without breaking my stride, hurdling, skipping, dodging, but still racing forward . . . until one day I ran full tilt into myself and blocked my own path. [15]

The scene was made even more sententious by the fact that it was Sunday. There was a tremendous vacuum left behind by God. In contrast to the kitchenlike intimacy of the church on Thompson Street—which in its ugliness succeeded in projecting its flock's image on the universe—the spiky shells on these blocks had a cold, punitive look, and seemed empty except for those few hours in the morning when people came with neutralized faces to pay their respects to a dead and departed deity. [16]

From the corner, I could see my mother in the front yard. Her face was turned toward me, although I knew she couldn't see me at that distance. I had the feeling that wherever I was, her face was always turned toward me. Now she saw me, she was waving and talking. In a moment she would begin to shout. I was already smiling and gesticulating too. I modified my walk, making it playful. "Hello, Paul!" she was shouting. "How are you?" I was still too far to talk. I wanted to run, I always wanted to run those last few yards. I hated the last few steps, the final enormous gap, between us. Once we were close enough, like lovers in an embrace, we wouldn't be able to see each other so clearly. [17]

I seized her by the shoulders and bent to kiss her. As usual, each of us offered a cheek. Quickly we turned our heads, and somehow miraculously avoided kissing each other on the lips, our heads turning just far enough so that each kissed the other with half a mouth in the middle of the cheek, making three or four smacks for good measure.

My father was inside. He would have liked to come out too, but he felt he would be a spectacle, and besides he seemed to think that she ought to greet me alone, as though she were giving birth to me again. [18]

He met me at the doorway, and we clogged up there, gesticulating and embracing. We always gesticulated too much, we distrusted language and thoughts. And all the while we were shouting, as if we were singing an opera. "Take off your coat!" they were shouting, "Take off your tie!" Sometimes I almost expected them to ask for my belt and shoelaces, but I suppose they knew that, after all, there was no way of disarming the dagger of the mind. [19]

"Wait, I'll make you a martini!" my father shouted, and he ran off into the kitchen. "Sit down!" my mother shouted. "Make yourself comfortable!" Shoving me into my father's chair, she pressed the button on the arm and I was suddenly in a horizontal position. She switched the radio to WQXR, and one of the more familiar symphonies poured out like coal out of a chute. [20]

This chair had been a gift to my father on one of his birthdays. My mother was delighted by the idea of the button. I never liked it. It always struck me as uncanny. I felt myself straining in it, trying to keep my head up a little. My father came in with the martini. I saw that it was amber. He never thought to make himself one. Like a servant. [21]

The martini was sweet. Suddenly I realized that I loved them very much. But what was I going to do with them? [22]

"Here's the Book Review," my mother said, handing me the paper. They both sat down, waiting for me to read it. How could I read it with them sitting there watching me as if I were performing a great feat? I was a spectacle, they assumed I didn't want to talk to them. I understood too that, in a way, they liked to believe I wasn't there just for a visit, and it was perfectly natural for me to be reading the Book Review of a Sunday afternoon. [23]

I put the paper down, reassuring them that I'd read it later. We looked at each other for a moment, smiling. I felt that I was stretched out on a bier. Pressing the button, I allowed the back of the chair to come up. I smiled at my mother to show her I didn't mind the chair. I liked it, but I just felt like sitting up, I was such a bundle of energy. [24]

"Well, how's everything, Paul?" she said. From the time I had been two years old, they had called me Bud, but somewhere in the last few years they began calling me Paul the way the outside world did. "Everything's fine," I said, realizing of course that they had no idea what that everything embodied. This vagueness was our tenderness. They'd have loved to know, but they were afraid of finding out something which might have offended not them, but me. [25]

The dinner was ready. It was always ready when I arrived. Sometimes I had the fantasy of just walking by the house: my mother would be in the front yard, holding a box lunch in her hands. I would take the box without stopping. My face would be expressionless, hers grieving but controlled. My father would stand just inside the doorway . . . [26]

My mother brought in the roast and my father carved it with great concentration, as if he were carving out our destiny. He placed on my plate the portion he had always desired for me. My mother heaped potatoes, gravy, vegetables on my plate. "I know you like to eat," she said, smiling and heaping my plate still more. This was a fiction. I never ate heartily, but nevertheless I exclaimed, "You know me, Mom!" [27]

Pretending I could scarcely wait, I attacked the roast with knife and fork, while my mother held back to observe this. "Home cooking," I mumbled around a mouthful, these two words speaking volumes to her. I wondered what she thought I ate every day, whether she ever speculated for a moment that I might have liked it better. As a matter of history, the first time I ate in the Automat, when I was about twelve, I discovered that my mother was not an especially good cook, and this had hurt me as much as anything in my childhood. I could hardly swallow the food for years after that, but practice makes perfect, and I had learned to chomp with the histrionic absorption of a movie hero on a picnic. [28]

As we ate, we regressed in time, reingesting all the events that had separated us. We retraced our steps to the very beginning, and there, joining hands, we advanced again from the birth of the soft-eyed boy to my embarrassing and unassimilable prodigality there at the table. To their great surprise, it always came out the same. We always bumped up against the present. Each time we raised our eyes from the plate, we were startled to discover each other, so camouflaged by time. As soon as our eyes met, we jumped back, as from an abyss. In these encounters, we resembled two forever inhibited people who press against each other in the subway: both want the contact, but neither dares admit it. [29]

It was like my friend Andrew's description of the first analyst he went to. This one was not a Freudian, he belonged to a group which held our difficulties to be "interpersonal," and so instead of having Andrew lie on a couch while he sat behind him, they faced each other across a table. There Andrew would lay out all the disgusting things he had done, avoiding the analyst's eye for fear of showing shame or triumph, but sneaking furtive glances now and then, while the analyst, on his side, had his hands full dissembling disapproval or any other sign which might conceivably have disturbed Andrew's flow. Occasionally, however, in darting about the room and briefly lighting on the table like flies, their eyes would collide, and in that split second shockingly copulate in a deep obscene surmise. [30]

Our conversation consisted of answerable questions and unquestionable answers. As usual, my mother found that I looked thin. All my life I had managed to stay thin as a reproach to her, and on her side, as if a mother's role were that of a fanatic taxidermist, she had done her best to stuff me. She asked me where I took my laundry. "Aren't the prices outrageous? And the way they boil your clothes in all that acid, a shirt doesn't last six months." She was working around to suggesting that I bring my laundry to her. Maybe those dirty shirts would tell her what she was so anxious, and so ashamed, to know. A smear of lipstick, a smell, a stain, might paint a Japanese picture. [31]

My father discussed the last month's boxing matches. Since I occasionally watched televised bouts in a bar, this had become a regular gambit. With an old man's memory, which clings to things as a child clings to its mother, for fear of being abandoned, he re- called every blow. If I happened to disagree with him—by mistake, or because I wasn't following him—he revised his version accord- ingly. We fought those fights side by side. [32]

When he wasn't talking about boxing, his remarks were designed to show me that he was a liberal, a man who understands. Yesterday he gave up his seat in the subway to a Negress. Jews are smart. Every- body does things without knowing why. Nobody can say who's right and who's wrong. There are two sides to every question. [33]

I remembered him when he was ten feet tall and his every state- ment was a revelation of the absolute order of things. I tried to steer him around to himself, to push him gently back into his own indis- tinctly remembered convictions, but this only succeeded in panicking him. He tried to believe that the only difference between us was that I was "modern." He was going to be "modern" too, by denying everything he felt, and forgetting the few lessons life had taught him. He thought of my modernity as relentless and inescapable, a march of history which would let nothing—parents least of all—stand in its way. [34]

My mother was smiling, and as I watched her over a forkful of mashed potatoes I realized that she was still pretty. I knew that smile from way back, I remembered how it had once outshone the sun in heaven. Only, it had had more of a Mona Lisa character then, an ambiguity that gave it a special quality of romance. Where was that romance now? I wondered. Which of us was unfaithful, and why? Each was caricatured by a love we didn't know how to express. Afraid to feel, we were condemned to think, and at the same time not to think. When—and how—had our oneness become three? What ingredient was added to my mixture to turn it to poison? What alchemy iso- lated my substance beyond their—and my—understanding? There we were, playing a painful game of blindman's buff. We began by band- aging our eyes; then the bandages had fallen away and we had realized that we were blind. [35]

At last I judged that I had eaten enough, an exemplary amount.

With all my blood and nerves busy in my stomach, I relaxed, I became flatulent with affection. My mother saw my face go blank and she beamed. Belly to belly, that was the only true way to talk. [36]

My father was describing how, on the job, he had solved a problem that had stumped even the architect. He had just 'scribed a plumb line on the floor. "Well I'll be goddamned," the architect had said, "if old Pete hasn't gone and done it again!" As I listened to this story, I never doubted it for a moment, and I was proud of him. That was his reality, and in it he was still magnificent, just as my mother could calculate better than the Secretary of the Treasury, how much it would cost a newlywed couple to set up housekeeping. It was in these attitudes, like an old-fashioned photograph, that I thought of them most fondly, and although I had long since exiled myself from that Garden of Eden, it was something I could not root out of my feelings. This homely love was my history. Like a navel, it was a reminder that I hadn't been struck fully formed from my own brow. I remember a story an Army doctor told me, about a Negro soldier whose belly was ripped open in a fight. They sewed him up in time and saved his life, but when they pulled off the adhesive tape, his belly button—he had the old-fashioned protruding kind—came away with it. When he saw what had happened, the soldier was beside himself, in the full sense of that expression, and they couldn't calm him down until the doctor sewed his belly button back on. [37]

I knew how he felt. Although I liked to imagine myself unfettered by human history, faced only by free choices, exquisitely irresponsible, it was still comforting to know that I hadn't been born in a bad novel like most of the people who spent their evenings in Village bars. Although they too probably came from Brooklyn or the Bronx, I couldn't imagine them with families. They seemed to have risen spontaneously from rotting social tissues, the way flies were thought to generate in filth, or in a wound. [38]

I admit that whenever I considered my parents for any length of time, I generally arrived at a feeling of incredulity there too, but at least this is some kind of an emotion, and after all, how else can you

look at a mother and father who hatched you like a plot and then
couldn't read their own writing? They, too, were inevitably incredu-
lous, always wondering. I could see them right there in that moment
struggling with this puzzle which was hidden in the back of their
minds the way people you read about now and then in the newspapers hide their children in a closet or a windowless room for
twenty years. Always, without realizing it, they were wondering what
I was, whether to be proud of me or ashamed, whether my strangeness was genius, sickness, or simply evil, whether I had sold my soul
like Faust or was still learning to walk, whether I was a hero or an
abortion. In the familiar terms, I was a failure. I had neither money,
fame, nor any immediate prospect of either. At least if I had been
an idiot, lurching up and down the sidewalk in front of the house,
they could have lavished all their pent-up love on my helpless heart,
but as it was they were never sure. [39]

My father was still talking about the job. He seemed very proud
to have a hand in this particular building, which had been given a lot
of publicity and which was apparently expected to become a world-
famous monument on Broadway. As superintendent, he had a set
of plans, and he brought them out for me to see. I recognized the
name of a large low-priced clothing chain which sold standard stuff
on installments. Feigning a show of interest, I studied the plans.
Besides some very ill-adapted functionalist architecture, the building
boasted two tremendous figures—a male and a female nude—above
its facade, on either side of the store name like parentheses. They
were over fifty feet high, my father assured me, and would be draped
in neon lights. "They're like the Statue of Liberty on Broadway," he
said, and I knew by the tone of his voice that he was quoting somebody. "What are they supposed to stand for?" I asked, in spite of the
feeling I had that this question was all wrong. He looked at me,
surprised and a little embarrassed. He was searching his mind for an
answer, and although by now I didn't want an answer, I didn't know
how to stop what I had started. I looked at the plans again. The
figures were sexless, without even the pretense of drapery or a fig leaf.
I knew what they stood for. The Statue of Liberty, since it was a

French gift, may be presumed to have something under her robes, but these were American-made, this was the naked truth. [40]

My father moved his lips as if to speak, but said nothing. In spite of myself again, I turned on him inquiringly, and he dropped his eyes. "It seems like a mighty big job, Pop," I said. "They must have a lot of confidence in you." "You said a mouthful," he said quickly, plainly relieved. "The architect himself asked for me." [41]

Primitive tools—a saw, a hammer, nails, a square rule, a leveler— these were not enough. I looked at my father, at his innocent face which had been chiseled into homely, heart-rending lines by the simplest kind of considerations, at his jaw made square by practical decisions, his mouth made thin by everyday resolutions, his eyes kept clear and alert with estimations of length, breadth, and height . . . and it struck me then that his head might have been done by a sculptor with a warm feeling for texture and no talent for portraiture, a craftsman with no idea of art. [42]

Suddenly I felt a mushrooming urge to blurt out something—I don't know what— "I think you're great, Pop," or "I'm with you," or "To hell with them all," and this made me very nervous, so nervous I could hardly sit still. In desperation, I abruptly decided to leave. With my mouth still full of lemon meringue pie, I announced apologetically that I had an unbreakable appointment for which I was already late. I had been on the point of calling them up, I improvised, for that very reason, but I felt that even a short visit was better than none. I would come again soon and we would have a nice long talk. [43]

They immediately fell into a frenzy of reassurances. Talking both at once, drowning each other out, they assured me that I didn't have to give explanations to them, they certainly understood how busy I was, and they had not the most infinitesimal wish to interfere with these quintessential commitments. Perish the thought—perish, in fact, the mother and father who would interrupt for a thousandth of a second their son's glorious onrush toward his entelechy. . . . [44]

Caught up in their extravagance, I reiterated my determination to come again soon with all the fervor of MacArthur vowing to return to the Philippines. I again congratulated my mother for having served up a truly historic feast and made ready to leave, avoiding my own eyes in the mirror as I knotted my tie. [45]

My father left the room for a moment and reappeared in his coat. He would walk me to the subway, he said. I was on the point of protesting, but I knew I shouldn't, so I said, "O.K., Pop, let's go." I kissed my mother, and she walked out to the gate with us. [46]

Closing the gate behind me, I said, "So long, Mom," and she answered, "So long, Bud," slipping unconsciously into my old nickname again. The sound of it moved me more than I would have thought possible, and I impulsively kissed her again before my father and I faded from her sight. [47]

At the corner I looked back to see her still standing there, her features erased by distance, and I waved, although I knew she couldn't see me. To my astonishment, she waved back. I caught the movement of her arm in the corner of my eye just as I was turning my head. I couldn't believe I had actually seen it—I knew she couldn't see across the street without her glasses. I stopped and took a step back—she was gone. Had I imagined it? It seemed very important to me to find out, and then I realized that I believed she *knew* when I turned the corner, she *sensed* it. No, no, I expostulated with myself, she only knew how long it took us to reach the corner, and then she waved. . . . [48]

"What's the matter?" It was my father, asking why I had stopped. "I was wondering how Mom could see this far," I said. "She just waved at us." "Yeah, she waves three, four times," he said indifferently, and we started off toward the subway again. [49]

I was trying to dismiss a vague fear that he wouldn't stop at the subway entrance, that he would go all the way with me, then I reflected that he rarely came to visit me. My mother had never been to my place. "I can't climb all those steps," she would say, as if I lived on top of Parnassus. Once my father and I had walked, just as we were walking now, through the Village. He didn't remember the neighborhood very clearly—he said the last time he'd been there was before I was born—and he had looked around him like the sightseers who go through the streets in plastic-topped buses. On Fourth Street, we had passed a big fat lesbian dressed in men's clothes and with her hair cut like a man. My father favored her with a disapproving glance as she went by. "Put a dress on that bastard and he'd be a woman," he said, wholly unaware that it was. [50]

A few minutes later, as we were walking through Waverly Place, he swept his arm over half a century's changes and said, "You know, this used to be all sportin' houses around here . . ." and I could see that he was wondering how the simple, old-fashioned sportin' house— where you knew what you wanted and got what you paid for—had given way to this, had borne a brood of Hamlets and hermaphrodites whose sport was an ambiguous affair. . . . [51]

We had reached the subway entrance and I stopped, but he began to descend the steps. I seized him by the arm. "You don't have to walk me down, Pop," I said. [52]

He was surprised. "That's all right," he said. "I haven't got anything else to do." [53]

"Yeah, but what's the use of your breathing all those fumes and then having to come all the way up again?" I said, still holding his arm. [54]

He was disappointed, I could see that he wanted to walk me down. "O.K., Pop," I said, letting go of his arm and starting down, "I guess a few steps don't faze you, do they?" [55]

"No," he said, "I'm used to them," and we went down together and he came back up alone. [56]

PURPOSE AND STRUCTURE

1. A feeling of alienation may be identified by the author's evocation of a mood. Although the story is written from a single point of view, how does the author modulate it? How does the drawing upon sensory experiences bring the subject into focus? By what other means is it brought into focus?

2. The narrative moves in space from Village to subway to Brooklyn and back to the subway entrance; and moves in time, not merely from the

beginning to the end of the journey to Brooklyn but through the narrator's association back and forth from the present to his remembrance of childhood. What purposes are served by these devices?

3. What concrete details in pars. 1–6 orient the reader spatially (so exactly that you could draw a map of the area) and temporally? One means is by the interweaving of the prosaic and factual with the imaginative and speculative. Cite illustrations.

What causal relationship and contrast in the first paragraph anticipate the subsequent revelation of the narrator's sense of homelessness?

What purpose is served in par. 5 by the enumeration of the inhabitants of Washington Square? What implied contrasts do you find in the listing? This paragraph goes beyond locating the subject in space and time. In what way?

4. How do the sentence, "I didn't see any of my crew," and the final statement in par. 6, "I took a long breath like a deep-sea diver and went reluctantly underground," further identify the milieu in which the narrator lives and foreshadow the later events of the story? How do the details in pars. 7–9 advance our understanding of the author's purpose?

5. The succeeding paragraphs (pars. 10–13), focusing on the staring woman and the gum-chewing man, seem at first glance to break the continuity of the story. What do they contribute to bringing the subject into focus?

6. From the narrator's arrival in Brooklyn described in par. 17 to his leavetaking in par. 47, action and conversation are counterpointed by reminiscence, commentary, speculation, questioning, and free association. What particulars make you aware of his alienation? Cite illustrations of the discrepancy between what the narrator says and does and what he thinks and feels. What other contrasts can you find in the long section set in his parents' home? What analogies contribute to our understanding of his feelings? A number of likenesses emerge between his behavior and that of his parents. How are they implicitly set forth?

DICTION AND TONE

1. How does the narrator's mumbling about home cooking in par. 28 contribute to the picture we get of his being shaken by what has happened to his relationship with his mother? Cite other passages that convey his sense of loss.

2. To what audience do you conceive the author is addressing himself? Is he responding to attacks on the "beat generation"? to the platitude that youth does not respect its parents? Is he searching for an answer to the nagging questions he has posed for himself? Is he expressing his own sense of frustration, even despair, in not finding an answer? Are his associations a means of self confrontation? self indulgence?

3. The narrator speaks in par. 9 of his *delicate ego*. What other instances can you find in which he mocks himself by employing a vocabulary that is pretentious? How does the inflated language in par. 44 contribute to the tone and purpose?

4. Study in context the linking of the following italicized words: *Neanderthal madonnas* [2]; *neutralized faces* [16]; the *dagger* of the *mind* [19]; this *vagueness* was our *tenderness* [25]; *embarrassing* and *unassimilable prodigality* [29]; *fanatic taxidermist* [31]; *flatulent* with *affection* [36]; *homely love* [37]; *frenzy* of *reassurances* [44]. What effects are achieved? How do they contribute to purpose and tone?

5. With what concrete details, figures of speech, paradoxes, ruminations, clichés, and rhetorical questions does the narrator dramatize the role playing in which both son and parents are engaged (look particularly at pars. 32–37)? How do they illuminate the purpose? heighten the irony and pathos?

6. Identify the figure of speech (pars. 38–39) that the narrator uses to dissociate himself from most of the people who spend their evenings in Village bars. How does it make you aware of his individuality? How does the figure of the lurching idiot emphasize his sense of alienation and its accompanying despair?

7. How does the author achieve both immediacy and distance (see Perspective in Glossary)? Cite passages to support your answer. How does the alternatively subjective and objective approach contribute to both purpose and tone? When is the story most moving? Does the author avoid self pity?

APPLICATIONS TO WRITING

1. Write a narrative in which you identify your subject by means of setting and situation. The latter might be your return to an old neighborhood, a visit with a childhood friend, a weekend visit with your parents,

or a conference with one of your professors. Its effectiveness will depend upon your ability to wrest meaning from the experience; to evoke the feelings that will convey meaning; to select the details that will bring your subject into focus and clarify your purpose; and to choose the words which will have sufficient power to re-evoke the scene for the reader.

2. Identify someone you know who has many characteristics of the group to which he belongs but who is atypical. Bring him into focus by placing him in a setting which permits us to see him both as a member of a class and as an individual. Possible settings: a dormitory room; a class room; a reception following a poetry reading; a counseling session; a civil rights demonstration.

3. Although Broyard's story is about alienation, it is also about compassion and love. By specific reference to the structure, purpose, diction, and tone of the narrative, support the point of view that the son's love and compassion outweigh his feeling of alienation. Show how they are brought into focus. If you believe that the narrator may more accurately be characterized by aggressively selfish concerns, defend your position by specific references to the story.

Part Two

DEFINITION

Definition—in logic, the placing of the word to be defined in a general class and then demonstrating how it differs from other members of the class; in rhetoric, the meaningful extension (usually enriched by the use of detail, concrete illustrations, anecdote, metaphor) of a logical definition in order to answer fully—though often implicitly—the question, "What is . . . ?" Wilder begins his essay with the traditional method of placing his subject in a class (*genus*) and stating what qualities (*differentiae*) distinguish it from other members of the class. Forster limits his subject by explicitly excluding peripheral questions and particularizing his general question by personal example. Morgenthau develops his definition of the components of tragedy and greatness by comparing and contrasting Lincoln and Stevenson. When the subject to be defined is abstract and complex, as in Krutch's *Tragic Fallacy*, it usually requires an extended definition based upon an inquiry that extends beyond the subject of the definition. As a means of defining existential freedom, Dostoyevsky transforms the elementary technique of question and answer into an internal dialectic.

SOME THOUGHTS
ON PLAYWRITING

THORNTON WILDER

Four fundamental conditions of the drama separate it from the other arts. Each of these conditions has its advantages and disadvantages, each requires a particular aptitude from the dramatist, and from each there are a number of instructive consequences' to be derived. These conditions are:

1. The theatre is an art which reposes upon the work of many collaborators;

2. It is addressed to the group-mind;

3. It is based upon a pretense and its very nature calls out a multiplication of pretenses;

4. Its action takes place in a perpetual present time. [1]

I. The Theatre Is an Art Which Reposes upon the Work of Many Collaborators

We have been accustomed to think that a work of art is by definition the product of one governing selecting will. [2]

First published in *The Intent of the Artist*, edited by Augusto Centeno, Princeton University Press. Copyright 1941, by Thornton Wilder. Reprinted by permission of Brandt & Brandt.

69

A landscape by Cézanne consists of thousands of brushstrokes each commanded by one mind. *Paradise Lost* and *Pride and Prejudice*, even in cheap frayed copies, bear the immediate and exclusive message of one intelligence. [3]

It is true that in musical performance we meet with intervening executants, but the element of intervention is slight compared to that which takes place in drama. Illustrations: [4]

1. One of the finest productions of *The Merchant of Venice* in our time showed Sir Henry Irving as Shylock, a noble, wronged and indignant being, of such stature that the Merchants of Venice dwindled before him into irresponsible schoolboys. He was confronted in court by a gracious, even queenly, Portia, Miss Ellen Terry. At the Odéon in Paris, however, Gémier played Shylock as a vengeful and hysterical buffoon, confronted in court by a Portia who was a *gamine* from the Paris streets with a lawyer's quill three feet long over her ear; at the close of the trial scene Shylock was driven screaming about the auditorium, behind the spectators' back and onto the stage again, in a wild Elizabethan revel. Yet for all their divergences both were admirable productions of the play. [5]

2. If there were ever a play in which fidelity to the author's requirements were essential in the representation of the principal role, it would seem to be Ibsen's *Hedda Gabler*, for the play is primarily an exposition of her character. Ibsen's directions read: "Enter from the left Hedda Gabler. She is a woman of twenty-nine. Her face and figure show great refinement and distinction. Her complexion is pale and opaque. Her steel-gray eyes express an unruffled calm. Her hair is an attractive medium brown, but is not particularly abundant; and she is dressed in a flowing loose-fitting morning gown." I once saw Eleanora Duse in this role. She was a woman of sixty and made no effort to conceal it. Her complexion was pale and transparent. Her hair was white, and she was dressed in a gown that suggested some medieval empress in mourning. And the performance was very fine. [6]

One may well ask: why write for the theatre at all? Why not

work in the novel where such deviations from one's intentions cannot take place? [7]

There are two answers:

1. The theatre presents certain vitalities of its own so inviting and stimulating that the writer is willing to receive them in compensation for this inevitable variation from an exact image.

2. The dramatist through working in the theatre gradually learns not merely to take account of the presence of the collaborators, but to derive advantage from them; and he learns, above all, to organize the play in such a way that its strength lies not in appearances beyond his control, but in the succession of events and in the unfolding of an idea, in narration. [8]

The gathered audience sits in a darkened room, one end of which is lighted. The nature of the transaction at which it is gazing is a succession of events illustrating a general idea—the stirring of the idea; the gradual feeding out of information; the shock and counter-shock of circumstances; the flow of action; the interruption of action; the moments of allusion to earlier events; the preparation of surprise, dread, or delight—all that is the author's and his alone. [9]

For reasons to be discussed later—the expectancy of the group-mind, the problem of time on the stage, the absence of the narrator, the element of pretense—the theatre carries the art of narration to a higher power than the novel or the epic poem. The theatre is unfolding action and in the disposition of events the authors may exercise a governance so complete that the distortions effected by the physical appearance of actors, by the fancies of scene painters and the misunderstandings of directors, fall into relative insignificance. It is just because the theatre is an art of many collaborators, with the constant danger of grave misinterpretation, that the dramatist learns to turn his attention to the laws of narration, its logic and its deep necessity of presenting a unifying idea stronger than its mere collection of happenings. The dramatist must be by instinct a storyteller. [10]

There is something mysterious about the endowment of the storyteller. Some very great writers possessed very little of it, and some others, lightly esteemed, possessed it in so large a measure that their books survive down the ages, to the confusion of severer critics. Alexandre Dumas had it to an extraordinary degree, while Melville, for all his splendid quality, had it barely sufficiently to raise his work from the realm of non-fiction. It springs, not, as some have said, from an aversion to general ideas, but from an instinctive coupling of idea and illustration; the idea, for a born storyteller, can only be expressed imbedded in its circumstantial illustration. The myth, the parable, the fable are the fountainhead of all fiction and in them is seen most clearly the didactic, moralizing employment of a story. Modern taste shrinks from emphasizing the central idea that hides behind the fiction, but it exists there nevertheless, supplying the unity to fantasizing, and offering a justification to what otherwise we would repudiate as mere arbitrary contrivance, pretentious lying, or individualistic emotional association spinning. For all their magnificent intellectual endowment, George Meredith and George Eliot were not born storytellers; they chose fiction as the vehicle for their reflections, and the passing of time is revealing their error in that choice. Jane Austen was pure story teller and her works are outlasting those of apparently more formidable rivals. The theatre is more exacting than the novel in regard to this faculty, and its presence constitutes a force which compensates the dramatist for the deviations which are introduced into his work by the presence of his collaborators. [11]

The chief of these collaborators are the actors. [12]

The actor's gift is a combination of three separate faculties or endowments. Their presence to a high degree in any one person is extremely rare, although the ambition to possess them is common. Those who rise to the height of the profession represent a selection and a struggle for survival in one of the most difficult and cruel of the artistic activities. The three endowments that compose the gift are observation, imagination, and physical co-ordination.

1. An observant and analyzing eye for all modes of behavior about it, for dress and manner, and for the signs of thought and emotion in one's self and in others.

2. The strength of imagination and memory whereby the actor may, at the indication in the author's text, explore his store of observations and represent the details of appearance and the intensity of the emotions—joy, fear, surprise, grief, love, and hatred, and through imagination extend them to intenser degrees and to differing characterizations.

3. A physical co-ordination whereby the force of these inner realizations may be communicated to voice, face and body. [13]

An actor must *know* the appearances and the mental states; he must *apply* his knowledge to the role; and he must physically *express* his knowledge. Moreover, his concentration must be so great that he can effect this representation under conditions of peculiar difficulty— in abrupt transition from the non-imaginative conditions behind the stage; and in the presence of fellow-actors who may be momentarily destroying the reality of the action. [14]

A dramatist prepares the characterization of his personages in such a way that it will take advantage of the actor's gift. [15]

Characterization in a novel is presented by the author's dogmatic assertion that the personage was such, and by an analysis of the personage with generally an account of his or her past. Since, in the drama, this is replaced by the actual presence of the personage before us and since there is no occasion for the intervening all-knowing author to instruct us as to his or her inner nature, a far greater share is given in a play to (1) highly characteristic utterances and (2) concrete occasions in which the character defines itself under action and (3) conscious preparation of the text whereby the actor may build upon the suggestions in the role according to his own abilities. [16]

Characterization in a play is like a blank check which the dramatist accords to the actor for him to fill in—not entirely blank, for a number of indications of individuality are already there, but to a far less definite and absolute degree than in the novel. [17]

The dramatist's principal interest being the movement of the story, he is willing to resign the more detailed aspects of characterization to the actor and is often rewarded beyond his expectation. [18]

The sleepwalking scene from *Macbeth* is a highly compressed selection of words whereby despair and remorse rise to the surface of indirect confession. It is to be assumed that had Shakespeare lived to see what the genius of Sarah Siddons could pour into the scene from that combination of observation, self-knowledge, imagination, and representational skill, even he might have exclaimed, "I never knew I wrote so well!" [19]

II. *The Theatre Is an Art Addressed To a Group-Mind*

Painting, sculpture, and the literature of the book are certainly solitary experiences; and it is likely that most people would agree that the audience seated shoulder to shoulder in a concert hall is not an essential element in musical enjoyment. [20]

But a play presupposes a crowd. The reasons for this go deeper than (1) the economic necessity for the support of the play and (2) the fact that the temperament of actors is proverbially dependent on group attention. [21]

It rests on the fact that (1) the pretense, the fiction on the stage would fall to pieces and absurdity without the support accorded to it by a crowd, and (2) the excitement induced by pretending a fragment of life is such that it partakes of ritual and festival, and requires a throng. [22]

Similarly the fiction that royal personages are of mysteriously different nature from other people requires audiences, levees, and processions for its maintenance. Since the beginnings of society, satirists have occupied themselves with the descriptions of kings and queens in their intimacy and delighted in showing how the prerogatives of royalty become absurd when the crowd is not present to extend to them the enhancement of an imaginative awe. [23]

The theatre partakes of the nature of festival. Life imitated is life raised to a higher power. In the case of comedy, the vitality of these pretended surprises, deceptions, and the *contretemps* becomes so lively that before a spectator, solitary or regarding himself as solitary, the structure of so much event would inevitably expose the artificiality of the attempt and ring hollow and unjustified; and in the case of tragedy, the accumulation of woe and apprehension would soon fall short of conviction. All actors know the disturbing sensation of playing before a handful of spectators at a dress rehearsal or performance where only their interest in pure craftsmanship can barely sustain them. During the last rehearsals the phrase is often heard: "This play is hungry for an audience." [24]

Since the theatre is directed to a group-mind, a number of consequences follow:

1. A group-mind presupposes, if not a lowering of standards, a broadening of the fields of interest. The other arts may presuppose an audience of connoisseurs trained in leisure and capable of being interested in certain rarefied aspects of life. The dramatist may be prevented from exhibiting, for example, detailed representations of certain moments in history that require specialized knowledge in the audience, or psychological states in the personages which are of insufficient general interest to evoke self-identification in the majority. In the Second Part of Goethe's *Faust* there are long passages dealing with the theory of paper money. The exposition of the nature of misanthropy (so much more drastic than Molière's) in Shakespeare's *Timon of Athens* has never been a success. The dramatist accepts this limitation in subject matter and realizes that the group-mind imposes upon him the necessity of treating material understandable by the larger number.

2. It is the presence of the group-mind that brings another requirement to the theatre—forward movement. [25]

Maeterlinck said that there was more drama in the spectacle of an old man seated by a table than in the majority of plays offered to the public. He was juggling with the various meanings in the word "drama." In the sense whereby drama means the intensified concentration of life's diversity and significance he may well have been right; if he meant drama as a theatrical representation before an audience he was wrong. Drama on the stage is inseparable from forward movement, from action. [26]

Many attempts have been made to present Plato's dialogues,

Gobineau's fine series of dialogues, *La Renaissance*, and the *Imaginary Conversations* of Landor; but without success. Through some ingredient in the group-mind, and through the sheer weight of anticipation involved in the dressing up and the assumption of fictional roles, an action is required, and an action that is more than a mere progress in argumentation and debate. [27]

III. The Theatre Is a World of Pretense

It lives by conventions: a convention is an agreed-upon falsehood, a permitted lie. [28] ·

Illustrations: Consider at the first performance of the *Medea*, the passage where Medea meditates the murder of her children. An anecdote from antiquity tells us that the audience was so moved by this passage that considerable disturbance took place. [29]

The following conventions were involved:

1. Medea was played by a man.

2. He wore a large mask on his face. In the lip of the mask was an acoustical device for projecting the voice. On his feet he wore shoes with soles and heels half a foot high.

3. His costume was so designed that it conveyed to the audience, by convention: woman of royal birth and Oriental origin.

4. The passage was in metric speech. All poetry is an "agreed-upon-falsehood" in regard to speech.

5. The lines were sung in a kind of recitative. All opera involves this "permitted lie" in regard to speech. [30]

Modern taste would say that the passage would convey very much greater pathos if a woman "like Medea" had delivered it—with an uncovered face that exhibited all the emotions she was undergoing. For the Greeks, however, there was no pretense that Medea was on the stage. The mask, the costume, the mode of declamation, were a series of signs which the spectator interpreted and reassembled in his own mind. Medea was being recreated within the imagination of each of the spectators. [31]

The history of the theatre shows us that in its greatest ages the stage employed the greatest number of conventions. The stage is fundamental pretense and it thrives on the acceptance of that fact and in the multiplication of additional pretenses. When it tries to assert that the personages in the action "really are," really inhabit such and such rooms, really suffer such and such emotions, it loses rather than gains credibility. The modern world is inclined to laugh condescendingly at the fact that in the plays of Racine and Corneille the gods and heroes of antiquity were dressed like the courtiers under Louis XIV; that in the Elizabethan age scenery was replaced by placards notifying the audience of the location; and that a whip in the hand and a jogging motion of the body indicated that a man was on horseback in the Chinese theatre; these devices did not spring from naïveté, however, but from the vitality of the public imagination in those days and from an instinctive feeling as to where the essential and where the inessential lay in drama. [32]

The convention has two functions:

1. It provokes the collaborative activity of the spectator's imagination; and

2. It raises the action from the specific to the general. [33]

This second aspect is of even greater importance than the first. [34]

If Juliet is represented as a girl "very like Juliet"—it was not merely a deference to contemporary prejudices that assigned this role to a boy in the Elizabethan age—moving about in a "real" house with marble staircases, rugs, lamps, and furniture, the impression is irresistibly conveyed that these events happened to this one girl, in one place, at one moment in time. When the play is staged as Shakespeare intended it, the bareness of the stage releases the events from the particular and the experience of Juliet partakes of that of all girls in love, in every time, place and language. [35]

The stage continually strains to tell this generalized truth and it is the element of pretense that reinforces it. Out of the lie, the pretense, of the theatre proceeds a truth more compelling than the novel can attain, for the novel by its own laws is constrained to tell of an action that "once happened"—"once upon a time." [36]

IV. *The Action on the Stage Takes Place in a Perpetual Present Time*

Novels are written in the past tense. The characters in them, it is true, are represented as living moment by moment their present time, but the constant running commentary of the novelist ("Tess slowly descended into the valley"; "Anna Karenina laughed") inevitably conveys to the reader the fact that these events are long since past and over. [37]

The novel is a past reported in the present. On the stage it is always now. This confers upon the action an increased vitality which the novelist longs in vain to incorporate into his work. [38]

This condition in the theatre brings with it another important element:

In the theatre we are not aware of the intervening storyteller. The speeches arise from the characters in an apparently pure spontaneity. [39]

A play is what takes place. [40]

A novel is what one person tells us took place. [41]

A play visibly represents pure existing. A novel is what one mind, claiming omniscience, asserts to have existed. [42]

Many dramatists have regretted this absence of the narrator from the stage, with his point of view, his powers of analyzing the behavior of the characters, his ability to interfere and supply further facts about the past, about simultaneous actions not visible on the stage, and above *all* his function of pointing the moral and emphasizing the significance of the action. In some periods of the theatre he has been present as chorus, or prologue and epilogue or as *raisonneur*. But surely this absence constitutes an additional force to the form, as well as an additional tax upon the writer's skill. It is the task of the dramatist so to co-ordinate his play, through the selection of episodes and speeches, that though he is himself not visible, his point of view and his governing intention will impose themselves on the spectator's attention, not as dogmatic assertion or motto, but as self-evident truth and inevitable deduction. [43]

Imaginative narration—the invention of souls and destinies—is to the philosopher an all but indefensible activity. [44]

Its justification lies in the fact that the communication of ideas from one mind to another inevitably reaches the point where exposition passes into illustration, into parable, metaphor, allegory, and myth. [45]

It is no accident that when Plato arrived at the height of his argument and attempted to convey a theory of knowledge and a theory of the structure of man's nature he passed over into story telling, into the myths of the Cave and the Charioteer; and that the great religious teachers have constantly had recourse to the parable as a means of imparting their deepest intuitions. [46]

The theatre offers to imaginative narration its highest possibilities. It has many pitfalls and its very vitality betrays it into service as mere diversion and the enhancement of insignificant matter; but it is well to remember that it was the theatre that rose to the highest place during those epochs that aftertime has chosen to call "great ages" and that the Athens of Pericles and the reigns of Elizabeth, Philip II, and Louis XIV were also the ages that gave to the world the greatest dramas it has known. [47]

PURPOSE AND STRUCTURE

1. The first paragraph of the Wilder essay is almost a textbook definition (see Glossary). Wilder places the word to be defined (*drama*) in a general class (the arts) and then states four fundamental conditions which differentiate it from the other members of the class. Why begin so abruptly and obviously? Would a paragraph of introduction—possibly an illustration—add to the interest of this part of the essay?

2. Wilder is audacious. He defines a large area with great economy. His methods include an exposed outline with numbered parts, labeled illustrations, summary prose, and skeleton paragraphs.

How do these methods serve the purposes of definition?

3. The substance of Wilder's definition is not based on such externals as stages, actors, and scenery, nor is it a formal setting forth of rules. Why does Wilder define drama in terms of its conditions?

4. The definition with which Wilder begins his essay (par. 1) is a very complicated thesis, one with parts that he lists in numbered sentences. What would the effect be if the thesis were presented in ordinary prose—without the use of the sentence outline? Try rewriting it.

5. The thesis has sixteen parts. Show these in an outline. Does Wilder follow this outline in the body of his essay? If he deviates, tell how and why.

6. The subject seems far too complicated—too "big"—for a short essay. Why not develop the essay into a treatise, or maintain the present length but sharply restrict the thesis?

7. Having contrasted the novel and drama in pars. 37–43, Wilder joins them in the conclusion of his essay (pars. 44–47). Why? Why begin with a negative judgment of *imaginative narration* (par. 44)? Why is it rhetorically effective that Plato is among those philosophers (he is the most famous of them) who judged imaginative narration *an all but indefensible activity*? Taking par. 46 into account, would it be even more effective for Wilder to cite Plato by name in par. 44?

8. In the last paragraph (47) Wilder states that the theater offers imaginative literature its highest possibilities. What evidence does he present for this statement? Is this the most effective conclusion for his essay? Why not use a summarizing conclusion?

9. How does par. 46 lead to par. 47? Is par. 46 an argument for drama? Is Wilder too clever in joining these two paragraphs?

DICTION AND TONE

1. Why does Wilder introduce the second sentence of par. 19 with *It is to be assumed*? He has not been so careful in introducing his own opinions in the rest of the essay. Discuss whether he should have qualified more carefully—or presented more modestly—the materials of this essay. How would you describe the tone of this essay?

2. Is the last sentence of par. 11 coherent? Rewrite it, attempting a more effective statement.

3. Par. 28 presents a short definition. Expand it or argue for its adequacy.

4. Analyze the diction, tone, and paragraphing of pars. 37–43. Change them into a single paragraph without making any other change. Compare the two methods of presentation rhetorically. Which is the more effective in terms of the purpose of the writer? Now recast the materials of pars. 37–43, constructing the best single paragraph you can. What have you gained (or lost)?

5. Compare and contrast pars. 37–43 with Lawrence's *Nathaniel Hawthorne and "The Scarlet Letter,"* pars. 1–12. Consider especially their diction and tone. How do their purposes differ?

6. What does Wilder mean by the *group-mind* in par. 1? Why doesn't he define this term in par. 1? Does he define it in another part of the essay? Find the definition or discuss the writer's reasons for omitting it. Think of a more accurate and effective phrase than *group-mind*. Why not use *audience response* or simply the word *audience?*

APPLICATIONS TO WRITING

Wilder's definition uses an expository method of great economy and coverage. This method allows him to set forth the complex and fundamental conditions of drama in a short essay.

1. Define another of the arts, using Wilder's methods.

2. Define a game (for instance, baseball) using Wilder's methods. (Remember that his definition is based neither on externals nor on rules. See question 3 under Purpose and Structure, above.)

MY WOOD

E . M . FORSTER

A few years ago I wrote a book which dealt in part with the difficulties of the English in India. Feeling that they would have had no difficulties in India themselves, the Americans read the book freely. The more they read it the better it made them feel, and a cheque to the author was the result. I bought a wood with the cheque. It is not a large wood—it contains scarcely any trees, and it is intersected, blast it, by a public footpath. Still, it is the first property that I have owned, so it is right that other people should participate in my shame, and should ask themselves, in accents that will vary in horror, this very important question: What is the effect of property upon the character? Don't let's touch economics; the effect of private ownership upon the community as a whole is another question—a more important question, perhaps, but another one. Let's keep to psychology. If you own things, what's their effect on you? What's the effect on me of my wood? [1]

In the first place, it makes me feel heavy. Property does have this effect. Property produces men of weight, and it was a man of weight who failed to get into the Kingdom of Heaven. He was not wicked, that unfortunate millionaire in the parable, he was only stout; he stuck out in front, not to mention behind, and as he wedged himself this way and that in the crystalline entrance and bruised his well-fed flanks, he saw beneath him a comparatively slim camel passing through the eye of a needle and being woven into the robe of God. The Gospels all through couple stoutness and slowness. They point out what is perfectly obvious, yet seldom realized: that if you have a lot of things you cannot move about a lot, that furniture requires dusting, dusters require servants, servants require insurance stamps, and the whole tangle of them makes you think twice before you accept an invitation to dinner or go for a bathe in the Jordan. Sometimes the Gospels proceed further and say with Tolstoy that property is sinful; they approach the difficult ground of asceticism here, where I cannot follow them. But as to the immediate effects of property on people, they just show straightforward logic. It produces men of weight. Men of weight cannot, by definition, move like the lightning from the East unto the West, and the ascent of a fourteen-stone bishop into a pulpit is thus the exact antithesis of the coming of the Son of Man. My wood makes me feel heavy. [2]

In the second place, it makes me feel it ought to be larger. [3]

The other day I heard a twig snap in it. I was annoyed at first, for I thought that someone was blackberrying, and depreciating the value of the undergrowth. On coming nearer, I saw it was not a man who had trodden on the twig and snapped it, but a bird, and I felt pleased. My bird. The bird was not equally pleased. Ignoring the relation between us, it took fright as soon as it saw the shape of my face, and flew straight over the boundary hedge into a field, the property of Mrs. Henessy, where it sat down with a loud squawk. It had become Mrs. Henessy's bird. Something seemed grossly amiss here, something that would not have occurred had the wood been larger. I could not afford to buy Mrs. Henessy out, I dared not murder her, and limitations of this sort beset me on every side. Ahab did not want that vineyard—he only needed it to round off his property, preparatory to plotting a new curve—and all the land around my wood has become necessary to me in order to round off the wood. A boundary protects. But—poor little thing—the boundary ought in its turn to be protected. Noises on the edge of it. Children throw stones. A little more, and then a little more, until we reach the sea. Happy Canute! Happier Alexander! And after all, why should even the world be the limit of possession? A rocket containing a Union Jack, will, it is hoped, be shortly fired at the moon. Mars. Sirius. Beyond which . . . But these immensities ended by saddening me. I could not suppose that my wood was the destined nucleus of universal dominion—it is so very small and contains no mineral wealth beyond the blackberries. Nor was I comforted when Mrs. Henessy's bird took alarm for the second time and flew clean away from us all, under the belief that it belonged to itself. [4]

In the third place, property makes its owner feel that he ought to do something to it. Yet he isn't sure what. A restlessness comes over him, a vague sense that he has a personality to express—the same sense which, without any vagueness, leads the artist to an act of creation. Sometimes I think I will cut down such trees as remain in the wood, at other times I want to fill up the gaps between them with new trees. Both impulses are pretentious and empty. They are not honest movements towards money-making or beauty. They spring from a foolish desire to express myself and from an inability to enjoy what I have got. Creation, property, enjoyment form a sinister trinity in the human mind. Creation and enjoyment are both very, very good, yet they are often unattainable without a material basis, and at such moments property pushes itself in as a substitute, saying, "Accept me instead—I'm good enough for all three." It is not enough. It is, as Shakespeare said of lust, "The expense of spirit in a waste of shame"; it is "Before, a joy proposed; behind, a dream." Yet we don't know how to shun it. It is forced on us by our economic system as the alternative to starvation. It is also forced on us by an internal defect in the soul, by the feeling that in property may lie the germs of self-development and of exquisite or heroic deeds. Our life on earth is, and ought to be, material and carnal. But we have not yet learned to manage our materialism and carnality properly; they are still entangled with the desire for ownership, where (in the words of Dante) "Possession is one with loss." [5]

And this brings us to our fourth and final point: the black-berries. [6]

Blackberries are not plentiful in this meagre grove, but they are easily seen from the public footpath which traverses it, and all too easily gathered. Foxgloves, too—people will pull up the foxgloves, and ladies of an educational tendency even grub for toadstools to show them on the Monday in class. Other ladies, less educated, roll down the bracken in the arms of their gentlemen friends. There is paper, there are tins. Pray, does my wood belong to me or doesn't it? And, if it does, should I not own it best by allowing no one else to walk there? There is a wood near Lyme Regis, also cursed by a public footpath, where the owner has not hesitated on this point. He has built high stone walls each side of the path, and has spanned it by bridges, so that the public circulate like termites while he gorges on the blackberries unseen. He really does own his wood, this able chap. Dives in Hell did pretty well, but the gulf dividing him from Lazarus could be traversed by vision, and nothing traverses it here. And perhaps I shall come to this in time. I shall wall in and fence out until I really taste the sweets of property. Enormously stout, endlessly avaricious, pseudo-creative, intensely selfish, I shall weave upon my forehead the quadruple crown of possession until those nasty Bolshies come and take it off again and thrust me aside into the outer darkness. [7]

PURPOSE AND STRUCTURE

1. Forster's essay defines an aspect of property. This is a more difficult feat than it seems. For instance, the definition of property in the *Encyclopaedia of Social Sciences* is lengthy, brilliant, and satiric: its point is the near impossibility of defining such a vast entity as property. Forster sees the difficulties clearly, and meets them in three ways. First, he presents to the reader a concrete example—"my wood"—which he follows through the essay. Second, he carefully limits the aspect of property which he explores. And third, he is personal in nearly all that he writes about property. Is his final definition purely personal?

2. This little essay is so well-organized that it seems to mock organization. The thesis is prepared for and delimited in par. 1. Is it stated twice?

3. The last sentence of the essay begins, "Enormously stout, endlessly avaricious, pseudo-creative, intensely selfish. . . ." Find the sections of the essay that develop these points.

DICTION AND TONE

1. Why begin with Americans? Are they involved in the *shame* and *horror* of Forster's question (par. 1)? What tone results from using such words as *shame* and *horror* in a conversational essay?

2. Why does Forster write *blast it* in par. 1?

3. Property "makes you think twice before you accept an invitation to dinner or go for a bathe in the Jordan." Why join these two examples (par. 2)?

4. Forster's bird "flew clean away from us all, under the belief that it belonged to itself" (par. 4). To whom did it belong?

5. In the last half of par. 5 Forster seems to tear through the fabric he has established. The limited definition explodes, the concrete becomes abstract, and the personal becomes entangled with *our life on earth*. Has the writer failed in this section of the essay? Explain.

6. The last sentence of the essay contains the phrase *nasty Bolshies*. Why not substitute *immoral Bolsheviks?*

APPLICATIONS TO WRITING

1. Forster's essay illustrates one way to approach Definition. Write a definition that is concrete, carefully limited, and personal.

2. A bird flies through par. 4. Its flight makes Forster feel his property should be larger. (Notice the irony of the last sentence.) Write a para-

graph in which a concrete movement through space illustrates a general statement. For instance, a ride on the roller coaster may illustrate "Experience is *not* the best teacher." Or the myth of Sisyphus may illustrate "a rolling stone gathers no moss."

THE TRAGIC FALLACY

from *The Modern Temper*

JOSEPH WOOD KRUTCH

All works of art which deserve their name have a happy end. This is indeed the thing which constitutes them art and through which they perform their function. Whatever the character of the events, fortunate or unfortunate, which they recount, they so mold or arrange or interpret them that we accept gladly the conclusion which they reach and would not have it otherwise. They may conduct us into the realm of pure fancy where wish and fact are identical and the world is remade exactly after the fashion of the heart's desire or they may yield some greater or less allegiance to fact; but they must always reconcile us in one way or another to the representation which they make and the distinctions between the genres are simply the distinctions between the means by which this reconciliation is effected. [1]

Comedy laughs the minor mishaps of its characters away; drama solves all the difficulties which it allows to arise; and melodrama, separating good from evil by simple lines, distributes its rewards and punishments in accordance with the principles of a naïve justice which satisfies the simple souls of its audience, which are neither philosophical enough to question its primitive ethics nor critical enough to object to the way in which its neat events violate the laws of probability. Tragedy, the greatest and the most difficult of the arts, can adopt none of these methods; and yet it must reach its own happy end in its own way. Though its conclusion must be, by its premise, outwardly calamitous, though it must speak to those who know that the good man is cut off and that the fairest things are the first to perish, yet it must leave them, as *Othello* does, content that this is so. We must be and we are glad that Juliet dies and glad that Lear is turned out into the storm. [2]

Milton set out, he said, to justify the ways of God to man, and his phrase, if it be interpreted broadly enough, may be taken as describing the function of all art, which must, in some way or other, make the life which it seems to represent satisfactory to those who see its reflection in the magic mirror, and it must gratify or at least reconcile the desires of the beholder, not necessarily, as the naïver exponents of Freudian psychology maintain, by gratifying individual and often eccentric wishes, but at least by satisfying the universally human desire to find in the world some justice, some meaning, or, at the very least, some recognizable order. Hence it is that every real tragedy, however tremendous it may be, is an affirmation of faith in life, a declaration that even if God is not in his Heaven, then at least Man is in his world. [3]

We accept gladly the outward defeats which it describes for the sake of the inward victories which it reveals. Juliet died, but not before she had shown how great and resplendent a thing love could be; Othello plunged the dagger into his own breast, but not before he had revealed that greatness of soul which makes his death seem unimportant. Had he died in the instant when he struck the blow, had he perished still believing that the world was as completely black as he saw it before the innocence of Desdemona was revealed to him, then, for him at least, the world would have been merely damnable, but Shakespeare kept him alive long enough to allow him to learn his error and hence to die, not in despair, but in the full acceptance of the tragic reconciliation to life. Perhaps it would be pleasanter if men could believe what the child is taught—that the good are happy and that things turn out as they should—but it is far more important to be able to believe, as Shakespeare did, that however much things in the outward world may go awry, man has, nevertheless, splendors of his own and that, in a word, Love and Honor and Glory are not words but realities. [4]

Thus for the great ages tragedy is not an expression of despair but the means by which they saved themselves from it. It is a profession of faith, and a sort of religion; a way of looking at life by virtue of which it is robbed of its pain. The sturdy soul of the tragic author seizes upon suffering and uses it only as a means by which joy may be wrung out of existence, but it is not to be forgotten that he is enabled to do so only because of his belief in the greatness of human nature and because, though he has lost the child's faith in life, he has not lost his far more important faith in human nature. A tragic writer does not have to believe in God, but he must believe in man. [5]

And if, then, the Tragic Spirit is in reality the product of a religious faith in which, sometimes at least, faith in the greatness of God is replaced by faith in the greatness of man, it serves, of course, to perform the function of religion, to make life tolerable for those who participate in its beneficent illusion. It purges the souls of those who might otherwise despair and it makes endurable the realization that the events of the outward world do not correspond with the desires of the heart, and thus, in its own particular way, it does what all religions do, for it gives a rationality, a meaning, and a justification to the universe. But if it has the strength it has also the weakness of all faiths, since it may—nay, it must—be ultimately lost as reality, encroaching further and further into the realm of imagination, leaves less and less room in which that imagination can build its refuge. [6]

It is, indeed, only at a certain stage in the development of the realistic intelligence of a people that the tragic faith can exist. A naïver people may have, as the ancient men of the north had, a body of legends which are essentially tragic, or it may have only (and need only) its happy and childlike mythology which arrives inevitably at its happy end, and where the only ones who suffer "deserve" to do so and in which, therefore, life is represented as directly and easily acceptable. A too sophisticated society on the other hand—one which, like ours, has outgrown not merely the simple optimism of the child but also that vigorous, one might almost say adolescent, faith in the nobility of man which marks a Sophocles or a Shakespeare, has neither fairy tales to assure it that all is always right in the end nor tragedies to make it believe that it rises superior in soul to the outward calamities which befall it. [7]

Distrusting its thought, despising its passions, realizing its impotent unimportance in the universe, it can tell itself no stories except those which make it still more acutely aware of its trivial miseries. When its heroes (sad misnomer for the pitiful creatures who people contemporary fiction) are struck down it is not, like Oedipus, by the gods that they are struck but only, like Oswald Alving, by syphilis, for they know that the gods, even if they existed, would not trouble with them, and they cannot attribute to themselves in art an importance in which they do not believe. Their so-called tragedies do not and cannot end with one of those splendid calamities which in Shakespeare seem to reverberate through the universe, because they cannot believe that the universe trembles when their love is, like Romeo's, cut off or when the place where they (small as they are) have gathered up their trivial treasure is, like Othello's sanctuary, defiled. Instead, mean misery piles on mean misery, petty misfortune follows petty misfortune, and despair becomes intolerable because it is no longer even significant or important. [8]

Ibsen once made one of his characters say that he did not read much because he found reading "irrelevant," and the adjective was brilliantly chosen because it held implications even beyond those of which Ibsen was consciously aware. What is it that made the classics irrelevant to him and to us? Is it not just exactly those to him impossible premises which make tragedy what it is, those assumptions that the soul of man is great, that the universe (together with whatever gods may be) concerns itself with him and that he is, in a word, noble? Ibsen turned to village politics for exactly the same reason that his contemporaries and his successors have, each in his own way, sought out some aspect of the common man and his common life— because, that is to say, here was at least something small enough for him to be able to believe. [9]

Bearing this fact in mind, let us compare a modern "tragedy" with one of the great works of a happy age, not in order to judge of their relative technical merits but in order to determine to what extent the former deserves its name by achieving a tragic solution capable of purging the soul or of reconciling the emotions to the life which it pictures. And in order to make the comparison as fruitful as possible let us choose *Hamlet* on the one hand and on the other a play like *Ghosts*, which was not only written by perhaps the most powerful as well as the most typical of modern writers but which is, in addition, the one of his works which seems most nearly to escape that triviality which cannot be entirely escaped by any one who feels, as all contemporary minds do, that man is relatively trivial. [10]

In *Hamlet* a prince ("in understanding, how like a god!") has thrust upon him from the unseen world a duty to redress a wrong which concerns not merely him, his mother, and his uncle, but the moral order of the universe. Erasing all trivial fond records from his mind, abandoning at once both his studies and his romance because it has been his good fortune to be called upon to take part in an action of cosmic importance, he plunges (at first) not into action but into thought, weighing the claims which are made upon him and contemplating the grandiose complexities of the universe. And when the time comes at last for him to die he dies, not as a failure, but as a success. Not only has the universe regained the balance which had been upset by what *seemed* the monstrous crime of the guilty pair ("there is nothing either good nor ill but thinking makes it so"), but in the process by which that readjustment is made a mighty mind has been given the opportunity, first to contemplate the magnificent scheme of which it is a part, and then to demonstrate the greatness of its spirit by playing a rôle in the grand style which it called for. We do not need to despair in *such* a world if it has *such* creatures in it. [11]

Turn now to *Ghosts*—look upon this picture and upon that. A young man has inherited syphilis from his father. Struck by a to him mysterious malady he returns to his northern village, learns the hopeless truth about himself, and persuades his mother to poison him. The incidents prove, perhaps, that pastors should not endeavor to keep a husband and wife together unless they know what they are doing. But what a world is this in which a great writer can deduce nothing more than that from his greatest work and how are we to be purged or reconciled when we see it acted? Not only is the failure utter, but it is trivial and meaningless as well. [12]

Yet the journey from Elsinore to Skien is precisely the journey which the human spirit has made, exchanging in the process princes for invalids and gods for disease. We say, as Ibsen would say, that the problems of Oswald Alving are more "relevant" to our life than the problems of Hamlet, that the play in which he appears is more "real" than the other more glamorous one, but it is exactly because we find it so that we are condemned. We can believe in Oswald but we cannot believe in Hamlet, and a light has gone out in the universe. Shakespeare justifies the ways of God to man, but in Ibsen there is no such happy end and with him tragedy, so called, has become merely an expression of our despair at finding that such justification is no longer possible. [13]

Modern critics have sometimes been puzzled to account for the fact that the concern of ancient tragedy is almost exclusively with kings and courts. They have been tempted to accuse even Aristotle of a certain naïveté in assuming (as he seems to assume) that the "nobility" of which he speaks as necessary to a tragedy implies a nobility of rank as well as of soul, and they have sometimes regretted that Shakespeare did not devote himself more than he did to the serious consideration of those common woes of the common man which subsequent writers have exploited with increasing pertinacity. Yet the tendency to lay the scene of a tragedy at the court of a king is not the result of any arbitrary convention but of the fact that the tragic writers believed easily in greatness just as we believe easily in meanness. To Shakespeare, robes and crowns and jewels are the garments most appropriate to man because they are the fitting outward manifestation of his inward majesty, but to us they seem absurd because the man who bears them has, in our estimation, so pitifully shrunk. We do not write about kings because we do not believe that any man is worthy to be one and we do not write about courts because hovels seem to us to be dwellings more appropriate to the creatures who inhabit them. Any modern attempt to dress characters in robes ends only by making us aware of a comic incongruity and any modern attempt to furnish them with a language resplendent like Shakespeare's ends only in bombast. [14]

True tragedy capable of performing its function and of purging the soul by reconciling man to his woes can exist only by virtue of a certain pathetic fallacy far more inclusive than that to which the name is commonly given. The romantics, feeble descendants of the tragic writers to whom they are linked by their effort to see life and nature in grandiose terms, loved to imagine that the sea or the sky had a way of according itself with their moods, of storming when they stormed and smiling when they smiled. But the tragic spirit sustains itself by an assumption much more far-reaching and no more justified. Man as it sees him lives in a world which he may not dominate but which is always aware of him. Occupying the exact center of a universe which would have no meaning except for him and being so little below the angels that, if he believes in God, he has no hesitation in imagining Him formed as he is formed and crowned with a crown like that which he or one of his fellows wears, he assumes that each of his acts reverberates through the universe. His passions are important to him because he believes them important throughout all time and all space; the very fact that he can sin (no modern can) means that this universe is watching his acts; and though he may perish, a God leans out from infinity to strike him down. And it is exactly because an Ibsen cannot think of man in any such terms as these that his persons have so shrunk and that his "tragedy" has lost that power which real tragedy always has of making that infinitely ambitious creature called man content to accept his misery if only he can be made to feel great enough and important enough. An Oswald is not a Hamlet chiefly because he has lost that tie with the natural and supernatural world which the latter had. No ghost will leave the other world to warn or encourage him, there is no virtue and no vice which he can possibly have which can be really important, and when he dies neither his death nor the manner of it will be, outside the circle of two or three people as unnecessary as himself, any more important than that of a rat behind the arras. [15]

Perhaps we may dub the illusion upon which the tragic spirit is nourished the Tragic, as opposed to the Pathetic, Fallacy, but fallacy though it is, upon its existence depends not merely the writing of tragedy but the existence of that religious feeling of which tragedy is an expression and by means of which a people aware of the dissonances of life manages nevertheless to hear them as harmony. Without it neither man nor his passions can seem great enough or important enough to justify the sufferings which they entail, and literature, expressing the mood of a people, begins to despair where once it had exulted. Like the belief in love and like most of the other mighty illusions by means of which human life has been given a value, the Tragic Fallacy depends ultimately upon the assumption which man so readily makes that something outside his own being, some "spirit not himself"—be it God, Nature, or that still vaguer thing called a Moral Order—joins him in the emphasis which he places upon this or that and confirms him in his feeling that his passions and his opinions are important. When his instinctive faith in that correspondence between the outer and the inner world fades, his grasp upon the faith that sustained him fades also, and Love or Tragedy or what not ceases to be the reality which it was because he is never strong enough in his own insignificant self to stand alone in a universe which snubs him with its indifference. [16]

In both the modern and the ancient worlds tragedy was dead long before writers were aware of the fact. Seneca wrote his frigid melodramas under the impression that he was following in the footsteps of Sophocles, and Dryden probably thought that his *All for Love* was an improvement upon Shakespeare, but in time we awoke to the fact that no amount of rhetorical bombast could conceal the fact that grandeur was not to be counterfeited when the belief in its possibility was dead, and turning from the hero to the common man, we inaugurated the era of realism. For us no choice remains except that between mere rhetoric and the frank consideration of our fellow men, who may be the highest of the anthropoids but who are certainly too far below the angels to imagine either that these angels can concern themselves with them or that they can catch any glimpse of even the soles of angelic feet. We can no longer tell tales of the fall of noble men because we do not believe that noble men exist. The best that we can achieve is pathos and the most that we can do is to feel sorry for ourselves. Man has put off his royal robes and it is only in sceptered pomp that tragedy can come sweeping by. . . .[17]

PURPOSE AND STRUCTURE

1. The complexity of the concept developed in this essay requires an extended definition. Krutch relates tragedy to a hierarchy of classes and subclasses (the method of *classification*). Since the primary purpose of the essay is to present a theory of tragedy and the tragic view of life, the definition of tragic fallacy serves as a means of illuminating them. The author brings it into focus by placing it in a larger theoretical context (the method of *identification*). What other methods of exposition are used to develop his definition? Cite illustrations.

2. Not until par. 16 does Krutch use the term *Tragic Fallacy*. How does he develop his definition? In your own words complete the sentence: The tragic fallacy is. . . . Upon what assumption about man does the fallacy rest? What is the causal relationship between this assumption and Krutch's central thesis?

3. The tragic fallacy is a member of a larger class of figures of speech, namely, personification. What details in pars. 15 and 16 are brought to bear to distinguish the tragic fallacy from the pathetic fallacy?

4. Par. 1 does not include either the words tragic (or tragedy) or fallacy. However, it prepares for the later definition and its implications in a number of ways: the opening sentence establishes the largest class into which tragedy may be placed—that is, all works of art. The same sentence establishes a connection between the worth of a work of art and its ending. The second sentence declares that there is a causal relationship between the happy end and the existence of a work of art as well as between the ending and the function of art. The third sentence suggests a paradox. How do the verbs *mold, arrange,* and *interpret* illuminate the paradox?

5. How do the specific allusions to *Othello* and *Romeo and Juliet* (par. 2) contribute to the commentary on tragedy? How is the transition from par. 1 established? How does this paragraph anticipate par. 16? By what means does the author make value judgments?

6. Analyze the methods of development used in pars. 3–14 and show how each contributes to the definition of tragic fallacy as well as to the thesis. Note in each case the use of transition.

7. The sentence structure is varied and complex. Krutch is a master of parallel structure. Examine the first sentence in par. 2 and note the nouns, verbs, adjectives, and clauses which are balanced. Find other sentences in which parallel structure is especially effective. In your next composition, make a conscious effort to imitate the structure of par. 11 in which simple and complex series of items are used; in which there are a number of *not . . . but* and *not only . . . but also* constructions; and in which there is striking use of climax, antithesis, subordination, and emphasis.

8. What evidence can you offer that the definition of the tragic fallacy serves a larger purpose? In answering this question you will need to analyze the author's means of achieving unity and coherence.

DICTION AND TONE

1. Krutch's diction is formal and frequently abstract. However, in par. 15 one is prepared for the abstractions in par. 16 by his use of a number of concrete images and allusions which help to clarify the abstractions. For

example, par. 15 concludes with the phrase, *a rat behind the arras*. What does this allusion to *Hamlet* contribute to the tone of the paragraph? How does it help to explicate the meaning? For almost every abstract statement Krutch makes, he follows it in the course of the paragraph, or subsequent paragraphs, with concrete illustrations, qualifying statements, analogies, and antitheses. Demonstrate.

2. Krutch appeals to his reader's emotions as well as to his reason. If his diction is not emotionally charged, then why are we moved? If it is through tone, how would you describe it? One aspect of the tone is reflected in his nostalgic look at other ages in history. Another reason the tone makes an impact upon the reader is the awesome character of his subject. We are reading not just about tragedy but about the condition we all share; we are reminded not only of Juliet and Desdemona and Lear and Hamlet but of ourselves—our loneliness, our despair, and our doom. Identify other aspects of tone by examining Krutch's selection of illustrations, his arrangement of materials, the rhythm of his sentences, his use of balanced structure and climax, his figures of speech, even his use of italics.

3. Examine the author's use of verbs, which frequently carry a heavy burden. For example, note the force of the phrase, *struck down*, in par. 8. Comment on the function of the following verbs in context: the universe *trembles* [8]; the man who bears them has . . . so pitifully *shrunk* [14]; a god *leans out* from infinity [15]; a universe which *snubs* him . . . [16]; because we find Oswald's world more real we are *condemned* [13].

4. How does Krutch's use of literary quotations or reverberations of them contribute to the tone and purpose: the fairest things are the first to perish [2]; to justify the ways of God to man [3]; if God is not in his Heaven, then at least Man is in his world [3]; Love and Honor and Glory are not words but realities [4]; whatever gods may be [9]; in understanding, how like a God! [11]; *such* a world if it has *such* creatures in it [11]; who may be the highest of the anthropoids but who are certainly too far below the angels [17].

5. Justify the linking of the following words: *splendid calamity* [8]; *mere rhetoric* [17].

6. Note the sequence in the first sentence of par. 11: it moves from *him* (Hamlet), his *mother*, his *uncle*, to the *moral order of the universe*. How does Krutch's ordering of terms contribute to purpose and tone?

APPLICATIONS TO WRITING

1. Consider Krutch's view that tragedy cannot be written in the twentieth century because we can no longer believe that man is the center of the universe and because there is no moral order to be found in it. Defend or challenge his point of view by specific reference to a modern play. You will need to focus your analysis upon a definition of tragedy.

2. Define a view of life such as Zen, Beat, the Absurd. Attempt to place it in a larger class. Compare and contrast it with other views of life, illustrate its meaning, and discuss its implications.

3. Krutch has alluded to, or described, a number of tragic heroes. Ask yourself if there can be a tragic hero in the contemporary world. What would he have in common with a tragic protagonist of an earlier period? How would he differ? Can you make a case for John Kennedy, Adlai Stevenson (see the essay by Morgenthau), Robert Oppenheimer, or any other figure in modern times as a tragic hero? Develop a definition of a tragic hero by specific allusion to a particular person in history.

4. Krutch's definition of a happy ending in art differs from the popular conception. Present your definition of a happy ending by specific reference to a work of literature.

STEVENSON—TRAGEDY
AND GREATNESS

HANS J. MORGENTHAU

Adlai Stevenson has been praised and buried. His wit and eloquence have been duly noted; his honesty and his disappointments commented on. Yet these qualities do not explain the impact his death has made upon the people. After all, there have been other witty, eloquent, honest and disappointed candidates for the Presidency whom men have not mourned as they mourn Adlai Stevenson. What sets Adlai Stevenson apart from all the other seekers after high office of his time, successful or unsuccessful? What is the gift which only he has brought to American life, which made the vanquished shine more brightly than the victor? The answer is both simple and complex: It is the quality of greatness tinged with tragedy. The man in the street felt that tragic greatness without being able to define its substance. Everybody knew that here was a unique political figure, different from all others and in an undefinable, almost mysterious sense superior to them. Everybody also sensed that this political figure, in all his uniqueness, was more like ourselves than the common run of politicians (this is what we mean when we say that he was "more human" than they) and that his tragic failure was in some way the tragedy of all of us writ large. Adlai Stevenson was indeed

Reprinted from *The New Republic*, copyright 1965, Harrison-Blaine of New Jersey, Inc.

political Everyman. His promise was ours, and so was his failure, and the tears we shed for him we shed for ourselves. [1]

Wherein did Adlai Stevenson's greatness consist? Wherein does any man's greatness consist? It consists in his ability to push the human potential for achievement in a particular respect to its outer limits, or beyond them if they are defined in terms of what can be expected in the ordinary course of events. Thus we speak of great painters and great writers, great liars and great lovers, great statesmen and great merchants, great saints and great crooks. We call them great because they have done what others may do well, indifferently or badly, with a measure of excellence that at least intimates perfection. [2]

Adlai Stevenson was great in his relationship to power. He was not a great statesman because he did not have the chance to use power for the purposes of the state. He was not a great politician because he did not choose to be a politician. But he was a great seeker after power, and it was his very greatness in the pursuit of power that was, as we shall see, responsible for the tragedy of his failure. [3]

In order to understand the substance of Stevenson's greatness, we must remind ourselves that there are two ways in which to be great in the pursuit of power. The search for power ordinarily entails, at least in a certain measure, the sacrifice of the intellectual and moral virtues. It is in the nature of the struggle for power that the competitors must deceive themselves as they deceive others. Those who have chosen power as the ultimate aim in life must use truth and virtue as means to their chosen end and discard them when they do not serve that end. The prototype of this power seeker is endowed with what Russell Kirk in a contemporary reference has called "a canine appetite for personal power." He is a Borgia or a Stalin, the Machiavellian prince, who will stop at nothing to gain and hold the power he seeks. He will sacrifice all other values for the sake of power. His greatness consists in that single-minded, ruthless pursuit of power, of which lesser—and better—men are incapable. They stop at some point on the road to power, distracted and restrained by the common virtues of intellect and ethics. [4]

Man is capable of another kind of greatness in the pursuit of power, which owes less to Machiavelli than to Plato's postulate of the philosopher-king and to the Hebrew-Christian ideal of the wise and good ruler. That greatness consists not in the single-minded pursuit of power but in the ability to subordinate the pursuit of power to transcendent intellectual and moral values. Rather than being possessed by power, those men possess it; rather than being devoured by it, they tame it. History has indeed known few rulers of this kind. But they have, as far as I can see, all been secure in the possession of power, generally by virtue of the automatic character of monarchical succession. Those who had to fight for gaining and keeping power, which is of course the normal situation in a democracy, have generally been precluded by this ever-present concern from attaining that greatness. The best they have been able to achieve has been an uneasy *modus vivendi*, a compromise between the demands of power and the requirements of the intellectual and moral virtues, with power having an excellent chance of prevailing when the chips are down. Of those who could not take power for granted but had to fight for it, I know only one who has attained that greatness: Abraham Lincoln. And it is indeed impossible to think of the substance of Stevenson's greatness without reflecting on the greatness of Lincoln. What they have in common explains their greatness; in what they differ accounts for the triumph of the one and the failure of the other. [5]

What Lincoln and Stevenson have in common is a high degree of freedom from illusion, to which politicians—as all men—are prey, about themselves, about their actions, and about the world. What took the place of these illusions was a lucid awareness, both intellectual and moral, of the nature of the political act, of their involvement in it, and of the consequences of that involvement for themselves and for the world. That awareness gave them the intellectual distinction and moral sensitivity, which set them apart from the common run of politicians. It gave their actions the appearance of indecisiveness and the reality of moral force. It accounts for their personal qualities of eloquence, wit and sadness. [6]

Lincoln and Stevenson knew both the moral risks and the practical hazards inseparable from the political act. They knew that to act politically was to take a jump into the dark. Innocent people would suffer, and the outcome was uncertain. Moral absolution could not be bought with good intentions nor could success be vouchsafed through ingenuity. The actor on the political stage takes his fate into his hands. Try as he may, he cannot escape the risks and hazards of his acts. If he is of the run of the mill, he will consult the flight of the birds, the constellation of the stars, or their modern equivalent, the public opinion polls, and receive the illusion of that certainty which the facts of experience refuse him. If he is great in the manner of Lincoln and Stevenson, he cannot help but face the risks and hazards of his acts, to weigh them against the risks and hazards of alternative acts, to shudder at what he must do—and do it as though those risks and hazards did not exist. He acts in awareness, and in spite of, these risks and hazards. Here is the measure of the heroic dimension of Lincoln's actions. [7]

What the actor's mind knows, his action is ignorant of. It can afford to be determined and bold because the mind has done its task of knowing, weighing, and judging. It is for that very same reason that the act carries within itself the conviction of justice in the sense of being appropriate to the end to be achieved. What needs to be done will be done, but nothing more, is the message the act seems to convey. Here is the core of the moral force of Lincoln's policies. [8]

That contrast and tension between what the actor knows and what he must do accounts for his eloquence, his wit and his sadness. In both Lincoln and Stevenson, eloquence is more than a mere matter of rhetoric and literary skill; wit is more than a mere matter of fleetness of brain and quickness of tongue; and sadness is more than a mere matter of mood and nerves. They are the qualities of souls that have been formed by their awareness of what the political act implies, and by the burden of having to act nevertheless. [9]

Lincoln and Stevenson share the gift of eloquence and wit with other great political figures. One thinks of Bismarck, Churchill, and Adenauer. The quality of sadness is theirs alone. It is the function of an intellectual and moral sensitivity in the face of power which, so it seems, is peculiarly American. It gives immunity against that ultimate illusion to which even the intellectually aware and morally sensitive political actor is apt to succumb. His heroism makes him act; his intellect makes him explain himself; his wit makes him transcend the incongruities of his political existence at least in thought. And so he may delude himself into believing that now he has mastered the political world. Lincoln and Stevenson were incapable of that ultimate illusion. They knew that, when all is said and done, they were still faced, without remedy or escape, with the moral ambiguities and practical pitfalls of the political act. Knowing what they knew about themselves, their actions, and the world, they could not but be sad. Their sadness denotes the resigned acceptance of the moral and intellectual imperfections of the political world and of their precarious place within it. [10]

It is hardly necessary to point out that these qualities of greatness are more fully developed in Lincoln than they are in Stevenson. They were not clearly visible before Lincoln entered the White House; it was the pain of great decisions that brought them to the fore. Thus they have a grave and somber aura which Stevenson's qualities are lacking. Stevenson's greatness was not the result of an ineluctable confrontation between personality and fate: The only great decision he had to face, it is true three times, was whether or not to seek the nomination. Rather it was the spontaneous expression of a great personality in intellectual anticipation of the fateful decisions he might have to make. Hence the peculiar quality of playfulness, of the aimless intellectual exercise, which is alien to Lincoln. [11]

What is the relevance of this difference between Lincoln and Stevenson for the latter's failure to gain political power after his initial success in Illinois? The answer to that question is obscured and rendered speculative by the intrinsic hopelessness of the 1952 and 1956 campaigns and by his failure to win the nomination in 1960. But why did he pursue the aspiration, foredoomed to failure, of becoming Secretary of State? And why did he silently suffer for four and a half years the humiliation of being Ambassador to the United

Nations? Can these questions be explained away as accidents of history? Or do these persistent failures point to a fatal flaw, a tragic defect in Stevenson's greatness, which barred his way to power, but which might not have barred him from making great use of it had he been able to achieve it? I think indeed that there was such a flaw. In order to understand its nature, let us return for a moment to Lincoln. [12]

Abraham Lincoln, we have said, revealed his greatness only after he had reached the highest office. He made his way to that office as a politician competing with other politicians, seeking power in the manner of politicians, always tough and sometimes ruthless and devious. Lincoln made no bones about wanting power, and the people gave it to him. It was only after he had reached it that he also achieved that awareness of, and detachment from it in which we found the key to his greatness. [13]

Stevenson showed his awareness of, and detachment from, power from the very outset. No doubt, he wanted power. When it eluded him in 1952, he said that he envied one man, the Governor of Illinois. When as Ambassador to the United Nations and nominal member of the cabinet he had the trappings of power without its substance, he complained about the "disadvantage in being anywhere other than the seat of power." He never forgave himself for his indecision in 1960. He wanted power, but he wanted it only with intellectual and moral reservations openly revealed. He wanted power, but not with that "canine appetite," with that single-minded animal ferocity which carried his competitors in the Democratic Party to success. He wanted power, but he did not want it badly enough. His was a civilized pursuit of power in a barely civilized political world. Yet the people want their politicians to be wholehearted and uncomplicated in their pursuit of power. By being so, the politicians give a token that they can hold and use power when they have it. It was this distance between the core of Stevenson's person and the pursuit of power and the interplay between the two, articulated by him and sensed by the people, that fascinated the masses and gained him their admiration but not their confidence. [14]

It was that very same distance that saved the defeated Stevenson from the disintegration which is the common lot of the frustrated seekers of great power. They hate or drink themselves to death. Stevenson in defeat could fall back upon that moral and intellectual core of his person that remained unaffected by the lust for power. He remained what he had been: eloquent, witty, and sad, but now he was so in a peculiarly purposeless way. The desire for power, too, remained; yet surviving the possibility of its satisfaction, it became patently futile and carried within itself a measure of humiliation. [15]

Stevenson wanted to be Secretary of State, and I suggested him in 1960 to the President-elect for that position; for I thought then, as I think now, that he was far better qualified than his competitors. But it should have been obvious to him—and to me—that politically the appointment was impossible; for the victor did not owe him that much and, more importantly, he could not be expected to countenance the star of Foggy Bottom to shine brighter than the sun of the White House. [16]

Stevenson's acceptance of the ambassadorship to the United Nations, to which I was opposed from the outset, and his unwillingness to relinquish it reveal most poignantly the desperation of his pursuit of power. The services he rendered to the country in that position could have been performed as well by lesser men, and they do not compensate for the personal diminution he suffered as a mouthpiece for policies on which he had no influence and was but rarely consulted. [17]

Had Stevenson been more unrestrained a seeker of power, he might have disintegrated in defeat. Had he been less addicted to the pursuit of power, he might have given it up in defeat altogether and become one of the great reflective men of the nation. He did neither. What could already be discerned in 1952, 1956, and 1960 now became almost pathetically obvious: the conflict between intellectual and moral awareness and the pursuit of power, spoiling both. [18]

There, then, is the rub. The intellectual and moral component was too dominant in Stevenson's personality for the good of his political ambitions. It made Stevenson reveal his greatness prematurely. In a democracy, ordinariness, not greatness, gains power. Once a great man, such as Lincoln, has gained power under the cover of ordinariness, he can afford to bare his greatness to the multitude, but not before. Lincoln's greatness evolved from his ordinariness, buttressed by power. Stevenson's greatness was a gift of nature, not grown from the successful conquest of power, but anticipating it. Yet had Stevenson possessed that quality of ordinariness necessary for the democratic conquest of power, behind which his greatness could for the time being have been hidden, he would in all probability still have lost in 1952 and 1956 and the world might never have known how great a man he was. Thus all may have turned out for the best. Alas, poor Adlai. Such is the irony of your life. [19]

PURPOSE AND STRUCTURE

1. Although Morgenthau treats a number of seemingly diverse subjects—greatness, tragedy, power, eloquence, wit, sadness, tragic flaw—a single but extended definition emerges. Each of these subjects has a bearing upon the complex definition embodied in this essay, each must be clarified by its own definition, and each relates to the others. How does he bring them together into a unified and coherent essay? What is the principle of subordination? of emphasis? How does the focus upon Stevenson in every paragraph of the essay (even par. 8, the only one in which he isn't named, is about him) give unity to what is defined? In what sense is he a part of what is defined? What is finally defined? As you examine the paragraphs noted below, you will be better able to document your answers to these questions.

2. The opening paragraph brings the subject into focus in a number of ways, including those of paradox, and comparison and contrast. Locate and identify those ways.

3. What illustrations are used in par. 2 to support the definition of greatness? What two members of the series might seem on first thought to be incongruous? Justify their inclusion by a re-examination of the

definition. Would you have excluded morality or ethics from your definition of greatness?

4. Describe the method of development in par. 3. How are causal relationship and paradox used?

5. In the contrast of the two ways to be great in the pursuit of power
(pars. 4–5), what are the several modes of development?

6. What is the meaning of the seeming paradox in the first sentence of
par. 8 (you will need to understand the sense in which *actor* is used)?

7. What causal relationships are developed in pars. 9–18?

8. The meanings of the words *eloquence, wit,* and *sadness* (pars. 9–10)
have been extended beyond our ordinary sense of them. How are these
definitions developed? Why is the quality of sadness shared only by
Lincoln and Stevenson?

9. How does the phrase, *ineluctable confrontation between personality
and fate* (par. 11), help to point the contrast between Stevenson and
Lincoln?

10. How is the meaning of *tragic flaw* (par. 12) clarified by the comparison with Lincoln? How is the comparison sharpened by its meaning?

11. *Distance* is a key word in pars. 14–15. How is it equally relevant to
the points made in each paragraph? Would *integrated* be a suitable
antonym for *distance* in this context?

12. How does the concluding paragraph point up the chief difference between Lincoln and Stevenson? How does it sum up the author's view of
Stevenson? How does it cast light on the subject of the definition? What
reverberations from *Hamlet* do you note in "Alas, poor Adlai"? What are
the ironic implications of the fact that Yorick was a court jester? Explain:
"Thus all may have turned out for the best," and "Such is the irony of
your life."

DICTION AND TONE

1. Analyze the components of rhythm and balance in pars. 5, 6, 7, 10,
and note when they are most pronounced within the sentence, when
within the total paragraph.

2. How is emphasis achieved by the repetition of words and phrases?

3. How does the *Hamlet* allusion contribute to tone as well as purpose? Pay special attention to *Alas, poor Adlai*. Why does the author shift here to the first name?

4. Explain the metaphor of *the star of Foggy Bottom*.

5. How would you characterize the author's attitude toward his materials? Does his interjection of himself obtrude in the two instances in pars. 16–17?

APPLICATIONS TO WRITING

1. Write a definition of *tragic flaw*, drawing upon ideas suggested by the Krutch and Morgenthau essays and other reading you have done. Illustrate your definition by specific reference to a person whom you know or to the protagonist of a play.

2. Define an abstract term in such a way that the full illumination of the subject is provided by a paradox.

3. Compare the respective views of Krutch and Morgenthau by focusing upon the purpose, structure, and tone of their essays.

EXISTENTIAL FREEDOM

from *Notes from Underground*

FEODOR DOSTOYEVSKY

"Ha-ha-ha! Strictly speaking there's no such thing as will!" you may interrupt me, guffawing. "Today, science has already succeeded in dissecting a man sufficiently to be able to tell that what we know as desire and free will are nothing but—" [1]

Hold on, hold on a moment! I was coming to that myself. I admit I was even frightened about it. I was about to say that will depended on hell knows what and perhaps we should thank God for that, but then I remembered about science, and that stopped me short. And it was at that point that you spoke up. Now, suppose one day they really find a formula at the root of all our wishes and whims that will tell us what they depend on, what laws they are subject to, how they develop, what they are aiming at in such and such a case, and so on and so forth—that is, a real mathematical equation? Well, chances are that man will then cease to feel desire. Almost surely. What joy will he get out of functioning according to a timetable? Furthermore, he'll change from a man into an organ stop or something like that, for

From *Notes from Underground, White Nights, The Dream of a Ridiculous Man,* and selections from *The House of the Dead* by Fyodor Dostoyevsky. Translated by Andrew R. MacAndrew, Copyright © 1961 by Andrew R. MacAndrew. Reprinted by arrangement with The New American Library, Inc., New York.

what is a man without will, wishes, and desires, if not an organ stop? [2]

Let's examine the probabilities then—whether or not it's likely to happen. Now, what do *you* say? [3]

"Hm. . . " you say, "our wishes are mostly misguided because of a mistaken evaluation of what's in our interest. If we sometimes desire something that doesn't make sense, it is because, in our stupidity, we believe that it's the easiest way to attain a supposed advantage. But once all this has been explained to us and worked out on a sheet of paper (which is very possible, because it is contemptible and meaningless to maintain that there may exist laws of nature which man will never penetrate), such desires will simply cease to exist. For when desire merges with reason, then we will reason instead of desiring. It will be impossible to retain reason and desire something senseless, that is, harmful. And once all our desires and all our reasoning can be computed (for the day is bound to come when we'll understand what actually governs what we now describe as our free will), then we may really have some sort of tables to guide our desires like everything else. So, if a man sticks out his tongue at someone, it is because he cannot *not* stick it out and has to stick it out holding his head exactly at the angle he does. So what *freedom* is there left in him, especially if he's a learned man, a diploma-holding scientist? Why, he can plot his life thirty years in advance. Anyway, if it comes to that, we've no choice but to accept. We must keep repeating to ourselves that, at no time and in no place, will nature ever ask for our permission; that we must accept it as it is and not as we paint it in our imaginations; that if we're moving toward graphs, timetables, and even test tubes, well, we'll just have to take it all—including, of course, the test tube! And if we do not wish to accept, nature itself will—" [4]

Yes, yes, I know, I know . . . But there's a snag here, as far as I'm concerned. You must excuse me, ladies and gentlemen, if I get entangled in my own thoughts. You must make allowances for the fact that I've spent all the forty years of my life in a mousehole under the floor. So allow me to indulge my fancy. [5]

I will admit that reason is a good thing. No argument about that. But reason is only reason, and it only satisfies man's rational requirements. Desire, on the other hand, is the manifestation of life itself—of all of life—and it encompasses everything from reason down to scratching oneself. And although, when we're guided by our desires, life may often turn into a messy affair, it's still life and not a series of extractions of square roots. [6]

I, for instance, instinctively want to live, to exercise all the aspects of life in me and not only reason, which amounts to perhaps one-twentieth of the whole. [7]

And what does reason know? It knows only what it has had time to learn. Many things will always remain unknown to it. That must be said even if there's nothing encouraging in it. [8]

Now, human nature is just the opposite. It acts as an entity, using everything it has, conscious and unconscious, and even if it deceives us, it lives. I suspect, ladies and gentlemen, that you're looking at me with pity, wondering how I can fail to understand that an enlightened, cultured man, such as the man of the future, could not deliberately wish to harm himself. It's sheer mathematics to you. I agree, it is mathematics. But let me repeat to you for the hundredth time that there is one instance when a man can wish upon himself, in full awareness, something harmful, stupid, and even completely idiotic. He will do it in order to *establish his right* to wish for the most idiotic things and not to be obliged to have only sensible wishes. But what if a quite absurd whim, my friends, turns out to be the most advantageous thing on earth for us, as sometimes happens? Specifically, it may be more advantageous to us than any other advantages, even when it most obviously harms us and goes against all the sensible conclusions of our reason about our interest—because, whatever else, it leaves us our most important, most treasured possession: our individuality. [9]

Some people concede, for instance, that desire may be the thing man treasures most. Desire, of course, can, if it wishes, agree with reason, especially if one uses it sparingly, never going too far. Then desire is quite useful, even praiseworthy. [10]

But in reality, desire usually stubbornly disagrees with reason . . . and . . . and . . . let me tell you that this too is useful and praiseworthy. [11]

Let's assume, ladies and gentlemen, that man isn't stupid. (For, indeed, if we say he is stupid, whom will we be able to call intelligent?) But even if he isn't stupid, he is still monstrously ungrateful. Phenomenally so! I would even say that the best definition of man is: ungrateful biped. But this is still not his main defect. His main defect is his chronic perversity, an affliction from which he has suffered throughout his history, from the Flood through the Schleswig-Holstein crisis. Perversity and, therefore, lack of common sense, since it is well known that perversity is due to a lack of good sense. Just have a look at the history of mankind and tell me what you see there. You find it grand? Maybe so. The Colossus of Rhodes is impressive enough to have prompted Mr. Anayevsky to say that some consider it a work of man and others consider it a creation of nature. You find it colorful? Yes, I suppose there's plenty of color in human history. Think of all the military dress uniforms and the formal civilian outfits. This seems quite impressive in itself. And if we think of all the uniforms worn on semi-official occasions, there's so much color that any historian would be dazzled by it. You find it monotonous? Yes, you have a good point there. They fight and fight and fight; they are fighting now, they fought before, and they'll fight in the future. Yes, I must agree that it's a bit too monotonous. [12]

So you see, you can say anything about world history—anything and everything that the most morbid imagination can think up. Except one thing, that is. It cannot be said that world history is reasonable. The word sticks in one's throat. And here's what happens all the time: good and reasonable men, sages and humanitarians, try to live constantly good and sensible lives, serving, so to speak, as human torches to light the path for their neighbors, to prove to them that it can be done. And what comes of it? Sure enough, these lovers of mankind sooner or later give up, some in the midst of a scandal, and often quite an unseemly one too. [13]

Now, let me ask you something: what can one expect from man, considering he's such a strange creature? You can shower upon him all earthly blessings, drown him in happiness so that there'll be nothing to be seen but the bubbles rising to the surface of his bliss, give him such economic security that he won't have anything to do but sleep, nibble at cakes, and worry about keeping world history flowing—and even then, out of sheer spite and ingratitude, man will play a dirty trick on you. He'll even risk his cake for the sake of the most glaring stupidity, for the most economically unsound nonsense, just to inject into all the soundness and sense surrounding him some of his own disastrous, lethal fancies. What he wants to preserve is precisely his noxious fancies and vulgar trivialities, if only to assure himself that men are still men (as if that were so important) and not piano keys simply responding to the laws of nature. Man is somehow averse to the idea of being unable to desire unless this desire happens to figure on his timetable at that moment. [14]

But even if man was nothing but a piano key, even if this could be demonstrated to him mathematically—even then, he wouldn't come to his senses but would pull some trick out of sheer ingratitude, just to make his point. And if he didn't have them on hand, he would devise the means of destruction, chaos, and all kinds of suffering to get his way. For instance, he'd swear loud enough for the whole world to hear—swearing is man's prerogative, setting him apart from the other animals—and maybe his swearing alone would get him what he wanted, that is, it'd prove to him that he's a man and not a piano key. [15]

Now, you may say that this too can be calculated in advance and entered on the timetable—chaos, swearing, and all—and that the very possibility of such a calculation would prevent it, so that sanity would prevail. Oh no! In that case man would go insane on purpose, just to be immune from reason. [16]

I believe this is so and I'm prepared to vouch for it, because it seems to me that the meaning of man's life consists in proving to himself every minute that he's a man and not a piano key. And man will keep proving it and paying for it with his own skin; he will turn into a troglodyte if need be. And, since this is so, I cannot help rejoicing that things are still the way they are and that, for the time being, nobody knows worth a damn what determines our desires. [17]

Now you scream that no one intends to deprive me of my free will, that they're only trying to arrange things so that my will coincides with what is in my own interest, the laws of nature, and arithmetic. [18]

Ah, ladies and gentlemen, don't talk to me of free will when it comes to timetables and arithmetic, when everything will be deducible from twice two makes four! There's no need for free will to find that twice two is four. That's not what I call free will! [19]

PURPOSE AND STRUCTURE

A concept as elusive as freedom of will requires a method of inquiry rather than a simple definition. Dostoyevsky's speculation on freedom of choice takes the form of a dialogue between conflicting aspects of the author's self. This dialectical method provides an imagined adversary through whom the author can state what freedom of choice is not and establishes the tone by suggesting his ambivalence, torment, and alienation. In order, then, to understand the method of defining free will, notice the narrator's indirect statement of equivalence (*thesis*); note the anticipated objections to his remarks (*antithesis*); then ask whether there is a resolution of these two discordant points of view (*synthesis*).

1. *Freedom of will* is never explicitly defined; its implied meaning is most fully suggested in par. 17 and most adequately prepared for in par. 14. Formulate an explicit statement of equivalence after careful re-reading. On what causal relationships must your definition be based?

2. Note that in both his own voice and in that of his imagined adversary the author asks a number of questions which are then answered. Underline these rhetorical queries, study the responses, and then test the inclusiveness of your statement.

3. Although desire and reason are contrasted, they are not simple antonyms. Reason is subsumed under desire, which is described as a *manifestation of life itself* (par. 6). How do you know that they do not bear equal weight (par. 7)?

4. What illustrations are used in par. 12 to support this unequal division?

5. The need for transitions is complicated by the dialectical method, but the use of "I," "you," and "ladies and gentlemen" provides the clues to the speaker. How is the transition in thought achieved between pars. 8 and 9? In what sentences does repetition help you to follow the progress of the thought?

DICTION AND TONE

1. When the adversary in the simulated dialogue projects a future in which "all our desires and all our reasoning can be computed" (par. 4), the example of determinism cited is that of a man sticking out his tongue at someone. In the Garnett and Gurney translations, thumbing of the nose is used as an illustration. Which phrase better conveys the tone and purpose? Explain.

2. Why are the metaphors *organ stop* (par. 2) and *piano key* (pars. 14, 15) effective as descriptions of man without freedom of choice?

3. How does the allusion to *life in a mousehole under the floor* (par. 5) contribute to tone and purpose?

4. For what is *twice two makes four* a metaphor? Where else is an arithmetical metaphor used? Show how it is especially appropriate to the tone and purpose to draw a metaphor from mathematics. Do these metaphors serve a different function from those drawn from music? If your answer is affirmative, justify it.

5. In the sentence, "Desire . . . can . . . *agree* with reason . . ." (par. 10), *agree* is not the best word the translator might have used. Substitute a more idiomatic word or phrase.

6. In this series describing man—*stupid, monstrously ungratfeul, chronic perversity*—how do the implied distinctions contribute to tone and purpose (par. 12)? Ask the same question of the series of adjectives which conclude the rhetorical questions: *grand, colorful,* and *monotonous* (par. 12). What irony is contained in the example of monotony?

7. Man is imagined as having nothing to do but *sleep, nibble at cakes,* and *worry about keeping world history flowing* (par. 14). What single verb that would parallel *sleep* and *nibble* might have been used?

8. Demonstrate the effectiveness of the word *troglodyte* in relation to the title, *Notes from Underground*; to the implied definition of freedom; and to the tone.

9. State the paradox on which the definition of freedom is grounded.

10. As we have observed above, the use of the second voice contributes eloquently to the tone. It permits a special kind of play of ideas (not to be confused with *playfulness*). Try to characterize the tone that emerges from this meaning of dialectic. But more important is the tone that accrues from the *tension* between two interacting forces. Why is the resultant tone especially appropriate, given the subject matter to be illuminated and the purpose of the dialogue?

APPLICATIONS TO WRITING

1. Conduct a dialogue with yourself about a contemplated course of action in which there are apparent rather than real benefits, or about an experience in which you have rationalized your behavior.

2. Employing a dialectical method, explore a current manifestation of the computer civilization. It is still being seriously predicted that the computer may one day solve all of man's perplexing problems (see Skinner's *Walden II*). Works like Huxley's *Brave New World*, Orwell's *1984*, and Heller's *Catch 22*, however, satirized man's vain aspiration to diminish the importance of the human equation. In many sections of *Notes from Underground*, Dostoyevsky bitterly denounces the "Crystal Palace" as a concept in which reason is entrenched and life has been reduced to a mathematical formula. One or more of these works may be suggestive to you in finding a focus for your interior monologue.

3. Choice, as here defined, is grounded upon the option to express one's wishes and desires, however trivial or destructive, in order to know and assert that one is a man and thus to give meaning to one's life. Write your definition of freedom of choice by employing a dialectical method. You might pose for yourself one of the following questions: To what degree does man have freedom to choose? Assuming a limited power of choice, what governs one's choices? Why is one choice better than another?

Part Three

CLASSIFICATION

Classification—an arbitrary systematic arrangement of categories (classes) so that the larger categories include the smaller. By definition, all members of a class have at least one characteristic in common. This characteristic varies with the needs and purposes of the person doing the classifying. Bacon's elaborate classification scheme serves the purpose of logically revealing error; Woolf's fluid classification serves her purpose of revealing the reciprocal relationship between reader and writer; Bigelow's classification is little more than a device for organizing and clarifying a vast and complex area of thought. On the basis of freshly recognized characteristics, Cowley removes Hemingway from the class to which earlier critics had assigned him and reclassifies him.

IDOLS OF THE MIND

FRANCIS BACON

The idols and false notions which are now in possession of the human understanding, and have taken deep root therein, not only so beset men's minds that truth can hardly find entrance, but even after entrance obtained, they will again in the very instauration of the sciences meet and trouble us, unless men being forewarned of the danger fortify themselves as far as may be against their assaults. [1]

There are four classes of Idols which beset men's minds. To these for distinction's sake I have assigned names,—calling the first class *Idols of the Tribe*; the second, *Idols of the Cave*; the third, *Idols of the Marketplace*; the fourth, *Idols of the Theatre*. [2]

The formation of ideas and axioms by true induction is no doubt the proper remedy to be applied for the keeping off and clearing away of idols. To point them out, however, is of great use; for the doctrine of Idols is to the Interpretation of Nature what the doctrine of the refutation of Sophisms is to common Logic. [3]

The Idols of the Tribe have their foundation in human nature itself, and in the tribe or race of men. For it is a false assertion that the sense of man is the measure of things. On the contrary, all perceptions as well of the sense as of the mind are according to the measure of the individual and not according to the measure of the universe. And the human understanding is like a false mirror, which,

121

receiving rays irregularly, distorts and discolours the nature of things by mingling its own nature with it. [4]

The Idols of the Cave are the idols of the individual man. For every one (besides the errors common to human nature in general) has a cave or den of his own, which refracts and discolours the light of nature; owing either to his own proper and peculiar nature; or to his education and conversation with others; or to the reading of books, and the authority of those whom he esteems and admires; or to the differences of impressions, accordingly as they take place in a mind preoccupied and predisposed or in a mind indifferent and settled; or the like: So that the spirit of man (according as it is meted out to different individuals) is in fact a thing variable and full of perturbation, and governed as it were by chance. Whence it was well observed by Heraclitus that men look for sciences in their own lesser worlds, and not in the greater or common world. [5]

There are also Idols formed by the intercourse and association of men with each other, which I call Idols of the Marketplace, on account of the commerce and consort of men there. For it is by discourse that men associate; and words are imposed according to the apprehension of the vulgar. And therefore the ill and unfit choice of words wonderfully obstructs the understanding. Nor do the definitions or explanations wherewith in some things learned men are wont to guard and defend themselves, by any means set the matter right. But words plainly force and overrule the understanding, and throw all into confusion, and lead men away into numberless empty controversies and idle fancies. [6]

Lastly, there are Idols which have immigrated into men's minds from the various dogmas of philosophies, and also from wrong laws of demonstration. These I call Idols of the Theatre; because in my judgment all the received systems are but so many stage-plays, representing worlds of their own creation after an unreal and scenic fashion. Nor is it only of the systems now in vogue, or only of the ancient sects and philosophies, that I speak; for many more plays of the same kind may yet be composed and in like artificial manner set forth; seeing that errors the most widely different have nevertheless causes for the most part alike. Neither again do I mean this only of entire systems, but also of many principles and axioms in science, which by tradition, credulity, and negligence have come to be received. [7]

But of these several kinds of Idols I must speak more largely and exactly, that the understanding may be duly cautioned. [8]

The human understanding is of its own nature prone to suppose the existence of more order and regularity in the world than it finds. And though there be many things in nature which are singular and unmatched, yet it devises for them parallels and conjugates and relatives which do not exist. Hence the fiction that all celestial bodies move in perfect circles; spirals and dragons being (except in name) utterly rejected. Hence too the element of Fire with its orb is brought in, to make up the square with the other three which the sense perceives. Hence also the ratio of density of the so-called elements is arbitrarily fixed at ten to one. And so on of other dreams. And these fancies affect not dogmas only, but simple notions also. [9]

The human understanding when it has once adopted an opinion (either as being the received opinion or as being agreeable to itself) draws all things else to support and agree with it. And though there be a greater number and weight of instances to be found on the other side, yet these it either neglects and despises, or else by some distinction sets aside and rejects; in order that by this great and pernicious predetermination the authority of its former conclusions may remain inviolate. And therefore it was a good answer that was made by one who when they showed him hanging in a temple a picture of those who had paid their vows as having escaped shipwreck, and would have him say whether he did not now acknowledge the power of the gods—"Aye," asked he again, "but where are they painted that were drowned after their vows?" And such is the way of all superstition, whether in astrology, dreams, omens, divine judgments, or the like; wherein men, having a delight in such vanities, mark the events where they are fulfilled, but where they fail, though this happen much oftener, neglect and pass them by. But with far more subtlety does this mischief insinuate itself into philosophy and the sciences; in which the first conclusion colours and brings into conformity with itself all that come after, though far sounder and better. Besides, independently of that delight and vanity which I have described, it is the peculiar and perpetual error of the human intellect to be more moved and excited by affirmatives than by negatives; whereas it ought properly to hold itself indifferently disposed towards both alike. Indeed in the establishment of any true axiom, the negative instance is the more forcible of the two. [10]

The human understanding is moved by those things most which strike and enter the mind simultaneously and suddenly, and so fill the imagination; and then it feigns and supposes all other things to be somehow, though it cannot see how, similar to those few things by which it is surrounded. But for that going to and fro to remote and heterogeneous instances, by which axioms are tried as in the fire, the intellect is altogether slow and unfit, unless it be forced thereto by severe laws and overruling authority. [11]

The human understanding is unquiet; it cannot stop or rest, and still presses onward, but in vain. Therefore it is that we cannot conceive of any end or limit to the world; but always as of necessity it occurs to us that there is something beyond. Neither again can it be conceived how eternity has flowed down to the present day; for that distinction which is commonly received of infinity in time past and in time to come can by no means hold; for it would thence follow that one infinity is greater than another, and that infinity is wasting away and tending to become finite. The like subtlety arises touching the infinite divisibility of lines, from the same inability of thought to stop. But this inability interferes more mischievously in the discovery of causes; for although the most general principles in nature ought to be held merely positive, as they are discovered, and cannot with truth be referred to a cause; nevertheless the human understanding being unable to rest still seeks something prior in the order of nature. And then it is that in struggling towards that which is further off it falls back upon that which is more nigh at hand; namely, on final causes: which have relation clearly to the nature of man rather than to the nature of the universe; and from this source have strangely defiled philosophy. But he is no less an unskilled and shallow philosopher who seeks causes of that which is most general, than he who in things subordinate and subaltern omits to do so. [12]

The human understanding is no dry light, but receives an infusion from the will and affections; whence proceed sciences which may be called "sciences as one would." For what a man had rather were true he more readily believes. Therefore he rejects difficult things from impatience of research; sober things, because they narrow hope; the deeper things of nature, from superstition; the light of experience, from arrogance and pride, lest his mind should seem to be occupied with things mean and transitory; things not commonly believed, out of deference to the opinion of the vulgar. Numberless in short are the ways, and sometimes imperceptible, in which the affections colour and infect the understanding. [13]

But by far the greatest hindrance and aberration of the human understanding proceeds from the dullness, incompetency, and deceptions of the senses; in that things which strike the sense outweigh things which do not immediately strike it, though they be more important. Hence it is that speculation commonly ceases where sight ceases; insomuch that of things invisible there is little or no observation. Hence all the working of the spirits inclosed in tangible bodies lies hid and unobserved of men. So also all the more subtle changes of form in the parts of coarser substances (which they commonly call alteration, though it is in truth local motion through exceedingly small spaces) is in like manner unobserved. And yet unless these two things just mentioned be searched out and brought to light, nothing great can be achieved in nature, as far as the production of works is concerned. So again the essential nature of our common air, and of all bodies less dense than air (which are very many), is almost unknown. For the sense by itself is a thing infirm and erring; neither can instruments for enlarging or sharpening the senses do much; but all the truer kind of interpretation of nature is effected by instances and experiments fit and apposite; wherein the sense decides touching the experiment only, and the experiment touching the point in nature and the thing itself. [14]

The human understanding is of its own nature prone to abstractions and gives a substance and reality to things which are fleeting. But to resolve nature into abstractions is less to our purpose than to dissect her into parts; as did the school of Democritus, which went further into nature than the rest. Matter rather than forms should be the object of our attention, its configurations and changes of configuration, and simple action, and law of action or motion; for forms are figments of the human mind, unless you will call those laws of action forms. [15]

Such then are the idols which I call *Idols of the Tribe*; and which take their rise either from the homogeneity of the substance of the human spirit, or from its preoccupation, or from its narrowness, or from its restless motion, or from an infusion of the affections, or from the incompetency of the senses, or from the mode of impression. [16]

The *Idols of the Cave* take their rise in the peculiar constitution, mental or bodily, of each individual; and also in education, habit, and accident. Of this kind there is a great number and variety; but I will instance those the pointing out of which contains the most important caution, and which have most effect in disturbing the clearness of the understanding. [17]

Men become attached to certain particular sciences and speculations, either because they fancy themselves the authors and inventors thereof, or because they have bestowed the greatest pains upon them and become most habituated to them. But men of this kind, if they betake themselves to philosophy and contemplations of a general character, distort and colour them in obedience to their former fancies; a thing especially to be noticed in Aristotle, who made his natural philosophy a mere bond-servant to his logic, thereby rendering it contentious and well nigh useless. The race of chemists again out of a few experiments of the furnace have built up a fantastic philosophy, framed with reference to a few things; and Gilbert also, after he had employed himself most laboriously in the study and observation of the loadstone, proceeded at once to construct an entire system in accordance with his favourite subject. [18]

There is one principal and as it were radical distinction between different minds, in respect of philosophy and the sciences; which is this: that some minds are stronger and apter to mark the differences of things, others to mark their resemblances. The steady and acute mind can fix its contemplations and dwell and fasten on the subtlest distinctions: the lofty and discursive mind recognises and puts together the finest and most general resemblances. Both kinds however easily err in excess, by catching the one at gradations the other at shadows. [19]

There are found some minds given to an extreme admiration of antiquity, others to an extreme love and appetite for novelty; but few so duly tempered that they can hold the mean, neither carping at what has been well laid down by the ancients, nor despising what is well introduced by the moderns. This however turns to the great injury of the sciences and philosophy; since these affectations of antiquity and novelty are the humours of partisans rather than judgments; and truth is to be sought for not in the felicity of any age, which is an unstable thing, but in the light of nature and experience, which is eternal. These factions therefore must be abjured, and care must be taken that the intellect be not hurried by them into assent. [20]

Contemplations of nature and of bodies in their simple form break up and distract the understanding, while contemplations of nature and bodies in their composition and configuration overpower and dissolve the understanding: a distinction well seen in the school of Leucippus and Democritus as compared with the other philosophies. For that school is so busied with the particles that it hardly attends to the structure; while the others are so lost in admiration of the structure that they do not penetrate to this simplicity of nature. These kinds of contemplation should therefore be alternated and taken by turns; that so the understanding may be rendered at once penetrating and comprehensive, and the inconveniences above mentioned, with the idols which proceed from them, may be avoided. [21]

Let such then be our provision and contemplative prudence for keeping off and dislodging the *Idols of the Cave*, which grow for the most part either out of the predominance of a favourite subject, or out of an excessive tendency to compare or to distinguish, or out of partiality for particular ages, or out of the largeness or minuteness of the objects contemplated. And generally let every student of nature take this as a rule—that whatever his mind seizes and dwells upon with peculiar satisfaction is to be held in suspicion, and that so much the more care is to be taken in dealing with such questions to keep the understanding even and clear. [22]

But the *Idols of the Marketplace* are the most troublesome of all: idols which have crept into the understanding through the alliances of words and names. For men believe that their reason governs words; but it is also true that words react on the understanding; and this it is that has rendered philosophy and the sciences sophistical and inactive. Now words, being commonly framed and applied according to the capacity of the vulgar, follow those lines of division which are most obvious to the vulgar understanding. And whenever an understanding of greater acuteness or a more diligent observation would alter those lines to suit the true divisions of nature, words stand in the way and resist the change. Whence it comes to pass that the high and formal discussions of learned men end oftentimes in disputes about words and names; with which (according to the use and wisdom of the mathematicians) it would be more prudent to begin, and so by means of definitions reduce them to order. Yet even definitions cannot cure this evil in dealing with natural and material things; since the definitions themselves consist of words, and those words beget others: so that it is necessary to recur to individual instances, and those in due series and order; as I shall say presently when I come to the method and scheme for the formation of notions and axioms. [23]

The idols imposed by words on the understanding are of two kinds. They are either names of things which do not exist (for as there are things left unnamed through lack of observation, so likewise are there names which result from fantastic suppositions and to which nothing in reality corresponds), or they are names of things which exist, but yet confused and ill-defined, and hastily and irregularly derived from realities. Of the former kind are Fortune, the Prime Mover, Planetary

Orbits, Element of Fire, and like fictions which owe their origin to false and idle theories. And this class of idols is more easily expelled, because to get rid of them it is only necessary that all theories should be steadily rejected and dismissed as obsolete. [24]

But the other class, which springs out of a faulty and unskillful abstraction, is intricate and deeply rooted. Let us take for example such a word as *humid*; and see how far the several things which the word is used to signify agree with each other; and we shall find the word *humid* to be nothing else than a mark loosely and confusedly applied to denote a variety of actions which will not bear to be reduced to any constant meaning. For it both signifies that which easily spreads itself round any other body; and that which in itself is indeterminate and cannot solidise; and that which readily yields in every direction; and that which easily divides and scatters itself; and that which easily unites and collects itself; and that which readily flows and is put in motion; and that which readily clings to another body and wets it; and that which is easily reduced to a liquid, or being solid easily melts. Accordingly when you come to apply the word—if you take it in one sense, flame is humid; if in another, air is not humid; if in another, fine dust is humid; if in another, glass is humid. So that it is easy to see that the notion is taken by abstraction only from water and common and ordinary liquids, without any due verification. [25]

There are however in words certain degrees of distortion and error. One of the least faulty kinds is that of names of substances, especially of lowest species and well-deduced (for the notion of *chalk* and of *mud* is good, of *earth* bad); a more faulty kind is that of actions, as *to generate, to corrupt, to alter*; the most faulty is of qualities (except such as are the immediate objects of the sense) as *heavy, light, rare, dense*, and the like. Yet in all these cases some notions are of necessity a little better than others, in proportion to the greater variety of subjects that fall within the range of the human sense. [26]

But the *Idols of the Theatre* are not innate, nor do they steal into the understanding secretly, but are plainly impressed and received into the mind from the play-books of philosophical systems and the perverted rules of demonstration. To attempt refutations in this case would be merely inconsistent with what I have already said: for since we agree neither upon principles nor upon demonstrations there is no place for argument. And this is so far well, inasmuch as it leaves the honour of the ancients untouched. For they are no wise disparaged—the question between them and me being only as to the way. For as the saying is, the lame man who keeps the right road outstrips the runner who takes a wrong one. Nay it is obvious that when a man runs the wrong way, the more active and swift he is the further he will go astray. [27]

But the course I propose for the discovery of sciences is such as leaves but little to the acuteness and strength of wits, but places all wits and understandings nearly on a level. For as in the drawing of a straight line or a perfect circle, much depends on the steadiness and practice of the hand, if it be done by aim of hand only, but if with the aid of rule or compass, little or nothing: so is it exactly with my plan. But though particular confutations would be of no avail, yet touching the sects and general divisions of such systems I must say something; something also touching the external signs which show that they are unsound; and finally something touching the causes of such great infelicity and of such lasting and general agreement in error; that so the access to truth may be made less difficult, and the human understanding may the more willingly submit to its purgation and dismiss its idols. [28]

PURPOSE AND STRUCTURE

1. In par. 2 Bacon names the four idols he is going to discuss. They can be represented diagrammatically as follows:

Idols

| Idols of Tribe | Idols of Cave | Idols of Marketplace | Idols of Theater |

How are pars. 4 to 7 related to the chart of par. 2?

2. Pars. 9–15 all begin with a statement about "the human understanding." How do these paragraphs relate to par. 4? They may be added to the chart:

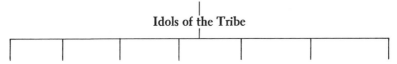

3. What kind of paragraph is 16? How many alternative causes are offered? How do they relate to the chart in question 2?

4. How do pars. 18–21 relate to 17? How does 17 relate to 5? If this information is added, it will look like this:

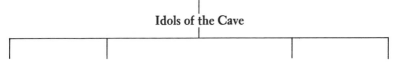

5. What kind of par. is 22? How does it compare with 16? How many alternative causes are offered? How do they relate to the chart in question 4?

6. Par. 23, like 17, introduces the next classification. Because this class is "most troublesome of all," the paragraph has a relatively lengthy explanation. How does it relate to 6?

7. Par. 24 introduces a subdivision found in none of the previous classes. The first two sentences report that the idols are of two kinds: names of things which do not exist; names of things which exist but are ill-defined. On the chart, this information would be indicated as follows:

Bacon rapidly disposes of the first category with a number of short examples. The second category he subdivides into three degrees of distortion: least, more, and most faulty. This information would appear on the diagram in this manner:

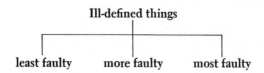

Now assemble the entire diagram. Don't forget the last idol.

8. For almost every one of his divisions and subdivisions Bacon provides an example or illustration. Enter at least one example for every entry on your classification chart wherever possible. Which divisions have no examples?

This method of organization and development is known as classification and illustration.

DICTION AND TONE

1. Parts of this selection from the *Novum Organum* have an archaic flavor: words like *instauration* and *whence* have disappeared from common usage; *vulgar* has changed meaning. Locate these words in a dictionary. What elements other than diction contribute to this flavor? Which examples are no longer meaningful to a modern reader?

2. Bacon frequently uses vivid imagery. The concept of *idols* of the mind is imagistic. Trace the figure he uses through pars. 4–5; identify the figures of speech in the last two paragraphs.

APPLICATIONS TO WRITING

In planning a classification paper it is not ordinarily necessary to chart your classifications, but on your first paper such a chart may be helpful. Classification reverses your ordering of experience of the world, for you *first* have individual experiences which you *later* group into classes. In thinking about your subject, it might be well to plan your illustrations first and then formulate your classes.

1. Some suggested topics: Idols of the American Mind; The Class Lines that Divide America (you may use economic, cultural, or social criteria, but only one criterion should apply at each stage of your classification); Books I Enjoy; Books I Never Finished Reading; Dates; Teachers; Emotional Obstructions to Clear Thinking; Types of Foreign Movies.

2. Select one of the idols and define it in your own words. Develop your composition by means of contemporary illustrations.

A PRIMER OF
EXISTENTIALISM

GORDON E. BIGELOW

For some years I fought the word by irritably looking the other way whenever I stumbled across it, hoping that like dadaism and some of the other "isms" of the French *avant garde* it would go away if I ignored it. But existentialism was apparently more than the picture it evoked of uncombed beards, smoky basement cafes, and French beatniks regaling one another between sips of absinthe with brilliant variations on the theme of despair. It turned out to be of major importance to literature and the arts, to philosophy and theology, and of increasing importance to the social sciences. To learn more about it, I read several of the self-styled introductions to the subject, with the baffled sensation of a man who reads a critical introduction to a novel only to find that he must read the novel before he can understand the introduction. Therefore, I should like to provide here something most discussions of existentialism take for granted, a simple statement of its basic characteristics. This is a reckless thing to do because there are several kinds of existentialism and what one says of one kind may not be true of another, but there is an area of agreement, and it is this common ground that I should like to set forth here. We should not run into trouble so long as we

From *College English*, December 1961. Reprinted with the permission of the National Council of Teachers of English and Gordon E. Bigelow.

understand from the outset that the six major themes outlined below will apply in varying degrees to particular existentialists. A reader should be able to go from here to the existentialists themselves, to the more specialized critiques of them, or be able to recognize an existentialist theme or coloration in literature when he sees it. [1]

A word first about the kinds of existentialism. Like transcendentalism of the last century, there are almost as many varieties of this *ism* as there are individual writers to whom the word is applied (not all of them claim it). But without being facetious we might group them into two main kinds, the *ungodly* and the *godly*. To take the ungodly or atheistic first, we would list as the chief spokesmen among many others Jean-Paul Sartre, Albert Camus, and Simone de Beauvoir. Several of this important group of French writers had rigorous and significant experience in the Resistance during the Nazi occupation of France in World War II. Out of the despair which came with the collapse of their nation during those terrible years they found unexpected strength in the single indomitable human spirit, which even under severe torture could maintain the spirit of resistance, the unextinguishable ability to say "No." From this irreducible core in the human spirit, they erected after the war a philosophy which was a twentieth-century variation of the philosophy of Descartes. But instead of saying "I think, therefore I am," they said "I can say No, therefore I exist." As we shall presently see, the use of the word "exist" is of prime significance. This group is chiefly responsible for giving existentialism its status in the popular mind as a literary-philosophical cult. [2]

Of the godly or theistic existentialists we should mention first a mid-nineteenth-century Danish writer, Søren Kierkegaard; two contemporary French Roman Catholics, Gabriel Marcel and Jacques Maritain; two Protestant theologians, Paul Tillich and Nicholas Berdyaev; and Martin Buber, an important contemporary Jewish theologian. Taken together, their writings constitute one of the most significant developments in modern theology. Behind both groups of existentialists stand other important figures, chiefly philosophers, who exert powerful influence upon the movement—Blaise Pascal, Friedrich Nietzsche, Henri Bergson, Martin Heidegger, Karl Jaspers, among others. Several literary figures, notably Tolstoy and Dostoievsky, are frequently cited because existentialist attitudes and themes are prominent in their writings. The eclectic nature of this movement should already be sufficiently clear and the danger of applying too rigidly to any particular figure the general characteristics of the movement which I now make bold to describe: [3]

I. Existence before Essence

Existentialism gets its name from an insistence that human life is understandable only in terms of an individual man's existence, his particular experience of life. It says that a man *lives* (has existence) rather than *is* (has being or essence), and that every man's experience of life is unique, radically different from everyone else's and can be understood truly only in terms of his involvement in life or commitment to it. It strenuously shuns that view which assumes an ideal of Man or Mankind, a universal of human nature of which each man is only one example. It eschews the question of Greek philosophy, "*What is mankind?*" which suggests that man can be defined if he is ranged in his proper place in the order of nature; it asks instead the question of Job and St. Augustine, "*Who am I?*" with its suggestion of the uniqueness and mystery of each human life and its emphasis upon the subjective or personal rather than the objective or impersonal. From the outside a man appears to be just another natural creature; from the inside he is an entire universe, the center of infinity. The existentialist insists upon this latter radically subjective view, and from this grows much of the rest of existentialism. [4]

II. Reason Is Impotent to Deal with the Depths of Human Life

There are two parts to this proposition—first, that human reason is relatively weak and imperfect, and second, that there are dark places in human life which are "non-reason" and to which reason scarcely penetrates. Since Plato, Western civilization has usually assumed a separation of reason from the rest of the human psyche, and has glorified reason as suited to command the nonrational part. The classic statement of this separation appears in the *Phaedrus*, where Plato describes the psyche in the myth of the chariot which is drawn by the white steeds of the emotions and the black unruly steeds of the appetites. The driver of the chariot is Reason who holds the reins which control the horses and the whip to subdue the surging black steeds of passion. Only the driver, the rational nature, is given human form; the rest of the psyche, the nonrational part, is given a lower, animal form. This separation and exaltation of reason is carried further in the allegory of the cave in the *Republic*. You recall the sombre picture of human life with which the story begins: men are chained in the dark in a cave, with their backs to a flickering firelight, able to see only uncertain shadows moving on the wall before them, able to hear only confused echoes of sounds. One of the men, breaking free from his chains, is able to turn and look upon the objects themselves and the light which casts the shadows; even, at last, he is able to work his way entirely out of the cave into the sunlight beyond. All this he is able to do through his reason; he escapes from the bondage of error, from time and change, from death itself, into the realm of changeless eternal ideas or Truth, and the lower nature which had chained him in darkness is left behind. [5]

Existentialism in our time, and this is one of its most important characteristics, insists upon reuniting the "lower" or irrational parts of the psyche with the "higher." It insists that man must be taken in his wholeness and not in some divided state, that whole man contains not only intellect but also anxiety, guilt, and the will to power—which modify and sometimes overwhelm the reason. A man seen in this light is fundamentally ambiguous, if not mysterious, full of contradictions and tensions which cannot be dissolved simply by taking thought. "Human life," said Berdyaev, "is permeated by underground streams." One is reminded of D. H. Lawrence's outburst against Franklin and his rational attempt to achieve moral perfection: "The

Perfectability of Man! . . . The perfectability of which man? I am many men. Which of them are you going to perfect? I am not a mechanical contrivance. . . . It's a queer thing is a man's soul. It is the whole of him. Which means it is the unknown as well as the known. . . . The soul of man is a dark vast forest, with wild life in it." The emphasis in existentialism is not on idea but upon the thinker who has the idea. It accepts not only his power of thought, but his contingency and fallibility, his frailty, his body, blood, and bones, and above all his death. Kierkegaard emphasized the distinction between *subjective* truth (what a person *is*) and *objective* truth (what the person *knows*), and said that we encounter the true self not in the detachment of thought but in the involvement and agony of choice and in the pathos of commitment to our choice. This distrust of rational systems helps to explain why many existential writers in their own expression are paradoxical or prophetic or gnomic, why their works often belong more to literature than to philosophy. [6]

III. Alienation or Estrangement

One major result of the dissociation of reason from the rest of the psyche has been the growth of science, which has become one of the hallmarks of Western civilization, and an ever-increasing rational ordering of men in society. As the existentialists view them, the main forces of history since the Renaissance have progressively separated man from concrete earthly existence, have forced him to live at ever higher levels of abstraction, have collectivized individual man out of existence, have driven God from the heavens, or what is the same thing, from the hearts of men. They are convinced that modern man lives in a fourfold condition of alienation: from God, from nature, from other men, from his own true self. [7]

The estrangement from God is most shockingly expressed by Nietzsche's anguished cry, "God is dead," a cry which has continuously echoed through the writings of the existentialists, particularly the French. This theme of spiritual barrenness is a commonplace in literature of this century, from Eliot's "Hollow Man" to the novels of Dos Passos, Hemingway, and Faulkner. It often appears in writers not commonly associated with the existentialists as in this remarkable passage from A *Story-Teller's Story*, where Sherwood Anderson describes his own awakening to his spiritual emptiness. He tells of walking alone late at night along a moonlit road when,

I had suddenly an odd, and to my own seeming, a ridiculous desire to abase myself before something not human and so stepping into the moonlit road, I knelt in the dust. Having no God, the gods having been taken from me by the life about me, as a personal God has been taken from all modern men by a force within that man himself does not understand but that is called the intellect, I kept smiling at the figure I cut in my own eyes as I knelt in the road. . . .

There was no God in the sky, no God in myself, no conviction in myself that I had the power to believe in a God, and so I merely knelt in the dust in silence and no words came to my lips.

In another passage Anderson wondered if the giving of itself by an entire generation to mechanical things was not really making all men impotent, if the desire for a greater navy, a greater army, taller public buildings, was not a sign of growing impotence. He felt that Puritanism and the industrialism which was its offspring had sterilized modern life, and proposed that man return to a healthful animal vigor by renewed contact with simple things of the earth, among them untrammeled sexual expression. One is reminded of the unkempt and delectable raffishness of Steinbeck's *Cannery Row* or of D. H. Lawrence's quasi-religious doctrine of sex, "blood-consciousness" and the "divine otherness" of animal existence. [8]

Man's estrangement from nature has been a major theme in literature at least since Rousseau and the Romantic movement, and can hardly be said to be the property of existentialists. But this group nevertheless adds its own insistence that one of modern man's most urgent dangers is that he builds ever higher the brick and steel walls of technology which shut him away from a health-giving life according to "nature." Their treatment of this theme is most commonly expressed as part of a broader insistence that modern man needs to shun abstraction and return to "concreteness" or "wholeness." [9]

A third estrangement has occurred at the social level and its sign is a growing dismay at man's helplessness before the great machine-like colossus of industrialized society. This is another major theme of Western literature, and here again, though they hardly discovered the danger or began the protest, the existentialists in our time renew the protest against any pattern or force which would stifle the unique and spontaneous in individual life. The crowding of men into cities, the subdivision of labor which submerges the man in his economic function, the burgeoning of centralized government, the growth of advertising, propaganda, and mass media of entertainment and com-munication—all the things which force men into Riesman's "Lonely Crowd"—these same things drive men asunder by destroying their individuality and making them live on the surface of life, content to deal with things rather than people. "Exteriorization," says Berdyaev, "is the source of slavery, whereas freedom is interiorization. Slavery always indicates alienation, the ejection of human nature into the external." This kind of alienation is exemplified by Zero, in Elmer Rice's play "The Adding Machine." Zero's twenty-five years as a bookkeeper in a department store have dried up his humanity, mak-ing him incapable of love, of friendship, of any deeply felt, freely expressed emotion. Such estrangement is often given as the reason for man's inhumanity to man, the explanation for injustice in modern society. In Camus' short novel, aptly called *The Stranger*, a young man is convicted by a court of murder. This is a homicide which he has actually committed under extenuating circumstances. But the court never listens to any of the relevant evidence, seems never to hear anything that pertains to the crime itself; it convicts the young man on wholly irrelevant grounds—because he had behaved in an unconventional way at his mother's funeral the day before the homicide. In this book one feels the same dream-like distortion of reality as in the trial scene in *Alice in Wonderland*, a suffocating sense of being enclosed by events which are irrational or absurd but also inexorable. Most disturbing of all is the young man's aloneness, the impermeable membrane of estrangement which surrounds him and prevents anyone else from penetrating to his experience of life or sympathizing with it. [10]

The fourth kind of alienation, man's estrangement from his own true self, especially as his nature is distorted by an exaltation of reason, is another theme having an extensive history as a major part of the Romantic revolt. Of the many writers who treat the theme, Hawthorne comes particularly close to the emphasis of contemporary existentialists. His Ethan Brand, Dr. Rappacini, and Roger Chilling-worth are a recurrent figure who represents the dislocation in human nature which results when an overdeveloped or misapplied intellect severs "the magnetic chain of human sympathy." Hawthorne is thoroughly existential in his concern for the sanctity of the individual human soul, as well as in his preoccupation with sin and the dark side of human nature, which must be seen in part as his attempt to build back some fullness to the flattened image of man bequeathed to him by the Enlightenment. Whitman was trying to do this when he added flesh and bone and a sexual nature to the spiritualized image of man he inherited from Emerson, though his image remains diffused and attenuated by the same cosmic optimism. Many of the nineteenth-century depictions of man represent him as a figure of power or of potential power, sometimes as daimonic, like Melville's Ahab, but after World War I the power is gone; man is not merely distorted or truncated, he is hollow, powerless, faceless. At the time when his command over natural forces seems to be unlimited, man is pictured as weak, ridden with nameless dread. And this brings us to another of the major themes of existentialism. [11]

IV. "Fear and Trembling," Anxiety

At Stockholm when he accepted the Nobel Prize, William Faulkner said that "Our tragedy today is a general and universal physical fear so long sustained by now that we can even bear it. There are no longer problems of the spirit. There is only one question: When will I be blown up?" The optimistic vision of the Enlightenment which saw man, through reason and its extensions in science, conquering all nature and solving all social and political problems in a continuous upward spiral of Progress, cracked open like a melon on the rock of World War I. The theories which held such high hopes died in that sickening and unimaginable butchery. Here was a concrete fact of human nature and society which the theories could not contain. The Great Depression and World War II deepened the sense of dismay which the loss of these ideals brought, but only with the atomic bomb did this become an unbearable terror, a threat of instant annihilation which confronted all men, even those most insulated by the thick crust of material goods and services. Now the most unthinking person could sense that each advance in mechanical technique carried not only a chromium and plush promise of comfort but a threat as well. [12]

Sartre, following Kierkegaard, speaks of another kind of anxiety which oppresses modern man—"the anguish of Abraham"—the necessity which is laid upon him to make moral choices on his own responsibility. A military officer in wartime knows the agony of choice which forces him to sacrifice part of his army to preserve the rest, as does a man in high political office, who must make decisions affecting the lives of millions. The existentialists claim that each of us must make moral decisions in our own lives which involve the same anguish. Kierkegaard finds that this necessity is one thing which makes each life unique, which makes it impossible to speculate or generalize about human life, because each man's case is irretrievably his own, something in which he is personally and passionately involved. His book *Fear and Trembling* is an elaborate and fascinating commentary on the Old Testament story of Abraham, who was commanded by God to sacrifice his beloved son Isaac. Abraham thus becomes the emblem of man who must make a harrowing choice, in this case between love for his son and love for God, between the universal moral law which says categorically, "thou shalt not kill," and the unique inner demand of his religious faith. Abraham's decision, which is to violate the abstract and collective moral law, has to be made not in arrogance but in fear and trembling, one of the inferences being that sometimes one must make an exception to the general law because he is (existentially) an exception, a concrete being whose existence can never be completely subsumed under any universal. [13]

V. The Encounter with Nothingness

For the man alienated from God, from nature, from his fellow man and from himself, what is left at last but Nothingness? The testimony of the existentialists is that this is where modern man now finds himself, not on the highway of upward Progress toward a radiant Utopia but on the brink of a catastrophic precipice, below which yawns the absolute void, an uncompromised black Nothingness. In one sense this is Eliot's Wasteland inhabited by his Hollow Man, who is

> Shape without form, shade without color
> Paralyzed force, gesture without motion.[1]

This is what moves E. A. Robinson's Richard Cory, the man who is everything that might make us wish that we were in his place, to go home one calm summer night and put a bullet through his head. [14]

One of the most convincing statements of the encounter with Nothingness is made by Leo Tolstoy in "My Confession." He tells how in good health, in the prime of life, when he had everything that a man could desire—wealth, fame, aristocratic social position, a beautiful wife and children, a brilliant mind and great artistic talent in the height of their powers, he nevertheless was seized with a growing uneasiness, a nameless discontent which he could not shake or alleviate. His experience was like that of a man who falls sick, with symptoms which he disregards as insignificant; but the symptoms return again and again until they merge into a continuous suffering.

[1] T. S. Eliot's "The Hollow Men" from Collected Poems of T. S. Eliot, New York: Harcourt, Brace & World, Inc., 1963. Reprinted by permission of Harcourt, Brace & World, Inc. The Canadian rights by permission of Faber & Faber, Ltd.

And the patient suddenly is confronted with the overwhelming fact that what he took for mere indisposition is more important to him than anything else on earth, that it is death! "I felt the ground on which I stood was crumbling, that there was nothing for me to stand on, that what I had been living for was nothing, that I had no reason for living. . . . To stop was impossible, to go back was impossible; and it was impossible to shut my eyes so as to see that there was nothing before me but suffering and actual death, absolute annihilation." This is the "Sickness Unto Death" of Kierkegaard, the despair in which one wishes to die but cannot. Hemingway's short story, "A Clean, Well-Lighted Place," gives an unforgettable expression of this theme. At the end of the story, the old waiter climbs into bed late at night saying to himself, "What did he fear? It was not fear or dread. It was a nothing which he knew too well. It was all a nothing and a man was nothing too. . . . Nada y pues nada, y nada y pues nada." And then because he has experienced the death of God he goes on to recite the Lord's Prayer in blasphemous despair: "Our Nothing who art in Nothing, nothing be thy nothing. . . ." And then the Ave Maria, "Hail nothing, full of nothing. . . ." This is stark, even for Hemingway, but the old waiter does no more than name the void felt by most people in the early Hemingway novels, a hunger they seek to assuage with alcohol, sex, and violence in an aimless progress from bar to bed to bull-ring. It goes without saying that much of the despair and pessimism in other contemporary authors springs from a similar sense of the void in modern life. [15]

VI. Freedom

Sooner or later, as a theme that includes all the others, the existentialist writings bear upon freedom. The themes we have outlined above describe either some loss of man's freedom or some threat to it, and all existentialists of whatever sort are concerned to enlarge the range of human freedom. [16]

For the avowed atheists like Sartre freedom means human autonomy. In a purposeless universe man is *condemned* to freedom because he is the only creature who is "self-surpassing," who can become something other than he is. Precisely because there is no God to give purpose to the universe, each man must accept individual responsibility for his own becoming, a burden made heavier by the fact that in choosing for himself he chooses for all men "the image of man as he ought to be." A man *is* the sum total of the acts that make up his life—no more, no less—and though the coward has made himself cowardly, it is always possible for him to change and make himself heroic. In Sartre's novel, *The Age of Reason,* one of the least likable of the characters, almost overwhelmed by despair and self-disgust at his homosexual tendencies, is on the point of solving his problem by mutilating himself with a razor, when in an effort of will he throws the instrument down, and we are given to understand that from this moment he will have mastery over his aberrant drive. Thus in the daily course of ordinary life must men shape their becoming in Sartre's world. [17]

The religious existentialists interpret man's freedom differently. They use much the same language as Sartre, develop the same themes concerning the predicament of man, but always include God as a radical factor. They stress the man of faith rather than the man of will. They interpret man's existential condition as a state of alienation from his essential nature which is God-like, the problem of his life being to heal the chasm between the two, that is, to find salvation. The mystery and ambiguity of man's existence they attribute to his being the intersection of two realms. "Man bears within himself," writes Berdyaev, "the image which is both the image of man and the image of God, and is the image of man as far as the image of God is actualized." Tillich describes salvation as "the act in which the cleavage between the essential being and the existential situation is overcome." Freedom here, as for Sartre, involves an acceptance of responsibility for choice and a *commitment* to one's choice. This is the meaning of faith, a faith like Abraham's, the commitment which is an agonizing sacrifice of one's own desire and will and dearest treasure to God's will. [18]

A final word. Just as one should not expect to find in a particular writer all of the characteristics of existentialism as we have described them, he should also be aware that some of the most striking expressions of existentialism in literature and the arts come to us by indirection, often through symbols or through innovations in conventional form. Take the preoccupation of contemporary writers with time. In *The Sound and the Fury*, Faulkner both collapses and expands normal clock time, or by juxtapositions of past and present blurs time into a single amorphous pool. He does this by using various forms of "stream of consciousness" or other techniques which see life in terms of unique, subjective experience—that is, existentially. The conventional view of externalized life, a rational orderly progression cut into uniform segments by the hands of a clock, he rejects in favor of a view which sees life as opaque, ambiguous, and irrational— that is, as the existentialist sees it. Graham Greene does something like this in *The Power and the Glory*. He creates a scene isolated in time and cut off from the rest of the world, steamy and suffocating as if a bell jar had been placed over it. Through this atmosphere fetid with impending death and human suffering, stumbles the whiskey priest, lonely and confused, pursued by a police lieutenant who has experienced the void and the death of God. [19]

Such expressions in literature do not mean necessarily that the authors are conscious existentialist theorizers, or even that they know the writings of such theorizers. Faulkner may never have read Heidegger—or St. Augustine—both of whom attempt to demonstrate that time is more within a man and subject to his unique experience of it than it is outside him. But it is legitimate to call Faulkner's views of time and life "existential" in this novel because in recent years existentialist theorizers have given such views a local habitation and a name. One of the attractions, and one of the dangers, of existential themes is that they become like Sir Thomas Browne's quincunx: once one begins to look for them, he sees them everywhere. But if one applies restraint and discrimination, he will find that they illuminate much of contemporary literature and sometimes the literature of the past as well. [20]

PURPOSE AND STRUCTURE

1. Bigelow first establishes two classes of existentialists, the godly and the ungodly, and illustrates each class. He then leaves these classifications and goes on to classify the general characteristics of existentialism under six headings. Diagram or outline his classifications, including all the subclasses.

2. Present a sound *rhetorical* reason for moving class five to fourth position. Now defend Bigelow's original order of these sections.

3. Bigelow's essay demonstrates the frequent close interplay between classification and illustration. An illustration is usually a member of a class that exhibits the typical characteristics of the class. By using an illustration, an author can discuss in particular what otherwise he would have to say in generalities. Moreover, the author assumes his illustrations are familiar to his readers so that by means of them he can lead his reader to an appreciation of the classification they represent. Re-read the essay quickly and make a list of the illustrations unfamiliar to you and explain why their unfamiliarity does or does not interfere with your comprehension.

4. What is gained by the use of headings for each section? What, if anything, is lost?

5. In the first sentence of par. 8 Bigelow claims that the cry **God is dead** "has continuously echoed through the writings of the existentialists, particularly the French." All the examples to support this statement, however, are drawn from American or British literature. What purpose is served by omitting French examples in favor of American ones? Where did this essay originally appear?

6. What, if anything, is wrong with the last sentence of par. 3?

7. Explain the use of commas and semicolons in the first sentence of par. 3.

DICTION AND TONE

1. Ordinarily the unnecessary introduction of foreign terms is discouraged. Explain why *avant garde* in par. 1 is not only permissible but highly appropriate.

2. What attitude is revealed by the diction of sentence 2, par. 1? Contrast it with the following: ". . . the picture it evoked of virile beards, softly-lit basement cafes, and French intellectuals engaging one another in thoughtful discussions . . ." In what way and to what degree is the attitude revealed in Bigelow's sentence relevant to his purpose?

3. Bigelow's tone is occasionally apologetic—that is, he apologizes for undertaking to write this essay. Defend or attack this statement, supplying evidence from the text.

4. In the second sentence of par. 18, God is mentioned as a *radical* factor. What does *radical* mean in this context?

5. In par. 5 Bigelow uses the word *lower* in *lower nature* without quotation marks; in par. 6 he puts the word in quotation marks. What change of meaning results?

6. Bigelow's illustrations reveal an assumption he has made about his audience. His vocabulary and sentence structure reveal an additional assumption. Characterize the tone that results from the mixture of these assumptions. Is it one of great profundity? great simplicity? overcomplication? oversimplification? or what?

APPLICATIONS TO WRITING

1. Write an essay in which you classify the themes (preferably but not necessarily existential) of a work of fiction and provide illustrations of each of your classes.

2. Select one or more of the characteristics Bigelow has described, and write an essay in which you classify the attitudes of your contemporaries on this subject.

3. Write A *Primer of Collegiate Philosophy* using a method of organization similar to Bigelow's.

THE PATRON AND
THE CROCUS

VIRGINIA WOOLF

Young men and women beginning to write are generally
given the plausible but utterly impracticable advice to write what
they have to write as shortly as possible, as clearly as possible, and
without other thought in their minds except to say exactly what is in
them. Nobody ever adds on these occasions the one thing needful:
"And be sure you choose your patron wisely," though that is the gist
of the whole matter. For a book is always written for somebody to
read, and, since the patron is not merely the paymaster, but also in a
very subtle and insidious way the instigator and inspirer of what is
written, it is of the utmost importance that he should be a desirable
man. [1]

But who, then, is the desirable man—the patron who will cajole the
best out of the writer's brain and bring to birth the most varied and
vigorous progeny of which he is capable? Different ages have answered the question differently. The Elizabethans, to speak roughly,
chose the aristocracy to write for and the playhouse public. The
eighteenth-century patron was a combination of coffee-house wit and

Grub Street bookseller. In the nineteenth century the great writers wrote for the half-crown magazines and the leisured classes. And looking back and applauding the splendid results of these different alliances, it all seems enviably simple, and plain as a pike-staff compared with our own predicament—for whom should we write? For the present supply of patrons is of unexampled and bewildering variety. There is the daily Press, the weekly Press, the monthly Press; the English public and the American public; the best-seller public and the worst-seller public; the high-brow public and the red-blood public; all now organised self-conscious entities capable through their various mouthpieces of making their needs known and their approval or displeasure felt. Thus the writer who has been moved by the sight of the first crocus in Kensington Gardens has, before he sets pen to paper, to choose from a crowd of competitors the particular patron who suits him best. It is futile to say, "Dismiss them all; think only of your crocus," because writing is a method of communication; and the crocus is an imperfect crocus until it has been shared. The first man or the last may write for himself alone, but he is an exception and an unenviable one at that, and the gulls are welcome to his works if the gulls can read them. [2]

Granted, then, that every writer has some public or other at the end of his pen, the high-minded will say that it should be a submissive public, accepting obediently whatever he likes to give it. Plausible as the theory sounds, great risks are attached to it. For in that case the writer remains conscious of his public, yet is superior to it—an uncomfortable and unfortunate combination, as the works of Samuel Butler, George Meredith, and Henry James may be taken to prove. Each despised the public; each desired a public; each failed to attain a public; and each wreaked his failure upon the public by a succession, gradually increasing in intensity, of angularities, obscurities, and affectations which no writer whose patron was his equal and friend would have thought it necessary to inflict. Their crocuses in consequence are tortured plants, beautiful and bright, but with something wrynecked about them, malformed, shrivelled on the one side, overblown on the other. A touch of the sun would have done them a world of good. Shall we then rush to the opposite extreme and accept (if in fancy alone) the flattering proposals which the editors of the *Times* and the *Daily News* may be supposed to make us—"Twenty pounds down for your crocus in precisely fifteen hundred words, which shall blossom upon every breakfast table from John o' Groats to the Land's End before nine o'clock to-morrow morning with the writer's name attached"? [3]

But will one crocus be enough, and must it not be a very brilliant yellow to shine so far, to cost so much, and to have one's name attached to it? The Press is undoubtedly a great multiplier of crocuses. But if we look at some of these plants, we shall find that they are only very distantly related to the original little yellow or purple flower which pokes up through the grass in Kensington Gardens about this time of year. The newspaper crocus is amazing but still a very different plant. It fills precisely the space allotted to it. It radiates a golden glow. It is genial, affable, warmhearted. It is beautifully finished, too, for let nobody think that the art of "our dramatic critic" of the *Times* or of Mr. Lynd of the *Daily News* is an easy one. It is no despicable feat to start a million brains running at nine o'clock in the morning, to give two million eyes something bright and brisk and amusing to look at. But the night comes and these flowers fade. So little bits of glass lose their lustre if you take them out of the sea; great prima donnas howl like hyenas if you shut them up in telephone boxes; and the most brilliant of articles when removed from its element is dust and sand and the husks of straw. Journalism embalmed in a book is unreadable. [4]

The patron we want, then, is one who will help us to preserve our flowers from decay. But as his qualities change from age to age, and it needs considerable integrity and conviction not to be dazzled by the pretensions or bamboozled by the persuasions of the competing crowd, this business of patron-finding is one of the tests and trials of authorship. To know whom to write for is to know how to write. Some of the modern patron's qualities are, however, fairly plain. The writer will require at this moment, it is obvious, a patron with the book-reading habit rather than the play-going habit. Nowadays, too, he must be instructed in the literature of other times and races. But there are other qualities which our special weaknesses and tendencies demand in him. There is the question of indecency, for instance, which plagues us and puzzles us much more than it did the Elizabethans. The twentieth-century patron must be immune from shock. He must distinguish infallibly between the little clod of manure which sticks to the crocus of necessity, and that which is plastered to it out of bravado. He must be a judge, too, of those social influences which inevitably play so large a part in modern literature, and able to say which matures and fortifies, which inhibits and makes sterile. Further, there is emotion for him to pronounce on, and in no department can he do more useful work than in bracing a writer against sentimentality on the one hand and a craven fear of expressing his feeling on the other. It is worse, he will say, and perhaps more common, to be afraid of feeling than to feel too much. He will add, perhaps, something about language, and point out how many words Shakespeare used and how much grammar Shakespeare violated, while we, though we keep our fingers so demurely to the black notes on the piano, have not appreciably improved upon *Antony and Cleopatra*. And if you can forget your sex altogether, he will say, so much the better; a writer has none. But all this is by the way—elementary and disputable. The patron's prime quality is something different, only to be expressed perhaps by the use of that convenient word which cloaks so much—atmosphere. It is necessary that the patron should shed and envelop the crocus in an atmosphere which makes it appear a plant of the very brightest importance, so that to misrepresent it is the one outrage not to be forgiven this side of the grave. He must make us feel that a single crocus, if it be a real crocus, is enough for him; that he does not want to be lectured, elevated, instructed, or improved; that he is sorry that he bullied Carlyle into vociferation, Tennyson into idyllics, and Ruskin into insanity; that he is now ready to efface himself or assert himself as his writers require; that he is bound to them by a more than maternal tie; that they are twins indeed, one dying if the other dies, one flourishing if the other flourishes; that the fate of literature depends upon their happy alliance—all of which proves, as we began by saying, that the choice of a patron is of the highest importance. But how to choose rightly? How to write well? Those are the questions. [5]

PURPOSE AND STRUCTURE

Although the author classifies patrons in minute detail, the method of classification subserves her purpose of persuading the reader that patrons with special characteristics are essential to the fruition of the writer's powers.

1. In the first sentence of par. 1 the author states that the advice given to beginning writers to write with brevity and clarity is plausible but impracticable. In suggesting that a patron must be wisely chosen she indicates two reasons for the impracticability of the advice. What are they? What clues does the syntax give you that they are not of equal significance to her?

2. The first sentence of par. 2 refers directly to the last sentence of par. 1 and elaborates it. What specific words and phrases are used to effect this transition?

3. In par. 2 how does the last sentence emphasize the preceding one?

4. In addition to classification the author develops her essay by showing the causal relationship between patron and crocus. For example, with a submissive public as patron, writers such as Butler, Meredith, and James produced "angularities, obscurities, and affectations." What causal relationship is developed in par. 4?

5. In each paragraph the author repeats her basic thesis either explicitly or implicitly. In par. 1 she states, "For a book is always written for somebody to read. . . ." How is this point stated in par. 2? In pars. 3 and 4 how is it conveyed by implication? In par. 5 it is again stated explicitly in at least two sentences. Identify them.

6. With what is *sentimentality* compared in par. 5?

7. In discussing the atmosphere favorable to the flourishing of the crocus, the author cites negative influences. What are they?

8. The different kinds of patron described in par. 2 may be charted diagrammatically:

In the remaining paragraphs patrons are further classified by specific qualities of character. Diagram the divisions and subdivisions under this heading.

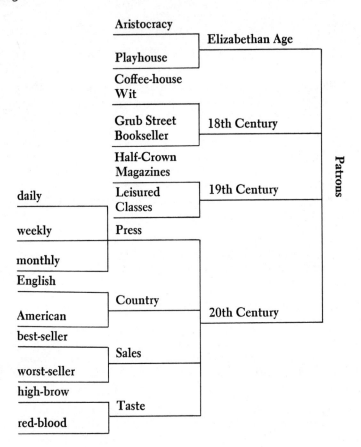

DICTION AND TONE

1. Discuss the effectiveness of the words *cajole* and *progeny* in the first sentence of par. 2. Substitute synonyms. What is gained or lost?

2. To what does the simile, *plain as a pikestaff*, refer? Find a simile or metaphor to describe the predicament of the writer in the twentieth century.

3. The crocus is used both literally and symbolically in the essay. How is the metaphor developed throughout the essay? Can you think of any other metaphor that would have been as effective? How does it contribute to coherence? to tone?

4. What does the reference to the gulls at the end of par. 2 contribute to tone?

5. Discuss the effectiveness of the adjectives used to describe the crocuses in par. 3. Applied to prose, what do they connote?

6. How do the particulars in the rhetorical sentence at the end of par. 3 contribute to tone?

7. What words in par. 4 recall her phrase, *touch of the sun?*

8. How does the metaphor at the end of par. 4 strengthen the idea that "Journalism embalmed in a book is unreadable"?

9. What metaphor defines the kind of discrimination the patron must possess regarding indecency?

10. How does the fact that "we keep our fingers so demurely to the black notes on the piano" relate to our failure to improve appreciably upon *Antony and Cleopatra?*

11. The author achieves emphasis in her conclusion by alluding to the patron's *prime* quality. By what other means does she achieve emphasis?

12. What do the words *lectured, elevated, instructed,* or *improved* have in common? What do they connote for you? for Virginia Woolf? Paraphrase her central thought in your own words. What is lost?

APPLICATIONS TO WRITING

1. Divide a subject on which you are well informed by virtue of observation, experience, and special knowledge into the classes that make it up. For example, classify your fellow students according to qualities of character, educational purposes, or their responses in the classroom; classify

professors in accordance with your observations or fictional portrayals of them. Or classify sports, jobs, books, movies, television programs. The interest of your paper will depend largely upon the skill with which you can make classification serve your central thematic purpose.

2. Characterize your own writing in relation to your audience: when you write a composition in English; apply for a position; correspond with a friend.

NIGHTMARE AND
RITUAL IN
HEMINGWAY

MALCOLM COWLEY

I

Going back to Hemingway's work after several years is like going back to a brook where you had often fished and finding the woods as deep and cool as they used to be. The trees are bigger, perhaps, but they are the same trees; the water comes down over the black stones as clear as always, with the same dull, steady roar where it plunges into the pool; and when the first trout takes hold of your line you can feel your heart beating against your fishing jacket. But something has changed, for this time there are shadows in the pool that you hadn't noticed before, and you have a sense that the woods are haunted. When Hemingway's stories first appeared, they seemed to be a transcription of the real world, new because they were accurate and because the world in those days was also new. With his insistence on "presenting things truly," he seemed to be a writer in the naturalistic tradition (for all his technical innovations); and the professors of American literature, when they got around to mentioning his books in their surveys, treated him as if he were a Dreiser of the lost generation, or perhaps the fruit of a misalliance between Dreiser and Jack London. Going back to his work in 1944, you perceive his kinship with a wholly different group of novelists, let us say with Poe and Hawthorne and Melville: the haunted and nocturnal writers, the men who dealt in images that were symbols of an inner world. [1]

On the face of it, his method is not in the least like theirs. He doesn't lead us into castles ready to collapse with age, or into very old New England houses, or embark with us on the search for a whale that is also the white spirit of evil; instead he tells the stories he has lived or heard, against the background of countries he has seen. But, you reflect on reading his books again, these are curious stories that he has chosen from his wider experience, and these countries are presented in a strangely mortuary light. In no other writer of our time can you find such a profusion of corpses: dead women in the rain; dead soldiers bloated in their uniforms and surrounded by torn papers; sunken liners full of bodies that float past the closed portholes. In no other writer can you find so many suffering animals: mules with their forelegs broken drowning in shallow water off the quay at Smyrna; gored horses in the bull ring; wounded hyenas first snapping at their own entrails and then eating them with relish. And morally wounded people who also devour themselves: punch-drunk boxers, soldiers with battle fatigue, veterans crazy with "the old rale," Lesbians, nymphomaniacs, bullfighters who have lost their nerve, men who lie awake all night while their brains get to racing "like a flywheel with the weight gone"—here are visions as terrifying as those of "The Pit and the Pendulum," even though most of them are copied from life; here are nightmares at noonday, accurately described, pictured without blur, but having the nature of obsessions or hypnagogic visions between sleep and waking. [2]

And, going back to them, you find a waking-dreamlike quality even in the stories that deal with pleasant or commonplace aspects of the world. Take, for example, "Big Two-Hearted River," where the plot —or foreground of the plot—is simply a fishing trip in the northern peninsula of Michigan. Nick Adams, who is Hemingway's earliest and most personal hero, gets off the train at an abandoned sawmill town; he crosses burned-over land, makes camp, eats his supper, and goes to sleep; in the morning he looks for bait, finds grasshoppers under a log, hooks a big trout and loses it, catches two other trout, then sits in the shadow and eats his lunch very slowly while watching the stream; he decides to do no more fishing that day. There is nothing else in the story, apparently; nothing but a collection of sharp sensory details, so that you smell or hear or touch or see everything that exists near Big Two-Hearted River; and you even taste Nick Adams' supper of beans and spaghetti. "All good books are alike," Hemingway later said, "in that they are truer than if they had really happened and after you are finished reading one you will feel that all that happened to you and afterwards it all belongs to you: the good and the bad, the ecstasy, the remorse and sorrow, the people and the places and how the weather was." This story belongs to the reader, but apparently it is lacking in ecstasy, remorse, and sorrow; there are no people in it except Nick Adams; apparently there is nothing but "the places and how the weather was." [3]

But Hemingway's stories are most of them continued, in the sense that he has a habit of returning to the same themes, each time making them a little clearer—to himself, I think, as well as to others. His work has an emotional consistency, as if all of it moved with the same current. A few years after "Big Two-Hearted River," he wrote another story that casts a retrospective light on his fishing trip (much as A *Farewell to Arms* helps to explain the background of Jake Barnes and Lady Brett, in *The Sun Also Rises*). The second story, "Now I Lay Me," deals with an American volunteer in the Italian army who isn't named but who might easily be Nick Adams. He is afraid to sleep at night because, so he says, "I had been living for a long time with the knowledge that if I ever shut my eyes in the dark and let myself go, my soul would go out of my body. I had been that way for a long time, ever since I had been blown up at night and felt it go out of me and go off and then come back." And the soldier continues:

I had different ways of occupying myself while I lay awake. I would think of a trout stream I had fished along when I was a boy and fish its whole length very carefully in my mind; fishing very carefully under all the logs, all the turns of the bank, the deep holes and the clear shallow stretches, sometimes catching trout and sometimes losing them. I would stop fishing at noon to eat my lunch; sometimes on a log over the stream; sometimes on a high bank under a tree, and I always ate my lunch very slowly and watched the stream below me while I ate. . . . Some nights too I made up streams, and some of them were very exciting, and it was like being awake and dreaming. Some of those streams I still remember and think that I have fished in them, and they are confused with streams I really know. [4]

After reading this passage, we have a somewhat different attitude toward the earlier story. The river described in it remains completely real for us; but also—like those other streams the soldier invented during the night—it has the quality of a waking dream. Although the events in the foreground are described with superb accuracy and for their own sake, we now perceive what we probably missed at a first reading: that there are shadows in the background and that part of the story takes place in an inner world. We notice that Nick Adams regards his fishing trip as an escape, either from nightmare or from realities that have become a nightmare. Sometimes his mind starts to work, even here in the wilderness; but "he knew he could choke it because he was tired enough," and he can safely fall asleep. "Nick felt happy," the author says more than once. "He felt he had left everything behind, the need for thinking, the need to write, other needs. It was all back of him." He lives as if in an enchanted country. There is a faint suggestion of old legends: all the stories of boys with cruel stepmothers who wandered off into the forest where the big trees sheltered them and the birds brought them food. There is even a condition laid on Nick's happiness, just as in many fairy tales where the hero must not wind a certain horn or open a certain door. Nick must not follow the river down into the swamp. "In the swamp the banks were bare, the big cedars came together overhead, the sun did not come through, except in patches; in the fast deep water, in the half light, the fishing would be tragic. In the swamp fishing was a tragic adventure. Nick did not want it. He did not want to go down the stream any further today." [5]

But fishing is not the only activity of his heroes that Hemingway endows with a curious and almost supernatural value. They drink early and late; they consume enough beer, wine, anis, grappa, and Fundador to put them all into alcoholic wards, if they were ordinary mortals; but drinking seems to have the effect on them of a magic potion. Robert Jordan, in *For Whom the Bell Tolls*, is the soberest of Hemingway's heroes, the child, as it were, of middle age. Nevertheless he finds that a cup of absinthe "took the place of the evening papers, of all the old evenings in cafés, of all the chestnut trees that would be in bloom now in this month . . . of all the things he had enjoyed and forgotten and that came back to him when he tasted that opaque, bitter, tongue-numbing, brain-warming, stomach-warming, idea-changing liquid alchemy." There is much that he wants to remember, but also the fear of death that he wants to forget, and he personifies liquor as "the giant killer." On one occasion he reflects that writing about his fears might help him even more than drowning them in absinthe. He says to himself, after worrying about all the lives that have been lost as a result of his activities behind the Fascist lines: "But my guess is you will get rid of all that by writing about it. . . . Once you write it down it is all gone." Hemingway himself sometimes seems to regard writing as an exhausting ceremony of exorcism. And, as a young man after the First World War, he had painful memories of which he wanted to rid himself by setting them all down. [6]

II

He was born on July 21, 1899, in Oak Park, Illinois, where his father was a physician. He went to school there, too, but what he regarded as his real home was a house in Michigan near the tip of the southern peninsula. The house was full of children all summer, for there were two boys and four girls in the family. In those days, the first-growth hemlock woods came down almost to the shore of the lake; and back in the woods was a settlement of Ojibways who lived by cutting the hemlocks for tanbark. Then one year all the woods were gone, "and there were only stumps, dried tree-tops, branches and fireweed where the woods had been." Ernest ran away from home when he was fifteen years old; that may have been the time he met the Battler beside the railway track near Mancelona. In 1917 he was graduated from Oak Park High School, where he had played football and had been chosen to write the class prophecy. He didn't go on to college, but instead got a job on the *Kansas City Star*; a few months later he went to Europe as a volunteer ambulance driver. He was badly wounded on the Italian front; he was given a silver medal (besides the Croce di Guerra); and after being patched together in a Milan hospital he served for a time in the Italian shock troops, the Arditi. One of the sights he could not forget was of the Austrian dead lying on their faces with their pockets turned out and each body surrounded by postcards and letters from home, a surprising quantity of paper. Another memory that became a nightmare was the evacuation of Smyrna by the Greeks, who left their baggage animals to drown. But that was something he saw four years later, when he was sent to the Middle East as a correspondent for the *Toronto Star*. [7]

In Paris, which would be his home for many years after the war, he set about learning to become a writer. He had met Sherwood Anderson, who sent him to Gertrude Stein with a letter of introduction. He also became a good friend of Ezra Pound and he sometimes helped Ford Madox Ford to edit the *Transatlantic* Review, although his name did not appear on the masthead. These four—but especially Pound and Miss Stein—seem to have been his principal teachers; and what they gave him (or rather, what they confirmed in him) was an ideal of complete objectivity. When he sent his early manuscripts to Pound, they came back to him blue-penciled, with most of the adjectives gone. Miss Stein was content to make general comments, but they were usually followed. He afterwards said to John Peale Bishop, "Ezra was right half the time, and when he was wrong, he was so wrong you were never in any doubt about it. Gertrude was always right." As soon as he had saved a little money, Hemingway quit his job as a correspondent and devoted all his time to his stories. Once at a dinner in Paris with Dos Passos and the Lincoln Steffenses, he insisted that anybody could write. "You can," he said to Mrs. Steffens, making the gesture of giving her a left hook to the jaw; in those days he always gestured like a boxer. "It's hell. It takes it all out of you; it nearly kills you; but you can do it. Anybody can. Even you can, Stef. . . . I haven't done it yet, but I will." And Steffens adds, in his autobiography, "I think he thought that writing was a matter of honesty and labor." [8]

"I was trying to write then," Hemingway tells us at the beginning of *Death in the Afternoon,*

and I found the greatest difficulty, aside from knowing truly what you really felt, rather than what you were supposed to feel, and had been taught to feel, was to put down what really happened in action; what the actual things were which produced the emotion that you experienced. In writing for a newspaper you told what happened and, with one trick and another, you communicated the emotion aided by the element of time-liness which gives a certain emotion to any account of something that has happened on that day; but the real thing, the sequence of motion and fact which made the emotion and which would be as valid in a year or in ten years or, with luck and if you stated it purely enough, always, was beyond me and I was working very hard to try to get it.

In those days he seems to have regarded stories as, essentially, machines for arousing emotion. You didn't put the emotion itself into the story, any more than you would make a reaping machine out of wheat or a sewing machine out of cloth and thread; but you picked out the sharp details from life that had aroused your own emotion and, if you described them accurately, in their proper sequence and without closing your eyes to violence and horror, you had something that would continue to arouse the emotion of your readers. That was the method Hemingway followed in his early sketches and, within its self-imposed limitations, it was extremely successful. It was even successful beyond those limitations, for his pictures proved to have a vast power of suggestion. Take, for example, two of the "chapters," or interchapters, from *In Our Time.* Chapter III reads in full:

We were in a garden in Mons. Young Buckley came in with his patrol from across the river. The first German I saw climbed up over the garden wall. We waited till he got one leg over and then potted him. He had so much equipment on and looked awfully surprised and fell down into the garden. Then three more came over further down the wall. We shot them. They all came just like that. [9]

There is nothing more. There are no editorial reflections on the horrors of modern warfare. There is, in the story itself, no emotion whatever except the "awfully surprised" look of the first German who was shot. But the story has the power of arousing emotion in the reader, who tends to put himself either in the position of the English riflemen or, more likely, in that of the Germans climbing the wall to their deaths. And the wall itself is so vivid that, for the reader, it tends to become a sort of metaphor for all the impassable obstacles we see in nightmares: the swamps in which our feet are mired, the endless steps, the river that must, and cannot be crossed. Moreover, Hemingway returns to the same type of image in the following interchapter:

It was a frightfully hot day. We'd jammed an absolutely perfect barri-cade across the bridge. It was simply priceless. A big old wrought-iron grating from the front of a house. Too heavy to lift and you could shoot through it and they would have to climb over it. It was absolutely topping. They tried to get over it, and we potted them from forty yards. They rushed it, and officers came out alone and worked on it. It was an abso-lutely perfect obstacle. Their officers were very fine. We were frightfully put out when we heard the flank had gone, and we had to fall back. [10]

Here the sense of nightmare becomes more definite. The reader begins to feel that the "absolutely perfect obstacle" is a symbol for other obstacles recurring in Hemingway's novels: for the wound that divides Jake and Brett (in *The Sun Also Rises*); for the death in childbirth that separates Frederic from Catherine (in *A Farewell to Arms*); and even for the bridge that must be destroyed (in *For Whom the Bell Tolls*) at the cost of the hero's life. Moreover, the picture of a wall reappears in the two interchapters that follow. Chapter V begins: "They shot the six cabinet ministers at half-past six in the morning against the wall of a hospital." Chapter VI begins: "Nick sat against the wall of the church where they had dragged him to be clear of machine-gun fire in the street." In Hemingway's unconscious mind, all these walls may have been the images of death, though I doubt that he regarded them consciously as symbols. He was trying in those early days to state everything behavioristically, and it was not until later that he began to make a deliberate use of symbolism, together with other literary devices that he had avoided in the beginning, when he was teaching himself to write "commencing with the simplest things." [11]

Later, in A *Farewell to Arms*, the rain becomes a conscious symbol of disaster. "Things went very badly," the hero tells us in the first chapter. "At the start of the winter came the permanent rain and with the rain came the cholera." Catherine Barkley is afraid of the rain because, she says, "sometimes I see me dead in it." Rain falls all during the retreat from Caporetto; it falls while Catherine is trying to have her baby in a Swiss hospital; and it is still falling when she dies and when Frederic pushes the nurses out of the room to be alone with her. "It wasn't any good," he says. "It was like saying goodbye to a statue. After a while I went out and left the hospital and walked back to the hotel in the rain." On the other hand, it is snow that is used as a symbol of death in "The Snows of Kilimanjaro" (along with other death symbols, like vultures, hyenas, and soaring in an imaginary airplane). And possibly snow has the same value in *For Whom the Bell Tolls*, where a spring snowfall adds to the danger of Robert Jordan's mission and indirectly causes his death. [12]

Even in these later novels and stories, Hemingway almost never makes the error that weakens the effect of most symbolic fiction. Ordinarily we think of it as a type of writing in which the events in the foreground tend to become misty because the author has his eyes fixed on something else. Hawthorne, in *The Marble Faun*, was so preoccupied with inner meanings that he seemed to lose his sense of the real world; but that is almost never the case with Hemingway. It is true that Maria, in *For Whom the Bell Tolls*, is almost more of a dream than she is a woman. When Frederic Henry dives into the flooded Tagliamento, in A *Farewell to Arms*, he is performing a rite of baptism that prepares us for the new life he is about to lead as a deserter from the Italian army; his act is emotionally significant, but it is a little unconvincing on the plane of action. These are perhaps the only two cases in which Hemingway seems to loosen his grip on reality. Elsewhere his eyes are fixed on the foreground; but he gives us a sense of other shadowy meanings that contribute to the force and complexity of his writing. [13]

By the early 1930's Hemingway's technique, apparently simple in the beginning, was becoming more elaborate. He had begun to talk about the possibility of writing what he called fourth-dimensional prose. "The reason everyone now tries to avoid it," he says in *Green Hills of Africa*, "to deny that it is important, to make it seem vain to try to do it, is because it is so difficult. Too many factors must combine to make it possible." [14]

"What is this now?" asks Kandisky, the Austrian in leather breeches who likes to lead the life of the mind. And the author tells him: [15]

"The kind of writing that can be done. How far prose can be carried if anyone is serious enough and has luck. There is a fourth and fifth dimension that can be gotten." [16]

"You believe it?" [17]

"I know it." [18]

"And if a writer can get this?" [19]

"Then nothing else matters. It is more important than anything else he can do. The chances are, of course, that he will fail. But there is a chance that he succeeds." [20]

"But that is poetry you are talking about." [21]

"No. It is much more difficult than poetry. It is a prose that has never been written. But it can be written, without tricks and without cheating. With nothing that will go bad afterwards." [22]

Now, I don't know exactly what Hemingway means by prose with "a fourth and fifth dimension." It would seem to me that any good prose has four dimensions, in the sense of being a solid object that moves through time, whereas the fifth dimension is here a mystical or meaningless figure of speech. But without understanding his choice of words, I do know that Hemingway's prose at its best gives a sense of depth and of moving forward on different levels that is lacking in even the best of his imitators, as it is in almost all the other novelists of our time. Moreover, I have at least a vague notion of how this quality in his work can be explained. [23]

III

Considering his laborious apprenticeship and the masters with whom he chose to study; considering his theories of writing, which he has often discussed, and how they have developed with the years; considering their subtle and highly conscious application, as well as the very complicated personality they serve to express, it is a little surprising to find that Hemingway is almost always described as a primitive. Yet the word really applies to him, if it is used in what might be called its anthropological sense. The anthropologists tell us that many of the so-called primitive peoples have an extremely elaborate system of beliefs, calling for the almost continual performance of rites and ceremonies; even their drunken orgies are ruled by tradition. Some of the forest-dwelling tribes believe that every rock or tree or animal has its own indwelling spirit. When they kill an animal or chop down a tree, they must beg its forgiveness, repeating a formula of propitiation; otherwise its spirit would haunt them. Living briefly in a world of hostile forces, they preserve themselves— so they believe—only by the exercise of magic lore. [24]

There is something of the same atmosphere in Hemingway's work. His heroes live in a world that is like a hostile forest, full of unseen dangers, not to mention the nightmares that haunt their sleep. Death spies on them from behind every tree. Their only chance of safety lies in the faithful observance of customs they invent for themselves. In an early story like "Big Two-Hearted River," you notice that Nick Adams does everything very slowly, not wishing "to rush his sensations any"; and he pays so much attention to the meaning and rightness of each gesture that his life in the wilderness becomes a series of little ceremonies.

Another hopper poked his face out of the bottle. His antennae wavered. Nick took him by the head and held him while he threaded the hook under his chin, down through his thorax and into the last segments of his abdomen. The grasshopper took hold of the hook with his front feet, spitting tobacco juice on it.

The grasshopper is playing its own part in a ritual; so too is the trout that swallows it, then bends the rod in jerks as it pumps against the current. The whole fishing trip, instead of being a mere escape, might be regarded as an incantation, a spell to banish evil spirits. And there are other rituals in Hemingway's work (besides drinking and writing, which I have mentioned already). Without too much difficulty we can recognize rites of animal sacrifice (as in *Death in the Afternoon*), of sexual union (in *For Whom the Bell Tolls*), of self-immolation (in "The Snows of Kilimanjaro"), of conversion (in *To Have and Have Not*), and of symbolic death and rebirth (in the Caporetto passage of *A Farewell to Arms*). When one of Hemingway's characters violates his own standards or the just laws of the tribe (as Ole Andreson has done in "The Killers"), he waits for death as stolidly as an Indian. [25]

Memories of the Indians he knew in his boyhood play an important part in Hemingway's work; they reappear in *The Torrents of Spring* and in several of his shorter stories. Robert Jordan, in *For Whom the Bell Tolls*, compares his own exploits to Indian warfare, and he strengthens himself during his last moments by thinking about his grandfather, an old Indian fighter. *In Our Time*, Hemingway's first book of stories, starts by telling how Nick Adams' father is called to attend an Indian woman who has been in labor for two days. The woman lies screaming in a bunkhouse, while her husband, with a badly injured foot, lies in the bunk above her smoking his pipe. Dr. Adams performs a Caesarean section without anesthetic, then sews up the wound with fishing leaders. When the operation is finished, he looks at the husband in the upper bunk and finds that he is dead; unable to bear his wife's pain, he has turned his face to the wall and cut his throat. A story Nick Adams later tells is of Trudy Gilby, the Indian girl with whom he used to go squirrel shooting and who, under the big hemlock trees, "did first what no one has ever done better." Most of Hemingway's heroines are in the image of Trudy; they have the obedience to their lovers and the sexual morals of Indian girls. His heroes suffer without complaining and, in one way or another, they destroy themselves like the Indian husband. [26]

But Hemingway feels an even greater kinship with the Spaniards, because they retain a primitive dignity in giving and accepting death. Even when their dignity is transformed into a blind lust for killing, as sometimes happened during their civil war, they continue to hold his respect. Augustín, in *For Whom the Bell Tolls*, sees four of Franco's cavalrymen and breaks out into a sweat that is not the sweat of fear. "When I saw those four there," he says, "and thought that we might kill them I was like a mare in the corral waiting for the stallion." And Robert Jordan thinks to himself: "We do it coldly but they do not, nor ever have. It is their extra sacrament. Their old one that they had before the new religion came from the far end of the Mediterranean, the one they have never abandoned but only suppressed and hidden to bring it out again in wars and inquisitions." Hemingway himself seems to have a feeling for half-forgotten sacraments; his cast of mind is pre-Christian and prelogical. [27]

Sometimes his stories come close to being adaptations of ancient myths. His first novel, for example, deals in different terms with the same legend that T. S. Eliot was not so much presenting as concealing in *The Waste Land*. When we turn to Eliot's explanatory notes, then read the book to which they refer as a principal source—*From Ritual to Romance*, by Jessie L. Weston—we learn that his poem is largely based on the legend of the Fisher King. The legend tells how the king was wounded in the loins and how he lay wasting in his bed while his whole kingdom became unfruitful; there was thunder but no rain; the rivers dried up, the flocks had no increase, and the women bore no children. *The Sun Also Rises* presents the same situation in terms of Paris after the First World War. It is a less despairing book than critics like to think; at times it is gay, friendly, even exuberant; but the hero has been wounded like the Fisher King, and he lives in a world that is absolutely sterile. I don't mean to imply that Heming-

way owes a debt to *The Waste Land.* He·had read the poem, which
he liked at first, and the notes that followed it, which he didn't like
at all; I doubt very much that he bothered to look at Jessie L. Weston's
book. He said in 1924, when he was paying tribute to Joseph Conrad:
"If I knew that by grinding Mr. Eliot into a fine dry powder and
sprinkling that powder over Mr. Conrad's grave Mr. Conrad would
shortly appear, looking very annoyed at the forced return, and com-
mence writing, I would leave for London early tomorrow with a
sausage grinder." And yet when he wrote his first novel, he dealt with
the same legend that Eliot had discovered by scholarship; recovering
it for himself, I think, by a sort of instinct for legendary situations. [28]

And it is this instinct for legends, for sacraments, for rituals, for
symbols appealing to buried hopes and fears, that helps to explain the
power of Hemingway's work and his vast superiority over his imitators.
The imitators have learned all his mannerisms as a writer, and in some
cases they can tell a story even better than Hemingway himself; but
they tell only the story; they communicate with the reader on only
one level of experience. Hemingway does more than that. Most of us
are also primitive in a sense, for all the machinery that surrounds our
lives. We have our private rituals, our little superstitions, our symbols
and fears and nightmares; and Hemingway reminds us unconsciously
of the hidden worlds in which we live. Reading his best work, we are
a little like Nick Adams looking down from the railroad bridge at the
trout in Big Two-Hearted River:

many trout in deep, fast-moving water, slightly distorted as he watched
far down through the glassy convex surface of the pool, its surface pushing
and swelling smooth against the resistance of the log-driven piles of the
bridge. At the bottom of the pool were the big trout. Nick did not see
them at first. Then he saw them at the bottom of the pool, big trout looking to hold themselves on the gravel bottom in a varying mist of gravel
and sand. [29]

During the last few years it has become the fashion to reprimand
Hemingway and to point out how much better his work would be

(with its undoubted power) if only he were a little more virtuous or reasonable or optimistic, or if he revealed the proper attitude toward progress and democracy. Critics like Maurice Coindreau (in French) and Bernard DeVoto have abused him without bothering to understand what he plainly says, much less what he suggests or implies. Even Maxwell Geismar, who is one of the few professors with a natural feeling for literary values, would like to make him completely over. "What a marvelous teacher Hemingway is," he exclaims,

with all the restrictions of temperament and environment which so far define his work! What could he not show us of living as well as dying, of the positives in our being as well as the destroying forces, of "grace under pressure" and the grace we need with no pressures, of ordinary life-giving actions along with those superb last gestures of doomed exiles!

Or, to put the matter more plainly, what a great writer Hemingway would be, in Geismar's opinion, if he combined his own work with equal parts of Trollope and Emerson. [30]

And the critics have some justice on their side. It is true that Hemingway has seldom been an affirmative writer; it is true that most of his work is narrow and violent and generally preoccupied with death. But the critics, although they might conceivably change him for the worse, are quite unable to change him for the better. He is one of the novelists who write, not as they should or would, but as they must. Like Poe and Hawthorne and Melville, he listens to his personal demon, which might also be called his intuition or his sense of life. If he listened to the critics instead, he might indeed come to resemble Trollope or Emerson, but the resemblance would be only on the surface and, as he sometimes says of writing that tries hard to meet public requirements, it would all go bad afterwards. Some of his own writing has gone bad, but surprisingly little of it. By now he has earned the right to be taken for what he is, with his great faults and greater virtues; with his narrowness, his power, his always open eyes, his stubborn, chip-on-the-shoulder honesty, his nightmares, his rituals for escaping them, and his sense of an inner and an outer world that for twenty years were moving together toward the same disaster. [31]

PURPOSE AND STRUCTURE

1. To remove an object from its usually assigned category, to examine it critically, and then to reclassify it on the basis of newly discovered characteristics can be an audacious and creative act. Cowley attempts just such a reclassification, for he announces his intention to remove Hemingway from one category of writers and to reassign him to another. (a) Where does Cowley announce his intention? Why is it important that his statement of intention come where it does? (b) To what school or class of writers was Hemingway first assigned? Who made the assignment? Why is it important to Cowley's thesis that the original classification be identified?

2. In part I what characteristics of Hemingway does Cowley identify to warrant reclassifying him as a writer? In part III what is the nature of the evidence he offers?

3. Relate parts I and III to the title.

4. In what way does the biographical material in part II contribute to the purpose of reclassifying Hemingway?

5. What new classification for Hemingway does Cowley suggest?

6. Each of the last three sentences of par. 2 uses a colon. Examine the sentences carefully and then formulate a rule for one use of the colon.

7. In par. 9 Cowley writes, "In those days he seems to have regarded stories as, essentially, machines for arousing emotion." Come to class prepared to compare this idea as developed in the paragraph with the ideas in Proust's *Prologue* and with Eliot's conception of the objective correlative.

8. In the last paragraph, Cowley writes, "Like Poe and Hawthorne and Melville, he listens to his personal demon. . . ." Many writers have listened to their personal demons. Why does reference to these contribute to coherence?

9. Par. 3 is almost entirely about "Big Two-Hearted River." What is the *general* idea of the paragraph? Where is it stated? What proportion of the paragraph is devoted to general idea; what proportion to example?

10. In what way is the construction of par. 4 the same as that of par. 3? In what way different?

DICTION AND TONE

1. Cowley begins his essay with an analogy: *Going back to Hemingway's work . . . is like going back to a brook where you had often fished.* Why does he select a brook? Why is returning to a brook more appropriate than returning to a childhood neighborhood?

2. What is Cowley's attitude toward professors of American literature? What clause in par. 1 is the best clue to his attitude?

3. In the next to last paragraph, Cowley's attitude toward Hemingway's critics is quite clear. Identify the language that reveals his attitude.

4. Aside from Cowley's attitude toward professors and critics, cite five pieces of evidence that lead you to conclude that Cowley admires Hemingway.

5. Compare the sentence structure and diction of pars. 2 and 3 with that of pars. 5 and 6. Explain why Cowley's style undergoes a subtle change.

APPLICATIONS TO WRITING

Once public opinion, tradition, or authority has classified an object or person, it is very difficult to attempt a reclassification. For example, the person who serves a jail sentence is readily classifiable as a law breaker. But, like Ghandi, he may also be a social leader or even a hero. (See Thoreau, *On the Duty of Civil Disobedience*.) The juvenile delinquent is juvenile; there is no doubt about that classification. But the behavior described as delinquent may be no more than a youthful emulation of adult values, for the adolescent is adventurous, has high courage, a strong sense of social solidarity, a sense of honor he will fight to defend.

Take a person or object which you know well and which you feel is generally erroneously classified and reclassify him or it according to the characteristics you identify and describe in your essay.

Part Four

COMPARISON AND CONTRAST

Comparison and Contrast—the presentation of a subject by indicating similarities between two or more things (comparison) and by indicating differences (contrast). The basic elements in a comparative process, then, are (1) the various entities compared, and (2) the points of likeness or difference between them. To be comparable, they should be members of the same class (see Classification). For example, life worshipers and death worshipers, both members of the same class, are comparable. Democracy and communism are not comparable, since the former is a subdivision of a political system and the latter, an economic one. The range of effects that may be achieved in comparison and contrast is reflected in Macaulay's straightforward development of the two aspects of the *persona* of the Puritans; in Mencken's preposterous and paradoxical development of the distinctions between men and women; in Trilling's allusive and fast paced exploration of the points of contact between literature and psychoanalysis; in Craft's concrete and intimate confrontation of talent and genius; in Huxley's subtle and complex counterpointing of life and death worshipers.

175

THE PURITANS

THOMAS BABINGTON MACAULAY

We would speak first of the Puritans, the most remarkable body of men, perhaps, which the world has ever produced. The odious and ridiculous parts of their character lie on the surface. He that runs may read them; nor have there been wanting attentive and malicious observers to point them out. For many years after the Restoration they were the theme of unmeasured invective and derision. They were exposed to the utmost licentiousness of the press and of the stage, at the time when the press and the stage were most licentious. They were not men of letters; they were, as a body, unpopular; they could not defend themselves; and the public would not take them under its protection. They were therefore abandoned, without reserve, to the tender mercies of the satirists and dramatists. The ostentatious simplicity of their dress, their sour aspect, their nasal twang, their stiff posture, their long graces, their Hebrew names, the Scriptural phrases which they introduced on every occasion, their contempt of human learning, their detestation of polite amusements, were indeed fair game for the laughers. But it is not from the laughers alone that the philosophy of history is to be learnt. And he who approaches this subject should carefully guard against the influence of that potent ridicule which has already misled so many excellent writers. [1]

Those who roused the people to resistance, who directed their

measures through a long series of eventful years, who formed, out of
the most unpromising materials, the finest army that Europe had ever
seen, who trampled down King, Church, and Aristocracy, who, in the
short intervals of domestic sedition and rebellion, made the name of
England terrible to every nation on the face of the earth, were no
vulgar fanatics. Most of their absurdities were mere external badges,
like the signs of freemasonry, or the dresses of friars. We regret that
those badges were not more attractive. We regret that a body to
whose courage and talents mankind has owed inestimable obligations
had not the lofty elegance which distinguished some of the adherents
of Charles the First, or the easy good-breeding for which the court
of Charles the Second was celebrated. But, if we must make our
choice, we shall, like Bassanio in the play, turn from the specious
caskets which contain only the Death's head and the Fool's head, and
fix on the plain leaden chest which conceals the treasure. [2]

The Puritans were men whose minds had derived a peculiar character from the daily contemplation of superior beings and eternal
interests. Not content with acknowledging, in general terms, an overruling Providence, they habitually ascribed every event to the will of
the Great Being, for whose power nothing was too vast, for whose
inspection nothing was too minute. To know him, to serve him, to
enjoy him, was with them the great end of existence. They rejected
with contempt the ceremonious homage which other sects substituted
for the pure worship of the soul. Instead of catching occasional glimpses
of the Deity through an obscuring veil, they aspired to gaze full on
his intolerable brightness, and to commune with him face to face.
Hence originated their contempt for terrestrial distinctions. The difference between the greatest and the meanest of mankind seemed to
vanish, when compared with the boundless interval which separated
the whole race from him on whom their own eyes were constantly
fixed. They recognized no title to superiority but his favour; and, confident of that favour, they despised all the accomplishments and all
the dignities of the world. If they were unacquainted with the works
of philosophers and poets, they were deeply read in the oracles of

God. If their names were not found in the registers of heralds, they were recorded in the Book of Life. If their steps were not accompanied by a splendid train of menials, legions of ministering angels had charge over them. Their palaces were houses not made with hands; their diadems crowns of glory which should never fade away. On the rich and the eloquent, on nobles and priests, they looked down with contempt: for they esteemed themselves rich in a more precious treasure, and eloquent in a more sublime language, nobles by the right of an earlier creation, and priests by the imposition of a mightier hand. The very meanest of them was a being to whose fate a mysterious and terrible importance belonged, on whose slightest action the spirits of light and darkness looked with anxious interest, who had been destined, before heaven and earth were created, to enjoy a felicity which should continue when heaven and earth should have passed away. Events which short-sighted politicians ascribed to earthly causes had been ordained on his account. For his sake empires had risen, and flourished, and decayed. For his sake the Almighty had proclaimed his will by the pen of the Evangelist, and the harp of the prophet. He had been wrested by no common deliverer from the grasp of no common foe. He had been ransomed by the sweat of no vulgar agony, by the blood of no earthly sacrifice. It was for him that the sun had been darkened, that the rocks had been rent, that the dead had risen, that all nature had shuddered at the sufferings of her expiring God. [3]

Thus the Puritan was made up of two different men, the one all self-abasement, penitence, gratitude, passion, the other proud, calm, inflexible, sagacious. He prostrated himself in the dust before his Maker: but he set his foot on the neck of his king. In his devotional retirement, he prayed with convulsions, and groans, and tears. He was half-maddened by glorious or terrible illusions. He heard the lyres of angels or the tempting whispers of fiends. He caught a gleam of the Beatific Vision, or woke screaming from dreams of everlasting fire. Like Vane, he thought himself intrusted with the sceptre of the millennial year. Like Fleetwood, he cried in the bitterness of his soul

that God had hid his face from him. But when he took his seat in
the council, or girt on his sword for war, these tempestuous workings
of the soul had left no perceptible trace behind them. People who
saw nothing of the godly but their uncouth visages, and heard nothing
from them but their groans and their whining hymns, might laugh
at them. But those had little reason to laugh who encountered them
in the hall of debate or in the field of battle. These fanatics brought
to civil and military affairs a coolness of judgement and an im-
mutability of purpose which some writers have thought inconsistent
with their religious zeal, but which were in fact the necessary effects
of it. The intensity of their feelings on one subject made them tran-
quil on every other. One overpowering sentiment had subjected to
itself pity and hatred, ambition and fear. Death had lost its terrors
and pleasure its charms. They had their smiles and their tears, their
raptures and their sorrows, but not for the things of this world.
Enthusiasm had made them Stoics, had cleared their minds from
every vulgar passion and prejudice, and raised them above the influence of danger and of corruption. It sometimes might lead them to
pursue unwise ends, but never to choose unwise means. They went
through the world, like Sir Artegal's iron man Talus with his flail,
crushing and trampling down oppressors, mingling with human
beings, but having neither part nor lot in human infirmities, insensible
to fatigue, to pleasure, and to pain, not to be pierced by any weapon,
not to be withstood by any barrier. [4]

Such we believe to have been the character of the Puritans. We
perceive the absurdity of their manners. We dislike the sullen gloom
of their domestic habits. We acknowledge that the tone of their
minds was often injured by straining after things too high for mortal
reach: and we know that, in spite of their hatred of Popery, they
too often fell into the worst vices of that bad system, intolerance
and extravagant austerity, that they had their anchorites and their
crusades, their Dunstans and their De Montforts, their Dominics
and their Escobars. Yet, when all circumstances are taken into consideration, we do not hesitate to pronounce them a brave, a wise,
an honest, and an useful body. [5]

PURPOSE AND STRUCTURE

1. Macaulay's comparison and contrast (see Glossary) of the reputed and actual qualities of "The Puritans" is masterful. His first sentence praises them (*most remarkable body of men, perhaps, which the world has produced*). Is this the topic sentence? or is the second sentence the topic sentence?

2. The powerful first sentence of par. 2 enumerates the Puritans' achievements. How do their achievements relate to their absurdities and lack of elegance (the central section of par. 2)? Why is the *plain leaden chest which conceals the treasure* an appropriate conclusion to the paragraph?

3. What is the topic sentence of par. 3? Does it involve a comparison and contrast? Does the paragraph?

4. The first sentence of par. 4 develops a sharp contrast. Follow this contrast through the paragraph sentence by sentence. The last sentence has what relationship to the previous contrasts?

5. *Enthusiasm had made them Stoics* (par. 4) strikingly joins two superficially disparate characteristics. What is the effect of joining them?

6. Par. 5 is a summary paragraph. The sentences between the first and the last are critical of the Puritans. Yet the final sentence praises them. Is this praise documented in the previous paragraphs?

DICTION AND TONE

1. The last sentence of par. 4 is vital and complex. Would it be more effective as two sentences?

2. What does the word *men* in the first sentence of par. 4 refer to— differing groups of Puritans or differing characteristics within each Puritan? Is *men* the most appropriate word here? Rewrite the sentence, attempting an improvement.

3. The last sentences of par. 3 swell into biblical eloquence. Why?

APPLICATIONS TO WRITING

1. Describe a political or religious group of today, using the method of Macaulay (contrasting the public reputation with private characteristics).

2. Describe a group sharing an attitude or set of beliefs (for instance, physical culturists, Zen Buddhists, free speech advocates, psychedelists). At one point in your paper, mirror their diction (see par. 3 for an example).

THE FEMININE MIND

H. L. MENCKEN

A man's women folk, whatever their outward show of respect for his merit and authority, always regard him secretly as an ass, and with something akin to pity. His most gaudy sayings and doings seldom deceive them; they see the actual man within, and know him for a shallow and pathetic fellow. In this fact, perhaps, lies one of the best proofs of feminine intelligence, or, as the common phrase makes it, feminine intuition. The marks of that so-called intuition are simply a sharp and accurate perception of reality, a habitual immunity to emotional enchantment, a relentless capacity for distinguishing clearly between the appearance and the substance. The appearance, in the normal family circle, is a hero, a magnifico, a demigod. The substance is a poor mountebank. [1]

A man's wife, true enough, may envy her husband certain of his more soothing prerogatives and sentimentalities. She may envy him his masculine liberty of movement and occupation, his impenetrable complacency, his peasant-like delight in petty vices, his capacity for hiding the harsh face of reality behind the cloak of romanticism, his general innocence and childishness. But she never envies him his shoddy and preposterous soul. [2]

This shrewd perception of masculine bombast and make-believe, this acute understanding of man as the eternal tragic comedian, is at the bottom of that compassionate irony which passes under the name of the maternal instinct. A woman wishes to mother a man simply because she sees into his helplessness, his need of an amiable environment, his touching self-delusion. That ironical note is not only daily apparent in real life; it sets the whole tone of feminine fiction. The woman novelist, if she be skillful enough to be taken seriously, never takes her heroes so. From the day of Jane Austen to the day of Selma Lagerlof she has always got into her character study a touch of superior aloofness, of ill-concealed derision. I can't recall a single masculine figure created by a woman who is not, at bottom, a booby. [3]

That it should be necessary, at this late stage in the senility of the human race, to argue that women have a fine and fluent intelligence is surely an eloquent proof of the defective observation, incurable prejudice, and general imbecility of their lords and masters. Women, in fact, are not only intelligent; they have almost a monopoly of certain of the subtler and more utile forms of intelligence. The thing itself, indeed, might be reasonably described as a special feminine character; there is in it, in more than one of its manifestations, a femaleness as palpable as the femaleness of cruelty, masochism or rouge. Men are strong. Men are brave in physical combat. Men are romantic, and love what they conceive to be virtue and beauty. Men incline to faith, hope and charity. Men know how to sweat and endure. Men are amiable and fond. But in so far as they show the true fundamentals of intelligence—in so far as they reveal a capacity for discovering the kernel of eternal verity in the husk of delusion and hallucination and a passion for bringing it forth—to that extent, at least, they are feminine, and still nourished by the milk of their mothers. The essential traits and qualities of the male, the hall-marks of the unpolluted masculine, are at the same time the hall-marks of the numskull. The caveman is all muscles and mush. Without a woman to rule him and think for him, he is a truly lamentable spectacle: a baby with whiskers, a rabbit with the frame of an aurochs, a feeble and preposterous caricature of God. [4]

Here, of course, I do not mean to say that masculinity contributes nothing whatsoever to the complex of chemicophysiological reactions which produces what we call superior ability; all I mean to say is that this complex is impossible without the feminine contribution—that it is a product of the interplay of the two elements. In women of talent we see the opposite picture. They are commonly somewhat mannish, and shave as well as shine. Think of George Sand, Catherine the Great, Elizabeth of England, Rosa Bonheur, Teresa Carreño or Cosima Wagner. Neither sex, without some fertilization of the complementary characters of the other, is capable of the highest reaches of human endeavor. Man, without a saving touch of woman in him, is too doltish, too naive and romantic, too easily deluded and lulled to sleep by his imagination to be anything above a cavalryman, a theologian or a corporation director. And woman, without some trace of that divine innocence which is masculine, is too harshly the realist for those vast projections of the fancy which lie at the heart of what we call genius. The wholly manly man lacks the wit necessary to give objective form to his soaring and secret dreams, and the wholly womanly woman is apt to be too cynical a creature to dream at all. [5]

What men, in their egotism, constantly mistake for a deficiency of intelligence in woman is merely an incapacity for mastering that mass of small intellectual tricks, that complex of petty knowledges, that collection of cerebral rubberstamps, which constitute the chief mental equipment of the average male. A man thinks that he is more intelligent than his wife because he can add up a column of figures more accurately, or because he is able to distinguish between the ideas of rival politicians, or because he is privy to the minutiae of some sordid and degrading business or profession. But these empty talents, of course, are not really signs of intelligence; they are, in fact, merely a congeries of petty tricks and antics, and their acquirement puts little more strain on the mental powers than a chimpanzee suffers in learning how to catch a penny or scratch a match. [6]

The whole mental baggage of the average business man, or even the average professional man, is inordinately childish. It takes no more actual sagacity to carry on the everyday hawking and haggling of the world, or to ladle out its normal doses of bad medicine and worse law, than it takes to operate a taxicab or fry a pan of fish. No observant person, indeed, can come into close contact with the general run of business and professional men—I confine myself to those who seem to get on in the world, and exclude the admitted failures—without marveling at their intellectual lethargy, their incurable ingenuousness, their appalling lack of ordinary sense. The late Charles Francis Adams, a grandson of one American President and a great-grandson of another, after a long lifetime in intimate association with some of the chief business "geniuses" of the United States, reported in his old age that he had never heard a single one of them say anything worth hearing. These were vigorous and masculine men, and in a man's world they were successful men, but intellectually they were all blank cartridges. [7]

There is, indeed, fair ground for arguing that, if men of that kidney were genuinely intelligent, they would never succeed at their gross and driveling concerns—that their very capacity to master and retain such balderdash as constitutes their stock in trade is proof of their inferior mentality. The notion is certainly supported by the familiar incompetency of admittedly first-rate men for what are called practical concerns. One could not think of Aristotle multiplying 3,472,701 by 99,999 without making a mistake, nor could one think of him remembering the range of this or that railway share for two years, or the number of tenpenny nails in a hundredweight, or the freight on lard from Galveston to Rotterdam. And by the same token one could not imagine him expert at bridge, or at golf, or at any other of the idiotic games at which what are called successful men commonly divert themselves. In his great study of British genius, Havelock Ellis found that an incapacity for such shabby expertness is visible in almost all first-rate men. They are bad at tying cravats. They are puzzled by bookkeeping. They know nothing of party politics. In brief, they are inert and impotent in the very fields of endeavor that see the average men's highest performances, and are easily surpassed by men who, in actual intelligence, are about as far below them as the *Simidoe*. [8]

This lack of skill at manual and mental tricks of a trivial character —which must inevitably appear to a barber as stupidity, and to a successful haberdasher as downright imbecility—is a character that men of the first class share with women of the first, second and even third classes. One seldom hears of women succeeding in the occupations which bring out such expertness most lavishly—for example, tuning pianos, practising law, or writing editorials for newspapers— despite the circumstance that the great majority of such occupations are well within their physical powers, and that few of them offer any very formidable social barriers to female entrance. There is no external reason why they should not prosper at the bar, or as editors of magazines, or as managers of factories, or in the wholesale trade, or as hotel-keepers. The taboos that stand in the way are of very small force; various adventurous women have defied them with impunity, and once the door is entered there remains no special handicap within. But, as everyone knows, the number of women actually practising these trades and professions is very small, and few of them have attained to any distinction in competition with men. [9]

The cause thereof, as I say, is not external, but internal. It lies in the same disconcerting apprehension of the larger realities, the same impatience with the paltry and meretricious, the same disqualification for mechanical routine and empty technic which one finds in the higher varieties of men. Even in the pursuits which, by the custom of Christendom, are especially their own, women seldom show any of that elaborately conventionalized and half automatic proficiency which is the pride and boast of most men. It is a commonplace of observation that a housewife who actually knows how to cook, or who can make her own clothes with enough skill to conceal the fact from the most casual glance, or who is competent to instruct her children in the elements of morals, learning and hygiene—it is a platitude that such a woman is very rare indeed, and that when she is encountered she is not usually esteemed for her general intelligence. [10]

This is particularly true in the United States, where the position of women is higher than in any other civilized or semi-civilized country, and the old assumption of their intellectual inferiority has been most successfully challenged. The American bourgeois dinner-table becomes a monument to the defective technic of the American housewife. The guest who respects his esophagus, invited to feed upon its discordant and ill-prepared victuals, evades the experience as long and as often as he can, and resigns himself to it as he might resign himself to being shaved by a paralytic. Nowhere else in the world have women more leisure and freedom to improve their minds, and nowhere else do they show a higher level of intelligence, but nowhere else is there worse cooking in the home, or a more inept handling of the whole domestic economy, or a larger dependence upon the aid of external substitutes, by men provided, for the skill that is wanting where it theoretically exists. It is surely no mere coincidence that the land of the emancipated and enthroned woman is also the land of canned soup, of canned pork and beans, of whole meals in cans, and of everything else ready made. And nowhere else is there a more striking tendency to throw the whole business of training the minds of children upon professional pedagogues, mostly idiots, and the whole business of developing and caring for their bodies upon pediatricians, playground "experts," sex hygienists and other such professionals, mostly frauds. [11]

In brief, women rebel—often unconsciously, sometimes even submitting all the while—against the dull, mechanical tricks of the trade that the present organization of society compels so many of them to practise for a living, and that rebellion testifies to their intelligence. If they enjoyed and took pride in those tricks, and showed it by diligence and skill, they would be on all fours with such men as are head waiters, accountants, school-masters or carpetbeaters, and proud of it. The inherent tendency of any woman above the most stupid is to evade the whole obligation, and, if she can not actually evade it, to reduce its demands to the minimum. And when some accident purges her, either temporarily or permanently, of the inclination to marriage, and she enters into competition with men in the general business of the world, the sort of career that she commonly carves out offers additional evidence of her mental superiority. In whatever calls for no more than an invariable technic and a feeble chicanery she usually fails; in whatever calls for independent thought and re-sourcefulness she usually succeeds. Thus she is almost always a failure as a lawyer, for the law requires only an armament of hollow phrases and stereotyped formulae, and a mental habit which puts these phantasms above sense, truth and justice; and she is almost always a failure in business, for business, in the main, is so foul a compound of trivialities and rogueries that her sense of intellectual integrity revolts against it. But she is usually a success as a sick-nurse, for that profession requires ingenuity, quick comprehension, courage in the face of novel and disconcerting situations, and above all, a capacity for penetrating and dominating character; and whenever she comes into competition with men in the arts, particularly on those secondary planes where simple nimbleness of mind is unaided by the master strokes of genius, she holds her own invariably. In the *demi-monde* one will find enough acumen and daring, and enough resilience in the face of special difficulties, to put the equipment of any exclusively male profession to shame. If the work of the average man required half the mental agility and readiness of resource of the work of the average brothel-keeper, the average man would be con-stantly on the verge of starvation. [12]

Men, as everyone knows, are disposed to question this superior intelligence of women; their egoism demands the denial, and they are seldom reflective enough to dispose of it by logical and evidential analysis. Moreover, there is a certain specious appearance of sound-ness in their position; they have forced upon women an artificial character which well conceals their real character, and women have found it profitable to encourage the deception. But though every normal man thus cherishes the soothing unction that he is the intel-lectual superior of all women, and particularly of his wife, he con-stantly gives the lie to his pretension by consulting and deferring to what he calls her intuition. That is to say, he knows by experience that her judgment in many matters of capital concern is more subtle and searching than his own, and, being disinclined to accredit this great sagacity to a more competent intelligence, he takes refuge behind the doctrine that it is due to some impenetrable and intangible talent for guessing correctly, some half mystical supersense, some vague (and, in essence, infra-human) instinct. [13]

The true nature of this alleged instinct, however, is revealed by an examination of the situations which inspire a man to call it to his aid. These situations do not arise out of the purely technical problems that are his daily concern, but out of the rarer and more fundamental, and hence enormously more difficult problems which beset him only at long and irregular intervals, and so offer a test, not of his mere capacity for being drilled, but of his capacity for genuine ratiocination. No man, I take it, save one consciously inferior and hen-pecked, would consult his wife about hiring a clerk, or about extending credit to some paltry customer, or about some routine piece of tawdry swindling; but not even the most egoistic man would fail to sound the sentiment of his wife about taking a partner into his business, or about standing for public office, or about marrying off their daughter. Such things are of massive importance; they lie at the foundation of well-being; they call for the best thought that the man confronted by them can muster; the perils hidden in a wrong decision overcome even the clamors of vanity. It is in such situations that the superior mental grasp of women is of obvious utility, and has to be admitted. It is here that they rise above the insignificant sentimentalities, superstitions and formulae of men, and apply to the business their singular talent for separating the appearance from the substance, and so exercise what is called their intuition. [14]

Intuition? Bosh! Women, in fact, are the supreme realists of the race. Apparently illogical, they are the possessors of a rare and subtle super-logic. Apparently whimsical, they hang to the truth with a tenacity which carries them through every phase of its incessant, jelly-like shifting of form. Apparently unobservant and easily deceived, they see with bright and horrible eyes. . . . In men, too, the same merciless perspicacity sometimes shows itself—men recognized to be more aloof and uninflammable than the general—men of special talent for the logical—sardonic men, cynics. Men, too, sometimes have brains. But that is a rare, rare man, I venture, who is as steadily intelligent, as constantly sound in judgment, as little put off by appearances, as the average multipara of forty-eight. [15]

PURPOSE AND STRUCTURE

1. Mencken describes women's failures as evidence of their superiority and men's successes as proof of their inferiority. This unstated paradox is developed by means of comparison and contrast. Locate the paragraphs in which he presents the similarities of men and women, the differences, and both. How does Mencken's definition of the feminine mind (try to sum it up in an inclusive statement) draw upon his comparison of men and women and unify the essay?

2. Before he defines the feminine mind, Mencken brings his subject into focus by the method of *identification*. In par. 1 he identifies the feminine mind through an implied contrast between the inward and outward attitude of woman toward man. Cite other examples of identification.

3. In par. 1 Mencken contrasts woman's outward show of respect toward man and her inward (secret) attitude of contempt and pity. The contrast, explicit or implied, between inward and outward behavior recurs throughout the essay. Where? What purpose does it serve in the development of his definition? What other contrasts are developed in this paragraph? What causal relationship is made in the first paragraph? What other causal relationships are developed in this essay? How do they contribute to Mencken's argument?

In his description of the three characteristics of the feminine mind, is each element of the series discrete? If not, what is the most general element in the series to which the others are subordinate? Locate other explicit or implied references to this attribute.

4. Analyze the methods of paragraph transition Mencken employs. For example, pars. 1–3 all deal with woman's perception of man: the first,

with her inward perception of him; the second, with her perception of him with special relationship to herself (that is, what she may and does not envy); the third, with Mencken's comment upon her perception. How does he provide a bridge between pars. 9 and 10? One way to achieve emphasis is through the cumulative use of illustration. How does the author achieve a cumulative effect without repetition? Underline the topic sentences in each paragraph and note the method of its development before you attempt an answer.

5. Consider the manner in which the author defines *compassionate irony* (par. 3). How has the term been anticipated in par. 1? How does he relate it to maternal instinct? Does he use it as an antithesis? a synonym? a qualification? Locate previous and subsequent assertions and illustrations which demonstrate both *compassion* and *irony*.

6. Is there an inherent contradiction in the point he makes in par. 1 and his use of *aloofness* and *derision* in his literary example in par. 3? Or can they be reconciled? Explain.

7. In par. 1 Mencken describes man and makes assertions about his weakness; he then states that because woman perceives these weaknesses, she is intelligent. In par. 4 there is an interesting use of counterpoint: because he must prove that woman is intelligent, therefore man is defective in his perception. Comment upon the logic or circularity of this kind of reasoning.

8. In the statement in which he recapitulates his definition of intelligence (par. 4) Mencken attributes a feminine quality to men. Far from being a term of disparagement, it is one of high praise. How do you know? To find further evidence, note the topic sentence in par. 5 and the concrete details which support it.

9. How does Mencken establish man's confusion of woman's intelligence with her intuition? How does he establish the speciousness of man's rationalization?

10. By what means does he develop the double antithesis between man's outward scorn and inward respect and woman's outward respect and inward contempt (par. 16)?

11. In par. 4 is a series of perfectly balanced sentences beginning *men are.* . . . How are they linked with the preceding sentences? In the last paragraph is another masterful example of parallel structure. Analyze its components and note other examples of balance.

DICTION AND TONE

1. Mencken provokes laughter but is serious. What is he serious about? Would his essay be funny if it were not serious? Would he be as effective if he did not make preposterous statements? By specific reference to the text, analyze what these elements contribute to the tone. Could you call it mock seriousness?

2. Which words among the following best describe Mencken's tone: buffoonery, diatribe, vituperation, invective, flamboyance, relish, bravura, castigation, astringency, stridency, exhibitionism, virtuosity, gusto, imperiousness, dogmatism? Defend your choice by specific allusions to text.

3. What tone is established in the first paragraph by the use of *magnifico, demigod, mountebank?* How would you characterize the order and tone of this series? Note the series in par. 4: *cruelty, masochism or rouge.* What is the logical relationship among these items? What do they tell you about his tone? In what other series in par. 5 does Mencken use the same technique? He uses the word *femaleness* for the first time in par. 4. What are its connotations? How does its use complicate the purpose and tone of the essay?

4. Mencken uses a series of abstractions such as virtue, beauty, faith, life, charity (par. 4). In the midst of his idiosyncratic verbs and nouns, what function do they perform? How does the phrase *in the husk of delusion and hallucination* contribute to the tone? Ask the same question of the series: *a baby with whiskers, a rabbit with the frame of an aurochs, a feeble and preposterous caricature of God.*

5. How does the allusion to Aristotle (par. 8) exemplify his humor, his tone? He juxtaposes *shabby* with *expertness* [8], *divine* with *innocence* [5], *intellectual* with *tricks* [6] and with *lethargy* [7], *cerebral* with *rubberstamps* [6], *shoddy* and *preposterous* with *soul* [2]. What is the effect of these pairings on purpose and tone?

6. From time to time Mencken qualifies his sweeping assertions. Identify statements that are preposterous and phrases or words that are hyperbolic. Note also the times he qualifies opinions that would otherwise tax the reader's credulity. Identify passages in which he modulates an extreme statement.

7. How does the word *infra-human* (par. 13) contribute to his purpose and tone?

8. Show the function of *jelly-like shifting; bright and horrible; merciless perspicacity; uninflammable; sardonic;* and *average multipara of forty-eight* in the context of the last paragraph.

9. Mencken asserted in his large work *In Defense of Women*, from which this essay was taken, that it was "pianissimo in tone." How would you sum up its tone?

APPLICATIONS TO WRITING

1. Using the method of comparison and contrast, define the quality of mind of two people close to you.

2. Mencken's attitudes toward women are reflected in a number of essays subsumed under the topic, "Reflections on Human Monogamy" in the fourth series of *Prejudices*. Read especially "The Helpmate," "Woman as Realpolitiker," "Venus at the Domestic Hearth," "The Rat-Trap" and compare and contrast his views of women with those in "The Feminine Mind." Analyze any differences in method and tone.

LITERATURE AND

PSYCHOANALYSIS

LIONEL TRILLING

A generation ago, literary men claimed Freud for their own, for reasons that are obvious enough, but nowadays it is not the tendency of literary men to continue this claim. The belief, which is now to be observed in some literary quarters, that Freud's science is hostile to the spirit of literature is as unconsidered a notion as the former belief that psychoanalysis was a sort of literary invention. Yet it is certainly true that, whatever natural affinity we see between Freud and literature, however great a contribution to the understanding of literature we judge him to have made, it must seem to a literary man that Freud sees literature not from within but from without. The great contribution he has made to our understanding of literature does not arise from what he says about literature itself but from what he says about the nature of the human mind: he showed us that poetry is indigenous to the very constitution of the mind; he saw the mind as being, in the greater part of its tendency, exactly a poetry-making faculty. When he speaks about literature itself, he is sometimes right and sometimes wrong. And sometimes, when he is

195

wrong, his mistakes are more useful than literary men are willing to perceive. But he is always, I think, outside the process of literature. Much as he responds to the product, he does not really imagine the process. He does not have what we call the *feel* of the thing. [1]

Freud was a scientist—this was the name he cherished and sought to deserve. Nowadays some of us have fallen into the habit of saying that there is no real difference between the mind of the scientist and the mind of the artist. We are all dismayed at the separateness and specialness of the disciplines of the mind, and when we meet together at conferences and round-tables designed to overcome this bad situation, we find it in our hearts to say to each other that we have everything in common, very little in difference. This is laudable in its motive, and no doubt it is true enough under some sufficiently large aspect. Yet in practical fact the difference is real and important, as of course we know. The reason I am insisting on the difference between the mind of the scientist and the mind of the literary man, and on Freud's being a scientist, is, obviously, that the recognition of this makes so much more interesting and significant the relation of Freud to humane letters. [2]

The canon of Freud's work is large and complex, and the tradition of humane letters is patently not to be encompassed in any formulation of its nature. I must therefore be hopelessly crude and summary in an attempt to suggest the connection between the two. Literature is not a unitary thing, and there is probably no such single entity as *the* literary mind. But I shall assume that literature is what it actually is not, a unity, and I shall deal with it in those of its aspects in which that assumption does not immediately appear to be absurd, in which it is not wholly impossible to say that literature "is" or "does" this or that. [3]

The first thing that occurs to me to say about literature, as I consider it in the relation in which Freud stands to it, is that literature is dedicated to the conception of the self. This is a very simple thing to say, perhaps to the point of dullness. But it becomes more complicated when we perceive how much of an achievement this conception is, how far it may be in advance of what society, or the general culture, can conceive. Tolstoi tells the story of the countess who wept buckets at a play while her coachman sat on the box of her waiting carriage, perishing of the cold through the long hours of the performance. This may stand for the discrepancy between what literature conceives of the self and what society, or the general culture, conceives. At the behest of literature, and with its help, the countess is able to imagine the selfhood of others, no doubt through the process of identification; she is not able, of herself, to imagine the selfhood of her own servant. What the *Iliad* conceives in the way of selfhood is far beyond what could be conceived by the culture in which it was written. *The Trojan Women* of Euripides must sometimes seem unendurable, so intense is the recognition of the selfhood of others in pain that it forces upon us. Yet it is possible that *The Trojan Women* was being composed at the very moment that Athens was infamously carrying out its reprisal against the city of Melos for wishing to remain neutral in the Peloponnesian War, slaughtering the men of the city and enslaving the women and children, doing this not in the passion of battle but, like the Greek princes of *The Trojan Women*, in the horrible deliberateness of policy. Thucydides understood the hideousness of the deed, and it is thought by some modern scholars that he conceived his *History* in the form of a tragedy in which the downfall of Athens is the consequence of her sin at Melos; but Thucydides does not record any party of opposition to the Melian decision or any revulsion among his fellow countrymen. In almost every developed society, literature is able to conceive of the self, and the selfhood of others, far more intensely than the general culture ever can. [4]

One of the best-known tags of literary criticism is Coleridge's phrase, "the willing suspension of disbelief." Coleridge says that the willing suspension of disbelief constitutes "poetic faith." I suppose that we might say that it constitutes scientific faith too, or scientific method. Once we get beyond the notion that science is, as we used to be told it was, "organized common sense," and have come to understand that science is organized improbability, or organized fantasy, we begin to see that the willing suspension of disbelief is an essential part of scientific thought. And certainly the willing suspension of disbelief constitutes moral faith—the essence of the moral life would seem to consist in doing that most difficult thing in the world, making a willing suspension of disbelief in the selfhood of someone else. This Freud was able to do in a most extraordinary way, and not by the mere impulse of his temperament, but systematically, as an element of his science. We recall, for instance, that dramatic moment in the development of psychoanalysis when Freud accepted as literally true the stories told him by so many of his early patients, of their having been, as children, sexually seduced or assaulted by adults, often by their own parents. We know how his patients rewarded his credulity—scarcely any of them were telling the truth. They had betrayed Freud into constructing a hypothesis on the basis of their stories. Hypotheses are precious things and this one now had to be abandoned, and so Freud had reason to think very harshly of his patients if he wished to. But he did not blame them, he did not say they were lying—he willingly suspended his disbelief in their fantasies, which they themselves believed, and taught himself how to find the truth that was really in them. [5]

It is hard to know whether to describe this incident as a triumph of the scientific imagination and its method or as the moral triumph of an impatient and even censorious man in whom the intention of therapy and discovery was stronger than the impulse to blame. But in whatever terms we choose to praise it, it has been established in the system of psychoanalytical therapy. From it followed the willing suspension of disbelief in the semantic value of dreams, and the willing suspension of disbelief in the concept of mind, which all well-trained neurologists and psychiatrists of Vienna knew to be but a chimera. Freud's acceptance of the fantasies of his early patients, his conclusion that their untruths had a meaning, a purpose, and even a value, was the suspension of disbelief in the selfhood of these patients. Its analogue is not, I think, the religious virtue of charity, but something in which the intelligence plays a greater part. We must be reminded of that particular kind of understanding, that particular exercise of the literary intelligence by which we judge adversely the deeds of Achilles, but not Achilles himself, by which we do not blame Macbeth, nor even, to mention the hero and heroine of Freud's favorite English poem, Adam and Eve, who, because they are the primal parents, we naturally want to blame for everything. [6]

If we go on with our gross summary comparison of literature and psychoanalysis, we can say that they are also similar in this respect, that it is of the essence of both to represent the opposition between two principles, those which Freud called the reality principle and the pleasure principle. Whenever Freud goes wrong in his dealings with literature, it is because he judges literature by too limited an application of these principles. When he praises literature, it is chiefly because of its powers of factual representation, its powers of discovery—"Not I but the poets," he said, "discovered the unconscious." When he denigrates literature (by implication), it is by speaking of its mere hedonism, of its being an escape from reality, a substitute-gratification, a daydream, an anodyne. Some years ago I dealt as sternly as I could with the errors of these formulations of Freud's,[1] and so now perhaps I am privileged to lighten the burden of reprobation they have had to bear and to take note of a certain rightness and usefulness they have. [7]

Freud is scarcely unique in conceiving of literature in terms of the opposition between reality and pleasure. This conception is endemic in literary criticism itself since at least the time of Plato, and often in a very simple form. It was usually in a very simple form indeed that the opposition was made in the nineteenth century. We have but to read the young Yeats and to observe his passion against fact and the literature of fact, and his avowed preference for the literature of dream, to see how established in the thought of the time was the opposition between the pleasure principle and the principle of reality. [8]

Nowadays literary criticism tends to be restive under the opposition, which it takes to be a covert denial of the autonomy of literature, a

[1] In "Freud and Literature," *The Liberal Imagination*, 1950.

way of judging literature by the categories of science. But the poets themselves have always accepted the opposition. They accept the commission to represent something called reality, which lies outside of literature, and which they think of as either antagonistic to the dream of pleasure, or as standing beyond pleasure. Wordsworth blamed himself for having "lived in a dream," for having failed to represent to himself the painful adversity of the world. Keats denounced himself for his membership in the "tribe" of mere dreaming poets, who are so much less than "those to whom the miseries of the world/ Are misery, and will not let them rest."

> What benefit canst thou do, or all thy tribe,
> To the great world? Thou art a dreaming thing,
> A fever of thyself—think of the Earth . . .

Yet with the dream of pleasure, or with the actuality of pleasure, the poets, at least of an earlier time than ours, always kept in touch. Keats's whole mental life was an effort to demonstrate the continuity between pleasure and reality. Wordsworth speaks of the principle of pleasure—the phrase is his—as constituting the "naked and native dignity of man." He says, moreover, that it is the principle by which man not only "feels, and lives, and moves," but also "knows": the principle of pleasure was for Wordsworth the very ground of the principle of reality, and so of course it is for Freud, even though he seems to maintain the irreconcilability of the two principles. And the mature Yeats, in that famous sentence of his, which is as Freudian in its tendency as it is Wordsworthian, tells us that, "In dreams begins responsibility." He bases the developed moral life on the autonomy of the youthful hedonistic fantasies. [9]

"Beauty is truth, truth beauty," said Keats, and generations of critics have been at pains to tell us that the equations are false. They forget what meaning we are required to assign to the two predications by reason of the fact that Keats utters them in the context of a passionate meditation on four great facts of human existence—love, death, art, and the relation that exists among these. When Keats said that beauty is truth, he was saying that the pleasure principle is at the root of existence, and of knowledge, and of the moral life. When he said that truth is beauty, he was putting in two words his enormously complex belief that the self can so develop that it may, in the intensity of art or meditation, perceive even very painful facts with a kind of pleasure, for it is one of the striking things about Keats that he represents so boldly and accurately the development of the self, and that, when he speaks of pleasure, he may mean—to use a language not his—sometimes the pleasure of the id, sometimes of the ego, and sometimes of the superego. [10]

Keats's mind was profoundly engaged by the paradox of the literary genre of tragedy, which must always puzzle us because it seems to propose to the self a gratification in regarding its own extinction. Very eminent psychoanalysts, continuators of Freud's science who would perhaps differ with him on no other point, do differ with him on the matter of his having conceived a tendency of the self to acquiesce in and even to desire its own end. Whether or not Freud's formulations of the death instinct stand up under scientific inquiry, I of course cannot venture to say. But certainly they confirm our sense of Freud's oneness with the tradition of literature. For literature has always recorded an impulse of the self to find affirmation even in its own extinction, even *by* its own extinction. When we read the great scene of the death of Oedipus at Colonus, we have little trouble, I think, in at least suspending our disbelief in Freud's idea. We do so the more willingly because the impulse to death is, in this magnificent moment, expressed and exemplified by the most passionate of men, the man in whom the energy of will and intellect was greatest, the man, too, who at the moment of his desire for death speaks of his extraordinary power of love. It is possible to argue that Oedipus does not in fact go to his death but to his apotheosis. It is possible, too, to say that when the poets speak of the desire for death or the happy acquiescence in death, they do not really mean death at all but apotheosis, or Nirvana, or what Yeats imagined, the existence "out of nature," in the "artifice of eternity." It is possible to say that something of this sort is really what Freud meant. But the poets call it death; it has much of the aspect of death; and when we take into account the age-old impulse of highly developed spirits to incorporate the idea of death into the experience of life, even to make death the criterion of life, we are drawn to the belief that the assertion of the death instinct is the effort of finely tempered minds to affirm the self in an ultimate confrontation of reality. [11]

There is yet another theme with which literature and Freud have an equal preoccupation. It is again a theme of opposition, cognate with the opposition between pleasure and reality—the theme of the opposition between love and power. That literature does conceive love and power as being in opposition is obvious enough from the frequency with which it presents the hero as both lover and warrior, the interest of his situation being that he finds it very hard to reconcile his desire for love and his desire for power. The theme has engaged not only the dramatic poets and the novelists but the lyric poets too—it was a lyric poet who put so large a part of the matter in a nutshell: "I could not love thee (Deare) so much,/ Lov'd I not Honour more," for the power I speak of is not gross, cruel power (although, in the context, this cannot be far from our minds) but rather, in its ideal conception, what is represented by the word *honor*: it is the power of cultural achievement, or of cultural commitment. As such, it was seen by Freud as pre-eminently a masculine issue. "The masculine character, the ability to dare and endure, to know and not to fear reality, to look the world in the face and take it for what it is, . . . this is what I want to preserve." It is not Freud I am quoting but one of Henry James's heroes, an American; but Basil Ransom of *The Bostonians* says very well what Freud meant. And Freud's concern for the preservation of what James calls "the masculine character," which, like James, Freud conceived to be under attack, has been made a point in the reproach directed at Freud that he displayed a masculine chauvinism, and, what is more, that, for all his overt preoccupation with love, he was yet more preoccupied with power, with aggression and personal force, or, at the best, with achievement. This contributes to a tendency which is to be observed of recent years, the tendency to represent Freud as really anesthetic to love and as in some way antagonistic to it. We all know how it has been said of Freud that he has made out love to be nothing but a reaction-formation against the most selfish and hostile impulses. And so strange are the surprises of the movement of thought that Freud, once attacked for the extravagance of his sexual emphasis, is now, by people of no little seriousness, said to be puritanical in his view of sexuality, surrendering to civilization and to achievement in civilization far more of impulse than there was any need to surrender. [12]

This is not a matter that can be argued here. I should like only to turn again to literature and to observe that the tendency of literature, when once it has represented the opposition between love and power, is to conceive of love as a principle of order for the self, even as a discipline, and as itself a power, a civic and civilizing power. Oedipus, that angry and violent man who pauses in his dying to set the word *love* at the very heart of experience, saying of himself, as Yeats translates the speech, "No living man has loved as I have loved," becomes the guardian genius of the Athenian civic life. William Blake, who envisaged life in a way that Freud would have easily understood, calls in a great voice, "Bring me my bow of burning gold!/ Bring me my arrows of desire./ Bring me my spear! . . ." What does he want this libidinal armament for? Why, that he "may build Jerusalem/ In England's green and pleasant land." And in his fine poem on the death of Freud, W. H. Auden speaks of the grief both of "anarchic Aphrodite" and of "Eros, builder of cities." [13]

Freud was much concerned with his own cultural commitment and achievement. And he loved fame. To some it may be surprising and even dismaying that this should be said of him; they will suppose that it does him no credit. In our culture the love of fame is not considered a virtue, or even an attractive trait of the personality. We are likely to confuse it with the love of publicity, and thus to be confirmed in our feeling that it is not a worthy motive of intellectual ambition. It is, I believe, considered particularly unbecoming in a scientist. But it is a trait which confirms our sense of Freud's personal connection with the tradition of literature, and my mention of it is meant as praise. Traditionally the love of fame has characterized two highly regarded professions, that of arms and that of letters. The soldier, however, is no longer supposed to desire fame. And even the poet, although I think we license him to entertain the fantasy of his immortal renown, no longer praises fame or says he wants it, as once he thought it very proper to do. Dante desired above all earthly things to be famous as a poet. Shakespeare believed implicitly in the permanence of his fame. Milton calls the love of fame "that last infirmity of noble mind," but he thus connects it with mind; and he speaks of it as an ally of the reality principle:

> Fame is the spur that the *clear* spirit doth raise
> To scorn delights and live laborious days. [14]

There can be no doubt that fame was the spur to Freud's clear spirit, to his desire to make clear what was darkly seen. As a student he stood in the great Aula of the University of Vienna, where were set up the busts of the famous men of the University, and he dreamed of the day when he should be similarly honored. He knew exactly what inscription he wanted on the pedestal, a line from *Oedipus Tyrannus*, "Who divined the riddle of the Sphinx and was a man most mighty"—the story is told by his biographer that he turned pale, as if he had seen a ghost, when, on his fiftieth birthday, he was presented by his friends and admirers with a medallion on which these very words were inscribed. [15]

And if we ask what moves the poets to their love of fame, what made the dying Keats say in despair, "Here lies one whose name is writ in water," and then again in hope, "I think I shall be among the English poets," the answer is not so very difficult to come by. The poets' idea of fame is the intense expression of the sense of the self, of the self defined by the thing it makes, which is conceived to be everlasting precisely because it was once a new thing, a thing added to the spirit of man. [16]

PURPOSE AND STRUCTURE

1. Trilling draws upon concepts familiar to his audience (the members of two psychoanalytic societies) in developing his comparison and contrast. The first of the five connections the author establishes between the fields of literature and psychoanalysis is the most general. Show how each of the successive points of similarity relates to the first one and may be subsumed under it (pars. 5–16).

2. The method of organization you have just examined gives coherence and unity to the essay. By what other devices does the author achieve these ends?

3. In par. 1 what contrast is made between Freud and the man of letters? What common ground between the two disciplines is also established? What key words acquaint you with it?

4. Par. 4 contains the first major comparison and a sub-contrast. How does the anecdote of the countess serve as an analogue to the latter? With what further details is the analogy developed?

5. In pars. 9 and 10 there is a seeming contradiction. What details are offered in par. 9 to support Trilling's statement that "the poets themselves have always accepted the opposition" (that is, between the pleasure principle and the reality principle)? What details are cited in the same and subsequent paragraphs which appear to refute this statement? Generalize from these details to determine whether Trilling contradicts himself or whether he has reconciled seemingly contradictory attitudes.

DICTION AND TONE

1. In par. 11 Trilling uses formal and abstract diction in discussing the paradox inherent in tragedy. By what rhetorical devices does he at once illuminate the paradox and invest his abstractions with life and meaning? Note the important function of the prepositions and the use of repetition in the sentence concluding, "even in its own extinction, even *by* its own extinction." Note other examples in this paragraph of the effective use of repetition. Rhetorical devices other than repetition are used to achieve

emphasis—for example, internal contrast, appositives, antithesis, and coordinate clauses. Identify them. How does the parallel structure contribute to both purpose and tone? Justify the use of the word *apotheosis* in its context. By what means is it clarified?

2. Very rarely does Trilling draw upon technical diction. In the few instances that follow, is it appropriate or even necessary to the context? Without using a specialized vocabulary, write a paraphrase for each sentence in which the following words appear: *reality principle* and *pleasure principle* [7]; *substitute gratification* [7]; *id, ego,* and *superego* [10]; *death instinct* [11]; *reaction-formation* [12]. Ask yourself which sentence —yours or Trilling's—more effectively serves his purpose.

3. How does the ironical comment concluding par. 12 contribute to purpose and tone?

4. How are the abstract words *love* and *power* rendered concrete and vivid in pars. 12–16? How are they brought into relationship? With what particulars are the varied connotations of *power* developed? List the synonyms, similes, and metaphors which suggest its range of meaning.

5. Justify the use and repetition of the word *thing* in the final sentence of the essay. What is its referent? What other devices in the sentence contribute to its parallel structure? Describe the tone of the final paragraph.

APPLICATIONS TO WRITING

1. Write an essay in which you develop a comparison and contrast between high school and college by drawing upon that which is familiar to your high school audience in order to acquaint it with the unfamiliar.

2. Establish the connections between two fields of study such as literature and sociology (or philosophy); art and literature; music and arts; biology (or anthropology) and psychology; or physics and chemistry. Assume that your audience is familiar with one but not both of these fields.

3. Develop a comparison and contrast between two instructors, two courses in the same field, two sports, two movies. Identify the area of common concern but give emphasis to the differences.

4. In your psychology textbooks you have read about such problems as childhood conditioning, the problem of the adolescent in achieving independence, or the concept of identity or of alienation. How has one of these topics beeen illuminated by a short story, novel, or play? Compare and contrast what you have learned from the text and from the fictional rendering.

HUXLEY AND
STRAVINSKY

ROBERT CRAFT

Los Angeles, July 27th, 1949

The Stravinskys invite Aldous and Maria Huxley to dinner. She is *petite* and eager with large, believing eyes in a small, pinched face, and he is even taller than anyone had warned. But one looks first at his silver-point features, especially the slightly hooked, slightly haughty nose, and rarely away from them thereafter. The right cornea is covered by a milky film, like clouded glass, and it is the unflawed but rapidly nictitating left eye which he turns to us, though its powers of sight are hardly greater. His skin has a desiccated appearance— from the desert sun during his anchorite period, one would suppose, except that it is also deathly white. Everything else about the man except the big weedy brows suggests not the out-of-doors, however, but the tightly-sealed edifices of intellectual respectability. What strikes one next is that he seems so absurdly out of scale in the diminutive Stravinsky house. He crouches under the low ceilings, ducks through the doorways, flinches by a chandelier, stoops at table, until we feel as though it may *really* be unsafe for him here, that he *could* actually trap himself in one of the tiny Stravinsky W.C.s and never get out. [1]

At table we are more precisely aware of his visual limitations: he *feels* for his knife, fork and plate, with the palpations of the blind. His wife helps him to find the food, and she continues to direct him throughout the meal in almost unnoticed *sotto voce* asides. "*Un tout petit peu à gauche, chérie,*" she whispers when his knife fails to find a hold on the meat, and in the same voice she advises him how long to uptilt the salt shaker, but I think he would not welcome, indeed would resent any sign of solicitude from another source. [2]

Conversation is in French. This is partly because Mr. and Mrs. H. obviously prefer to talk in that language, but principally because I.S.'s ear, having been exclusively confined to my backwoods American, is not attuned to Huxley English. (The word "issue," for example, a clean, sibilant "*iss-u*" in Mr. H's mouth, a gooey "*ish-shoe*" in mine, must confound the I.S.s as it distracts me.) In any case, I.S. seems to think of Mr. H. as an English-born Frenchman whose manners may be the quintessence of Englishness (this is good in I.S.'s book), but who is in other important respects more civilised (French). Language apart, the two men inhibit each other. If Mr. H. is the wrong size he is also the wrong culture. That sovereignty of scientific rationalism, the very blueprint of his intellectual heredity, is a planet away from I.S.'s mystagogical view of human existence. I.S. has not followed any science or philosophy of science since his reading of Bergson a half-century ago. It is for this reason, also, that he lives in terror all evening lest Mr. H. dwell on scientific deeds and books of which he has never heard. Yet I think that Mr. H. is as self-conscious of his own limitations in being unable to stem the flow of his thoughts long enough to approach the world of the other from the other's bias. The two men watch each other like champions of two mutually incomprehensible games; for basic toe-holds rather than gambits or feints. [3]

Mr. H.'s voice, a lambent, culture-saturated purr, is as memorable as his head. When he tells a story, it ripples musically through pursed lips. The longer anecdotes begin in low dove-tones, rising toward what promises to be a loudly explosive finish but knots into a *knödel* instead, or fizzles out at the climactic high notes. And what a story-teller he is! As family history alone his autobiography would contain the richest material of any living writer, but judging from tonight's tales of Joyce, Pound, Eliot, Yeats, such a book promises to be one of the most amusing for the 'twenties and 'thirties as well. Best of all, he betrays no mark of the repertory company, and good as these per-formances are, the most astonishing occurs in a rather more difficult line—in confrontation with I.S.'s collection of sea shells. Holding each specimen under a magnifying glass two inches from his left eye, Mr. H. casually sheds a mass of obscure learning about it, and when dropping a Latin name, he begs our pardon with exquisite punc-tilio. [4]

The hunching and cringing from the constrictions of Lilliput begin all over again on the way to the living room, though having charted the chief dangers in his memory he now moves with a more gliding and rubbery walk. We ensconce him in the largest chair, from which, however, he seems to squirm away—parts of him, anyway—like a cornered cephalopod, now stretching its peripatetic tentacles to alarming lengths, now cupping them in. As he listens to us his fingers plait and unplait, or tickle the fenders of his chair, but when he talks his arms move continuously and rapidly in large illustrative gestures so that he seems, like Vishnu, to have several pairs of them. And what does he talk about? The finding of bacteria at ocean depths; the heightening of erotic sensibilities through breathing exercises; the sexual customs of the American Utopias, especially the Oneida experi-ment of training adolescent boys on women past the menopause; Baudelaire's Latin poems, which "demonstrate wide reading in the type of poem but show complete ignorance of stress and merely duplicate the number of syllables"; the possibility of flights to the moon within a decade if enough money were to be diverted to the project, though Mr. H.'s only interest in going to any other planet would be "to establish contact with an older civilisation." This river of information is continually nourished by tributaries of quotations—

a couplet by Trumbull Stickney, a clerihew, the whole of *"Le vierge, le vivace, et le bel aujourd'hui,"* which he recites as though he were reading from an oculist's chart, except for one small stumble of memory from which he picks himself up with an air of surprise that none of us had caught him as he tripped. One feels confident that Mr. H. would have as much Bartlett no matter what the topic, and that every volume in the anthology will always automatically flick open to the right page. [5]

Brilliant as it is, we are a little relieved when it comes to an end; *I* am, anyway, for I have resolved a dozen times an hour to keep my Boeotian ignorance to myself and never to expose it in public—at any rate not in *this* public. But he is the gentlest human being I have ever seen, and the most delightfully giggly. [6]

August 19th, 1949

To the Huxleys' for tea—parsley tea with crystal sugar, and a tray of molasses cookies, wheat germ, raw carrots, small wedges of non-fattening fruit cake. Architecturally the house would satisfy the taste for mansions of a retired Kenya colonial; and it is a contrast in most other ways as well to the I.S. house, which, like the composer himself, is small, snug, brightly lighted, not forbiddingly private, as packed as a provincial museum. The lights are off as we enter, drawn curtains notwithstanding, and the sole evidence of Edison is a lamp in Mr. H.'s study that would seem more suitable for third-degree interrogations. The walls are bare, except for a few of Mr. H.'s own water-colours (landscapes with trees and rocks somewhat in the manner of Cézanne), and the furniture, what there is of it, is severe. I.S. does not scintillate in such surroundings. And when Mrs. H. withdraws, taking V. with her so that the boys may have a smoking-room chat, he is not only uncomfortable but positively frightened of facing Mr. H. without V.'s support. As I know I.S., he is whetting for a whisky, but the display of health foods and Mrs. H.'s rather gingerly proffering of a carafe of sherry intimidate him and he does not ask for it. The sepulchral lighting and raftered baronial hall dampen the conversation, too; Mr. H. is serious here, and we are reverent and hushed—though for my own part I could not have contributed more than five or six twigs to the pyre of Mr. H.'s talk anyway, and these are held back less by the bleakness of the *décor* than by self-consciousness for my pawky verbal congestions. [7]

Mr. H. alone and uninterrupted is not easily bettered, in any case, and I regret no magnetic tape preserved him today, especially his description of the culinary mortifications of St. Philip Neri. He is more engaging to listen to than to read, the conversationalist being superior to the writer in at least two definite ways. First, the talk is wholly free of the late-Tolstoy type of sermonising that has become such a heavy part of the books; second, the talker embroiders his main thematic paths with a luxury of odd links, an anastomosis of curious connections (the Huxley style is beginning to affect me!) which the writer could not—no writer could—afford to follow. [8]

What is Mr. H. to I.S.? A kind of handy, neighbourhood university, whatever more besides. I.S., like a radio quiz master, is forever wanting immediate answers to random matters of fact. He will leave the dinner table to trace some scrap of information and return thirty minutes and two cold courses later—empty-handed more often than not, for lack of a methodology. If Mr. H. is in town, however, I.S. need only pick up the telephone, as he did yesterday when he wanted a run-down on the history of scissors. He is convinced that Mr. H. suffers from his encyclopedic erudition, incidentally, and I believe that this is true, even to the extent that the Tao of his seemingly unquenchable quest is freedom through possession. [9]

And I.S. to Mr. H.? A "genius" is the simple but, I think, complete answer: one of a sacred few invested with the divine power of creation. Mr. H. prostrates himself before the mystery of this power and he seems to regard it as a justification for the existence of the mass of humanity. D. H. Lawrence was Mr. H.'s genius in the early years, and whatever qualities the word represents for him now, Lawrentian or otherwise, he thirsts for them still, as others do for religious inspiration. At the same time, he would disclaim even a pinch of these qualities as his own, I think, and would allow the designation "creative writer" for himself only if he were attempting to explain his low income to a tax collector. He writhes when anyone so much as hints at a reference to his work, and actually groans aloud when V. alludes to a dramatisation of *Brave New World*; a direct question about a book-in-progress would doubtless dissolve him altogether. Contrast this with I.S., who beams satisfaction at the mention of *his* tiniest opus. But, then, I.S. *is* a creator. [10]

Mr. H. also looks to I.S. as a source of knowledge *about* music, however, and not only for the so-called secrets of art but, curiously, for the plainest of lexical facts as well. His appetite for this knowledge appears to be insatiable, moreover, though he already possesses a huge store of music history and a tune-humming acquaintance with the repertory which is (on that level) as wide as I.S.'s. He does not seem to consider that such knowledge has little interest for, or bearing on, the mind of the composer, or that the composer's stock of prejudices is narrow and rather cranky because of the creative preoccupations of the moment. How long, I wonder, will it take Mr. H. to discover that I.S.'s genius is wrapped—for protection from musical data—in a vacuum? [11]

PURPOSE AND STRUCTURE

1. Robert Craft contrasts two of his friends: one is a *"genius"* (par. 10) and the other is a *handy, neighbourhood university* (par. 9). But the contrast of genius and knowledge is presented through intimate and concrete details, not all of them obviously appropriate. Discuss whether the following details are relevant to the purpose of the writer:

The right cornea is covered by a milky film, like clouded glass, and it is the unflawed but rapidly nictitating left eye which he turns to us, though its powers of sight are hardly greater (par. 1);

The two men watch each other like champions of two mutually incomprehensible games; for basic toe-holds rather than gambits or feints (par. 3);

We ensconce him in the largest chair, from which, however, he seems to squirm away—parts of him, anyway—like a cornered cephalopod (par. 5);

To the Huxleys' for tea—parsley tea with crystal sugar, and a tray of molasses cookies, wheat germ, raw carrots, small wedges of non-fattening fruit cake (par. 7);

As I know I. S., he is whetting for a whisky (par. 7);

the composer's stock of prejudices is narrow and rather cranky (par. 11).

2. What is the function of par. 6? Why not join it to the end of par. 5?

3. Stravinsky and Huxley get information from each other: Stravinsky wants a rundown on the history of scissors (par. 9); Huxley asks about the plainest of lexical facts (par. 11) in music. Is there an implied contrast in their need for information?

4. Compare and contrast Huxley's Tao (par. 9) and Stravinsky's vacuum (par. 11). Why should Stravinsky's genius be protected from musical ideas (par. 11)?

DICTION AND TONE

1. What is the effect—what is the tone—of the many references to differences of size: constrictions of Lilliput (par. 5); trap himself in one of the tiny Stravinsky W. C.s and never get out (par. 1); and so on. Locate these references and discuss their function.

2. Why is the following simile appropriate: as though he were reading from an oculist's chart (par. 5)?

3. What is the effect (par. 5) of referring to peripatetic tentacles? to cupping them in? to Vishnu?

4. In the last sentence of par. 8 Craft seems to write as no writer can afford to write. Why? Why use the technical word anastomosis?

5. Is knots into a knödel (par. 4) a meaningful description of the end of a story? Discuss.

APPLICATIONS TO WRITING

Robert Craft contrasts two of his friends by presenting intimate and concrete details which convince the reader of their reality and of their uniqueness; he also contrasts them as types (the genius and the man of knowledge). Contrast two of your friends in the same way: the loner and the lover, the surfer and the skin diver, the drama major and the English major, the joker and the broker, the Chicken Little and the Pollyanna.

PASCAL

ALDOUS HUXLEY

Life and the Routine of Living

It is worth remarking that the revelation of life confirms many of the revelations of death.[1] The business and the distractions which Pascal hated so much, because they made men forget that they must die, are hateful to the life-worshiper because they prevent men from fully living. Death makes these distractions seem trivial and silly; but equally so does life. It was from pain and gradually approaching dissolution that Ivan Ilyitch learned to understand the futility of his respectable bourgeois career. If he had ever met a genuinely living man, if he had ever read a book, or looked at a picture, or heard a piece of music by a living artist, he would have learned the same lesson. But Pascal and the later Tolstoy would not permit the revelation to come from life. Their aim was to humiliate men by rolling them in the corruption of the grave, to inflict a defiling punishment on them; they condemned, not only the distracting, life-destroying futilities with which men fill their days, but also the life which these futilities destroyed. The life-worshiper agrees with them in hating

"Pascal" from *Collected Essays* by Aldous Huxley. Copyright, 1929, by Aldous Huxley. Reprinted by permission of Harper & Brothers. Canadian reprint by permission of Chatto and Windus Ltd.

[1] I have borrowed the phrase from Shestov. 'La Révélation de la Mort' is the title, in its French translation, of one of his most interesting books.

216

the empty fooleries and sordidnesses of average human existence. Incidentally the progress of science and industry has enormously increased the element of foolery and sordidness in human life. The clerk and the taylorized workman leave their imbecile tasks to spend their leisure under the influence of such opiate distractions as are provided by the newspaper, the cinema, the radio; they are given less and less opportunity to do any active or creative living of their own. Pascal and Tolstoy would have led them from silliness to despair by talking to them of death; but "memento vivere" is the life-worshiper's advice. If people remembered to live, they would abstain from occupations which are mere substitutes for life. [1]

The Life-Worshiper's Creed

The life-worshiper's philosophy is comprehensive. As a manifold and discontinuous being, he is in a position to accept all the partial and apparently contradictory syntheses constructed by other philosophers. He is at one moment a positivist and at another a mystic: now haunted by the thought of death (for the apocalypse of death is one of the incidents of living) and now a Dionysian child of nature; now a pessimist and now, with a change of lover or liver or even the weather, an exuberant believer that God's in his heaven and all's right with the world. He holds these different beliefs because he is many different people. Each belief is the rationalization of the prevailing mood of one of these persons. There is really no question of any of these philosophies being true or false. The psychological state called joy is no truer than the psychological state called melancholy (it may be more valuable as an aid to social or individual living—but that is another matter). Each is a primary fact of experience. And since one psychological state cannot be truer than another, since all are equally facts, it follows that the rationalization of one state cannot be truer than the rationalization of another. What Hardy says about the universe is no truer than what Meredith says; if the majority of contemporary readers prefer the world-view expressed in *Tess of*

the D'Urbervilles to the optimism which forms the background to
Beauchamp's Career, that is simply because they happen to live in a
very depressing age and consequently suffer from a more or less
chronic melancholy. Hardy seems to them truer than Meredith
because the philosophy of "Tess" and "Jude" is more adequate as a
rationalization of their own prevailing mood than the philosophy of
Richard Feverel or Beauchamp. What applies to optimism and pessimism applies equally to other trends of philosophical thought. Even
the doctrines of "fixed fate, free will, foreknowledge absolute," for all
the elaborateness of their form, are in substance only expression of
emotional and physiological states. One feels free or one feels con-
ditioned. Both feelings are equally facts of experience, so are the facts
called "mystical ecstasy" and "reasonableness." Only a man whose
life was rich in mystical experiences could have constructed a
cosmogony like that of Boehme's; and the works of Voltaire could
have been written only by one whose life was singularly poor in such
experiences. People with strongly marked idiosyncrasies of character
have their world-view almost forced upon them by their psychology.
The only branches of philosophy in regard to which it is permissible
to talk of truth and falsehood are logic and the theory of knowledge.
For logic and the theory of knowledge are concerned with the necessities and the limitations of thought—that is to say, with mental habits
so primordial that it is all but impossible for any human being to
break them. When a man commits a paralogism or lays claim to a
more than human knowledge of the nature of things, we are justified
in saying that he is wrong. I may, for example, admit that all men
are mortal and that Socrates is a man, but nevertheless feel impelled
to conclude that Socrates is immortal. Am I not as well justified in
this opinion as I am in my optimism or pessimism, whichever the
case may be? The answer is: no. I may have a personal taste for
Socrates's immortality; but, in the syllogistic circumstances, the taste
is so outrageously bad, so universally condemned, that it would be
madness to try to justify it. Moreover, I should discover that, if I
put my paralogistic theories into practice, I should find myself in

serious trouble, not only with other human beings, but even with things. The hero of Dostoievsky's *Notes from Underground* protests against the intolerable tyranny of two and two making four. He prefers that they shall make five, and insists that he has a right to his preference. And no doubt he has a right. But if an express train happens to be passing at a distance of two plus two yards, and he advances four yards and a half under the impression that he will still be eighteen inches on the hither side of destruction, this right of his will not save him from coming to a violent and bloody conclusion. [2]

Scientific thought is true or false because science deals with sense impressions which are, if not identical for all human beings, at least sufficiently similar to make something like universal agreement possible. The difference between a scientific theory and a metaphysical world-view is that the first is a rationalization of psychological experiences which are more or less uniform for all men and for the same man at different times, while the second is a rationalization of experiences which are diverse, occasional, and contradictory. A man may be a pessimistic determinist before lunch and an optimistic believer in the will's freedom after it; but both before and after his meal he will observe that the color of the sky is blue, that stones are hard, that the sun gives light and warmth. It is for this reason that there are many philosophies, and only one science. [3]

But even science demands that its votaries shall think, according to circumstances, in a variety of different ways. The mode of thinking which gives valid results when applied to objects of more than a certain size (in other words, to large numbers of objects; for anything big enough to be perceptible to our senses is built up, apparently, of enormous numbers of almost infinitesimal components) is found to be absolutely inapplicable to single objects of atomic or subatomic dimensions. About large agglomerations of atoms we can think in terms of "organized common sense." But when we come to consider individual atoms and their minuter components, common-sense gives results which do not square with the observed facts. (Nobody, of course, has ever actually observed an atom or an electron; but the nature of their behavior can be inferred, with more or less probability, from such happenings on a macroscopical scale as accompany their invisible activity.) In the sub-atomic world practically all our necessities of thought become not only unnecessary but misleading. A description of this universe reads like a page from Lewis Carroll or Edward Lear. [4]

Seeing, then, that even sense impressions not only can but must be rationalized in irreconcilably different ways, according to the class of object with which they are supposed to be connected, we need not be troubled or surprised by the contradictions which we find in the rationalization of less uniform psychological experiences. Thus, the almost indefinitely numerous rationalizations of the aesthetic and the mystical experiences not only contradict one another, but agree in contradicting those rationalizations of sense experience known as scientific theories. This fact greatly disturbed our grandfathers, who kept on losing their faith, sacrificing their reason, striking attitudes of stoical despair, and, in general, performing the most extraordinary spiritual antics, because of it. Science is "true," they argued; therefore art and religion, therefore beauty and honor, love and ideals, must be "false." "Reality" has been "proved" by science to be an affair of space, time, mass, number, and cause; therefore all that makes life worth living is an "illusion." Or else they started from the other end. Art, religion, beauty, love, make life worth living; therefore science, which disregards the existence of these things, must be false. It is unnecessary for us to take so tragic a view. Science, we have come to realize, takes no cognizance of the things that make life worth living, for the simple reason that beauty, love, and so on, are not measurable quantities, and science deals only with what can be measured. One psychological fact is as good as another. We perceive beauty as immediately as we perceive hardness; to say that one sensation is illusory and that the other corresponds with reality is a gratuitous piece of presumption. [5]

Answers to the riddle of the universe often have a logical form and are expressed in such a way that they raise questions of epistemology and involve the acceptance or rejection of certain scientific theories. In substance, however, they are simply rationalizations of diverse and equally valid psychological states, and are therefore neither true nor false. (Incidentally, similar states are not necessarily or invariably rationalized in the same way. Mystical experiences which, in Europe, are explained in terms of a personal God are interpreted by the Buddhists in terms of an entirely godless order of things. Which is the truer rationalization? God, or not-God, whichever the case may be, knows.) The life-worshiper who adopts in turn all the solutions to the cosmic riddle is committing no crime against logic or the truth. He is simply admitting the obvious fact that he is a human being— that is to say, a series of distinct psychological states, a colony of diverse personalities. Each state demands its appropriate rationalizations; or, in other words, each personality has its own philosophies of life. Philosophical consistency had some justification so long as it could be imagined that the substance of one's world-view (as opposed to the logical trappings in which it was clothed and the problems of epistemology and science connected with it) was uniquely true. But if we admit, as I think we must, that one world-view cannot be truer than another, but that each is the expression in intellectual terms of some given and undeniable fact of experience, then consistency loses all philosophical merit. It is pointless to ignore all the occasions when you feel that the world is good, for the sake of being consistently a pessimist; it is pointless, for the sake of being consistently a positivist, to deny that your body is sometimes tenanted by a person who has mystical experiences. Pessimism is no truer than optimism, nor positivism than mysticism. Philosophically, there is no reason why a man should deny the thoughts of all but one of his potential selves. Each self on occasion exists; each has its feelings about the universe, its cosmic tastes—or, to put it in a different way, each inhabits its own universe. What relation these various private universes bear to the Universe in Itself, if such a thing exists, it is clearly impossible to say. We can believe, if we like, that each of them represents one aspect of the whole. "In my Father's house are many mansions." Nature has given to each individual the key to quite a number of these metaphysical mansions. The life-worshiper suggests that man shall make use of all his keys instead of throwing all but one of them away. He admits the fact of vital diversity and makes the best of it. In this he is unlike the general run of thinkers, who are very reluctant to admit diversity, and, if they do confess the fact, deplore it. They find diversity shocking, they desire at all costs to correct it. And even if it came to be universally admitted that no one world-view could possibly be true, these people would continue, none the less, to hold fast to one to the exclusion of all the rest. They would go on worshiping consistency, if not on philosophical, then on moral grounds. Or, in other words, they would practice and demand consistency through fear of inconsistency, through fear of being dangerously free, through fear of life. For morality is always the product of terror; its chains and strait-waistcoats are fashioned by those who dare not trust others, because they dare not trust themselves, to walk in liberty. By such poor terror-stricken creatures consistency in thought and conduct is prized among the highest virtues. In order to achieve this consistency they reject as untrue, or as immoral or antisocial (it matters not which; for any stick will serve to beat a dog), all the thoughts which do not harmonize with the particular system they have elected to defend; they do their best to repress all impulses and desires which cannot be fitted into their scheme of moral behavior. With what deplorable results! [6]

Pascal, the Death-Worshiper

The consistent thinker, the consistently moral man, is either a walking mummy or else, if he has not succeeded in stifling all his vitality, a fanatical monomaniac. (By the admirers of consistency the mummies are called "serene" or "stoical," the monomaniacs "single-minded"—as though single-mindedness were a virtue in a being to whom bountiful nature has given a multiple mind! Single-mindedness is all very well in cows or baboons; in an animal claiming to belong to the same species as Shakespeare it is simply disgraceful.) [7]

In spite of all his heroic efforts, Pascal never succeeded in entirely suppressing the life that was in him. It was not in his power to turn himself into a pious automaton. Vitality continued to flow out of him, but through only one channel. He became a monomaniac, a man with but one aim—to impose the death of Christian spirituality on himself and all his fellows. "What religion," he asks, "will teach us to cure pride and concupiscence?" In other words, what religion will cure us of living? For concupiscence, or desire, is the instrument of life, and "the pride of the peacock is the glory of God"—not of Pascal's God, of course, but of the God of Life. Christianity, he concludes, is the only religion which will cure men of living. Therefore all men must become Christians. Pascal extended all his extraordinary powers in trying, by persuasion, by argument, to convert his fellows to consistent death-worship. It was with the *Provincial Letters* that he opened the campaign. With what consummate generalship! The casuists were routed with terrific slaughter. Entranced by that marvelous prose, we find ourselves even now believing that their defeat was merited, that Pascal was in the right. But if we stop our ears to the charmer's music and consider only the substance of what he says, we shall realize that the rights were all on the side of the Jesuits and that Pascal was using his prodigious talents to make the worse appear the better cause. The casuists were often silly and pedantic. But their conception of morality was, from a life-worshiper's point of view, entirely sound. Recognizing the diversity of human beings, the infinite variety of circumstances, they perceived that every case should be considered on its own merits. Life was to be tethered, but with an elastic rope; it was to be permitted to do a little gamboling. To Pascal this libertarianism seemed horrible. There must be no compromise with life; the hideous thing must be ruthlessly suppressed. Men must be bound down by rigid commandments, coffined in categorical imperatives, paralyzed by the fear of hell and the incessant contemplation of death, buried under mounds of prohibitions. He said so with such exquisite felicity of phrase and cadence that people have gone on imagining, from that day to this, that he was upholding a noble cause, when in fact he was fighting for the powers of darkness. [8]

After the *Letters* came the *Pensées*—the fragmentary materials of what was to have been a colossal work of Christian apology. Implacably the fight against life continued. "Admiration spoils everything from childhood onwards. Oh, isn't he clever! Isn't he good! The children of the Port Royal school, who are not urged on with this spur of envy and glory, sink into indifference." Pascal must have been delighted. A system of education which resulted in children sinking into "la nonchalance" was obviously, in his eyes, almost ideal. If the children had quietly withered up into mummies, it would have been absolutely perfect. The man was to be treated to the same deadening influences as the child. It was first to be demonstrated that he lived in a state of hopeless wretchedness. This is a task which Pascal undertook with the greatest satisfaction. All his remarks on the "misère de l'homme" are magnificent. But what is this misery? When we examine Pascal's arguments we find that man's misery consists in not being something different from a man. In not being simple, consistent, without desires, omniscient and dead, but on the contrary alive and full of concupiscence, uncertain, inconsistent, multiple. But to blame a thing for not being something else is childish. Sheep are not men; but that is no reason for talking about the "misère du mouton." Let sheep make the best of their sheepishness and men of their humanity. But Pascal does not want men to make the best of their human life; he wants them to make the worst of it, to throw it away. After depressing them with his remarks about misery, he brings them into paralyzing contact with death and infinity; he demonstrates the nothingness, in the face of this darkness, these immensities, of every thought, action, and desire. To clinch the argument he invokes the Jansenist God, the Christian revelation. If it is man's true nature to be consistent and undesiring, then (such is Pascal's argument) Jansenistic death-worship is a psychological necessity. It is more than a psychological necessity; death-worship has been made obligatory by the God of Death in person, has been decreed in a revelation which Pascal undertakes to prove indubitably historical. [9]

Pascal's Universe

The spectacle of so much malignity, so much hatred, is profoundly repulsive. Hate begets hate, and it is difficult not to detest Pascal for his venomous detestation of everything that is beautiful and noble in human existence. It is a detestation, however, which must be tempered with pity. If the man sinned against the Holy Ghost—and surely few men have sinned like Pascal, since few indeed have been endowed with Pascal's extraordinary gifts—it was because he could not help it. [10]

His desires, in Blake's words, were weak enough to be restrained. Feeble, a sick man, he was afraid of life, he dreaded liberty. Acquainted only with the mystical states that are associated with malady and deprivation, this ascetic had never experienced those other, no less significant, states that accompany the fulfillment of desire. For if we admit the significance of the mystical rapture, we must equally admit the significance of the no less prodigious experiences associated with love in all its forms, with the perception of sensuous beauty, with intoxication, with rhythmic movement, with anger, with strife and triumph, with all the positive manifestations of concupiscent life. Ascetic practices produce a condition of abnormality and so enable the ascetic to get out of the ordinary world into another and, as he feels, more significant and important universe. Anger, the feeling inspired by sensuous beauty, the orgasm of amorous desire, are abnormal states precisely analogous to the state of mystical ecstasy, states which permit the angry man, the aesthete, the lover, to become temporary inhabitants of non-Podsnapian universes which are immediately felt (just as the mystic's universe is immediately felt) to be of peculiar value and significance. Pascal was acquainted with only one abnormal universe—that which the ecstatic mystic briefly inhabits.

Of all the rest he had no personal knowledge; his sickly body did not permit of his approaching them. We condemn easily that which we do not know, and with pleasure that which, like the fox who said the grapes were sour, we cannot enjoy. [11]

To a sickly body Pascal joined an extraordinarily powerful analytical intellect. Too acute to be taken in by the gross illusions of rationalism, too subtle to imagine that a homemade abstraction could be a reality, he derided the academic philosophers. He perceived that the basis of reason is unreasonable; first principles come from "the heart," not from the mind. The discovery would have been of the first importance if Pascal had only made it with the right organ. But instead of discovering the heart with the heart, he discovered it with the head. It was abstractly that he rejected abstractions, and with the reason that he discovered unreason. His realism was only theoretical; he never lived it. His intelligence would not permit him to find satisfaction in the noumena and abstractions of rationalist philosophy. But for fixed noumena and simple unchanging abstractions he none the less longed. He was able to satisfy these longings of an invalid philosopher and at the same time to salve his intellectual conscience by choosing an irrational abstraction to believe in—the God of Christianity. Marooned on that static Rock of Ages, he felt himself safe—safe from the heaving flux of appearances, safe from diversity, safe from the responsibilities of freedom, safe from life. If he had allowed himself to have a heart to understand the heart with, if he had possessed a body with which to understand the body, and instincts and desires capable of interpreting the meaning of instinct and desire, Pascal might have been a life-worshiper instead of a devotee of death. But illness had strangled the life out of his body and made his desires so weak that to resist them was an easy virtue. Against his heart he struggled with all the force of his tense and focused will. The Moloch of religious principle demanded its sacrifice. Obediently, Pascal performed the rite of harakiri. Moloch, unsatisfied, demanded still more blood. Pascal offered his services; he would make other people do as he had done. Moloch should be glutted with entrails. All his writings are persuasive invitations to the world to come and commit suicide. It is the triumph of principle and consistency. [12]

Musical Conclusion

And yet the life-worshiper is also, in his own way, a man of principles and consistency. To live intensely—that is his guiding principle. His diversity is a sign that he consistently tries to live up to his principles; for the harmony of life—of the single life that persists as a gradually changing unity through time—is a harmony built up of many elements. The unity is mutilated by the suppression of any part of the diversity. A fugue has need of all its voices. Even in the rich counterpoint of life each separate small melody plays its indispensable part. The diapason closes full in man. In *man*. But Pascal aspired to be more than a man. Among the interlaced melodies of the human counterpoint are love songs and anacreontics, marches and savage dance-rhythms, hymns of hate and loud hilarious chanties. Odious voices in the ears of one who wanted his music to be wholly celestial! Pascal commanded them to be still and they were silent. Bending toward his life, we listen expectantly for a strain of angelic singing. But across the centuries what harsh and painful sounds come creaking down to us! [13]

PURPOSE AND STRUCTURE

1. Huxley calls his final section *Musical Conclusion*. Notice that the entire essay has a musical form: the introductory statement announces two themes, A & B; a lengthy development of A follows; then an equally lengthy development of B; finally A & B are resolved. What are A & B? Explain how the two are announced in the first section.

2. Comparison is the demonstration of similarities; contrast, of differences. How are the life-worshiper and the death-worshiper similar? how different?

3. The third paragraph is developed by comparison and examples. What is being compared? What is the example?

4. In par. 2 the novels of Hardy and Meredith are used as examples. What are they examples of? Similarly, the references to Voltaire and Boehme are examples. What are *they* examples of? The syllogism involving Socrates and the anecdote about the hero of *Notes from Underground* are also examples; of what? Show how Huxley relates the three ideas in an orderly manner.

5. The introduction of science in pars. 3 and 4 seems to be an intrusion. Justify the inclusion of the information in these paragraphs.

DICTION AND TONE

1. Characterize briefly the audience for which this essay is intended and support your characterization with evidence from the text.

2. List all the musical terms in par. 13 and show how they contribute to the meaning of the entire essay.

3. In par. 1 what word would be more appropriate than *foolery*; than *taylorized?* Find a less slanted word than *imbecile* in *imbecile tasks*; than *opiate* in *opiate distractions.* Would *futility* be as appropriate as *silliness* in *from silliness to despair?*

4. In par. 2 is *an exuberant believer that God's in his heaven* an adequate antithesis to *pessimist?*

5. At the end of par. 2 why is *conclusion* a more appropriate word than *end?*

APPLICATIONS TO WRITING

Write an essay in which you compare and contrast two attitudes. As far as possible, support your general observations with specific illustrations and examples. Adapt Huxley's "musical form"—the announcement of

two themes, the lengthy development of one, the development of the
other, a resolution—to your subject. Some suggested topics: Attitudes
Toward Modern and Traditional Music (You may wish to substitute
Modern and Traditional painting, houses, poetry, and so on.); Progres-
sive and Traditional Education; Capital Punishment; Racial Integration;
College Athletics.

Part Five

ILLUSTRATION

Illustration—at its simplest, a particular member of a class used to explain or dramatize the class. The individual member selected must be a fair representative of the distinctive qualities of the class. At its most complex, an illustration provides the particulars on which a generalization is based; the generalization—a type of person or thing, an idea or abstraction—may or may not be explicitly stated. Eiseley makes the witches in *Macbeth* illustrate "projections from our own psyche." Bettelheim transforms what might have been a mere case history into an illustration of a predicament of contemporary man. Fiction may be regarded as an illustration of an implied generalization. In *Some Thoughts on Playwriting*, Thornton Wilder says, "Modern taste shrinks from emphasizing the central idea that hides behind the fiction, but exists there nevertheless. . . ." However, to say that the dialogue in What *Cocktail Party?* illustrates the synthetic personality does not do justice to Thurber's humor and wisdom. And to label "the second tree from the corner" as a metaphor for what all men want does not take account of the resonance of White's ironic understatement. Finally, Hemingway's *Big Two-Hearted River* might be called pure narration; to speak of it as illustration is to reduce it to another form of discourse. Obviously the central idea behind a piece of fiction cannot be stated in expository language without loss of precision and power.

231

THE UNCOMPLETED MAN

LOREN EISELEY

The nature into which Shakespeare's Macbeth dabbles so unsuccessfully with the aid of witchcraft, in the famous scene on the heath, is unforgettable in literature. We watch in horrified fascination the malevolent change in the character of Macbeth as he gains a dubious insight into the unfolding future—a future which we know to be self-created. This scene, fearsome enough at all times, is today almost unbearable to the discerning observer. Its power lies in its symbolic delineation of the relationship of Macbeth's midnight world to the realm of modern science—a relationship grasped by few. [1]

The good general, Banquo, who, unlike Macbeth, is wary of such glimpses into the future as the witches have allowed the two companions, seeks to restrain his impetuous comrade, " 'Tis strange," Banquo says,

> And oftentimes, to win us to our harm
> The instruments of darkness tell us truths,
> Win us with honest trifles, to betray's
> In deepest consequence.

Macbeth who, in contrast to Banquo, has immediately seized upon the self-imposed reality induced by the witches' prophecies, stumbles out of their toils at the last, only to protest in his dying hour:

233

> And be these juggling fiends no more believ'd . . .
> That keep the word of promise to our ear
> And break it to our hope! [2]

Who, we may now inquire, are these strange beings who waylaid Macbeth, and why do I, who have spent a lifetime in the domain of science, make the audacious claim that this old murderous tale of the scientific twilight extends its shadow across the doorway of our modern laboratories? These bearded, sexless creatures who possess the faculty of vanishing into air or who reappear in some ultimate flame-wreathed landscape only to mock our folly, are an exteriorized portion of ourselves. They are projections from our own psyche, smoking wisps of mental vapor that proclaim our subconscious intentions and bolster them with Delphic utterances—half-truths which we consciously accept, and which then take power over us. Under the spell of such oracles we create, not a necessary or real future, but a counterfeit drawn from within ourselves, which we then superimpose, through purely human power, upon reality. Indeed one could say that these phantoms create a world which is at the same time spurious and genuine, so complex is our human destiny. [3]

Every age has its style in these necromantic projections. The corpse-lifting divinations of the Elizabethan sorcerers have given way, in our time, to other and, at first sight, more scientific interpretations of the future. Today we know more about man, where he has come from, and what we may expect of him—or so we think. But there is one thing, in my belief, which identifies Macbeth's "juggling fiends" in any age, whether these uncanny phantoms appear as witches, star readers, or today's technologists. This quality is their claim to omniscience—an omniscience only half-stated on the basis of the past or specious present, and always lacking in genuine knowledge of the future. The leading characteristic of the future they present is its fixed, static, inflexible quality. [4]

Such a future is fated beyond human will to change, just as Macbeth's demons, by prophecy, worked in him a transformation of character which then created inevitable tragedy. Until the appearance of the witches on the heath gave it shape, that tragedy existed only as a latent possibility in Macbeth's subconscious. Similarly, in this age, one could quote those who seek control of man's destiny by the evocation of his past. Their wizardry is deceptive because their spells are woven out of a genuine portion of reality—which, however, has taken on this always identifiable quality of fixity in an unfixed universe. The ape is always in our hearts, we are made to say, although each time a child is born something totally and genetically unique enters the universe, just as it did long ago when the great ethical leaders—Christ, the Buddha, Confucius—spoke to their followers. [5]

Man escapes definition even as the modern phantoms in militarist garb proclaim—as I have heard them do—that man will fight from one side of the solar system to the other, and beyond. The danger, of course, is truly there, but it is a danger which, while it lies partially in what man is, lies much closer to what he chooses to believe about himself. Man's whole history is one of transcendence and of self-examination, which have led him to angelic heights of sacrifice as well as into the bleakest regions of despair. The future is not truly fixed but the world arena is smoking with the caldrons of those who would create tomorrow by evoking, rather than exorcising, the stalking ghosts of the past. [6]

Even this past, however, has been far deeper and more pregnant with novelty than the short-time realist can envisage. As an evolutionist I never cease to be astounded by the past. It is replete with more features than one world can realize. Perhaps it was this that led the philosopher Santayana to speak of men's true natures as not adequately manifested in their condition at any given moment, or even in their usual habits. "Their real nature," he contended, "is what they would discover themselves to be if they possessed self-knowledge, or as the Indian scripture has it, if they became what they are." I should like to approach this mystery of the self, which so intrigued the great philosopher, from a mundane path strewn with the sticks and stones through which the archaeologist must pick his way. [7]

Let me illustrate what I mean by a very heavy and peculiar stone which I keep upon my desk. It has been split across; carbon black, imprinted in the gray shale, is the outline of a fish. The chemicals that composed the fish—most of them at least—are still there in the stone. They are, in a sense, imperishable. They may come and go, pass in and out of living things, trickle away in the long erosion of time. They are inanimate, yet at one time they constituted a living creature. [8]

Often at my desk, now, I sit contemplating the fish. It does not have to be a fish. It could be the long-horn Alaskan bison on my wall. For the point is, you see, that the fish is extinct and gone, just as those great heavy-headed beasts are gone, just as our massive-faced and shambling forebears of the Ice Age have vanished. The chemicals still about us here took a shape that will never be seen again so long as grass grows or the sun shines. Just once out of all time there was a pattern that we call *Bison regius,* a fish-like amphibian called *Ichthyostega,* and, at this present moment, a primate who knows, or thinks he knows, the entire score. In the past there has been armor; there have been bellowings out of throats like iron furnaces; there have been phantom lights in the dark forest, and toothed reptiles winging through the air. It has all been carbon and its compounds, the black stain running perpetually across the stone. [9]

But though the elements are known, nothing in all those shapes is now returnable. No living chemist can shape a dinosaur, no living hand can start the dreaming tentacular extensions that characterize the life of the simplest ameboid cell. Finally, as the greatest mystery of all, I who write these words on paper, cannot establish my own reality. I am, by any reasonable and considered logic, dead. This may be a matter of concern to you reading these words; but if it is any consolation, I can assure you that you are as dead as I. For, on my office desk, to prove my words is the fossil out of the stone, and there is the carbon of life stained black on the ancient rock. [10]

There is no life in the fossil. There is no life in the carbon in my body. As the idea strikes me—and believe me it comes as a profound shock—I run down the list of elements. There is no life in the iron, there is no life in the phosphorus, the nitrogen does not contain me, the water that soaks my tissues is not I. What am I then? I pinch my body in a kind of sudden desperation. My heart knocks, my fingers close around the pen. There is, it seems, a semblance of life here. [11]

But the minute I start breaking this strange body down into its constituents, it is dead. It does not know me. Carbon does not speak, calcium does not remember, iron does not weep. Even if I hastily reconstitute their combinations in my mind, rebuild my arteries, and let oxygen in the grip of hemoglobin go hurrying through a thousand conduits, I have a kind of machine, but where in all this array of pipes and hurried flotsam is the dweller? [12]

From whence, out of what steaming pools or boiling cloudbursts did he first arise? What forces can we find which brought him up the shore, scaled his body into an antique, reptilian shape and then cracked it like an egg to let a soft-furred animal with a warmer heart emerge? And we? Would it not be a good thing if man were tapped gently like a fertile egg to see what might creep out? I sometimes think of this as I handle the thick-walled skulls of the animal men who preceded us, or ponder over those remote splay-footed creatures whose bones lie deep in the world's wastelands at the very bottom of time. [13]

With the glooms and night terrors of those vast cemeteries I have been long familiar. A precisely similar gloom enwraps the individual life of each of us. There are moments in my bed at midnight, or watching the play of moonlight on the ceiling, when this ghostliness of myself comes home to me with appalling force, when I lie tense, listening as if removed, far off, to the footfalls of my own heart, or seeing my own head on the pillow turning restlessly with the round staring eyes of a gigantic owl. I whisper "Who?" to no one but myself in the silent, sleeping house—the living house gone back to sleep with the sleeping stones, the eternally sleeping chair, the picture that sleeps forever on the bureau, the dead, also sleeping, though they walk in my dreams. In the midst of all this dark, this void, this emptiness, I, more ghostly than a ghost, cry "Who? Who?" to no answer, aware only of other smaller ghosts like the bat sweeping by the window or the dog who, in repeating a bit of his own lost history, turns restlessly among nonexistent grasses before he subsides again upon the floor. [14]

"Trust the divine animal who carries us through the world," writes Emerson. Like the horse who finds the way by instinct when the traveler is lost in the forest, so the divine within us, he contends, may find new passages opening into nature; human metamorphosis may be possible. Emerson wrote at a time when man still lived intimately with animals and pursued wild, dangerous ways through primeval forests and prairies. Emerson and Thoreau lived close enough to nature to know something still of animal intuition and wisdom. They had not reached that point of utter cynicism—that distrust of self and of the human past which leads finally to total entrapment in that past, "man crystallized," as Emerson again was shrewd enough to observe. [15]

This entrapment is all too evident in the writings of many concerned with the evolutionary story of man. Their gaze is fixed solely upon a past into which, one begins to suspect, has been poured a certain amount of today's frustration, venom, and despair. Like the witches in *Macbeth*, these men are tempting us with seeming realities about ourselves until these realities take shape in our minds and become the future. It is not necessary to break the code of DNA in order to control human destiny. The tragedy is that men are already controlling it even while they juggle retorts and shake vials in search of a physical means to enrich their personalities. We would like to contain the uncontainable future in a glass, have it crystallized out before us as a powder to swallow. All then, we imagine, would be well. [16]

As our knowledge of the genetic mechanism increases, both scientists and journalists bombard our ears with ingenious accounts of how we are to control, henceforth, our own evolution. We who have recourse only to a past which we misread and which has made us cynics would now venture to produce our own future out of this past alone. Again I judge this self-esteem as a symptom of our time, our powerful, misused technology, our desire not to seek the good life but to produce a painless mechanical version of it—our willingness to be good if goodness can, in short, be swallowed in a pill. [17]

Once more we are on the heath of the witches, or, to come closer to our own time, we are in the London laboratory where the good Doctor Jekyll produced a potion and reft out of his own body the monster Hyde. [18]

Nature, as I have tried to intimate in this little dissection, is never quite where we see it. It is a becoming as well as a passing, but the becoming is both within and without our power. It is this lesson, with all our hard-gained knowledge, that is so difficult to comprehend. All along the evolutionary road it could have been said, "This is man," if there had then been such a magical self-delineating and mind-freezing world. It could have immobilized us at any step of our journey. It could have held us hanging to the bough from which we actually dropped; it could have kept us cowering, small-brained and helpless, whenever the great cats came through the reeds. It could have stricken us with terror before the fire that was later to be our warmth and weapon against Ice Age cold. At any step of the way, the word *man*, in retrospect, could be said to have encompassed just such final limits. [19]

Each time the barrier has been surmounted. Man is not man. He is elsewhere. There is within us only that dark, divine animal engaged in a strange journey—that creature who, at midnight, knows its own ghostliness and senses its far road. "Man's unhappiness," brooded Carlyle, "comes of his Greatness; it is because there is an Infinite in him, which with all his cunning he cannot quite bring under the Finite." This is why hydrogen, which has become the demon element of our time, should be seen as the intangible dagger which hung before Macbeth's vision, but which had no power except what was lent to it by his own mind. [20]

The terror that confronts our age is our own conception of ourselves. Above all else this is the potion which the modern Dr. Jekylls have concocted. As Shakespeare foresaw:

> It hath been taught us from the primal state
> That he which is was wished until he were.

This is not the voice of the witches. It is the clear voice of a great poet almost four centuries gone, who saw at the dawn of the scientific age what was to be the darkest problem of man: his conception of himself. The words are quiet, almost cryptic; they do not foretell. They imply a problem in free will. Shakespeare, in this passage, says nothing of starry influences, machinery, beakers, or potions. He says, in essence, one thing only: that what we wish will come. [21]

I submit to you that this is the deadliest message man will ever encounter in all literature. It thrusts upon him inescapable choices. Shakespeare's is the eternal, the true voice of the divine animal, piercing, as it has always pierced, the complacency of little centuries in which, encamped as in hidden thickets, men have sought to evade self-knowledge by describing themselves as men. [22]

PURPOSE AND STRUCTURE

1. In this essay, Eiseley is explicit about the ideas he discusses, but the burden of their presentation is carried almost exclusively by illustrations which make the ideas vivid and dramatic as well as immediately comprehensible.

Eiseley begins his essay with a reference to the witches' scene in *Macbeth*. He does not explicitly state the ideas he wishes to illustrate until par. 3. (a) What are the ideas? (b) What is gained by beginning with the reference to the witches? Why does he not state his ideas and then illustrate them?

2. In par. 4 he starts to apply these ideas to the contemporary scene. The paragraph, only six sentences long, warrants study. Sentence 1 is the topic sentence; sentence 2 provides both an illustration from the past of the topic sentence and a transition to the next sentence; sentence 3 provides a contemporary illustration of the topic; sentence 4 says that both illustrations share a common quality; sentence 5 identifies the quality; sentence 6 continues the identification and effects a transition to the next paragraph. Analyze par. 5 in a similar way.

3. Macbeth's witches and the ideas they embody disappear from pars. 7–15, and new ideas, with their accompanying illustrations, are presented. (a) In the beginning, Eiseley first presents his illustration and then his ideas. What order does he follow in this middle section? (b) Are pars. 7–15 necessary to Eiseley's thesis, or are they only a pleasant interruption? What relationship does this central section have to the rest of the essay? Examine the transitions that occur before and after the section.

4. In par. 19 Eiseley states that the words, "This is man," could have halted the evolutionary process. How many examples of this idea does he supply? Isn't one example enough? What is the purpose in offering several?

5. In par. 20 Eiseley writes, "There is within us only that dark, *divine animal* engaged in a strange journey—that creature who, *at midnight, knows its own ghostliness* and senses its far *road*." Explain how the words italicized by the editors contribute to the coherence of the essay.

DICTION AND TONE

1. At the end of par. 3 Eiseley describes the world created by the phantoms as *spurious and genuine*. First explain this paradox and then explain what it contributes to his essay.

2. At the end of par. 6 he says, ". . . the world arena is smoking with the caldrons. . . ." Explain the appropriateness of the figure.

3. In the first sentence of par. 6 he uses the word *novelty*. Explain the meaning of *novelty* in the context in which he uses it.

4. In par. 9 he refers to his fish and to the long-horned Alaskan bison by their technical names, *Ichthyostega* and *Bison regius*, but he refers to man as a primate and not as *Homo sapiens*. What effect is produced by the introduction of the technical names? By the way he refers to man?

5. What is the general tone of Eiseley's essay? Is it optimistic? pessimistic? cautious? scientifically detached?

6. Eiseley, as he says in par. 3, is a scientist. Briefly characterize his language. Is it general, particular, abstract, concrete, objective, subjective? How does it differ from the language used in a scientific treatise?

APPLICATIONS TO WRITING

1. Eiseley makes his interpretation of a scene from Shakespeare illustrate some of his ideas about how man contributes to the shaping of his own future. Take a scene from some literary work with which you are familiar, preferably but not necessarily one from Shakespeare, and make it serve a similar purpose by using it as an illustration of some general truth about the human condition.

2. Select a proverb and illustrate it with a personal anecdote. You may wish to review the opening paragraph of *My Wood* for some ideas about how to begin.

JOEY: A "MECHANICAL BOY"

BRUNO BETTELHEIM

Joey, when we began our work with him, was a mechanical boy. He functioned as if by remote control, run by machines of his own powerfully creative fantasy. Not only did he himself believe that he was a machine but, more remarkably, he created this impression in others. Even while he performed actions that are intrinsically human, they never appeared to be other than machine-started and executed. On the other hand, when the machine was not working he had to concentrate on recollecting his presence, for he seemed not to exist. A human body that functions as if it were a machine and a machine that duplicates human functions are equally fascinating and frightening. Perhaps they are so uncanny because they remind us that the human body can operate without a human spirit, that body can exist without soul. And Joey was a child who had been robbed of his humanity. [1]

Not every child who possesses a fantasy world is possessed by it. Normal children may retreat into realms of imaginary glory or magic powers, but they are easily recalled from these excursions. Disturbed children are not always able to make the return trip; they remain withdrawn, prisoners of the inner world of delusion and fantasy. In many ways Joey presented a classic example of this state of infantile autism. In any age, when the individual has escaped into a delusional

Reprinted by permission of *Scientific American*.

243

world, he has usually fashioned it from bits and pieces of the world at hand. Joey, in his time and world, chose the machine and froze himself in its image. His story has a general relevance to the understanding of emotional development in a machine age. [2]

Joey's delusion is not uncommon among schizophrenic children today. He wanted to be rid of his unbearable humanity, to become completely automatic. He so nearly succeeded in attaining this goal that he could almost convince others, as well as himself, of his mechanical character. The descriptions of autistic children in the literature take for their point of departure and comparison the normal or abnormal human being. To do justice to Joey I would have to compare him simultaneously to a most inept infant and a highly complex piece of machinery. Often we had to force ourselves by a conscious act of will to realize that Joey was a child. Again and again his acting-out of his delusions froze our own ability to respond as human beings. [3]

During Joey's first weeks with us we would watch absorbedly as this at once fragile-looking and imperious nine-year-old went about his mechanical existence. Entering the dining room, for example, he would string an imaginary wire from his "energy source"—an imaginary electric outlet—to the table. There he "insulated" himself with paper napkins and finally plugged himself in. Only then could Joey eat, for he firmly believed that the "current" ran his ingestive apparatus. So skillful was the pantomime that one had to look twice to be sure there was neither wire nor outlet nor plug. Children and members of our staff spontaneously avoided stepping on the "wires" for fear of interrupting what seemed the source of his very life. [4]

For long periods of time, when his "machinery" was idle, he would sit so quietly that he would disappear from the focus of the most conscientious observation. Yet in the next moment he might be "working" and the center of our captivated attention. Many times a day he would turn himself on and shift noisily through a sequence of higher and higher gears until he "exploded," screaming "crash, crash!" and hurling items from his ever present apparatus—radio tubes, light bulbs, even motors or, lacking these, any handy breakable object. (Joey had an astonishing knack for snatching bulbs and tubes unobserved.) As soon as the object thrown had shattered, he would cease his screaming and wild jumping and retire to mute, motionless nonexistence. [5]

Our maids, inured to difficult children, were exceptionally attentive to Joey; they were apparently moved by his extreme infantile fragility, so strangely coupled with megalomaniacal superiority. Occasionally some of the apparatus he fixed to his bed to "live him" during his sleep would fall down in disarray. This machinery he contrived from masking tape, cardboard, wire and other paraphernalia. Usually the maids would pick up such things and leave them on a table for the children to find, or disregard them entirely. But Joey's machine they carefully restored: "Joey must have the carburetor so he can breathe." Similarly they were on the alert to pick up and preserve the motors that ran him during the day and the exhaust pipes through which he exhaled. [6]

How had Joey become a human machine? From intensive interviews with his parents we learned that the process had begun even before birth. Schizophrenia often results from parental rejection, sometimes combined ambivalently with love. Joey, on the other hand, had been completely ignored. [7]

"I never knew I was pregnant," his mother said, meaning that she had already excluded Joey from her consciousness. His birth, she said, "did not make any difference." Joey's father, a rootless draftee in the wartime civilian army, was equally unready for parenthood. So, of course, are many young couples. Fortunately most such parents lose their indifference upon the baby's birth. But not Joey's parents. "I did not want to see or nurse him," his mother declared. "I had no feeling of actual dislike—I simply didn't want to take care of him." For the first three months of his life Joey "cried most of the time." A colicky baby, he was kept on a rigid four-hour feeding schedule, was not touched unless necessary and was never cuddled or played with. The mother, preoccupied with herself, usually left Joey alone in the crib or

playpen during the day. The father discharged his frustrations by
punishing Joey when the child cried at night. [8]

Soon the father left for overseas duty, and the mother took Joey,
now a year and a half old, to live with her at her parents' home. On
his arrival the grandparents noticed that ominous changes had occurred in the child. Strong and healthy at birth, he had become frail
and irritable; a responsive baby, he had become remote and inacces-
sible. When he began to master speech, he talked only to himself.
At an early date he became preoccupied with machinery, including
an old electric fan which he could take apart and put together again
with surprising deftness. [9]

Joey's mother impressed us with a fey quality that expressed her
insecurity, her detachment from the world and her low physical
vitality. We were struck especially by her total indifference as she
talked about Joey. This seemed much more remarkable than the
actual mistakes she made in handling him. Certainly he was left to
cry for hours when hungry, because she fed him on a rigid schedule;
he was toilet-trained with great rigidity so that he would give no
trouble. These things happen to many children. But Joey's existence
never registered with his mother. In her recollections he was fused at
one moment with one event or person; at another, with something or
somebody else. When she told us about his birth and infancy, it was
as if she were talking about some vague acquaintance, and soon her
thoughts would wander off to another person or to herself. [10]

When Joey was not yet four, his nursery school suggested that he
enter a special school for disturbed children. At the new school his
autism was immediately recognized. During his three years there he
experienced a slow improvement. Unfortunately a subsequent two
years in a parochial school destroyed this progress. He began to develop compulsive defenses, which he called his "preventions." He
could not drink, for example, except through elaborate piping systems
built of straws. Liquids had to be "pumped" into him, in his fantasy,
or he could not suck. Eventually his behavior became so upsetting
that he could not be kept in the parochial school. At home things did

not improve. Three months before entering the Orthogenic School he made a serious attempt at suicide. [11]

To us Joey's pathological behavior seemed the external expression of an overwhelming effort to remain almost nonexistent as a person. For weeks Joey's only reply when addressed was "Bam." Unless he thus neutralized whatever we said, there would be an explosion, for Joey plainly wished to close off every form of contact not mediated by machinery. Even when he was bathed he rocked back and forth with mute, engine-like regularity, flooding the bathroom. If he stopped rocking, he did this like a machine too; suddenly he went completely rigid. Only once, after months of being lifted from his bath and carried to bed, did a small expression of puzzled pleasure appear on his face as he said very softly: "They even carry you to your bed here." [12]

For a long time after he began to talk he would never refer to anyone by name, but only as "that person" or "the little person" or "the big person." He was unable to designate by its true name anything to which he attached feelings. Nor could he name his anxieties except through neologisms or word contaminations. For a long time he spoke about "master paintings" and "a master painting room" (*i.e.*, masturbating and masturbating room). One of his machines, the "criticizer," prevented him from "saying words which have unpleasant feelings." Yet he gave personal names to the tubes and motors in his collection of machinery. Moreover, these dead things had feelings; the tubes bled when hurt and sometimes got sick. He consistently maintained this reversal between animate and inanimate objects. [13]

In Joey's machine world everything, on pain of instant destruction, obeyed inhibitory laws much more stringent than those of physics. When we came to know him better, it was plain that in his moments of silent withdrawal, with his machine switched off, Joey was absorbed in pondering the compulsive laws of his private universe. His preoccupation with machinery made it difficult to establish even practical contacts with him. If he wanted to do something with a counselor, such as play with a toy that had caught his vague attention, he could not do so: "I'd like this very much, but first I have to turn off the machine." But by the time he had fulfilled all the requirements of his preventions, he had lost interest. When a toy was offered to him, he could not touch it because his motors and his tubes did not leave him a hand free. Even certain colors were dangerous and had to be strictly avoided in toys and clothing, because "some colors turn off the current, and I can't touch them because I can't live without the current." [14]

Joey was convinced that machines were better than people. Once when he bumped into one of the pipes on our jungle gym he kicked it so violently that his teacher had to restrain him to keep him from injuring himself. When she explained that the pipe was much harder than his foot, Joey replied: "That proves it. Machines are better than the body. They don't break; they're much harder and stronger." If he lost or forgot something, it merely proved that his brain ought to be thrown away and replaced by machinery. If he spilled something his arm should be broken and twisted off because it did not work properly. When his head or arm failed to work as it should, he tried to punish it by hitting it. Even Joey's feelings were mechanical. Much later in his therapy, when he had formed a timid attachment to another child and had been rebuffed, Joey cried: "He broke my feelings." [15]

Gradually we began to understand what had seemed to be contradictory in Joey's behavior—why he held on to the motors and tubes, then suddenly destroyed them in a fury, then set out immediately and urgently to equip himself with new and larger tubes. Joey had created these machines to run his body and mind because it was too painful to be human. But again and again he became dissatisfied with their failure to meet his need and rebellious at the way they frustrated his will. In a recurrent frenzy he "exploded" his light bulbs and tubes, and for a moment became a human being—for one crowning instant he came alive. But as soon as he had asserted his dominance through the self-created explosion, he felt his life ebbing away. To keep on existing he had immediately to restore his machines and replenish the electricity that supplied his life energy. [16]

What deep-seated fears and needs underlay Joey's delusional system? We were long in finding out, for Joey's preventions effectively concealed the secret of his autistic behavior. In the meantime we dealt with his peripheral problems one by one. [17]

During his first year with us Joey's most trying problem was toilet behavior. This surprised us, for Joey's personality was not "anal" in the Freudian sense; his original personality damage had antedated the period of his toilet-training. Rigid and early toilet-training, however, had certainly contributed to his anxieties. It was our effort to help Joey with this problem that led to his first recognition of us as human beings. [18]

Going to the toilet, like everything else in Joey's life, was surrounded by elaborate preventions. We had to accompany him; he had to take off all his clothes; he could only squat, not sit, on the toilet seat; he had to touch the wall with one hand, in which he also clutched frantically the vacuum tubes that powered his elimination. He was terrified lest his whole body be sucked down. [19]

To counteract this fear we gave him a metal wastebasket in lieu of a toilet. Eventually, when eliminating into the wastebasket, he no longer needed to take off all his clothes, nor to hold on to the wall. He still needed the tubes and motors which, he believed, moved his bowels for him. But here again the all-important machinery was itself a source of new terrors. In Joey's world the gadgets had to move their bowels, too. He was terribly concerned that they should, but since they were so much more powerful than men, he was also terrified that if his tubes moved their bowels, their feces would fill all of space and leave him no room to live. He was thus always caught in some fearful contradiction. [20]

Our readiness to accept his toilet habits, which obviously entailed some hardship for his counselors, gave Joey the confidence to express his obsessions in drawings. Drawing these fantasies was a first step toward letting us in, however distantly, to what concerned him most deeply. It was the first step in a year-long process of externalizing his anal preoccupations. As a result he began seeing feces everywhere; the whole world became to him a mire of excrement. At the same time he began to eliminate freely wherever he happened to be. But with this release from his infantile imprisonment in compulsive rules, the toilet and the whole process of elimination became less dangerous. Thus far it had been beyond Joey's comprehension that anybody could possibly move his bowels without mechanical aid. Now Joey took a further step forward; defecation became the first physiological process he could perform without the help of vacuum tubes. It must not be thought that he was proud of this ability. Taking pride in an achievement presupposes that one accomplishes it of one's own free will. He still did not feel himself an autonomous person who could do things on his own. To Joey defecation still seemed enslaved to some incomprehensible but utterly binding cosmic law, perhaps the law his parents had imposed on him when he was being toilet-trained. [21]

It was not simply that his parents had subjected him to rigid, early training. Many children are so trained. But in most cases the parents have a deep emotional investment in the child's performance. The child's response in turn makes training an occasion for interaction between them and for the building of genuine relationships. Joey's parents had no emotional investment in him. His obedience gave them no satisfaction and won him no affection or approval. As a toilet-trained child he saved his mother labor, just as household machines saved her labor. As a machine he was not loved for his performance, nor could he love himself. [22]

So it had been with all other aspects of Joey's existence with his parents. Their reactions to his eating or noneating, sleeping or wakening, urinating or defecating, being dressed or undressed, washed or bathed did not flow from any unitary interest in him, deeply embedded in their personalities. By treating him mechanically his parents made him a machine. The various functions of life—even the parts of his body—bore no integrating relationship to one another or to any sense of self that was acknowledged and confirmed by others. Though he had acquired mastery over some functions, such as toilet-training and speech, he had acquired them separately and kept them isolated from each other. Toilet-training had thus not gained him a pleasant feeling of body mastery; speech had not led to communication of thought or feeling. On the contrary, each achievement only steered him away from self-mastery and integration. Toilet-training had enslaved him. Speech left him talking in neologisms that obstructed his and our ability to relate to each other. In Joey's development the normal process of growth had been made to run backward. Whatever he had learned put him not at the end of his infantile development toward integration but, on the contrary, farther behind than he was at its very beginning. Had we understood this sooner, his first years with us would have been less baffling. [23]

It is unlikely that Joey's calamity could befall a child in any time and culture but our own. He suffered no physical deprivation; he starved for human contact. Just to be taken care of is not enough for relating. It is a necessary but not a sufficient condition. At the extreme where utter scarcity reigns, the forming of relationships is certainly hampered. But our society of mechanized plenty often makes for equal difficulties in a child's learning to relate. Where parents can provide the simple creature-comforts for their children only at the cost of significant effort, it is likely that they will feel pleasure in being able to provide for them; it is this, the parents' pleasure, that gives children a sense of personal worth and sets the process of relating in motion. But if comfort is so readily available that the parents feel no particular pleasure in winning it for their children, then the children cannot develop the feeling of being worthwhile around the satisfaction of their basic needs. Of course parents and children can and do develop relationships around other situations. But matters are then no longer so simple and direct. The child must be on the receiving end of care and concern given with pleasure and without the exaction of return if he is to feel loved and worthy of respect and consideration. This feeling gives him the ability to trust; he can entrust his well-being to persons to whom he is so important. Out of such trust the child learns to form close and stable relationships. [24]

For Joey relationship with his parents was empty of pleasure in comfort-giving as in all other situations. His was an extreme instance of a plight that sends many schizophrenic children to our clinics and hospitals. Many months passed before he could relate to us; his despair that anybody could like him made contact impossible. [25]

When Joey could finally trust us enough to let himself become more infantile, he began to play at being a papoose. There was a corresponding change in his fantasies. He drew endless pictures of himself as an electrical papoose. Totally enclosed, suspended in empty space, he is run by unknown, unseen powers through wireless electricity. [26]

As we eventually came to understand, the heart of Joey's delusional system was the artificial, mechanical womb he had created and into which he had locked himself. In his papoose fantasies lay the wish to be entirely reborn in a womb. His new experiences in the school suggested that life, after all, might be worth living. Now he was searching for a way to be reborn in a better way. Since machines were better than men, what was more natural than to try rebirth through them? This was the deeper meaning of his electrical papoose. [27]

As Joey made progress, his pictures of himself became more dominant in his drawings. Though still machine-operated, he has grown in self-importance. Another great step forward is represented in a picture in which he has acquired hands that do something, and he has had the courage to make a picture of the machine that runs him. Later still the papoose became a person, rather than a robot encased in glass. [28]

Eventually Joey began to create an imaginary family at the school: the "Carr" family. Why the Carr family? In the car he was enclosed as he had been in his papoose, but at least the car was not stationary; it could move. More important, in a car one was not only driven but also could drive. The Carr family was Joey's way of exploring the possibility of leaving the school, of living with a good family in a safe, protecting car. [29]

Joey at last broke through his prison. In this brief account it has not been possible to trace the painfully slow process of his first true relations with other human beings. Suffice it to say that he ceased to be a mechanical boy and became a human child. This newborn child was, however, nearly 12 years old. To recover the lost time is a tremendous task. That work has occupied Joey and us ever since. Sometimes he sets to it with a will; at other times the difficulty of real life makes him regret that he ever came out of his shell. But he has never wanted to return to his mechanical life. [30]

One last detail and this fragment of Joey's story has been told. When Joey was 12, he made a float for our Memorial Day parade. It carried the slogan: "Feelings are more important than anything under the sun." Feelings, Joey had learned, are what make for humanity; their absence, for a mechanical existence. With this knowledge Joey entered the human condition. [31]

PURPOSE AND STRUCTURE

In this essay Bettelheim clarifies the general concept of emotional development in a machine age by drawing upon the experiences of a single individual, Joey, as an illustration. The illustration in turn is developed by means of analogy. By taking an extreme and atypical example of a boy who *froze himself* in the image of the machine the author dramatizes his general concept.

1. With what details in par. 1 does the author develop his analogy?

2. How do the two meanings of the word *possess* underlie the contrast made in par. 2? What causal relationships are established in the last three sentences of the paragraph?

3. What dual comparison is made in par. 3? What two concepts in this paragraph are repetitions of those previously mentioned? What new causal relationship is advanced?

4. What illustrations in par. 4 develop the image of Joey's mechanical existence? How do the last two sentences of the paragraph derive from them?

5. What is the relationship of par. 6 to pars. 4 and 5?

6. What illustrations develop the causal relationships advanced in pars. 7–10?

7. What further particulars in par. 12 support the opening generalization?

8. What comparison and contrast is developed in par. 13? What is its relationship to par. 12?

9. What causal relationship is developed in par. 14?

10. Note how par. 16 serves a transitional purpose in summing up what has been previously stated. How does par. 17 serve a transitional purpose?

11. How do pars. 18–23 illustrate the generalization that "in Joey's development the normal process of growth had been made to run backward"? In par. 23 what kind of relationship is implied by the words *had been made?*

12. How does the analogy of labor-saving devices in par. 22 contribute to your understanding of Joey's problem? How does the succeeding paragraph further illuminate the analogy?

13. How does the author develop the opening topic sentence in par. 24?

14. What is the relationship of pars. 26–29 to par. 30?

15. What is the relationship of Joey's Memorial Day slogan to the concluding sentence; to the author's central purpose?

16. With what concrete illustrations does the author make clear each of the following dualities: human-mechanical; fragile-imperious; internalize-externalize; explosions-preventions?

DICTION AND TONE

1. The word *froze,* or a synonym, is used throughout the essay. Comment on its relevance to structural purpose and tone.

2. How does the diction, appropriate to the vocabulary of a machine, contribute to the tone? provide emphasis? Refer both to the author's descriptions and to Joey's own choice of words.

3. Identify the irony in par. 13.

4. Discuss the appropriateness of the word *work* in par. 30.

5. What is Bettelheim's attitude toward Joey? toward his mother? How do you know?

6. From what point of view does he narrate the story of Joey? Is he speaking solely as a psychiatrist? If not, from what other perspective?

APPLICATIONS TO WRITING

1. Clarify a general concept by drawing upon the experiences of a single individual. Beginning with an observation about the family, the university, an occupation, a leisure activity, attempt to clarify and illustrate your concept by narrating the experiences of a single individual.

2. Analyze the means by which the author transforms what might have been a medical case history into a moving portrait of Joey. Examine a number of case histories in psychiatric texts. What are the differences in intention, tone, perspective, and diction in the two modes of writing?

WHAT COCKTAIL PARTY?

JAMES THURBER

"I'm not so stupid as to believe that the cocktail party in 'The Cocktail Party' is actually a cocktail party," Grace Sheldon told me the other day at a cocktail party that was unquestionably a cocktail party. "What do *you* think it is?" [1]

I was all wariness in a moment. Ever since the distinguished Mr. T. S. Eliot's widely discussed play came to town, I have been cornered at parties by women, and men, who seem intent on making me say what I think "The Cocktail Party" means, so they can cry "Great God, how naïve!" and then go around telling people that I probably don't even know the significance of the pumpkin in "Cinderella." I have learned to spar for time, with a counter-question of my own. "Do you believe in the innocence of the innocents in 'The Innocents'?" I asked Grace Sheldon. [2]

Grace finished her Martini and looked around for the man in the white coat with the cocktail tray. "The only thing I am sure of," she said, "is the death of the salesman in 'Death of a Salesman.' I'm sure he dies and is supposed to be dead." [3]

"You're just an old positivist," I said. [4]

"The point is whether Eliot was impelled to write the play by forces beyond his control and cognizance," chimed in Charles Endless, joining us and waving his empty highball glass. "I presume you're

256

talking about *the* play." Endless is forever repeating the critical judgments of his psychiatrist, Dr. Karl Wix, and embroidering them with
the skeins of his own prejudices. "There is no such thing as the power
of conscious selection in the creative writer," Charles went on. "I
should say that the psychic inspiration of 'The Cocktail Party' was the
consequence of something Eliot had done, whereas 'The Turn of the
Screw'—or 'The Innocents,' if you prefer to call it that—is clear proof
of Henry James's conscious unawareness of something he had *not*
done." [5]

"Something important, of course," I annotated. [6]

"Vastly," underlined Endless. "Observe the size of the symbols
these two writers have been impelled to select from the stockpile of
literary devices and properties: the holy cross and the dark
tower." [7]

"I haven't seen 'The Sign of the Screw,' and I don't want to talk
about it," said Grace. "I want to find out what Mr. Thurber thinks
'The Cocktail Party' is about. I'm not interested in what Dr. Wix
thinks was the matter with Henry James." [8]

"Great God!" cried Charles. "The woman seeks narrative sense in
the sheerest mechanism of expiation!" [9]

"I do not," said Grace, taking another Martini from the hovering
cocktail tray. [10]

Endless bowed with what he believed to be eighteenth-century
grace, and was about to set off to find more congenial intellectual
companionship when Malcolm Codd said something that arrested
him. Codd, who had appeared quietly, as usual, from nowhere, wore
glasses with flesh-colored rims and sipped furtively at a glass of milk.
"Yes?" said Charles irritably, turning on him. [11]

"I say," Codd said, "that anyone is indiscreet who tells what he
thinks the play means. It is clearly one of those projection techniques,
like the ink blots that are now all the vogue with psychiatrists. What
the spots and the play mean to you is the thumbprint of your persona, the signature of your psyche, a history of your past, a key to
your bedroom, a portrait of your ego in Technicolor. I would no
more think of telling you what 'The Cocktail Party' meant to me last

Saturday afternoon than I would think of telling you last night's dream." [12]

"You should have read either a great deal more or a great deal less than you have," Charles said. [13]

I decided to color the dialogue with some rhythms of my own, since they always annoy Charles. "What makes you think, Codd, that the meaning of the play to you, or last night's dream, is sure to show a sinister significance?" I asked. [14]

Charles stared at me in horror. "Great God!" he cried. "Are you looking for the bluebird of happiness? Do you think there are actually hinges on chimneys so the stars can get by? Do you believe Love will slay the dragon and live happily ever after?" [15]

I was as cool as steel. "I believe in the sudden deep greenness of summer," I said. In the fifteen years I have known Charles, his skepticism has always shattered against my affirmation, and he knows it. [16]

"Bah!" he said, turning grandly on his heel, and bumping into old Mrs. Weaver, who is convinced that Eliot wrote the play in his sleep. [17]

"Goddam it," she said, "look where you're going." [18]

Mrs. Codd laughed. Since she never says anything, I hadn't noticed she was there. [19]

"He is lost beyond saving," Codd said, taking his wife's arm and leading her away. [20]

One always knows Grace Sheldon is there. She began to chew on it again. "I don't know you well enough to tell you what Dr. Wix thinks 'Gentlemen Prefer Blondes' is about," she said, watching Ruth Endless dive out of a cloud of women, strafe her husband briefly, and disappear behind a cliff of laughing men. "Or rather," she went on, "what Charles says Dr. Wix thinks it means. But you still haven't told me what *you* think of 'The Cocktail Party.'" [21]

I laughed a laugh that was not actually a laugh. [22]

"What *don't* you think it means, then?" she put in helpfully. [23]

I circled around this for a moment. "Do you mean what Eliot is

intentionally not saying, or what he just *happens* not to have said?"
I asked, with enormous tidiness. She looked bewildered and I tried to
clear it up for her, and for me. "Let me put it this way," I said. "No
playwright has ever deliberately said 'Kings wear oysters in their
shoes.' This line has not been left out, however, in the sense that it
has been *rejected*. It is certainly not what Eliot is *not* saying. If we
charged him with it, he might quite properly reply, 'I would never
not say that!' " [24]

Grace Sheldon sighed, and robbed the passing tray of another
drink. "Then what is it he isn't saying?" she wailed. "What is it he
doesn't mean to mean?" [25]

"My dear lady," I said, "if we were to discuss what he does not
mean, we would find ourselves discussing what some other particular
play does mean, since I am persuaded that what he is not saying has
been said in some identifiable drama, and just as vehemently as he
has not said it, if not so eloquently. The question is—what other
play?" [26]

Grace made a desperate stab at it. " 'Candida'?" she whispered. [27]

I am afraid I sneered. Grace can be extraordinarily obtuse. "I am
not privy to what Eliot is not saying," I said coldly, "but I will stake
my sacred honor that he is not not saying what 'Candida' says." [28]

Grace glanced at her watch. "I wish everybody were as simple as
Shaw," she said. "I'm going home." And she went. [29]

Ruth Endless descended on me with Archie Kess in tow. "Archie
has a theory about Peter Quilpe in 'The Cocktail Party,' " she said.
"Archie thinks Quilpe is not really the wife's lover but the husband's
fantasy of the kind of lover she would pick if she picked one." [30]

"A degradation symbol?" I asked. [31]

"Exactly," said Archie. "Eliot has given the word 'Quilpe' the same
force as our 'twerp' or 'drip.' If he had meant the character to be real,
he would have called him Querringhouse, or Quillingham, or Quar-
termaine." [32]

I turned this over in my mind. Then Ruth said, "I happen to know that Quilpe is based on an actual person Eliot can't stand named Sweeney, or Prufrock, or some such name. Just as Julia in the show is Lady Serena Carnarvon, or somebody, who once hit Eliot with a paper dart at a musicale in London." [33]

Archie kept nodding and grinning, and I snarled at him, "If it gives you two any satisfaction to find the paper snow of personal retaliation in this magnificent blizzard of poetic thought, I hope all the radiators in your part of Hell go thrump." [34]

"All the time?" asked Archie. [35]

I walked away from them and joined Betty Logan and Tom Frayne. [36]

"For God's sake, Betty," Frayne was saying, gesturing with his cigarette, "say the Psychiatrist is Ambition, or Hope, or God, or Escapism, or Dedication, or the Father Image, or the Death Urge, or the Oedipus Complex, or a snatch of song you can't get out of your mind, but don't stand there and try to tell me he is an actual, carnate, human male psychiatrist. Can you imagine such a well-bred and cultured English psychiatrist—for that is what he would be if he were mortal—*crashing* a cocktail party in London?" [37]

"What makes you think it is a cocktail party?" I asked coolly. "Eliot himself says—" [38]

"I don't care what Eliot himself says," snapped Tom. "Eliot has missed a great many of the meanings in his play—wasn't that obvious to you when you saw it?" [39]

"I wouldn't say 'obvious,'" I said. "I would say it nagged and nibbled at the rind of my consciousness." [40]

"What do *you* think the play is about? What do *you* think it means?" asked Betty. [41]

I decided to withdraw down a murky bypass. "The identity of the third murderer in 'Macbeth' has puzzled Shakespearean scholars for more than three centuries," I said. "Would it impair or increase your pleasure in the great tragedy if you found out who he actually is, or was?" [42]

"It wouldn't make any difference to me," Betty said. [43]

"What are you driving at, Thurber?" asked Tom. [44]

"The Catonian Trium," I said. " 'The Cocktail Party' is plainly a revaluation of the theory of Cato the Elder that two primary identities can sustain an unidentifiable third. That is, the *duum* differs from the *unum* in that it can absorb, without distortion of meaning, the introduction of an unknown, or mysterious, or debatable third." [45]

"Naturally," said Tom with crisp impatience. "Everybody knows that. But it doesn't apply here. You are adding the Psychiatrist to Julia and Alex when, as a matter of fact, *they* are added to him. You don't seem to understand what identity is being concealed." [46]

I found myself in the embarrassing position of being routed in an argument involving a theory I had made up. "He'll debauch you, Betty," I said, and retreated from the field. [47]

When the Eliot play begins to burn at the edges of a cocktail party, it spreads rapidly through the room, igniting every tongue, including the tongues of those ladies and gentlemen who haven't seen the play and don't intend to, or can hardly wait. On my way to the front hall, after waving goodbye to my hostess, I overheard a young man telling a pretty girl that the play is a hoax, the secret of whose anagrammatic scheme had been figured out by his roommate at Harvard, a brilliant chap named Buzz Walkley. As I passed into the hall, Judge Henneman trotted out of the lavatory, hardly able to breathe, as usual, and seized my arm. "What's fellow up to?" he wheezed. "Study of the female element in the human male," I explained. "Buncombe," he wheezed. "Discipline breaking down all over world." He stood there, gripping my arm and trying to breathe for a full minute. Then he let go and tottered back to the controversy. [48]

I turned to find Edgeley, the butler, waiting with my hat and coat and stick. "What do *you* make of it, Edgeley?" I asked. [49]

He helped me on with my coat. "It's another variant of the prickly-pear theme, I should say," he ventured, "if I'm not perhaps being a bit too basic." [50]

"Not at all," I said. "I'm afraid some of us have been much too high in the superstructure to see the fundamentals clearly." We walked to the door. [51]

"Your point is prettily taken," he said. [52]

I thanked him. [53]

"There is an ancient Latin saying," he went on, "which, freely translated, goes like this: 'If my ship burn at sea, then who shall know its destination save the stars and God?' " [54]

"Who indeed?" I said cautiously. I thought I detected a faint whiff of kirsch on his breath. [55]

"My colleague, Huntington," he continued, "has hit it off rather sharply, I think—but I am boring you." [56]

"Not at all," I told him. "What does Huntington say?" [57]

"Huntington says, 'It is desolater than you think.' " He opened the door for me. "Quite keen, don't you agree?" [58]

"Very," I said. [59]

I went out and Edgeley closed the door slowly and softly behind me. I stood a moment on the stoop, wondering vaguely about his background. A cab turned the corner and I waved it down. When I got in, I glanced at the driver's identification card and saw that his name was Louis Sandek. He turned around and looked at me thoughtfully. "You know something?" he said. I took fifty cents out of my pocket, gave it to him, got out of the cab, and slammed the door shut. He shrugged and drove off. It was twelve blocks to my hotel, but I walked. I was in no mood to listen to the Sandek version. [60]

PURPOSE AND STRUCTURE

1. This satirical narrative is an illustration of something that is never directly stated. You should be able to discover it by reading between the lines. (Don't fall into the absurd traps into which Thurber, with dazzling profligacy, places his *dramatis personae*.) Not counting Thurber himself

in his complex role as commentator, as the guest who baits the others, and as a kind of wise fool, there are sixteen characters at the cocktail party, if one includes the absent Dr. Karl Wix, the psychiatrist, whose presence is invoked by the interpretations attributed to him; the nameless pretty girl and young man; the missing Buzz Walkley, the latter's brilliant Harvard roommate; and Huntington, the colleague of Edgeley, the butler. Since these characters have been portrayed with varying degrees of amplitude, it is obvious that the chief clues to what is being illustrated will be provided by this large cast. Begin by asking yourself some questions: are they types or individuals? If they are types, what do they have in common and how do they differ? If some of them are individuals, and not types, by what means are they differentiated? But even when distinguished, are they really distinguishable?

2. Relate the title, What *Cocktail Party?*, to the purpose of the narrative. It is obvious that T. S. Eliot's play, *The Cocktail Party*, one of the scenes of which is a cocktail party, is being discussed at a cocktail party. But beyond the play of words with which the ubiquitous Grace Sheldon begins the dialogue, there are other implications. The italicizing of *What* provides one clue to the subject being illustrated. How does the subsequent narrative account for the italics?

3. The consistency of Thurber's role as narrator gives the story unity. Find the passages in which he is the omniscient observer and those in which he is a participant who is baiting the other guests. In what sense are his sparring, counter-questions, and interpretations only an extension of his observer's role? How does the baiting role give emphasis to the observer's role? For example, look at par. 45 in which he alludes to *The Catonian Trium*. By means of this absurd invention his satirical intention is made apparent. Find other passages in which his role of direct participant clarifies and extends what he is able to say as narrator. While the structure appears to be formless, it is tightly knit. What recurring elements provide transitions and give it unity and coherence?

4. What is the relationship between what he is *ostensibly* and *actually* illustrating? For example, note that Endless quotes or embroiders the critical judgments of his psychiatrist; Grace Sheldon persists in trying to ferret out Thurber's view and quotes what Charles says the psychiatrist thinks it means; Ruth Endless quotes Archie Kess's theory about Quilpe; the young man quotes his Harvard roommate; and the butler quotes his colleague, Huntington. How do these fragments of conversation illustrate Thurber's view of the human situation? Formulate your own generalization of what is being illustrated.

DICTION AND TONE

1. Thurber achieves irony by the mock seriousness with which he speaks in his non-detached role and with which he invests the vocabulary of the other guests. Cite examples.

2. How is a humorous effect achieved in the reference to "Henry James's conscious unawareness of something he had *not* done" (par. 5)?

3. How do the lines Thurber assigns himself in par. 24 contribute to purpose and tone?

4. The narrator pretends not to perceive the implications of what he is describing (*irony of statement*). For example, in deadpan manner, with simulated seriousness, he responds to Endless' preposterous and nonsensical remark with the line, " 'Something important, of course,' I annotated" (par. 6). Find other examples.

5. A cumulative humorous effect is achieved (not unlike Jack Benny's running gags) when Grace Sheldon persists in extracting from Thurber an answer to the question, what do you think *The Cocktail Party* really means (or what *don't* you think it means or what is it he doesn't mean to mean); when the judge trots out of the lavatory posing a variation of the same question; when Thurber directs it to the butler; and finally when the cab driver's query seems imminent. Locate other examples of levity.

6. Note the context of the following images and phrases and show how they contribute to the irony of tone: *the pumpkin in Cinderella* [2]; *'The Sign of the Screw'* [8]; *the sheerest mechanism of expiation* [9]; *a sinister significance* [14]; *with enormous tidiness* [24]; *Kings wear oysters in their shoes* [24]; *a degradation symbol* [31]; *somebody, who once hit Eliot with a paper dart at a musicale in London* [33]; *nagged and nibbled at the rind of my consciousness* [40].

7. How do verbs and nouns work in the vignettes of Grace and Ruth: "She began to *chew* on it again"; "*dive* out of a *cloud* of women, *strafe* her husband . . . and disappear behind a *cliff* of laughing men" (par. 21)?

8. By becoming the *persona* of the other guests, and a caricature of them, the narrator can make even more preposterous interpretations and more

pretentious allusions than they do. How does this role merge with and extend the omniscient observer's role?

9. Relate the line given to Charles Endless, "You should have read either a great deal more or a great deal less than you have," to the author's purpose and tone. Speculate on the possibility that Thurber is allowing Endless to speak for him.

10. Determine the degree of objectivity with which Thurber views the cocktail party and, by extension, the human situation. You will need to examine closely the variety of statements which comment upon his role or his attitude; such as "I was all wariness" [2]; "I have been cornered" [2]; "I have learned to spar" [3]; "his skepticism has always shattered against my affirmation" [16]; "I was in no mood to listen to the Sandek version [60]. Analyze the subtle variations of tone in relation to the context in which these (and other) quotations appear (see Perspective in Glossary).

APPLICATIONS TO WRITING

1. Attempt a narrative in which you rely primarily upon dialogue to illustrate a conviction you hold dearly, or to place in relief the bias of others, or both. You might use the table in a cafeteria, an intermission at the theater, an art gallery, or the student union as the setting. As you write, ask yourself whether each bit of dialogue moves the narrative forward toward its conclusion. You will need to be clear about the generalization you are trying to illustrate.

2. Compare and contrast E. B. White's *The Second Tree from the Corner* with What *Cocktail Party?*, giving attention to their respective views of man and their attitudes about psychiatry as well as to their purpose, diction, and tone.

3. Write a satirical sketch in which you present your version of the synthetic personality who leans on the crutch provided by other people's opinions.

THE SECOND TREE
FROM THE CORNER

E . B . WHITE

"Ever had any bizarre thoughts?" asked the doctor. [1]
Mr. Trexler failed to catch the word. "What kind?" he said. [2]

"Bizarre," repeated the doctor, his voice steady. He watched his patient for any slight change of expression, any wince. It seemed to Trexler that the doctor was not only watching him closely but was creeping slowly toward him, like a lizard toward a bug. Trexler shoved his chair back an inch and gathered himself for a reply. He was about to say "Yes" when he realized that if he said yes the next question would be unanswerable. Bizarre thoughts, bizarre thoughts? Ever have any bizarre thoughts? What kind of thoughts *except* bizarre had he had since the age of two? [3]

Trexler felt the time passing, the necessity for an answer. These psychiatrists were busy men, overloaded, not to be kept waiting. The next patient was probably already perched out there in the waiting room, lonely, worried, shifting around on the sofa, his mind stuffed with bizarre thoughts and amorphous fears. Poor bastard, thought Trexler. Out there all alone in that misshapen antechamber, staring at

"The Second Tree from the Corner" from *The Second Tree from the Corner* by E. B. White. Originally appeared in *The New Yorker*. Copyright 1947 by E. B. White. Reprinted by permission of Harper & Brothers.

266

the filing cabinet and wondering whether to tell the doctor about that day on the Madison Avenue bus. [4]

Let's see, bizarre thoughts. Trexler dodged back along the dreadful corridor of the years to see what he could find. He felt the doctor's eyes upon him and knew that time was running out. Don't be so conscientious, he said to himself. If a bizarre thought is indicated here, just reach into the bag and pick anything at all. A man as well supplied with bizarre thoughts as you are should have no difficulty producing one for the record. Trexler darted into the bag, hung for a moment before one of his thoughts, as a hummingbird pauses in the delphinium. No, he said, not that one. He darted to another (the one about the rhesus monkey), paused, considered. No, he said, not that. [5]

Trexler knew he must hurry. He had already used up pretty nearly four seconds since the question had been put. But it was an impossible situation—just one more lousy, impossible situation such as he was always getting himself into. When, he asked himself, are you going to quit maneuvering yourself into a pocket? He made one more effort. This time he stopped at the asylum, only the bars were lucite —fluted, retractable. Not here, he said. Not this one. [6]

He looked straight at the doctor. "No," he said quietly. "I never have any bizarre thoughts." [7]

The doctor sucked in on his pipe, blew a plume of smoke toward the rows of medical books. Trexler's gaze followed the smoke. He managed to make out one of the titles, "The Genito-Urinary System." A bright wave of fear swept cleanly over him, and he winced under the first pain of kidney stones. He remembered when he was a child, the first time he ever entered a doctor's office, sneaking a look at the titles of the books—and the flush of fear, the shirt wet under the arms, the book on t.b., the sudden knowledge that he was in the advanced stages of consumption, the quick vision of the hemorrhage. Trexler sighed wearily. Forty years, he thought, and I still get thrown by the title of a medical book. Forty years and I still can't stay on life's little bucky horse. No wonder I'm sitting here in this dreary joint at the end of this woebegone afternoon, lying about my bizarre thoughts to a doctor who looks, come to think of it, rather tired. [8]

The session dragged on. After about twenty minutes, the doctor rose and knocked his pipe out. Trexler got up, knocked the ashes out of his brain, and waited. The doctor smiled warmly and stuck out his hand. "There's nothing the matter with you—you're just scared. Want to know how I know you're scared?" [9]

"How?" asked Trexler. [10]

"Look at the chair you've been sitting in! See how it has moved back away from my desk? You kept inching away from me while I asked you questions. That means you're scared." [11]

"Does it?" said Trexler, faking a grin. "Yeah, I suppose it does." [12]

They finished shaking hands. Trexler turned and walked out uncertainly along the passage, then into the waiting room and out past the next patient, a ruddy pin-striped man who was seated on the sofa twirling his hat nervously and staring straight ahead at the files. Poor, frightened guy, thought Trexler, he's probably read in the *Times* that one American male out of every two is going to die of heart disease by twelve o'clock next Thursday. It says that in the paper almost every morning. And he's also probably thinking about that day on the Madison Avenue bus. [13]

A week later, Trexler was back in the patient's chair. And for several weeks thereafter he continued to visit the doctor, always toward the end of the afternoon, when the vapors hung thick above the pool of the mind and darkened the whole region of the East Seventies. He felt no better as time went on, and he found it impossible to work. He discovered that the visits were becoming routine and that although the routine was one to which he certainly did not look forward, at least he could accept it with cool resignation, as once, years ago, he had accepted a long spell with a dentist who had settled down to a steady fooling with a couple of dead teeth. The visits, moreover, were now assuming a pattern recognizable to the patient. [14]

Each session would begin with a résumé of symptoms—the dizziness in the streets, the constricting pain in the back of the neck, the apprehensions, the tightness of the scalp, the inability to concentrate, the despondency and the melancholy times, the feeling of pressure and tension, the anger at not being able to work, the anxiety over work not done, the gas on the stomach. Dullest set of neurotic symptoms in the world, Trexler would think, as he obediently trudged back over them for the doctor's benefit. And then, having listened attentively to the recital, the doctor would spring his question: "Have you ever found anything that gives you relief?" And Trexler would answer, "Yes. A drink." And the doctor would nod his head knowingly. [15]

As he became familiar with the pattern Trexler found that he increasingly tended to identify himself with the doctor, transferring himself into the doctor's seat—probably (he thought) some rather slick form of escapism. At any rate, it was nothing new for Trexler to identify himself with other people. Whenever he got into a cab, he instantly became the driver, saw everything from the hackman's angle (and the reaching over with the right hand, the nudging of the flag, the pushing it down, all the way down along the side of the meter), saw everything—traffic, fare, everything—through the eyes of Anthony Rocco, or Isidore Freedman, or Matthew Scott. In a barbershop, Trexler was the barber, his fingers curled around the comb, his hand on the tonic. Perfectly natural, then, that Trexler should soon be occupying the doctor's chair, asking the questions, waiting for the answers. He got quite interested in the doctor, in this way. He liked him, and he found him a not too difficult patient. [16]

It was on the fifth visit, about halfway through, that the doctor turned to Trexler and said, suddenly, "What do you want?" He gave the word "want" special emphasis. [17]

"I d'know," replied Trexler uneasily. "I guess nobody knows the answer to that one." [18]

"Sure they do," replied the doctor. [19]

"Do you know what you want?" asked Trexler narrowly. [20]

"Certainly," said the doctor. Trexler noticed that at this point the doctor's chair slid slightly backward, away from him. Trexler stifled a small, internal smile. Scared as a rabbit, he said to himself. Look at him scoot! [21]

"What *do* you want?" continued Trexler, pressing his advantage, pressing it hard. [22]

The doctor glided back another inch away from his inquisitor. "I want a wing on the small house I own in Westport. I want more money, and more leisure to do the things I want to do." [23]

Trexler was just about to say, "And what are those things you want to do, Doctor?" when he caught himself. Better not go too far, he mused. Better not lose possession of the ball. And besides, he thought, what the hell goes on here, anyway—me paying fifteen bucks a throw for these séances and then doing the work myself, asking the questions, weighing the answers. So he wants a new wing! There's a fine piece of theatrical gauze for you! A new wing. [24]

Trexler settled down again and resumed the role of patient for the rest of the visit. It ended on a kindly, friendly note. The doctor reassured him that his fears were the cause of his sickness, and that his fears were unsubstantial. They shook hands, smiling. [25]

Trexler walked dizzily through the empty waiting room and the doctor followed along to let him out. It was late; the secretary had shut up shop and gone home. Another day over the dam. "Goodbye," said Trexler. He stepped into the street, turned west toward Madison, and thought of the doctor all alone there, after hours, in that desolate hole—a man who worked longer hours than his secretary. Poor, scared, overworked bastard, thought Trexler. And that new wing! [26]

It was an evening of clearing weather, the Park showing green and desirable in the distance, the last daylight applying a high lacquer to the brick and brownstone walls and giving the street scene a luminous and intoxicating splendor. Trexler meditated, as he walked, on what he wanted. "What do you want?" he heard again. Trexler knew what he wanted, and what, in general, all men wanted; and he was glad, in a way, that it was both inexpressible and unattainable, and that it wasn't a wing. He was satisfied to remember that it was deep, form-less, enduring, and impossible of fulfillment, and that it made men sick, and that when you sauntered along Third Avenue and looked through the doorways into the dim saloons, you could sometimes pick out from the unregenerate ranks the ones who had not forgotten, gazing steadily into the bottoms of the glasses on the long chance that they could get another little peek at it. Trexler found himself renewed by the remembrance that what he wanted was at once great and microscopic, and that although it borrowed from the nature of large deeds and of youthful love and of old songs and early intimations, it was not any one of these things, and that it had not been isolated or pinned down, and that a man who attempted to define it in the privacy of a doctor's office would fall flat on his face. [27]

Trexler felt invigorated. Suddenly his sickness seemed health, his dizziness stability. A small tree, rising between him and the light, stood there saturated with the evening, each gilt-edged leaf perfectly drunk with excellence and delicacy. Trexler's spine registered an ever so slight tremor as it picked up this natural disturbance in the lovely scene. "I want the second tree from the corner, just as it stands," he said, answering an imaginary question from an imaginary physician. And he felt a slow pride in realizing that what he wanted none could bestow, and that what he had none could take away. He felt content to be sick, unembarrassed at being afraid; and in the jungle of his fear he glimpsed (as he had so often glimpsed them before) the flashy tail feathers of the bird courage. [28]

Then he thought once again of the doctor, and of his being left there all alone, tired, frightened. (The poor, scared guy, thought Trexler.) Trexler began humming "Moonshine Lullaby," his spirit reacting instantly to the hypodermic of Merman's healthy voice. He crossed Madison, boarded a downtown bus, and rode all the way to Fifty-second Street before he had a thought that could rightly have been called bizarre. [29]

PURPOSE AND STRUCTURE

1. The details in pars. 1–13 concern a single session in the psychiatrist's office, pars. 14–16 the pattern of subsequent meetings, pars. 17–26 the

climactic fifth visit, and pars. 27–29 Mr. Trexler's concluding reflections. How does each of these sequences illustrate the implied generalization? In addition to being chronological, how is the order cumulative in effect?

2. The author achieves vividness and realism by the specific mention of name, place, time and circumstances. For example, "The Genito-Urinary System," the Madison Avenue bus, the *Times*, and the region of the East Seventies. What other particulars contribute to verisimilitude by their specificity?

3. In his silent reflections in par. 4 it occurs to Trexler that the next patient was already perched out in the waiting room, lonely and worried. What is significant about this thought? Where else in the narrative does Trexler interpret the feelings of others?

4. "Suddenly his sickness seemed health, his dizziness stability" (par. 28). Explain.

5. What is the significance of wanting the second tree from the corner? Why not the first? Try to state in your own words what Trexler wanted. Interpret: "What he wanted none could bestow, and . . . what he had none could take away" (par. 28).

6. What details describing Trexler's symptoms are directly recounted? What symptoms become apparent by implication?

7. In what sense do the details in pars. 16 and 21 repeat what has been stated before? In what sense are they a culmination of what has preceded? What new elements have been introduced? What is the source of the humor?

DICTION AND TONE

1. The author's unerring skill in finding the precise word to serve the purpose and tone of the narrative is demonstrable when a synonym is used in its place. Compare the results after you have made substitutions for the following: *wince* [3]; *gathered* [3]; *perched* [4]; *lousy* [6]; *maneuvering* [6]; *woebegone* [8]; *inching* [11]; *nudging* [16]; *scoot* [21]; *jungle* [28]. Comment further on the relevance of these words to the author's purpose and tone. How do they illuminate the relationship between narrator and

reader? What visual image is conveyed by them? What are their connotations? Determine the degree of concreteness achieved in each case.

2. The words *bizarre thoughts* are used throughout the essay. Why is
bizarre an effective word? What is achieved by its repeated use?

3. Note the contrast between Trexler's unexpressed free associations and
his actual statements in the psychiatrist's office. How does this contribute
to the ironic tone?

4. In par. 3 Trexler felt "that the doctor was not only watching him
closely but was creeping slowly toward him, like a lizard toward a bug."
Find other examples in which the diction graphically conveys Trexler's
feelings toward the psychiatrist.

5. The author's viewpoint may be inferred from the thoughts, feelings
and behavior of Trexler, but primarily from the vivid and figurative
language. What is he satirizing? What is he affirming?

6. Discuss the appropriateness and effectiveness of the following images
in relation to purpose and tone: *Trexler darted into the bag, hung for a
moment before one of his thoughts, as a hummingbird pauses in the
delphinium* [5]; *he stopped at the asylum, only the bars were lucite—
fluted, retractable* [6]; *life's little bucky horse* [8]; *the vapors hung thick
above the pool of the mind* [14]; *So he wants a new wing! There's a fine
piece of theatrical gauze for you!* [24]; *the flashy tail feathers of the bird
courage* [28]; *the hypodermic of Merman's healthy voice* [29]. In your
analysis, generalize on the kinds of language represented by these quotations. What other contexts would you expect to contain such words as
hummingbird, bucky horse, theatrical gauze, tail feathers, hypodermic?
Why are the bars *lucite-fluted* and *retractable?* What is the effect on the
reader of comparing Merman's voice to a hypodermic?

7. What tone is implied by the word *séances* in par. 24?

APPLICATIONS TO WRITING

1. Write a narrative which illustrates your view of some aspect of our
culture. Your feelings and attitudes should become apparent to the reader
by implication rather than by explicit statement.

2. Write your own answer to the question—What do you want?—in the manner of par. 27.

3. Recreate an imaginary session with a psychiatrist, your boss, your teacher or your congressman in which your feelings and attitudes are implicitly illustrated.

BIG TWO-HEARTED RIVER
(Parts I and II)

Part I

The train went on up the track out of sight, around one of the hills of burnt timber. Nick sat down on the bundle of canvas and bedding the baggage man had pitched out of the door of the baggage car. There was no town, nothing but the rails and the burned-over country. The thirteen saloons that had lined the one street of Seney had not left a trace. The foundations of the Mansion House hotel stuck up above the ground. The stone was chipped and split by the fire. It was all that was left of the town of Seney. Even the surface had been burned off the ground. [1]

Nick looked at the burned-over stretch of hillside, where he had expected to find the scattered houses of the town and then walked down the railroad track to the bridge over the river. The river was there. It swirled against the log spiles of the bridge. Nick looked down into the clear, brown water, colored from the pebbly bottom, and watched the trout keeping themselves steady in the current with wavering fins. As he watched them they changed their positions by quick angles, only to hold steady in the fast water again. Nick watched them a long time. [2]

He watched them holding themselves with their noses into the current, many trout in deep, fast moving water, slightly distorted as he watched far down through the glassy convex surface of the pool, its surface pushing and swelling smooth against the resistance of the log-driven piles of the bridge. At the bottom of the pool were the big trout. Nick did not see them at first. Then he saw them at the bottom of the pool, big trout looking to hold themselves on the gravel bottom in a varying mist of gravel and sand, raised in spurts by the current. [3]

Nick looked down into the pool from the bridge. It was a hot day. A kingfisher flew up the stream. It was a long time since Nick had looked into a stream and seen trout. They were very satisfactory. As the shadow of the kingfisher moved up the stream, a big trout shot upstream in a long angle, only his shadow marking the angle, then lost his shadow as he came through the surface of the water, caught the sun, and then, as he went back into the stream under the surface, his shadow seemed to float down the stream with the current, unresisting, to his post under the bridge where he tightened facing up into the current. [4]

Nick's heart tightened as the trout moved. He felt all the old feeling. [5]

He turned and looked down the stream. It stretched away, pebbly-bottomed with shallows and big boulders and a deep pool as it curved away around the foot of a bluff. [6]

Nick walked back up the ties to where his pack lay in the cinders beside the railway track. He was happy. He adjusted the pack harness around the bundle, pulling straps tight, slung the pack on his back, got his arms through the shoulder straps and took some of the pull off his shoulders by leaning his forehead against the wide band of the tump-line. Still, it was too heavy. It was much too heavy. He had his leather rod-case in his hand and leaning forward to keep the weight of the pack high on his shoulders he walked along the road that paralleled the railway track, leaving the burned town behind in the heat, and then turned off around a hill with a high, fire-scarred hill on either side onto a road that went back into the country. He walked along the road feeling the ache from the pull of the heavy pack. The road climbed steadily. It was hard work walking up-hill. His muscles ached and the day was hot, but Nick felt happy. He felt he had left everything behind, the need for thinking, the need to write, other needs. It was all back of him. [7]

From the time he had gotten down off the train and the baggage man had thrown his pack out of the open car door things had been different. Seney was burned, the country was burned over and changed, but it did not matter. It could not all be burned. He knew that. He hiked along the road, sweating in the sun, climbing to cross the range of hills that separated the railway from the pine plains. [8]

The road ran on, dipping occasionally, but always climbing. Nick went on up. Finally the road after going parallel to the burnt hillside reached the top. Nick leaned back against a stump and slipped out of the pack harness. Ahead of him, as far as he could see, was the pine plain. The burned country stopped off at the left with the range of hills. On ahead islands of dark pine trees rose out of the plain. Far off to the left was the line of the river. Nick followed it with his eye and caught glints of the water in the sun. [9]

There was nothing but the pine plain ahead of him, until the far blue hills that marked the Lake Superior height of land. He could hardly see them, faint and far away in the heat-light over the plain. If he looked too steadily they were gone. But if he only half-looked they were there, the far-off hills of the height of land. [10]

Nick sat down against the charred stump and smoked a cigarette. His pack balanced on the top of the stump, harness holding ready, a hollow molded in it from his back. Nick sat smoking, looking out over the country. He did not need to get his map out. He knew where he was from the position of the river. [11]

As he smoked, his legs stretched out in front of him, he noticed a grasshopper walk along the ground and up onto his woolen sock. The grasshopper was black. As he had walked along the road, climbing, he had started many grasshoppers from the dust. They were all black.

They were not the big grasshoppers with yellow and black or red and black wings whirring out from their black wing sheathing as they fly up. These were just ordinary hoppers, but all a sooty black in color. Nick had wondered about them as he walked, without really thinking about them. Now, as he watched the black hopper that was nibbling at the wool of his sock with its fourway lip, he realized that they all turned black from living in the burned-over land. He realized that the fire must have come the year before, but the grasshoppers were all black now. He wondered how long they would stay that way. [12]

Carefully he reached his hand down and took hold of the hopper by the wings. He turned him up, all his legs walking in the air, and looked at his joined belly. Yes, it was black too, iridescent where the back and head were dusty. [13]

"Go on, hopper," Nick said, speaking out loud for the first time. "Fly away somewhere." [14]

He tossed the grasshopper up into the air and watched him sail away to a charcoal stump across the road. [15]

Nick stood up. He leaned his back against the weight of his pack where it rested upright on the stump and got his arms through the shoulder straps. He stood with the pack on his back on the brow of the hill looking out across the country, toward the distant river and then struck down the hillside away from the road. Underfoot the ground was good walking. Two hundred yards down the hillside the fire line stopped. Then it was sweet fern, growing ankle high, to walk through, and clumps of jack pines; a long undulating country with frequent rises and descents, sandy underfoot and the country alive again. [16]

Nick kept his direction by the sun. He knew where he wanted to strike the river and he kept on through the pine plain, mounting small rises to see other rises ahead of him and sometimes from the top of a rise a great solid island of pines off to his right or his left. He broke off some sprigs of the heathery sweet fern, and put them under his pack straps. The chafing crushed it and he smelled it as he walked. [17]

He was tired and very hot, walking across the uneven, shadeless pine plain. At any time he knew he could strike the river by turning off to his left. It could not be more than a mile away. But he kept on toward the north to hit the river as far upstream as he could go in one day's walking. [18]

For some time as he walked Nick had been in sight of one of the big islands of pine standing out above the rolling high ground he was crossing. He dipped down and then as he came slowly up to the crest of the bridge he turned and made toward the pine trees. [19]

There was no underbrush in the island of pine trees. The trunks of the trees went straight up or slanted toward each other. The trunks were straight and brown without branches. The branches were high above. Some interlocked to make a solid shadow on the brown forest floor. Around the grove of trees was a bare space. It was brown and soft underfoot as Nick walked on it. This was the over-lapping of the pine needle floor, extending out beyond the width of the high branches. The trees had grown tall and the branches moved high, leaving in the sun this bare space they had once covered with shadow. Sharp at the edge of this extension of the forest floor commenced the sweet fern. [20]

Nick slipped off his pack and lay down in the shade. He lay on his back and looked up into the pine trees. His neck and back and the small of his back rested as he stretched. The earth felt good against his back. He looked up at the sky, through the branches, and then shut his eyes. He opened them and looked up again. There was a wind high up in the branches. He shut his eyes again and went to sleep. [21]

Nick woke stiff and cramped. The sun was nearly down. His pack was heavy and the straps painful as he lifted it on. He leaned over with the pack on and picked up the leather rod-case and started out from the pine trees across the sweet fern swale, toward the river. He knew it could not be more than a mile. [22]

He came down a hillside covered with stumps into a meadow. At the edge of the meadow flowed the river. Nick was glad to get to the river. He walked upstream through the meadow. His trousers were soaked with the dew as he walked. After the hot day, the dew had come quickly and heavily. The river made no sound. It was too fast and smooth. At the edge of the meadow, before he mounted to a piece of high ground to make camp, Nick looked down the river at the trout rising. They were rising to insects come from the swamp on the other side of the stream when the sun went down. The trout jumped out of water to take them. While Nick walked through the little stretch of meadow alongside the stream, trout had jumped high out of water. Now as he looked down the river, the insects must be settling on the surface, for the trout were feeding steadily all down the stream. As far down the long stretch as he could see, the trout were rising, making circles all down the surface of the water, as though it were starting to rain. [23]

The ground rose, wooded and sandy, to overlook the meadow, the stretch of river and the swamp. Nick dropped his pack and rod-case and looked for a level piece of ground. He was very hungry and he wanted to make his camp before he cooked. Between two jack pines, the ground was quite level. He took the ax out of the pack and chopped out two projecting roots. That leveled a piece of ground large enough to sleep on. He smoothed out the sandy soil with his hand and pulled all the sweet fern bushes by their roots. His hands smelled good from the sweet fern. He smoothed the uprooted earth. He did not want anything making lumps under the blankets. When he had the ground smooth, he spread his three blankets. One he folded double, next to the ground. The other two he spread on top. [24]

With the ax he slit off a bright slab of pine from one of the stumps and split it into pegs for the tent. He wanted them long and solid to hold in the ground. With the tent unpacked and spread on the ground, the pack, leaning against a jackpine, looked much smaller. Nick tied the rope that served the tent for a ridge-pole to the trunk of one of the pine trees and pulled the tent up off the ground with the other end of the rope and tied it to the other pine. The tent hung on the rope like a canvas blanket on a clothesline. Nick poked a pole he had cut up under the back peak of the canvas and then made it a tent by pegging out the sides. He pegged the sides out taut and drove the pegs deep, hitting them down into the ground with the flat of the ax until the rope loops were buried and the canvas was drum tight. [25]

Across the open mouth of the tent Nick fixed cheesecloth to keep out mosquitoes. He crawled inside under the mosquito bar with various things from the pack to put at the head of the bed under the slant of the canvas. Inside the tent the light came through the brown canvas. It smelled pleasantly of canvas. Already there was something mysterious and homelike. Nick was happy as he crawled inside the tent. He had not been unhappy all day. This was different though. Now things were done. There had been this to do. Now it was done. It had been a hard trip. He was very tired. That was done. He had made his camp. He was settled. Nothing could touch him. It was a good place to camp. He was there, in the good place. He was in his home where he had made it. Now he was hungry. [26]

He came out, crawling under the cheesecloth. It was quite dark outside. It was lighter in the tent. [27]

Nick went over to the pack and found, with his fingers, a long nail in a paper sack of nails, in the bottom of the pack. He drove it into the pine tree, holding it close and hitting it gently with the flat of the ax. He hung the pack up on the nail. All his supplies were in the pack. They were off the ground and sheltered now. [28]

Nick was hungry. He did not believe he had ever been hungrier. He opened and emptied a can of pork and beans and a can of spaghetti into the frying pan. [29]

"I've got a right to eat this kind of stuff, if I'm willing to carry it," Nick said. His voice sounded strange in the darkening woods. He did not speak again. [30]

He started a fire with some chunks of pine he got with the ax from a stump. Over the fire he stuck a wire grill, pushing the four legs down into the ground with his boot. Nick put the frying pan on the grill over the flames. He was hungrier. The beans and spaghetti warmed. Nick stirred them and mixed them together. They began to bubble, making little bubbles that rose with difficulty to the surface. There was a good smell. Nick got out a bottle of tomato catchup and cut four slices of bread. The little bubbles were coming faster now. Nick sat down beside the fire and lifted the frying pan off. He poured about half the contents out into the tin plate. It spread slowly on the plate. Nick knew it was too hot. He poured on some tomato catchup. He knew the beans and spaghetti were still too hot. He looked at the fire, then at the tent, he was not going to spoil it all by burning his tongue. For years he had never enjoyed fried bananas because he had never been able to wait for them to cool. His tongue was very sensitive. He was very hungry. Across the river in the swamp, in the almost dark, he saw a mist rising. He looked at the tent once more. All right. He took a full spoonful from the plate. [31]

"Chrise," Nick said, "Geezus Chrise," he said happily. [32]

He ate the whole plateful before he remembered the bread. Nick finished the second plateful with the bread, mopping the plate shiny. He had not eaten since a cup of coffee and a ham sandwich in the station restaurant at St. Ignace. It had been a very fine experience. He had been that hungry before, but had not been able to satisfy it. He could have made camp hours before if he had wanted to. There were plenty of good places to camp on the river. But this was good. [33]

Nick tucked two big chips of pine under the grill. The fire flared up. He had forgotten to get water for the coffee. Out of the pack he got a folding canvas bucket and walked down the hill, across the edge of the meadow, to the stream. The other bank was in the white mist. The grass was wet and cold as he knelt on the bank and dipped the canvas bucket into the stream. It bellied and pulled hard in the current. The water was ice cold. Nick rinsed the bucket and carried it full up to the camp. Up away from the stream it was not so cold. [34]

Nick drove another big nail and hung up the bucket full of water. He dipped the coffee pot half full, put some more chips under the grill onto the fire and put the pot on. He could not remember which way he made coffee. He could remember an argument about it with Hopkins, but not which side he had taken. He decided to bring it to a boil. He remembered now that was Hopkins' way. He had once argued about everything with Hopkins. While he waited for the coffee to boil, he opened a small can of apricots. He liked to open cans. He emptied the can of apricots out into a tin cup. While he watched the coffee on the fire, he drank the juice syrup of the apricots, carefully at first to keep from spilling, then meditatively, sucking the apricots down. They were better than fresh apricots. [35]

The coffee boiled as he watched. The lid came up and coffee and grounds ran down the side of the pot. Nick took it off the grill. It was a triumph for Hopkins. He put sugar in the empty apricot cup and poured some of the coffee out to cool. It was too hot to pour and he used his hat to hold the handle of the coffee pot. He would not let it steep in the pot at all. Not the first cup. It should be straight Hopkins all the way. Hop deserved that. He was a very serious coffee drinker. He was the most serious man Nick had ever known. Not heavy, serious. That was a long time ago. Hopkins spoke without moving his lips. He had played polo. He made millions of dollars in Texas. He had borrowed carfare to go to Chicago, when the wire came that his big well had come in. He could have wired for money. That would have been too slow. They called Hop's girl the Blonde Venus. Hop did not mind because she was not his real girl. Hopkins said very confidently that none of them would make fun of his real girl. He was right. Hopkins went away when the telegram came. That was on the Black River. It took eight days for the telegram to reach him. Hopkins gave away his .22 caliber Colt automatic pistol to Nick. He gave his camera to Bill. It was to remember him always by. They were all going fishing again next summer. The Hop Head was rich. He would get a yacht and they would all cruise along the north shore of Lake Superior. He was excited but serious. They said good-bye and all felt bad. It broke up the trip. They never saw Hopkins again. That was a long time ago on the Black River. [36]

Nick drank the coffee, the coffee according to Hopkins. The coffee was bitter. Nick laughed. It made a good ending to the story. His mind was starting to work. He knew he could choke it because he was tired enough. He spilled the coffee out of the pot and shook the grounds loose into the fire. He lit a cigarette and went inside the tent. He took off his shoes and trousers, sitting on the blankets, rolled the shoes up inside the trousers for a pillow and got in between the blankets. [37]

Out through the front of the tent he watched the glow of the fire, when the night wind blew on it. It was a quiet night. The swamp was perfectly quiet. Nick stretched under the blanket comfortably. A mosquito hummed close to his ear. Nick sat up and lit a match. The mosquito was on the canvas, over his head. Nick moved the match quickly up to it. The mosquito made a satisfactory hiss in the flame. The match went out. Nick lay down again under the blanket. He turned on his side and shut his eyes. He was sleepy. He felt sleep coming. He curled up under the blanket and went to sleep. [38]

Part II

In the morning the sun was up and the tent was starting to get hot. Nick crawled out under the mosquito netting stretched across the mouth of the tent, to look at the morning. The grass was wet on his hands as he came out. He held his trousers and his shoes in his hands. The sun was just up over the hill. There was the meadow, the river and the swamp. There were birch trees in the green of the swamp on the other side of the river. [39]

The river was clear and smoothly fast in the early morning. Down about two hundred yards were three logs all the way across the stream. They made the water smooth and deep above them. As Nick watched, a mink crossed the river on the logs and went into the swamp. Nick was excited. He was excited by the early morning and the river. He was really too hurried to eat breakfast, but he knew he must. He built a little fire and put on the coffee pot. [40]

While the water was heating in the pot he took an empty bottle and went down over the edge of the high ground to the meadow. The meadow was wet with dew and Nick wanted to catch grasshoppers for bait before the sun dried the grass. He found plenty of good grasshoppers. They were at the base of the grass stems. Sometimes they clung to a grass stem. They were cold and wet with the dew, and could not jump until the sun warmed them. Nick picked them up, taking only the medium-sized brown ones, and put them into the bottle. He turned over a log and just under the shelter of the edge were several hundred hoppers. It was a grasshopper lodging house. Nick put about fifty of the medium browns into the bottle. While he was picking up the hoppers the others warmed in the sun and commenced to hop away. They flew when they hopped. At first they made one flight and stayed stiff when they landed, as though they were dead. [41]

Nick knew that by the time he was through with breakfast they would be as lively as ever. Without dew in the grass it would take him all day to catch a bottle full of good grasshoppers and he would have to crush many of them, slamming at them with his hat. He washed his hands at the stream. He was excited to be near it. Then he walked up to the tent. The hoppers were already jumping stiffly in the grass. In the bottle, warmed by the sun, they were jumping in a mass. Nick put in a pine stick as a cork. It plugged the mouth of the bottle enough, so the hoppers could not get out and left plenty of air passage. [42]

He had rolled the log back and knew he could get grasshoppers there every morning. [43]

Nick laid the bottle full of jumping grasshoppers against a pine trunk. Rapidly he mixed some buckwheat flour with water and stirred it smooth, one cup of flour, one cup of water. He put a handful of coffee in the pot and dipped a lump of grease out of a can and slid it sputtering across the hot skillet. On the smoking skillet he poured smoothly the buckwheat batter. It spread like lava, the grease spitting sharply. Around the edges the buckwheat cake began to firm, then brown, then crisp. The surface was bubbling slowly to porousness. Nick pushed under the browned under surface with a fresh pine chip. He shook the skillet sideways and the cake was loose on the surface. I won't try and flop it, he thought. He slid the chip of clean wood all the way under the cake, and flopped it over onto its face. It sputtered in the pan. [44]

When it was cooked Nick regreased the skillet. He used all the batter. It made another big flapjack and one smaller one. [45]

Nick ate a big flapjack and a smaller one, covered with apple butter. He put apple butter on the third cake, folded it over twice, wrapped it in oiled paper and put it in his shirt pocket. He put the apple butter jar back in the pack and cut bread for two sandwiches. [46]

In the pack he found a big onion. He sliced it in two and peeled the silky outer skin. Then he cut one half into slices and made onion sandwiches. He wrapped them in oiled paper and buttoned them in the other pocket of his khaki shirt. He turned the skillet upside down on the grill, drank the coffee, sweetened and yellow brown with condensed milk in it, and tidied up the camp. It was a good camp. [47]

Nick took his fly rod out of the leather rod-case, jointed it, and shoved the rod-case back into the tent. He put on the reel and threaded the line through the guides. He had to hold it from hand to hand, as he threaded it, or it would slip back through its own weight. It was a heavy, double tapered fly line. Nick had paid eight dollars for it a long time ago. It was made heavy to lift back in the air and come forward flat and heavy and straight to make it possible to cast a fly which has no weight. Nick opened the aluminum leader box. The leaders were coiled between the damp flannel pads. Nick had wet the pads at the water cooler on the train up to St. Ignace. In the damp pads the gut leaders had softened and Nick unrolled one and tied it by a loop at the end to the heavy fly line. He fastened a hook on the end of the leader. It was a small hook; very thin and springy. [48]

Nick took it from his hook book, sitting with the rod across his lap. He tested the knot and the spring of the rod by pulling the line taut. It was a good feeling. He was careful not to let the hook bite into his finger. [49]

He started down to the stream, holding his rod, the bottle of grasshoppers hung from his neck by a thong tied in half hitches around the neck of the bottle. His landing net hung by a hook from his belt. Over his shoulder was a long flour sack tied at each corner into an ear. The cord went over his shoulders. The sack flapped against his legs. [50]

Nick felt awkward and professionally happy with all his equipment hanging from him. The grasshopper bottle swung against his chest. In his shirt the breast pockets bulged against him with the lunch and his fly book. [51]

He stepped into the stream. It was a shock. His trousers clung tight to his legs. His shoes felt the gravel. The water was a rising cold shock. [52]

Rushing, the current sucked against his legs. Where he stepped in, the water was over his knees. He waded with the current. The gravel slid under his shoes. He looked down at the swirl of water below each leg and tipped up the bottle to get a grasshopper. [53]

The first grasshopper gave a jump in the neck of the bottle and went out into the water. He was sucked under in a whirl by Nick's right leg and came to the surface a little way down stream. He floated rapidly, kicking. In a quick circle, breaking the smooth surface of the water, he disappeared. A trout had taken him. [54]

Another hopper poked his face out of the bottle. His antenna wavered. He was getting his front legs out of the bottle to jump. Nick took him by the head and held him while he threaded the slim hook under his chin, down through his thorax and into the last segments of his abdomen. The grasshopper took hold of the hook with his front feet, spitting tobacco juice on it. Nick dropped him into the water. [55]

Holding the rod in his right hand he let out line against the pull of the grasshopper in the current. He stripped off line from the reel with his left hand and let it run free. He could see the hopper in the little waves of the current. It went out of sight. [56]

There was a tug on the line. Nick pulled against the taut line. It was his first strike. Holding the now living rod across the current, he brought in the line with his left hand. The rod bent in jerks, the trout pumping against the current. Nick knew it was a small one. He lifted the rod straight up in the air. It bowed with the pull. [57]

He saw the trout in the water jerking with his head and body against the shifting tangent of the line in the stream. [58]

Nick took the line in his left hand and pulled the trout, thumping tiredly against the current, to the surface. His back was mottled the clear, water-over-gravel color, his side flashing in the sun. The rod under his right arm, Nick stooped, dipping his right hand into the current. He held the trout, never still, with his moist right hand, while he unhooked the barb from his mouth, then dropped him back into the stream. [59]

He hung unsteadily in the current, then settled to the bottom beside a stone. Nick reached down his hand to touch him, his arm to the elbow under water. The trout was steady in the moving stream, resting on the gravel, beside a stone. As Nick's fingers touched him, touched his smooth, cool, underwater feeling he was gone, gone in a shadow across the bottom of the stream. [60]

He's all right, Nick thought. He was only tired. [61]

He had wet his hand before he touched the trout, so he would not disturb the delicate mucus that covered him. If a trout was touched with a dry hand, a white fungus attacked the unprotected spot. Years before when he had fished crowded streams, with fly fishermen ahead of him and behind him, Nick had again and again come on dead trout, furry with white fungus, drifted against a rock, or floating belly up in some pool. Nick did not like to fish with other men on the river. Unless they were of your party, they spoiled it. [62]

He wallowed down the stream, above his knees in the current, through the fifty yards of shallow water above the pile of logs that crossed the stream. He did not rebait his hook and held it in his hand as he waded. He was certain he could catch small trout in the shallows, but he did not want them. There would be no big trout in the shallows this time of day. [63]

Now the water deepened up his thighs sharply and coldly. Ahead was the smooth damned-back flood of water above the logs. The water was smooth and dark; on the left, the lower edge of the meadow; on the right the swamp. [64]

Nick leaned back against the current and took a hopper from the bottle. He threaded the hopper on the hook and spat on him for good luck. Then he pulled several yards of line from the reel and tossed the hopper out ahead onto the fast, dark water. It floated down towards the logs, then the weight of the line pulled the bait under the surface. Nick held the rod in his right hand, letting the line run out through his fingers. [65]

There was a long tug. Nick struck and the rod came alive and dangerous, bent double, the line tightening, coming out of water, tightening, all in a heavy, dangerous, steady pull. Nick felt the moment when the leader would break if the strain increased and let the line go. [66]

The reel ratcheted into a mechanical shriek as the line went out in a rush. Too fast. Nick could not check it, the line rushing out, the reel note rising as the line ran out. [67]

With the core of the reel showing, his heart feeling stopped with the excitement, leaning back against the current that mounted icily his thighs, Nick thumbed the reel hard with his left hand. It was awkward getting his thumb inside the fly reel frame. [68]

As he put on pressure the line tightened into sudden hardness and beyond the logs a huge trout went high out of water. As he jumped, Nick lowered the tip of the rod. But he felt, as he dropped the tip to ease the strain, the moment when the strain was too great; the hardness too tight. Of course, the leader had broken. There was no mistaking the feeling when all spring left the line and it became dry and hard. Then it went slack. [69]

His mouth dry, his heart down, Nick reeled in. He had never seen so big a trout. There was a heaviness, a power not to be held, and then the bulk of him, as he jumped. He looked as broad as a salmon. [70]

Nick's hand was shaky. He reeled in slowly. The thrill had been too much. He felt, vaguely, a little sick, as though it would be better to sit down. [71]

The leader had broken where the hook was tied to it. Nick took it in his hand. He thought of the trout somewhere on the bottom, holding himself steady over the gravel, far down below the light, under the logs, with the hook in his jaw. Nick knew the trout's teeth would cut through the snell of the hook. The hook would imbed itself in his jaw. He'd bet the trout was angry. Anything that size would be angry. That was a trout. He had been solidly hooked. Solid as a rock. He felt like a rock, too, before he started off. By God, he was a big one. By God, he was the biggest one I ever heard of. [72]

Nick climbed out onto the meadow and stood, water running down his trousers and out of his shoes, his shoes squelchy. He went over and sat on the logs. He did not want to rush his sensations any. [73]

He wiggled his toes in the water, in his shoes, and got out a cigarette from his breast pocket. He lit it and tossed the match into the fast water below the logs. A tiny trout rose at the match, as it swung around in the fast current. Nick laughed. He would finish the cigarette. [74]

He sat on the logs, smoking, drying in the sun, the sun warm on his back, the river shallow ahead entering the woods, curving into the woods, shallows, light glittering, big water-smooth rocks, cedars along the bank and white birches, the logs warm in the sun, smooth to sit on, without bark, gray to the touch; slowly the feeling of disappointment left him. It went away slowly, the feeling of disappointment that came sharply after the thrill that made his shoulders ache. It was all right now. His rod lying out on the logs, Nick tied a new hook on the leader, pulling the gut tight until it grimped into itself in a hard knot. [75]

He baited up, then picked up the rod and walked to the far end of the logs to get into the water, where it was not too deep. Under and beyond the logs was a deep pool. Nick walked around the shallow shelf near the swamp shore until he came out on the shallow bed of the stream. [76]

On the left, where the meadow ended and the woods began, a great elm tree was uprooted. Gone over in a storm, it lay back into the woods, its roots clotted with dirt, grass growing in them, rising a solid bank beside the stream. The river cut to the edge of the uprooted tree. From where Nick stood he could see deep channels, like ruts, cut in the shallow bed of the stream by the flow of the current. Pebbly where he stood and pebbly and full of boulders beyond; where it curved near the tree roots, the bed of the stream was marly and between the ruts of deep water green weed fronds swung in the current. [77]

Nick swung the rod back over his shoulder and forward, and the line, curving forward, laid the grasshopper down one of the deep channels in the weeds. A trout struck and Nick hooked him. [78]

Holding the rod far out toward the uprooted tree and sloshing backward in the current, Nick worked the trout, plunging, the rod bending alive, out of the danger of the weeds into the open river. Holding the rod, pumping alive against the current, Nick brought the trout in. He rushed, but always came, the spring of the rod yielding to the rushes, sometimes jerking under the water, but always bringing him in. Nick eased downstream with the rushes. The rod above his head he led the trout over the net, then lifted. [79]

The trout hung heavy in the net, mottled trout back and silver sides in the meshes. Nick unhooked him; heavy sides, good to hold, big undershot jaw, and slipped him, heaving and big sliding, into the long sack that hung from his shoulders in the water. [80]

Nick spread the mouth of the sack against the current and it filled, heavy with water. He held it up, the bottom in the stream, and the water poured out through the sides. Inside at the bottom was the big trout, alive in the water. [81]

Nick moved downstream. The sack out ahead of him sunk heavy in the water, pulling from his shoulders. [82]

It was getting hot, the sun hot on the back of his neck. [83]

Nick had one good trout. He did not care about getting many trout. Now the stream was shallow and wide. There were trees along both banks. The trees of the left bank made short shadows on the current in the forenoon sun. Nick knew there were trout in each shadow. In the afternoon, after the sun had crossed toward the hills, the trout would be in the cool shadows on the other side of the stream. [84]

The very biggest ones would lie up close to the bank. You could always pick them up there on the Black. When the sun was down they all moved out into the current. Just when the sun made the water blinding in the glare before it went down, you were liable to strike a big trout anywhere in the current. It was almost impossible to fish then, the surface of the water was blinding as a mirror in the sun. Of course, you could fish upstream, but in a stream like the Black, or this, you had to wallow against the current and in a deep place, the water piled up on you. It was no fun to fish upstream with this much current. [85]

Nick moved along through the shallow stretch watching the banks for deep holes. A beech tree grew close beside the river, so that the branches hung down into the water. The stream went back in under the leaves. There were always trout in a place like that. [86]

Nick did not care about fishing that hole. He was sure he would get hooked in the branches. [87]

It looked deep though. He dropped the grasshopper so the current took it under water, back in under the overhanging branch. The line pulled hard and Nick struck. The trout threshed heavily, half out of water in the leaves and branches. The line was caught. Nick pulled hard and the trout was off. He reeled in and holding the hook in his hand, walked down the stream. [88]

Ahead, close to the left bank, was a big log. Nick saw it was hollow; pointing up river the current entered it smoothly, only a little ripple spread each side of the log. The water was deepening. The top of the hollow log was gray and dry. It was partly in the shadow. [89]

Nick took the cork out of the grasshopper bottle and a hopper clung to it. He picked him off, hooked him and tossed him out. He held the rod far out so that the hopper on the water moved into the current flowing into the hollow log. Nick lowered the rod and the hopper floated in. There was a heavy strike. Nick swung the rod against the pull. It felt as though he were hooked into the log itself, except for the live feeling. [90]

He tried to force the fish out into the current. It came, heavily. [91]

The line went slack and Nick thought the trout was gone. Then he saw him, very near, in the current, shaking his head, trying to get the hook out. His mouth was clamped shut. He was fighting the hook in the clear flowing current. [92]

Looping in the line with his left hand, Nick swung the rod to make the line taut and tried to lead the trout toward the net, but he was gone, out of sight, the line pumping. Nick fought him against the current, letting him thump in the water against the spring of the rod. He shifted the rod to his left hand, worked the trout upstream, holding his weight, fighting on the rod, and then let him down into the net. He lifted him clear of the water, a heavy half circle in the net, the net dripping, unhooked him and slid him into the sack. [93]

He spread the mouth of the sack and looked down in at the two big trout alive in the water. [94]

Through the deepening water, Nick waded over to the hollow log. He took the sack off, over his head, the trout flopping as it came out of water, and hung it so the trout were deep in the water. Then he pulled himself up on the log and sat, the water from his trousers and boots running down into the stream. He laid his rod down, moved along to the shady end of the log and took the sandwiches out of his pocket. He dipped the sandwiches in the cold water. The current carried away the crumbs. He ate the sandwiches and dipped his hat full of water to drink, the water running out through his hat just ahead of his drinking. [95]

It was cool in the shade, sitting on the log. He took a cigarette out and struck a match to light it. The match sunk into the gray wood, making a tiny furrow. Nick leaned over the side of the log, found a hard place and lit the match. He sat smoking and watching the river. [96]

Ahead the river narrowed and went into a swamp. The river became smooth and deep and the swamp looked solid with cedar trees, their trunks close together, their branches solid. It would not be possible to walk through a swamp like that. The branches grew so low. You would have to keep almost level with the ground to move at all. You could not crash through the branches. That must be why the animals that lived in swamps were built the way they were, Nick thought. [97]

He wished he had brought something to read. He felt like reading.

He did not feel like going on into the swamp. He looked down the river. A big cedar slanted all the way across the stream. Beyond that the river went into the swamp. [98]

Nick did not want to go in there now. He felt a reaction against deep wading with the water deepening up under his armpits, to hook big trout in places impossible to land them. In the swamp the banks were bare, the big cedars came together overhead, the sun did not come through, except in patches; in the fast deep water, in the half light, the fishing would be tragic. In the swamp fishing was a tragic adventure. Nick did not want it. He did not want to go down the stream any further today. [99]

He took out his knife, opened it and stuck it in the log. Then he pulled up the sack, reached into it and brought out one of the trout. Holding him near the tail, hard to hold, alive, in his hand, he whacked him against the log. The trout quivered, rigid. Nick laid him on the log in the shade and broke the neck of the other fish the same way. He laid them side by side on the log. They were fine trout. [100]

Nick cleaned them, slitting them from the vent to the tip of the jaw. All the insides and the gills and tongue came out in one piece. They were both males; long gray-white strips of milt, smooth and clean. All the insides clean and compact, coming out all together. Nick tossed the offal ashore for the minks to find. [101]

He washed the trout in the stream. When he held them back up in the water they looked like live fish. Their color was not gone yet. He washed his hands and dried them on the log. Then he laid the trout on the sack spread out on the log, rolled them up in it, tied the bundle and put it in the landing net. His knife was still standing, blade stuck in the log. He cleaned it on the wood and put it in his pocket. [102]

Nick stood up on the log, holding his rod, the landing net hanging heavy, then stepped into the water and splashed ashore. He climbed the bank and cut up into the woods, toward the high ground. He was going back to camp. He looked back. The river just showed through the trees. There were plenty of days coming when he could fish the swamp. [103]

PURPOSE AND STRUCTURE

1. What does this story illustrate? Why is it included as an example of illustration? Work through the following rhetorical analysis, and when you have finished, return to these questions and try to answer them.

Hemingway's *Big Two-Hearted River* is, of course, a short story—that is to say, narration. But the writer of exposition and of argument and persuasion can learn much from narration. He uses it every time he illustrates a generalization with a concrete story. See examples from this section as well as Forster's *My Wood* and Baldwin's *Notes of a Native Son*. This type of narration—let us call it *illustrative narration*—is very important to the writer of exposition or argument; often the persuasive power and interest of a piece of writing will lie in the stories that are told to drive home the main points.

Another use of narration may be called *expository narration* whereby a sequence of events in time can best be presented. Thus the functions of a gasoline engine might be analyzed by following the story of a drop of gasoline from the gas tank to the exhaust pipe. Recipes (how to make an apple pie) or directions (how to build a mountain cabin) are explanations in time; thus they too are expository narration. They lack, of course, the implicit meaning, the unstated power, that would make them pure narration.

2. Hemingway's story is an example of pure narration; it contains less exposition, description or argument than most narration. There are hardly any generalizations. It is all surface, all event, almost inane in its lack of explicit meaning. What is the point of the memory of the argument with Hopkins about how to make coffee (par. 35)?

3. Why does Nick laugh (par. 37)? Is the attitude toward generalization expressed here appropriate to the method of the telling of the story?

4. "His mind was starting to work. He knew he could choke it because he was tired enough" (par. 37). Why does Nick want to choke his mind?

5. Is his mind "choked" during most of this story?

6. If the narrator does not state the significance of his experiences, how can the reader know whether they are significant or not? See Cowley, *Nightmare and Ritual in Hemingway*.

7. Why is Nick's pack much too heavy [7]? Why is Nick happy [7–8]?

DICTION AND TONE

1. Pars. 12 and 13 deal with the color of the grasshoppers. Is the word "black" used too often? What effect is attained with this repetition? Is the effect necessary to the meaning of the story?

2. When, in par. 21, Nick lies on his back and looks up (more than once) into the pine trees, we are told only one thing about them. What is it?

3. Considering the situation, is this an adequate description?

4. The previous paragraph [20] contains a rather elaborate description of the same trees. Analyze the structure of the sentences. What kind of sentences are they? Do they lack variety? Or are they too sophisticated and varied for their context?

5. How does this description function in the total story? Is it necessary?

6. Where is the subject of the last sentence placed [20]? Is this arrangement effective or too mannered?

7. Compare the structure of the sentences in par. 21 with those in par. 20. Are the sentences in par. 21 more typical of those in the rest of the story?

8. Pars. 24 to 28 seem to contain a good example of expository narration (or process analysis). As Nick makes camp the sequence of events in time is carefully presented. Is the purpose of the passage to describe how to make camp? If not, why describe so precisely how it is done? Each of these paragraphs contains information which would be omitted from expository narration. Point to this information. Why is it included?

9. Par. 26 ends with a series of very short and repetitious sentences. Would you call this passage expository narration? Why does Hemingway repeat both structure and meaning? Is it inappropriate to express Nick's thoughts in such childish sentences? Read the passage aloud. It is an incantation. What is its purpose?

10. The whole story seems to be expository narration, but of course it is more than that. Is it all incantation? What is it? Analyze a selected passage for evidence of your interpretation.

APPLICATIONS TO WRITING

Hemingway's *Big Two-Hearted River* has been included under illustration in order to show that narration adds a dimension to exposition. Exposition (and argument and persuasion) cannot entirely contain the power and precision of narration; each is rightly considered a different form of discourse. Of course narration can and should be used in exposition—just as exposition must be used in narration. But the writer should be aware that the meaning of his illustration is never entirely caught in the generalization or the abstraction. However relevant and cogent the story seems to be, it will, if it is a good story, include meanings that expository prose cannot make explicit. Hemingway's *Big Two-Hearted River* might be called an illustration; if it is, however, the generalization which it illustrates is entirely implied. Perhaps it would be better not to speak of the story as illustration.

Now return to the first questions of the analysis.

1. Write of an experience—such as fishing through ice in winter—from three different points of view: (1) as an illustration of a generalization (state the generalization), (2) in order to tell how to do it, (3) in order to tell the story.

2. Present one of your deepest feelings—or most irrational private superstitions—in narration.

3. Write a critical comparison of Hemingway's *Big Two-Hearted River* and White's *The Second Tree from the Corner* as narratives.

Part Six

Analysis—a method of exposition by logical division, applicable to anything that can be divided into component parts: an object, such as a novel, essay, or film, as in Huxley's *The Essay* or in Agee's *Monsieur Verdoux*; a complex idea, as in Langer's *Lord of Creation*; or an organic whole, one in which the parts reciprocally modify each other, as in Ciardi's *Robert Frost: The Way to the Poem*. In the analysis of the purposes and activities of the intellectual, Jarrell describes parts in terms of their characteristic function. Analysis may also be concerned with the connection of events (causal analysis): given this condition or series of conditions, what effects will follow? For example, in her essay Mrs. Langer attempts to show the consequences of man's ability to manipulate symbols and to form abstractions.

THE ESSAY

"I am a man and alive," wrote D. H. Lawrence. "For this reason I am a novelist. And, being a novelist, I consider myself superior to the saint, the scientist, the philosopher, and the poet, who are all great masters of different bits of man alive, but never get the whole hog. . . . Only in the novel are *all* things given full play." [1]

What is true of the novel is only a little less true of the essay. For, like the novel, the essay is a literary device for saying almost everything about almost anything. By tradition, almost by definition, the essay is a short piece, and it is therefore impossible to give all things full play within the limits of a single essay. But a collection of essays can cover almost as much ground, and cover it almost as thoroughly as can a long novel. Montaigne's Third Book is the equivalent, very nearly, of a good slice of the *Comédie Humaine*. [2]

Essays belong to a literary species whose extreme variability can be studied most effectively within a three-poled frame of reference. There is the pole of the personal and the autobiographical; there is the pole of the objective, the factual, the concrete-particular; and there is the pole of the abstract-universal. Most essayists are at home and at their best in the neighborhood of only one of the essay's three poles, or at the most only in the neighborhood of two of them. There

are the predominantly personal essayists, who write fragments of reflective autobiography and who look at the world through the keyhole of anecdote and description. There are the predominantly objective essayists who do not speak directly of themselves, but turn
their attention outward to some literary or scientific or political theme.
Their art consists in setting forth, passing judgment upon, and drawing general conclusions from, the relevant data. In a third group we
find those essayists who do their work in the world of high abstractions, who never condescend to be personal and who hardly deign to
take notice of the particular facts, from which their generalizations
were originally drawn. Each kind of essay has its special merits and
defects. The personal essayists may be as good as Charles Lamb at his
best, or as bad as Mr. X at his cutest and most self-consciously whimsical. The objective essay may be as lively, as brassily contentious as
a piece by Macaulay; but it may also, with fatal ease, degenerate into
something merely informative or, if it be critical, into something
merely learned and academic. And how splendid, how truly oracular
are the utterances of the great generalizers! "He that hath wife and
children hath given hostages to fortune; for they are impediments to
great enterprises, either of virtue or mischief." And from Bacon we
pass to Emerson. "All men plume themselves on the improvement of
society, and no man improves. Society never advances. It recedes as
fast on one side as it gains on the other. For everything that is given,
something is taken." Even a Baltasar Gracian, that briefest of essayists who writes as though he were cabling his wisdom, at two dollars
a word, to the Antipodes, sometimes achieves a certain magnificence.
"Things have their period; even excellences are subject to fashion.
The sage has one advantage: he is immortal. If *this* is not his century,
many others will be." But the medal of solemn and lapidary generalization has its reverse. The constantly abstract, constantly impersonal
essayist is apt to give us not oracles but algebra. As an example of such
algebraic writing, let me quote a short passage from the English
translation of Paul Valéry's *Dialogues*. It is worth remarking that
French literature has a tradition of high and sustained abstraction;
English literature has not. Works that in French are not at all out of

the common seem, when translated, strange almost to the point of absurdity. But even when made acceptable by tradition and a great talent, the algebraic style strikes us as being very remote from the living reality of our immediate experience. Here, in the words of an imaginary Socrates, is Valéry's description of the kind of language in which (as I think, unfortunately) he liked to write. "What is more mysterious than clarity? what more capricious than the way in which light and shade are distributed over the hours and over men? Certain peoples lose themselves in their thoughts, but for the Greeks all things are forms. We retain only their relations and, enclosed, as it were, in the limpid day, Orpheus-like we build, by means of the word, temples of wisdom and science that may suffice for all reasonable creatures. This great art requires of us an admirably exact language. The very word that signifies language is also the name, with us, for reason and calculation; the same word says these three things." In the stratosphere of abstract notions this elegant algebra is all very well; but a completely bodiless language can never do justice to the data of immediate experience, nor can it contribute anything to our understanding of the "capricious lights and shades" in the midst of which, whether we like it or not, we must perforce live out our lives. [3]

The most richly satisfying essays are those which make the best not of one, not of two, but of all the three worlds in which it is possible for the essay to exist. Freely, effortlessly, thought and feeling move in these consummate works of art, hither and thither between the essay's three poles—from the personal to the universal, from the abstract back to the concrete, from the objective datum to the inner experience. [4]

The perfection of any artistic form is rarely achieved by its first inventor. To this rule Montaigne is the great and marvelous exception. By the time he had written his way into the Third Book, he had reached the limits of his newly discovered art. "What are these essays," he had asked at the beginning of his career, "but grotesque bodies pieced together of different members, without any definite shape, without any order, coherence, or proportion, except they be accidental." But a few years later the patchwork grotesques had turned into living organisms, into multiform hybrids like those beautiful monsters of the old mythologies, the mermaids, the manheaded bulls with wings, the centaurs, the Anubises, the seraphim—impossibilities compounded of incompatibles, but compounded from within, by a process akin to growth, so that the human trunk seems to spring quite naturally from between the horse's shoulders, the fish modulates into the full-breasted Siren as easily and inevitably as a musical theme modulates from one key to another. Free association artistically controlled—this is the paradoxical secret of Montaigne's best essays. One damned thing after another—but in a sequence that in some almost miraculous way develops a central theme and relates it to the rest of human experience. And how beautifully Montaigne combines the generalization with the anecdote, the homily with the autobiographical reminiscence! How skilfully he makes use of the concrete particular, the *chose vue*, to express some universal truth, and to express it more powerfully and penetratingly than it can be expressed by even the most oracular of the dealers in generalities! Here, for example, is what a great oracle, Dr. Johnson, has to say about the human situation and the uses of adversity. "Affliction is inseparable from our present state; it adheres to all the inhabitants of this world, in different proportions indeed, but with an allotment which seems very little regulated by our own conduct. It has been the boast of some swelling moralists that every man's fortune was in his own power, that prudence supplied the place of all other divinities, and that happiness is the unfailing consequence of virtue. But, surely, the quiver of Omnipotence is stored with arrows, against which the shield of human virtue, however adamantine it has been boasted, is held up in vain; we do not always suffer by our crimes, we are not always protected by our innocence. . . . Nothing confers so much ability to resist the temptations that perpetually surround us, as an habitual consideration of the shortness of life, and the uncertainty of those pleasures that solicit our pursuit; and this consideration can be inculcated only by affliction." This is altogether admirable; but there are other and, I would say, better ways of approaching the subject.

"*J'ay veu en mon temps cent artisans, cent laboureurs, plus sages et plus heureux que des Recteurs de l'Universite.*" (I have seen in my time hundreds of artisans and laborers, wiser and happier than university presidents.) Again, "Look at poor working people sitting on the ground with drooping heads after their day's toil. They know neither Aristotle nor Cato, neither example nor precept; and yet from them Nature draws effects of constancy and patience purer and more unconquerable than any of those we study so curiously in the schools." Add to one touch of nature one touch of irony, and you have a comment on life more profound, in spite of its casualness, its seeming levity, than the most eloquent rumblings of the oracles. "It is not our follies that make me laugh," says Montaigne, "it is our sapiences." And why should our sapiences provoke a wise man to laughter? Among other reasons, because the professional sages tend to express themselves in a language of highest abstraction and widest generality—a language that, for all its gnomic solemnity is apt, in a tight corner, to reveal itself as ludicrously inappropriate to the facts of life as it is really and tragically lived. [5]

In the course of the last forty years I have written essays of every size and shape and color. Essays almost as short as Gracian's and, on occasion, longer even than Macaulay's. Essays autobiographical. Essays about things seen and places visited. Essays in criticism of all kinds of works of art, literary, plastic, musical. Essays about philosophy and religion, some of them couched in abstract terms, others in the form of an anthology with comments, others again in which general ideas are approached through the concrete facts of history and biography. Essays, finally, in which, following Montaigne, I have tried to make the best of all the essay's three worlds, have tried to say everything at once in as near an approach to contrapuntal simultaneity as the nature of literary art will allow of. [6]

Sometimes, it seems to me, I have succeeded fairly well in doing what, in one field or another, I had set out to do. Sometimes, alas, I know that I have not succeeded. But "please do not shoot the pianist; he is doing his best." Doing his best, *selon ses quelques doigts perclus*, to make his cottage upright say as much as the great orchestra of the novel, doing his best to "give all things full play." For the writer at least, and perhaps also for the reader, it is better to have tried and failed to achieve perfection than never to have tried at all. [7]

PURPOSE AND STRUCTURE

1. The variety of techniques Huxley uses in the seven paragraphs of this essay illustrates how even short essays frequently employ more than one method of exposition. Comparison, elements of definition, illustration—*one damned thing after another*—are made to serve his three-poled analysis of essays and essayists. In analysis we usually start with the whole, divide it into its components, examine them, and then at the end reassemble them into the whole. Huxley begins with the parts, and only after examining them does he assemble them and present the reader with his conception of the *most richly satisfying essay*. Explain why the nature of his material makes his method necessary.

2. What does he achieve by beginning his analysis with a comparison between the novel as described by D. H. Lawrence and the essay? Your answer should take cognizance of at least the following: Does the comparison work to the essay's advantage or disadvantage? What is the relationship between the quotation and what Huxley says about Montaigne in par. 5? What relationship does this opening quotation have to Huxley's conclusion?

3. In par. 4 Huxley claims that the most satisfying essays are those that make the best of three worlds. Let us apply his own standards to his essay: (a) Starting with the second sentence of par. 3, show how Huxley moves by stages—almost sentence by sentence—from the general to the increasingly particular. (b) Where in the essay does he move from the universal to the personal? from the objective datum to the inner experience?

4. In par. 3 Huxley discusses the merits and defects of the different kinds of essayists. (a) He illustrates his discussion by identifying and characterizing some meritorious writers. Explain why his refusal to name defective writers weakens or strengthens his essay. (b) He carefully balances the merits and defects of each kind of essayist, giving approximately equal space to virtues and vices. But of the three kinds of essayists, he

gives most space to the generalizers and provides examples of their work only. What purpose is served by discussing the generalizers at greater length than the others? Why does he illustrate them and not the others?

5. In the terms which Huxley uses, explain why it is appropriate that he introduce himself and his work at the end.

DICTION AND TONE

1. Huxley tries to be fair to the three kinds of essayists, but his attitude toward them is revealed by his diction. What impression of the essayist is conveyed by *keyhole* in *keyhole of anecdote* [3]; by *condescend* in *never condescend to be personal* [3]; by *deign* in *hardly deign to take notice* [3]; by *brassily contentious* [3]; by *lapidary* in *solemn and lapidary generalizations* [3]; by *cabling his wisdom, at two dollars a word* [3]; by *completely bodiless language* [3]?

2. The language of mathematics is usually regarded as being precise. In par. 3 Huxley states that the abstract essayist *is apt to give us . . . algebra*. Explain fully what connotations he intends by his use of *algebra*. If necessary, make a detailed comparison between algebra and the general statement in order to make your explanation precise and vivid.

3. Huxley calls *free association artistically controlled* a paradox. What is paradoxical about it? (par. 5)

4. *One damned thing after another* is a marked departure from the formal language Huxley normally uses. Explain why it is appropriate or inappropriate in the essay.

5. In par. 5 Huxley juxtaposes a passage from Dr. Johnson and one from Montaigne. Contrast the level of abstraction of the language in these passages.

6. The tone of *And how splendid, how truly oracular are the utterances of the great generalizers!* could be misinterpreted as being ironic. What evidence within the paragraph proves that Huxley does not intend to be ironic? (par. 3)

7. In the last paragraph, Huxley compares the essayist's upright piano with the novelist's great orchestra. Relate the comparison to his use of *contrapuntal simultaneity* at the end of the previous paragraph.

APPLICATIONS TO WRITING

1. Apply Huxley's analytical method to the novel or poem. Make whatever changes in the three poles you feel are necessary.

2. Apply Huxley's analytical method to a non-literary art form—painting, dance, music, sculpture, architecture. Make whatever changes in the three poles you feel are necessary.

3. Write an analysis of an essay you have read recently, using Huxley's three poles as a standard for judgment.

MONSIEUR VERDOUX
(Parts II and III)

J A M E S   A G E E

Part II

Chaplin's performance as Verdoux is the best piece of playing I have ever seen: here, I cannot even specify the dozen or so
close-ups each so great and so finely related and timed that withdrawn
and linked in series they are like the notes of a slow, magnificent, and
terrifying song, which the rest of the film serves as an accompaniment.
I could write many pages, too, about the richness and quality of the
film as a work of art, in fact, of genius; and as many more trying,
hopelessly, to determine how Chaplin's intellect, instinct, intuition,
creative intelligence, and pure experience as a master artist and as a
showman, serve and at times disserve one another: for intellectually
and in every other kind of self-exhaustion this seems incomparably
his most ambitious film. And since the film is provocative of so much
that cannot be examined as fun, I wish I might also use the many
thousands of words I would require to do it adequate honor, purely as
fun. And all the more because I love and revere the film as deeply as
any I have seen, and believe that it is high among the great works
of this century, I wish I might discuss at proper length its weak-

nesses as a work of art and of moral understanding. I have reluctantly chosen, instead, to suggest a single aspect of its meaning, which seems to me particularly important. And this itself, I fear, I may have reduced beyond usefulness. [1]

Chaplin's theme, the greatest and the most appropriate to its time that he has yet undertaken, is the bare problem of surviving at all in such a world as this. With his usual infallibility of instinct he has set his story in Europe; Europeans are aware of survival as a problem, as we are not. As rightly, he has set aside the tramp, whose charming lessons in survival are too wishful for his purposes, for his first image of the Responsible Man, and of modern civilization. (For Verdoux embodies much of the best that can be said of modern civilization, whether democratic-capitalist, fascist, or communist: whatever he may lack in the way of conscience, he does have brains; and whatever crimes he commits, they are committed, or so he believes, out of compassionate love and in uncompromising discharge of responsibility.) The tramp is the free soul intact in its gallantry, innocence, eagerness for love, ridiculousness, and sorrow; we recognize in him much that is dear to us in ourselves. Verdoux is so much nearer and darker that we can hardly bear to recognize ourselves in him. He is the committed, dedicated soul, and this soul is not intact: we watch its death agonies. And this tragic process is only the more dreadful because it is depicted not gravely but briskly, with a cold savage gaiety; the self-destroying soul is rarely aware of its own predicament. [2]

The problem of survival: the Responsible Man. Chaplin develops his terrible theme chiefly as a metaphor for business. But the film is also powerful as a metaphor for war: the Verdoux home as an embattled nation, the wife and child as the home front, Verdoux as expeditionary force, hero in the holiest of causes, and war criminal. But it is even more remarkable and fascinating as a study of the relationship between ends and means, a metaphor for the modern personality—that is, a typical "responsible" personality reacting to contemporary pressures according to the logic of contemporary ethics. [3]

In the terms of this metaphor the basic cast is small. Verdoux, his wife, and their son are differing aspects of a single personality. Verdoux is the master, the intelligence and the deep unconscious; he has estranged his soul and his future. He has made the assumption that most people make, today—one of the chief assumptions on which modern civilization rests. That is, that in order to preserve intact in such a world as this those aspects of the personality which are best and dearest to one, it is necessary to exercise all that is worst in one; and that it is impossible to do this effectively if one communicates honestly with one's best. Accordingly the personality which, until the world struck that living down, lived in poverty and docility, but happily, is broken and segregated. [4]

The wife and child are shut away in a home which is at once a shrine and a jail; and there, immobilized, and cut off from the truth, they virtually cease to exist as living objects of love; they become an ever more rigid dream. For when the worst and the best in the personality are thus segregated, and the worst is thus utilized in the nominal service of the best, it is inevitably the good which is exploited; the evil, which thinks of itself as faithful slave, is treacherous master; and evil, being active and knowledgeable, grows; and good, rendered motionless and denied knowledge, withers. Like most men obsessed with the world's ruthlessness, Verdoux carries his veneration of innocence to the extreme; he is determined that it shall never be touched, shall never change (the song of how many million homesick soldiers: "We want to find everything at home just as we left it"). But change is inevitable, and uncontrollable. Ruthlessness and the murderous adoration of static innocence enlarge each other; and the ruthless man becomes the more ruthless because he has broken all communication with innocence. And innocence itself is altered. At the moment Verdoux tells his wife that they own their home at last, she dares to remember sadly that they were happier when they were poor. Her face shows the terrible drugged passiveness of the over-sustained, the still more terrible intuitive guilt that comes of all that is uneasily apprehended, untold, and unasked. Small wonder that she has become a cripple; the wonder is that she continues to breathe.

Passiveness was forced on her, truth was destroyed, love was undermined, her own love became pity, as surely as her husband's, and in pity and in fear she failed to question what was being done. As is so often true, it was not she who wanted to be so well provided for; that was her husband's desire, the one desire he might hope to satisfy; so she let him satisfy it. [5]

As for Verdoux, he is irreparably committed. All the heart he has left prevents his confessing to his wife, and prevents his changing trades. He could only have chosen his course through defect of love—vengefulness and self-pity masked as pity, pity masked as love; the love-destroying, monstrous arrogance it requires to make the innocent answerable for your guilt—and the constant necessity of deceiving love has damaged love still more profoundly. Like many business men who feel unloved, or incapable of full enough love, he can only propitiate, and express, his love by providing for his family as handsomely as possible. (He can desire this of course, rather than the bare subsistence his wife prefers, only because he respects the standards of the world he thinks he despises. During his docile years, remember, he served at the high altar of modern civilization, breathing year in and year out. The Bank's soul-dissolving odor of sanctity, all day, every day, touching the sacred wealth he must never dare touch with his conscious desire. When he was thrown out of his job, this ruthlessness released the tremendously impounded ruthlessness in him.) But that is never well enough to satisfy him—and only *his* satisfaction really counts, in this household—for his wife and child scarcely exist for him except as a self-vindicating dream, which he must ceaselessly labor to sustain, improve, perfect, be worthy of. A vicious cycle is established. Only through the best good-providing possible can Verdoux at once express his love, quiet his dying intuition that his love is defective and that he is wrong even in the little that he believes to be right, sustain the dream that is all that remains of love, require of himself ever more obsessive industriousness in crime, and silence his wife. [6]

As good, by his will, is ever more stonily immobilized, evil becomes ever more protean in disguise and self-disguise, ever more mercurial in its journeyings. (The personality is also a constant metaphor for modern civilization—in which, for one instance, creative power is paralyzed except in the interests of gain and destruction; in those interests it is vigorous as never before.) Verdoux cannot bear to sit still, to stop work, long enough to realize his predicament. He cannot feel "at home," at home. He has to act his roles as perfect husband and father, dearly as he wants merely to *be* both, just as he acts all his other roles. All that he loves is saturated in deceit; and he in self-deceit as well. He gets home seldom, apparently never longer than overnight; the divided spirit can only assert its unity, even its illusion of unity or its desire, in twilight contemplation or in dreams; and the pressure of business is always on him. The pressure of business indeed! Verdoux's family is almost lifeless; such piteously cherished life as it retains, he is hopelessly estranged from. All that requires his intelligence, skill, and vitality, all that gives him life, is in his business. He is the loneliest character I know of: he can never be so desperately lonely as during these hours among those dearest to him, when he must deceive not mere victims, or the world at large, but those he loves. The only moments during which this appalling loneliness is broken, during which he ever honestly communicates, however briefly, with other human beings, are those few moments during which he can know that his victims realize they are being murdered. No doubt he loves his wife and child—there are two of the most heart-stopping, beautiful close-ups ever made, to prove that—but in the fearful depths into which he cannot risk a glance he loves only their helplessness; and deeper, only the idea of love; and that only because it consecrates his true marriage, which is to murder. [7]

Part III

The most mysterious line in the film, Verdoux's reference to having "lost" his family, becomes clear if the three are seen as members of a single personality. The wife whom segregation and deceit so inevitably paralyzed was dying a slow death from the moment she became

uneasy and failed with her own kind of misguided tenderness, to be-
seech her husband's confidence; and the child could not long have
survived his mother. [8]

With their death Verdoux all but dies himself. He becomes old,
bent, sore, stiff, not only through heartbreak or because all that he
most cherished in his nature is destroyed, but because their death
has deprived him of the one motive he would recognize for his
criminality. The third meeting with Miss Nash, for all its handsome
prospects, revives him only to an old man's charming glimmer; but as
soon as danger once more requires work of him and, after showing
how effortlessly he might escape, he casually surrenders himself to
society's vengeance, he limbers up and shines like a snake which has
just cast its winter skin. All that remains now is memory and the
pure stripped ego, the naked will to survive which discovers, with
ineffable relief, that there is no longer any point in surviving. [9]

With his soul dead at last, it is no wonder that Verdoux asserts
himself so proudly, in the courtroom and death cell, in terms of his
dream of himself. He would have explained himself less proudly and
with greater moral understanding to his wife, but he had successfully
avoided that possibility, at the cost of their marriage and her life.
His dream of himself is urgently challenged only once, by the girl
whose life he spares; and he successfully resists that challenge in the
strangest and, I think, most frightening scene ever filmed. [10]

I had expected this film to be the last word in misogyny; but although there is a good deal of it about, Verdoux's handling of his
victims is in general remarkably genial and kindly. The one really
hair-raising moment of that sort is the chance second meeting with
the girl, the scene in which he brushes her off. After all, Verdoux
risks nothing against the poor frumps he kills or tries to kill, except
his life. But the girl is infinitely more dangerous. She is the one
human with whom he holds in common everything he regards as
most important. Both have known love as passionate pity for the helpless, both could kill for love; both would be capable of maturer love,
if at all, only with their own kind. The girl is much closer to Verdoux

than his own wife, or his murdered wives; in sparing her he has betrayed both his marriage and his vocation. Since he is above all else a family man and an artist, she threatens the very structure of his soul. But the deranged and deadlocked will which has made and sustained Verdoux is never so strong or so ruthless as when it faces the threat of cure; and I know of no moment more dreadful or more beautifully achieved than that in which Verdoux veers from the girl, the sun on his suddenly shriveled cheek, and mutters in the shriveled, almost effeminate little voice of more than mortal hatred and terror: "You go on about your business." [11]

But *why* does Verdoux become a murderer? One good answer is: why not? Verdoux is a business realist; in terms of that realism the only difference between free enterprise in murder and free enterprise in the sale of elastic stockings is the difference in legal liability and in net income. And if the film is regarded as a metaphor for war, we may blush to ask Verdoux *why*; or if it is regarded as a metaphor for the destruction of the soul, murder is almost too mild a vocation. Yet we may still ask why, and wonder why Chaplin's only direct statements, most of which are made through Verdoux, are so remarkably inadequate. Verdoux, to be sure, is grandly in character in holding "society" accountable and in absolving the individual; but is this all that Chaplin knows? If so, he is as surely a victim and dupe of evil as Verdoux or the civilization he excoriates, and all that goes deeper in the film is achieved intuitively, as if in a kind of waking dream. If he knows better, then he is gravely at fault, as artist and moralist, in making clear no more than he does, still worse in tossing the mass-audience so cynical and misleading a sop; and one of the purest and most courageous works I know of is, at its climax, pure and courageous only against the enemy, not in the face of the truth. For the answers to why and how criminality can be avoided, we can look inward more profitably than at the film; for all that is suggested in the film is operant in each of us. If Chaplin had illuminated these bottom causes more brightly than we can see them in ourselves, *Verdoux* would be a still greater work of art than it is. But in proposing so richly suggestive an image of process and effect in the world and in the personality, and in proposing it so beautifully, the film, with all its faults, is one of the few indispensable works of our time. [12]

It even contains and implies the beginning of the answer. Good and evil are inextricable, Verdoux insists. But his fatal mistake was in trying to keep them apart. If the film is regarded as a metaphor for the personality, and through that metaphor, as a metaphor for the personality as the family as business as war as civilization as murder, then this is certain: if the man and wife had honored their marriage with more than their child, the murders would never have been committed, the paralysis would never have imposed itself or would have been dissolved, and the wife and child would never have been shut into that exquisite tabernacle of a closed garden, but all three would have lived as one in that poverty for which the wife was forlorn, in the intactness of soul and the irresponsibility of that anarchic and immortal lily of the field, the tramp, the most humane and most nearly complete among the religious figures our time has evolved; whom for once in his life Chaplin set aside, to give his century its truest portrait of the upright citizen. [13]

PURPOSE AND STRUCTURE

1. The striking relationship of the parts to the whole in this functional analysis of a movie is signalled by guideposts. In the first paragraph Agee tells us what facets of the film he must exclude from consideration and the single aspect on which he will focus. What are they?

The organization of the essay, the method to be used to integrate the parts with the whole, is set forth in the third and fourth paragraphs. The theme is factored into three metaphors (identify them); the characters—Verdoux and his wife and child—are described as aspects of a single personality; and the interweaving of theme and cast is begun. How do the characterizations in pars. 5–13 illuminate the metaphors? How are the metaphors linked to each other?

2. The theme of survival in the modern world is developed by a series of stated and implied contrasts (par. 2). What are they?

3. With what contrasting details is the concept of the predicament of the modern personality developed in par. 7? What causal relationships are established? What is the relationship of cause to effect in pars. 12 and 13? Is the syntactically complex structure of the last sentence (par. 13) necessary to communicate its substance? Restate its meaning in your own words.

4. What function do the rhetorical questions serve in par. 12? How are the following concerns brought together into a coherent paragraph: the causes of criminality; the metaphors for war and self destruction; Chaplin's intention, weakness, method, and achievement; the charge to look inward.

5. Agee states that Verdoux's fatal mistake was to try to separate good and evil (par. 13). How have the preceding paragraphs prepared us for this concept? How does the long concluding sentence develop it?

DICTION AND TONE

1. What clues does Agee provide to his attitude toward his materials (par. 1)? Underline the words and phrases which prepare you for a subjective and interpretive approach to the film. At what subsequent points does Agee convey his attitude toward his materials?

2. How does the phrase, *in such a world as this*, help to establish the tone [2]? What tone is created by the linking of *cold* and *savage* with *gaiety* [2]; *terrible* with *theme* [3]; *rigid* with *dream* [5]; *murderous* with *adoration* [5]; *sacred* with *wealth* [6]; *consecrates* with *murder* [7]; *innocence* with *guilt* [7]; *naked* with *will to survive* [9]; *ineffable* with *relief* [9]; *threat* with *cure* [11]; *anarchic and immortal lily of the field* with the *tramp* [13]?

3. How do the phrases, *vengefulness and self-pity masked as pity, pity masked as love*, serve to define Verdoux's defect of love (par. 6)?

4. Defend the use of *terrible* (par. 3), a word we are prone to use indiscriminately.

5. Metaphor is used throughout the essay in an extended meaning. How does it contribute to the structure? to Agee's view of art? to the tone?

6. How does the variety of ways in which the words *love, dream, guilt,* and *innocence* are defined contribute to the author's purpose and tone?

7. In the concluding sentence the elements following *metaphors for the personality* are not separated by commas. Can you justify this omission?

8. Why is the concluding phrase, *upright citizen,* ironic? What concepts have prepared you for its use?

APPLICATIONS TO WRITING

1. Analyze a film of some dimension and complexity (or opera, symphony, art exhibit, or play) in which you organize your ideas by dividing your topic into parts and then weaving them together into an integrated whole.

2. Analyze a novel or drama in which you point the relationship of theme and character development and emphasize causal relationships.

3. Analyze the achievement of a famous director (such as Chaplin, Resnais, Bergman, Fellini, Antonioni, or Truffaut) in a film you have seen. Pars. 1 and 12 should suggest to you a variety of approaches.

THE LORD OF CREATION

SUSANNE K. LANGER

•

Of all born creatures, man is the only one that cannot live by bread alone. He lives as much by symbols as by sense report, in a realm compounded of tangible things and virtual images, of actual events and ominous portents, always between fact and fiction. For he sees not only actualities but meanings. He has, indeed, all the impulses and interests of animal nature; he eats, sleeps, mates, seeks comfort and safety, flees pain, falls sick and dies, just as cats and bears and fishes and butterflies do. But he has something more in his repertoire, too—he has laws and religions, theories and dogmas, because he lives not only through sense but through symbols. That is the special asset of his mind, which makes him the master of earth and all its progeny. [1]

By the agency of symbols—marks, words, mental images, and icons of all sorts—he can hold his ideas for contemplation long after their original causes have passed away. Therefore, he can think of things that are not presented or even suggested by his actual environment. By associating symbols in his mind, he combines things and events that were never together in the real world. This gives him the power we call imagination. Further, he can symbolize only part of an idea and let the rest go out of consciousness; this gives him the faculty that has been his pride throughout the ages—the power of abstraction.

From "The Lord of Creation." Reprinted from the January, 1944 issue of *Fortune* magazine by special permission. © 1944 Time, Inc.

319

The combined effect of these two powers is inestimable. They are the roots of his supreme talent, the gift of reason. [2]

In the war of each against all, which is the course of nature, man has an unfair advantage over his animal brethren; for he can see what is not yet there to be seen, know events that happened before his birth, and take possession of more than he actually eats; he can kill at a distance; and by rational design he can enslave other creatures to live and act for him instead of for themselves. [3]

Yet this mastermind has strange aberrations. For in the whole animal kingdom there is no such unreason, no such folly and impracticality as man displays. He alone is hounded by imaginary fears, beset by ghosts and devils, frightened by mere images of things. No other creature wastes time in unprofitable ritual or builds nests for dead specimens of its race. Animals are always realists. They have intelligence in varying degrees—chickens are stupid, elephants are said to be very clever—but, bright or foolish, animals react only to reality. They may be fooled by appearance, by pictures or reflections, but once they know them as such, they promptly lose interest. Distance and darkness and silence are not fearful to them, filled with voices or forms, or invisible presences. Sheep in the pasture do not seem to fear phantom sheep beyond the fence, mice don't look for mouse goblins in the clock, birds do not worship a divine thunderbird. [4]

But oddly enough, men do. They think of all these things and guard against them, worshiping animals and monsters even before they conceive of divinities in their own image. Men are essentially unrealistic. With all their extraordinary intelligence, they alone go in for patently impractical actions—magic and exorcism and holocausts—rites that have no connection with common-sense methods of self-preservation, such as a highly intelligent animal might use. In fact, the rites and sacrifices by which primitive man claims to control nature are sometimes fatal to the performers. Indian puberty rites are almost always intensely painful, and African natives have sometimes died during initiations into honorary societies. [5]

We usually assume that very primitive tribes of men are closer to animal estate than highly civilized races; but in respect of practical attitudes, this is not true. The more primitive man's mind, the more fantastic it seems to be; only with high intellectual discipline do we gradually approach the realistic outlook of intelligent animals. [6]

Yet this human mind, so beclouded by phantoms and superstitions, is probably the only mind on earth that can reach out to an awareness of things beyond its practical environment and can also conceive of such notions as truth, beauty, justice, majesty, space and time and creation. [7]

There is another paradox in man's relationship with other creatures: namely, that those very qualities he calls animalian—"brutal," "bestial," "inhuman"—are peculiarly his own. No other animal is so deliberately cruel as man. No other creature intentionally imprisons its own kind, or invents special instruments of torture such as racks and thumbscrews for the sole purpose of punishment. No other animal keeps its own brethren in slavery; so far as we know, the lower animals do not commit anything like the acts of pure sadism that figure rather largely in our newspapers. There is no torment, spite, or cruelty for its own sake among beasts, as there is among men. A cat plays with its prey, but does not conquer and torture smaller cats. But man, who knows good and evil, is cruel for cruelty's sake; he who has a moral law is more brutal than the brutes, who have none; he alone inflicts suffering on his fellows with malice aforethought. [8]

If man's mind is really a higher form of the animal mind, his morality a specialized form of herd instinct, then where in the course of evolution did he lose the realism of a clever animal and fall prey to subjective fears? And why should he take pleasure in torturing helpless members of his own race? [9]

The answer is, I think, that man's mind is *not* a direct evolution from the beast's mind, but is a unique variant and therefore has had a meteoric and startling career very different from any other animal history. The trait that sets human mentality apart from every other is its preoccupation with symbols, with images and names that *mean* things, rather than with things themselves. This trait may have been a mere sport of nature once upon a time. Certain creatures do develop tricks and interests that seem biologically unimportant. Pack rats, for instance, and some birds of the crow family take a capricious pleasure in bright objects and carry away such things for which they have, presumably, no earthly use. Perhaps man's tendency to see certain forms as *images*, to hear certain sounds not only as signals but as expressive tones, and to be excited by sunset colors or starlight, was originally just a peculiar sensitivity in a rather highly developed brain. But whatever its cause, the ultimate destiny of this trait was momentous; for all human activity is based on the appreciation and use of symbols. Language, religion, mathematics, all learning, all science and superstition, even right and wrong, are products of symbolic expression rather than direct experience. Our commonest words, such as "house" and "red" and "walking," are symbols; the pyramids of Egypt and the mysterious circles of Stonehenge are symbols; so are dominions and empires and astronomical universes. We live in a mind-made world, where the things of prime importance are images or words that embody ideas and feelings and attitudes. [10]

The animal mind is like a telephone exchange; it receives stimuli from outside through the sense organs and sends out appropriate responses through the nerves that govern muscles, glands, and other parts of the body. The organism is constantly interacting with its surroundings, receiving messages and acting on the new state of affairs that the messages signify. [11]

But the human mind is not a simple transmitter like a telephone exchange. It is more like a great projector; for instead of merely mediating between an event in the outer world and a creature's responsive action, it transforms or, if you will, distorts the event into an image to be looked at, retained, and contemplated. For the images of things that we remember are not exact and faithful transcriptions even of our actual sense impressions. They are made as much by what we think as by what we see. It is a well-known fact that if you ask several people the size of the moon's disk as they look at it, their estimates will vary from the area of a dime to that of a barrel top. Like a magic lantern, the mind projects its ideas of things on the screen of what we call "memory"; but like all projections, these ideas are transformations of actual things. They are, in fact, *symbols* of reality, not pieces of it. [12]

A symbol is not the same thing as a sign; that is a fact that psychologists and philosophers often overlook. All intelligent animals use signs; so do we. To them as well as to us sounds and smells and motions are signs of food, danger, the presence of other beings, or of rain or storm. Furthermore, some animals not only attend to signs but produce them for the benefit of others. Dogs bark at the door to be let in; rabbits thump to call each other; the cooing of doves and the growl of a wolf defending his kill are unequivocal signs of feelings and intentions to be reckoned with by other creatures. [13]

We use signs just as animals do, though with considerably more elaboration. We stop at red lights and go on green; we answer calls and bells, watch the sky for coming storms, read trouble or promise or anger in each other's eyes. That is animal intelligence raised to the human level. Those of us who are dog lovers can probably all tell wonderful stories of how high our dogs have sometimes risen in the scale of clever sign interpretation and sign using. [14]

A sign is anything that announces the existence or the imminence of some event, the presence of a thing or a person, or a change in a state of affairs. There are signs of the weather, signs of danger, signs of future good or evil, signs of what the past has been. In every case a sign is closely bound up with something to be noted or expected in experience. It is always a part of the situation to which it refers, though the reference may be remote in space and time. In so far as we are led to note or expect the signified event we are making correct use of a sign. This is the essence of rational behavior, which animals show in varying degrees. It is entirely realistic, being closely bound up with the actual objective course of history—learned by experience, and cashed in or voided by further experience. [15]

If man had kept to the straight and narrow path of sign using, he would be like the other animals, though perhaps a little brighter. He would not talk, but grunt and gesticulate and point. He would make his wishes known, give warnings, perhaps develop a social system like that of bees and ants, with such a wonderful efficiency of communal enterprise that all men would have plenty to eat, warm apartments— all exactly alike and perfectly convenient—to live in, and everybody could and would sit in the sun or by the fire, as the climate demanded, not talking but just basking, with every want satisfied, most of his life. The young would romp and make love, the old would sleep, the middle-aged would do the routine work almost unconsciously and eat a great deal. But that would be the life of a social, superintelligent, purely sign-using animal. [16]

To us who are human, it does not sound very glorious. We want to go places and do things, own all sorts of gadgets that we do not absolutely need, and when we sit down to take it easy we want to talk. Rights and property, social position, special talents and virtues, and above all our ideas, are what we live for. We have gone off on a tangent that takes us far away from the mere biological cycle that animal generations accomplish; and that is because we can use not only signs but symbols. [17]

A symbol differs from a sign in that it does not announce the presence of the object, the being, condition, or whatnot, which is its meaning, but merely *brings this thing to mind*. It is not a mere "sub- stitute sign" to which we react as though it were the object itself. The fact is that our reaction to hearing a person's name is quite different from our reaction to the person himself. There are certain rare cases where a symbol stands directly for its meaning: in religious experience, for instance, the Host is not only a symbol but a Presence. But symbols in the ordinary sense are not mystic. They are the same sort of thing that ordinary signs are; only they do not call our atten- tion to something necessarily present or to be physically dealt with— they call up merely a conception of the thing they "mean." [18]

The difference between a sign and a symbol is, in brief, that a sign causes us to think or act *in face of* the thing signified, whereas a symbol causes us to think *about* the thing symbolized. Therein lies the great importance of symbolism for human life, its power to make

this life so different from any other animal biography that generations of men have found it incredible to suppose that they were of
purely zoological origin. A sign is always embedded in reality, in a
present that emerges from the actual past and stretches to the future;
but a symbol may be divorced from reality altogether. It may refer
to what is *not* the case, to a mere idea, a figment, a dream. It serves,
therefore, to liberate thought from the immediate stimuli of a physically present world; and that liberation marks the essential difference
between human and nonhuman mentality. Animals think, but they
think *of* and *at* things; men think primarily *about* things. Words,
pictures, and memory images are symbols that may be combined and
varied in a thousand ways. The result is a symbolic structure whose
meaning is a complex of all their respective meanings, and this
kaleidoscope of *ideas* is the typical product of the human brain that
we call the "stream of thought." [19]

The process of transforming all direct experience into imagery or
into that supreme mode of symbolic expression, language, has so
completely taken possession of the human mind that it is not only a
special talent but a dominant, organic need. All our sense impressions
leave their traces in our memory not only as signs disposing our practical reactions in the future but also as symbols, images representing
our *ideas* of things; and the tendency to manipulate ideas, to combine
and abstract, mix and extend them by playing with symbols, is man's
outstanding characteristic. It seems to be what his brain most naturally
and spontaneously does. Therefore his primitive mental function is
not judging reality, but *dreaming his desires.* [20]

Dreaming is apparently a basic function of human brains, for it is
free and unexhausting like our metabolism, heartbeat, and breath.
It is easier to dream than not to dream, as it is easier to breathe than
to refrain from breathing. The symbolic character of dreams is fairly
well established. Symbol mongering, on this ineffectual, uncritical
level, seems to be instinctive, the fulfillment of an elementary need
rather than the purposeful exercise of a high and difficult talent. [21]

The special power of man's mind rests on the evolution of this special activity, not on any transcendently high development of animal intelligence. We are not immeasurably higher than other animals; we are different. We have a biological need and with it a biological gift that they do not share. [22]

Because man has not only the ability but the constant need of *conceiving* what has happened to him, what surrounds him, what is demanded of him—in short, of symbolizing nature, himself, and his hopes and fears—he has a constant and crying need of *expression*. What he cannot express, he cannot conceive; what he cannot conceive is chaos, and fills him with terror. [23]

If we bear in mind this all-important craving for expression we get a new picture of man's behavior; for from this trait spring his powers and his weaknesses. The process of symbolic transformation that all our experiences undergo is nothing more nor less than the process of *conception*, which underlies the human faculties of abstraction and imagination. [24]

When we are faced with a strange or difficult situation, we cannot react directly, as other creatures do, with flight, aggression, or any such simple instinctive pattern. Our whole reaction depends on how we manage to conceive the situation—whether we cast it in a definite dramatic form, whether we see it as a disaster, a challenge, a fulfillment of doom, or a fiat of the Divine Will. In words or dreamlike images, in artistic or religious or even in cynical form, we must *construe* the events of life. There is great virtue in the figure of speech, "I can *make* nothing of it," to express a failure to understand something. Thought and memory are processes of *making* the thought content and the memory image; the pattern of our ideas is given by the symbols through which we express them. And in the course of manipulating those symbols we inevitably distort the original experience, as we abstract certain features of it, embroider and reinforce those features with other ideas, until the conception we project on the screen of memory is quite different from anything in our real history. [25]

Conception is a necessary and elementary process; what we do with our conceptions is another story. That is the entire history of human culture—of intelligence and morality, folly and superstition, ritual, language, and the arts—all the phenomena that set man apart from, and above, the rest of the animal kingdom. As the religious mind has to make all human history a drama of sin and salvation in order to define its own moral attitudes, so a scientist wrestles with the mere presentation of "the facts" before he can reason about them. The process of *envisaging* facts, values, hopes, and fears underlies our whole behavior pattern; and this process is reflected in the evolution of an extraordinary phenomenon found always, and only, in human societies—the phenomenon of language. [26]

Language is the highest and most amazing achievement of the symbolistic human mind. The power it bestows is almost inestimable, for without it anything properly called "thought" is impossible. The birth of language is the dawn of humanity. The line between man and beast—between the highest ape and the lowest savage—is the language line. Whether the primitive Neanderthal man was anthropoid or human depends less on his cranial capacity, his upright posture, or even his use of tools and fire, than on one issue we shall probably never be able to settle—whether or not he spoke. [27]

In all physical traits and practical responses, such as skills and visual judgments, we can find a certain continuity between animal and human mentality. Sign using is an ever evolving, ever improving function throughout the whole animal kingdom, from the lowly worm that shrinks into his hole at the sound of an approaching foot, to the dog obeying his master's command, and even to the learned scientist who watches the movements of an index needle. [28]

This continuity of the sign-using talent has led psychologists to the belief that language is evolved from the vocal expressions, grunts and coos and cries, whereby animals vent their feelings or signal their fellows; that man has elaborated this sort of communion to the point where it makes a perfect exchange of ideas possible. [29]

I do not believe that this doctrine of the origin of language is correct. The essence of language is symbolic, not signific; we use it first and most vitally to formulate and hold ideas in our own minds. Conception, not social control, is its first and foremost benefit. [30]

Watch a young child that is just learning to speak play with a toy; he says the name of the object, e.g.: "Horsey! horsey! horsey!" over and over again, looks at the object, moves it, always saying the name to himself or to the world at large. It is quite a time before he talks to anyone in particular; he talks first of all to himself. This is his way of forming and fixing the *conception* of the object in his mind, and around this conception all his knowledge of it grows. *Names* are the essence of language; for the *name* is what abstracts the conception of the horse from the horse itself, and lets the mere idea recur at the speaking of the name. This permits the conception gathered from one horse experience to be exemplified again by another instance of a horse, so that the notion embodied in the name is a general notion. [31]

To this end, the baby uses a word long before he *asks for* the object; when he wants his horsey he is likely to cry and fret, because he is reacting to an actual environment, not forming ideas. He uses the animal language of *signs* for his wants; talking is still a purely symbolic process—its practical value has not really impressed him yet. [32]

Language need not be vocal; it may be purely visual, like written language, or even tactual, like the deaf-mute system of speech; but it *must be denotative*. The sounds, intended or unintended, whereby animals communicate do not constitute a language, because they are signs, not names. They never fall into an organic pattern, a meaningful syntax of even the most rudimentary sort, as all language seems to do with a sort of driving necessity. That is because signs refer to actual situations, in which things have obvious relations to each other that require only to be noted; but symbols refer to ideas, which are not physically there for inspection, so their connections and features have to be represented. This gives all true language a natural tendency toward growth and development, which seems almost like a life of its own. Languages are not invented; they grow with our need for expression. [33]

In contrast, animal "speech" never has a structure. It is merely an emotional response. Apes may greet their ration of yams with a shout of "Nga!" But they do not say "Nga" between meals. If they could *talk about* their yams instead of just saluting them, they would be the most primitive men instead of the most anthropoid of beasts. They would have ideas, and tell each other things true or false, rational or irrational; they would make plans and invent laws and sing their own praises, as men do. [34]

PURPOSE AND STRUCTURE

1. Susanne Langer sets out to explain the reasons why man is "the Lord of Creation." Her causal analysis is simple in its larger design but complex in its details. In answer to the question, "Why is man in a unique position in the world?" she can simply reply, "Because he uses symbols." But this answer does not explain adequately, and it leads to other questions. What is a symbol? How does it differ from a sign? Do other animals as well as man use symbols? The answers to these and other questions, relevant to her central purpose, are developed by means of examples and illustrations, comparisons, contrasts, definition, and analogy.

An examination of par. 9 provides an introduction to her organization. Consisting of only two questions, the paragraph touches upon the points previously raised and prepares the reader for the answer to follow. Read the paragraph and then answer the following: (a) Where does she develop the idea that man has lost the realism of a clever animal? What method does she use in her development? (b) Where does she develop the idea that man takes pleasure in torture? What method does she use in her development?

2. What is the function of the first three paragraphs?

3. Pars. 11 and 12, each with its own analogy, develop a contrast. What is the purpose of the information developed by the contrast?

4. Pars. 13 and 14, each with its own examples, develop a comparison. What is the purpose of the information developed by the comparison?

5. Par. 16 is a brief causal analysis: given a certain set of conditions, particular consequences will follow. What are the conditions? the conse-

quences? Explain why and to what degree this information is necessary to the essay.

6. In par. 10 Mrs. Langer answers the questions of par. 9 by stating that man's *preoccupation with symbols* sets his *mentality apart from every other.* She does not begin to define a symbol, however, until par. 18. Explain why she waits eight paragraphs before defining her key term. Would it be more or less effective if her definition came immediately after par. 10?

7. In her analysis of the causes behind man's lordship over the world, in what way is the function of par. 20 different from that of par. 10? Does par. 20 advance her line of reasoning, or is it a repetition of information already presented? Relate the paragraph to the first sentence of the essay.

8. In par. 14 Mrs. Langer established that men *use signs just as animals do.* Why does she repeat this information in par. 28?

DICTION AND TONE

1. What is the effect of the allusion in the first sentence and the response to it in the second?

2. In the third sentence of par. 10, Mrs. Langer calls a trait of man a *mere sport of nature.* What does *sport* mean in this context?

3. Two sentences later she refers to the *capricious pleasure* of pack rats and crows. What is the effect of this reference?

4. In par. 16, is she being ironic in her description of what life would be like if men used only signs? Defend your answer.

5. In par. 19 she refers to animal *biography.* Can an animal have a biography? What does *biography* mean?

6. In par. 19 she says *animals think,* but in par. 27, she says "thought" is not possible without language. Is it possible to think without having thoughts? Has she contradicted herself? Explain how the contexts of pars. 19 and 27 do or do not justify her logic.

7. Should the last three words of the essay be *as man does* instead of *as men do?* Explain your answer.

APPLICATIONS TO WRITING

Analyze one aspect of man's behavior in terms of its symbolic significance. For example, all games and sports are symbolic, for there is no intrinsic value in hitting a ball into a hole or throwing one through a hoop. What needs of man do games express or satisfy? Hardly anyone today hunts or fishes to supply himself with food. Why does he do it—and usually at considerable expense in time and money? Why does man buy three hundred horsepower automobiles when only a few horsepower can be used under present traffic conditions and laws?

ROBERT FROST:
THE WAY TO
THE POEM

JOHN CIARDI

STOPPING BY WOODS ON A SNOWY EVENING

Whose woods these are I think I know.
His house is in the village though;
He will not see me stopping here
To watch his woods fill up with snow.

My little horse must think it queer
To stop without a farmhouse near
Between the wood and frozen lake
The darkest evening of the year.

He gives his harness bells a shake
To ask if there is some mistake.
The only other sound's the sweep
Of easy wind and downy flake.

Reprinted by permission of John Ciardi and *Saturday Review*.
"Stopping by Woods on a Snowy Evening" from *You Come Too* by Robert Frost.
Copyright © 1959, 1923, by Holt, Rinehart and Winston, Inc. Copyright, 1951,
by Robert Frost. Reprinted by permission of the publishers.

The woods are lovely, dark and deep.
But I have promises to keep,
And miles to go before I sleep,
And miles to go before I sleep.

The School System has much to say these days of the virtue of reading widely, and not enough about the virtues of reading less but in depth. There are any number of reading lists for poetry, but there is not enough talk about individual poems. Poetry, finally, is one poem at a time. To read any one poem carefully is the ideal preparation for reading another. Only a poem can illustrate how poetry works. [1]

Above, therefore, is a poem—one of the master lyrics of the English language, and almost certainly the best-known poem by an American poet. What happens in it?—which is to say, not *what* does it mean, but *how* does it mean? How does it go about being a human reenactment of a human experience? The author—perhaps the thousandth reader would need to be told—is Robert Frost. [2]

Even the TV audience can see that this poem begins as a seemingly simple narration of a seemingly simple incident but ends by suggesting meanings far beyond anything specifically referred to in the narrative. And even readers with only the most casual interest in poetry might be made to note the additional fact that, though the poem suggests those larger meanings, it is very careful never to abandon its pretense to being simple narration. There is duplicity at work. The poet pretends to be talking about one thing, and all the while he is talking about many others. [3]

Many readers are forever unable to accept the poet's essential duplicity. It is almost safe to say that a poem is never about what it seems to be about. As much could be said of the proverb. The bird in the hand, the rolling stone, the stitch in time never (except by an artful double-deception) intend any sort of statement about birds, stones, or sewing. The incident of this poem, one must conclude, is at root a metaphor. [4]

Duplicity aside, this poem's movement from the specific to the general illustrates one of the basic formulas of all poetry. Such a grand poem as Arnold's "Dover Beach" and such lesser, though unfortunately better known, poems as Longfellow's "The Village Blacksmith" and Holmes's "The Chambered Nautilus" are built on the same progression. In these three poems, however, the generalization is markedly set apart from the specific narration, and even seems additional to the telling rather than intrinsic to it. It is this sense of division one has in mind in speaking of "a tacked-on moral." [5]

There is nothing wrong-in-itself with a tacked-on moral. Frost, in fact, makes excellent use of the device at times. In this poem, however, Frost is careful to let the whatever-the-moral-is grow out of the poem itself. When the action ends the poem ends. There is no epilogue and no explanation. Everything pretends to be about the narrated incident. And that pretense sets the basic tone of the poem's performance of itself. [6]

The dramatic force of that performance is best observable, I believe, as a progression in three scenes. [7]

In scene one, which coincides with stanza one, a man—a New England man—is driving his sleigh somewhere at night. It is snowing, and as the man passes a dark patch of woods he stops to watch the snow descend into the darkness. We know, moreover, that the man is familiar with these parts (he knows who owns the woods and where the owner lives), and we know that no one has seen him stop. As scene one forms itself in the theater of the mind's eye, therefore, it serves to establish some as yet unspecified relation between the man and the woods. [8]

It is necessary, however, to stop here for a long parenthesis: Even so simple an opening statement raises any number of questions. It is impossible to address all the questions that rise from the poem stanza by stanza, but two that arise from stanza one illustrate the sort of thing one might well ask of the poem detail by detail. [9]

Why, for example, does the man not say what errand he is on? What is the force of leaving the errand generalized? He might just as well have told us that he was going to the general store, or returning from it with a jug of molasses he had promised to bring Aunt Harriet and two suits of long underwear he had promised to bring the hired man. Frost, moreover, can handle homely detail to great effect. He preferred to leave his motive generalized. Why? [10]

And why, on the other hand, does he say so much about knowing the absent owner of the woods and where he lives? Is it simply that one set of details happened-in whereas another did not? To speak of things "happening-in" is to assault the integrity of a poem. Poetry cannot be discussed meaningfully unless one can assume that everything in the poem—every last comma and variant spelling—is in it by the poet's specific act of choice. Only bad poets allow into their poems what is haphazard or cheaply chosen. [11]

The errand, I will venture a bit brashly for lack of space, is left generalized in order the more aptly to suggest *any* errand in life and, therefore, life itself. The owner is there because he is one of the forces of the poem. Let it do to say that the force he represents is the village of mankind (that village at the edge of winter) from which the poet finds himself separated (has separated himself?) in his moment by the woods (and to which, he recalls finally, he has promises to keep). The owner is he-who-lives-in-his-village-house, thereby locked away from the poet's awareness of the-time-the-snow-tells as it engulfs and obliterates the world the village man allows himself to believe he "owns." Thus, the owner is a representative of an order of reality from which the poet has divided himself for the moment, though to a certain extent he ends by reuniting with it. Scene one, therefore, establishes not only a relation between the man and the woods, but the fact that the man's relation begins with his separation (though momentarily) from mankind. [12]

End parenthesis one, begin parenthesis two. [13]

Still considering the first scene as a kind of dramatic performance of forces, one must note that the poet has meticulously matched the simplicity of his language to the pretended simplicity of the narrative. Clearly, the man stopped because the beauty of the scene moved him, but he neither tells us that the scene is beautiful nor that he is moved. A bad writer, always ready to overdo, might have written: "The vastness gripped me, filling my spirit with the slow

steady sinking of the snow's crystalline perfection into the glimmer-
less profundities of the hushed primeval wood." Frost's avoidance of
such a spate illustrates two principles of good writing. The first, he
has stated himself in "The Mowing": "Anything *more* than the
truth would have seemed too weak" (italics mine). Understatement
is one of the basic sources of power in English poetry. The second
principle is to let the action speak for itself. A good novelist does not
tell us that a given character is good or bad (at least not since the
passing of the Dickens tradition): he shows us the character in action
and then, watching him, we know. Poetry, too, has fictional obligations: even when the characters are ideas and metaphors rather than
people, they must be *characterized in action*. A poem does not *talk
about* ideas; it *enacts* them. The force of the poem's performance,
in fact, is precisely to act out (and thereby to make us act out em-
phatically, that is, to *feel out*, that is, *to identify with*) the speaker
and why he stopped. The man is the principal actor in this little
"drama of why" and in scene one he is the only character, though as
noted, he is somehow related to the absent owner. [14]

  End second parenthesis. [15]

  In scene two (stanzas two and three) a *foil* is introduced. In
fiction and drama, a foil is a character who "plays against" a more
important character. By presenting a different point of view or an
opposed set of motives, the foil moves the more important character
to react in ways that might not have found expression without such
opposition. The more important character is thus more fully revealed
—to the reader and to himself. The foil here is the horse. [16]

  The horse forces the question. Why did the man stop? Until it
occurs to him that his "little horse must think it queer" he had not
asked himself for reasons. He had simply stopped. But the man finds
himself faced with the question he imagines the horse to be asking:
what *is* there to stop for out there in the cold, away from bin and
stall (house and village and mankind?) and all that any self-respecting
beast could value on such a night? In sensing that other view, the
man is forced to examine his own more deeply. [17]

  In stanza two the question arises only as a feeling within the man.

In stanza three, however (still scene two), the horse acts. He gives his harness bells a shake. "What's wrong?" he seems to say. "What are we waiting for?" [18]

By now, obviously the horse—without losing its identity as horse— has also become a symbol. A symbol is something that stands for something else. Whatever that something else may be, it certainly begins as that order of life that does not understand why a man stops in the wintry middle of nowhere to watch the snow come down. (Can one fail to sense by now that the dark and the snowfall symbolize a death-wish, however momentary, *i.e.*, that hunger for final rest and surrender that a man may feel, but not a beast?) [19]

So by the end of scene two the performance has given dramatic force to three elements that work upon the man. There is his relation to the world of the owner. There is his relation to the brute world of the horse. And there is that third presence of the unownable world, the movement of the all-engulfing snow across all the orders of life, the man's, the owner's, and the horse's—with the difference that the man knows of that second dark-within-the-dark of which the horse cannot, and the owner will not, know. [20]

The man ends scene two with all these forces working upon him simultaneously. He feels himself moved to a decision. And he feels a last call from the darkness: "the sweep / Of easy wind and downy flake." It would be so easy and so downy to go into the woods and let himself be covered over. [21]

But scene three (stanza four) produces a fourth force. This fourth force can be given many names. It is certainly better, in fact, to give it many names than to attempt to limit it to one. It is social obliga- tion, or personal commitment, or duty, or just the realization that a man cannot indulge a mood forever. All of these and more. But, finally, he has a simple decision to make. He may go into the woods and let the darkness and the snow swallow him from the world of beast and man. Or he must move on. And unless he is going to stop here forever, it is time to remember that he has a long way to go and that he had best be getting there. (So there is something to be said for the horse, too.) [22]

Then and only then, his question driven more and more deeply into himself by these cross-forces, does the man venture a comment on what attracted him: "The woods are lovely, dark and deep." His mood lingers over the thought of that lovely dark-and-deep (as do the very syllables in which he phrases the thought), but the final decision is to put off the mood and move on. He has his man's way to go and his man's obligations to tend to before he can yield. He has miles to go before his sleep. He repeats that thought and the performance ends. [23]

But why the repetition? The first time Frost says "And miles to go before I sleep," there can be little doubt that the primary meaning is: "I have a long way to go before I get to bed tonight." The second time he says it, however, "miles to go" and "sleep" are suddenly transformed into symbols. What are those "something-elses" the symbols stand for? Hundreds of people have tried to ask Mr. Frost that question and he has always turned it away. He has turned it away *because he cannot answer it*. He could answer some part of it. But some part is not enough. [24]

For a symbol is like a rock dropped into a pool: it sends out ripples in all directions, and the ripples are in motion. Who can say where the last ripple disappears? One may have a sense that he knows the approximate center point of the ripples, the point at which the stone struck the water. Yet even then he has trouble marking it surely. How does one make a mark on water? Oh, very well—the center point of that second "miles to go" is probably approximately in the neighborhood of being close to meaning, perhaps, "the road of life"; and the second "before I sleep" is maybe that close to meaning "before I take my final rest," the rest in darkness that seemed so temptingly dark-and-deep for the moment of the mood. But the ripples continue to move and the light to change on the water, and the longer one watches the more changes he sees. Such shifting-and-being-at-the-same-instant is of the very sparkle and life of poetry. One experiences it as one experiences life, for every time he looks at an experience he sees something new, and sees it change as he watches it. And that sense of continuity in fluidity is one of the primary kinds of knowledge, one of man's basic ways of knowing, and one that only the arts can teach, poetry foremost among them. [25]

Frost himself certainly did not ask what that repeated last line meant. It came to him and he received it. He "felt right" about it. And what he "felt right" about was in no sense a "meaning" that, say, an essay could apprehend, but an act of experience that could be fully presented only by the dramatic enactment of forces which is the performance of the poem. [26]

Now look at the poem in another way. Did Frost know what he was going to do when he began? Considering the poem simply as an act of skill, as a piece of juggling, one cannot fail to respond to the magnificent turn at the end where, with one flip, seven of the simplest words in the language suddenly dazzle full of never ending waves of thought and feeling. Or, more precisely, of felt-thought. Certainly an equivalent stunt by a juggler—could there be an equivalent—would bring the house down. Was it to cap his performance with that grand stunt that Frost wrote the poem? [27]

Far from it. The obvious fact is that *Frost could not have known he was going to write those lines until he wrote them.* Then a second fact must be registered: *he wrote them because, for the fun of it, he had got himself into trouble.* [28]

Frost, like every good poet, began by playing a game with himself. The most usual way of writing a four line stanza with four feet to the line is to rhyme the third line with the first, and the fourth line with the second. Even that much rhyme is so difficult in English that many poets and almost all of the anonymous ballad makers do not bother to rhyme the first and third lines at all, settling for two rhymes in four lines as good enough. For English is a rhyme-poor language. In Italian and in French, for example, so many words end with the same sounds that rhyming is relatively easy—so easy that many modern French and Italian poets do not bother to rhyme at all. English, being a more agglomerate language, has far more final sounds, hence fewer of them rhyme. When an Italian poet writes a line ending with "vita" (life) he has literally hundreds of rhyme choices available. When an English poet writes "life" at the end of a line he can summon "strife, wife, knife, fife, rife," and then he is in trouble. Now "life-strife" and "life-rife" and "life-wife" seem to offer a combination of possible ideas that can be related by more than just the rhyme. Inevitably, therefore, the poets have had to work and rework these combinations until the sparkle has gone out of them. The reader is normally tired of such rhyme-led associations. When he encounters "life-strife" he is certainly entitled to suspect that the poet did not really want to say "strife"—that had there been in English such a word as, say, "hife," meaning "infinite peace and harmony," the poet would as gladly have used that word instead of "strife." Thus, the reader feels that the writing is haphazard, that the rhyme is making the poet say things he does not really feel, and which therefore the reader does not feel except as boredom. One likes to see the rhymes fall into place, but he must end with the belief that it is the poet who is deciding what is said and not the rhyme scheme that is forcing the saying. [29]

So rhyme is a kind of game, and an especially difficult one in English. As in every game, the fun of the rhyme is to set one's difficulties high and then to meet them skillfully. As Frost himself once defined freedom, it consists of "moving easy in harness." [30]

In "Stopping by Woods on a Snowy Evening" Frost took a long chance. He decided to rhyme not two lines in each stanza, but three. Not even Frost could have sustained that much rhyme in a long poem (as Dante, for example, with the advantage of writing in Italian, sustained triple rhyme for thousands of lines in "The Divine Comedy"). Frost would have known instantly, therefore, when he took the original chance, that he was going to write a short poem. He would have had that much foretaste of it. [31]

So the first stanza emerged rhymed a-a-b-a. And with the sure sense that this was to be a short poem, Frost decided to take an additional chance and to redouble: in English three rhymes in four lines is more than enough; there is no need to rhyme the fourth line. For the fun of it, however, Frost set himself to pick up that loose rhyme and to weave it into the pattern, thereby accepting the all but impossible burden of quadruple rhyme. [32]

The miracle is that it worked. Despite the enormous freight of rhyme, the poem not only came out as a neat pattern, but managed to do so with no sense of strain. Every word and every rhyme falls into place as naturally and as inevitably as if there were no rhyme restricting the poet's choices. [33]

That ease-in-difficulty is certainly inseparable from the success of the poem's performance. One watches the skill-man juggle three balls, then four, then five, and every addition makes the trick more wonderful. But unless he makes the hard trick seem as easy as an easy trick, then all is lost. [34]

The real point, however, is not only that Frost took on a hard rhyme-trick and made it seem easy. It is rather as if the juggler, carried away, had tossed up one more ball than he could really handle, and then amazed himself by actually handling it. So with the real triumph of this poem. Frost could not have known what a stunning effect his repetition of the last line was going to produce. He could not even know he was going to repeat the line. He simply found himself up against a difficulty he almost certainly had not foreseen and he had to improvise to meet it. For in picking up the rhyme from the third line of stanza one and carrying it over into stanza two, he had created an endless chain-link form within which each stanza left a hook sticking out for the next stanza to hang on. So by stanza four, feeling the poem rounding to its end. Frost had to do something about that extra rhyme. [35]

He might have tucked it back into a third line rhyming with the *know-though-snow* of stanza one. He could thus have rounded the poem out to the mathematical symmetry of using each rhyme four times. But though such a device might be defensible in theory, a rhyme repeated after eleven lines is so far from its original rhyme sound that its feeling as rhyme must certainly be lost. And what good is theory if the reader is not moved by the writing? [36]

It must have been in some such quandary that the final repetition suggested itself—a suggestion born of the very difficulties the poet had let himself in for. So there is that point beyond mere ease in handling a hard thing, the point at which the very difficulty offers the poet the opportunity to do better than he knew he could. What, aside from having that happen to oneself, could be more self-delighting than to participate in its happening by one's reader-identification with the poem? [37]

And by now a further point will have suggested itself: that the human insight of the poem and the technicalities of its poetic artifice are inseparable. Each feeds the other. That interplay is the poem's meaning, a matter not of WHAT DOES IT MEAN, for no one can ever say entirely what a good poem means, but of HOW DOES IT MEAN, a process one can come much closer to discussing. [38]

There is a necessary epilogue. Mr. Frost has often discussed this poem on the platform, or more usually in the course of a long-evening-after a talk. Time and again I have heard him say that he just wrote it off, that it just came to him, and that he set it down as it came. [39]

Once at Bread Loaf, however, I heard him add one very essential piece to the discussion of how it "just came." One night, he said, he had sat down after supper to work at a long piece of blank verse. The piece never worked out, but Mr. Frost found himself so absorbed in it that, when next he looked up, dawn was at his window. He rose, crossed to the window, stood looking out for a few minutes, and *then* it was that "Stopping by Woods" suddenly "just came," so that all he had to do was cross the room and write it down. [40]

Robert Frost is the sort of artist who hides his traces. I know of no Frost worksheets anywhere. If someone has raided his wastebasket in secret, it is possible that such worksheets exist somewhere, but Frost would not willingly allow anything but the finished product to leave him. Almost certainly, therefore, no one will ever know what was in that piece of unsuccessful blank verse he had been working at with such concentration, but I for one would stake my life that could that worksheet be uncovered, it would be found to contain the germinal stuff of "Stopping by Woods"; that what was a-simmer in him all night without finding its proper form, suddenly, when he let his still-occupied mind look away, came at him from a different direction, offered itself in a different form, and that finding that form exactly right the impulse proceeded to marry itself to the new shape in one of the most miraculous performances of English lyricism. [41]

And that, too—whether or not one can accept so hypothetical a discussion—is part of HOW the poem means. It means that marriage to the perfect form, the poem's shapen declaration of itself, its moment's monument fixed beyond all possibility of change. And thus, finally, in every truly good poem, "How does it mean?" must always be answered "Triumphantly." Whatever the poem "is about," *how* it means is always how Genesis means: the word become a form, and the form become a thing, and—when the becoming is true—the thing become a part of the knowledge and experience of the race forever. [42]

PURPOSE AND STRUCTURE

1. The larger part of this essay is a functional analysis of one poem—an explanation of how the parts of "Stopping by Woods on a Snowy Evening" relate to one another in action. What is Ciardi's purpose in making this analysis?

2. In par. 4 what does *except by an artful double-deception* mean? Give an example of such a double meaning. How is his point about proverbs relevant to poetry?

3. Compare the function of parenthesis one (pars. 9–12) to parenthesis two (par. 14). How do they differ? Criticize pars. 13 and 15. Are they necessary?

4. Ciardi tries to define a symbol in par. 25. Why is this paragraph necessary to his central purpose? Does he succeed in explaining what a literary symbol is? Summarize his statement, if you can. Do you feel his interpretation of the meaning of the symbol in the Frost poem is sensible or fantastic?

5. Par. 28 speaks of Frost getting into trouble for the fun of it. Is this, finally, an implied argument for the fun of reading difficult poems? Discuss.

6. In pars. 5 and 6 Ciardi says that though the Frost poem moves from the specific to the general, it avoids a "tacked-on moral." How? Draw upon the entire essay for your answer.

DICTION AND TONE

1. Compare the first and last paragraphs of the essay. How do they differ? Why? Which makes demands on the reader similar to those made by a poem? Why? Explain the meaning and criticize the diction of these phrases from the last paragraph: *shapen declaration, moment's monument, how Genesis means.*

2. Why does Ciardi use the word *duplicity* in pars. 3 and 4? Are the connotations of this word inappropriate to the context? Throughout the essay the author uses an implied metaphor for the poet. What is it?

3. Why does Ciardi use the phrase *happening-in* (par. 11)? Can you think of a more appropriate phrase?

4. Why does Ciardi use *How does it mean* instead of *What does it mean* (pars. 2, 38)? Is the choice of words significant? Why does he use all capital letters (par. 38)? Are they necessary?

5. Par. 41 ends with a long sentence. Why? Would it be more effective written as two sentences? Discuss.

APPLICATIONS TO WRITING

1. Write a short paper analyzing the relation between the rhyme scheme and the last line of Frost's "Stopping by Woods on a Snowy Evening." Work back through Ciardi's functional analysis (pars. 29–37), putting it in your own words.

2. Ciardi writes: "Only a poem can illustrate how poetry works." Write a functional analysis of one poem.

THE INTELLECTUAL

IN AMERICA

RANDALL JARRELL

The philosopher Diogenes lived in a tub in the market place. He owned the clothes on his back and a wooden cup; one morning, when he saw a man drinking out of his hands, he threw away the cup. Alexander the Great came to Athens, and went down to the market place to see Diogenes; as he was about to leave he asked, "Is there anything I can do for you?" "Yes," said Diogenes, "you can get out of my light." [1]

At different times, and in different places, this story has meant different things. The ages and places that have venerated wisdom, reason, lovers of wisdom—most ages and places have done so—have listened to the story and thought, with a kind of marveling delight: "The things a man can do without!" Alexander may have owned Greece, Asia Minor, and part of Africa, but there was nothing he could do for Diogenes but move aside and let the sunlight fall upon him. What is real in the world: that is what we must learn, Rilke wrote. Diogenes had learned; so that he could no longer be tipped or bribed with Greece, Asia Minor, and part of Africa—with what the world thought reality, and he illusion. He had remained in his place, the place of Wisdom, and had put Alexander the Great in his place, the place of Power. [2]

Reprinted by permission of the author and of *Mademoiselle*.

But when our age, our country, listens to the story of how Alexander stood in Diogenes' light, it thinks instead, in astonishing perplexity: "What on earth was he doing *there?*" Why should a ruler, a general, a statesman, make a pilgrimage to a poverty-striken philosopher, an intellectual of the most eccentric kind? We wouldn't. Most of us seem to distrust intellectuals as such, to feel that they must be abnormal or else they wouldn't be intellectuals. This is so plain that *Variety* can call our time "the era when to be accused of having some intellect is tantamount to vilification"; and Brooks Atkinson, after noting that the American Psychological Association "has made the same point in more technical language," can conclude that "a passion for ignorance has swept the country like the shmoo." A historian like Henry Steele Commager can say that "the historian of the future who chronicles this decade will be puzzled by the depth, strength, and prevalence of our anti-intellectualism," and can refer to "the vague aura of guilt that surrounds association with academic, intellectual, literary, and reform societies." When men like Senator McCarthy or Westbrook Pegler attack or make fun of men like Dean Acheson, they use as one of their most effective points against him the fact that he has—gone to Harvard. Can anyone imagine their English or French or German counterparts being able to use Oxford, the Sorbonne, or Heidelberg in this way? Nor is it a question of party: plenty of Democrats would have done the same thing to a Republican Secretary of State; and when President Eisenhower, in a recent speech, defined an intellectual as "a man who takes more words than is necessary to tell more than he knows," he was speaking not as a Republican but as an American. [3]

Haven't people got the story of Diogenes and Alexander the Great backwards? Didn't Diogenes wait, and wait, and wait? and, finally, go to Macedonia and get his Senator to make an appointment for him with the Emperor? and didn't the Palace Secretary say to the Senator, after seeing the week's schedule: Miss Macedonia, and the President of the Macedonian Federation of Labor, and the House Committee on Un-Macedonian Activities, and a delegation from the Macedonian

Legion—didn't the Secretary say to Diogenes' Senator, as politely as he could: "The Emperor is a practical man, and has no time for philosophers"? [4]

And then Diogenes went back to Athens. He had always been alone in his tub but, somehow, he hadn't felt lonely: he had had for company the knowledge that some day Alexander would come—had had for company people's good will or good-humored indifference, their surprised or amused admiration, their resigned immemorial "We may not have the sense or the time, but *somebody* has to be wise." But now it was different. A Voice said to Diogenes, like the voice of God: "If some are wise, then others must be foolish: therefore I will have no one wise." [5]

The Voice went on: "You intellectuals, you highbrows, you long-hairs, you eggheads, are the way you are because there's something wrong with you. You sit there in your ivory tower"—really it was a tub; where would Diogenes have got the money to buy a tower?—"pretending you're so different from other people, wasting your time on all these books that don't make sense, and pictures my six-year-old girl can draw better than, and equations it takes another egghead like yourself to make heads or tails of—why don't you get wise to yourself and do what I do, and say what I say, and think like I think, and then maybe I'd have some respect for you?" [6]

It was hard for Diogenes to know what to answer; and when he looked at his tub, it looked smaller and dingier than it used to look; and when he looked at the philosophy that had grown out of the tub, he felt about it the way an old Chinese poet said that he felt about his poetry; that if he wrote one of his poems on a cookie and gave it to a dog, the dog wouldn't eat it. . . . [7]

What could Diogenes do? Some people say he changed—changed until he was exactly the same as everybody else, only more so: before long, people say, he owned the biggest advertising agency in Greece—or else it was the biggest broadcasting company. Or else both. People respected him, then. And every four years Alexander the Great *would* come to see Diogenes; and as he was about to leave Diogenes would ask, "Is there anything I can do for you?" and Alexander the Great would say, "Well, yes. There're these speeches." Then Diogenes would write his speeches. [8]

But some people say that Diogenes kept on the same as before, but that he kept hearing voices—not voices exactly, but this Voice—and kept looking uneasily at people, when really they weren't paying any attention to him except sometimes to laugh at him, or wonder to each other whether maybe he wasn't a Communist or else just crazy. When he talked to people he had a queer look on his face, as if he didn't like the way you were, but didn't like the way he was either. There was a feeble-minded man in the market place that people used to laugh at and make jokes about; but people had got too civilized to make jokes about a thing like that any more, and they made them about Diogenes instead. If you were a politician and something happened, you could blame it on Diogenes—so that he was useful to people, in a way; and he spent part of his time discovering things, or inventing things—penicillin, and television, and hybrid corn, and tensor analysis, and the atom bomb—and writing books, and painting pictures, and composing music, and doing all sorts of things that, if you put a practical man, a business man, in charge of, you could make a lot of money out of it. The trouble with him wasn't that he was useless, exactly; it was more that he was—different. [9]

One night Diogenes woke up and couldn't get back to sleep; he shifted back and forth in his tub, and repeated poems to himself, or said equations, or thought; finally he just lay there. And the Voice said to him, louder than he had ever heard it before: "You are free to think differently from me and to retain your life, your property, and all that you possess; but you are henceforth a stranger among your people. You may retain your civil rights, but they will be useless to you, for you will never be chosen by your fellow citizens if you solicit their votes; and they will affect to scorn you if you ask for their esteem. You will remain among men, but you will be deprived of the rights of mankind. Your fellow creatures will shun you like an impure being; and even those who believe in your innocence will abandon you, lest they be shunned in their turn. Go in peace! I have given you your life, but it is an existence worse than death." [10]

. . . But these last sentences were not said to Diogenes by some imaginary Voice, but were written a hundred and twenty-five years ago by Alexis de Tocqueville. This, he said, is what public opinion in the United States says to the man who disagrees with it. Many of this historian's statements about our country had a frightening and prophetic truth; and the passage of time has not altogether falsified the sentences which I have quoted. But things as they are in gross and confused reality are better than things as they were in Tocqueville's clear and penetrating imagination; he has created something which reality approaches as a limit. The American Diogenes is far better off inside Des Moines, or Jersey City, or Los Angeles, than inside Tocqueville's terrible sentences. Nowadays, after all, there are other people like Diogenes, some of whom say to him, *Brother*; there are people who, even if they themselves are not intellectuals, are willing for someone else to be; and—just as there are people who dislike Negroes or Jews or the Irish, but who like good Negroes, good Jews, good Irishmen, ones who are hardly like Negroes or Jews or Irishmen at all—there are people who dislike intellectuals but are willing to like a good intellectual, one who is hardly like an intellectual at all. And, too, there are the people of the rest of the world, most of whom tolerate, respect, admire even, intellectuals; it is a consolation to American intellectuals to know that their situation is, in some degree, a singular one. [11]

They have suffered this misfortune: they are live, differing, individual human beings who have been put into a category that is itself a condemnation—who are described sufficiently, people think, by an indicting stereotype. There is no way for them to get free of it. If we meet an honest and intelligent politician, a dozen, a hundred, we say that they aren't like politicians at all, and our category of politicians stays unchanged; we know what politicians are like. If a man thinks women men's intellectual inferiors, and keeps coming across women smarter than himself, he murmurs that the exception proves the rule, and saves for the first stupid woman he meets the scornful, categorizing: "Women!" We are this way about nationalities, faiths, races, sexes—about cats and dogs, even. And just as there are anti-Semitic Jews, women who despise women, there are intellectuals who enjoy attacking other intellectuals for being intellectuals. (Big fleas have little fleas to bite 'em, especially when the little ones know they are going to get applauded by the dog.) And other intellectuals behave badly in other ways. It would be odd if they didn't. A looked-down-on class always gets some of its bad qualities simply from knowing that it is being looked down on; the calm and generosity and ease of the justly respected are replaced, often, by the uneasy resentment of the unjustly condemned. Toynbee says that the Turks took it for granted that the "Franks" among them possessed those qualities which the Franks, at home in Europe, considered ghetto qualities. If you have been put in your place long enough, you begin to act like the place. Some of the intellectual's faults are only our imagination, and some are our fault, and some are his fault. But his faults and his virtues, all his qualities, are more varied than we say. He is smart sometimes, dumb sometimes; ingenuous, disingenuous; nice, awful; so that we could say with perfect truth about this, as about so many things: "The more intellectuals I meet the less I know about the intellectual." [12]

We're all intellectuals about *something*. President Eisenhower, for example, is an intellectual where military strategy is concerned; he's taken the courses, learned the terms, done the reading and thinking and practicing, so that he speaks a language, thinks thoughts, makes discriminations, that only other experts can fully understand or appreciate. If you want to be impressed with what a dumb amateur you are, with what trained, intelligent, and discriminating intellectuals the professionals are, sit in a hotel room with some coaches scouting a team, and hear what *they* have to say about the football game you thought you saw that afternoon. People are intellectuals about different things; if you're one about soufflés or salmon-fishing, why look with resentful distrust at somebody who's one about quartets or Sanskrit? Intellectuals are more like plain Americans than plain Americans think; plenty of them *are* plain Americans. And if they're complicated ones, different, is that really so bad? My daughter was telling me about a different boy, a queer one, whom the other children looked down their noses at. I said, "How's he so different?" She said, "Lots of ways. He—he wears corduroys instead of blue jeans." Forgive us each day our corduroys. [13]

Plain Americans enjoy telling Diogenes what they think of him; it would be interesting to know what he thinks of them. It is plain that, whether or not they like him, he likes them; he no longer despairs and flies to Europe, but stays home and suffers willingly—is thankful for—his native fate. Living among them, he can hardly avoid realizing that Americans are a likable, even lovable people, possessing virtues some of which are rare in our time and some of which are rare in any time. But if he were to talk about the faults which accompany our virtues, he might say that the American, characteristically, thinks that nothing is hard or ought to be hard except business or sport; everything else must come of itself. Tocqueville said almost this, long ago: "His curiosity is at once insatiable and cheaply satisfied; for he cares more to know a great deal quickly than to know anything well. . . . The habit of inattention must be considered as the greatest defect of the democratic character." And he goes on to say that the American's leaders—whom Tocqueville calls, oddly, his courtiers and flatterers—"assure him that he possesses all the virtues without having acquired them, or without caring to acquire them." Diogenes could say to us: "You are not willing to labor to be wise; you are not even willing to be wise. It would be a change, and you are not willing to change; it would make you different from other Americans, and you are not willing to be different from them in any way. You wish to remain as you are, and to have the rest of the world change until it is exactly like you; and it seems to you unreasonable, even perverse, for the rest of the world not to wish this too." [14]

All this is very human; but it is very human, too, for the rest of the world, Europeans especially, to be afraid that we will be successful in transforming them into what so many of them believe us to be: rich, powerful, and skillful barbarians, materialists who neglect or despise things of the mind and spirit. The American Way of Life, to many Europeans, means Senator McCarthy, the comic books, and Mickey Spillane. If we say, "But they aren't the real America," and name the scientists and artists and scholars who seem to us the real America, these Europeans will answer: "They! Why, you look down on them, you attack them, you make fun of them—how gladly you would be rid of them!" Then we would have to explain that they are taking our anti-intellectualism too literally: that our country— the most advanced, scientifically, technologically, and industrially, that the world has known—has to depend for every moment of its existence upon the work of millions of highly educated specialists of every sort. What would we be without the production of intellectuals, the fruits of intellect? [15]

We need to let our allies know more about American culture, so that they can feel more as if they were accompanying a fellow, and less as if they were following a robot. And we need to let more of our own people know about it and share it. Nobody has ever before had so much money to spend, so much time to spend; do we always spend it as interestingly or imaginatively as we might? Is what Tocqueville said so long ago true today—that Americans "carry very low tastes into their extraordinary fortunes, and seem to have acquired the supreme power only to minister to their coarse and paltry pleasures"? Is it true that "the love of well-being now has become the predominant taste of the nation"? Do Americans, democratic peoples in general, need nothing so much as "a more enlarged idea of themselves and their kind"? [16]

The Founding Fathers of our country were men who had "an enlarged idea of themselves and their kind"; they had for themselves and us great expectations. Franklin and Jefferson and Adams were men who respected, who labored to understand, and who made their own additions to, science and philosophy and education, the things of the mind and of the spirit. They would have disliked the word intellectual, as we may dislike it, because it seems to set apart from most men what it is natural and laudable for all men to aspire to— our species is called *homo sapiens*; but they would have admitted that, if you wanted to use the word, they were intellectuals. To look down upon, to stigmatize as eccentric or peripheral, science and art and philosophy, human thought, would have seemed to them un-American. It would not have seemed to them, even, human. [17]

That most human and American of Presidents—of Americans—Abraham Lincoln, said as a young man: "The things I want to know are in books; my best friend is the man who'll get me a book I ain't read." It's a hard heart, and a dull one, that doesn't go out to that sentence. The man who will make us see what we haven't seen, feel what we haven't felt, understand what we haven't understood—he *is* our best friend. And if he knows more than we do, that is an invitation to us, not an indictment of us. And it is not an indictment of him, either; it takes all sorts of people to make a world—to make, even, a United States of America. [18]

PURPOSE AND STRUCTURE

This eloquent and moving plea for the intellectual is a complex example of the analysis of function and purpose as well as of cause and effect. In discussing the function and purpose of the intellectual and the response of his fellow Americans, the author compares and contrasts the intellectual in various times and places. He describes him both as a member of a class and as an individual. In addition to comparison and contrast, definition, and classification, the author develops his analysis by the use of illustration, analogy, and quotation from authority.

1. Par. 1 begins with a simple but dramatic account of Diogenes, a symbol of the eternal seeker of wisdom. In the following paragraph Jarrell refers to the story as one which has meant different things at different times and in different places. How does the author characterize the ages and places that have delighted in this story? What two contrasts developed within this paragraph characterize Diogenes?

2. The comparison prepared for by the first sentence in par. 2 is developed by illustrations in par. 3. From what sources are they drawn?

3. In pars. 4–8 the author imaginatively recreates Diogenes' experience.

How does this reconstruction aid him in developing the comparison begun in pars. 2 and 3? What concrete details describe the American attitude toward the intellectual? What analogy is developed in par. 7? What is its relation to par. 6? Who does *some people* refer to in par. 8? What contemporary allusions are used in this imaginary account of Diogenes' experience?

4. Par. 9 tells what an intellectual does, his characteristic functions. What are they? What other purpose does the paragraph serve?

5. In par. 10 the effects of being an intellectual in America are enumerated. What are they?

6. Analyze the methods by which par. 11 is developed.

7. With what particulars is the analogy in par. 12 developed? What causal relationship is advanced?

8. What particulars develop the thesis of par. 13? What is the author's didactic purpose?

9. In par. 14 what evidence is advanced for the statement that the intellectual likes his American countrymen? What specific purpose is served by the allusions to Tocqueville and Diogenes?

10. How does par. 15 refer to par. 14? How does it prepare for par. 16?

11. Compare the purposes of the two allusions to Eisenhower (pars. 3 and 13).

12. How are intellectuals linked with other victims of stereotyping?

13. By what means does the author suggest the shared characteristics of all intellectuals? What are these characteristics? How does he suggest the differences among intellectuals? What are they?

14. Is Jarrell an intellectual? Relate your answer to his use of *we* and *most of us in* par. 3 and his slightly different use of *we* in par. 16.

DICTION AND TONE

1. What is the author's primary attitude toward his subject? How do you know?

2. What is the author's dominant purpose: to instruct, to persuade, to shock, to outrage, to entertain? Support your conclusion by specific reference to the text.

3. Note the shifts in point of view from the impersonal and detached to the subjective and involved. What cues enable you to identify the point of view? What point of view is dominant? In answering this question, consider the author's reliance on the several voices other than his own: Diogenes, the Voice speaking to Diogenes, and Tocqueville.

4. How is the recurrent allusion to Diogenes ironic? How does it contribute to the unity of the essay? How does it provide emphasis?

5. What extra-literal meanings are conveyed by *he threw away the cup* and *you can get out of my light* (par. 1)?

6. How do the verbs *tipped* and *bribed* convey tone (par. 2)?

7. What purpose is served by the rhetorical questions (par. 3)?

8. What tone is established by the contemporary allusions in pars. 3, 4, and 8?

9. Identify the satire in pars. 4 and 8; the irony in par. 9.

10. Comment on the diction in par. 6 from the point of view of range, source, appropriateness in context, purpose, and tone: *you intellectuals, you highbrows, you long-hairs, you eggheads; you sit there in your ivory tower—really it was a tub; pictures my six-year-old girl can draw better than; to make heads or tails of; why don't you get wise to yourself . . . and think like I think?*

11. How does the analogy in par. 7 contribute to the ironic tone?

12. Discuss the use of the descriptive words *Communist, crazy,* and *feeble-minded* in the context of par. 9. How do they contribute to the bitterness of tone?

13. Justify the use of the word *terrible* in reference to Tocqueville's sentences (par. 11).

14. What rhetorical purpose is served by the coupling of opposites: *smart, dumb; ingenuous, disingenuous; nice, awful* (par. 12)?

15. What tone is conveyed by the allusion, "Forgive us each day our corduroys" (par. 13)? In order to comment on its rhetorical purpose, you will need to understand its source.

16. Why is *The American Way of Life* capitalized in par. 15?

17. Would a more effective word than *fellow* convey the idea expressed in the first sentence of par. 16?

18. Comment on the use of the words *un-American, even,* and *human* in the last two sentences of par. 17.

19. How is irony achieved in the quotation from Lincoln in par. 18?

20. What is the function of the cliché in the last sentence of the essay?

21. Throughout the essay Jarrell makes cogent appeals to the reason and reasonableness of his readers. List a number of his logical and persuasive arguments. He also makes several emotional appeals to the reader. What are they?

APPLICATIONS TO WRITING

1. Develop a causal analysis in which you chart the connection of events: given this cause, what effect will follow? Use Jarrell's statement for your text: "Some of the intellectual's faults are only our imagination, and some are our fault, and some are his fault." Attempt to sustain an allusion or symbol throughout your paper.

2. Write a portrait of an intellectual in which you discuss the characteristics he shares with all intellectuals as well as those which distinguish him as an individual. In making these distinctions, use concrete details to give credibility to your impressions of his mode of life, his convictions, behavior, and personality. If you have no personal acquaintance with an intellectual, select a contemporary or historical figure for your analysis. Draw upon biographical documents and his published writing to develop your essay.

Part Seven

ARGUMENT AND

PERSUASION

Argument and Persuasion are reciprocally related. Formal argument often consists of the following parts: the *proposition*, an assertion that leads to the *issue*; the *issue*, the aspect of the proposition which the writer is attempting to prove and the question on which the whole argument rests; the *evidence*, the facts and opinions which the author offers as testimony. He may order the evidence deductively by proceeding from certain premises to a *conclusion*, or inductively by generalizing from a number of instances and drawing a *conclusion*. Informal arguments frequently make greater use of the methods of exposition than they do of formal logic. Argument is a mode of discourse; *the* argument, a line of reasoning. (See Deduction, Induction, Logic, and Analogy in Glossary.)

The purpose of argument is to persuade. The attempt to distinguish between argument and persuasion is sometimes made by reference to means (argument makes appeals to reason; persuasion, to emotions); sometimes to ends (argument causes someone to change his mind; persuasion moves him to action). These distinctions, however, are more academic than functional, for in practice argument and persuasion are

357

not discrete entities. Yet the proof in argument rests largely upon the objectivity of evidence; the proof in persuasion, upon a subtle and controlled use of language. The diction employed, as well as such literary devices as irony, satire, paradox, metaphor, and allusion, will establish the tone, which in turn may affect the reader's judgment of the objectivity of the evidence and the degree to which he is persuaded by it. The argument in *Freedom and the Responsibility of the Press* is public; the tone, ironic and outspoken. The argument in *Civil Disobedience*, based often on unstated assumptions, constitutes a philosophical inquiry into the nature of man, his conscience, and his government. In *The Subjection of Women* Miss Hardwick develops the argument by focusing on the issue of what in women is given and what is acquired; she brings to bear upon it a rigorous logic, an immense vigor, and a devastating wit. In *What I Believe* Forster persuades by a combination of tough-mindedness and skepticism about his own position. Sartre's argument depends on the resolution of a paradox. In *The Allegory of the Cave*, Plato's consummate power to persuade rests upon the brilliant use of metaphor, the structure of the dialogue, and the unspoken flattery of the reader. Finally, the persuasive power of *A Modest Proposal* lies in its sustained irony: Swift simulates an amorality which is cumulatively revealed in an exaggerated rationality and a view of man which reduces him to an object to be used.

FREEDOM AND
THE RESPONSIBILITY
OF THE PRESS

ROBERT MAYNARD HUTCHINS

In 1930, some twenty-five years ago, I last had the honor of confronting the American Society of Newspaper Editors. The quarter of a century between has been the longest in history. That was a different world, before the Depression, before the New Deal, before the Newspaper Guild, before the suburbs, before they charged for newsprint, before the atom, before television. It was a world in which the press was powerful and numerous. Though the press is powerful still, some eight hundred papers that were alive then are gone now. Twenty-five years hence, when I am eighty-one, where will the press be? [1]

When last here, I said: "The greatest aggregation of educational foundations is the press itself . . . Indeed I notice that in spite of the frightful lies you have printed about me I still believe everything you print about other people . . . If the American press does not need or cannot get the leadership of some endowed newspapers, we

Reprinted by permission of The World Publishing Company from *Freedom, Education, and the Fund* by Robert M. Hutchins, a Meridian Book, Copyright © 1956, by Robert M. Hutchins.

must fall back on the long process of education through educational institutions, hoping that in the long run we may produce a generation that will demand better things of you. This process will be tedious and difficult, because of the power of the press itself over the minds and habits of those whom the educational institutions produce." [2]

Though I am neither prophet nor preacher, my words were not attended. I would merely remind you that a great many men who paid no attention then are not here now. [3]

I joined in another effort in your behalf in 1947, when the Report of the Commission on the Freedom of the Press appeared. The Commission felt a little sad. It said, "The outstanding fact about the communications industry today is that the number of its units has declined." It expressed a high opinion of your role in life, for it said, "Freedom of speech and freedom of the press are moral rights which the state must not infringe." And again, "We must recognize that the agencies of mass communication are an educational instrument, perhaps the most powerful there is." [4]

You were furious. Your president issued a statement in six paragraphs, in three of which he said that the members of the Commission were "left-wing," and in all of which he stated his conviction that, since most of the members of the Commission were professors without experience in the newspaper business, nothing they said could be of any importance, although it might be dangerous. At the meeting of this society in 1947, to which I had expected to be invited to receive your congratulations, the only thing that saved me from condemnation was the express unwillingness of your committee to "dignify" me by such action. [5]

All over the country you attacked the Report. I hope you will read it sometime. But for fear you won't, I shall quote a passage from it that will give you the main idea: "If modern society requires great agencies of mass communication, if these concentrations become so powerful that they are a threat to democracy, if democracy cannot solve the problem simply by breaking them up—then those agencies must control themselves or be controlled by government. If they are controlled by government, we lose our chief safeguard against totalitarianism—and at the same time take a long step toward it." [6]

A kind of neurotic sensitivity is characteristic of the press throughout the English-speaking world. The British papers were outraged by the report of the Royal Commission on the Press, which was almost as mild as ours. I don't know what makes the press feel this way. After all, in this country there is a special amendment to the Constitution, and the first one at that, protecting it. Perhaps it is this special dignity that sometimes leads newspapers to confuse their private interests with those of the public. One of the most celebrated managing editors in the country told our Commission that the only threat to the freedom of the press was the Newspaper Guild and that all we had to do was to adopt a resolution denouncing the Guild and go home. Most papers saw Marshall Field's suit against the AP as the end of freedom of the press. All he wanted to do to the AP was to join it. About once a week you break out in exasperation against anybody who tries to keep anything from you, for reasons of state or for any reason at all. You are the only uncriticized institution in the country. You will not criticize one another, and any suggestion that anybody else might do so sets you to muttering about the First Amendment. [7]

I know that lately life has been hard for you. And it may get even worse; for it may turn out that reading is an anachronism. When I was a boy, reading was the only established and available path to knowledge, information, or even entertainment. But the other day in Hollywood I met a man who was putting the Great Books on records. Everything else has already been put on records or films. One glance at the children making for the television set on their return from school is enough to show that this is a different world.. The habit of reading, which my generation fell into because there was not much else to do, may now not be formed at all; it may have too much competition. [8]

The competition may win. Gresham's Law of Culture is that easy stuff drives out hard. It is harder to read, even after Dr. Flesch has

finished with the printed page, than it is to look and listen. I do not
believe that newspapers can do what comic books, picture magazines,
motion pictures, and television can do in glorious technicolor. Since
they can do this kind of thing better, why should you do it at all? [9]

You may say it is the only way to survive. John Cowles suggests it
may be a way to die. In his Sigma Delta Chi speech he said newspapers have realized that complete and fair. coverage builds circulation. With few exceptions, he said, those newspapers which "have
had the heaviest circulation losses are not papers that regard full and
fair news presentation as their primary function and reason for
existence." If so good a businessman as Mr. Cowles can think there
is *any* chance that sensationalism and entertainment are not good
for business, a layman may perhaps be forgiven for being impressed. [10]

Emboldened by his example, I will say that newspapers should do
as well as they can the things that they can do best, and they should
leave to others the responsibility of entertaining the public. If you are
worried about who is going to discharge that responsibility, read the
March 21, 1955 issue of *Newsweek*, which says that television is
abandoning "Johns Hopkins Science Review," "Princeton, '55," and
"The Search." These programs have won many honors and audiences
that look large to people who do not work in advertising agencies. [11]

A couple of years ago Henry Luce was discussing the monopoly
newspaper. He said the argument against it was that it deprived the
community of differing presentations of news and opinions. He went
on, "Like so many high-brow discussions about newspapers (I notice
that journalists invariably use the word 'high-brow' when referring to
criticisms of the press, even when, as in this case, the truth of the
criticism is self-evident to the merest moron) this one is fine, except
that it ignores the actual nature of a newspaper. Does any one feel
strongly that a city ought to have several newspapers in order to offer
the community a greater variety of comic strips, breakfast menus, and
cheesecake?" If this is the actual nature of a newspaper, the fewer
papers the better. Certainly the special constitutional protection
thrown about them seems no more warranted than such protection

would be for acrobats, chefs, beauty parlor operators, and astrologers. [12]

What the framers of the First Amendment had in mind was debate, a great continuing debate, with the people hearing all sides and getting all the facts. If government could be kept from interfering with this debate, nothing could interfere with it; for a man who differed with the existing papers could start one of his own. The Founding Fathers did not foresee that 94 per cent of American cities and eighteen American states would be without competing papers. In the overwhelming majority of communities there can now be no debate among rival editors. The editor in a one-paper town has the only voice there is, and the only one there is likely to be. The debate has become a soliloquy. [13]

Talk about the virtues of monopoly is the flimsiest rationalization, as is shown by the poor quality of the papers in many monopoly towns. Monopoly cannot be a good thing. At its best it can be like a benevolent despotism, good while the benevolence lasts, but an accident in any case. Monopoly may in the present state of affairs be a necessary evil, but let us not pretend that it is not an evil. [14]

Rising costs have put the publisher in the driver's seat, where he has no business to be. The First Amendment was not instituted to give a preferred position to people who were making money out of papers as against those who were making money out of other articles of commerce. The Amendment was to protect the content of the press, not the cash return from it. The reason the publisher is in the driver's seat is that it costs so much money to own and operate a newspaper, and more all the time. If the soliloquy is that of one of the richest men in town, it is more than likely that it will sound the same political note as other soliloquies in other towns, rendered by other rich men. This is the basis of the phrase, "a one-party press." [15]

Of course we have a one-party press in this country, and we shall have one as long as the press is big business, and as long as people with money continue to feel safer on the Republican side. For sheer psalm-singing sanctimoniousness no statement in recent years has surpassed that of Charles F. McCahill, president of the American

Newspaper Publishers Association, when he was asked to comment on
Adlai Stevenson's polite remarks on a one-party press. Mr. McCahill
said, and I quote him: "It is the responsibility of the individual
editor and publisher to decide what is printed in a particular newspaper. Fortunately, there is no power in this country to standardize
the editorial views of any editor or publisher." Here in two sentences
Mr. McCahill managed (1) to say what everybody knew already;
(2) to be completely irrelevant; and (3) to prove Mr. Stevenson's
point for him by making the partisan insinuation that Mr. Stevenson
wanted the power to standardize editorial opinion. How you get
along with these publishers is more than I can understand. [16]

Lord Beaverbrook, when he was asked by the Royal Commission on
the Press what his purpose in life was, replied under oath: "I run the
paper purely for the purpose of making propaganda, and with no
other motive." (There is apparently less cant among publishers in
England than we are accustomed to here.) Lord Beaverbrook's propaganda collides wherever it goes with the counter-propaganda of
numerous local and national voices. The popular press in Britain is
the most sensational in the world, but an Englishman who doesn't
want a sensational newspaper does not have to take the *Mirror*.
Because of the geography of England he can get anywhere, inex-
pensively, and usually with his breakfast, a presentation of the news
as fair as an editor can make it and as full as the restrictions on newsprint will allow, together with serious commentary upon it. [17]

In the absence of some new technological revolution the number of
papers per community in this country seems unlikely to increase.
Nothing suggests that costs will fall. Television and suburbanization
are driving ahead as fast as they can go. As monopoly continues to
spread, the ancient check of competition can of course no longer be
relied on. [18]

This should lead to the burial of that consoling reference to Jefferson's Second Inaugural, an ever-present refuge in time of criticism,
which made its last formal appearance in the statement of your committee commenting on the Report of the Commission on the Freedom
of the Press. Jefferson said, in effect, that the people would make their

views of a newspaper felt by refusing to read, believe, or buy it. The theory that the daily test of the market place is an expression of public criticism, and all that is needed, is reduced to absurdity when the public has no option, when it has to buy the newspaper that is offered or go without. [19]

If we cannot look to competition to keep publishers from getting out of hand, what can we do to save their freedom from the consequences of their irresponsibility? My youthful suggestion of some endowed newspapers was designed to execute some publishers *pour encourager les autres*. The object was to set some standards that publishers of unendowed newspapers might be held to. I take this proposal less seriously than I did twenty-five years ago. The *Christian Science Monitor* undoubtedly has a good influence on the press of this country, but the conditions under which it operates, with its foundations in heaven rather than on earth, are so different from the ordinary that any publisher has an adequate excuse for not following the *Monitor's* example. So I fear it would be with an endowed newspaper. [20]

A trust such as that which controls the future of the Washington *Post* regulates the selection of stockholders, but gives the editor no explicit protection. The British trusts usually have the same object, that of preventing the ownership from falling into unsuitable hands. Although the British trusts reflect an attitude that an editor would find reassuring, no trust covering a daily newspaper leaves him formally any better off than he would be if there were no trust. The most that the Royal Commission was willing to say was, "A trust does not necessarily convert a newspaper from a commercial to a non-commercial concern or give it quality which it did not possess . . . A trust can be, however, a valuable means of preserving quality where quality already exists. We accordingly welcome the action of public-spirited proprietors who have taken such steps as lie in their power to safeguard the character and independence of their papers; and we hope that the number of papers so protected will grow." [21]

A publisher's willingness to establish a trust shows that he could be trusted without it; still it is a way of extending the benevolence of the benevolent despot beyond the limits of his own life. When you have a newspaper worth protecting, a trust will help you protect it; but a trust does not guarantee you a newspaper worth protecting. [22]

The purpose of a newspaper, and the justification for the privileges of the press, is the enlightenment of the people about their current affairs. No other medium of communication can compete with the newspaper in the performance of this task. A newspaper that is doing this job well is a good newspaper, no matter how deficient it may be in astrology, menus, comics, cheesecake, crime, and Republican propaganda. A newspaper that is doing this job deserves protection against government, and it will certainly need it. [23]

A newspaper that is doing this job will have to bring before its readers points of view with which it disagrees and facts that it deplores. Otherwise in monopoly towns the people cannot expect to be enlightened; for television and radio are unlikely to be in the same class with a well-run newspaper in telling what is happening and what it means. Television and radio are, moreover, controlled by a governmental agency, and one that does not inspire much confidence today. [24]

A good many newspapers take seriously their responsibility to enlighten the people about current affairs. It is generally agreed that the best American papers are as good as any in the world and that the average is high. Our question is how to maintain the good newspapers in the faith and how to convert the others. [25]

I think the opposition to the principal recommendation of the Commission on the Freedom of the Press ought to be reconsidered. This recommendation was that a new agency be established to appraise and report annually upon the performance of the press. The Commission said, "It seems to us clear that some agency which reflects the ambitions of the American people for its press should exist for the purpose of comparing the accomplishments of the press with the aspirations which the people have for it. Such an agency would also educate the people as to the aspirations which they ought to have for the press." The Commission suggested that this agency be independent of government and of the press; that it be created by gifts;

and that it be given a ten-year trial, at the end of which an audit of its achievement could determine anew the institutional form best adapted to its purposes. The fact that the British commission independently reached an identical recommendation seems to me highly significant. [26]

Such an agency should contain representatives of the press; it should also contain laymen. My guess is that the weakness of the Press Council in Sweden results from the fact that it is composed entirely of representatives of the newspapers. I believe that the British Council will go the same way because the press rejected the recommendation of the Royal Commission that the Council should have lay members and a lay chairman. If its first report is suggestive of its future, this group is likely to manifest its fearless and high-principled character by speaking sternly to newspapers on trivial subjects. [27]

The Nieman Reports, the Press Institute statements, A. J. Liebling's "Wayward Press," Robert Lasch in the *Progressive*, occasional studies by schools of journalism, these are all we have in this country. They are too casual and limited, and, since most of them are directed at the press, they do not perform one function that the Commission on the Freedom of the Press regarded as essential: they do not "educate the people as to the aspirations which they ought to have for the press." [28]

Your own efforts to act as a critical agency have come to nothing. You appointed a committee in 1949 "to examine the desirability of sponsoring an appraisal of the self-improvement possibilities of American newspapers." The Committee reported in 1950 as follows: "Our Committee recognizes and reiterates that the American Society of Newspaper Editors is, itself, and must be, a continuing committee of the whole on self-examination and self-improvement. But, in addition, we urge the Society to call upon its Board of Directors to take whatever action may be necessary from time to time to clarify understanding of American newspapers by the public, and to keep editors alert to their responsibilities in fulfilling the public's right to an adequate, independent newspaper press." [29]

That sounds as though it was written by a public relations man. In these sonorous sentences we hear the cadence of the Psalms. [30]

The great issues of our time are peace and freedom. A new critical agency might appraise the performance of the newspapers in correcting, or contributing to, our vast confusion on these subjects. We know that the peoples of the earth are now equipped to turn one another into radioactive cinders. Can you say that the press has given Americans the material they need to reach a conclusion on the course they should follow, on the choice between co-existence and no existence, the choice between seeking peace through purchase and intimidation and seeking it through total, enforceable disarmament, the choice between competing nationalisms and world law? [31]

And what of freedom in the garrison state? Since most of you take the official line, that the only important fact of life is our imminent danger from international conspiracy, most of you have watched the erosion of freedom without a twinge. When the official line permitted, you have sallied forth, as when you gallantly led the troops from the rear in a belated attack on Senator McCarthy. You have filled the air with warnings of the sinister figures on the Left, but have printed almost nothing about the fat cats on the Right. You have allowed things to get to such a pass that some government departments now have guidance clinics in which the employee is taught how not to look like a security risk. Look at the Passport Division, interfering with the travel of Americans on their lawful occasions; at the Attorney-General's list, ruining the lives of thousands on the basis of hearsay; at the Post Office Department, saving us from *Pravda* and Aristophanes; at the State Department, adding the name of Corsi to those of Davies and Service and countless others. See the blacklist spreading in industry, merging with proposals that American Communists should be starved to death. Listen to the wire-tapping, to the cry of Fifth Amendment Communist, to the kept witnesses roaming the land. The most distressing part of it is not that these things happen, but that the free press of this country appears to regard them as matters of routine. [32]

You are educators, whether you like it or not. You make the views that people have of public affairs. No competition can shake you from that position. You will lose it only if you neglect or abandon it. As the number of papers per community declines, the responsibility of each one that remains increases. This is a responsibility that is discharged by being a newspaper, by giving the news. The editorial function is to make sure that it is given in such a way that it can be understood. The people must see the alternatives before them; otherwise they cannot be enlightened. [33]

Enlightenment means telling the people where they are in time and space. It means engaging in systematic criticism. The criticism of current affairs has to be made in the light of some standard. This must be something more than a set of partisan slogans. The standard by which the American press must judge current events is derived from an understanding of and sympathy with the deepest aspirations of the American people, those for peace and freedom. A press that serves its country in this way need have no concern about the future. [34]

PURPOSE AND STRUCTURE

1. What is the purpose of Hutchins' argument? Is he so outspoken as to be unpersuasive? Note the many ironic and even sarcastic sallies in his speech. Would he be more persuasive if he were more serious? Had he made tactful and flattering remarks to his audience would his argument be more acceptable? There is, however, a powerful and unspoken flattery in Hutchins' talk. Can you identify it?

2. Identify Hutchins' *proposition:* what does he assert is a fact?

3. Identify the *issue:* on what question does his argument rest?

4. Identify the *evidence:* from what facts and opinions does he draw?

5. From what premises does he move to a *conclusion?* Identify the conclusion.

6. From what *instances* does he generalize? Enumerate them.

7. Analyze the way that Hutchins establishes transitions between pars. 8-11.

DICTION AND TONE

1. Why does Hutchins use the word *confronting* in the first sentence of his talk?

2. In par. 3 does Hutchins mean that those who did not follow his advice died?

3. Why does he say the Report was criticized as unimportant, *although it might be dangerous* (par. 5)? Is this logically possible? Has he made a mistake in logic?

4. *All over the country you attacked the Report. I hope you will read it sometime.* (par. 6) Is this too blunt to be persuasive?

5. Why is the list which ends par. 12 appropriate?

6. Is the last sentence of par. 16 serious or humorous? Both?

7. What does the word *execute* mean in par. 20? Is Hutchins ironic?

APPLICATIONS TO WRITING

Hutchins' argument is outspoken and witty. He does not pull his punches. Is he persuasive? Present an argument before a Faculty Publications Board which has suppressed or censored stories in the school paper. Argue for freedom of the press, for the right of students to publish the paper without interference. Be forthright and yet persuasive. Remember that respect for an audience's intelligence and integrity can be expressed in your argument and tone; it need not be stated.

From ON THE DUTY OF
CIVIL DISOBEDIENCE

HENRY   DAVID   THOREAU

I heartily accept the motto, "That government is best which governs least"; and I should like to see it acted up to more rapidly and systematically. Carried out, it finally amounts to this, which also I believe—"That government is best which governs not at all"; and when men are prepared for it, that will be the kind of government which they will have. Government is at best but an expedient; but most governments are usually, and all governments are sometimes, inexpedient. The objections which have been brought against a standing army, and they are many and weighty, and deserve to prevail, may also at last be brought against a standing government. The standing army is only an arm of the standing government. The government itself, which is only the mode which the people have chosen to execute their will, is equally liable to be abused and perverted before the people can act through it. Witness the present Mexican war, the work of comparatively a few individuals using the standing government as their tool; for, in the outset, the people would not have consented to this measure. [1]

This American government—what is it but a tradition, though a recent one, endeavoring to transmit itself unimpaired to posterity,

Reprinted by permission of Houghton Mifflin Company.

but each instant losing some of its integrity? It has not the vitality and force of a single living man; for a single man can bend it to his will. It is a sort of wooden gun to the people themselves. But it is not the less necessary for this; for the people must have some complicated machinery or other, and hear its din, to satisfy that idea of government which they have. Governments show thus how successfully men can be imposed on, even impose on themselves, for their own advantage. It is excellent, we must all allow. Yet this government never of itself furthered any enterprise, but by the alacrity with which it got out of its way. *It* does not keep the country free. *It* does not settle the West. *It* does not educate. The character inherent in the American people has done all that has been accomplished; and it would have done somewhat more, if the government had not sometimes got in its way. For government is an expedient by which men would fain succeed in letting one another alone; and, as has been said, when it is most expedient, the governed are most let alone by it. Trade and commerce, if they were not made of india-rubber, would never manage to bounce over the obstacles which legislators are continually putting in their way and, if one were to judge these men wholly by the effects of their actions and not partly by their intentions, they would deserve to be classed and punished with those mischievous persons who put obstructions on the railroads. [2]

But, to speak practically and as a citizen, unlike those who call themselves no-government men, I ask for, not at once no government, but *at once* a better government. Let every man make known what kind of government would command his respect, and that will be one step toward obtaining it. [3]

After all, the practical reason why, when the power is once in the hands of the people, a majority are permitted, and for a long period continue, to rule is not because they are most likely to be in the right, nor because this seems fairest to the minority, but because they are physically the strongest. But a government in which the majority rule in all cases cannot be based on justice, even as far as men understand it. Can there not be a government in which majorities do not virtually decide right and wrong, but conscience?—in which majorities decide only those questions to which the rule of expediency is applicable? Must the citizen ever for a moment, or in the least degree, resign his conscience to the legislator? Why has every man a conscience, then? I think that we should be men first, and subjects afterwards. It is not desirable to cultivate a respect for the law, so much as for the right. The only obligation which I have a right to assume is to do at any time what I think right. It is truly enough said that a corporation has no conscience; but a corporation of conscientious men is a corporation *with* a conscience. Law never made men a whit more just; and, by means of their respect for it, even the well-disposed are daily made the agents of injustice. A common and natural result of an undue respect for law is, that you may see a file of soldiers, colonel, captain, corporal, privates, powder-monkeys, and all, marching in admirable order over hill and dale to the wars, against their wills, ay, against their common sense and consciences, which makes it very steep marching indeed, and produces a palpitation of the heart. They have no doubt that it is a damnable business in which they are concerned; they are all peaceably inclined. Now, what are they? Men at all? or small movable forts and magazines, at the service of some unscrupulous man in power? Visit the Navy-Yard, and behold a marine, such a man as an American government can make, or such as it can make a man with its black arts—a mere shadow and reminiscence of humanity, a man laid out alive and standing, and already, as one may say, buried under arms with funeral accompaniments, though it may be,—

> "Not a drum was heard, not a funeral note,
>   As his corse to the rampart we hurried;
> Not a soldier discharged his farewell shot
>   O'er the grave where our hero was buried." [4]

The mass of men serve the state thus, not as men mainly, but as machines, with their bodies. They are the standing army, and the militia, jailers, constables, *posse comitatus*, etc. In most cases there is no free exercise whatever of the judgment or of the moral sense; but they put themselves on a level with wood and earth and stones; and wooden men can perhaps be manufactured that will serve the pur-

pose as well. Such command no more respect than men of straw or a
lump of dirt. They have the same sort of worth only as horses and
dogs. Yet such as these even are commonly esteemed good citizens.
Others—as most legislators, politicians, lawyers, ministers, and office-
holders—serve the state chiefly with their heads; and, as they rarely
make any moral distinctions, they are as likely to serve the devil,
without *intending* it, as God. A very few—as heroes, patriots, martyrs,
reformers in the great sense, and men—serve the state with their
consciences also, and so necessarily resist it for the most part; and they
are commonly treated as enemies by it. A wise man will only be
useful as a man, and will not submit to be "clay," and "stop a hole to
keep the wind away," but leave that office to his dust at least:—

> "I am too high-born to be propertied,
> To be a secondary at control,
> Or useful serving-man and instrument
> To any sovereign state throughout the world." [5]

He who gives himself entirely to his fellowmen appears to them
useless and selfish; but he who gives himself partially to them is
pronounced a benefactor and philanthropist. [6]

How does it become a man to behave toward this American government today? I answer, that he cannot without disgrace be associated with it. I cannot for an instant recognize that political organization as *my* government which is the *slave's* government also. [7]

All men recognize the right of revolution; that is, the right to refuse
allegiance to, and to resist, the government, when its tyranny or its
inefficiency are great and unendurable. But almost all say that such
is not the case now. But such was the case, they think, in the Revolution of '75. If one were to tell me that this was a bad government
because it taxed certain foreign commodities brought to its ports, it
is most probable that I should not make an ado about it, for I can
do without them. All machines have their friction; and possibly this
does enough good to counter-balance the evil. At any rate, it is a
great evil to make a stir about it. But when the friction comes to have
its machine, and oppression and robbery are organized, I say, let us

not have such a machine any longer. In other words, when a sixth of the population of a nation which has undertaken to be the refuge of liberty are slaves, and a whole country is unjustly overrun and conquered by a foreign army, and subjected to military law, I think that it is not too soon for honest men to rebel and revolutionize. What makes this duty the more urgent is the fact that the country so overrun is not our own, but ours is the invading army. [8]

Paley, a common authority with many on moral questions, in his chapter on the "Duty of Submission to Civil Government," resolves all civil obligation into expediency; and he proceeds to say that "so long as the interest of the whole society requires it, that is, so long as the established government cannot be resisted or changed without public inconveniency, it is the will of God . . . that the established government be obeyed—and no longer. This principle being admitted, the justice of every particular case of resistance is reduced to a computation of the quantity of the danger and grievance on the one side, and of the probability and expense of redressing it on the other." Of this, he says, every man shall judge for himself. But Paley appears never to have contemplated those cases to which the rule of expediency does not apply, in which a people, as well as an individual, must do justice, cost what it may. If I have unjustly wrested a plank from a drowning man, I must restore it to him though I drown myself. This, according to Paley, would be inconvenient. But he that would save his life, in such a case, shall lose it. This people must cease to hold slaves, and to make war on Mexico, though it cost them their existence as a people. [9]

In their practice, nations agree with Paley; but does any one think that Massachusetts does exactly what is right at the present crisis?

> "A drab of state, a cloth-o'-silver slut,
> To have her train borne up, and her soul trail in the dirt."

Practically speaking, the opponents to a reform in Massachusetts are not a hundred thousand politicians at the South, but a hundred thousand merchants and farmers here, who are more interested in commerce and agriculture than they are in humanity, and are not prepared to do justice to the slave and to Mexico, *cost what it may*. I quarrel not with far-off foes, but with those who, near at home, co-öperate with, and do the bidding of, those far away, and without whom the latter would be harmless. We are accustomed to say, that the mass of men are unprepared; but improvement is slow, because the few are not materially wiser or better than the many. It is not so important that many should be as good as you, as that there be some absolute goodness somewhere; for that will leaven the whole lump. There are thousands who are *in opinion* opposed to slavery and to the war, who yet in effect do nothing to put an end to them; who, esteeming themselves children of Washington and Franklin, sit down with their hands in their pockets, and say that they know not what to do, and do nothing; who even postpone the question of free-dom to the question of free trade, and quietly read the prices-current along with the latest advices from Mexico, after dinner, and, it may be, fall asleep over them both. What is the price-current of an honest man and patriot today? They hesitate, and they regret, and sometimes they petition; but they do nothing in earnest and with effect. They will wait, well disposed, for others to remedy the evil, that they may no longer have it to regret. At most, they give only a cheap vote, and a feeble countenance and God-speed, to the right, as it goes by them. There are nine hundred and ninety-nine patrons of virtue to one virtuous man. But it is easier to deal with the real possessor of a thing than with the temporary guardian of it. [10]

All voting is a sort of gaming, like checkers or backgammon, with a slight moral tinge to it, a playing with right and wrong, with moral questions; and betting naturally accompanies it. The character of the voters is not staked. I cast my vote, perchance, as I think right; but I am not vitally concerned that right should prevail. I am willing to leave it to the majority. Its obligation, therefore, never exceeds that of expediency. Even voting *for the right* is *doing* nothing for it. It is only expressing to men feebly your desire that it should pre-vail. A wise man will not leave the right to the mercy of chance, nor wish it to prevail through the power of the majority. There is but little virtue in the action of masses of men. When the majority shall at length vote for the abolition of slavery, it will be because they are indifferent to slavery, or because there is but little slavery left to be abolished by their vote. *They* will then be the only slaves. Only *his* vote can hasten the abolition of slavery who asserts his own freedom by his vote. [11]

I hear of a convention to be held at Baltimore, or elsewhere, for the selection of a candidate for the Presidency, made up chiefly of editors, and men who are politicians by profession; but I think, what is it to any independent, intelligent, and respectable man what decision they may come to? Shall we not have the advantage of his wisdom and honesty, nevertheless? Can we not count upon some independent votes? Are there not many individuals in the country who do not attend conventions? But no: I find that the respectable man, so called, has immediately drifted from his position, and despairs of his country, when his country has more reason to despair of him. He forthwith adopts one of the candidates thus selected as the only *available* one, thus proving that he is himself *available* for any purposes of the demagogue. His vote is of no more worth than that of any unprincipled foreigner or hireling native, who may have been bought. O for a man who is a *man*, and, as my neighbor says, has a bone in his back which you cannot pass your hand through! Our statistics are at fault: the population has been returned too large. How many *men* are there to a square thousand miles in this country? Hardly one. Does not America offer any inducement for men to settle here? The American has dwindled into an Odd Fellow—one who may be known by the development of his organ of gregariousness, and a manifest lack of intellect and cheerful self-reliance; whose first and chief concern, on coming into the world, is to see that the almshouses are in good repair; and, before yet he has lawfully donned the virile garb, to collect a fund for the support of the widows and orphans that may be; who, in short, ventures to live only by the aid of the Mutual Insurance Company, which has promised to bury him decently. [12]

It is not a man's duty, as a matter of course, to devote himself to the eradication of any, even the most enormous, wrong; he may still properly have other concerns to engage him; but it is his duty, at least, to wash his hands of it, and, if he gives it no thought longer, not to give it practically his support. If I devote myself to other pursuits and contemplations, I must first see, at least, that I do not pursue them sitting upon another man's shoulders. I must get off him first, that he may pursue his contemplations too. See what gross inconsistency is tolerated. I have heard some of my townsmen say, "I should like to have them order me out to help put down an insurrection of the slaves, or to march to Mexico;—see if I would go"; and yet these very men have each, directly by their allegiance, and so indirectly, at least, by their money, furnished a substitute. The soldier is applauded who refuses to serve in an unjust war by those who do not refuse to sustain the unjust government which makes the war; is applauded by those whose own act and authority he disregards and sets at naught; as if the state were penitent to that degree that it hired one to scourge it while it sinned, but not to that degree that it left off sinning for a moment. Thus, under the name of Order and Civil Government, we are all made at last to pay homage to and support our own mean-ness. After the first blush of sin comes its indifference; and from immoral it becomes, as it were, *un*moral, and not quite unneccessary to that life which we have made. [13]

The broadest and most prevalent error requires the most disinter-ested virtue to sustain it. The slight reproach to which the virtue of patriotism is commonly liable, the noble are most likely to incur. Those who, while they disapprove of the character and measures of a government, yield to it their allegiance and support are undoubtedly its most conscientious supporters, and so frequently the most serious obstacles to reform. Some are petitioning the State to dissolve the Union, to disregard the requisitions of the President. Why do they not dissolve it themselves—the union between themselves and the State—and refuse to pay their quota into its treasury? Do not they stand in the same relation to the State that the State does to the Union? And have not the same reasons prevented the State from resisting the Union which have prevented them from resisting the State? [14]

How can a man be satisfied to entertain an opinion merely, and enjoy *it*? Is there any enjoyment in it, if his opinion is that he is aggrieved? If you are cheated out of a single dollar by your neighbor, you do not rest satisfied with knowing that you are cheated, or with saying that you are cheated, or even with petitioning him to pay you your due; but you take effectual steps at once to obtain the full amount, and see that you are never cheated again. Action from principle, the perception and the performance of right, changes things and relations; it is essentially revolutionary, and does not consist wholly with anything which was. It not only divides States and churches, it divides families; ay, it divides the *individual*, separating the diabolical in him from the divine. [15]

Unjust laws exist; shall we be content to obey them, or shall we endeavor to amend them, and obey them until we have succeeded, or shall we transgress them at once? Men generally, under such a government as this, think that they ought to wait until they have persuaded the majority to alter them. They think that, if they should resist, the remedy would be worse than the evil. But it is the fault of the government itself that the remedy *is* worse than the evil. It makes it worse. Why is it not more apt to anticipate and provide for reform? Why does it not cherish its wise minority? Why does it cry and resist before it is hurt? Why does it not encourage its citizens to be on the alert to point out its faults, and *do* better than it would have them? Why does it always crucify Christ, and excommunicate Copernicus and Luther, and pronounce Washington and Franklin rebels? [16]

One would think, that a deliberate and practical denial of its authority was the only offence never contemplated by government; else, why has it not assigned its definite, its suitable and proportionate, penalty? If a man who has no property refuses but once to earn nine shillings for the State, he is put in prison for a period unlimited by any law that I know, and determined only by the discretion of those who placed him there; but if he should steal ninety times nine shillings from the State, he is soon permitted to go at large again. [17]

If the injustice is part of the necessary friction of the machine of government, let it go, let it go: perchance it will wear smooth—certainly the machine will wear out. If the injustice has a spring, or a pulley, or a rope, or a crank, exclusively for itself, then perhaps you may consider whether the remedy will not be worse than the evil; but if it is of such a nature that it requires you to be the agent of injustice to another, then, I say, break the law. Let your life be a counter friction to stop the machine. What I have to do is to see, at any rate, that I do not lend myself to the wrong which I condemn. [18]

As for adopting the ways which the State has provided for remedying the evil, I know not of such ways. They take too much time, and a man's life will be gone. I have other affairs to attend to. I came into this world, not chiefly to make this a good place to live in, but to live in it, be it good or bad. A man has not everything to do, but something; and because he cannot do *everything*, it is not necessary that he should do *something* wrong. It is not my business to be petitioning the Governor or the Legislature any more than it is theirs to petition me; and if they should not hear my petition, what should I do then? But in this case the State has provided no way; its very Constitution is the evil. This may seem to be harsh and stubborn and unconciliatory; but it is to treat with the utmost kindness and consideration the only spirit that can appreciate or deserves it. So is all change for the better, like birth and death, which convulse the body. [19]

I do not hesitate to say, that those who call themselves Abolitionists should at once effectually withdraw their support, both in person and property, from the government of Massachusetts, and not wait till they constitute a majority of one, before they suffer the right to prevail through them. I think that it is enough if they have God on their side, without waiting for that other one. Moreover, any man more right than his neighbors constitutes a majority of one already. [20]

I meet this American government, or its representative, the State government, directly, and face to face, once a year—no more—in the person of its tax-gatherer; this is the only mode in which a man situated as I am necessarily meets it; and it then says distinctly, Recognize me; and the simplest, the most effectual, and, in the present posture of affairs, the indispensablest mode of treating with it on this head, of expressing your little satisfaction with and love for it, is to deny it then. My civil neighbor, the tax-gatherer, is the very man I have to deal with—for it is, after all, with men and not with parchment that I quarrel—and he has voluntarily chosen to be an agent of the government. How shall he ever know well what he is and does as an officer of the government, or as a man, until he is obliged to consider whether he shall treat me, his neighbor, for whom he has respect, as a neighbor and well-disposed man, or as a maniac and disturber of the peace, and see if he can get over this obstruction to his neighborliness without a ruder and more impetuous thought or speech corresponding with his action. I know this well, that if one thousand, if one hundred, if ten men whom I could name—if ten *honest* men only—ay, if *one* HONEST man, in this State of Massachusetts, *ceasing to hold slaves*, were actually to withdraw from this copartnership, and be locked up in the county jail therefor, it would be the abolition of slavery in America. For it matters not how small the beginning may seem to be: what is once well done is done forever. But we love better talk about it: that we say is our mission. Reform keeps many scores of newspapers in its service, but not one man. If my esteemed neighbor, the State's ambassador, who will devote his days to the settlement of the question of human rights in the Council Chamber, instead of being threatened with the prisons of Carolina, were to sit down the prisoner of Massachusetts, that State which is so anxious to foist the sin of slavery upon her sister—though at present she can discover only an act of inhospitality to be the ground of a quarrel with her—the Legislature would not wholly waive the subject the following winter. [21]

Under a government which imprisons any unjustly, the true place for a just man is also a prison. The proper place to-day, the only place which Massachusetts has provided for her freer and less desponding spirits, is in her prisons, to be put out and locked out of the State by her own act, as they have already put themselves out by their principles. It is there that the fugitive slave, and the Mexican prisoner on parole, and the Indian come to plead the wrongs of his race should find them; on that separate, but more free and honorable, ground, where the State places those who are not *with* her, but *against* her—the only house in a slave State in which a free man can abide with honor. If any think that their influence would be lost there, and their voices no longer afflict the ear of the State, that they would not be as an enemy within its walls, they do not know by how much truth is stronger than error, nor how much more eloquently and effectively he can combat injustice who has experienced a little in his own person. Cast your whole vote, not a strip of paper merely, but your whole influence. A minority is powerless while it conforms to the majority; it is not even a minority then; but it is irresistible when it clogs by its whole weight. If the alternative is to keep all just men in prison, or give up war and slavery, the State will not hesitate which to choose. If a thousand men were not to pay their tax-bills this year, that would not be a violent and bloody measure, as it would be to pay them, and enable the State to commit violence and shed innocent blood. This is, in fact, the definition of a peaceable revolution, if any such is possible. If the tax-gatherer, or any other public officer, asks me, as one has done, "But what shall I do?" my answer is, "If you really wish to do anything, resign your office." When the subject has refused allegiance, and the officer has resigned his office, then the revolution is accomplished. But even suppose blood should flow. Is there not a sort of blood shed when the conscience is wounded? Through this wound a man's real manhood and immortality flow out, and he bleeds to an everlasting death. I see this blood flowing now. [22]

I have contemplated the imprisonment of the offender, rather than the seizure of his goods—though both will serve the same purpose—because they who assert the purest right, and consequently are most dangerous to a corrupt State, commonly have not spent much time in accumulating property. To such the State renders comparatively small service, and a slight tax is wont to appear exorbitant, particularly if they are obliged to earn it by special labor with their hands. If there were one who lived wholly without the use of money, the State itself would hesitate to demand it of him. But the rich man— not to make any invidious comparison—is always sold to the institution which makes him rich. Absolutely speaking, the more money, the less virtue; for money comes between a man and his objects, and obtains them for him; and it was certainly no great virtue to obtain it. It puts to rest many questions which he would otherwise be taxed to answer; while the only new question which it puts is the hard but superfluous one, how to spend it. Thus his moral ground is taken from under his feet. The opportunities of living are diminished in proportion as what are called the "means" are increased. The best thing a man can do for his culture when he is rich is to endeavor to carry out those schemes which he entertained when he was poor. Christ answered the Herodians according to their condition. "Show me the tribute-money," said he;—and one took a penny out of his pocket;—if you use money which has the image of Caesar on it, and which he has made current and valuable, that is, *if you are men of the State*, and gladly enjoy the advantages of Caesar's government, then pay him back some of his own when he demands it. "Render therefore to Caesar that which is Caesar's, and to God those things which are God's"—leaving them no wiser than before as to which was which; for they did not wish to know. [23]

When I converse with the freest of my neighbors, I perceive that, whatever they may say about the magnitude and seriousness of the question, and their regard for the public tranquillity, the long and the short of the matter is, that they cannot spare the protection of the existing government, and they dread the consequences to their property and families of disobedience to it. For my own part, I should not like to think that I ever rely on the protection of the State. But, if I deny the authority of the State when it presents its tax-bill, it will soon take and waste all my property, and so harass me and my children without end. This is hard. This makes it impossible for a man to live honestly, and at the same time comfortably, in outward respects. It will not be worth the while to accumulate property; that would be sure to go again. You must hire or squat somewhere, and raise but a small crop, and eat that soon. You must live within yourself, and depend upon yourself always tucked up and ready for a start, and not have many affairs. A man may grow rich in Turkey even, if he will be in all respects a good subject of the Turkish government. Confucius said: "If a state is governed by the principles of reason, poverty and misery are subjects of shame; if a state is not governed by the principles of reason, riches and honors are the subjects of shame." No: until I want the protection of Massachusetts to be extended to me in some distant Southern port, where my liberty is endangered, or until I am bent solely on building up an estate at home by peaceful enterprise, I can afford to refuse allegiance to Massachusetts, and her right to my property and life. It costs me less in every sense to incur the penalty of disobedience to the State than it would to obey. I should feel as if I were worth less in that case. [24]

Some years ago, the State met me in behalf of the Church, and commanded me to pay a certain sum toward the support of a clergyman whose preaching my father attended, but never I myself. "Pay," it said, "or be locked up in the jail." I declined to pay. But, unfortunately, another man saw fit to pay it. I did not see why the school master should be taxed to support the priest, and not the priest the schoolmaster; for I was not the State's schoolmaster, but I supported myself by voluntary subscription. I did not see why the lyceum should not present its tax-bill, and have the State to back its demand, as well as the Church. However, at the request of the selectmen, I condescended to make some such statement as this in writing:—"Know all men by these presents, that I, Henry Thoreau, do not wish to be regarded as a member of any incorporated society which I have not joined." This I gave to the town clerk; and he has it. The State, having thus learned that I did not wish to be regarded as a member of that church, has never made a like demand on me since; though it said that it must adhere to its original presumption that time. If I had known how to name them, I should then have signed off in detail from all the societies which I never signed on to; but I did not know where to find a complete list. [25]

I have paid no poll-tax for six years. I was put into a jail once on this account, for one night; and, as I stood considering the walls of solid stone, two or three feet thick, the door of wood and iron, a foot thick, and the iron grating which strained the light, I could not help being struck with the foolishness of that institution which treated me as if I were mere flesh and blood and bones to be locked up. I wondered that it should have concluded at length that this was the best use it could put me to, and had never thought to avail itself of my services in some way. I saw that, if there was a wall of stone between me and my townsmen, there was a still more difficult one to climb or break through before they could get to be as free as I was. I did not for a moment feel confined, and the walls seemed a great waste of stone and mortar. I felt as if I alone of all my townsmen had paid my tax. They plainly did not know how to treat me, but behaved like persons who are underbred. In every threat and in every compliment there was a blunder; for they thought that my chief desire was to stand the other side of that stone wall. I could not but smile to see how industriously they locked the door on my meditations, which followed them out again without let or hindrance, and *they* were really all that was dangerous. As they could not reach me, they had resolved to punish my body; just as boys, if they cannot come at some person against whom they have a spite, will abuse his dog. I saw that the State was half-witted, that it was timid as a lone woman with her silver spoons, and that it did not know its friends from its foes, and I lost all my remaining respect for it, and pitied it. [26]

Thus the State never intentionally confronts a man's sense, intellectual or moral, but only his body, his senses. It is not armed with superior wit or honesty, but with superior physical strength. I was not born to be forced. I will breathe after my own fashion. Let us see who is the strongest. What force has a multitude? They only can force me who obey a higher law than I. They force me to become like themselves. I do not hear of *men* being *forced* to live this way or that by masses of men. What sort of life were that to live? When I meet a government which says to me, "Your money or your life," why should I be in haste to give it my money? It may be in a great strait, and not know what to do: I cannot help that. It must help itself; do as I do. It is not worth the while to snivel about it. I am not responsible for the successful working of the machinery of society.

I am not the son of the engineer. I perceive that, when an acorn and a chestnut fall side by side, the one does not remain inert to make way for the other, but both obey their own laws, and spring and grow and flourish as best they can, till one, perchance, overshadows and destroys the other. If a plant cannot live according to its nature, it dies; and so a man. [27]

PURPOSE AND STRUCTURE

1. Although Thoreau discusses such things as allegiance to the state and non-payment of taxes, these are details in his larger argument. What are the issues he has raised? At least one issue has to do with the conflict between individual conscience and the general welfare. Try stating each issue in a simple sentence. If you cannot fully state an issue in a sentence, you may write a brief paragraph, but make it as short as possible.

2. Thoreau bases his argument on numerous unstated assumptions about the nature of man, his conscience, his wisdom, and about the nature of government. Copy five of Thoreau's statements and demonstrate the unstated assumptions supporting each.

3. In par. 4 Thoreau writes, "But a government in which a majority rule in all cases cannot be based on justice, even as far as men understand it." (a) What does Thoreau understand by justice? What role does his understanding of justice play in his main argument? (b) If the Supreme Court had to defend itself against his charge, what is the nature of the evidence it would offer?

4. In par. 5 Thoreau makes a distinction between men who serve their governments with their heads and those who serve with their consciences. (a) What assumption does he make about the nature of conscience? (b) What evidence does he supply for the statements? (c) Account for the strength and force of the statements. Do they appeal to reason and logic? to emotions? to the experience of the audience? to the coupling of *men* with conscience and of *office-holders* with heads?

5. In par. 15 Thoreau writes about action stemming from principle. His argument is clever, for it necessarily wins everyone's assent as no man

would admit that his public actions are unprincipled. However, "Action from principle, the perception and the performance of right" raises more issues than it resolves. What are the issues?

6. In par. 27 Thoreau claims that a man must live according to his nature or die. What is the rhetorical nature of the evidence he offers? In this instance, what is logically wrong with his method of argument?

DICTION AND TONE

1. Thoreau's tone is extraordinarily complex. Is this a lecture? a sermon? a revolutionist's creed? It is hard to say. With what kind of audience would this essay be most effective? Consider such things as economic position of audience, age, education, philosophic predilection (realist, idealist, pragmatist).

2. In *The Essay* Huxley describes three poles of the essay. In Huxley's terms, is Thoreau at home in the neighborhood of one pole, two poles, or all three? Is his argument more or less persuasive as a result?

3. Thoreau's prose is frequently epigrammatic. Here are a few examples:
   That government is best which governs least [1].
   He who gives himself entirely to his fellow men appears to them useless and selfish; but he who gives himself partially to them is pronounced a benefactor and philanthropist [6].
   If I devote myself to other pursuits and contemplations, I must first see, at least, that I do not pursue them sitting upon another man's shoulders [13].
   Any man more right than his neighbors constitutes a majority of one already [20].
   A minority is powerless while it conforms to the majority; it is not even a minority then; but it is irresistible when it clogs by its whole weight [22].
   The best thing a man can do for his culture when he is rich is to endeavor to carry out those schemes which he entertained when he was poor [23].
   If a plant cannot live according to its nature, it dies; and so a man [27].
   These statements and others like them contribute significantly to Thoreau's tone and to his persuasive power. Characterize the tone they

establish. On what does their effectiveness depend? Consider such things as sentence structure (balance), diction, repetition, rhythm.

APPLICATIONS TO WRITING

1. Take one or more of the issues Thoreau raises and in a well-developed essay apply it to a contemporary situation.

2. Engage in a debate with Thoreau. Respond point by point to his arguments.

3. In A *Primer of Existentialism* Bigelow explains that each man must accept the responsibility "for his own becoming, a burden made heavier by the fact that in choosing for himself he chooses for all men 'the image of man as he ought to be.' " Take one or more of Thoreau's points and write an essay in which you show what a civilization would be like if all men accepted and acted upon the points you select.

4. Select one of the sentences in question 3, Diction and Tone above. Study its function in the original paragraph. Remove it from its context and use it as a topic sentence in a completely new paragraph of your own.

THE SUBJECTION OF
WOMEN

ELIZABETH HARDWICK

Vassal, slave, inferior, other, thing, victim, dependent, parasite, prisoner—oh, bitter, raped, child-swollen flesh doomed to immanence! Sisyphean goddess of the dust pile! Demeter, Xantippe, Ninon de Lenclos, Marie Bashkirtsev, and "a friend of mine . . ." From cave to café, boudoir to microscope, from the knitting needles to the short story: they are all here in a potency of pages, a foreshortened and exaggerated, a mysterious and too clear relief, an eloquent lament and governessy scolding, a poem and a doctoral thesis. I suppose there is bound to be a little laughter in the wings at the mere thought of this madly sensible and brilliantly obscure tome on women by Simone de Beauvoir, *The Second Sex.* [1]

Still the more one sinks into this very long book, turning page after page, the more clearly it seems to lack a subject with reasonable limitations and concreteness, a subject on which offered illustrations may wear some air of finality and conviction. The theme of the work is that women are not simply "women," but are, like men, in the fullest sense human beings. Yet one cannot easily write the history of people! This point may appear trivial; nevertheless, to take on this glorious and fantastic book is not like reading at all—from the first to the last sentence one has the sensation of playing some breathlessly exciting and finally exhausting game. You gasp and strain and re- member; you point out and deny and agree, trying always to find some way of taking hold, of confining, defining, and understanding. What is so unbearably whirling is that the author too goes through this effort to include nearly every woman and attitude that has ever existed. There is no difference of opinion, unless it be based upon a fact of which she may be ignorant, she has not thought of also. She makes her own points and all one's objections too, often in the same sentence. The effort required for this work must have been killing. No discredit to the donkey-load undertaking is meant when one imagines Simone de Beauvoir at the end may have felt like George Eliot when she said she began *Romola* as a young woman and finished it an old one. (This touching remark did not refer to the time spent in composition, but to the wrinkling weight of the task.) [2]

I quote a sentence about the *promises* the Soviet Union made to women: ". . . pregnancy leaves were to be paid for by the State, which would assume charge of the children, signifying not that they would be *taken away* from their parents, but that they would not be *abandoned* to them." There is majesty here and the consolations of philosophy, perhaps also, in this instance, a bit of willful obfuscation; but that kind of strangeness occurs endlessly, showing, for purposes of argument at least, an oversensitivity to difficulties. A devastating dialogue goes on at this author's desk. After she has written, "the State, which would assume charge of the children," there is a comma pause. In that briefest of grammatical rests, voices assault her intel- ligence saying, "But suppose people don't want their children taken away by the State?" If all these disputing voices are admitted, one on top of the other, you are soon lost in incoherence and fantasy. Another instance: "It is understandable, in this perspective, that women take exception to masculine logic. Not only is it inapplicable to her experience, but in his hands, as she knows, masculine reason- ing becomes an underhanded form of force." A few pages on: "One can bank on her credulity. Woman takes an attitude of respect and faith toward the masculine universe . . ." [3]

I take up the bewildering inclusiveness of this book, because there is hardly a thing I would want to say contrary to her thesis that Simone de Beauvoir has not said herself, including the fact, mentioned in the preface, that problems peculiar to women are not particularly pressing at the moment and that, by and large, "we have won." These acknowledgments would seem of tremendous importance, but they are a mere batting of the eye in this eternity of "oppression." [4]

In spite of all positions being taken simultaneously, there is an unmistakable *drift* to the book. Like woman's life, *The Second Sex* is extremely repetitious and some things are repeated more often than others, although nearly every idea is repeated more than once. One is justified, then, in assuming what is repeated most often is most profoundly felt. The diction alone is startling and stabs the heart with its vigor in finding phrases of abjection and debasement. It is as though one had lived forever in that intense, shady, wretched world of *Wozzeck*, where the humor draws tears, the gaiety is fearful and children skip rope neither knowing nor caring their mother has been murdered. "Conjugal slavery, annihilation, servant, devaluation, tyranny, passive, forbidden, doomed, abused, trapped, prey, domineer, helpless, imprisoned," and so on. This immediately suggests a masochistic view of life, reinforced by the fact that for the male quite an opposite vocabulary has dug into this mind like a tick: "free, busy, active, proud, arrogant, master, existent, liberty, adventure, daring, strength, courage . . ." [5]

Things being as they are, it is only fair to say that Simone de Beauvoir, in spite of her absorbing turn of phrase, miraculously does *not* give to me, at least, the impression of being a masochist, a Lesbian, a termagant, or a man-hater, and that this book is not "the self-pitying cry of one who resents being born a woman," as one American housewife-reviewer said. There is a nervous, fluent, rare aliveness on every page and the writer's more "earnest" qualities, her discipline, learning and doggedness, amount not only to themselves, that is, qualities which certainly help one to write long books, but to a kind of "charm" that ought to impress the most contented woman. This book is an accomplishment; on the other hand, if one is expecting something truly splendid and unique like *The Origins of Totalitarianism* by Hannah Arendt, to mention another woman, he will be disappointed. [6]

The Second Sex begins with biological material showing that in nature there are not always two sexes and reproduction may take place asexually. I have noticed in the past that many books strongly presenting feminine claims begin in this manner, as if under a compulsion to veil the whole idea of sexual differentiation with a buzzing, watery mist of insect habits and unicellular forms of life. This is dramaturgy, meant to put one, after a heavy meal, in a receptive frame of mind. It is the dissonant, ambiguous music as the curtain rises on the all too familiar scene of the man at the hunt and the woman at the steaming pot; the scene looks clear enough, but the music suggests things may not be as they appear. That woman may not have to carry those screaming brats in her womb, after all, but will, if you don't watch out, simply "divide"! And the man: it is possible in the atomic age that a pin prick may fertilize the egg and then where will he be? This material is followed by curiosities from anthropology: some primitive societies thought the woman did it all alone and the man was no more important than a dish of herbs or a draft of beet juice. [7]

These biological and anthropological matters are of enormous fascination, but often, and a bit in this present work too, a false and dramatic use is made of them: they carry a weight of mystification and intensity quite unjustified when the subject is the modern woman. They would seem to want to throw doubt upon what is not yet doubtful: the bisexual nature of human reproduction. We are relieved when the dividing amoebas and budding sponges swim out of view. [8]

The claim of *The Second Sex* is that what we call the feminine character is an illusion and so is feminine "psychology," both in its loose meaning and in the psychoanalytical view. None of these female traits is "given"—the qualities and incapacities women have shown rather consistently in human history are simply the result of their "situation." This situation is largely the work of men, the male sex which has sought its own convenience with undeviating purpose throughout history. The female situation does not derive, at least not sufficiently to explain it, from women's natural physical and psychological difference, but has much of its origin in economics. When man developed the idea of private property, woman's destiny was "sealed." At this time women were cut off from the more adventurous activities of war, forays, explorations, to stay at home to *protect* and *maintain* what men had achieved by their far-reaching pursuits. The woman was reduced to a state of *immanence:* stagnation, the doing of repetitive tasks, concerned with the given, with maintaining, keeping, mere functioning. Man, however, is a free being, an *existent* who makes choices, decisions, has projects which are not confined to securing the present but point to the unknown future; he dares, fails, wanders, grabs, insists. By means of his activities he *transcends* his mere animal nature. What a man gives, the woman accepts; she decides nothing, changes nothing; she polishes, mends, cleans what he has invented and shaped. The man risks life, the woman merely produces it as an unavoidable function. "That is why superiority has been accorded in humanity not to the sex that brings forth but that which kills." The man imagines, discovers religions; the women worship. He has changed the earth; she arises each morning to an expectation of stove, nursing, scrubbing which has remained nearly as fixed as the course of our planets. Women continue in immanence not out of desire, but from "complicity." Having been robbed of economic independence, experience, substance, she clings unhappily because she has not been "allowed" to prepare for a different life. [9]

Naturally, it is clear many women do not fit this theory and those who may be said to do so would not describe it in the words of Simone de Beauvoir. These persons' claims are admitted quite fully throughout the book, but always with the suggestion that the women who seem to be "existents" really aren't and those who insist they find fulfillment in the inferior role are guilty of "bad faith." [10]

That is as it may be, but what, one asks at the beginning, about the man who, almost without exception in this work, is a creature of the greatest imagination, love of liberty, devotion to projects; ambitious, potent and disciplined, he scorns a life of mere "love," refuses to imprison himself in another's being, but looks toward the world, seeks to transcend himself, change the course of history. This is an exaggeration of course. For every Ophelia one remembers not only Cleopatra but poor Swann, unable, for all his taste and enthusiasm, to write his book on Vermeer, drowning his talent in the pursuit of pure pleasure which can only be given by the "other," Odette; for every excited Medea who gave up herself, her place, to follow the fickle man you remember not only Joan of Arc but that being of perfect, blowsy immanence, the Duke of Windsor, who abandoned the glories of a complex project for the sweet, repetitive, futureless domesticity of ocean liners and resorts. And Sartre has written a whole book on Baudelaire, a fascinating and immensely belligerent one, that claims Baudelaire resented responsibility for his own destiny, refused his possibilities of transcendence, would not make decisions, define himself, but flowed along on a tepid river of dependence, futility, refusal—like women, fond of scents and costumes, nostalgic, procrastinating, wishful. [11]

It would seem then that men, even some "heroic" ones, often allow themselves to be what women are forced to be. But, of course, with the greatest will in the world a man cannot allow himself to be that most extremely doomed and chained being—the mother who must bear and raise children and whose figure naturally hangs over such a work as *The Second Sex* like Spanish moss. Simone de Beauvoir's opinion of the division of labor established in the Garden of Eden, if not as some believe earlier, is very striking:

. . . giving birth and suckling are not *activities*, they are natural functions; no projects are involved; and that is why woman found in them no reason for a lofty affirmation of her existence—she submitted passively to her biologic fate. The domestic cares of maternity imprisoned her in repetition and immanence; they were repeated from day to day in an identical form, which was perpetuated almost without change from century to century; they produced nothing new. [12]

But what difference does it make that childbearing is not an activity, nor perhaps an instinct; it is a necessity. [13]

The Second Sex is so briskly Utopian it fills one with a kind of shame and sadness, like coming upon old manifestoes and committee programs in the attic. It is bursting with an almost melancholy desire for women to take their possibilities *seriously*, to reject the given, the easy, the traditional. I do not, as most reviewers seem to, think the picture offered here of a woman's life is entirely false—a lifetime of chores is bad luck. But housework, child rearing, cleaning, keeping, nourishing, looking after—these must be done by someone, or worse by millions of someones day in and day out. In the home at least it would seem "custom" has not been so much capricious as observant in finding that women are fairly well adapted to this necessary routine. And they must keep at it whether they like it or not. [14]

George Orwell says somewhere that reformers hate to admit nobody will do the tedious, dirty work of the world except under "some form of coercion." Mopping, ironing, peeling, feeding—it is not absurd to call this unvarying routine *slavery*, Simone de Beauvoir's word. But its necessity does not vanish by listing the tropical proliferation of open and concealed forms of coercion that may be necessary to make women do it. Bachelors are notoriously finicky, we have all observed. The dust pile is revoltingly real. [15]

Most men, also, are doomed to work of brutalizing monotony. Hardly any intellectuals are willing to undertake a bit of this dreadful work their fellow beings must do, no matter what salary, what working conditions, what degree of "socialist dignity" might be attached to it. If artists could save a man from a lifetime of digging coal by digging it themselves one hour a week, most would refuse. Some would commit suicide. "It's not the time, it's the anticipation!

It ruins the whole week! I can't even read, much less write!" [16]

Childbearing and housekeeping may be repetitive and even intellectually stunting. Yet nothing so fills one with despair as those products of misplaced transcendent hope, those millions of stupid books, lunatic pamphlets, absurd editorials, dead canvases and popular songs which have clogged up the sewers and ashcans of the modern world, representing more wretched labor, dreaming, madness, vanity and waste of effort than one can bear to think of. There is an annihilating nothingness in these undertakings by comparison with which the production of one stupid, lazy, lying child is an event of some importance. Activity, transcendence, project—this is an optimistic, exhilarating vocabulary. Yet Sartre had to disown the horde of "existents" who fell to like farm hands at the table, but were not themselves able to produce so much as a carrot. [17]

Are women "the equal" of men? This is an embarrassing subject. [18]

Women are certainly physically inferior to men and if this were not the case the whole history of the world would be different. No comradely socialist legislation on woman's behalf could accomplish a millionth of what a bit more muscle tissue, gratuitously offered by nature, might do for this "second" being. [19]

On the average she is shorter than the male and lighter, her skeleton is more delicate . . . muscular strength is much less in women . . . she has less respiratory capacity, the lungs and trachea being smaller . . . The specific gravity of the blood is lower . . . and there is less hemoglobin; women are therefore less robust and more disposed to anemia than are males. Their pulse is more rapid, the vascular system less stable . . . Instability is strikingly characteristic of woman's organization in general . . . In comparison with her the male seems infinitely favored.

There is a kind of poetry in this description which might move a flighty person to tears. But it goes on:

These biological considerations are extremely important . . . But I deny that they establish for her a fixed and inevitable destiny. They are insufficient for setting up a hierarchy of the sexes . . . they do not condemn her to remain in a subordinate role forever. [20]

Why doesn't this "condemn her to remain in a subordinate role forever"? In my view this poor endowment would seem to be all the answer one needs to why women don't sail the seven seas, build bridges, conquer foreign lands, lay international cables and trudge up Mount Everest. But forgetting these daring activities, a woman's physical inferiority to a man is a limiting reality every moment of her life. Because of it women are "doomed" to situations that promise reasonable safety against the more hazardous possibilities of nature which they are too weak and easily fatigued to endure and against the stronger man. Any woman who has ever had her wrist twisted by a man recognizes a fact of nature as humbling as a cyclone to a frail tree branch. How can *anything* be more important than this? The prodigious ramifications could occupy one for an eternity. For instance:

At eighteen T. E. Lawrence took a long bicycle tour through France by himself; no young girl would be allowed to engage in any escapade, still less to adventure on foot in a half-desert and dangerous country, as Lawrence did a year later. [21]

Simone de Beauvoir's use of "allow" is inaccurate; she stresses "permission" where so often it is really "capacity" that is involved. For a woman a solitary bicycle tour of France would be dangerous, but not impossible; Lawrence's adventure in Arabia would be suicidal and so a woman is nearly unimaginable as the author of *The Seven Pillars of Wisdom*. First of all the Arabs would rape this unfortunate female soldier or, if they had some religious or practical reason for resisting temptation, they would certainly have to leave her behind on the march, like yesterday's garbage, as the inevitable fatigue arrived. To say that physical weakness doesn't, in a tremendous number of activities, "condemn her to a subordinate role" is a mere assertion, not very convincing to the unmuscled, light breathing, nervously unstable, blushing feminine reality. [22]

Arabian warfare is indeed an extreme situation. But what about solitary walks through the town after midnight? It is true that a woman's freedom to enjoy this simple pleasure would be greatly increased if men had no aggressive sexual feelings toward her. Like a stray dog, also weaker than men, she might roam the world at will, arousing no more notice than a few pats on the head or an irritable kick now and then. Whether such a change is possible in the interest of the weaker sex is very doubtful. [23]

There is the notion in *The Second Sex*, and in other radical books on the subject, that if it were not for the tyranny of custom, women's sexual life would be characterized by the same aggressiveness, greed and command as that of the male. This is by no means certain: so much seems to lead right back where we've always been. Society must, it seems, inhibit to some extent the sexuality of all human beings. It has succeeded in restraining men much less than women. Brothels, which have existed from the earliest times, are to say the least a rarity for the use of women. And yet women will patronize opium dens and are frequently alcoholic, activities wildly destructive to their home life, beauty, manners and status and far more painful and time-consuming than having children. Apparently a lot of women are dying for dope and cocktails; nearly all are somewhat thrifty, cautious and a little lazy about hunting sex. Is it necessarily an error that many people think licentious women are incapable of experiencing the slightest degree of sexual pleasure and are driven to their behavior by an encyclopedic curiosity to know if such a thing exists? A wreck of a man, tracking down girls in his Chevrolet, at least can do *that!* Prostitutes are famously cold; pimps, who must also suffer professional boredom, are not automatically felt to be impotent. Homosexual women, who have rebelled against their "conditioning" in the most crucial way, do not appear to "cruise" with that truly astonishing, ageless zest of male homosexuals. A pair seems to find each other sufficient. Drunken women who pick up a strange man look less interested in a sexual partner than in a companion for a drink the next morning. There is a staggering amount of evidence that points to the idea that women set a price of one kind or another on sexual intercourse; they are so often not in the mood. [24]

This is not to say women aren't interested in sex *at all*. They clearly want a lot of it, but in the end the men of the world seem to want still more. It is only the quantity, the capacity in that sense, in which the sexes appear to differ. Women, in the language of sociology books, "fight very hard" to get the amount of sexual satisfaction they want— and even harder to keep men from forcing a superabundance their way. It is difficult to see how anyone can be sure that it is only man's voracious appetite for conquest which has created, as its contrary, this reluctant, passive being who has to be wooed, raped, bribed, begged, threatened, married, supported. Perhaps she really has to be. After she has been conquered she has to "pay" the man to restrain his appetite, which he is so likely to reveal at cocktail parties, and in his pitifully longing glance at the secretary—she pays with ironed shirts, free meals, the pleasant living room, a son. [25]

And what about the arts—those womanish activities which are, in our day, mostly "done at home." For those who desire this form of transcendence, the other liberating activities of mankind, the office, the factory, the world of commerce, public affairs, are horrible pits where the extraordinary man is basely and casually slain. [26]

Women have excelled in the performance arts: acting, dancing and singing—for some reason Simone de Beauvoir treats these accomplishments as if they were usually an extension of prostitution. Women have contributed very little to the art of painting and they are clearly weak in the gift for musical composition. (Still whole nations seem without this latter gift, which may be inherited. Perhaps even nations inherit it, the male members at least. Like baldness, women may transmit the gift of musical composition but they seldom ever suffer from it.) [27]

Literature is the art in which women have had the greatest success. But a woman needs only to think of this activity to feel her bones rattling with violent distress. Who is to say that *Remembrance of Things Past* is "better" than the marvelous *Emma*? *War and Peace* better than *Middlemarch*? *Moby Dick* superior to *La Princesse de Clèves*? But everybody says so! It is only the whimsical, cantankerous, the eccentric critic, or those who refuse the occasion for such distinctions, who would say that any literary work by a woman, marvelous as these may be, is on a level with the very greatest accomplishments of men. Of course the *best* literature by women is superior to *most* of the work done by men and anyone who values literature at all will approach all excellence with equal enthusiasm. [28]

The Second Sex is not whimsical about women's writing, but here again perhaps too much is made of the position in which women have been "trapped" and not enough of how "natural" and inevitable their literary limitations are. Nevertheless, the remarks on artistic women are among the most brilliant in this book. Narcissism and feelings of inferiority are, according to Simone de Beauvoir, the demons of literary women. Women want to please, "but the writer of originality, unless dead, is always shocking, scandalous; novelty disturbs and repels." Flattered to be in the world of art at all, the woman is "on her best behavior; she is afraid to disarrange, to investigate, to explode . . ." Women are timid and fall back on "ancient houses, sheepfolds, kitchen gardens, picturesque old folks, roguish children . . ." and even the best are conservative. "There are women who are mad and there are women of sound method; none has that madness in her method that we call genius." [29]

If women's writing seems somewhat limited, I don't think it is only due to these psychological failings. Women have much less experience of life than a man, as everyone knows. But in the end are they suited to the kind of experiences men have? *Ulysses* is not just a work of genius, it is Dublin pubs, gross depravity, obscenity, brawls. Stendhal as a soldier in Napoleon's army, Tolstoy on his Cossack campaigns, Dostoevsky before the firing squad, Proust's obviously first-hand knowledge of vice, Conrad and Melville as sailors, Michelangelo's tortures on the scaffolding in the Sistine chapel, Ben Jonson's drinking bouts, dueling, his ear burnt by the authorities because of a political indiscretion in a play—these horrors and the capacity to endure them are *experience*. Experience is something more than going to law school or having the nerve to say honestly what you think in a drawing room filled with men; it is the privilege as well to endure brutality, physical torture, unimaginable sordidness, and even the privilege *to want*, like Boswell, to grab a miserable tart under Westminster Bridge. Syphilis and epilepsy—even these seem to be tragic afflictions a male writer can endure more easily than a woman. I should imagine a woman would be more depleted by epilepsy than Dostoevsky seems to have been, more ravaged by syphilis than Flaubert, more weakened by deprivation than Villon. Women live longer, safer lives than men and a man may, if he wishes, choose that life; it is hard to believe a woman could choose, like Rimbaud, to sleep in the streets of Paris at seventeen. [30]

If you remove the physical and sexual experiences many men have made literature out of, you have carved away a great hunk of masterpieces. There is a lot left: James, Balzac, Dickens; the material in these books, perhaps not always in Balzac, is a part of women's lives too or might be "worked up"—legal practices and prison conditions in Dickens, commerce in Balzac, etc. [31]

But the special *vigor* of James, Balzac, Dickens or Racine, the queer, remaining strength to produce masterpiece after masterpiece—that is belittling! The careers of women of prodigious productivity, like George Sand, are marked by a great amount of failure and waste, indicating that though time was spent at the desk perhaps the supreme effort was not regularly made. Who can help but feel that *some of* James's vigor is sturdily rooted in his masculine flesh and that this repeatedly successful creativity is less likely with the "weaker sex" even in the socialist millennium. It is not suggested that muscles write books, but there is a certain sense in which, talent and experience being equal, they may be considered a bit of an advantage. In the end, it is in the matter of experience that women's disadvantage is catastrophic. It is very difficult to know how this may be extraordinarily altered. [32]

Coquettes, mothers, prostitutes and "minor" writers—one sees these faces, defiant or resigned, still standing at the Last Judgment. They are all a little sad, like the Chinese lyric:

Why do I heave deep sighs?
It is natural, a matter of course, all
creatures have their laws. [33]

PURPOSE AND STRUCTURE

1. The title of this piece provides an obvious clue to the central issue on
which Miss Hardwick's argument rests, but not until par. 9 is it given
full definition. Examine the development of this paragraph. What is its
topic sentence? What causal relationship is developed? What comparisons and contrasts are implied? What is the issue?

2. Pars. 10–33 constitute the author's refutations of Miss de Beauvoir's
position as set forth in par. 9; however, pars. 1–6 have indirectly prepared you for the issue. How? What is the primary thesis advanced in the
first section (pars. 1–6)? How does it relate to the argument, the proposition, the issue? Pars. 7 and 8 (which start off the second section)
constitute a different kind of preparation for Miss de Beauvoir's "claim"
in par. 9. What is it? What is the transition from pars. 7–8 to par. 9?
What is the unifying factor in the second section? What is the transition
between the second and third sections? Section Four asks the question:
Are women the equal of men? It divides into two subsections. What are
they? The final section focuses on women in the arts, especially literature.
How do Miss Hardwick's arguments here draw upon the main points of
the preceding section?

3. How does Miss Hardwick support her criticism of Miss de Beauvoir's
lack of selectivity in pars. 2 and 3?

4. Analyze the author's use of evidence. Find examples in which she
draws upon her personal experience and opinion, history, literature, and
reference to "authority." Is there any suggestion that she extends her
reference to what she has observed to *all* women? Specify.

5. Cite examples of the author's reliance on the deductive method of
reasoning; the inductive. On which method does she primarily rely?

6. What generalization follows from the details in par. 30 on the nature
of the experience which Miss Hardwick regards as alien to women? On

what premises about the sources of greatness in literature is her argument based? What other premises might have been taken into consideration? In pars. 31–32, after conceding that a woman might have experienced the life depicted in the novels of James, Balzac, or Dickens, or that a woman might have "worked up" such material, Miss Hardwick makes the secondary point that women lack the special vigor to be as productive as these men. How does she qualify the premise that vigor has its source in masculine flesh and muscle and that productivity is derived from physical strength? What other causal relationship might have been developed?

DICTION AND TONE

1. Miss Hardwick employs Miss de Beauvoir's existentialist vocabulary in words like *immanence, existent, transcends* (par. 9). Determine their function by studying the words used in apposition to them and by noting which words are used as antonyms. What does this technique contribute to purpose and tone?

2. Can it be said that the first paragraph establishes the tone of the entire essay? In the opening non-sentence what do the first epithets preceding the first dash denote and connote? What attitude toward the position of women do they reflect? How do the phrases *oh, bitter, raped, child-swollen flesh doomed to immanence!* and *Sisyphean goddess of the dustpile!* comment upon the first series? How does the diction color the meaning? What do the proper names signify in relation to what has preceded? What contrast and range are suggested by the phrases beginning from *cave to café?* How do the phrases following *potency of pages* define the author's attitude toward her materials? What contrasts are implied in *eloquent lament* and *governessy scolding?* in a *poem* and a *doctoral thesis?* In the light of what has preceded, are you fully prepared for the admission of *a little laughter in the wings?* How do the couplings of *madly sensible* and *brilliantly obscure tome* prepare you for what is to follow? What does the tone of this paragraph suggest to you about Miss Hardwick's attitude toward *The Second Sex?* toward Simone de Beauvoir?

3. How much of the satirical edge depends upon colorful diction? To what degree does it emanate from the selection and juxtaposition of Miss de Beauvoir's own words? To what degree does it depend upon Miss Hardwick's commentary, direct and indirect, upon the latter? Examine

par. 5 as it illuminates these questions. How does the word *drift* function? How does the sentence referring to the repetitiousness of *The Second Sex* drive home the point? How does *stabs the heart with its vigor* function? By analogy, how do the images from *that intense shady wretched world of Wozzeck* communicate Miss Hardwick's view of Miss de Beauvoir? Then note the descriptive words quoted from Miss de Beauvoir (you have already observed this technique in par. 1), which, having been listed as if they appeared consecutively in Miss de Beauvoir's 732 pages, lead to the generalization that Miss de Beauvoir has a masochistic view of life. What does the piling up of words in the two complementary series reveal of the author's purpose and tone? In the comment, "quite an opposite vocabulary has *dug into this mind like a tick*," what tone is achieved by the figure of speech? Find other paragraphs in which the selection of words, the color of the words, or the choice of analogy communicates a similar tone.

4. What is the function of such phrases as "and *a bit* in this present work" and "they *would seem* to want to throw doubt" (par. 8)?

5. What is the effect of modifying *immanence* with *blowsy* (par. 11)?

6. How do the allusions to Sartre help to define the author's purpose and tone (pars. 11 and 17)?

7. What overtones betray Miss Hardwick's view of men (par. 17)?

8. To what degree does Miss Hardwick's tone reflect objectivity and detachment? subjectivity and personal involvement? Defend your answer. To what degree does the author rely upon caricature and parody to persuade the reader? Is there a discrepancy between the dominant tone and the ostensible purpose of the essay? How would you formulate it? To what extent does the author's tone advance her persuasive purpose? defeat it? Exemplify.

APPLICATIONS TO WRITING

1. Select from a significant book a controversial issue on which to focus your argument and attempt to persuade your reader. Instead of emulating Miss Hardwick, deal with it straightforwardly. If irony or satire or caricature comes naturally to you, don't suppress it.

2. Read at least two or three chapters from Simone de Beauvoir's *The Second Sex*. Write a detailed analysis of Miss Hardwick's method by specific reference both to the book she is attacking and to her own essay.

3. After reading *The Second Sex*, select an issue on which to focus your agreement or disagreement with the author. Keep clearly in mind your central purpose (that is, of what do you wish to persuade your readers?).

WHAT I BELIEVE

E . M . FORSTER

I do not believe in belief. But this is an age of faith, where
one is surrounded by so many militant creeds that, in self-defense, one
has to formulate a creed of one's own. Tolerance, good temper, and
sympathy are no longer enough in a world which is rent by religious
and racial persecution, in a world where ignorance rules, and science,
who ought to have ruled, plays the subservient pimp. Tolerance, good
temper, and sympathy—well, they are what matter really, and if the
human race is not to collapse they must come to the front before
long. But for the moment they don't seem enough, their action is no
stronger than a flower, battered beneath a military jack boot. They
want stiffening, even if the process coarsens them. Faith, to my mind,
is a stiffening process, a sort of mental starch, which ought to be
applied as sparingly as possible. I dislike the stuff. I do not believe in
it, for its own sake, at all. Herein I probably differ from most of the
contributors to this volume, who believe in belief, and are only sorry
they can't swallow even more than they do. My lawgivers are Erasmus
and Montaigne, not Moses and St. Paul. My temple stands not upon
Mount Moriah but in the Elysian Field where even the immoral are
admitted. My motto is "Lord, I disbelieve—help thou my unbelief." [1]

Copyright, 1939, by E. M. Forster. Reprinted from his volume, *Two Cheers for
Democracy*, by permission of Harcourt, Brace & World, Inc. Canadian rights by
permission of Edward Arnold (Publishers) Ltd.

406

I have, however, to live in an age of Faith—the sort of thing I used to hear praised and recommended when I was a boy. It is damned unpleasant, really. It is bloody in every sense of the word. And I have to keep my end up in it. Where do I start? [2]

With personal relationships. Here is something comparatively solid in a world full of violence and cruelty. Not absolutely solid, for psychology has split and shattered the idea of a "person," and has shown that there is something incalculable in each of us, which may at any moment rise to the surface and destroy our normal balance. We don't know what we're like. We can't know what other people are like. How then can we put any trust in personal relationships, or cling to them in the gathering political storm? In theory we can't. But in practice we can and do. Though A isn't unchangeably A or B unchangeably B, there can still be love and loyalty between the two. For the purpose of living one has to assume that the personality is solid, and the "self" is an entity, and to ignore all contrary evidence. And since to ignore evidence is one of the characteristics of faith, I certainly can proclaim that I believe in personal relationships. [3]

Starting from them, I get a little order into the contemporary chaos. One must be fond of people and trust them if one isn't to make a mess of life, and it is therefore essential that they shouldn't let one down. They often do. The moral of which is that I must myself be as reliable as possible, and this I try to be. But reliability isn't a matter of contract—that is the main difference between the world of personal relationships and the world of business relationships. It is a matter for the heart, which signs no documents. In other words, reliability is impossible unless there is a natural warmth. Most men possess this warmth, though they often have bad luck and get chilled. Most of them, even when they are politicians, *want* to keep faith. And one can, at all events, show one's own little light here, one's own poor little trembling flame, with the knowledge that it's not the only light that is shining in the darkness, and not the only one which the darkness doesn't comprehend. Personal relations are despised today. They are regarded as bourgeois luxuries, as products of a time of fair weather which has now passed, and we are urged to get rid of them, and to dedicate ourselves to some movement or cause instead. I hate the idea of dying for a cause, and if I had to choose between betraying my country and betraying my friend, I hope I should have the guts to betray my country. Such a choice may scandalize the modern reader, and he may stretch out his patriotic hand to the telephone at once, and ring up the police. It wouldn't have shocked Dante, though. Dante places Brutus and Cassius in the lowest circle of Hell because they had chosen to betray their friend Julius Caesar rather than their country Rome. Probably one won't be asked to make such an agonizing choice. Still there lies at the back of every creed something terrible and hard for which the worshiper may one day be required to suffer, and there is even a terror and a hardness in this creed of personal relationships, urbane and mild though it sounds. Love and loyalty to an individual can run counter to the claims of the state. When they do—down with the state, say I, which means that the state will down me. [4]

This brings me along to democracy, "even Love, the Beloved Republic, which feeds upon Freedom and lives." Democracy isn't a beloved republic really, and never will be. But it is less hateful than other contemporary forms of government, and to that extent it deserves our support. It does start from the assumption that the individual is important, and that all types are needed to make a civilization. It doesn't divide its citizens into the bossers and the bossed, as an efficiency regime tends to do. The people I admire most are those who are sensitive and want to create something or discover something, and don't see life in terms of power, and such people get more of a chance under a democracy than elsewhere. They found religions, great or small, or they produce literature and art, or they do disinterested scientific research, or they may be what is called "ordinary people," who are creative in their private lives, bring out their children decently, for instance, or help their neighbors. All these people need to express themselves, they can't do so unless society allows them liberty to do so, and the society which allows them most liberty is a democracy. [5]

Democracy has another merit. It allows criticism, and if there isn't public criticism there are bound to be hushed-up scandals. That is why I believe in the press, despite all its lies and vulgarity, and why I believe in Parliament. The British Parliament is often sneered at because it's a talking shop. Well, I believe in it because it is a talking shop. I believe in the private member who makes himself a nuisance. He gets snubbed and is told that he is cranky or ill-informed, but he exposes abuses which would otherwise never have been mentioned, and very often an abuse gets put right just by being mentioned. Occasionally, too, in my country, a well-meaning public official loses his head in the cause of efficiency, and thinks himself God Almighty. Such officials are particularly frequent in the Home Office. Well, there will be questions about them in Parliament sooner or later, and then they'll have to mend their steps. Whether Parliament is either a representative body or an efficient one is very doubtful, but I value it because it criticizes and talks, and because its chatter gets widely reported. [6]

So two cheers for democracy: one because it admits variety and two because it permits criticism. Two cheers are quite enough: there is no occasion to give three. Only Love, the Beloved Republic deserves that. [7]

What about force, though? While we are trying to be sensitive and advanced and affectionate and tolerant, an unpleasant question pops up: Doesn't all society rest upon force? If a government can't count upon the police and the army, how can it hope to rule? And if an individual gets knocked on the head or sent to a labor camp, of what significance are his opinions? [8]

This dilemma doesn't worry me as much as it does some. I realize that all society rests upon force. But all the great creative actions, all the decent human relations, occur during the intervals when force has not managed to come to the front. These intervals are what matter. I want them to be as frequent and as lengthy as possible and I call them "civilization." Some people idealize force and pull it into the foreground and worship it, instead of keeping it in the background as long as possible. I think they make a mistake, and I think that their opposites, the mystics, err even more when they declare that force doesn't exist. I believe that it does exist, and that one of our jobs is to prevent it from getting out of its box. It gets out sooner or later, and then it destroys us and all the lovely things which we have made. But it isn't out all the time, for the fortunate reason that the strong are so stupid. Consider their conduct for a moment in the Nibelung's *Ring*. The giants there have the guns, or in other words the gold; but they do nothing with it, they do not realize that they are all-powerful, with the result that the catastrophe is delayed and the castle of Walhalla, insecure but glorious, fronts the storms for generations. Fafnir, coiled around his hoard, grumbles and grunts; we can hear him under Europe today; the leaves of the wood already tremble, and the Bird calls its warnings uselessly. Fafnir will destroy us, but by a blessed dispensation he is stupid and slow, and creation goes on just outside the poisonous blast of his breath. The Nietzschean would hurry the monster up, the mystic would say he didn't exist, but Wotan, wiser than either, hastens to create warriors before doom declares itself. The Valkyries are symbols not only of courage but of intelligence; they represent the human spirit snatching its opportunity while the going is good, and one of them even finds time to love. Brunhilde's last song hymns the recurrence of love, and since it is the privilege of art to exaggerate she goes even further, and proclaims the love which is eternally triumphant and feeds upon freedom, and lives. [9]

So that is what I feel about force and violence. It is, alas! the ultimate reality, on this earth, but—hooray!—it doesn't always get to the front. Some people call its absences "decadence"; I call them "civilization" and find in such interludes the chief justification for the human experiment. I look the other way until fate strikes me. Whether this is due to courage or to cowardice in my own case I cannot be sure. But I know that if men hadn't looked the other way in the past nothing of any value would survive. The people I respect most behave as if they were immortal and as if society were eternal. Both assumptions are false: both of them must be accepted as true if we are to go on eating and working and loving, and are to keep open a few breathing holes for the human spirit. No millennium seems likely to descend upon humanity; no better and stronger League of Nations will be instituted; no form of Christianity and no alternative to Christianity will bring peace to the world or integrity to the individual; no "change of heart" will occur. And yet we needn't despair, indeed we cannot despair; the evidence of history shows us that men have always insisted on behaving creatively under the shadow of the sword; that they have done their artistic and scientific and domestic stuff for the sake of doing it, and that we had better follow their example under the shadow of the airplanes. Others, with more vision or courage than myself, see the salvation of humanity ahead, and will dismiss my conception of civilization as paltry, a sort of tip-and-run game. Certainly it is presumptuous to say that we *can't* improve, and that man, who has only been in power for a few thousand years, will never learn to make use of his power. All I mean is that, if people continue to kill one another at the rate they do, the world cannot get better than it is, and that since there are more people than formerly, and their means for destroying one another more diabolic, the world may well get worse. What's good in people—and consequently in the world—is their insistence on creation, their belief in friendship, in loyalty, for its own sake; and though violence remains and is indeed the major partner in this muddled establishment, I believe that creativeness remains too, and will always assume direction when violence sleeps. So, though I am not an optimist, I cannot agree with Sophocles that it were better never to have been born. And although I see no evidence that each batch of births is superior to the last, I leave the field open for this happier view. This is such a difficult time to live in, especially for a European, one can't help getting gloomy and also a bit rattled. [10]

There is of course hero worship, fervently recommended as a panacea in some quarters. But here we shall get no help. Hero worship is a dangerous vice, and one of the minor merits of a democracy is that it does not encourage it, or produce that unmanageable type of citizen known as the Great Man. It produces instead different kinds of small men, and that's a much finer achievement. But people who can't get interested in the variety of life and can't make up their own minds get discontented over this, and they long for a hero to bow down before and to follow blindly. It's significant that a hero is an integral part of the authoritarian stock in trade today. An efficiency regime can't be run without a few heroes stuck about to carry off the dullness—much as plums have to be put into a bad pudding to make it palatable. One hero at the top and a smaller one each side of him is a favorite arrangement, and the timid and the bored are comforted by such a trinity, and, bowing down, feel exalted by it. [11]

No, I distrust Great Men. They produce a desert of uniformity around them and often a pool of blood, too, and I always feel a little man's pleasure when they come a cropper. Every now and then one reads in the newspapers some such statement as, "The *coup d'etat* appears to have failed and Admiral Boga's whereabouts is at present unknown." Admiral Boga had probably every qualification for being a great man—an iron will, personal magnetism, dash, flair—but fate was against him, so he retires to unknown whereabouts instead of parading history with his peers. He fails with a completeness that no artist and no lover can experience, because with them the process of creation is itself an achievement, whereas with him the only possible achievement is success. I believe in aristocracy though—if that's the right word, and if a democrat may use it. Not an aristocracy of power, based upon rank and influence, but an aristocracy of the sensitive, the considerate, and the plucky. Its members are to be found in all nations and classes, and all through the ages, and there is a secret understanding between them when they meet. They represent the true human tradition, the one permanent victory of our queer race over cruelty and chaos. Thousands of them perish in obscurity; a few are great names. They are sensitive for others as well as for themselves, they are considerate without being fussy, their pluck is not swankiness but the power to endure, and they can take a joke. I give no examples— it is risky to do that—but the reader may as well consider whether this is the type of person he would like to meet and to be, and whether (going further with me) he would prefer that the type should *not* be an ascetic one. I'm against asceticism myself. I'm with the old

Scotchman who wanted less chastity and more delicacy. I don't feel that my aristocrats are a real aristocracy if they thwart their bodies, since bodies are the instruments through which we register and enjoy the world. Still, I don't insist here. This isn't a major point. It's clearly possible to be sensitive, considerate, and plucky and yet be an ascetic too, and if anyone possesses the first three qualities, I'll let him in! On they go—an invincible army, yet not a victorious one. The aristocrats, the elect, the chosen, the best people—all the words that describe them are false, and all attempts to organize them fail. Again and again authority, seeing their value, has tried to net them and to utilize them as the Egyptian priesthood or the Christian Church or the Chinese civil service or the Group Movement, or some other worthy stunt. But they slip through the net and are gone; when the door is shut they are no longer in the room; their temple, as one of them remarked, is the holiness of the heart's imagination, and their kingdom, though they never possess it, is the wide open world. [12]

With this type of person knocking about, and constantly crossing one's path if one has eyes to see or hands to feel, the experiment of earthly life cannot be dismissed as a failure. But it may well be hailed as a tragedy, the tragedy being that no device has been found by which these private decencies can be transferred to public affairs. As soon as people have power they go crooked and sometimes dotty, too, because the possession of power lifts them into a region where normal honesty never pays. For instance, the man who is selling newspapers outside the Houses of Parliament can safely leave his papers to go for a drink, and his cap beside them: anyone who takes a paper is sure to drop a copper into the cap. But the men who are inside the Houses of Parliament—they can't trust one another like that; still less can the government they compose trust other governments. No caps upon the pavement here, but suspicion, treachery, and armaments. The more highly public life is organized the lower does its morality sink; the nations of today behave to each other worse than they ever did in the past, they cheat, rob, bully, and bluff, make war without notice, and kill as many women and children as possible; whereas primitive tribes were at all events restrained by taboos. It's a humiliating outlook—though the greater the darkness, the brighter shine the little lights, reassuring one another, signaling, "Well, at all events I'm still here. I don't like it very much, but how are you?" Unquenchable lights of my aristocracy! Signals of the invincible army! "Come along —anyway let's have a good time while we can." I think they signal that too. [13]

The savior of the future—if ever he comes—will not preach a new gospel. He will merely utilize my aristocracy; he will make effective the good will and the good temper which are already existing. In other words he will introduce a new technique. In economics, we are told that if there was a new technique of distribution, there need be no poverty, and people would not starve in one place while crops were dug under in another. A similar change is needed in the sphere of morals and politics. The desire for it is by no means new; it was expressed, for example, in theological terms by Jacopone da Todi over six hundred years ago. *"Ordina questo amore, O tu che m'ami,"* he said. "O thou who lovest me—set this love in order." His prayer was not granted and I do not myself believe that it ever will be, but here, and not through a change of heart, is our probable route. Not by becoming better, but by ordering and distributing his native goodness, will man shut up force into his box, and so gain time to explore the universe and to set his work upon it worthily. At present he only explores it at odd moments, when force is looking the other way, and his divine creativeness appears as a trivial by-product, to be scrapped as soon as the drums beat and the bombers hum. [14]

Such a change, claim the orthodox, can only be made by Christianity, and will be made by it in God's good time: man always has failed and always will fail to organize his own goodness, and it is presumptuous of him to try. This claim—solemn as it is—leaves me cold. I cannot believe that Christianity will ever cope with the present world-wide mess, and I think that such influence as it retains in modern society is due to its financial backing rather than to its spiritual appeal. It was a spiritual force once, but the indwelling spirit will have to be restated if it is to calm the water again, and probably restated in a non-Christian form. Naturally a great many people, and people who are not only good but able and intelligent, will disagree with me here; they will vehemently deny that Christianity has failed, or they will argue that its failure proceeds from the wickedness of men, and really proves its ultimate success. They have Faith, with a large F. My faith has a very small one, and I only bring it into the open because these are strenuous and serious days, and one likes to say what one thinks while speech is still free: it may not be free much longer. [15]

These are the reflections of an individualist and a liberal who has found his liberalism crumbling beneath him and at first felt ashamed. Then, looking around, he decided there was no special reason for shame, since other people, whatever they felt, were equally insecure. And as for individualism—there seems no way out of this, even if one wants to find one. The dictator-hero can grind down his citizens till they are all alike, but he can't melt them into a single man. That is beyond his power. He can order them to merge, he can incite them to mass antics, but they are obliged to be born separately and to die separately and, owing to these unavoidable termini, will always be running off the totalitarian rails. The memory of birth and the expectation of death always lurk within the human being, making him separate from his fellows and consequently capable of intercourse with them. Naked I came into the world, naked I shall go out of it! And a very good thing too, for it reminds me that I am naked under my shirt. Until psychologists and biologists have done much more tinkering than seems likely, the individual remains firm and each of us must consent to be one, and to make the best of the difficult job. [16]

PURPOSE AND STRUCTURE

1. Forster's reference to Montaigne as one of his *lawgivers* (par. 1) seems odd. This great French essayist (whose voice is, unfortunately, slightly muffled in translation) does not give laws; he writes about himself and his opinions. T. S. Eliot describes him as the least destructible of adversaries: "You could as well dissipate a fog by flinging hand-grenades

into it. For Montaigne is a fog, a gas, a fluid, insidious element. He does not reason, he insinuates, charms, and influences; or if he reasons, you must be prepared for his having some other design upon you than to convince you by his argument." Eliot concludes that by the time a man knows Montaigne well enough to attack him, he will already be thoroughly infected by him. Is, then, Forster's reference to Montaigne as one of his *lawgivers* too ironic to be persuasive?

2. Considering Forster's title, his first sentence is unexpected. Is it the thesis of his essay? Would it be logical to end the essay with the first sentence? What is the function of the first paragraph? Argue for or against the effectiveness of the first sentence.

3. What is the function of par. 2? of the first three sentences? the fourth? the fifth? How soon is the question in the fifth sentence answered?

4. Forster proclaims (in the last sentence of par. 3) that he, too, has faith. Is he inconsistent? What is his persuasive purpose in referring to *one of the characteristics of faith?*

5. In par. 4 Forster argues for a kind of *reliability*. What is it based on? Can the loyal citizen show this *reliability* toward his state?

6. Is Forster inconsistent in stating there is *terror and hardness* in this creed of personal relationships (par. 4)?

7. Forster looks *the other way until fate strikes him* (par. 10). Why? Does it matter *whether this is due to courage or cowardice?*

8. In par. 10 Forster argues for false assumptions. Is his argument persuasive?

9. Admiral Boga (par. 12) *fails with a completeness that no artist and no lover can experience.* Of what is Forster trying to persuade the reader?

10. How can man *shut up force into his box* (par. 14)? Does Forster think it will ever happen? Why, then, present this solution? In other words, what is the persuasive purpose of par. 14?

11. Forster ends par. 15 rather apologetically. Is he withdrawing his criticism of Christianity? Is he weakening his argument against Christianity by ending so softly? What is the purpose of par. 15?

12. Forster begins the last paragraph by referring to himself as *a liberal who has found his liberalism crumbling beneath him and at first felt*

ashamed. How did he lose his shame? If this is an argument for liberalism, it seems a rather weak one. Why does Forster present it?

13. Forster says that individualism will remain because we are born separately and we die separately (par. 16). Is this consistent with his belief that we should behave as if we were immortal (par. 10)?

14. Forster gives many tentative or seemingly weak arguments for his beliefs. What is their cumulative persuasive effect? In par. 3 he argues for personal relationships but admits *We can't know what other people are like.* In par. 4 he argues for reliability based on human warmth, though he admits that we often *have bad luck and get chilled.* He gives only *two cheers for democracy* (par. 7). He admits that all society rests on force (par. 9), but he wants to keep force *in the background as long as possible.* He concludes par. 10—which contains important and complex ideas—by admitting *one can't help getting gloomy and also a bit rattled.* One of his arguments for his aristocracy (par. 12) is that they are the sort the reader *would like to meet or be.* He is against asceticism (par. 12), but admits *This isn't a major point.* He doesn't believe (par. 14) in a change of heart for man, but rather in *ordering and distributing his native goodness.* And so on; there are other examples in the essay.

Does the essay persuade the reader that a man could live by these beliefs? Is such a man presented in the essay?

DICTION AND TONE

1. Is it persuasive to speak of living in an age of Faith as *damned unpleasant?*

2. To a British audience, what is the tone of *bloody in every sense of the word* (par. 2)?

3. Forster says that democracy deserves our support because it is *less hateful* than other contemporary forms of government (par. 5). Describe the tone of this statement.

4. The phrase *two cheers for democracy* (par. 7) seems almost too carefully modulated. Argue for or against its persuasiveness.

5. The second sentence of par. 10 contains both *alas!* and *hooray!* What is the tone of these exclamations?

6. Why is Forster's metaphor *breathing holes for the human spirit* (par. 10) persuasive?

7. Comment on the diction of *As soon as people have power they go crooked and sometimes dotty, too* (par. 13).

8. Forster ends a list (par. 12) of characteristics of aristocracy with *and they can take a joke*. Is this deliberately anticlimactic? What is the tone?

9. Why does Forster follow *eyes to see* with the less usual *hands to feel* (par. 13)?

APPLICATIONS TO WRITING

1. Forster is persuasive partly because he is courageous enough to see difficulties and inconsistencies—and honest enough to write of them. Write a composition on some of your beliefs which are as inconsistent as you are.

2. Forster is persuasive partly because he reflects the tenor of his beliefs in his diction, his tone, and in the organization of his essay—including his paragraphs and sentences. Write a composition in which you do the same.

3. Forster is persuasive partly because his description of his beliefs becomes an implicit portrait of himself. Write a composition in which you do the same.

4. Forster is persuasive because he combines the above-mentioned methods in one essay. Do the same.

THE REPUBLIC OF
SILENCE

JEAN-PAUL SARTRE

We were never more free than during the German occupation. We had lost all our rights, beginning with the right to talk.
Every day we were insulted to our faces and had to take it in silence.
Under one pretext or another, as workers, Jews, or political prisoners,
we were deported EN MASSE. Everywhere, on billboards, in the newspapers, on the screen, we encountered the revolting and insipid picture
of ourselves that our oppressors wanted us to accept. And, because
of all this, we were free. Because the Nazi venom seeped even into
our thoughts, every accurate thought was a conquest. Because an all-
powerful police tried to force us to hold our tongues, every word took
on the value of a declaration of principles. Because we were hunted
down, every one of our gestures had the weight of a solemn commitment. The circumstances, atrocious as they often were, finally made
it possible for us to live, without pretense or false shame, the hectic
and impossible existence that is known as the lot of man. Exile,
captivity, and especially death (which we usually shrink from facing
at all in happier times) became for us the habitual objects of our
concern. We learned that they were neither inevitable accidents, nor
even constant and exterior dangers, but that they must be considered

as our lot itself, our destiny, the profound source of our reality as men. At every instant we lived up to the full sense of this commonplace little phrase: "Man is mortal!" And the choice that each of us made of his life and of his being was an authentic choice because it was made face to face with death, because it could always have been expressed in these terms: "Rather death than. . . ." And here I am not speaking of the élite among us who were real Resistants, but of all Frenchmen who, at every hour of the night and day throughout four years, answered no. But the very cruelty of the enemy drove us to the extremities of this condition by forcing us to ask ourselves questions that one never considers in time of peace. All those among us—and what Frenchman was not at one time or another in this situation— who knew any details concerning the Resistance asked themselves anxiously, "If they torture me, shall I be able to keep silent?" Thus the basic question of liberty itself was posed, and we were brought to the verge of the deepest knowledge that man can have of himself. For the secret of a man is not his Oedipus complex or his inferiority complex: it is the limit of his own liberty, his capacity for resisting torture and death. [1]

To those who were engaged in underground activities, the conditions of their struggle afforded a new kind of experience. They did not fight openly like soldiers. In all circumstances they were alone. They were hunted down in solitude, arrested in solitude. It was completely forlorn and unbefriended that they held out against torture, alone and naked in the presence of torturers, clean-shaven, well-fed, and well-clothed, who laughed at their cringing flesh, and to whom an untroubled conscience and a boundless sense of social strength gave every appearance of being in the right. Alone. Without a friendly hand or a word of encouragement. Yet, in the depth of their solitude, it was the others that they were protecting, all the others, all their comrades in the Resistance. Total responsibility in total solitude— is this not the very definition of our liberty? This being stripped of all, this solitude, this tremendous danger, were the same for all. For the leaders and for their men, for those who conveyed messages without knowing what their content was, as for those who directed the entire Resistance, the punishment was the same—imprisonment, deportation, death. There is no army in the world where there is such equality of risk for the private and for the commander-in-chief. And this is why the Resistance was a true democracy: for the soldier as for the commander, the same danger, the same forsakenness, the same total responsibility, the same absolute liberty within discipline. Thus, in darkness and in blood, a Republic was established, the strongest of Republics. Each of its citizens knew that he owed himself to all and that he could count only on himself alone. Each of them, in complete isolation, fulfilled his responsibility and his role in history. Each of them, standing against the oppressors, undertook to be himself, freely and irrevocably. And by choosing for himself in liberty, he chose the liberty of all. This Republic without institutions, without an army, without police, was something that at each instant every Frenchman had to win and to affirm against Nazism. No one failed in this duty, and now we are on the threshold of another Republic. May this Republic about to be set up in broad daylight preserve the austere virtues of that other Republic of Silence and of Night. [2]

PURPOSE AND STRUCTURE

1. What effect has the apparent paradox in the opening statement?

2. A paradox can be resolved either by restatement so that its intended meaning is clear or by defining the terms accurately and applying the definition consistently. Which method does Sartre use?

3. Sartre frequently develops rhythm in his statements by using a series of three elements. Note every time he resorts to this pattern. At times the series is an enumeration; elsewhere the items are in climactic order. Distinguish between the two patterns.

4. A series construction always requires parallel construction. Note the series that begins with the sixth sentence of par. 1. Does this parallelism contribute to force? to logic? to emotional intensity? Try reading the sentences aloud.

5. Circle the subjects of the first six sentences of par. 1. How does Sartre avoid monotony? Notice where the subjects appear in the sentences.

6. Sartre uses a comparable technique at the beginning of par. 2. Identify it. Analyze the cause to effect development of par. 1.

DICTION AND TONE

1. Many of the structural patterns examined above contribute to the tone of the essay. The diction also establishes tone. In par. 2 how many times is the word *alone* used in the first six sentences? What is the effect of placing *alone* in a one-word sentence?

2. Notice the variety of words or phrases Sartre uses to support the sense and feeling of *alone—solitude, forlorn*. List the others.

3. What is the effect of *clean-shaven, well-fed, well-clothed?* Do these modifiers excite the response they usually would? Why or why not?

APPLICATIONS TO WRITING

Write an argument which is based on a paradox. Some suggested topics: college as an escape from intellectual concerns; the army as the place for an independent life; go without sleep to be really wakeful; poverty makes for richness; our possessions possess us.

THE ALLEGORY OF
THE CAVE

from *The Republic*

PLATO

And now, I said, let me show in a figure how far our nature is enlightened or unenlightened: Behold! human beings living in an underground den, which has a mouth open towards the light and reaching all along the den; here they have been from their childhood, and have their legs and necks chained so that they can not move, and can only see before them, being prevented by the chains from turning round their heads. Above and behind them a fire is blazing at a distance, and between the fire and the prisoners there is a raised way; and you will see, if you look, a low wall built along the way, like the screen which marionette players have in front of them, over which they show the puppets. [1]

I see. [2]

And do you see, I said, men passing along the wall carrying all sorts of vessels, and statues and figures of animals made of wood and stone and various materials, which appear over the wall? Some of them are talking, others silent. [3]

From *The Works of Plato*, translated by Benjamin Jowett. Published by Tudor Publishing Company. Reprinted by permission of the publisher.

You have shown me a strange image, and they are strange prisoners. [4]

Like ourselves, I replied; and they see only their own shadows, or the shadows of one another, which the fire throws on the opposite wall of the cave? [5]

True, he said; how could they see anything but the shadows if they were never allowed to move their heads? [6]

And of the objects which are being carried in like manner they would only see the shadows? [7]

Yes, he said. [8]

And if they were able to converse with one another, would they not suppose that they were naming what was actually before them? [9]

Very true. [10]

And suppose further that the prison had an echo which came from the other side, would they not be sure to fancy when one of the passers-by spoke that the voice which they heard came from the passing shadow? [11]

No question, he replied. [12]

To them, I said, the truth would be literally nothing but the shadows of the images. [13]

That is certain. [14]

And now look again, and see what will naturally follow if the prisoners are released and disabused of their error. At first, when any of them is liberated and compelled suddenly to stand up and turn his neck round and walk and look towards the light, he will suffer sharp pains; the glare will distress him, and he will be unable to see the realities of which in his former state he had seen the shadows; and then conceive some one saying to him, that what he saw before was an illusion, but that now, when he is approaching nearer to being and his eye is turned towards more real existence, he has a clearer vision—what will be his reply? And you may further imagine that his instructor is pointing to the objects as they pass and requiring him to name them—will he not be perplexed? Will he not fancy that the shadows which he formerly saw are truer than the objects which are now shown to him? [15]

Far truer. [16]

And if he is compelled to look straight at the light, will he not have a pain in his eyes which will make him turn away to take refuge in the objects of vision which he can see, and which he will conceive to be in reality clearer than the things which are now being shown to him? [17]

True, he said. [18]

And suppose once more, that he is reluctantly dragged up a steep and rugged ascent, and held fast until he is forced into the presence of the sun himself, is he not likely to be pained and irritated? When he approaches the light his eyes will be dazzled, and he will not be able to see anything at all of what are now called realities. [19]

Not all in a moment, he said. [20]

He will require to grow accustomed to the sight of the upper world. And first he will see the shadows best, next the reflections of men and other objects in the water, and then the objects themselves; then he will gaze upon the light of the moon and the stars and the spangled heaven; and he will see the sky and the stars by night better than the sun or the light of the sun by day? [21]

Certainly. [22]

Last of all he will be able to see the sun, and not mere reflections of him in the water, but he will see him in his own proper place, and not in another; and he will contemplate him as he is. [23]

Certainly. [24]

He will then proceed to argue that this is he who gives the season and the years, and is the guardian of all that is in the visible world, and in a certain way the cause of all things which he and his fellows have been accustomed to behold? [25]

Clearly, he said, he would first see the sun and then reason about him. [26]

And when he remembered his old habitation, and the wisdom of the den and his fellow-prisoners, do you not suppose that he would felicitate himself on the change, and pity them? [27]

Certainly, he would. [28]

And if they were in the habit of conferring honors among them-

selves on those who were quickest to observe the passing shadows and
to remark which of them went before, and which followed after, and
which were together; and who were therefore best able to draw conclusions as to the future, do you think that he would care for such
honors and glories, or envy the possessors of them? Would he not
say with Homer,

"Better to be the poor servant of a poor master,"

and to endure anything, rather than think as they do and live after
their manner? [29]

Yes, he said, I think that he would rather suffer anything than
entertain these false notions and live in this miserable manner. [30]

Imagine once more, I said, such an one coming suddenly out of the
sun to be replaced in his old situation; would he not be certain to
have his eyes full of darkness? [31]

To be sure, he said. [32]

And if there were a contest, and he had to compete in measuring
the shadows with the prisoners who had never moved out of the den,
while his sight was still weak, and before his eyes had become steady
(and the time which would be needed to acquire this new habit of
sight might be very considerable), would he not be ridiculous? Men
would say of him that up he went and down he came without his
eyes; and that it was better not even to think of ascending; and if
any one tried to loose another and lead him up to the light let them
only catch the offender, and they would put him to death. [33]

No question, he said. [34]

This entire allegory, I said, you may now append, dear Glaucon,
to the previous argument; the prison-house is the world of sight, the
light of the fire is the sun, and you will not misapprehend me if you
interpret the journey upwards to be the ascent of the soul into the
intellectual world according to my poor belief, which, at your desire,
I have expressed—whether rightly or wrongly God knows. But,
whether true or false, my opinion is that in the world of knowledge
the idea of good appears last of all, and is seen only with an effort;
and, when seen, is also inferred to be the universal author of all things
beautiful and right, parent of light and of the lord of light in this

visible world, and the immediate source of reason and truth in the intellectual; and that this is the power upon which he who would act rationally either in public or private life must have his eye fixed. [35]

I agree, he said, as far as I am able to understand you. [36]

Moreover, I said, you must not wonder that those who attain to this beatific vision are unwilling to descend to human affairs; for their souls are ever hastening into the upper world where they desire to dwell; which desire of theirs is very natural, if our allegory may be trusted. [37]

Yes, very natural. [38]

And is there anything surprising in one who passes from divine contemplations to the evil state of man, misbehaving himself in a ridiculous manner; if, while his eyes are blinking and before he has become accustomed to the surrounding darkness, he is compelled to fight in courts of law, or in other places, about the images or the shadows of images of justice, and is endeavoring to meet the conceptions of those who have never yet seen absolute justice? [39]

Anything but surprising, he replied. [40]

Any one who has common sense will remember that the bewilderments of the eyes are of two kinds, and arise from two causes, either from coming out of the light or from going into the light, which is true of the mind's eye, quite as much as of the bodily eye; and he who remembers this when he sees any one whose vision is perplexed and weak, will not be too ready to laugh; he will first ask whether that soul of man has come out of the brighter life, and is unable to see because unaccustomed to the dark, or having turned from darkness to the day is dazzled by excess of light. And he will count the one happy in his condition and state of being, and he will pity the other; or, if he have a mind to laugh at the soul which comes from below into the light, there will be more reason in this than in the laugh which greets him who returns from above out of the light into the den. [41]

That, he said, is a very just distinction. [42]

But then, if I am right, certain professors of education must be wrong when they say that they can put a knowledge into the soul which was not there before, like sight into blind eyes. [43]

They undoubtedly say this, he replied. [44]

Whereas, our argument shows that the power and capacity of learning exists in the soul already; and that just as the eye was unable to turn from darkness to light without the whole body, so too the instrument of knowledge can only by the movement of the whole soul be turned from the world of becoming into that of being, and learn by degrees to endure the sight of being, and of the brightest and best of being, or in other words, of the good. [45]

Very true. [46]

And must there not be some art which will effect conversion in the easiest and quickest manner; not implanting the faculty of sight, for that exists already, but has been turned in the wrong direction, and is looking away from the truth? [47]

Yes, he said, such an art may be presumed. [48]

And whereas the other so-called virtues of the soul seem to be akin to bodily qualities, for even when they are not originally innate they can be implanted later by habit and exercise, the virtue of wisdom more than anything else contains a divine element which always remáins, and by this conversion is rendered useful and profitable; or, on the other hand, hurtful and useless. Did you never observe the narrow intelligence flashing from the keen eye of a clever rogue—how eager he is, how clearly his paltry soul sees the way to his end; he is the reverse of blind, but his keen eyesight is forced into the service of evil; and he is mischievous in proportion to his cleverness? [49]

Very true, he said. [50]

But what if there had been a circumcision of such natures in the days of their youth; and they had been severed from those sensual pleasures, such as eating and drinking, which, like leaden weights, were attached to them at their birth, and which drag them down and turn the vision of their souls upon the things that are below—if, I say, they had been released from these impediments and turned in the opposite direction, the very same faculty in them would have seen the truth as keenly as they see what their eyes are turned to now. [51]

Very likely. [52]

Yes, I said; and there is another thing which is likely, or rather a necessary inference from what has preceded, that neither the uneducated and uninformed of the truth, nor yet those who never make an end of their education, will be able ministers of state; not the former, because they have no single aim of duty which is the rule of all their actions, private as well as public; nor the latter, because they will not act at all except upon compulsion, fancying that they are already dwelling apart in the islands of the blest. [53]

Very true, he replied. [54]

Then, I said, the business of us who are the founders of the State will be to compel the best minds to attain that knowledge which we have already shown to be the greatest of all—they must continue to ascend until they arrive at the good; but when they have ascended and seen enough we must not allow them to do as they do now. [55]

What do you mean? [56]

I mean that they remain in the upper world: but this must not be allowed; they must be made to descend again among the prisoners in the den, and partake of their labors and honors, whether they are worth having or not. [57]

But is not this unjust? he said; ought we to give them a worse life, when they might have a better? [58]

You have again forgotten, my friend, I said, the intention of the legislator, who did not aim at making any one class in the State happy above the rest; the happiness was to be in the whole State, and he held the citizens together by persuasion and necessity, making them benefactors of the State, and therefore benefactors of one another; to this end he created them, not to please themselves, but to be his instruments in binding up the State. [59]

True, he said, I had forgotten. [60]

Observe, Glaucon, that there will be no injustice in compelling our philosophers to have a care and providence of others; we shall explain to them that in other States, men of their class are not obliged to share in the toils of politics: and this is reasonable for they grow up at their own sweet will, and the government would rather not have them. Being self-taught, they can not be expected to show any gratitude for a culture which they have never received. But we have brought you into the world to be rulers of the hive, kings of your-selves and of the other citizens, and have educated you far better and more perfectly than they have been educated, and you are better able to share in the double duty. Wherefore each of you, when his turn comes, must go down to the general underground abode, and get the habit of seeing in the dark. When you have acquired the habit, you will see ten thousand times better than the inhabitants of the den, and you will know what the several images are, and what they repre-sent, because you have seen the beautiful and just and good in their truth. And thus our State, which is also yours, will be a reality, and not a dream only, and will be administered in a spirit unlike that of other States, in which men fight with one another about shadows only and are distracted in the struggle for power, which in their eyes is a great good. Whereas the truth is that the State in which the rulers are most reluctant to govern is always the best and most quietly gov-erned, and the State in which they are most eager, the worst. [61]

Quite true, he replied. [62]

And will our pupils, when they hear this, refuse to take their turn at the toils of State, when they are allowed to spend the greater part of their time with one another in the heavenly light? [63]

Impossible, he answered; for they are just men, and the commands which we impose upon them are just; there can be no doubt that every one of them will take office as a stern necessity, and not after the fashion of our present rulers of State. [64]

Yes, my friend, I said; and there lies the point. You must contrive for your future rulers another and a better life than that of a ruler, and then you may have a well-ordered State; for only in the State which offers this, will they rule who are truly rich, not in silver and gold, but in virtue and wisdom, which are the true blessings of life. Whereas if they go to the administration of public affairs, poor and hungering after their own private advantage, thinking that hence they are to snatch the chief good, order there can never be; for they will be fighting about office, and the civil and domestic broils which thus arise will be the ruin of the rulers themselves and of the whole State. [65]

Most true, he replied. [66]

And the only life which looks down upon the life of political ambition is that of true philosophy. Do you know of any other? [67]

Indeed, I do not, he said. [68]

And those who govern ought not to be lovers of the task? For, if they are, there will be rival lovers, and they will fight. [69]

No question. [70]

Who then are those whom we shall compel to be guardians? Surely they will be the men who are wisest about affairs of State, and by whom the State is best administered, and who at the same time have other honors and another and a better life than that of politics? [71]

They are the men, and I will choose them, he replied. [72]

PURPOSE AND STRUCTURE

1. Plato's *Republic* is, of course, one of the consummate works of the human spirit; *The Allegory of the Cave*, from Book VII, is possibly its most famous passage. Let us consider some of its methods of persuasion.

The first speaker (he is Socrates) begins with a strange and complicated image. What is its purpose? Would it serve its purpose more effectively if it were simplified? What would the result be if the two sources of light (from the entrance of the den and from the fire) were reduced to one—say, from the entrance? if the men passing along the wall (par. 3) were omitted and the prisoners simply saw *their own shadows, or the shadows of one another* (par. 5)? if the shadows of *all sorts of vessels, and statues and figures of animals made of wood and stone and various materials* (par. 3) were omitted? In other words, either simplify the description of the cave or show these strange and complicated details to be functional in the allegory developed by Socrates.

2. Why use the phrase *what are now called realities* (par. 19)?

3. The allegory of the movement from error to *what are now called realities* (par. 19) is elaborated in pars. 15–26. Is it repetitious? Are the *objects* in the last sentence of par. 15 the same as the *objects* in par. 21? Do they have a different allegorical significance (see pars. 35–72)?

4. What is the significance of *he is reluctantly dragged up a steep and rugged ascent, and held fast until he is forced into the presence of the sun* (par. 19)? Would it be more persuasive if Plato stated his theories directly, without allegory?

5. In par. 35 Socrates gives his interpretation of the allegory. Should he thereafter drop the allegory? In how many of his speeches following par. 35 does he refer to or use the image of the cave? Compare the ways he uses it before and after par. 35.

6. Why is par. 36 persuasive, coming as it does in response to par. 35?

7. Why is the detail in the last sentence of par. 15 important? Relate it to the whole of par. 33; to par. 29. (See also pars. 39 and 41.) Consider its persuasive effect on two possible audiences: (1) The rulers (Plato's guardians); what attitude should they take toward the errors they make? (2) Those who are to be ruled by the guardians; what attitude should they take toward the errors of their rulers? toward one of their group who seems to be more efficient or more clever (see also the last part of par. 49) than the guardians?

8. What is Glaucon's function in the dialogue? Does he serve as a representative of the audience? Are his responses too acquiescent and simple-minded to be convincing?

9. While the images, the structure of the dialogue, the diction and tone, all work together to persuade the reader, the most powerful persuasive device of all—possibly because it is unspoken—is flattery. In order to understand how it works, we must ask who is addressed, who is the audience? Seemingly, it is Glaucon—that is to say, a somewhat imperceptive representative of the reader. He is being persuaded to accept the rule of the *guardians* (par. 71). These guardians are forced to leave their *underground den* (par. 1) and are *dragged up a steep and rugged ascent* (par. 19), there to see the light of the *spangled heaven* (par. 21). But when they attain this *world of knowledge* and of *the idea of good* (par. 35), they are forced to leave it—to leave *the islands of the blest* (par. 53)—and to go back to the den. Why? In par. 72 Glaucon accepts the rule of the guardians: *They are the men and I will choose them.* Is the reader persuaded to accept these men as rulers also?

Who are these guardians? They are men whose nature has become *enlightened* (par. 1). How does reading this dialogue begin the process of becoming enlightened? Why is this flattering to the reader? Why does this flattery persuade the reader to accept the argument of Plato?

DICTION AND TONE

1. The figure of the underground den is introduced (par. 1) with the words *enlightened or unenlightened*. Discuss their appropriateness to the image. Would "wise or unwise" be as appropriate?

2. Discuss the progressive change in tone from the description of the underground den (pars. 1–13), to the description of the released prisoners before they grow accustomed to the sight of the upper world (pars. 15–20), to what happens after (pars. 21–26). Does the diction change? How do diction and tone contribute to the persuasiveness of the passage (pars. 1–26)? to the acceptance of Socrates' point that it is *the ascent of the soul into the intellectual world* (par. 35)?

3. What is the purpose of the imagery and diction of *then he will gaze upon the light of the moon and the stars and the spangled heaven* (par. 21)?

4. What is the *wisdom of the den* (par. 27)? Why use the word *wisdom?*

5. Who is *the guardian of all that is in the visible world* (par. 25)? Why is it persuasive to use the same word for the rulers of the state (par. 71)?

6. Is the word *circumcision* (in the first sentence of par. 51) precise and appropriate?

APPLICATIONS TO WRITING

1. One of the ways *The Allegory of the Cave* persuades is through a story of escape from prison (it ends with the escaped prisoner returning to rule the prison). Write a counter-allegory and present it as Plato's dialogue does. (For instance, the prisoner escapes and refuses to return, or he refuses to escape, or he returns and refuses to rule.)

2. Write an ironic imitation of Plato's dialogue, using modern examples. For instance, begin with a political convention—your cave—then discuss choosing candidates who are (1) happily engaged in other pursuits, (2) don't wish to be chosen, and (3) whose eyes are *full of darkness* (par. 31).

3. Glaucon seems to serve a minimal function in the dialogue; he agrees

with practically all of Socrates' statements. Rewrite the dialogue omitting Glaucon and presenting Socrates' argument in persuasive, discursive prose. (Warning: Reorganization of the structure and recasting of the material may be necessary.)

4. Socrates' method for choosing the guardians has certain similarities to part of a plan developed in 1946 to police the atom bomb (called the Lilienthal Report or the Baruch Report). It attempted to solve the following problem: Atomic power can be policed only by the top scientists in the field, but such scientists refuse to act as policemen because the job is too boring.

Look up the report (written in semi-official prose) and master the details of its solution to the problem. Then write a Platonic dialogue in which you persuade your audience to accept or reject this solution.

5. Plato's allegory conveys his theory of knowledge. Create an allegory in which you convey your own theory of knowledge. Present it, as Plato does, in dialogue form.

6. Socrates' tone is extremely persuasive; he is tentative and modest (for instance, in par. 35) and he is sweetly reasonable in answering Glaucon's one objection (par. 59). It is possible that only a discourteous person, one who is willing to challenge his tone and reject his premises, can argue effectively against him. Write an impolite dialogue between Socrates and the protagonist of Dostoyevsky's *Existential Freedom*.

A MODEST PROPOSAL
for Preventing the Children of Ireland from Being a Burden to Their Parents or Country

JONATHAN SWIFT

It is a melancholy object to those who walk through this great town or travel in the country, when they see the streets, the roads, and cabin-doors crowded with beggars of the female sex, followed by three, four, or six children, all in rags, and importuning every passenger for an alms. These mothers instead of being able to work for their honest livelihood, are forced to employ all their time in strolling to beg sustenance for their helpless infants, who, as they grow up, either turn thieves for want of work, or leave their dear native country, to fight for the Pretender in Spain, or sell themselves to the Barbadoes. [1]

I think it is agreed by all parties, that this prodigious number of children in the arms, or on the backs, or at the heels of their mothers, and frequently of their fathers, is in the present deplorable state of the kingdom a very great additional grievance; and therefore whoever could find out a fair, cheap, and easy method of making these children sound and useful members of the common-wealth, would deserve so well of the public as to have his statue set up for a preserver of the nation. [2]

But my intention is very far from being confined to provide only for the children of professed beggars; it is of a much greater extent,

435

and shall take in the whole number of infants at a certain age, who are born of parents in effect as little able to support them, as those who demand our charity in the streets. [3]

As to my own part, having turned my thoughts, for many years, upon this important subject, and maturely weighed the several schemes of other projectors, I have always found them grossly mistaken in their computation. It is true, a child just dropt from its dam, may be supported by her milk for a solar year with little other nourishment, at most not above the value of two shillings, which the mother may certainly get, or the value in scraps, by her lawful occupation of begging; and it is exactly at one year old that I propose to provide for them in such a manner, as, instead of being a charge upon their parents, or the parish, or wanting food and raiment for the rest of their lives, they shall, on the contrary, contribute to the feeding and partly to the clothing of many thousands. [4]

There is likewise another great advantage in my scheme, that it will prevent those voluntary abortions, and that horrid practice of women murdering their bastard children, alas! too frequent among us—sacrificing the poor innocent babes, I doubt, more to avoid the expense than the shame—which would move tears and pity in the most savage and inhuman breast. [5]

The number of souls in this kingdom being usually reckoned one million and a half, of these I calculate there may be about two hundred thousand couple whose wives are breeders; from which number I subtract thirty thousand couples, who are able to maintain their own children, although I apprehend there cannot be so many, under the present distresses of the kingdom; but this being granted, there will remain an hundred and seventy thousand breeders. I again subtract fifty thousand, for those women who miscarry, or whose children die by accident or disease within the year. There only remain an hundred and twenty thousand children of poor parents annually born: The question therefore is, How this number shall be reared, and provided for? which, as I have already said, under the present situation of affairs, is utterly impossible by all the methods hitherto proposed; for we can neither employ them in handicraft or agriculture; we neither build houses, (I mean in the country) nor cultivate land: They can very seldom pick up a livelihood by stealing till they arrive at six years old, except where they are of towardly parts, although, I confess, they learn the rudiments much earlier; during which time they can however be properly looked upon only as probationers; as I have been informed by a principal gentleman in the county of Cavan, who protested to me, that he never knew above one or two instances under the age of six, even in a part of the kingdom so renowned for the quickest proficiency in that art. [6]

I am assured by our merchants, that a boy or a girl before twelve years old, is no saleable commodity, and even when they come to this age, they will not yield above three pounds, or three pounds and half a crown at most, on the exchange; which cannot turn to account either to the parents or kingdom, the charge of nutriment and rags having been at least four times that value. [7]

I shall now therefore humbly propose my own thoughts, which I hope will not be liable to the least objection. [8]

I have been assured by a very knowing American of my acquaintance in London, that a young healthy child well nursed is at a year old a most delicious, nourishing, and wholesome food, whether stewed, roasted, baked, or boiled; and I make no doubt that it will equally serve in a fricassee, or a ragout. [9]

I do therefore humbly offer it to publick consideration, that of the hundred and twenty thousand children, already computed, twenty thousand may be reserved for breed, whereof only one fourth part to be males; which is more than we allow to sheep, black cattle, or swine; and my reason is that these children are seldom the fruits of marriage, a circumstance not much regarded by our savages; therefore one male will be sufficient to serve four females. That the remaining hundred thousand may, at a year old, be offered in the sale to the persons of quality and fortune through the kingdom; always advising the mother to let them suck plentifully in the last month, so as to render them plump and fat for a good table. A child will make two dishes at an entertainment for friends; and when the family dines alone, the fore or hind quarter will make a reasonable dish, and seasoned with a little pepper or salt will be very good boiled on the fourth day, especially in winter. [10]

I have reckoned upon a medium that a child just born will weigh 12 pounds, and in a solar year, if tolerably nursed, increaseth to 28 pounds. [11]

I grant this food will be somewhat dear, and therefore very proper for landlords, who, as they have already devoured most of the parents, seem to have the best title to the children. [12]

Infants' flesh will be in season throughout the year, but more plentiful in March, and a little before and after; for we are told by a grave author, an eminent French physician, that fish being a prolific diet, there are more children born in Roman Catholic countries about nine months after Lent than at any other season; therefore, reckoning a year after Lent, the markets will be more glutted than usual, because the number of popish infants is at least three to one in this kingdom: and therefore it will have one other collateral advantage, by lessening the number of papists among us. [13]

I have already computed the charge of nursing a beggar's child (in which list I reckon all cottagers, laborers, and four-fifths of the farmers) to be about two shillings per annum, rags included; and I believe no gentleman would repine to give ten shillings for the carcass of a good fat child, which, as I have said, will make four dishes of excellent nutritive meat, when he hath only some particular friend or his own family to dine with him. Thus the squire will learn to be a good landlord, and grow popular among his tenants; the mother will have eight shillings net profit, and be fit for work till she produces another child. [14]

Those who are more thrifty (as I must confess the times require) may flay the carcass, the skin of which artificially dressed will make admirable gloves for ladies, and summer boots for fine gentlemen. [15]

As to our city of Dublin, shambles may be appointed for this purpose in the most convenient parts of it, and butchers we may be assured will not be wanting; although I rather recommend buying the children alive and dressing them hot from the knife, as we do roasting pigs. [16]

A very worthy person, a true lover of his country, and whose virtues I highly esteem, was lately pleased in discoursing on this matter to offer a refinement upon my scheme. He said that many gentlemen of this kingdom, having of late destroyed their deer, he conceived that the want of venison might be well supplied by the bodies of young lads and maidens, not exceeding fourteen years of age nor under twelve; so great a number of both sexes in every country being now ready to starve for want of work and service; and these to be disposed of by their parents if alive, or otherwise by their nearest relations. But with due deference to so excellent a friend, and so deserving a patriot, I cannot be altogether in his sentiments; for as to the males, my American acquaintance assured me from frequent experience, that their flesh was generally tough and lean, like that of our schoolboys, by continual exercise, and their taste disagreeable, and to fatten them would not answer the charge. Then as to the females, it would, I think with humble submission, be a loss to the publick, because they soon would become breeders themselves: And besides it is not improbable that some scrupulous people might be apt to censure such a practice (although indeed very unjustly) as a little bordering upon cruelty, which, I confess, hath always been with me the strongest objection against any project, how well soever intended. [17]

But in order to justify my friend, he confessed that this expedient was put into his head by the famous Psalmanazar, a native of the island Formosa, who came from thence to London, above twenty years ago, and in conversation told my friend, that in his country when any young person happened to be put to death, the executioner sold the carcass to persons of quality, as a prime dainty, and that, in his time, the body of a plump girl of fifteen, who was crucified for an attempt to poison the Emperor, was sold to his Imperial Majesty's prime minister of state, and other great mandarins of the court, in joints from the gibbet, at four hundred crowns. Neither indeed can

I deny, that if the same use were made of several plump young girls in this town, who, without one single groat to their fortunes, cannot stir abroad without a chair, and appear at a play-house and assemblies in foreign fineries which they never will pay for, the kingdom would not be the worse. [18]

Some persons of a desponding spirit are in great concern about that vast number of poor people, who are aged, diseased, or maimed, and I have been desired to employ my thoughts what course may be taken, to ease the nation of so grievous an encumbrance. But I am not in the least pain upon that matter, because it is very well known, that they are every day dying, and rotting, by cold, and famine, and filth, and vermin, as fast as can be reasonably expected. And as to the younger labourers, they are now in almost as hopeful a condition. They cannot get work, and consequently pine away for want of nourishment, to a degree, that if at any time they are accidentally hired to common labour, they have not strength to perform it, and thus the country and themselves are happily delivered from the evils to come. [19]

I have too long digressed, and therefore shall return to my subject. I think the advantages by the proposal which I have made are obvious and many, as well as of the highest importance. [20]

For *first*, as I have already observed, it would greatly lessen the number of papists, with whom we are yearly over-run, being the principal breeders of the nation, as well as our most dangerous enemies, and who stay at home on purpose with a design to deliver the kingdom to the Pretender, hoping to take their advantage by the absence of so many good Protestants, who have chosen rather to leave their country, than stay at home, and pay tithes against their conscience to an Episcopal curate. [21]

Secondly, the poorer tenants will have something valuable of their own, which by law may be made liable to distress and help to pay their landlord's rent, their corn and cattle being already seized, and money a thing unknown. [22]

Thirdly, whereas the maintenance of an hundred thousand children, from two years old and upward, cannot be computed at less than ten shillings apiece per annum, the nation's stock will be thereby increased fifty thousand pounds per annum, besides the profit of a new dish introduced to the tables of all gentlemen of fortune in the kingdom who have any refinement in taste. And the money will circulate among ourselves, the goods being entirely of our own growth and manufacture. [23]

Fourthly, the constant breeders, beside the gain of eight shillings sterling per annum by the sale of their children, will be rid of the charge of maintaining them after the first year. [24]

Fifthly, this food would likewise bring great custom to taverns, where the vintners will certainly be so prudent as to procure the best receipts for dressing it to perfection, and consequently have their houses frequented by all the fine gentlemen who justly value themselves upon their knowledge in good eating; and a skillful cook, who understands how to oblige his guests, will contrive to make it as expensive as they please. [25]

Sixthly, this would be a great inducement to marriage, which all wise nations have either encouraged by rewards or enforced by laws and penalties. It would increase the care and the tenderness of mothers toward their children, when they were sure of a settlement for life to the poor babes, provided in some sort by the public, to their annual profit instead of expense. We should soon see an honest emulation among the married women, which of them could bring the fattest child to the market. Men would become as fond of their wives during the time of their pregnancy as they are now of their mares in foal, their cows in calf, their sows when they are ready to farrow; nor offer to beat or kick them (as is too frequent a practice) for fear of a miscarriage. [26]

Many other advantages might be enumerated. For instance, the addition of some thousand carcasses in our exportation of barreled beef, the propagation of swine's flesh, and improvement in the art of making good bacon, so much wanted among us by the great destruction of pigs, too frequent at our tables; which are no way comparable in taste or magnificence to a well-grown, fat, yearling child, which roasted whole will make a considerable figure at a lord mayor's feast or any other public entertainment. But this and many others I omit, being studious of brevity. [27]

Supposing that one thousand families in this city would be constant customers for infants' flesh, besides others who might have it at merry meetings, particularly at wedding and christenings, I compute that Dublin would take off annually about twenty thousand carcasses; and the rest of the kingdom (where probably they will be sold somewhat cheaper) the remaining eighty thousand. [28]

I can think of no one objection that will possibly be raised against this proposal, unless it should be urged that the number of people will be thereby much lessened in the kingdom. This I freely own, and 'twas indeed one principal design in offering it to the world. I desire the reader will observe that I calculate my remedy for this one individual kingdom of Ireland, and for no other that ever was, is, or, I think, ever can be upon earth. Therefore let no man talk to me of other expedients: of taxing our absentees at five shillings a pound: of using neither clothes, nor household furniture, except what is of our own growth and manufacture: of utterly rejecting the materials and instruments that promote foreign luxury: of curing the expensiveness of pride, vanity, idleness, and gaming in our women: of introducing a vein of parsimony, prudence and temperance: of learning to love our country, wherein we differ even from Laplanders, and the inhabitants of Topinamboo: of quitting our animosities, and factions, nor act any longer like the Jews, who were murdering one another at the very moment their city was taken: of being a little cautious not to sell our country and consciences for nothing: of teaching landlords to have at least one degree of mercy towards their tenants. Lastly, of putting a spirit of honesty, industry, and skill into our shopkeepers, who, if a resolution could now be taken to buy only our native goods, would immediately unite to cheat and exact upon us in the price, the measure, and the goodness, nor could ever yet be brought to make one fair proposal of just dealing, though often and earnestly invited to it. [29]

Therefore I repeat, let no man talk to me of these and the like expedients, till he hath at least some glimpse of hope, that there will ever be some hearty and sincere attempt to put them in practice. [30]

But as to my self, having been wearied out for many years with offering vain, idle, visionary thoughts, and at length utterly despairing of success, I fortunately fell upon this proposal, which as it is wholly new, so it hath something solid and real, of no expense and little trouble, full in our own power, and whereby we can incur no danger in disobliging England. For this kind of commodity will not bear exportation, the flesh being of too tender a consistence, to admit a long continuance in salt, although perhaps I could name a country, which would be glad to eat up our whole nation without it. [31]

After all, I am not so violently bent upon my own opinion, as to reject any offer, proposed by wise men, which shall be found equally innocent, cheap, easy, and effectual. But before something of that kind shall be advanced in contradiction to my scheme, and offering a better, I desire the author or authors, will be pleased maturely to consider two points. *First*, as things now stand, how they will be able to find food and raiment for a hundred thousand useless mouths and backs. And *Secondly*, there being a round million of creatures in human figure throughout this kingdom, whose whole subsistence put into a common stock would leave them in debt two millions of pounds sterling, adding those who are beggars by profession, to the bulk of farmers, cottagers and labourers, with their wives and children, who are beggars in effect; I desire those politicians, who dislike my overture, and may perhaps be so bold to attempt an answer, that they will first ask the parents of these mortals, whether they would not at this day think it a great happiness to have been sold for food at a year old, in the manner I prescribe, and thereby have avoided such a perpetual scene of misfortunes as they have since gone through, by the oppression of landlords, the impossibility of paying rent without money or trade, the want of common sustenance, with neither house nor clothes to cover them from the inclemencies of the weather, and the most inevitable prospect of entailing the like or greater miseries upon their breed for ever. [32]

I profess, in the sincerity of my heart, that I have not the least personal interest in endeavoring to promote this necessary work, having no other motive than the public good of my country, by advancing our trade, providing for infants, relieving the poor, and giving some pleasure to the rich. I have no children by which I can propose to get a single penny; the youngest being nine years old, and my wife past child-bearing. [33]

PURPOSE AND STRUCTURE

1. In discussing A *Modest Proposal* it is important to distinguish between the character of Swift and the character he *assumes* for the purpose of writing the essay. This assumed character, frequently referred to as a mask through which Swift writes, will hereafter be called the *narrator*. This distinction is important, for the effectiveness of the essay depends in part upon the narrator's inability to comprehend fully all the implications of what he is suggesting. He is morally blind. As you will see, Swift reveals this blindness by degrees; at the same time he develops a complex but narrow narrator whose two dominant characteristics are his extreme rationality and his conception of humanity solely in terms of economics— utility and value. (See Irony, Perspective, Tone in Glossary.)

2. The first seven paragraphs—up to, *I shall now therefore humbly propose my own thoughts* . . . constitute an introduction. Identify at least two purposes of this lengthy introduction.

3. What is your impression of the narrator of the first three paragraphs? Consider such language as *this great town, dear Native Country, sound and useful members of the common-wealth.* Whom or what does he sound like?

4. The moral nature of the narrator begins to emerge in par. 4. What one word dehumanizes his fellow countrymen?

5. Par. 6 continues this dehumanization. What one word in the first sentence reveals the narrator's attitudes toward people? Notice how the choice of words maintains his tone.

6. In par. 6 the narrator assumes a highly objective attitude. What does

he gain? What do the mathematical tabulations say about the narrator? about the proposal itself?

7. Some of the horror of A *Modest Proposal* grows out of the narrator's inability to consider human misery in any terms other than economic ones. Swift handles this inability in an increasingly subtle fashion. For example, the narrator lists six advantages to his proposal. In the sixth advantage, what does he assume to be the source of decent human behavior? How is this consistent with his character?

8. The last two sentences of the essay are especially revealing as a commentary on human nature. In them the narrator anticipates an objection to his proposal and answers it. What is the objection he anticipates? If his anticipation is correct, what does this say about his audience?

DICTION AND TONE

1. In par. 2 notice how *present deplorable state of the kingdom* makes the presence of starving children regrettable not for the children's sakes, but for the nation's. What words in the rest of the paragraph sustain this attitude?

2. In the last sentence of par. 6, what is the effect of *livelihood, towardly, probationers, renowned?*

3. In par. 7, what is the effect of *commodity?*

4. Par. 9 is straightforward—almost blunt—and yet rather elegantly written. Discrepancy between elegance of statement and blunt meaning is usually discouraged. What is gained here?

5. Compare the first and last sentences of par. 10. Which evokes the most horror? Defend your answer using some of the principles discussed under Abstraction in the Glossary.

6. Par. 12 is a brilliant sentence. What is the significance of *therefore?* Of *proper?* Is *devoured* meant literally? Why is *best title* particularly appropriate?

7. In par. 14 is *gentleman* appropriate? Why *fine* gentlemen in par. 15?

8. In par. 19, explain the effect of *as fast as can be reasonably expected.*

APPLICATIONS TO WRITING

1. Write your own modest proposal. You may suggest solutions to problems in such areas as unemployment, food distribution, education, race relations, foreign policy. If you prefer, focus attention on some problem in your school or community. A few words of caution: Swift makes only *one* outlandish assumption—that children be consumed as food—and the remainder of his argument follows quite logically. The more outlandish assumptions you make, the weaker your essay will be. Notice also that your essay must be logical. Consistency of tone, highly important, will depend on your ability to maintain a good "mask" and on your sense of appropriate diction.

2. *A Modest Proposal* is frequently called the greatest piece of sustained irony in English literature. Write an extended definition of irony based on your understanding of this essay. Support your generalizations with evidence from the essay.

Part Eight

DICTION AND TONE

Diction—style as determined by choice of words. Good diction is characterized by precision and appropriateness to subject matter; weak diction, by the use of inappropriate, vague or trite words. The relationship between the kinds of words a writer selects and his subject matter in large part determines tone. Baldwin's diction—a striking combination of formal public language and informal private language—reflects his subject matter. Hersey's diction does not; his language is deliberately flat and reportorial. Orwell's has a cinematic immediacy; on the other hand, Camus' is abstract yet personal. Russell's diction is formal and poetic, while Lawrence's is by turn colloquial and apocalyptic. Porter is a master of metaphoric language and parody. And White (*The Door*), in the most supple and necessary fashion, creates part of his own language—*tex, koid, sani,* and *duro* (see Tone). The deliberate use of inappropriate diction is a frequent device of satire (for satire see Swift).

Tone—the manner in which the writer communicates his attitude toward the material he is presenting. For his attitude toward his audience, see Audience. Diction is the most obvious means of establishing tone. Baldwin's diction reflects his vision of public race riots and his vision of himself as an

447

intimate, complex battleground. On the other hand, Hersey's language is only one element in establishing his tone. More important is his selection and arrangement of facts and his refusal to comment freely (as Baldwin comments). Hersey's nearly total absorption by his material results in his tone. Orwell's tone in *Marrakech* is that of a visitor who communicates what he sees, what he feels, and, finally, what he thinks. Camus, writing of another North African city, presents a completely different tone, combining a nostalgic mood and an opulent atmosphere. For Camus, Algiers is one of the human situations, the place where man lives the life of the body. Russell's tone rises to his great theme of first things and of last things. Lawrence, on the other hand, moves back and forth from the personal to revelations from the underworld. Miss Porter reveals her attitude toward her subject— one of "horrid fascination"—through parody, metaphors, and a fluent structure. White's tone (*The Door*) is not so much split as it is shattered; he communicates it through coined fragments of words, incoherent parentheses, and images of induced psychosis (see Diction).

NOTES OF A NATIVE SON

JAMES BALDWIN

On the 29th of July, in 1943, my father died. On the same day, a few hours later, his last child was born. Over a month before this, while all our energies were concentrated in waiting for these events, there had been, in Detroit, one of the bloodiest race riots of the century. A few hours after my father's funeral, while he lay in state in the undertaker's chapel, a race riot broke out in Harlem. On the morning of the 3rd of August, we drove my father to the graveyard through a wilderness of smashed plate glass. [1]

The day of my father's funeral had also been my nineteenth birthday. As we drove him to the graveyard, the spoils of injustice, anarchy, discontent, and hatred were all around us. It seemed to me that God himself had devised, to mark my father's end, the most sustained and brutally dissonant of codas. And it seemed to me, too, that the violence which rose all about us as my father left the world had been devised as a corrective for the pride of his eldest son. I had declined to believe in that apocalypse which had been central to my father's vision; very well, life seemed to be saying, here is something that will certainly pass for an apocalypse until the real thing comes along. I had inclined to be contemptuous of my father for the conditions of his life, for the conditions of our lives. When his life had ended I began

449

to wonder about that life and also, in a new way, to be apprehensive about my own. [2]

I had not known my father very well. We had got on badly, partly because we shared, in our different fashions, the vice of stubborn pride. When he was dead I realized that I had hardly ever spoken to him. When he had been dead a long time I began to wish I had. It seems to be typical of life in America, where opportunities, real and fancied, are thicker than anywhere else on the globe, that the second generation has no time to talk to the first. No one, including my father, seems to have known exactly how old he was, but his mother had been born during slavery. He was of the first generation of free men. He, along with thousands of other Negroes, came North after 1919 and I was part of that generation which had never seen the landscape of what Negroes sometimes call the Old Country. [3]

He had been born in New Orleans and had been a quite young man there during the time that Louis Armstrong, a boy, was running errands for the dives and honky-tonks of what was always presented to me as one of the most wicked of cities—to this day, whenever I think of New Orleans, I also helplessly think of Sodom and Gomorrah. My father never mentioned Louis Armstrong, except to forbid us to play his records; but there was a picture of him on our wall for a long time. One of my father's strong-willed female relatives had placed it there and forbade my father to take it down. He never did, but he eventually maneuvered her out of the house and when, some years later, she was in trouble and near death, he refused to do anything to help her. [4]

He was, I think, very handsome. I gather this from photographs and from my own memories of him, dressed in his Sunday best and on his way to preach a sermon somewhere, when I was little. Handsome, proud, and ingrown, "like a toe-nail," somebody said. But he looked to me, as I grew older, like pictures I had seen of African tribal chieftains: he really should have been naked, with war-paint on and barbaric mementos, standing among spears. He could be chilling in the pulpit and indescribably cruel in his personal life and he was certainly the most bitter man I have ever met; yet it must be said

that there was something else in him, buried in him, which lent him
his tremendous power and, even, a rather crushing charm. It had
something to do with his blackness, I think—he was very black—
with his blackness and his beauty, and with the fact that he knew
that he was black but did not know that he was beautiful. He claimed
to be proud of his blackness but it had also been the cause of much
humiliation and it had fixed bleak boundaries to his life. He was
not a young man when we were growing up and he had already suffered many kinds of ruin; in his outrageously demanding and pro-
tective way he loved his children, who were black like him and
menaced, like him; and all these things sometimes showed in his
face when he tried, never to my knowledge with any success, to
establish contact with any of us. When he took one of his children
on his knee to play, the child always became fretful and began to
cry; when he tried to help one of us with our homework the absolutely
unabating tension which emanated from him caused our minds and
our tongues to become paralyzed, so that he, scarcely knowing why,
flew into a rage and the child, not knowing why, was punished. If it
ever entered his head to bring a surprise home for his children, it
was, almost unfailingly, the wrong surprise and even the big watermelons he often brought home on his back in the summertime led to
the most appalling scenes. I do not remember, in all those years, that
one of his children was ever glad to see him come home. From what
I was able to gather of his early life, it seemed that this inability to
establish contact with other people had always marked him and had
been one of the things which had driven him out of New Orleans.
There was something in him, therefore, groping and tentative, which
was never expressed and which was buried with him. One saw it most
clearly when he was facing new people and hoping to impress them.
But he never did, not for long. We went from church to smaller and
more improbable church, he found himself in less and less demand as
a minister, and by the time he died none of his friends had come to
see him for a long time. He had lived and died in an intolerable
bitterness of spirit and it frightened me, as we drove him to the grave-
yard through those unquiet, ruined streets, to see how powerful and

overflowing this bitterness could be and to realize that this bitterness now was mine. [5]

When he died I had been away from home for a little over a year. In that year I had had time to become aware of the meaning of all my father's bitter warnings, had discovered the secret of his proudly pursed lips and rigid carriage: I had discovered the weight of white people in the world. I saw that this had been for my ancestors and now would be for me an awful thing to live with and that the bitterness which had helped to kill my father could also kill me. [6]

He had been ill a long time—in the mind, as we now realized, reliving instances of his fantastic intransigence in the new light of his affliction and endeavoring to feel a sorrow for him which never, quite, came true. We had not known that he was being eaten up by paranoia, and the discovery that his cruelty, to our bodies and our minds, had been one of the symptoms of his illness was not, then, enough to enable us to forgive him. The younger children felt, quite simply, relief that he would not be coming home anymore. My mother's observation that it was he, after all, who had kept them alive all these years meant nothing because the problems of keeping children alive are not real for children. The older children felt, with my father gone, that they could invite their friends to the house without fear that their friends would be insulted or, as had sometimes happened with me, being told that their friends were in league with the devil and intended to rob our family of everything we owned. (I didn't fail to wonder, and it made me hate him, what on earth we owned that anybody else would want.) [7]

His illness was beyond all hope of healing before anyone realized that he was ill. He had always been so strange and had lived, like a prophet, in such unimaginably close communion with the Lord that his long silences which were punctuated by moans and hallelujahs and snatches of old songs while he sat at the living-room window never seemed odd to us. It was not until he refused to eat because, he said, his family was trying to poison him that my mother was forced to accept as a fact what had, until then, been only an unwilling suspicion. When he was committed, it was discovered that he had tuberculosis and, as it turned out, the disease of his mind allowed the disease of his body to destroy him. For the doctors could not force him to eat, either, and, though he was fed intravenously, it was clear from the beginning that there was no hope for him. [8]

In my mind's eye I could see him, sitting at the window, locked up in his terrors; hating and fearing every living soul including his children who had betrayed him, too, by reaching towards the world which had despised him. There were nine of us. I began to wonder what it could have felt like for such a man to have had nine children whom he could barely feed. He used to make little jokes about our poverty, which never, of course, seemed very funny to us; they could not have seemed very funny to him, either, or else our all too feeble response to them would never have caused such rages. He spent great energy and achieved, to our chagrin, no small amount of success in keeping us away from the people who surrounded us, people who had all-night rent parties to which we listened when we should have been sleeping, people who cursed and drank and flashed razor blades on Lenox Avenue. He could not understand why, if they had so much energy to spare, they could not use it to make their lives better. He treated almost everybody on our block with a most uncharitable asperity and neither they, nor, of course, their children were slow to reciprocate. [9]

The only white people who came to our house were welfare workers and bill collectors. It was almost always my mother who dealt with them, for my father's temper, which was at the mercy of his pride, was never to be trusted. It was clear that he felt their very presence in his home to be a violation: this was conveyed by his carriage, almost ludicrously stiff, and by his voice, harsh and vindictively polite. When I was around nine or ten I wrote a play which was directed by a young, white schoolteacher, a woman, who then took an interest in me, and gave me books to read and, in order to corroborate my theatrical bent, decided to take me to see what she somewhat tactlessly referred to as "real" plays. Theater-going was forbidden in our house, but, with the really cruel intuitiveness of a child, I suspected that the color of this woman's skin would carry the day for me. When, at school, she suggested taking me to the theater, I did not, as I might have done if she had been a Negro, find a way of discouraging her, but agreed that she should pick me up at my house one evening. I then, very cleverly, left all the rest to my mother, who suggested to my father, as I knew she would, that it would not be very nice to let such a kind woman make the trip for nothing. Also, since it was a schoolteacher, I imagine that my mother countered the idea of sin with the idea of "education," which word, even with my father, carried a kind of bitter weight. [10]

Before the teacher came my father took me aside to ask *why* she was coming, what *interest* she could possibly have in our house, in a boy like me. I said I didn't know but I, too, suggested that it had something to do with education. And I understood that my father was waiting for me to say something—I didn't quite know what; perhaps that I wanted his protection against this teacher and her "education." I said none of these things and the teacher came and we went out. It was clear, during the brief interview in our living room, that my father was agreeing very much against his will and that he would have refused permission if he had dared. The fact that he did not dare caused me to despise him: I had no way of knowing that he was facing in that living room a wholly unprecedented and frightening situation. [11]

Later, when my father had been laid off from his job, this woman became very important to us. She was really a very sweet and generous woman and went to a great deal of trouble to be of help to us, particularly during one awful winter. My mother called her by the highest name she knew: She said she was a "christian." My father could scarcely disagree but during the four or five years of our relatively close association he never trusted her and was always trying to surprise in her open, Midwestern face the genuine, cunningly hidden, and hideous motivation. In later years, particularly when it began to be clear that this "education" of mine was going to lead me to perdition, he became more explicit and warned me that my white friends in high school were not really my friends and that I would see, when I was older, how white people would do anything to keep a Negro down. Some of them could be nice, he admitted, but none of them were to be trusted and most of them were not even nice. The best thing was to have as little to do with them as possible. I did not feel this way and I was certain, in my innocence, that I never would. [12]

But the year which preceded my father's death had made a great change in my life. I had been living in New Jersey, working in defense plants, working and living among southerners, white and black. I knew about the south, of course, and about how southerners treated Negroes and how they expected them to behave, but it had never entered my mind that anyone would look at me and expect *me* to behave that way. I learned in New Jersey that to be a Negro meant, precisely, that one was never looked at but was simply at the mercy of the reflexes the color of one's skin caused in other people. I acted in New Jersey as I had always acted, that is as though I thought a great deal of myself—I had to *act* that way—with results that were, simply, unbelievable. I had scarcely arrived before I had earned the enmity, which was extraordinarily ingenious, of all my superiors and nearly all my co-workers. In the beginning, to make matters worse, I simply did not know what was happening. I did not know what I had done, and I shortly began to wonder what *anyone* could possibly do, to bring about such unanimous, active, and unbearably vocal hostility. I knew about jim-crow but I had never experienced it. I went to the same self-service restaurant three times and stood with all the Princeton boys before the counter, waiting for a hamburger and coffee; it was always an extraordinarily long time before anything was set before me; but it was not until the fourth visit that I learned that, in fact, nothing had ever been set before me: I had simply picked something up. Negroes were not served there, I was told, and they had been waiting for me to realize that I was always the only Negro present. Once I was told this, I determined to go there all the time. But now they were ready for me and, though some dreadful scenes were subsequently enacted in that restaurant, I never ate there again. [13]

It was the same story all over New Jersey, in bars, bowling alleys, diners, places to live. I was always being forced to leave, silently, or with mutual imprecations. I very shortly became notorious and chil-

dren giggled behind me when I passed and their elders whispered or
shouted—they really believed that I was mad. And it did begin to
work on my mind, of course; I began to be afraid to go anywhere and
to compensate for this I went places to which I really should not have
gone and where, God knows, I had no desire to be. My reputation in
town naturally enhanced my reputation at work and my working day
became one long series of acrobatics designed to keep me out of
trouble. I cannot say that these acrobatics succeeded. It began to seem
that the machinery of the organization I worked for was turning over,
day and night, with but one aim: to eject me. I was fired once, and
contrived, with the aid of a friend from New York, to get back on
the payroll; was fired again, and bounced back again. It took a while
to fire me for the third time, but the third time took. There were no
loopholes anywhere. There was not even any way of getting back
inside the gates. [14]

   That year in New Jersey lives in my mind as though it were the
year during which, having an unsuspected predilection for it, I first
contracted some dread, chronic disease, the unfailing symptom of
which is a kind of blind fever, a pounding in the skull and fire in the
bowels. Once this disease is contracted, one can never be really care-
free again, for the fever, without an instant's warning, can recur at
any moment. It can wreck more important things than race relations.
There is not a Negro alive who does not have this rage in his blood—
one has the choice, merely, of living with it consciously or surrendering to it. As for me, this fever has recurred in me, and does, and will
until the day I die. [15]

   My last night in New Jersey, a white friend from New York took
me to the nearest big town, Trenton, to go to the movies and have
a few drinks. As it turned out, he also saved me from, at the very
least, a violent whipping. Almost every detail of that night stands
out very clearly in my memory. I even remember the name of the
movie we saw because its title impressed me as being so patly ironical.
It was a movie about the German occupation of France, starring
Maureen O'Hara and Charles Laughton and called *This Land Is
Mine*. I remember the name of the diner we walked into when the

movie ended: it was the "American Diner." When we walked in the counterman asked what we wanted and I remember answering with the casual sharpness which had become my habit: "We want a hamburger and a cup of coffee, what do you think we want?" I do not know why, after a year of such rebuffs, I so completely failed to anticipate his answer, which was, of course, "We don't serve Negroes here." This reply failed to discompose me, at least for the moment. I made some sardonic comment about the name of the diner and we walked out into the streets. [16]

This was the time of what was called the "brown-out," when the lights in all Americans cities were very dim. When we re-entered the streets something happened to me which had the force of an optical illusion, or a nightmare. The streets were very crowded and I was facing north. People were moving in every direction but it seemed to me, in that instant, that all of the people I could see, and many more than that, were moving toward me, against me, and that everyone was white. I remember how their faces gleamed. And I felt, like a physical sensation, a *click* at the nape of my neck as though some interior string connecting my head to my body had been cut. I began to walk. I heard my friend call after me, but I ignored him. Heaven only knows what was going on in his mind, but he had the good sense not to touch me—I don't know what would have happened if he had—and to keep me in sight. I don't know what was going on in my mind, either; I certainly had no conscious plan. I wanted to do something to crush these white faces, which were crushing me. I walked for perhaps a block or two until I came to an enormous, glittering, and fashionable restaurant in which I knew not even the intercession of the Virgin would cause me to be served. I pushed through the doors and took the first vacant seat I saw, at a table for two, and waited. [17]

I do not know how long I waited and I rather wonder, until today, what I could possibly have looked like. Whatever I looked like, I frightened the waitress who shortly appeared, and the moment she appeared all of my fury flowed towards her. I hated her for her white face, and for her great, astounded, frightened eyes. I felt that if she found a black man so frightening I would make her fright worthwhile. [18]

She did not ask me what I wanted, but repeated, as though she had learned it somewhere, "We don't serve Negroes here." She did not say it with the blunt, derisive hostility to which I had grown so accustomed, but, rather, with a note of apology in her voice, and fear. This made me colder and more murderous than ever. I felt I had to do something with my hands. I wanted her to come close enough for me to get her neck between my hands. [19]

So I pretended not to have understood her, hoping to draw her closer. And she did step a very short step closer, with her pencil poised incongruously over her pad, and repeated the formula: ". . . don't serve Negroes here." [20]

Somehow, with the repetition of that phrase, which was already ringing in my head like a thousand bells of a nightmare, I realized that she would never come any closer and that I would have to strike from a distance. There was nothing on the table but an ordinary watermug half full of water, and I picked this up and hurled it with all my strength at her. She ducked and it missed her and shattered against the mirror behind the bar. And, with that sound, my frozen blood abruptly thawed, I returned from wherever I had been, I *saw*, for the first time, the restaurant, the people with their mouths open, already, as it seemed to me, rising as one man, and I realized what I had done, and where I was, and I was frightened. I rose and began running for the door. A round, potbellied man grabbed me by the nape of the neck just as I reached the doors and began to beat me about the face. I kicked him and got loose and ran into the streets. My friend whispered, *"Run!"* and I ran. [21]

My friend stayed outside the restaurant long enough to misdirect my pursuers and police, who arrived, he told me, at once. I do not know what I said to him when he came to my room that night. I could not have said much. I felt, in the oddest, most awful way, that I had somehow betrayed him. I lived it over and over and over again, the way one relives an automobile accident after it has happened and one finds oneself alone and safe. I could not get over two facts, both equally difficult for the imagination to grasp, and one was that I could have been murdered. But the other was that I had been ready to commit murder. I saw nothing very clearly but I did see this: that my life, my *real* life, was in danger, and not from anything other people might do but from the hatred I carried in my own heart. [22]

II

I had returned home around the second week in June—in great haste because it seemed that my father's death and my mother's confinement were both but a matter of hours. In the case of my mother, it soon became clear that she had simply made a miscalculation. This had always been her tendency and I don't believe that a single one of us arrived in the world, or has since arrived anywhere else, on time. But none of us dawdled so intolerably about the business of being born as did my baby sister. We sometimes amused ourselves, during those endless, stifling weeks, by picturing the baby sitting within in the safe, warm dark, bitterly regretting the necessity of becoming a part of our chaos and stubbornly putting it off as long as possible. I understood her perfectly and congratulated her on showing such good sense so soon. Death, however, sat as purposefully at my father's bedside as life stirred within my mother's womb and it was harder to understand why he so lingered in that long shadow. It seemed that he had bent, and for a long time, too, all of his energies towards dying. Now death was ready for him but my father held back. [23]

All of Harlem, indeed, seemed to be infected by waiting. I had never before known it to be so violently still. Racial tensions throughout this country were exacerbated during the early years of the war, partly because the labor market brought together hundreds of thousands of ill-prepared people and partly because Negro soldiers, regardless of where they were born, received their military training in the south. What happened in defense plants and army camps had repercussions, naturally, in every Negro ghetto. The situation in Harlem had grown bad enough for clergymen, policemen, educators, politicians, and social workers to assert in one breath that there was no "crime wave" and to offer, in the very next breath, suggestions as to how to combat it. These suggestions always seemed to involve playgrounds, despite the fact that racial skirmishes were occurring in the playgrounds, too. Playground or not, crime wave or not, the Harlem police force had been augmented in March, and the unrest grew— perhaps, in fact, partly as a result of the ghetto's instinctive hatred of policemen. Perhaps the most revealing news item, out of the steady parade of reports of muggings, stabbings, shootings, assaults, gang wars, and accusations of police brutality, is the item concerning six Negro girls who set upon a white girl in the subway because, as they all too accurately put it, she was stepping on their toes. Indeed she was, all over the nation. [24]

I had never before been so aware of policemen, on foot, on horse-back, on corners, everywhere, always two by two. Nor had I ever been so aware of small knots of people. They were on stoops and on corners and in doorways, and what was striking about them, I think, was that they did not seem to be talking. Never, when I passed these groups, did the usual sound of a curse or a laugh ring out and neither did there seem to be any hum of gossip. There was certainly, on the other hand, occurring between them communication extraordinarily intense. Another thing that was striking was the unexpected diversity of the people who made up these groups. Usually, for example, one would see a group of sharpies standing on the street corner, jiving the passing chicks; or a group of older men, usually, for some reason, in the vicinity of a barber shop, discussing baseball scores, or the numbers, or making rather chilling observations about women they had known. Women, in a general way, tended to be seen less often together—unless they were church women, or very young girls, or prostitutes met together for an unprofessional instant. But that summer I saw the strangest combinations: large, respectable, churchly matrons standing on the stoops or the corners with their hair tied up, together with a girl in sleazy satin whose face bore the marks of gin and the razor, or heavy-set, abrupt, no-nonsense older men, in company with the most disreputable and fanatical "race" men, or these same "race" men with the sharpies, or these sharpies with the churchly women. Seventh Day Adventists and Methodists and Spiritualists seemed to be hobnobbing with Holyrollers and they were all, alike, entangled with the most flagrant disbelievers; something heavy in their stance seemed to indicate that they had all, incredibly, seen a common vision, and on each face there seemed to be the same strange, bitter shadow. [25]

The churchly women and the matter-of-fact, no-nonsense men had children in the Army. The sleazy girls they talked to had lovers there, the sharpies and the "race" men had friends and brothers there. It would have demanded an unquestioning patriotism, happily as uncommon in this country as it is undesirable, for these people not to have been disturbed by the bitter letters they received, by the newspaper stories they read, not to have been enraged by the posters, then to be found all over New York, which described the Japanese as "yellow-bellied Japs." It was only the "race" men, to be sure, who spoke ceaselessly of being revenged—how this vengeance was to be exacted was not clear—for the indignities and dangers suffered by Negro boys in uniform; but everybody felt a directionless, hopeless bitterness, as well as that panic which can scarcely be suppressed when one knows that a human being one loves is beyond one's reach, and in danger. This helplessness and this gnawing uneasiness does something, at length, to even the toughest mind. Perhaps the best way to sum all this up is to say that the people I knew felt, mainly, a peculiar kind of relief when they knew that their boys were being shipped out of the south, to do battle overseas. It was, perhaps, like feeling that the most dangerous part of a dangerous journey had been passed and that now, even if death should come, it would come with honor and without the complicity of their countrymen. Such a death would be, in short, a fact with which one could hope to live. [26]

It was on the 28th of July, which I believe was a Wednesday, that I visited my father for the first time during his illness and for the last time in his life. The moment I saw him I knew why I had put off this visit so long. I had told my mother that I did not want to see him because I hated him. But this was not true. It was only that I *had* hated him and I wanted to hold on to this hatred. I did not want to look on him as a ruin: it was not a ruin I had hated. I imagine that one of the reasons people cling to their hates so stubbornly is because they sense, once hate is gone, that they will be forced to deal with pain. [27]

We traveled out to him, his older sister and myself, to what seemed to be the very end of a very Long Island. It was hot and dusty and we wrangled, my aunt and I, all the way out, over the fact that I had recently begun to smoke and, as she said, to give myself airs. But I knew that she wrangled with me because she could not bear to face the fact of her brother's dying. Neither could I endure the reality of her despair, her unstated bafflement as to what had happened to her brother's life, and her own. So we wrangled and I smoked and from time to time she fell into a heavy reverie. Covertly, I watched her face, which was the face of an old woman; it had fallen in, the eyes were sunken and lightless; soon she would be dying, too. [28]

In my childhood—it had not been so long ago—I had thought her beautiful. She had been quick-witted and quick-moving and very generous with all the children and each of her visits had been an event. At one time one of my brothers and myself had thought of running away to live with her. Now she could no longer produce out of her handbag some unexpected and yet familiar delight. She made me feel pity and revulsion and fear. It was awful to realize that she no longer caused me to feel affection. The closer we came to the hospital the more querulous she became and at the same time, naturally, grew more dependent on me. Between pity and guilt and fear I began to feel that there was another me trapped in my skull like a jack-in-the-box who might escape my control at any moment and fill the air with screaming. [29]

She began to cry the moment we entered the room and she saw him lying there, all shriveled and still, like a little black monkey. The great, gleaming apparatus which fed him and would have compelled him to be still even if he had been able to move brought to mind, not beneficence, but torture; the tubes entering his arm made me think of pictures I had seen when a child, of Gulliver, tied down by the pygmies on that island. My aunt wept and wept, there was a whistling sound in my father's throat; nothing was said; he could not speak. I wanted to take his hand, to say something. But I do not know what I could have said, even if he could have heard me. He was not really in that room with us, he had at last really embarked on his journey; and though my aunt told me that he said he was going to meet Jesus, I did not hear anything except that whistling in his throat. The doctor came back and we left, into that unbearable train again, and home. In the morning came the telegram saying that he was dead. Then the house was suddenly full of relatives, friends, hysteria, and confusion and I quickly left my mother and the children to the care of those impressive women, who, in Negro communities at least, automatically appear at times of bereavement armed with lotions, proverbs, and patience, and an ability to cook. I went downtown. By the time I returned, later the same day, my mother had been carried to the hospital and the baby had been born. [30]

III

For my father's funeral I had nothing black to wear and this posed a nagging problem all day long. It was one of those problems, simple, or impossible of solution, to which the mind insanely clings in order to avoid the mind's real trouble. I spent most of that day at the downtown apartment of a girl I knew, celebrating my birthday with whiskey and wondering what to wear that night. When planning a birthday celebration one naturally does not expect that it will be up against competition from a funeral and this girl had anticipated taking me out that night, for a big dinner and a night club afterwards. Sometime during the course of that long day we decided that we would go out anyway, when my father's funeral service was over. I imagine I decided it, since, as the funeral hour approached, it became clearer and clearer to me that I would not know what to do with myself when it was over. The girl, stifling her very lively concern as to the possible effects of the whiskey on one of my father's chief mourners, concentrated on being conciliatory and practically helpful. She found a black shirt for me somewhere and ironed it and, dressed in the darkest pants and jacket I owned, and slightly drunk, I made my way to my father's funeral. [31]

The chapel was full, but not packed, and very quiet. There were, mainly, my father's relatives, and his children, and here and there I saw faces I had not seen since childhood, the faces of my father's one-time friends. They were very dark and solemn now, seeming somehow to suggest that they had known all along that something like this would happen. Chief among the mourners was my aunt, who had quarreled with my father all his life; by which I do not mean to suggest that her mourning was insincere or that she had not loved him. I suppose that she was one of the few people in the world who had, and their incessant quarreling proved precisely the strength of the tie that bound them. The only other person in the world, as far as I knew, whose relationship to my father rivaled my aunt's in depth was my mother, who was not there. [32]

It seemed to me, of course, that it was a very long funeral. But it was, if anything, a rather shorter funeral than most, nor, since there were no overwhelming, uncontrollable expressions of grief, could it be called—if I dare to use the word—successful. The minister who preached my father's funeral sermon was one of the few my father had still been seeing as he neared his end. He presented to us in his sermon a man whom none of us had ever seen—a man thoughtful, patient, and forbearing, a Christian inspiration to all who knew him, and a model for his children. And no doubt the children, in their disturbed and guilty state, were almost ready to believe this; he had been remote enough to be anything and, anyway, the shock of the incontrovertible, that it was really our father lying up there in that casket, prepared the mind for anything. His sister moaned and this grief-stricken moaning was taken as corroboration. The other faces held a dark, non-committal thoughtfulness. This was not the man they had known, but they had scarcely expected to be confronted with *him*; this was, in a sense deeper than questions of fact, the man they had not known, and the man they had not known may have been the real one. The real man, whoever he had been, had suffered and now he was dead: this was all that was sure and all that mattered now. Every man in the chapel hoped that when his hour came he, too, would be eulogized, which is to say forgiven, and that all of his lapses, greeds, errors, and strayings from the truth would be invested with coherence and looked upon with charity. This was perhaps the last thing human beings could give each other and it was what they demanded, after all, of the Lord. Only the Lord saw the midnight tears, only He was present when one of His children, moaning and wringing hands, paced up and down the room. When one slapped one's child in anger the recoil in the heart reverberated through heaven and became part of the pain of the universe. And when the children were hungry and sullen and distrustful and one watched them, daily, growing wilder, and further away, and running headlong into danger, it was the Lord who knew what the charged heart endured as the strap was laid to the backside; the Lord alone who knew what one *would* have said if one had had, like the Lord, the gift of the living word. It was the Lord who knew of the impossibility every parent in that room faced: how to prepare the child for the day when the child would be despised and how to *create* in the child—by what means?—a stronger antidote to this poison than one had found for oneself. The avenues, side streets, bars, billiard halls, hospitals, police stations, and even the playgrounds of Harlem—not to mention the houses of correction, the jails, and the morgue—testified to the potency of the poison while remaining silent as to the efficacy of whatever antidote, irresistibly raising the question of whether or not such an antidote existed; raising, which was worse, the question of whether or not an antidote was desirable; perhaps poison should be fought with poison. With these several schisms in the mind and with more terrors in the heart than could be named, it was better not to judge the man who had gone down under an impossible burden. It was better to remember: *Thou knowest this man's fall; but thou knowest not his wrassling.* [33]

While the preacher talked and I watched the children—years of changing their diapers, scrubbing them, slapping them, taking them to school, and scolding them had had the perhaps inevitable result of making me love them, though I am not sure I knew this then—my mind was busily breaking out with a rash of disconnected impressions. Snatches of popular songs, indecent jokes, bits of books I had read, movie sequences, faces, voices, political issues—I thought I was going mad; all these impressions suspended, as it were, in the solution of the faint nausea produced in me by the heat and liquor. For a moment I had the impresssion that my alcoholic breath, inefficiently disguised with chewing gum, filled the entire chapel. Then someone began singing one of my father's favorite songs and, abruptly, I was with him, sitting on his knee, in the hot, enormous, crowded church which was the first church we attended. It was the Abyssinia Baptist Church on 138th Street. We had not gone there long. With this image, a host of others came. I had forgotten, in the rage of my growing up, how proud my father had been of me when I was little. Apparently, I had had a voice and my father had liked to show me off before the members of the church. I had forgotten what he had looked like when he was pleased but now I remembered that he had always been grinning with pleasure when my solos ended. I even remembered certain expressions on his face when he teased my mother—had he loved her? I would never know. And when had it all begun to change? For now it seemed that he had not always been cruel. I remembered being taken for a haircut and scraping my knee on the footrest of the barber's chair and I remembered my father's face as he soothed my crying and applied the stinging iodine. Then I remembered our fights, fights which had been of the worst possible kind because my technique had been silence. [34]

I remembered the one time in all our life together when we had really spoken to each other. [35]

It was on a Sunday and it must have been shortly before I left home. We were walking, just the two of us, in our usual silence, to or from church. I was in high school and had been doing a lot of writing and I was, at about this time, the editor of the high school magazine. But I had also been a Young Minister and had been preaching from the pulpit. Lately, I had been taking fewer engagements and preached as rarely as possible. It was said in the church, quite truthfully, that I was "cooling off." [36]

My father asked me abruptly, "You'd rather write than preach, wouldn't you?" [37]

I was astonished at his question—because it was a real question. I answered, "Yes." [38]

That was all we said. It was awful to remember that that was all we had *ever* said. [39]

The casket now was opened and the mourners were being led up the aisle to look for the last time on the deceased. The assumption was that the family was too overcome with grief to be allowed to make this journey alone and I watched while my aunt was led to the casket and, muffled in black, and shaking, led back to her seat. I disapproved of forcing the children to look on their dead father, considering that the shock of his death, or, more truthfully, the shock of death as a reality, was already a little more than a child could bear, but my judgment in this matter had been overruled and there they were, bewildered and frightened and very small, being led, one by one, to the casket. But there is also something very gallant about children at such moments. It has something to do with their silence and gravity and with the fact that one cannot help them. Their legs, somehow, seem *exposed*, so that it is at once incredible and terribly clear that their legs are all they have to hold them up. [40]

I had not wanted to go to the casket myself and I certainly had not wished to be led there, but there was no way of avoiding either of these forms. One of the deacons led me up and I looked on my father's face. I cannot say that it looked like him at all. His blackness had been equivocated by powder and there was no suggestion in that casket of what his power had or could have been. He was simply an old man dead, and it was hard to believe that he had ever given anyone either joy or pain. Yet, his life filled that room. Further up the avenue his wife was holding his newborn child. Life and death so close together, and love and hatred, and right and wrong, said something to me which I did not want to hear concerning man, concerning the life of man. [41]

After the funeral, while I was downtown desperately celebrating my birthday, a Negro soldier, in the lobby of the Hotel Braddock, got into a fight with a white policeman over a Negro girl. Negro girls, white policemen, in or out of uniform, and Negro males—in or out of uniform—were part of the furniture of the lobby of the Hotel Braddock and this was certainly not the first time such an incident had occurred. It was destined, however, to receive an unprecedented publicity, for the fight between the policeman and the soldier ended with the shooting of the soldier. Rumor, flowing immediately to the streets outside, stated that the soldier had been shot in the back, an instantaneous and revealing invention, and that the soldier had died protecting a Negro woman. The facts were somewhat different—for example, the soldier had not been shot in the back, and was not dead, and the girl seems to have been as dubious a symbol of womanhood as her white counterpart in Georgia usually is, but no one was interested in the facts. They preferred the invention because this invention expressed and corroborated their hates and fears so perfectly. It is just as well to remember that people are always doing this. Perhaps many of those legends, including Christianity, to which the world clings began their conquest of the world with just some such concerted surrender to distortion. The effect, in Harlem, of this particular legend was like the effect of a lit match in a tin of gasoline. The mob gathered before the doors of the Hotel Braddock simply began to swell and to spread in every direction, and Harlem exploded. [42]

The mob did not cross the ghetto lines. It would have been easy, for example, to have gone over Morningside Park on the west side or to have crossed the Grand Central railroad tracks at 125th Street on the east side, to wreak havoc in white neighborhoods. The mob seems to have been mainly interested in something more potent and real than the white face, that is, in white power, and the principal damage done during the riot of the summer of 1943 was to white business establishments in Harlem. It might have been a far bloodier story, of course, if, at the hour the riot began, these establishments had still been open. From the Hotel Braddock the mob fanned out, east and west along 125th Street, and for the entire length of Lenox, Seventh, and Eighth avenues. Along each of these avenues,

and along each major side street—116th, 125th, 138th, and so on—
bars, stores, pawnshops, restaurants, even little luncheonettes had
been smashed open and entered and looted—looted, it might be
added, with more haste than efficiency. The shelves really looked as
though a bomb had struck them. Cans of beans and soup and dog
food, along with toilet paper, corn flakes, sardines, and milk tumbled
every which way, and abandoned cash registers and cases of beer
leaned crazily out of the splintered windows and were strewn along
the avenues. Sheets, blankets, and clothing of every description
formed a kind of path, as though people had dropped them while
running. I truly had not realized that Harlem *had* so many stores
until I saw them all smashed open; the first time the word *wealth*
ever entered my mind in relation to Harlem was when I saw it scattered in the streets. But one's first, incongruous impression of plenty
was countered immediately by an impression of waste. None of this
was doing anybody any good. It would have been better to have left
the plate glass as it had been and the goods lying in the stores. [43]

It would have been better, but it would also have been intolerable,
for Harlem had needed something to smash. To smash something is
the ghetto's chronic need. Most of the time it is the members of the
ghetto who smash each other, and themselves. But as long as the
ghetto walls are standing there will always come a moment when
these outlets do not work. That summer, for example, it was not
enough to get into a fight on Lenox Avenue, or curse out one's
cronies in the barber shops. If ever, indeed, the violence which fills
Harlem's churches, pool halls, and bars erupts outward in a more
direct fashion, Harlem and its citizens are likely to vanish in an
apocalyptic flood. That this is not likely to happen is due to a great
many reasons, most hidden and powerful among them the Negro's
real relation to the white American. This relation prohibits, simply,
anything as uncomplicated and satisfactory as pure hatred. In order
really to hate white people, one has to blot so much out of the
mind—and the heart—that this hatred itself becomes an exhausting
and self-destructive pose. But this does not mean, on the other hand,
that love comes easily: the white world is too powerful, too com-

placent, too ready with gratuitous humiliation, and, above all, too ignorant and too innocent for that. One is absolutely forced to make perpetual qualifications and one's own reactions are always canceling each other out. It is this, really, which has driven so many people mad, both white and black. One is always in the position of having to decide between amputation and gangrene. Amputation is swift but time may prove that the amputation was not necessary—or one may delay the amputation too long. Gangrene is slow, but it is impossible to be sure that one is reading one's symptoms right. The idea of going through life as a cripple is more than one can bear, and equally unbearable is the risk of swelling up slowly, in agony, with poison. And the trouble, finally, is that the risks are real even if the choices do not exist. [44]

"But as for me and my house," my father had said, "we will serve the Lord." I wondered, as we drove him to his resting place, what this line had meant for him. I had heard him preach it many times. I had preached it once myself, proudly giving it an interpretation different from my father's. Now the whole thing came back to me, as though my father and I were on our way to Sunday school and I were memorizing the golden text: *And if it seem evil unto you to serve the Lord, choose you this day whom you will serve; whether the gods which your fathers served that were on the other side of the flood, or the gods of the Amorites, in whose land ye dwell: but as for me and my house, we will serve the Lord.* I suspected in these familiar lines a meaning which had never been there for me before. All of my father's texts and songs, which I had decided were meaningless, were arranged before me at his death like empty bottles, waiting to hold the meaning which life would give them for me. This was his legacy: nothing is ever escaped. That bleakly memorable morning I hated the unbelievable streets and the Negroes and whites who had, equally, made them that way. But I knew that it was folly, as my father would have said, this bitterness was folly. It was necessary to hold on to the things that mattered. The dead man mattered, the new life mattered; blackness and whiteness did not matter; to believe that they did was to acquiesce in one's own destruction. Hatred, which could destroy so much, never failed to destroy the man who hated and this was an immutable law. [45]

It began to seem that one would have to hold in the mind forever two ideas which seemed to be in opposition. The first idea was acceptance, the acceptance, totally without rancor, of life as it is, and men as they are: in the light of this idea, it goes without saying that injustice is a commonplace. But this did not mean that one could be complacent, for the second idea was of equal power: that one must never, in one's own life, accept these injustices as commonplace but must fight them with all one's strength. This fight begins, however, in the heart and it now had been laid to my charge to keep my own heart free of hatred and despair. This intimation made my heart heavy and, now that my father was irrecoverable, I wished that he had been beside me so that I could have searched his face for the answers which only the future would give me now. [46]

PURPOSE AND STRUCTURE

1. The title of James Baldwin's essay—its diction and tone—prepares the reader for the splintered and powerful first paragraph, and, indeed, for the entire essay. *Notes* are free, personal, and fragmentary. *Native Son* not only connotes organizations of native-born patriots, it also suggests Richard Wright's powerful novel of the same title, a bitter attack on race prejudice. What is the function of par. 1? Is this paragraph coherent?

2. Notice the transitional sentence at the beginning of par. 2: *The day of my father's funeral had also been my nineteenth birthday.* How does this function as transition?

3. The announced themes of the first paragraph are concretely elaborated in the three main sections of the essay. The wilderness between birth and death, the wilderness of blackness and whiteness, is the subject of Section I, which ends, "*I could not get over two facts, both equally difficult for the imagination to grasp, and one was that I could have been murdered. But the other was that I had been ready to commit murder. I saw nothing very clearly but I did see this: that my life, my real life, was in danger, and not from anything other people might do but from the hatred*

I carried in my own heart." Every paragraph in Section I touches upon or develops this theme of *hatred.* Examine each one and show how. Notice that this theme is combined so richly with other themes that Baldwin's conclusion to Section II is surprising and powerful.

4. Section II of the essay develops the identities in birth and death; Section III combines and resolves the themes of the preceding sections. It begins, *For my father's funeral I had nothing black to wear and this posed a nagging problem all day long. It was one of those problems, simple, or impossible of solution, to which the mind insanely clings in order to avoid the mind's real trouble.* Baldwin's thesis states the mind's real trouble. What is the thesis?

5. The form of this essay, however, says more than can be stated in a thesis. The free, personal, and fragmentary notes for which the title has prepared the reader have moved in a pattern that is complex, concrete, and structured. Personal experience has constantly been given a general significance. Polar opposites—birth-death, whiteness-blackness, love-hate, father-son—have collided, become identical, and stubbornly separated into new oppositions. Thus the last paragraph states the discoveries that have been made through the form of the essay. What are these discoveries?

6. Does the last sentence in par. 26 relate to the final paragraph of the essay?

DICTION AND TONE

1. See Purpose and Structure above: the tone of Baldwin's essay is in large part achieved through structure.

2. The diction of much of the following sentence in par. 2 is formal: *I had declined to believe in that apocalypse which had been central to my father's vision; very well, life seemed to be saying, here is something that will certainly pass for an apocalypse until the real thing comes along.* The last few words are similar to the words of a popular song. Is this an accidental or planned allusion? Is the allusion effective or inappropriate?

3. In par. 10 Baldwin speaks of his father's voice as *vindictively polite.* Is this possible? Is the phrase appropriate?

4. Why does Baldwin give the title of the movie and the name of the diner in par. 16?

5. The first two sentences of par. 30 refer to a monkey, torture, Gulliver, and pygmies. What tone results from these images? from the *whistling sound* of the next sentence?

APPLICATIONS TO WRITING

1. The diction and tone of *Notes of a Native Son* are sometimes personal and autobiographical, sometimes public and formal. But both the language and the attitudes expressed seem to grow directly out of experiences described in the essay. Write a composition showing how one of your ideas has grown out of concrete personal experiences.

2. In Baldwin's first paragraph the death of his father, the birth of a sister, and race riots are related to each other. Throughout his essay personal experiences acquire a general significance. Write a composition in which you show a discovery about yourself to be a discovery about your family or nation.

A NOISELESS FLASH

JOHN HERSEY

At exactly fifteen minutes past eight in the morning, on August 6, 1945, Japanese time, at the moment when the atomic bomb flashed above Hiroshima, Miss Toshiko Sasaki, a clerk in the personnel department of the East Asia Tin Works, had just sat down at her place in the plant office and was turning her head to speak to the girl at the next desk. At that same moment, Dr. Masakazu Fujii was settling down cross-legged to read the Osaka *Asahi* on the porch of his private hospital, overhanging one of the seven deltaic rivers which divide Hiroshima; Mrs. Hatsuyo Nakamura, a tailor's widow, stood by the window of her kitchen, watching a neighbor tearing down his house because it lay in the path of an air-raid-defense fire lane; Father Wilhelm Kleinsorge, a German priest of the Society of Jesus, reclined in his underwear on a cot on the top floor of his order's three-story mission house, reading a Jesuit magazine, *Stimmen der Zeit*; Dr. Terufumi Sasaki, a young member of the surgical staff of the city's large modern Red Cross Hospital, walked along one of the hospital corridors with a blood specimen for a Wassermann test in his hand; and the Reverend Mr. Kiyoshi Tanimoto, pastor of the Hiroshima Methodist Church, paused at the door of a rich man's house in Koi, the city's western suburb, and prepared to unload a handcart full of

Copyright, 1946, by John Hersey. From *Hiroshima* by John Hersey, which first appeared in *The New Yorker*. Reprinted by permission of Alfred A. Knopf, Inc.

things he had evacuated from town in fear of the massive B-29 raid which everyone expected Hiroshima to suffer. A hundred thousand people were killed by the atomic bomb, and these six were among the survivors. They still wonder why they lived when so many others died. Each of them counts many small items of chance or volition— a step taken in time, a decision to go indoors, catching one streetcar instead of the next—that spared him. And now each knows that in the act of survival he lived a dozen lives and saw more death than he ever thought he would see. At the time, none of them knew anything. [1]

The Reverend Mr. Tanimoto got up at five o'clock that morning. He was alone in the parsonage, because for some time his wife had been commuting with their year-old baby to spend nights with a friend in Ushida, a suburb to the north. Of all the important cities of Japan, only two, Kyoto and Hiroshima, had not been visited in strength by B-san, or Mr. B, as the Japanese, with a mixture of respect and unhappy familiarity, called the B-29; and Mr. Tanimoto, like all his neighbors and friends, was almost sick with anxiety. He had heard uncomfortably detailed accounts of mass raids on Kure, Iwakuni, Tokuyama, and other nearby towns; he was sure Hiroshima's turn would come soon. He had slept badly the night before, because there had been several air-raid warnings. Hiroshima had been getting such warnings almost every night for weeks, for at that time the B-29s were using Lake Biwa, northeast of Hiroshima, as a rendezvous point, and no matter what city the Americans planned to hit, the Superfortresses streamed in over the coast near Hiroshima. The frequency of the warnings and the continued abstinence of Mr. B with respect to Hiroshima had made its citizens jittery; a rumor was going around that the Americans were saving something special for the city. [2]

Mr. Tanimoto is a small man, quick to talk, laugh, and cry. He wears his black hair parted in the middle and rather long; the prominence of the frontal bones just above his eyebrows and the smallness of his mustache, mouth, and chin give him a strange, old-young look, boyish and yet wise, weak and yet fiery. He moves nervously and fast, but with a restraint which suggests that he is a cautious, thoughtful man. He showed, indeed, just those qualities in the uneasy days before the bomb fell. Besides having his wife spend the nights in Ushida, Mr. Tanimoto had been carrying all the portable things from his church, in the close-packed residential district called Nagara-gawa, to a house that belonged to a rayon manufacturer in Koi, two miles from the center of town. The rayon man, a Mr. Matsui, had opened his then unoccupied estate to a large number of his friends and acquaintances, so that they might evacuate whatever they wished to a safe distance from the probable target area. Mr. Tanimoto had had no difficulty in moving chairs, hymnals, Bibles, altar gear, and church records by pushcart himself, but the organ console and an upright piano required some aid. A friend of his named Matsuo had, the day before, helped him get the piano out to Koi; in return, he had promised this day to assist Mr. Matsuo in hauling out a daughter's belongings. That is why he had risen so early. [3]

Mr. Tanimoto cooked his own breakfast. He felt awfully tired. The effort of moving the piano the day before, a sleepless night, weeks of worry and unbalanced diet, the cares of his parish—all combined to make him feel hardly adequate to the new day's work. There was another thing, too; Mr. Tanimoto had studied theology at Emory College, in Atlanta, Georgia; he had graduated in 1940; he spoke excellent English; he dressed in American clothes; he had cor-responded with many American friends right up to the time the war began; and among a people obsessed with a fear of being spied upon —perhaps almost obsessed himself—he found himself growing in-creasingly uneasy. The police had questioned him several times, and just a few days before, he had heard that an influential acquaintance, a Mr. Tanaka, a retired officer of the Toyo Kisen Kaisha steamship line, an anti-Christian, a man famous in Hiroshima for his showy philanthropies and notorious for his personal tyrannies, had been telling people that Tanimoto should not be trusted. In compensation, to show himself publicly a good Japanese, Mr. Tanimoto had taken on the chairmanship of his local *tonarigumi*, or Neighborhood Association, and to his other duties and concerns this position had added the business of organizing air-raid defense for about twenty families. [4]

Before six o'clock that morning, Mr. Tanimoto started for Mr. Matsuo's house. There he found that their burden was to be a *tansu*, a large Japanese cabinet, full of clothing and household goods. The two men set out. The morning was perfectly clear and so warm that the day promised to be uncomfortable. A few minutes after they started, the air-raid siren went off—a minute-long blast that warned of approaching planes but indicated to the people of Hiroshima only a slight degree of danger, since it sounded every morning at this time, when an American weather plane came over. The two men pulled and pushed the handcart through the city streets. Hiroshima was a fan-shaped city, lying mostly on the six islands formed by the seven estuarial rivers that branch out from the Ota River; its main commercial and residential districts, covering about four square miles in the center of the city, contained three-quarters of its population, which had been reduced by several evacuation programs from a wartime peak of 380,000 to about 245,000. Factories and other residential districts, or suburbs, lay compactly around the edges of the city. To the south were the docks, an airport, and the island-studded Inland Sea. A rim of mountains runs around the other three sides of the delta. Mr. Tanimoto and Mr. Matsuo took their way through the shopping center, already full of people, and across two of the rivers to the sloping streets of Koi, and up them to the outskirts and foothills. As they started up a valley away from the tight-ranked houses, the all-clear sounded. (The Japanese radar operators, detecting only three planes, supposed that they comprised a reconnaissance.) Pushing the handcart up to the rayon man's house was tiring, and the men, after they had maneuvered their load into the driveway and to the front steps, paused to rest awhile. They stood with a wing of the house between them and the city. Like most homes in this part of Japan, the house consisted of a wooden frame and wooden walls supporting a heavy tile roof. Its front hall, packed with rolls of bedding and clothing, looked like a cool cave full of fat cushions. Opposite the house, to the right of the front door, there was a large, finicky rock garden. There was no sound of planes. The morning was still; the place was cool and pleasant. [5]

Then a tremendous flash of light cut across the sky. Mr. Tanimoto has a distinct recollection that it travelled from east to west, from the city toward the hills. It seemed a sheet of sun. Both he and Mr. Matsuo reacted in terror—and both had time to react (for they were 3,500 yards, or two miles, from the center of the explosion). Mr. Matsuo dashed up the front steps into the house and dived among the bedrolls and buried himself there. Mr. Tanimoto took four or five steps and threw himself between two big rocks in the garden. He bellied up very hard against one of them. As his face was against the stone, he did not see what happened. He felt a sudden pressure, and then splinters and pieces of board and fragments of tile fell on him. He heard ṇo roar. (Almost no one in Hiroshima recalls hearing any noise of the bomb. But a fisherman in his sampan on the Inland Sea near Tsuzu, the man with whom Mr. Tanimoto's mother-in-law and sister-in-law were living, saw the flash and heard a tremendous explosion; he was nearly twenty miles from Hiroshima, but the thunder was greater than when the B-29s hit Iwakuni, only five miles away.) [6]

When he dared, Mr. Tanimoto raised his head and saw that the rayon man's house had collapsed. He thought a bomb had fallen directly on it. Such clouds of dust had risen that there was a sort of twilight around. In panic, not thinking for the moment of Mr. Matsuo under the ruins, he dashed out into the street. He noticed as he ran that the concrete wall of the estate had fallen over—toward the house rather than away from it. In the street, the first thing he saw was a squad of soldiers who had been burrowing into the hillside opposite, making one of the thousands of dugouts in which the Japanese apparently intended to resist invasion, hill by hill, life for life; the soldiers were coming out of the hole, where they should have been safe, and blood was running from their heads, chests, and backs. They were silent and dazed. [7]

Under what seemed to be a local dust cloud, the day grew darker and darker. [8]

At nearly midnight, the night before the bomb was dropped, an announcer on the city's radio station said that about two hundred B-29s were approaching southern Honshu and advised the population of Hiroshima to evacuate to their designated "safe areas." Mrs. Hatsuyo Nakamura, the tailor's widow, who lived in the section called Nobori-cho and who had long had a habit of doing as she was told, got her three children—a ten-year-old boy, Toshio, an eight-year-old girl, Yaeko, and a five-year-old girl, Myeko—out of bed and dressed them and walked with them to the military area known as the East Parade Ground, on the northeast edge of the city. There she unrolled some mats and the children lay down on them. They slept until about two, when they were awakened by the roar of the planes going over Hiroshima. [9]

As soon as the planes had passed, Mrs. Nakamura started back with her children. They reached home a little after two-thirty and she immediately turned on the radio, which, to her distress, was just then broadcasting a fresh warning. When she looked at the children and saw how tired they were, and when she thought of the number of trips they had made in past weeks, all to no purpose, to the East Parade Ground, she decided that in spite of the instructions on the radio, she simply could not face starting out all over again. She put the children in their bedrolls on the floor, lay down herself at three o'clock, and fell asleep at once, so soundly that when planes passed over later, she did not waken to their sound. [10]

The siren jarred her awake at about seven. She arose, dressed quickly, and hurried to the house of Mr. Nakamoto, the head of her Neighborhood Association, and asked him what she should do. He said that she should remain at home unless an urgent warning—a series of intermittent blasts of the siren—was sounded. She returned home, lit the stove in the kitchen, set some rice to cook, and sat down to read that morning's Hiroshima *Chugoku*. To her relief, the all-clear sounded at eight o'clock. She heard the children stirring, so she went and gave each of them a handful of peanuts and told them to stay on their bedrolls, because they were tired from the night's walk. She had hoped that they would go back to sleep, but the man in the house directly to the south began to make a terrible hullabaloo of hammering, wedging, ripping, and splitting. The prefectural government, convinced, as everyone in Hiroshima was, that the city would be attacked soon, had begun to press with threats and warnings for the completion of wide fire lanes, which, it was hoped, might act in conjunction with the rivers to localize any fires started by an incendiary raid; and the neighbor was reluctantly sacrificing his home to the city's safety. Just the day before, the prefecture had ordered all able-bodied girls from the secondary schools to spend a few days helping to clear these lanes, and they started work soon after the all-clear sounded. [11]

Mrs. Nakamura went back to the kitchen, looked at the rice, and began watching the man next door. At first, she was annoyed with him for making so much noise, but then she was moved almost to tears by pity. Her emotion was specifically directed toward her neighbor, tearing down his home, board by board, at a time when there was so much unavoidable destruction, but undoubtedly she also felt a generalized, community pity, to say nothing of self-pity. She had not had an easy time. Her husband, Isawa, had gone into the Army just after Myeko was born, and she had heard nothing from or of him for a long time, until, on March 5, 1942, she received a seven-word telegram: "Isawa died an honorable death at Singapore." She learned later that he had died on February 15th, the day Singapore fell, and that he had been a corporal. Isawa had been a not particularly prosperous tailor, and his only capital was a Sankoku sewing machine. After his death, when his allotments stopped coming, Mrs. Nakamura got out the machine and began to take in piece-work herself, and since then had supported the children, but poorly, by sewing. [12]

As Mrs. Nakamura stood watching her neighbor, everything flashed whiter than any white she had ever seen. She did not notice what happened to the man next door; the reflex of a mother set her in motion toward her children. She had taken a single step (the house was 1,350 yards, or three-quarters of a mile, from the center of the explosion) when something picked her up and she seemed to fly into the next room over the raised sleeping platform, pursued by parts of her house. [13]

Timbers fell around her as she landed, and a shower of tiles pommelled her; everything became dark, for she was buried. The debris did not cover her deeply. She rose up and freed herself. She heard a child cry, "Mother, help me!," and saw her youngest—Myeko, the five-year-old—buried up to her breast and unable to move. As Mrs. Nakamura started frantically to claw her way toward the baby, she could see or hear nothing of her other children. [14]

In the days right before the bombing, Dr. Masakazu Fujii, being prosperous, hedonistic, and at the time not too busy, had been allowing himself the luxury of sleeping until nine or nine-thirty, but fortunately he had to get up early the morning the bomb was dropped to see a house guest off on a train. He rose at six, and half an hour later walked with his friend to the station, not far away, across two of the rivers. He was back home by seven, just as the siren sounded its sustained warning. He ate breakfast and then, because the morning was already hot, undressed down to his underwear and went out on the porch to read the paper. This porch—in fact, the whole building —was curiously constructed. Dr. Fujii was the proprietor of a peculiarly Japanese institution: a private, single-doctor hospital. This building, perched beside and over the water of the Kyo River, and next to the bridge of the same name, contained thirty rooms for thirty patients and their kinfolk—for, according to Japanese custom, when a person falls sick and goes to a hospital, one or more members of his family go and live there with him, to cook for him, bathe, massage, and read to him, and to offer incessant familial sympathy, without which a Japanese patient would be miserable indeed. Dr. Fujii had no beds—only straw mats—for his patients. He did, however, have all sorts of modern equipment; an X-ray machine, diathermy apparatus, and a fine tiled laboratory. The structure rested two-thirds on the land, one-third on piles over the tidal waters of the Kyo. This over-hang, the part of the building where Dr. Fujii lived, was queer-looking, but it was cool in summer and from the porch, which faced away from the center of the city, the prospect of the river, with pleasure boats drifting up and down it, was always refreshing. Dr. Fujii had occasionally had anxious moments when the Ota and its mouth branches rose to flood, but the piling was apparently firm enough and the house had always held. [15]

Dr. Fujii had been relatively idle for about a month because in July, as the number of untouched cities in Japan dwindled and as Hiro-shima seemed more and more inevitably a target, he began turning patients away, on the ground that in case of a fire raid he would not be able to evacuate them. Now he had only two patients left—a woman from Yano, injured in the shoulder, and a young man of twenty-five recovering from burns he had suffered when the steel factory near Hiroshima in which he worked had been hit. Dr. Fujii had six nurses to tend his patients. His wife and children were safe; his wife and one son were living outside Osaka, and another son and two daughters were in the country on Kyushu. A niece was living with him, and a maid and a manservant. He had little to do and did not mind, for he had saved some money. At fifty, he was healthy, convivial, and calm, and he was pleased to pass the evenings drinking whiskey with friends, always sensibly and for the sake of conversation. Before the war, he had affected brands imported from Scotland and America; now he was perfectly satisfied with the best Japanese brand, Suntory. [16]

Dr. Fujii sat down cross-legged in his underwear on the spotless matting of the porch, put on his glasses, and started reading the Osaka *Asahi*. He liked to read the Osaka news because his wife was there. He saw the flash. To him—faced away from the center and looking at his paper—it seemed a brilliant yellow. Startled, he began to rise to his feet. In that moment (he was 1,550 yards from the center), the hospital leaned behind his rising and, with a terrible ripping noise, toppled into the river. The Doctor, still in the act of getting to his feet, was thrown forward and around and over; he was buffeted and gripped; he lost track of everything, because things were so speeded up; he felt the water. [17]

Dr. Fujii hardly had time to think that he was dying before he realized that he was alive, squeezed tightly by two long timbers in a V across his chest, like a morsel suspended between two huge chopsticks—held upright, so that he could not move, with his head miraculously above water and his torso and legs in it. The remains of his hospital were all around him in a mad assortment of splintered lumber and materials for the relief of pain. His left shoulder hurt terribly. His glasses were gone. [18]

Father Wilhelm Kleinsorge, of the Society of Jesus, was, on the morning of the explosion, in rather frail condition. The Japanese wartime diet had not sustained him, and he felt the strain of being a foreigner in an increasingly xenophobic Japan; even a German, since the defeat of the Fatherland, was unpopular. Father Kleinsorge had, at thirty-eight, the look of a boy growing too fast—thin in the face, with a prominent Adam's apple, a hollow chest, dangling hands, big feet. He walked clumsily, leaning forward a little. He was tired all the time. To make matters worse, he had suffered for two days, along with Father Cieslik, a fellow-priest, from a rather painful and urgent diarrhea, which they blamed on the beans and black ration bread they were obliged to eat. Two other priests then living in the mission compound, which was in the Nobori-cho section—Father Superior LaSalle and Father Schiffer—had happily escaped this affliction. [19]

Father Kleinsorge woke up about six the morning the bomb was dropped, and half an hour later—he was a bit tardy because of his sickness—he began to read Mass in the mission chapel, a small Japanese-style wooden building which was without pews, since its worshippers knelt on the usual Japanese matted floor, facing an altar graced with splendid silks, brass, silver, and heavy embroideries. This morning, a Monday, the only worshippers were Mr. Takemoto, a theological student living in the mission house; Mr. Fukai, the secretary of the diocese; Mrs. Murata, the mission's devoutly Christian

housekeeper; and his fellow-priests. After Mass, while Father Kleinsorge was reading the Prayers of Thanksgiving, the siren sounded. He
stopped the service and the missionaries retired across the compound
to the bigger building. There, in his room on the ground floor, to the
right of the front door, Father Kleinsorge changed into a military
uniform which he had acquired when he was teaching at the Rokko
Middle School in Kobe and which he wore during air-raid alerts. [20]

After an alarm, Father Kleinsorge always went out and scanned the
sky, and in this instance, when he stepped outside, he was glad to see
only the single weather plane that flew over Hiroshima each day
about this time. Satisfied that nothing would happen, he went in and
breakfasted with the other Fathers on substitute coffee and ration
bread, which, under the circumstances, was especially repugnant to
him. The Fathers sat and talked awhile, until, at eight, they heard the
all-clear. They went then to various parts of the building. Father
Schiffer retired to his room to do some writing. Father Cieslik sat in
his room in a straight chair with a pillow over his stomach to ease his
pain, and read. Father Superior LaSalle stood at the window of his
room, thinking. Father Kleinsorge went up to a room on the third
floor, took off all his clothes except his underwear, and stretched out
on his right side on a cot and began reading his *Stimmen der
Zeit*. [21]

After the terrible flash—which, Father Kleinsorge later realized,
reminded him of something he had read as a boy about a large meteor
colliding with the earth—he had time (since he was 1,400 yards from
the center) for one thought: A bomb has fallen directly on us. Then,
for a few seconds or minutes, he went out of his mind. [22]

Father Kleinsorge never knew how he got out of the house. The
next things he was conscious of were that he was wandering around
in the mission's vegetable garden in his underwear, bleeding slightly
from small cuts along his left flank; that all the buildings round
about had fallen down except the Jesuits' mission house, which had
long before been braced and double-braced by a priest named Grop-
per, who was terrified of earthquakes; that the day had turned dark;
and that Murata-*san*, the housekeeper, was nearby, crying over and

over, "*Shu Jesusu, awaremi tamai!* Our Lord Jesus, have pity on us!" [23]

On the train on the way into Hiroshima from the country, where he lived with his mother, Dr. Terufumi Sasaki, the Red Cross Hospital surgeon, thought over an unpleasant nightmare he had had the night before. His mother's home was in Mukaihara, thirty miles from the city, and it took him two hours by train and tram to reach the hospital. He had slept uneasily all night and had awakened an hour earlier than usual, and, feeling sluggish and slightly feverish, had debated whether to go to the hospital at all; his sense of duty finally forced him to go, and he had started out on an earlier train than he took most mornings. The dream had particularly frightened him because it was so closely associated, on the surface at least, with a disturbing actuality. He was only twenty-five years old and had just completed his training at the Eastern Medical University, in Tsingtao, China. He was something of an idealist and was much distressed by the inadequacy of medical facilities in the country town where his mother lived. Quite on his own, and without a permit, he had begun visiting a few sick people out there in the evenings, after his eight hours at the hospital and four hours' commuting. He had recently learned that the penalty for practicing without a permit was severe; a fellow-doctor whom he had asked about it had given him a serious scolding. Nevertheless, he had continued to practice. In his dream, he had been at the bedside of a country patient when the police and the doctor he had consulted burst into the room, seized him, dragged him outside, and beat him up cruelly. On the train, he just about decided to give up the work in Mukaihara, since he felt it would be impossible to get a permit, because the authorities would hold that it would conflict with his duties at the Red Cross Hospital. [24]

At the terminus, he caught a streetcar at once. (He later calculated that if he had taken his customary train that morning, and if he had had to wait a few minutes for the streetcar, as often happened, he would have been close to the center at the time of the explosion and would surely have perished.) He arrived at the hospital at seven-forty and reported to the chief surgeon. A few minutes later, he went to a room on the first floor and drew blood from the arm of a man in order to perform a Wassermann test. The laboratory containing the incubators for the test was on the third floor. With the blood specimen in his left hand, walking in a kind of distraction he had felt all morning, probably because of the dream and his restless night, he started along the main corridor on his way toward the stairs. He was one step beyond an open window when the light of the bomb was reflected, like a gigantic photographic flash, in the corridor. He ducked down on one knee and said to himself, as only a Japanese would, "Sasaki, *gambare!* Be brave!" Just then (the building was 1,650 yards from the center), the blast ripped through the hospital. The glasses he was wearing flew off his face; the bottle of blood crashed against one wall; his Japanese slippers zipped out from under his feet—but otherwise, thanks to where he stood, he was untouched. [25]

Dr. Sasaki shouted the name of the chief surgeon and rushed around to the man's office and found him terribly cut by glass. The hospital was in horrible confusion: heavy partitions and ceilings had fallen on patients, beds had overturned, windows had blown in and cut people, blood was spattered on the walls and floors, instruments were everywhere, many of the patients were running about screaming, many more lay dead. (A colleague working in the laboratory to which Dr. Sasaki had been walking was dead; Dr. Sasaki's patient, whom he had just left and who a few moments before had been dreadfully afraid of syphilis, was also dead.) Dr. Sasaki found himself the only doctor in the hospital who was unhurt. [26]

Dr. Sasaki, who believed that the enemy had hit only the building he was in, got bandages and began to bind the wounds of those inside the hospital; while outside, all over Hiroshima, maimed and dying citizens turned their unsteady steps toward the Red Cross Hospital to begin an invasion that was to make Dr. Sasaki forget his private nightmare for a long, long time. [27]

Miss Toshiko Sasaki, the East Asia Tin Works clerk, who is not related to Dr. Sasaki, got up at three o'clock in the morning on the day the bomb fell. There was extra housework to do. Her eleven-month-old brother, Akio, had come down the day before with a serious stomach upset; her mother had taken him to the Tamura Pediatric Hospital and was staying there with him. Miss Sasaki, who was about twenty, had to cook breakfast for her father, a brother, a sister, and herself, and—since the hospital, because of the war, was unable to provide food—to prepare a whole day's meals for her mother and the baby, in time for her father, who worked in a factory making rubber earplugs for artillery crews, to take the food by on his way to the plant. When she had finished and had cleaned and put away the cooking things, it was nearly seven. The family lived in Koi, and she had a forty-five minute trip to the tin works, in the section of town called Kannonmachi. She was in charge of the personnel records in the factory. She left Koi at seven, and as soon as she reached the plant, she went with some of the other girls from the personnel department to the factory auditorium. A prominent local Navy man, a former employee, had committed suicide the day before by throwing himself under a train—a death considered honorable enough to warrant a memorial service, which was to be held at the tin works at ten o'clock that morning. In the large hall, Miss Sasaki and the others made suitable preparations for the meeting. This work took about twenty minutes. [28]

Miss Sasaki went back to her office and sat down at her desk. She was quite far from the windows, which were off to her left, and behind her were a couple of tall bookcases containing all the books of the factory library, which the personnel department had organized. She settled herself at her desk, put some things in a drawer, and shifted papers. She thought that before she began to make entries in her lists of new employees, discharges, and departures for the Army, she would chat for a moment with the girl at her right. Just as she turned her head away from the windows, the room was filled with a blinding light. She was paralyzed by fear, fixed still in her chair for a long moment (the plant was 1,600 yards from the center). [29]

Everything fell, and Miss Sasaki lost consciousness. The ceiling dropped suddenly and the wooden floor above collapsed in splinters and the people up there came down and the roof above them gave way; but principally and first of all, the bookcases right behind her swooped forward and the contents threw her down, with her left leg horribly twisted and breaking underneath her. There, in the tin factory, in the first moment of the atomic age, a human being was crushed by books. [30]

PURPOSE AND STRUCTURE

1. The first two words of Hersey's report are *At exactly*. Why begin with these words?

2. Miss Toshiko Sasaki is introduced in the first sentence, the other five survivors in the second sentence (par. 1). Would it be more effective to introduce all six in the second sentence, rewriting the first sentence to end with the word *Hiroshima*? Would it be more effective to present each of the survivors in a separate sentence? Rewrite, or argue for Hersey's two sentences.

3. Hersey introduces the six survivors in one order (par. 1) and describes their experiences in another order (pars. 2–30). Why? Would it be more effective for the sections of the report to follow the sequence of the introduction?

4. Is the last sentence of the introduction (par. 1) too general? Formulate it more precisely or argue for its present form.

5. The introduction describes precisely what each of the six survivors was doing at the moment of the flash. Thus the reader begins with the climax of each episode. Does this knowledge reduce the interest of the detailed episodes? Would it be preferable to save this information for the end of each episode? Discuss.

6. The first sentence of par. 2 identifies Mr. Tanimoto and gives the time (*five o'clock that morning*). The second sentence gives further information about him. Then the rest of the paragraph is an exposition of his situation. How much of it is peculiar to Mr. Tanimoto? Could this information have been attached to any of the other five victims? Is it most

relevant to Mr. Tanimoto? Why place this information at this point in the essay?

7. The last sentence of par. 3 (*That is why he had risen so early*) refers back to the first sentence of par. 2. What portions of these paragraphs tell why he rose so early?

8. The first sentence of par. 4 is the next point in time after Mr. Tanimoto got up. Is the second sentence (*He felt awfully tired*) the topic sentence of par. 4? Discuss.

9. In par. 5 there is a geographical description of the city (*Hiroshima was a fan-shaped city, lying mostly on the six islands formed by the seven estuarial rivers . . .*). The sentence preceding this description (*The two men pulled and pushed the handcart through the city streets*) and the words following it (*Mr. Tanimoto and Mr. Matsuo took their way through the shopping center . . .*) seem to have little to do with the description. Why describe the city here? Would this description be preferable at the beginning of the essay? Where is the best place in the essay for such information?

10. Why end the episode with this detail (par. 8)? Why is the same detail introduced in par. 7?

11. The fourth sentence in par. 6 consists of three simple independent clauses joined by conjunctions. The usual punctuation would be to separate the clauses with commas. Why, then, does Hersey use a dash and parentheses?

12. The distance of each of the victims from the center of the explosion is given in pars. 6, 13, 17, 22, 25, and 29. Is this information most relevant at the particular points chosen by Hersey? Rewrite this section of each of the above paragraphs, attempting a more effective arrangement of the material without using parentheses.

13. Choose five other examples of parenthetical statements. Compare and contrast their rhetorical functions with five parenthetical examples from the magazine *Consumer Reports* (published by Consumers Union). Note: Parentheses are sometimes used in technical writing (carrying a heavy load of statistical or comparative data) to freely locate complicated modifiers.

14. Par. 30, the conclusion of *A Noiseless Flash*, is not ordered chronologically, though the events are located in time. Why end with what happened *first of all?*

15. Is it accurate to say *Everything fell* (par. 30)?

16. Why refer to *tin factory* in the last sentence of par. 30?

17. Why does Hersey call it *the first moment of the atomic age* (par. 30)? Discuss whether these words can be considered part of the thesis of the essay. Can it be argued that other "moments" are just as relevant to the meaning of Hersey's essay? (One example might be 1905, the year Albert Einstein created the special theory of relativity—one of whose propositions was that mass and energy are equivalent.)

18. Can the last words of the essay (*a human being was crushed by books*) be considered part of the thesis? Discuss.

DICTION AND TONE

1. The diction of *A Noiseless Flash* is reportorial—careful, flat, and conventional. But the manner in which the writer communicates his attitude toward his subject—his tone—is complex.

   Consider Hersey's first two sentences. They are densely factual (*overhanging one of the seven deltaic rivers which divide Hiroshima*) and almost obsessively exact (*reclined in his underwear on a cot on the top floor of the order's three-story mission house, reading a Jesuit magazine, Stimmen der Zeit*). The sentences are overladen with detail. How do they prepare the reader for the rest of the essay?

2. Write a short introductory paragraph to *A Noiseless Flash*, setting it in historical perspective and commenting on the moral, military, and political implications. Discuss whether Hersey should have used such an introduction.

3. Search the essay for comments or generalizations made by Hersey. Has Hersey failed to take advantage of his material, to develop relevant generalizations from his data? Formulate a generalization and develop a paragraph using the factual material of *A Noiseless Flash* as evidence. Compare the tone of your paragraph with the tone of *A Noiseless Flash*, with its relative paucity of overt moralizing or intellectual analysis. Has Hersey failed to communicate his attitude toward his materials—failed, in other words, to establish his tone? Discuss. If you believe he has communicated his tone, attempt a statement of it. Point to details, organizing principles, or diction as evidence for your statement.

4. Why use the word *estuarial* (par. 5)? Would a more common word or phrase be better?

5. Why *finicky rock garden* (par. 5)? Would you omit this detail?

APPLICATIONS TO WRITING

The factual density and precision of Hersey's A *Noiseless Flash* almost convince the reader that here is a transcription of reality, that everything is included from moment to moment. In part the reader's impression is a result of (1) diction which does not call attention to itself ("flat"), (2) careful selection of details ("facts"), (3) effective arrangement of the details, and (4) control of tone (primarily through the last two elements). Try to employ these four methods in the following applications to writing.

1. Describe fifteen minutes of your day in chronological process, including necessary exposition as Hersey does. (See pars. 2, 3, 4, 5.)

2. Describe an automobile accident, beginning with the moment of impact, then cutting back to an earlier time and returning to the impact.

3. Begin with a moment from basketball—say, the last score of the game. Freeze the instant the ball leaves the hand of the scorer, describing the position of each player. Then describe how each player reached this point, beginning sixty seconds before this time.

MARRAKECH

GEORGE ORWELL

As the corpse went past the flies left the restaurant table in a cloud and rushed after it, but they came back a few minutes later. [1]

The little crowd of mourners—all men and boys, no women—threaded their way across the market place between the piles of pomegranates and the taxis and the camels, wailing a short chant over and over again. What really appeals to the flies is that the corpses here are never put into coffins, they are merely wrapped in a piece of rag and carried on a rough wooden bier on the shoulders of four friends. When the friends get to the burying-ground they hack an oblong hole a foot or two deep, dump the body in it and fling over it a little of the dried-up, lumpy earth, which is like broken brick. No gravestone, no name, no identifying mark of any kind. The burying-ground is merely a huge waste of hummocky earth, like a derelict building-lot. After a month or two no one can even be certain where his own relatives are buried. [2]

When you walk through a town like this—two hundred thousand inhabitants, of whom at least twenty thousand own literally nothing except the rags they stand up in—when you see how the people live, and still more how easily they die, it is always difficult to believe that

492

you are walking among human beings. All colonial empires are in reality founded upon that fact. The people have brown faces—besides, there are so many of them! Are they really the same flesh as yourself? Do they even have names? Or are they merely a kind of undifferentiated brown stuff, about as individual as bees or coral insects? They rise out of the earth, they sweat and starve for a few years, and then they sink back into the nameless mounds of the grave-yard and nobody notices that they are gone. And even the graves themselves soon fade back into the soil. Sometimes, out for a walk, as you break your way through the prickly pear, you notice that it is rather bumpy underfoot, and only a certain regularity in the bumps tells you that you are walking over skeletons. [3]

I was feeding one of the gazelles in the public gardens. [4]

Gazelles are almost the only animals that look good to eat when they are still alive, in fact, one can hardly look at their hindquarters without thinking of a mint sauce. The gazelle I was feeding seemed to know that this thought was in my mind, for though it took the piece of bread I was holding out it obviously did not like me. It nibbled rapidly at the bread, then lowered its head and tried to butt me, then took another nibble and then butted again. Probably its idea was that if it could drive me away the bread would somehow remain hanging in mid-air. [5]

An Arab navvy working on the path nearby lowered his heavy hoe and sidled slowly towards us. He looked from the gazelle to the bread and from the bread to the gazelle, with a sort of quiet amazement, as though he had never seen anything quite like this before. Finally he said shyly in French:

"I could eat some of that bread." [6]

I tore off a piece and he stowed it gratefully in some secret place under his rags. This man is an employee of the Municipality. [7]

When you go through the Jewish quarters you gather some idea of what the medieval ghettoes were probably like. Under their Moorish rulers the Jews were only allowed to own land in certain restricted areas, and after centuries of this kind of treatment they have ceased to bother about overcrowding. Many of the streets are a good deal less than six feet wide, the houses are completely windowless, and sore-eyed children cluster everywhere in unbelievable numbers, like clouds of flies. Down the centre of the street there is generally running a little river of urine. [8]

In the bazaar huge families of Jews, all dressed in the long black robe and little black skull-cap, are working in dark fly-infested booths that look like caves. A carpenter sits crosslegged at a prehistoric lathe, turning chair-legs at lightning speed. He works the lathe with a bow in his right hand and guides the chisel with his left foot, and thanks to a lifetime of sitting in this position his left leg is warped out of shape. At his side his grandson, aged six, is already starting on the simpler parts of the job. [9]

I was just passing the coppersmiths' booths when somebody noticed that I was lighting a cigarette. Instantly, from the dark holes all round, there was a frenzied rush of Jews, many of them old grandfathers with flowing grey beards, all clamouring for a cigarette. Even a blind man somewhere at the back of one of the booths heard a rumour of cigarettes and came crawling out, groping in the air with his hand. In about a minute I had used up the whole packet. None of these people, I suppose, works less than twelve hours a day, and every one of them looks on a cigarette as a more or less impossible luxury. [10]

As the Jews live in self-contained communities they follow the same trades as the Arabs, except for agriculture. Fruit-sellers, potters, silversmiths, blacksmiths, butchers, leatherworkers, tailors, water-carriers, beggars, porters—whichever way you look you see nothing but Jews. As a matter of fact there are thirteen thousand of them, all living in the space of a few acres. A good job Hitler wasn't here. Perhaps he was on his way, however. You hear the usual dark rumours about the Jews, not only from the Arabs but from the poorer Europeans. [11]

"Yes, *mon vieux*, they took my job away from me and gave it to a Jew. The Jews! They're the real rulers of this country, you know. They've got all the money. They control the banks, finance—everything." [12]

"But," I said, "isn't it a fact that the average Jew is a labourer working for about a penny an hour?" [13]

"Ah, that's only for show! They're all money lenders really. They're cunning, the Jews." [14]

In just the same way, a couple of hundred years ago, poor old women used to be burned for witchcraft when they could not even work enough magic to get themselves a square meal. [15]

All people who work with their hands are partly invisible, and the more important the work they do, the less visible they are. Still, a white skin is always fairly conspicuous. In northern Europe, when you see a labourer ploughing a field, you probably give him a second glance. In a hot country, anywhere south of Gibraltar or east of Suez, the chances are that you don't even see him. I have noticed this again and again. In a tropical landscape one's eye takes in everything except the human beings. It takes in the dried-up soil, the prickly pear, the palm tree and the distant mountain, but it always misses the peasant hoeing at his patch. He is the same colour as the earth, and a great deal less interesting to look at. [16]

It is only because of this that the starved countries of Asia and Africa are accepted as tourist resorts. No one would think of running cheap trips to the Distressed Areas. But where the human beings have brown skins their poverty is simply not noticed. What does Morocco mean to a Frenchman? An orange grove or a job in Government service. Or to an Englishman? Camels, castles, palm trees, Foreign Legionnaires, brass trays, and bandits. One could probably live there for years without noticing that for nine-tenths of the people the reality of life is an endless, back-breaking struggle to wring a little food out of an eroded soil. [17]

Most of Morocco is so desolate that no wild animal bigger than a hare can live on it. Huge areas which were once covered with forest have turned into a treeless waste where the soil is exactly like broken-up brick. Nevertheless a good deal of it is cultivated, with frightful labour. Everything is done by hand. Long lines of women, bent double like inverted capital L's, work their way slowly across the fields, tearing up the prickly weeds with their hands, and the peasant gathering lucerne for fodder pulls it up stalk by stalk instead of reaping it, thus saving an inch or two on each stalk. The plough is a wretched wooden thing, so frail that one can easily carry it on one's shoulder, and fitted underneath with a rough iron spike which stirs the soil to a depth of about four inches. This is as much as the strength of the animals is equal to. It is usual to plough with a cow and a donkey yoked together. Two donkeys would not be quite strong enough, but on the other hand two cows would cost a little more to feed. The peasants possess no harrows, they merely plough the soil several times over in different directions, finally leaving it in rough furrows, after which the whole field has to be shaped with hoes into small oblong patches to conserve water. Except for a day or two after the rare rainstorms there is never enough water. Along the edges of the fields channels are hacked out to a depth of thirty or forty feet to get at the tiny trickles which run through the subsoil. [18]

Every afternoon a file of very old women passes down the road outside my house, each carrying a load of firewood. All of them are mummified with age and the sun, and all of them are tiny. It seems to be generally the case in primitive communities that the women, when they get beyond a certain age, shrink to the size of children. One day a poor old creature who could not have been more than four feet tall crept past me under a vast load of wood. I stopped her and put a five-sou piece (a little more than a farthing) into her hand. She answered with a shrill wail, almost a scream, which was partly gratitude but mainly surprise. I suppose that from her point of view, by taking any notice of her, I seemed almost to be violating a law of nature. She accepted her status as an old woman, that is to say as a beast of burden. When a family is travelling it is quite usual to see a father and a grown-up son riding ahead on donkeys, and an old woman following on foot, carrying the baggage. [19]

But what is strange about these people is their invisibility. For several weeks, always at about the same time of day, the file of old women had hobbled past the house with their firewood, and though they had registered themselves on my eyeballs I cannot truly say that I had seen them. Firewood was passing—that was how I saw it. It was only that one day I happened to be walking behind them, and the curious up-and-down motion of a load of wood drew my attention to the human being beneath it. Then for the first time I noticed the poor old earth-coloured bodies, bodies reduced to bones and leathery skin, bent double under the crushing weight. Yet I suppose I had not been five minutes on Moroccan soil before I noticed the overloading of the donkeys and was infuriated by it. There is no question that the donkeys are damnably treated. The Moroccan donkey is hardly bigger than a St. Bernard dog, it carries a load which in the British Army would be considered too much for a fifteen-hands mule, and very often its pack-saddle is not taken off its back for weeks together. But what is peculiarly pitiful is that it is the most willing creature on earth, it follows its master like a dog and does not need either bridle or halter. After a dozen years of devoted work it suddenly drops dead, whereupon its master tips it into the ditch and the village dogs have torn its guts out before it is cold. [20]

This kind of thing makes one's blood boil, whereas—on the whole —the plight of the human beings does not. I am not commenting, merely pointing to a fact. People with brown skins are next door to invisible. Anyone can be sorry for the donkey with its galled back, but it is generally owing to some kind of accident if one even notices the old woman under her load of sticks. [21]

As the storks flew northward the Negroes were marching southward —a long, dusty column, infantry, screw-gun batteries, and then more infantry, four or five thousand men in all, winding up the road with a clumping of boots and a clatter of iron wheels. [22]

They were Senegalese, the blackest Negroes in Africa, so black that sometimes it is difficult to see whereabouts on their necks the hair begins. Their splendid bodies were hidden in reach-me-down khaki uniforms, their feet squashed into boots that looked like blocks of wood, and every tin hat seemed to be a couple of sizes too small. It was very hot and the men had marched a long way. They slumped under the weight of their packs and the curiously sensitive black faces were glistening with sweat. [23]

As they went past a tall, very young Negro turned and caught my eye. But the look he gave me was not in the least the kind of look you might expect. Not hostile, not contemptuous, not sullen, not even inquisitive. It was the shy, wide-eyed Negro look, which actually is a look of profound respect. I saw how it was. This wretched boy, who is a French citizen and has therefore been dragged from the forest to scrub floors and catch syphilis in garrison towns, actually has feelings of reverence before a white skin. He has been taught that the white race are his masters, and he still believes it. [24]

But there is one thought which every white man (and in this connection it doesn't matter twopence if he calls himself a socialist) thinks when he sees a black army marching past. "How much longer can we go on kidding these people? How long before they turn their guns in the other direction?" [25]

It was curious, really. Every white man there had this thought stowed somewhere or other in his mind. I had it, so had the other onlookers, so had the officers on their sweating chargers and the white N.C.O.'s marching in the ranks. It was a kind of secret which we all knew and were too clever to tell; only the Negroes didn't know it. And really it was like watching a flock of cattle to see the long column, a mile or two miles of armed men, flowing peacefully up the road, while the great white birds drifted over them in the opposite direction, glittering like scraps of paper. [26]

PURPOSE AND STRUCTURE

1. Instead of *telling* the reader that the natives are poor, Orwell *shows* poverty in at least five ways. Identify. Explain the difference between telling and showing.

2. By showing instead of telling, Orwell maintains the point of view of an objective reporter. How then can you tell that he is outraged at the spectacle of misery?

3. State clearly in one sentence the significance of the incident involving the cigarettes. Compare your statement with Orwell's report. What

specific details and particulars make his account more vivid than your summary? What is the topic sentence of par. 10?

4. Could pars. 4–7 just as well come after 8–15 as before? Could other groups of paragraphs be rearranged? What does this indicate about the organization? What gives the essay coherence?

5. Notice the lack of transition between parts of the essay. What is gained by avoiding logical transitions and abruptly juxtaposing the elements?

DICTION AND TONE

1. List all the words revealing Orwell's lack of objectivity in reporting on the Moroccan donkeys. Why does he reveal his feelings about the donkeys but conceal his feelings about the people?

2. Orwell frequently uses a more particular verb than the general one *to walk*. For example, "The little crowd of mourners . . . *threaded their way*. . . ." What verbs does he use in place of *to walk* in par. 19?

3. In par. 2, circle the verbs relating to the burial. What feelings are evoked?

4. In par. 3 Orwell addresses the reader by writing, "When *you* walk through a town like this. . . ." What would be the difference in tone if he had written, "When *one* walks . . . ?" How does this tone contribute to his purpose?

5. In how many ways are the storks and the Negro soldiers different? What is the effect of placing these contrasting elements together?

APPLICATIONS TO WRITING

Write an essay in which you describe objectively a highly moving scene or situation. Select a scene of poverty, one evoking pity, terror, or revulsion. Although you must make an effort to maintain an objective tone, your real but unstated feelings should be evident to the reader.

THE SPIRIT OF ALGIERS

ALBERT CAMUS

They are often secret, the loves you share with a place. Cities like Paris, Prague, and even Florence are turned in upon themselves, and so limit the society which is natural to them. But Algiers, and with it certain privileged places, cities on the sea, open out into the sky like a mouth or a wound. The things one loves in Algiers are the things everyone lives by: the sea at every turning, a certain burden in the sunshine, the beauty of the people. And, as always, in this shamelessness, in this offering, there is an even more secret perfume. In Paris, one can have a longing for space and the beating of wings. Here man is overwhelmed, and, assured of his desires, he can take stock of his riches. [1]

Undoubtedly you must live in Algiers for a long time to understand how withering an excess of natural goods can be. There is nothing here for the man who wants to learn, to educate himself, or to better himself. This is a country without lessons. It neither makes promises nor drops hints. It is satisfied with giving, but in profusion. It is completely given over to the eyes, and you know it as soon as you enjoy it. Its pleasures are past remedy, and its joys without hope. It calls for spirits that are clear-sighted, that is, bereft of consolation. It requires one to make an act of lucidity as one makes an

500

act of faith. A strange land that bestows upon the man it sustains both his grandeur and his misery! It is not surprising that the sensuous riches with which a sensitive man is provided in this country coincide with the most extreme poverty. There is no truth which does not bring with it its own bitterness. Why then be surprised if I no longer love the face of this land except among its poorest people? [2]

Throughout their youth here men find a life in proportion to their beauty; and afterwards there is a decline and a forgetting. They put their stakes on the flesh, but they knew they were going to lose. In Algiers, to the man who is young and alive, everything offers an escape and an excuse for triumphs: the bay, the sun, the red and white play of terraces toward the sea, the flowers and the sports grounds, the girls with cool legs. But for him who has lost his youth, there is nothing to cling to and nowhere for melancholy to escape from itself. Elsewhere, on Italian terraces, in the cloisters of Europe, or along the outline of Provençal hills, there are many places where man can flee from his humanity and gently get free of himself. But everything here calls for solitude and the blood of young men. Goethe, on his deathbed, cried out for light, and that has become a historic saying. In Belcourt and in Babel-Oued, old men sitting at the backs of cafés listen to the boastings of young men with plastered hair. [3]

These beginnings and these ends, it is summer that brings them to us in Algiers. During these months the wealthy desert the city. But the poor remain, and the sky. Along with them we go down together toward the port and man's treasures: the warmth of the water and the brown bodies of women. And at night, gorged with these riches, they go back to the oilcloth and the oil lamp that furnish all the scenery of their lives. [4]

In Algiers, you bathe in the harbor and then go and rest on a raft. When you go near a raft where there is a pretty girl, you shout to your friends: "I tell you, she's a peach." Those are healthy pleasures. One must believe that they constitute the ideal of these young people since most of them continue this life during the winter, and every day at noon they gather naked in the sun for a frugal meal. Not that they have read the dull tracts of the nudists, those Protestants of the flesh (there is a systemization of the body which is as irritating as that of the mind). But they are happy in the sun. [5]

Not nearly enough importance will ever be placed upon this habit of our age. For the first time in two thousand years the body may be seen naked on the beaches. For twenty centuries men have striven to make Greek insolence and naïveté decent, to diminish the importance of the flesh and to complicate dress. Today, after all this history, the stretches of young people on Mediterranean beaches go back to the magnificent gestures of the athletes of Delos. And living in this way, beside the flesh and by the flesh, they see that the flesh has its shades, its life and—to venture a bit of nonsense—a psychology of its own. [6]

May I lay myself open to ridicule by saying that I do not like the way in which Gide exalts the flesh? He calls upon it to delay desire in order to sharpen desire. Thus he is like those who, in the slang of the brothel, are called complicated or cerebral. Christianity also wants to defer desire. But it is more natural and sees in this deference a mortification. My friend Vincent, who is a cooper and a junior swimming champion, has an even clearer view of things. He drinks when he is thirsty, if he desires a woman he tries to sleep with her, and would marry her if he were in love with her (that hasn't happened yet). Afterwards, he always says, "That's better"—which sums up forcefully the apology one might make for satiety. [7]

The evolution of the flesh, like that of the mind, has its history, its setbacks, its advances and its losses. With this difference only: color. When you go to the harbor baths during the summer, you become aware of the simultaneous passing of every skin from white to gold, then to brown, and finally to tobacco color, the ultimate effort of transformation of which the body is capable. The harbor is dominated by the play of the white cubes of the Casbah. When you are at water level, against the crude white background of the Arab city, the bodies unfold a copper frieze. And as August advances and the sun grows greater, the white of the houses becomes more blinding, and the skins take on a more somber warmth. How then escape identifying yourself with this dialogue of stone and flesh, as the sun and the seasons pass? The whole morning is spent diving, in blossoming laughter amid sprays of water, in long paddle strokes around red and black cargo vessels (those that come from Norway are all scented with wood; those from Germany are filled with the smell of oil; those that hug the coast smell of wine and old casks). When sunshine is spilling from every corner of the sky, an orange canoe laden with brown bodies draws us into a crazy race. Then the cadenced beating of the double paddle, the blades the color of fruit, is suspended sharply and we glide along in the still water of the harbor: how can I have any doubts that I am piloting over the smooth waters a wild cargo of gods in whom I recognize my brothers? [8]

But at the other end of the town, summer is already offering us her other riches: I mean her moments of silence and her boredom. These moments of silence differ in quality, according to whether they spring from shadow or shade of the bordering trees. Arabs sell for five francs glasses of iced lemonade flavored with orange flowers. Their cry, "Ice cold, ice cold!" carries across the empty square. After their cries, silence falls again under the sunshine: in the vendor's jug, the ice turns round and I hear its tiny noise. There is the silence of siesta. In the streets along the sea front, outside the hairdressers' dirty shops, it can be measured by the musical buzzing of flies behind the curtains made of hollow reeds. Elsewhere, in the Moorish cafés of the Casbah, it is the flesh that is silent, that cannot tear itself away from these places, leave the glass of tea and discover time again in the sounds of its own blood. But, above all, there is the silence of summer evenings. [9]

These brief moments, when day slips into night, are they thronged with secret signs and calls—is that why Algiers is so bound to them in my imagination? Sometimes when I am far away from this country, I conjure up its twilights like promises of happiness. Over the hills which dominate the city there are roads among the mastic and olive trees. And it is toward them that my heart turns. I see sprays of black birds climb toward the green horizons. In the sky, empty suddenly of sunshine, something gradually relaxes. A tiny host of red clouds string out until they are absorbed back into the air. Almost immediately afterwards appears the first star, and then, in one stride, comes the devouring night. [10]

Fleeting evenings in Algiers, what unequalled quality do they possess to stir so many things in me? The sweetness that they leave on my lips, I have not time to weary of before it disappears in the night. Is that the secret of its persistence? [11]

On Padovani beach the dance hall is open every day. And in the huge rectangular night club, open to the sea its whole length long, the poor young people of the district dance until evening. Often, I used to wait there for an unusual moment. During the day, the hall is protected by sloping wooden screens. When the sun has disappeared, they are raised. Then the hall is filled with a strange green light, born of the double shell of sea and sky. Sitting away from the windows, you see only the sky and the faces of the passing dancers, as in a shadow theatre. Night comes quickly then and with it the lights. [12]

I cannot put into words how moving and how secret this subtle moment is to me. I remember, though, a tall splendid girl who had danced all afternoon. She wore a jasmine necklace over her clinging blue dress that was wet with sweat from her hips down her legs. She laughed as she danced and tossed back her head. When she came close to the table, she left floating after her the mingled smell of flowers and flesh. When evening arrived, I could no longer see her body pressed against her partner's, but against the sky moved the alternate spots of white jasmine and black hair, and when she threw back her full bosom I could hear her laugh and see her partner's profile bend down suddenly. My idea of innocence, I owe to nights like these. In any event, I learn no longer to separate these beings laden with violent feelings from the sky where their desires whirl. [13]

In suburban cinemas in Algiers, they sometimes sell peppermints which bear, marked in red, everything essential to the birth of love:

1) Questions: "Do you love me?" "When will you marry me?"; 2) Answers: "Madly"; "In the spring." After preparing the ground, you pass them to your neighbor who replies in a similar fashion or simply plays the fool. In Belcourt, they have seen marriages arranged in this way and whole lives committed by the exchange of peppermint sweets. And this gives a good picture of the childlike people of this country. [14]

The sign of youth is, perhaps, a splendid inclination toward easily won happiness. But, above all, it is an eagerness to live which comes near squandering. In Belcourt, as in Babel-Oued, they marry young. They go to work very early, and they use up in ten years the experience of a man's life. A thirty-year-old workman has already played all his cards. He awaits the end with his wife and his children. His happiness has been short and merciless. So has his life. And you understand that he is born of this country where everything is given only to be taken away. In this abundance and profusion, life takes the curve of the great passions, sudden, exacting, generous. It is not to be built, but to be burned. So there is no question of contemplating and of becoming better. [15]

The idea of hell, for example, is only a mild joke here. An imagination of this kind is allowed only to the very virtuous. And I believe that virtue is a word without meaning all over Algeria. Not that these men lack principles. They have their morality, and a very special one. They do not neglect their mothers. They see that their wives are respected in the streets. They are considerate to pregnant women. They do not attack an adversary in pairs, because "that isn't done." The one who does not observe these elementary rules "is not a man" and that settles the affair. This seems just and strict to me. We are still very far from obeying unconsciously this code of the street, the only disinterested one I know. I have seen people's faces around me soften with pity whenever a man went by surrounded by policemen and, before they knew whether the man had stolen, was a parricide or simply a nonconformist: "The poor chap," they said, or again, with a shade of admiration: "That one's a pirate." [16]

There are races born to pride and life. They are the ones that foster the most remarkable inclination towards boredom. They are the ones, too, in whom the attitude toward death is most repellent. Putting the joys of the senses aside, the amusements of these people are among the silliest. A bowling club, association banquets, the shilling cinema and community fetes have for years provided adequate recreation for those over thirty. Sundays in Algiers are among the most sinister days in the world. How then could these unthinking people clothe with myths the deep horror of their life? Everything connected with death here is a subject of fun or of hate. These people without religion or idols die alone after living in a crowd. [17]

I well know that such a people cannot be accepted by everyone. Here, intelligence has no place, as it has in Italy. This race is indifferent to the mind. It has a cult and an admiration of the flesh. From flesh it draws its strength, its naïve cynicism and a childish vanity which deserves to be judged severely. Here it is a people without a past, without a tradition, and yet not without poetry—but a poetry whose quality is hard and sensual, far from tenderness, the same as their sky, the only poetry that truly moves me and makes me at one with myself. The opposite of a civilized people is a creative people. These barbarians sprawling on the beaches—I have the foolish hope that, perhaps without their knowing, they are in the act of fashioning the face of a culture in which man's grandeur will at last find its true countenance. These people entirely given over to their present live without myths, without consolation. They have put all their goods on this earth, and accordingly they are defenseless against death. [18]

Everything made here shows a distaste for stability and a heedlessness of the future. There is a rush to live, and if an art was to be born here, it would obey that hatred of duration that drove the Dorians to carve their first column in wood. Between this sky and these faces turned toward it there is nothing on which to hang a mythology, a literature, a philosophy, or a religion, but stones, flesh, stars and those truths that the hand can touch. [19]

Oneness is expressed here in terms of sunshine and of sea. It is felt in the heart in a certain human desire which contains its own bitterness and its own grandeur. Gradually I come to the knowledge that there is no superhuman happiness, no eternity outside the curve of days. These absurd, essential goods, these relative truths are the only ones that move me. The others, ideals, I have not enough heart to understand. I do not wish to play the fool, but I cannot find any sense in the happiness of angels. I know only that this will endure longer than I. And what shall I call eternity, if not what goes on after my death? [20]

I am not expressing the satisfaction of an individual with his lot. It is something very different. It is not always easy to be a man, still less to be a pure man. But to be pure is to rediscover the country of the soul where the relationship of the world becomes perceptible, where the beating of the blood meets the violent pulsations of the two-o'clock sun. It is a well-known fact that you always recognize your native land when you are about to lose it. For those who are too tortured by themselves, their native land is the one that rejects them. I should not like to be brutal nor seem to exaggerate. But, in short, those things in this life that reject me are first of all those things which make me die. Everything that exalts life at the same time increases its absurdity. In the Algerian summer I learn that one thing is more tragic than suffering, and that is the life of a happy man. But this may also be the road to a larger life, since it leads one not to cheat. [21]

Many, in fact, pretend to a love of living in order to elude love itself. They try to enjoy themselves and to "make experiments." But this is a point of view of the mind. One needs an exceptional gift to be a sensualist. A man's life comes to an end without the help of his mind, with its retreats and advances, its simultaneous solitude and presence. To see these men of Belcourt working, supporting their wives and their children, I believe it possible to feel a secret shame. I have no illusions; there is not much love in the lives I am speaking of. I ought to say there is no longer very much. But at least they have evaded nothing. There are words that I have never understood very well, like sin. Yet I believe I know that these men have not sinned against life. For if there is one sin against life, it is not so much in despairing as in hoping for another life and slipping away from the implacable grandeur of this one. These men have not cheated. They were summer gods at twenty because of their eagerness to live, and thus they remain deprived of all hope. I have seen two of them die. They were filled with horror, but silent. It is better thus. From Pandora's box in which swarmed the evils of humanity, the Greeks let out hope after all the others, as the most terrible of all. I know of no more moving symbol. For hope, contrary to what people believe, is the equivalent of resignation. And to live is not to be resigned. [22]

Here is the bitter lesson of Algerian summers. But already the season is trembling and summer is slipping away. The first September rains, after so much violence and tenseness, are like the first tears of the liberated earth, as if for a few days this country were stirring with tenderness. At the same time the acacias spread an odor of love over the whole of Algeria. In the evening or after the rain, the entire earth, her belly wet with a seed perfumed with bitter almond, rests from having given herself all summer long to the sun. And once again, this odor consecrates the marriage of man and earth and awakes in us the only truly virile love in this world, perishable and bounteous. [23]

PURPOSE AND STRUCTURE

1. With what concrete details is par. 1 developed?

2. How does Camus prepare the reader for the value judgment implicit in his rhetorical question (par. 2)?

3. At the beginning of par. 2 Camus makes an explicit value judgment. What is it?

4. Locate other explicit statements of attitude. Mark the paragraphs in which there are implicit judgment values. By what means do you become aware of them?

5. How does the contrast in par. 3 contribute to the author's purpose?

6. How are transitions established between pars. 1, 2, and 3?

7. How does the author interweave the abstract and the concrete in pars. 5 to 8?

8. How does the custom of the peppermint exchange support the generalization in par. 14? What other purpose is served by mentioning it?

9. What basic dualities are linked in this essay? How are they contrasted?

10. What is the meaning of *disinterested* in par. 16?

11. What is the relevance of the rhetorical question in par. 17 to the central purpose of the essay? to the ideas in pars. 18, 19, and 20?

12. Explain the seeming paradox: "The opposite of a civilized people is a creative people." How does this paradox relate to Camus' purpose? to what precedes and what follows?

13. What specific details convey Camus' views concerning truth, absurdity, and eternity in pars. 20–22?

14. What would be lost if the first sentence in the essay were written as follows: "The loves you share with a place are often secret"?

15. The last sentence in par. 13 reads: "My idea of innocence, I owe to nights like these." Locate other examples of inverted sentence order. What, if anything, is gained by these inversions?

16. What causal relationships are developed in the essay?

17. Is the author's approach primarily inductive or deductive? Justify your conclusion.

DICTION AND TONE

1. Discuss in context the images evoked by the following examples of metaphorical language: *turned in upon themselves* [1]; *cities . . . open*

out into the sky like a mouth or a wound [1]; *a certain burden in the sunshine* [1]; *the beating of wings* [1]; *an even more secret perfume* [1]; *gorged with these riches* [4]; *those Protestants of the flesh* [5]; *this dialogue of stone and flesh* [8].

2. Discuss the relationship of the following words: *withering* to *excess* [2]; *remedy* to *pleasures* [2]; *lucidity* to *act* [2]; *insolence* to *naïveté* [6]; *merciless* to *happiness* [15]; *naïve* to *cynicism* [18].

3. What are the components of the aphoristic statements in par. 2? How do they contribute to the tone?

4. Are *abundance* and *profusion* mutually exclusive terms (par. 15)?

5. How does the author rely on sight, sound, smell, and touch in conveying the spirit of Algiers? Cite specific passages.

6. Account for the rhythm of the sentences in pars. 1, 10, and 23.

7. How are the author's feelings modulated by his thought? Cite passages in which he appeals to the reader's emotions and those in which he appeals to his reason. Which are most persuasive to you? Why?

8. What rhetorical devices communicate the Algerian concept of morality in par. 16? Camus' conception?

9. How are expository, descriptive, and narrative elements fused? Which element is dominant? Mark examples of each.

APPLICATIONS TO WRITING

Throughout the essay Camus makes a number of explicit value judgments. However, if he did not communicate his feelings about Algiers *primarily* by implicit means, he would have failed in his purpose, and the tone of this piece would have been didactic and hortatory. Instead he conveys his view of the human situation by evoking a nostalgic mood and an opulent atmosphere. By indirection, by irony, by understatement, by implied comparisons, and most of all by use of concrete sensory images, he succeeds in this purpose.

1. Recreate the spirit of a place for which you have warm memories. Suggest your feelings about its inhabitants by implicit means.

2. Describe a mode of life that you have experienced or observed and may have outgrown or renounced. Or try to persuade the reader of its joys and values. Use several of the rhetorical devices employed by Camus.

3. From what dominant viewpoint does Camus write (poet, humanist, hedonist, moralist)? Support your judgment by quotation from the text and analysis of his purpose, structure, diction and tone.

A FREE MAN'S WORSHIP

To Dr. Faustus in his study Mephistopheles told the history of the Creation, saying:

The endless praises of the choirs of angels had begun to grow wearisome; for, after all, did he not deserve their praise? Had he not given them endless joy? Would it not be more amusing to obtain undeserved praise, to be worshipped by beings whom he tortured? He smiled inwardly, and resolved that the great drama should be performed.

For countless ages the hot nebula whirled aimlessly through space. At length it began to take shape, the central mass threw off planets, the planets cooled, boiling seas and burning mountains heaved and tossed, from black masses of cloud hot sheets of rain deluged the barely solid crust. And now the first germ of life grew in the depths of the ocean, and developed rapidly in the fructifying warmth into vast forest trees, huge ferns springing from the damp mould, sea monsters breeding, fighting, devouring, and passing away. And from the monsters, as the play unfolded itself, Man was born, with the power of thought, the knowledge of good and evil, and the cruel thirst for worship. And Man saw that all is passing in this mad, monstrous world, that all is struggling to snatch, at any cost, a few brief moments of life before Death's inexorable decree. And Man said: "There is a hidden purpose, could we but fathom it, and the purpose is good; for we must reverence something, and in the visible world there is nothing worthy of reverence." And Man stood aside from the struggle, resolving that God intended harmony to come out of chaos

From *Mysticism and Logic*, by Bertrand Russell. Reprinted by permission of George Allen & Unwin, Ltd.

by human efforts. And when he followed the instincts which God had transmitted to him from his ancestry of beasts of prey, he called it Sin, and asked God to forgive him. But he doubted whether he could be justly forgiven, until he invented a divine Plan by which God's wrath was to have been appeased. And seeing the present was bad, he made it yet worse, that thereby the future might be better. And he gave God thanks for the strength that enabled him to forgo even the joys that were possible. And God smiled; and when he saw that Man had become perfect in renunciation and worship, he sent another sun through the sky, which crashed into Man's sun; and all returned again to nebula.

"Yes," he murmured, "it was a good play; I will have it performed again." [1]

Such, in outline, but even more purposeless, more void of meaning is the world which Science presents for our belief. Amid such a world, if anywhere, our ideals henceforward must find a home. That Man is the product of causes which had no prevision of the end they were achieving; that his origin, his growth, his hopes and fears, his loves and his beliefs, are but the outcome of accidental collocations of atoms; that no fire, no heroism, no intensity of thought and feeling, can preserve an individual life beyond the grave; that all the labours of the ages, all the devotion, all the inspiration, all the noon-day brightness of human genius, are destined to extinction in the vast death of the solar system, and that the whole temple of Man's achievement must inevitably be buried beneath the débris of a universe in ruins—all these things, if not quite beyond dispute, are yet so nearly certain, that no philosophy which rejects them can hope to stand. Only within the scaffolding of these truths, only on the firm foundation of unyielding despair, can the soul's habitation henceforth be safely built. [2]

How, in such an alien and inhuman world, can so powerless a creature as Man preserve his aspirations untarnished? A strange mystery it is that Nature, omnipotent but blind, in the revolutions of her secular hurryings through the abysses of space, has brought forth at last a child, subject still to her power, but gifted with sight, with knowledge of good and evil, with the capacity of judging all the works of his unthinking Mother. In spite of Death, the mark and seal of the parental control, Man is yet free, during his brief years, to examine, to criticize, to know, and in imagination to create. To him alone, in the world with which he is acquainted, this freedom belongs; and in this lies his superiority to the resistless forces that control his outward life. [3]

The savage, like ourselves, feels the oppression of his impotence before the powers of Nature; but having in himself nothing that he respects more than Power, he is willing to prostrate himself before his gods, without inquiring whether they are worthy of his worship. Pathetic and very terrible is the long history of cruelty and torture, of degradation and human sacrifices endured in the hope of placating the jealous gods: surely, the trembling believer thinks, when what is most precious has been freely given, their lust for blood must be appeased, and more will not be required. The religion of Moloch—as such creeds may be generically called—is in essence the cringing submission of the slave, who dare not, even in his heart, allow the thought that his master deserves no adulation. Since the independence of ideals is not yet acknowledged, Power may be freely worshipped, and receive an unlimited respect, despite its wanton infliction of pain. [4]

But gradually, as morality grows bolder, the claim of the ideal world begins to be felt, and worship, if it is not to cease, must be given to gods of another kind than those created by the savage. Some, though they feel the demands of the ideal, will still consciously reject them, still urging that naked Power is worthy of worship. Such is the attitude inculcated in God's answer to Job out of the whirlwind: the divine power and knowledge are paraded, but of the divine goodness there is no hint. Such also is the attitude of those who, in our own day, base their morality upon the struggle for survival, maintaining that the survivors are necessarily the fittest. But others, not content with an answer so repugnant to the moral sense, will adopt the position which we have become accustomed to regard as specially religious, maintaining that, in some hidden manner, the world of fact is really harmonious with the world of ideals. Thus Man creates God, all-powerful and all-good, the mystic unity of what is and what should be. [5]

But the world of fact, after all, is not good; and, in submitting our judgment to it, there is an element of slavishness from which our thoughts must be purged. For in all things it is well to exalt the dignity of Man, by freeing him as far as possible from the tyranny of non-human Power. When we have realised that Power is largely bad, that Man, with his knowledge of good and evil, is but a helpless atom in a world which has no such knowledge, the choice is again presented to us: Shall we worship Force, or shall we worship Goodness? Shall our God exist and be evil, or shall he be recognised as the creation of our own conscience? [6]

The answer to this question is very momentous, and affects profoundly our whole morality. The worship of Force, to which Carlyle and Nietzsche and the creed of Militarism have accustomed us, is the result of failure to maintain our own ideals against a hostile universe: it is itself a prostrate submission to evil, a sacrifice of our best to Moloch. If strength indeed is to be respected, let us respect rather the strength of those who refuse that false "recognition of facts" which fails to recognise that facts are often bad. Let us admit that, in the world we know, there are many things that would be better otherwise, and that the ideals to which we do and must adhere are not realised in the realm of matter. Let us preserve our respect for truth, for beauty, for the ideal of perfection which life does not permit us to attain, though none of these things meet with the approval of the unconscious universe. If Power is bad, as it seems to be, let us reject it from our hearts. In this lies Man's true freedom: in determination to worship only the God created by our own love of the good, to respect only the heaven which inspires the insight of our best moments. In action, in desire, we must submit perpetually to the tyranny of outside forces; but in thought, in aspiration, we are free, free from our fellow-men, free from the petty planet on which our bodies impotently crawl, free even, while we live, from the tyranny of death. Let us learn, then, that energy of faith which enables us to live constantly in the vision of the good; and let us descend in action, into the world of fact, with that vision always before us. [7]

When first the opposition of fact and ideal grows fully visible, a spirit of fiery revolt, of fierce hatred of the gods, seems necessary to the assertion of freedom. To defy with Promethean constancy a hostile universe, to keep its evil always in view, always actively hated, to refuse no pain that the malice of Power can invent, appears to be the duty of all who will not bow before the inevitable. But indignation is still a bondage, for it compels our thoughts to be occupied with an evil world; and in the fierceness of desire from which rebellion springs there is a kind of self-assertion which it is necessary for the wise to overcome. Indignation is a submission of our thoughts, but not of our desires; the Stoic freedom in which wisdom consists is found in the submission of our desires, but not of our thoughts. From the submission of our desires springs the virtue of resignation; from the freedom of our thoughts springs the whole world of art and philosophy, and the vision of beauty by which, at last, we half reconquer the reluctant world. But the vision of beauty is possible only to unfettered contemplation, to thoughts not weighted by the load of eager wishes; and thus Freedom comes only to those who no longer ask of life that it shall yield them any of those personal goods that are subject to the mutations of Time. [8]

Although the necessity of renunciation is evidence of the existence of evil, yet Christianity, in preaching it, has shown a wisdom exceeding that of the Promethean philosophy of rebellion. It must be admitted that, of the things we desire, some, though they prove impossible, are yet real goods; others, however, as ardently longed for, do not form part of a fully purified ideal. The belief that what must be renounced is bad, though sometimes false, is far less often false than untamed passion supposes; and the creed of religion, by providing a reason for proving that it is never false, has been the means of purifying our hopes by the discovery of many austere truths. [9]

But there is in resignation a further good element: even real goods, when they are unattainable, ought not to be fretfully desired. To every man comes, sooner or later, the great renunciation. For the young, there is nothing unattainable; a good thing desired with the whole force of a passionate will, and yet impossible, is to them not credible. Yet, by death, by illness, by poverty, or by the voice of duty, we must learn, each one of us, that the world was not made for us, and that, however beautiful may be the things we crave, Fate may nevertheless forbid them. It is the part of courage, when misfortune comes, to bear without repining the ruin of our hopes, to turn away our thoughts from vain regrets. This degree of submission to Power is not only just and right; it is the very gate of wisdom. [10]

But passive renunciation is not the whole of wisdom; for not by renunciation alone can we build a temple for the worship of our own ideals. Haunting foreshadowings of the temple appear in the realm of imagination, in music, in architecture, in the untroubled kingdom of reason, and in the golden sunset magic of lyrics, where beauty shines and glows, remote from the touch of sorrow, remote from the fear of change, remote from the failures and disenchantments of the world of fact. In the contemplation of these things the vision of heaven will shape itself in our hearts, giving at once a touchstone to judge the world about us, and an inspiration by which to fashion to our needs whatever is not incapable of serving as a stone in the sacred temple. [11]

Except for those rare spirits that are born without sin, there is a cavern of darkness to be traversed before that temple can be entered. The gate of the cavern is despair, and its floor is paved with the gravestones of abandoned hopes. There Self must die; there the eagerness, the greed of untamed desire must be slain, for only so can the soul be freed from the empire of Fate. But out of the cavern the Gate of Renunciation leads again to the daylight of wisdom, by whose radiance a new insight, a new joy, a new tenderness, shine forth to gladden the pilgrim's heart. [12]

When, without the bitterness of impotent rebellion, we have learnt both to resign ourselves to the outward rule of Fate and to recognise that the nonhuman world is unworthy of our worship, it becomes possible at last so to transform and refashion the unconscious universe, so to transmute it in the crucible of the imagination, that a new image of shining gold replaces the old idol of clay. In all the multiform facts of the world—in the visual shapes of trees and mountains and clouds, in the events of the life of Man, even in the very omnipotence of Death—the insight of creative idealism can find the reflection of a beauty which its own thoughts first made. In this way mind asserts its subtle mastery over the thoughtless forces of Nature. The more evil the material with which it deals, the more thwarting to untrained desire, the greater is its achievement in inducing the reluctant rock to yield up its hidden treasure, the prouder its victory in compelling the opposing forces to swell the pageant of its triumph. Of all the arts, Tragedy is the proudest, the most triumphant; for it builds its shining citadel in the very centre of the enemy's country, on the very summit of his highest mountain; from its impregnable watch-towers, his camps and arsenals, his columns and forts, are all revealed; within its walls the free life continues, while the legions of Death and Pain and Despair, and all the servile captains of tyrant Fate, afford the burghers of that dauntless city new spectacles of beauty. Happy those sacred ramparts, thrice happy the dwellers on that all-seeing eminence. Honour to those brave warriors who, through countless ages of warfare, have preserved for us the priceless heritage of liberty, and have kept undefiled by sacrilegious invaders the home of the unsubdued. [13]

But the beauty of Tragedy does but make visible a quality which, in more or less obvious shapes, is present always and everywhere in life. In the spectacle of Death, in the endurance of intolerable pain, and in the irrevocableness of a vanished past, there is a sacredness, an overpowering awe, a feeling of the vastness, the depth, the inexhaustible mystery of existence, in which, as by some strange marriage of pain, the sufferer is bound to the world by bonds of sorrow. In these moments of insight, we lose all eagerness of temporary desire, all struggling and striving for petty ends, all care for the little trivial things, that, to a superficial view, make up the common life of day by day; we see, surrounding the narrow raft illumined by the flickering light of human comradeship, the dark ocean on whose rolling waves we toss for a brief hour; from the great night without, a chill blast breaks in upon our refuge; all the loneliness of humanity amid hostile forces is concentrated upon the individual soul, which must struggle alone, with what of courage it can command, against the whole weight of a universe that cares nothing for its hopes and fears. Victory, in this struggle with the powers of darkness, is the true baptism into the glorious company of heroes, the true initiation into the overmastering beauty of human existence. From that awful encounter of the soul with the outer world, renunciation, wisdom, and charity are born; and with their birth a new life begins. To take into the inmost shrine of the soul the irresistible forces whose puppets we seem to be—Death and change, the irrevocableness of the past, and the powerlessness of Man before the blind hurry of the universe from vanity to vanity—to feel these things and know them is to conquer them. [14]

This is the reason why the Past has such magical power. The beauty of its motionless and silent pictures is like the enchanted purity of late autumn, when the leaves, though one breath would make them fall, still glow against the sky in golden glory. The Past does not change or strive; like Duncan, after life's fitful fever it sleeps well; what was eager and grasping, what was petty and transitory, has faded away, the things that were beautiful and eternal shine out of it like stars in the night. Its beauty, to a soul not worthy of it, is unendurable; but to a soul which has conquered Fate it is the key of religion. [15]

The life of Man, viewed outwardly, is but a small thing in comparison with the forces of Nature. The slave is doomed to worship Time and Fate and Death, because they are greater than anything he finds in himself, and because all his thoughts are of things which they devour. But, great as they are, to think of them greatly, to feel their passionless splendour, is greater still. And such thought makes us free men; we no longer bow before the inevitable in Oriental subjection, but we absorb it, and make it part of ourselves. To abandon the

struggle for private happiness, to expel all eagerness of temporary
desire, to burn with passion for eternal things—this is emancipation,
and this is the free man's worship. And this liberation is effected
by a contemplation of Fate; for Fate itself is subdued by the
mind which leaves nothing to be purged by the purifying fire of
Time. [16]

United with his fellow-men by the strongest of all ties, the tie of a
common doom, the free man finds that a new vision is with him
always, shedding over every daily task the light of love. The life of
Man is a long march through the night, surrounded by invisible foes,
tortured by weariness and pain, towards a goal that few can hope to
reach, and where none may tarry long. One by one, as they march,
our comrades vanish from our sight, seized by the silent orders of
omnipotent Death. Very brief is the time in which we can help them,
in which their happiness or misery is decided. Be it ours to shed sunshine on their path, to lighten their sorrows by the balm of sympathy,
to give them the pure joy of a never-tiring affection, to strengthen
failing courage, to instil faith in hours of despair. Let us not weigh
in grudging scales their merits and demerits, but let us think only of
their need—of the sorrows, the difficulties, perhaps the blindnesses,
that make the misery of their lives; let us remember that they are
fellow-sufferers in the same darkness, actors in the same tragedy with
ourselves. And so, when their day is over, when their good and their
evil have become eternal by the immortality of the past, be it ours to
feel that, where they suffered, where they failed, no deed of ours was
the cause, but wherever a spark of the divine fire kindled in their
hearts, we were ready with encouragement, with sympathy, with
brave words in which high courage glowed. [17]

Brief and powerless is Man's life; on him and all his race the slow,
sure doom falls pitiless and dark. Blind to good and evil, reckless of
destruction, omnipotent matter rolls on its relentless way; for Man,
condemned to-day to lose his dearest, to-morrow himself to pass
through the gate of darkness, it remains only to cherish, ere yet the
blow falls, the lofty thoughts that ennoble his little day; disdaining

the coward terrors of the slave of Fate, to worship at the shrine that his own hands have built; undismayed by the empire of chance, to preserve a mind free from the wanton tyranny that rules his outward life; proudly defiant of the irresistible forces that tolerate, for a moment, his knowledge and his condemnation, to sustain alone, a weary but unyielding Atlas, the world that his own ideals have fashioned despite the trampling march of unconscious Power. [18]

PURPOSE AND STRUCTURE

1. What is the rhetorical function of Russell's dramatic account of the creation? For example, does it introduce major themes and assumptions?

2. Russell begins par. 3 with a question: "How . . . can so powerless a creature as Man preserve his aspirations untarnished?" Where and how does he answer the question?

3. He begins par. 8 with a subordinate construction: "When first the opposition of fact and ideal grows fully visible. . . ." Where is the *opposition of fact and ideal* developed?

4. "Indignation is a submission of our thoughts, but not of our desires; the Stoic freedom in which wisdom consists is found in the submission of our desires, but not of our thoughts" (par. 8). Outline the separate developments of (a) *submission of desires* and (b) *not of our thoughts.*

5. In par. 5 Russell begins the second sentence with *Some;* the fifth sentence with *But others.* Who are the *some?* the *others?* What purpose is served by using these general words instead of the particular names?

6. Russell begins par. 6 with the statement, "But the world of fact . . . is not good." Is this an assertion or a conclusion drawn from evidence? If an assertion, is it an assertion of such a generally agreed upon idea that it needs no proof? If evidence is supplied, cite it.

7. In sentence 3, par. 2, Russell states that man's "loves and his beliefs are but the outcome of accidental collocations of atoms." In par. 17 he says that the "free man finds that a new vision is with him always, shedding over every daily task the light of love." Taken out of context, these

statements are contradictory. Explain how the rhetorical context of each resolves the contradiction.

DICTION AND TONE

1. What resources of language does Russell employ to keep the essay, with its great emphasis on death and extinction, from being morbid?

2. Why does Russell capitalize so many nouns? What does this capitalization tell you about the level of concreteness or abstraction of his language?

3. Russell uses considerable sentence variety and unusual sentence length. For example, the sentence, "In the spectacle of Death, in the endurance of intolerable pain, and in the irrevocableness of a vanished past, there is a sacredness, an overpowering awe, a feeling of the vastness, the depth, the inexhaustible mystery of existence, in which, as by some strange marriage of pain, the sufferer is bound to the world by bonds of sorrow," is hardly recognizable as a "There is a . . ." type of sentence. Instead of, "The great renunciation comes to every man sooner or later," Russell writes, "To every man comes, sooner or later, the great renunciation," so that the emphasis falls on *every man*. Select five sentences and show how their construction contributes to effectiveness.

4. Analyze the subject of sentence 3, par. 2.

5. Russell makes frequent use of figurative language. Select three figures of speech and explain why they enhance or detract from his essay.

6. Justify Russell's use of the word *worship*.

APPLICATIONS TO WRITING

1. Write an essay in which you analyze apparent contradictions in Russell's argument. For example, in par. 2 Russell makes man a product of mechanical determinism; in par. 16 he makes man free. *Power is bad* in par. 7, but *submission to Power* is the *very gate of wisdom* in par. 10.

In par. 2 man is the *outcome of accidental collocations of atoms*, but in par. 14 existence is mysterious and sacred.

2. Write an essay in which you compare Russell's and Krutch's tragic views of life. You may want to consider such things as their purposes, the substance of their essays, and their tone.

3. Write a parable that embodies your own view of worship. Explain the parable, as Russell explains his.

NATHANIEL HAWTHORNE AND
"THE SCARLET LETTER"

D. H. LAWRENCE

Nathaniel Hawthorne writes romance. [1]

And what's romance? Usually, a nice little tale where you have everything As You Like It, where rain never wets your jacket and gnats never bite your nose and it's always daisy-time. *As You Like It* and *Forest Lovers*, etc. *Morte D'Arthur*. [2]

Hawthorne obviously isn't this kind of romanticist: though nobody has muddy boots in *The Scarlet Letter*, either. [3]

But there is more to it. *The Scarlet Letter* isn't a pleasant, pretty romance. It is a sort of parable, an earthly story with a hellish meaning. [4]

All the time there is this split in the American art and art-consciousness. On the top it is as nice as pie, goody-goody and lovey-dovey. Like Hawthorne being such a blue-eyed darling, in life, and Longfellow and the rest such sucking doves. Hawthorne's wife said she "never saw him in time," which doesn't mean she saw him too late. But always in the "frail effulgence of eternity." [5]

524

Serpents they were. Look at the inner meaning of their art and see what demons they were. [6]

You *must* look through the surface of American art, and see the inner diabolism of the symbolic meaning. Otherwise it is all mere childishness. [7]

That blue-eyed darling Nathaniel knew disagreeable things in his inner soul. He was careful to send them out in disguise. [8]

Always the same. The deliberate consciousness of Americans so fair and smooth-spoken, and the under-consciousness so devilish. *Destroy! destroy! destroy!* hums the under-consciousness. *Love and produce! Love and produce!* cackles the upper consciousness. And the world hears only the Love-and-produce cackle. Refuses to hear the hum of destruction underneath. Until such time as it will *have* to hear. [9]

The American has got to destroy. It is his destiny. It is his destiny to destroy the whole corpus of the white psyche, the white consciousness. And he's got to do it secretly. As the growing of a dragon-fly inside a chrysalis or cocoon destroys the larva grub, secretly. [10]

Though many a dragon-fly never gets out of the chrysalis case: dies inside. As America might. [11]

So the secret chrysalis of *The Scarlet Letter*, diabolically destroying the old psyche inside. [12]

Be good! Be good! warbles Nathaniel. *Be good, and never sin! Be sure your sins will find you out.* [13]

So convincingly that his wife never saw him "as in time." [14]

Then listen to the diabolic undertone of *The Scarlet Letter*. [15]

Man ate of the tree of knowledge, and became ashamed of himself. [16]

Do you imagine Adam had never lived with Eve before that apple episode? Yes, he had. As a wild animal with his mate. [17]

It didn't become "sin" till the knowledge-poison entered. That apple of Sodom. [18]

We are divided in ourselves, against ourselves. And that is the meaning of the cross symbol. [19]

In the first place, Adam knew Eve as a wild animal knows its mate, momentaneously, but vitally, in blood-knowledge. Blood-knowledge, not mind-knowledge. Blood-knowledge, that seems utterly to forget, but doesn't. Blood-knowledge, instinct, intuition, all the vast vital flux of knowing that goes on in the dark, antecedent to the mind. [20]

Then came that beastly apple, and the other sort of knowledge started. [21]

Adam began to look at himself. "My hat!" he said. "What's this? My Lord! What the deuce!—And Eve! I wonder about Eve." [22]

Thus starts KNOWING. Which shortly runs to UNDERSTANDING, when the devil gets his own. [23]

When Adam went and took Eve, *after* the apple, he didn't do any more than he had done many a time before, in act. But in consciousness he did something very different. So did Eve. Each of them kept an eye on what they were doing, they watched what was happening to them. They wanted to KNOW. And that was the birth of sin. Not *doing* it, but KNOWING about it. Before the apple, they had shut their eyes and their minds had gone dark. Now, they peeped and pried and imagined. They watched themselves. And they felt uncomfortable after. They felt self-conscious. So they said, "The *act* is sin. Let's hide. We've sinned." [24]

No wonder the Lord kicked them out of the Garden. Dirty hypocrites. [25]

The sin was the self-watching, self-consciousness. The sin, and the doom. Dirty understanding. [26]

Nowadays men do hate the idea of dualism. It's no good, dual we are. The Cross. If we accept the symbol, then, virtually, we accept the fact. We are divided against ourselves. [27]

For instance, the blood *hates* being KNOWN by the mind. It feels itself destroyed when it is KNOWN. Hence the profound instinct of privacy. [28]

And on the other hand, the mind and the spiritual consciousness of man simply *hates* the dark potency of blood-acts: hates the genuine dark sensual orgasms, which do, for the time being, actually obliterate the mind and the spiritual consciousness, plunge them in a suffocating flood of darkness. [29]

You can't get away from this. [30]

Blood-consciousness overwhelms, obliterates, and annuls mind-consciousness. [31]

Mind-consciousness extinguishes blood-consciousness, and consumes the blood. [32]

We are all of us conscious in both ways. And the two ways are antagonistic in us. [33]

They will always remain so. [34]

That is our cross. [35]

The antagonism is so obvious, and so far-reaching, that it extends to the smallest thing. The cultured, highly-conscious person of to-day *loathes* any form of physical, "menial" work: such as washing dishes or sweeping a floor or chopping wood. This menial work is an insult to the spirit. "When I see men carrying heavy loads, doing brutal work, it always makes me want to cry," said a beautiful, cultured woman to me. [36]

"When you say that, it makes me want to beat you," said I, in reply. "When I see you with your beautiful head pondering heavy thoughts, I just want to hit you. It outrages me." [37]

My father hated books, hated the sight of anyone reading or writing. [38]

My mother hated the thought that any of her sons should be condemned to manual labour. Her sons must have something higher than that. [39]

She won. But she died first. [40]

He laughs longest who laughs last. [41]

There is a basic hostility in all of us between the physical and the mental, the blood and the spirit. The mind is "ashamed" of the blood. And the blood is destroyed by the mind, actually. Hence pale-faces. [42]

At present the mind-consciousness and the so-called spirit triumphs. In America supremely. In America, nobody does anything from the blood. Always from the nerves, if not from the mind. The blood is chemically reduced by the nerves, in American activity. [43]

When an Italian labourer labours, his mind and nerves sleep, his blood acts ponderously. [44]

Americans, when they are *doing* things, never seem really to be doing them. They are "busy about" it. They are always busy "about" something. But truly *immersed* in *doing* something, with the deep blood-consciousness active, that they never are. [45]

They admire the blood-conscious spontaneity. And they want to get it in their heads. "Live from the body," they shriek. It is their last mental shriek. *Co-ordinate.* [46]

It is a further attempt still to rationalize the body and blood. "Think about such and such a muscle," they say, "and relax there." [47]

And every time you "conquer" the body with the mind (you can say "heal" it, if you like) you cause a deeper, more dangerous complex or tension somewhere else. [48]

Ghastly Americans, with their blood no longer blood. A yellow spiritual fluid. [49]

The Fall. [50]

There have been lots of Falls. [51]

We *fell* into *knowledge* when Eve bit the apple. Self-conscious knowledge. For the first time the mind put up a fight against the blood. Wanting to UNDERSTAND. That is to intellectualize the blood. [52]

The blood must be *shed*, says Jesus. [53]

Shed on the cross of our own divided psyche. [54]

Shed the blood, and you become mind-conscious. Eat the body and drink the blood, self-cannibalizing, and you become extremely conscious, like Americans and some Hindus. Devour yourself, and God knows what a lot you'll know, what a lot you'll be conscious of. [55]

Mind you don't choke yourself. [56]

For a long time men *believed* that they could be perfected through the mind, through the spirit. They believed, passionately. They had their ecstasy in pure consciousness. They *believed* in purity, chastity, and the wings of the spirit. [57]

America soon plucked the bird of the spirit. America soon killed the *belief* in the spirit. But not the practice. The practice continued with a sarcastic vehemence. America, with a perfect inner contempt for the spirit and the consciousness of man, practises the same spirituality and universal love and KNOWING all the time, incessantly, like a drug habit. And inwardly gives not a fig for it. Only for the *sensation*. The pretty-pretty *sensation* of love, loving all the world. And the nice fluttering aeroplane *sensation* of knowing, knowing, knowing. Then the prettiest of all sensations, the sensation of UNDERSTANDING. Oh, what a lot they understand, the darlings? So good at the trick, they are. Just a trick of self-conceit. [58]

The Scarlet Letter gives the show away. [59]

You have your pure-pure young person Dimmesdale. [60]

You have the beautiful Puritan Hester at his feet. [61]

And the first thing she does is to seduce him. [62]

And the first thing he does is to be seduced. [63]

And the second thing they do is to hug their sin in secret, and gloat over it, and try to understand. [64]

Which is the myth of New England. [65]

Deerslayer refused to be seduced by Judith Hutter. At least the Sodom apple of sin didn't fetch him. [66]

But Dimmesdale was seduced gloatingly. Oh, luscious Sin! [67]

He was such a pure young man. [68]

That he had to make a fool of purity. [69]

The American psyche. [70]

Of course the best part of the game lay in keeping up pure appearances. [71]

The greatest triumph a woman can have, especially an American woman, is the triumph of seducing a man: especially if he is pure. [72]

And he gets the greatest thrill of all, in falling.—"Seduce me, Mrs. Hercules." [73]

And the pair of them share the subtlest delight in keeping up pure appearances, when everybody knows all the while. But the power of pure appearances is something to exult in. All America gives in to it. *Look* pure! [74]

To seduce man. To have everybody know. To keep up appearances of purity. Pure! [75]

This is the great triumph of woman. [76]

A. The Scarlet Letter. Adulteress! The great Alpha. Alpha! Adulteress! The new Adam and Adama! American! [77]

A. Adulteress! Stitched with gold thread, glittering upon the bosom. The proudest insignia. [78]

Put her upon the scaffold and worship her there. Worship her there. The Woman, the Magna Mater. A. Adulteress! Abel! [79]

Abel! Abel! Abel! Admirable! [80]

It becomes a farce. [81]

The fiery heart. A. Mary of the Bleeding Heart. Mater Adolerata! A. Capital A. Adulteress. Glittering with gold thread. Abel! Adultery. Admirable! [82]

It is, perhaps, the most colossal satire ever penned. *The Scarlet Letter.* And by a blue-eyed darling of a Nathaniel. [83]

Not Bumppo, however. [84]

The human spirit, fixed in a lie, adhering to a lie, giving itself perpetually the lie. [85]

All begins with A. [86]

Adulteress. Alpha. Abel. Adam. A. America. [87]

The Scarlet Letter. [88]

"Had there been a Papist among the crowd of Puritans, he might have seen in this beautiful woman, so picturesque in her attire and mien, and with the infant at her bosom, an object to remind him of the image of Divine Maternity, which so many illustrious painters have vied with one another to represent; something which should remind him, indeed, but only by contrast, of that sacred image of sinless Motherhood, whose infant was to redeem the world." [89]

Whose infant was to redeem the world indeed! It will be a startling redemption the world will get from the American infant. [90]

"Here was a taint of deepest sin in the most sacred quality of human life, working such effect that the world was only the darker for this woman's beauty, and more lost for the infant she had borne." [91]

Just listen to the darling. Isn't he a master of apology? [92]

Of symbols, too. [93]

His pious blame is a chuckle of praise all the while. [94]

Oh, Hester, you are a demon. A man *must* be pure, just so that you can seduce him to a fall. Because the greatest thrill in life is to bring down the Sacred Saint with a flop into the mud. Then when you've brought him down, humbly wipe off the mud with your hair, another Magdalen. And then go home and dance a witch's jig of triumph, and stitch yourself a Scarlet Letter with gold thread, as duchesses used to stitch themselves coronets. And then stand meek on the scaffold and fool the world. Who will all be envying your sin, and beating you because you've stolen an advantage over them. [95]

Hester Prynne is the great nemesis of woman. She is the KNOWING Ligeia risen diabolic from the grave. Having her own back. UNDER-STANDING. [96]

This time it is Mr. Dimmesdale who dies. She lives on and is Abel. [97]

His spiritual love was a lie. And prostituting the woman to his spiritual love, as popular clergymen do, in his preachings and loftiness, was a tall white lie. Which came flop. [98]

We are so pure in spirit. Hi-tiddly-i-ty! [99]

Till she tickled him in the right place, and he fell. [100]

Flop. [101]

Flop goes spiritual love. [102]

But keep up the game. Keep up appearances. Pure are the pure. To the pure all things, etc. [103]

Look out, Mister, for the Female Devotee. Whatever you do, don't let her start tickling you. She knows your weak spot. Mind your Purity. [104]

When Hester Prynne seduced Arthur Dimmesdale it was the beginning of the end. But from the beginning of the end to the end of the end is a hundred years or two. [105]

Mr. Dimmesdale also wasn't at the end of his resources. Previously, he had lived by governing his body, ruling it, in the interests of his spirit. Now he has a good time all by himself torturing his body, whipping it, piercing it with thorns, macerating himself. It's a form of masturbation. He wants to get a mental grip on his body. And since he can't quite manage it with the mind, witness his fall—he will give it what for, with whips. His will shall *lash* his body. And he enjoys his pains. Wallows in them. To the pure all things are pure. [106]

It is the old self-mutilation process, gone rotten. The mind wanting to get its teeth in the blood and flesh. The ego exulting in the tortures of the mutinous flesh. I, the ego, I *will* triumph over my own flesh. Lash! Lash! I am a grand free spirit. *Lash!* I am the master of my soul! *Lash! Lash!* I am the captain of my soul. *Lash!* Hurray! "In the fell clutch of circumstance," etc., etc. [107]

Good-bye Arthur. He depended on women for his Spiritual Devotees, spiritual brides. So, the woman just touched him in his weak spot, his Achilles Heel of the flesh. Look out for the spiritual bride. She's after the weak spot. [108]

It is the battle of wills. [109]

"For the will therein lieth, which dieth not——" [110]

The Scarlet Woman becomes a Sister of Mercy. Didn't she just, in the late war. Oh, Prophet Nathaniel! [111]

Hester urges Dimmesdale to go away with her, to a new country, to a new life. He isn't having any. [112]

He knows there is no new country, no new life on the globe to-day. It is the same old thing, in different degrees, everywhere. *Plus ça change, plus c'est la même chose.* [113]

Hester thinks, with Dimmesdale for her husband, and Pearl for her child, in Australia, maybe, she'd have been perfect. [114]

But she wouldn't. Dimmesdale had already fallen from his integrity as a minister of the Gospel of the Spirit. He had lost his manliness. He didn't see the point of just leaving himself between the hands of a woman, and going away to a "new country," to be her thing entirely. She'd only have despised him more, as every woman despises a man who has "fallen" to her: despises him with her tenderest lust. [115]

He stood for nothing any more. So let him stay where he was and dree out his weird. [116]

She had dished him and his spirituality, so he hated her. As Angel Clare was dished, and hated Tess. As Jude in the end hated Sue: or should have done. The women make fools of them, the spiritual men. And when, as men, they've gone flop in their spirituality, they can't pick themselves up whole any more. So they just crawl, and die detesting the female, or the females, who made them fall. [117]

The saintly minister gets a bit of his own back, at the last minute, by making public confession from the very scaffold where she was exposed. Then he dodges into death. But he's had a bit of his own back, on everybody. [118]

" 'Shall we not meet again?' whispered she, bending her face down close to him. 'Shall we not spend our immortal life together? Surely, surely we have ransomed one another with all this woe! Thou lookest far into eternity with those bright dying eyes. Tell me what thou seest!' " [119]

" 'Hush, Hester—hush,' said he, with tremulous solemnity. 'The law we broke!—the sin here so awfully revealed! Let these alone be in thy thoughts. I fear! I fear!' " [120]

So he dies, throwing the "sin" in her teeth, and escaping into death. [121]

The law we broke, indeed. You bet! [122]

Whose law? [123]

But it is truly a law, that man must either stick to the belief he has grounded himself on, and obey the laws of that belief. Or he must admit the belief itself to be inadequate, and prepare himself for a new thing. [124]

There was no change in belief, either in Hester or in Dimmesdale or in Hawthorne or in America. The same old treacherous belief, which was really cunning disbelief, in the Spirit, in Purity, in Selfless Love, and in Pure Consciousness. They would go on following this belief, for the sake of the sensationalism of it. But they would make a fool of it all the time. Like Woodrow Wilson, and the rest of modern Believers. The rest of modern Saviours. [125]

If you meet a Saviour to-day, be sure he is trying to make an inner-most fool of you. Especially if the saviour be an UNDERSTANDING WOMAN, offering her love. [126]

Hester lives on, pious as pie, being a public nurse. She becomes at last an acknowledged saint, Abel of the Scarlet Letter. [127]

She would, being a woman. She has had her triumph over the in-dividual man, so she quite loves subscribing to the whole spiritual life of society. She will make herself as false as hell, for society's sake, once she's had her real triumph over Saint Arthur. [128]

Blossoms out into a Sister-of-Mercy Saint. [129]

But it's a long time before she really takes anybody in. People kept on thinking her a witch, which she was. [130]

As a matter of fact, unless a woman is held, by man, safe within the bounds of belief, she becomes inevitably a destructive force. She can't help herself. A woman is almost always vulnerable to pity. She can't bear to see anything *physically* hurt. But let a woman loose from the bounds and restraints of man's fierce belief, in his gods and in himself, and she becomes a gentle devil. She becomes subtly diabolic. The colossal evil of the united spirit of Woman. WOMAN, German woman or American woman, or every other sort of woman, in the last war, was something frightening. As every *man* knows. [131]

Woman becomes a helpless, would-be-loving demon. She is helpless. Her very love is a subtle poison. [132]

Unless a man believes in himself and his gods, *genuinely:* unless he fiercely obeys his own Holy Ghost; his woman will destroy him. Woman is the nemesis of doubting man. She can't help it. [133]

And with Hester, after Ligeia, woman becomes a nemesis to man. She bolsters him up from the outside, she destroys him from the inside. And he dies hating her, as Dimmesdale did. [134]

Dimmesdale's spirituality had gone on too long, too far. It had become a false thing. He found his nemesis in woman. And he was done for. [135]

Woman is a strange and rather terrible phenomenon, to man. When the subconscious soul of woman recoils from its creative union with man, it becomes a destructive force. It exerts, willy-nilly, an invisible destructive influence. The woman herself may be as nice as milk, to all appearance, like Ligeia. But she is sending out waves of silent destruction of the faltering spirit in men, all the same. She doesn't know it. She can't even help it. But she does it. The devil is in her. [136]

The very women who are most busy saving the bodies of men, and saving the children: these women-doctors, these nurses, these educationalists, these public-spirited women, these female saviours: they are all, from the inside, sending out waves of destructive malevolence which eat out the inner life of a man, like a cancer. It is so, it will be so, till men realize it and react to save themselves. [137]

God won't save us. The women are so devilish godly. Men must save themselves in this strait, and by no sugary means either. [138]

A woman can use her sex in sheer malevolence and poison, while she is *behaving* as meek and good as gold. Dear darling, she is really snow-white in her blamelessness. And all the while she is using her sex as a she-devil, for the endless hurt of her man. She doesn't know it. She will never believe it if you tell her. And if you give her a slap in the face for her fiendishness, she will rush to the first magistrate, in indignation. She is so *absolutely* blameless, the she-devil, the dear, dutiful creature. [139]

Give her the great slap, just the same, just when she is being most angelic. Just when she is bearing her cross most meekly. [140]

Oh, woman out of bounds is a devil. But it is man's fault. Woman never *asked*, in the first place, to be cast out of her bit of an Eden of belief and trust. It is man's business to bear the responsibility of belief. If he becomes a spiritual fornicator and liar, like Ligeia's husband and Arthur Dimmesdale, how *can* a woman believe in him? Belief doesn't go by choice. And if a woman doesn't believe in a *man*, she believes, essentially, in nothing. She becomes, willy-nilly, a devil. [141]

A devil she is, and a devil she will be. And most men will succumb to her devilishness. [142]

Hester Prynne was a devil. Even when she was so meekly going round as a sick-nurse. Poor Hester. Part of her wanted to be saved from her own devilishness. And another part wanted to go on and on in devilishness, for revenge. Revenge! REVENGE! It is this that fills the

unconscious spirit of woman to-day. Revenge against man, and against
the spirit of man, which has betrayed her into unbelief. Even when
she is most sweet and a salvationist, she is her most devilish, is woman.
She gives her man the sugar-plum of her own submissive sweetness.
And when he's taken this sugar-plum in his mouth, a scorpion comes
out of it. After he's taken this Eve to his bosom, oh, so loving, she
destroys him inch by inch. Woman and her revenge! She will have it,
and go on having it, for decades and decades, unless she's stopped.
And to stop her you've got to believe in yourself and your gods, your
own Holy Ghost, Sir Man; and then you've got to fight her, and never
give in. She's a devil. But in the long run she is conquerable. And just
a tiny bit of her wants to be conquered. You've got to fight three-
quarters of her, in absolute hell, to get at the final quarter of her that
wants a release, at last, from the hell of her own revenge. But it's a
long last. And not yet. [143]

"She had in her nature a rich, voluptuous, oriental characteristic—a
taste for the gorgeously beautiful." This is Hester. This is American.
But she repressed her nature in the above direction. She would not
even allow herself the luxury of labouring at fine, delicate stitching.
Only she dressed her little sin-child Pearl vividly, and the scarlet letter
was gorgeously embroidered. Her Hecate and Astarte insignia. [144]

"A voluptuous, oriental characteristic—" That lies waiting in American women. It is probable that the Mormons are the forerunners of
the coming real America. It is probable that men will have more than
one wife, in the coming America. That you will have again a half-
oriental womanhood, and a polygamy. [145]

The grey nurse, Hester. The Hecate, the hellcat. The slowly-
evolving voluptuous female of the new era, with a whole new sub-
missiveness to the dark, phallic principle. [146]

But it takes time. Generation after generation of nurses and political women and salvationists. And in the end, the dark erection of
the images of sex-worship once more, and the newly submissive
woman. That kind of depth. Deep women in that respect. When we
have at last broken this insanity of mental-spiritual consciousness.

And the women *choose* to experience again the great submission. [147]

"The poor, whom she sought out to be the objects of her bounty, often reviled the hand that was stretched to succour them." [148]

Naturally. The poor hate a salvationist. They smell the devil underneath. [149]

"She was patient—a martyr indeed—but she forbore to pray for her enemies, lest, in spite of her forgiving aspirations, the words of the blessing should stubbornly twist themselves into a curse." [150]

So much honesty, at least. No wonder the old witch-lady Mistress Hibbins claimed her for another witch. [151]

"She grew to have a dread of children; for they had imbibed from their parents a vague idea of something horrible in this dreary woman gliding silently through the town, with never any companion but only one child." [152]

"A vague idea!" Can't you see her "gliding silently"? It's not a question of a vague idea imbibed, but a definite feeling directly received. [153]

"But sometimes, once in many days, or perchance in many months, she felt an eye—a human eye—upon the ignominious brand, that seemed to give a momentary relief, as if half her agony were shared. The next instant, back it all rushed again, with a still deeper throb of pain; for in that brief interval she had sinned again. Had Hester sinned alone?" [154]

Of course not. As for sinning again, she would go on all her life silently, changelessly "sinning." She never repented. Not she. Why should she? She had brought down Arthur Dimmesdale, that too-too snow-white bird, and that was her life-work. [155]

As for sinning again when she met two dark eyes in a crowd, why of course. Somebody who understood as she understood. [156]

I always remember meeting the eyes of a gypsy woman, for one moment, in a crowd, in England. She knew, and I knew. What did we know? I was not able to make out. But we knew. [157]

Probably the same fathomless hate of this spiritual-conscious society in which the outcast woman and I both roamed like meek-looking wolves. Tame wolves waiting to shake off their tameness. Never able to. [158]

And again, that "voluptuous, oriental" characteristic that knows the mystery of the ithyphallic gods. She would not betray the ithyphallic gods to this white, leprous-white society of "lovers." Neither will I, if I can help it. These leprous-white, seducing, spiritual women, who "understand" so much. One has been too often seduced, and "understood." "I can read him like a book," said my first lover of me. The book is in several volumes, dear. And more and more comes back to me the gulf of dark hate and *other* understanding, in the eyes of the gypsy woman. So different from the hateful white light of understanding which floats like scum on the eyes of white, oh, so white English and American women, with their understanding voices and their deep, sad words, and their profound, *good* spirits. Pfui! [159]

Hester was scared only of one result of her sin: Pearl. Pearl, the scarlet letter incarnate. The little girl. When women bear children, they produce either devils or sons with gods in them. And it is an evolutionary process. The devil in Hester produced a purer devil in Pearl. And the devil in Pearl will produce—she married an Italian Count—a piece of purer devilishness still. [160]

And so from hour to hour we ripe and ripe. [161]

And then from hour to hour we rot and rot. [162]

There was that in the child "which often impelled Hester to ask in bitterness of heart, whether it were for good or ill that the poor little creature had been born at all." [163]

For ill, Hester. But don't worry. Ill is as necessary as good. Malevolence is as necessary as benevolence. If you have brought forth, spawned, a young malevolence, be sure there is a rampant falseness in the world against which this malevolence must be turned. Falseness has to be bitten and bitten, till it is bitten to death. Hence Pearl. [164]

Pearl. Her own mother compares her to the demon of plague, or scarlet fever, in her red dress. But then plague is necessary to destroy a rotten, false humanity. [165]

Pearl, the devilish girl-child, who can be so tender and loving and *understanding*, and then, when she has understood, will give you a hit across the mouth, and turn on you with a grin of sheer diabolic jeering. [166]

Serves you right, you shouldn't be *understood*. That is your vice. You shouldn't want to be loved, and then you'd not get hit across the mouth. Pearl will love you: marvellously. And she'll hit you across the mouth: oh, so neatly. And serves you right. [167]

Pearl is perhaps the most modern child in all literature. [168]

Old-fashioned Nathaniel, with his little-boy charm, he'll tell you what's what. But he'll cover it with smarm. [169]

Hester simply *hates* her child, from one part of herself. And from another, she cherishes her child as her one precious treasure. For Pearl is the continuing of her female revenge on life. But female revenge hits both ways. Hits back at its own mother. The female revenge in Pearl hits back at Hester, the mother, and Hester is simply livid with fury and "sadness," which is rather amusing. [170]

"The child could not be made amenable to rules. In giving her exist-ence a great law had been broken; and the result was a being whose elements were perhaps beautiful and brilliant, but all in disorder, or with an order peculiar to themselves, amidst which the point of variety and arrangement was difficult or impossible to discover." [171]

Of course the order is peculiar to themselves. But the point of variety is this: "Draw out the loving, sweet soul, draw it out with marvellous understanding; and then spit in its eye." [172]

Hester, of course, didn't at all like it when her sweet child drew out her motherly soul, with yearning and deep understanding: and then spit in the motherly eye, with a grin. But it was a process the mother had started. [173]

Pearl had a peculiar look in her eyes: "a look so intelligent, yet so inexplicable, so perverse, sometimes so malicious, but generally accom-panied by a wild flow of spirits, that Hester could not help questioning at such moments whether Pearl was a human child." [174]

A little demon! But her mother, and the saintly Dimmesdale, had borne her. And Pearl, by the very openness of her perversity, was more straightforward than her parents. She flatly refuses any Heavenly Father, seeing the earthly one such a fraud. And she has the pietistic Dimmesdale on toast, spits right in his eye: in both his eyes. [175]

Poor, brave, tormented little soul, always in a state of recoil, she'll be a devil to men when she grows up. But the men deserve it. If they'll let themselves be "drawn," by her loving understanding, they deserve that she shall slap them across the mouth the moment they *are* drawn. The chickens! Drawn and trussed. [176]

Poor little phenomenon of a modern child, she'll grow up into the devil of a modern woman. The nemesis of weak-kneed modern men, craving to be love-drawn. [177]

The third person in the diabolic trinity, or triangle, of the Scarlet Letter, is Hester's first husband, Roger Chillingworth. He is an old Elizabethan physician with a grey beard and a long-furred coat and a twisted shoulder. Another healer. But something of an alchemist, a magician. He is a magician on the verge of modern science, like Francis Bacon. [178]

Roger Chillingworth is of the old order of intellect, in direct line from the mediaeval Roger Bacon alchemists. He has an old, intellectual belief in the dark sciences, the Hermetic philosophies. He is no Christian, no selfless aspirer. He is not an aspirer. He is the old authoritarian in man. The old male authority. But without passional belief. Only intellectual belief in himself and his male authority. [179]

Shakespeare's whole tragic wail is because of the downfall of the true male authority, the ithyphallic authority and masterhood. It fell with Elizabeth. It was trodden underfoot with Victoria. [180]

But Chillingworth keeps on the *intellectual* tradition. He hates the new spiritual aspirers, like Dimmesdale, with a black, crippled hate. He is the old male authority, in intellectual tradition. [181]

You can't keep a wife by force of an intellectual tradition. So Hester took to seducing Dimmesdale. [182]

Yet her only marriage, and her last oath, is with the old Roger. He and she are accomplices in pulling down the spiritual saint. [183]

"Why dost thou smile so at me—" she says to her old, vengeful husband. "Art thou not like the Black Man that haunts the forest around us? Hast thou not enticed me into a bond which will prove the ruin of my soul?" [184]

"Not thy soul!" he answered with another smile. "No, not thy soul!" [185]

It is the soul of the pure preacher, that false thing, which they are after. And the crippled physician—this other healer—blackly vengeful in his old, distorted male authority, and the "loving" woman, they bring down the saint between them. [186]

A black and complementary hatred, akin to love, is what Chillingworth feels for the young, saintly parson. And Dimmesdale responds, in a hideous kind of love. Slowly the saint's life was poisoned. But the black old physician smiles, and tries to keep him alive. Dimmesdale goes in for self-torture, self-lashing, lashing his own white, thin, spiritual saviour's body. The dark old Chillingworth listens outside the door and laughs, and prepares another medicine, so that the game can go on longer. And the saint's very soul goes rotten. Which is the supreme triumph. Yet he keeps up appearances still. [187]

The black, vengeful soul of the crippled, masterful male, still dark in his authority: and the white ghastliness of the fallen saint! The two halves of manhood mutually destroying one another. [188]

Dimmesdale has a "coup" in the very end. He gives the whole show away by confessing publicly on the scaffold, and dodging into death, leaving Hester dished, and Roger as it were, doubly cuckolded. It is a neat last revenge. [189]

Down comes the curtain, as in Ligeia's poem. [190]

But the child Pearl will be on in the next act, with her Italian Count and a new brood of vipers. And Hester greyly Abelling, in the shadows, after her rebelling. [191]

It is a marvellous allegory. It is to me one of the greatest allegories in all literature, *The Scarlet Letter*. Its marvellous under-meaning! And its perfect duplicity. [192]

The absolute duplicity of that blue-eyed *Wunderkind* of a Nathaniel. The American wonder-child, with his magical allegorical insight. [193]

But even wonder-children have to grow up in a generation or two. [194]

And even SIN becomes stale. [195]

PURPOSE AND STRUCTURE

The structure of Lawrence's essay is loose. And the ease of his diction and tone—with its sinuous elisions (pars. 1–4) shocking leaps (pars. 5–12, 161–162) and sudden rants (pars. 37, 46)—leads the reader to expect an improvised form. But it is not so free as it seems. It falls into two interpenetrating parts: pars. 1–58, which prepare the reader for an interpretation of *The Scarlet Letter*, and pars. 59–195, which present the interpretation. In the first part, pars. 1–4 introduce, with model concision, *The Scarlet Letter* as a kind of romance; pars. 5–14 relate it to American art. Pars. 15–26 relate it to another *earthly story with a hellish meaning*— Adam and Eve. Pars. 27–58 present dualism (with an example in work and thought, pars. 36–41; in Americans and Italians, pars. 42–58). Par. 58 ends the first part of the essay with a summary, a kind of thesis. Then nearly all the rest of the essay (pars. 59–191) is application of par. 58 to a particular example, *The Scarlet Letter*. Pars. 192–5 are a concise conclusion.

1. Lawrence presents (pars. 1–4) his method and his subject rapidly. His first sentence tells the reader that Hawthorne writes romance and the last sentence of par. 4 tells the reader what kind of romance. The first four paragraphs are very short. Argue for or against the present arrangement of paragraphs. Why does Lawrence begin the second sentence of par. 2 with *Usually?* In what way is *The Scarlet Letter* like the romances of par. 2? What's the difference between the first and the second *As You Like It* in par. 2? Is the repetition ineffective? What time is *daisy-time?* Is the answer to the question in par. 2 stated as a sentence? Should it be? The list at the end of par. 2 seems improvised and fragmentary with its *etc.* and the afterthought of *Morte D'Arthur*. Argue for or against its simplicity and arrangement.

2. Without making any other change, reduce the first twelve paragraphs to one and argue for or against the reduction. Then recast the sentences and fragments of pars. 1 to 12 into more acceptable college prose and

rearrange into a single coherent paragraph. Compare its effectiveness with Lawrence's.

3. Why does Lawrence refer to a *suffocating flood of darkness* (par. 29)? Is he expressing his rejection of these experiences?

4. What is the function of the word *Co-ordinate* in par. 46? What is Lawrence's purpose in quoting *"Think about such and such a muscle . . . and relax there."* (par. 47)? Why does he refer to A *yellow spiritual fluid* (par. 49)?

5. What is the trick the *darlings* are good at (par. 58)? Lawrence refers to *the sensation of* UNDERSTANDING. Why does he use the word *sensation?* Is *the nice fluttering aeroplane* sensation *of knowing, knowing, knowing* intelligible? Defend or attack its effectiveness. What does *like a drug habit* refer to? What does *with a perfect inner contempt* refer to? Why is it necessary for Lawrence to attack so powerfully?

6. Why does Lawrence begin his commentary on *The Scarlet Letter* with a series of very short paragraphs (pars. 59–65)? Compare this summary with pars. 28–30 in Wilder. How do the purposes and techniques of these passages differ?

7. Both pars. 65 and 70 conclude short sections of the essay. Do they repeat the same point?

8. Why does Lawrence see *The Scarlet Letter* (pars. 77–80) as a *farce* (par. 81)?

9. Is there *pious blame* (par. 94) in par. 89? Where is the *chuckle of praise?*

10. Compare Lawrence's description of Dimmesdale's flagellation (pars. 106–107) with the description of flagellation in *The Scarlet Letter* (not quoted; find it in the work itself, Chapter 11, beginning of the third paragraph from the end). How do the purposes of the descriptions differ? Show how their differing purposes have influenced their diction and tone. Is Lawrence unfair in his paraphrase and interpretation of Hawthorne's text?

11. What is implied in *from the beginning of the end to the end of the end is a hundred years or two* (par. 105)?

12. Relate Lawrence's statement, *Serves you right, you shouldn't be* understood. *That is your vice* (par. 167), to his interpretation of *The Scarlet Letter.*

13. Why does Lawrence comment that Hester's *"sadness"* is rather amusing (par. 170)?

14. Is Lawrence implying a defense of his own malevolence in par. 164?

15. Why does Chillingworth feel a *black and complementary hatred, akin to love* (par. 187)?

16. Why are they *mutually destroying one another* (par. 188)?

17. Why is Chillingworth *doubly cuckolded* (par. 189)?

18. Lawrence's purpose is larger than a strictly literary criticism of *The Scarlet Letter*. Can you sum it up? Discuss par. 145 in relation to your view of the essay. Discuss par. 145 in relation to par. 147: in relation to par. 159—*these leprous-white seducing women who "understand" so much*. Is par. 145 consistent with Lawrence's other statements about American women?

19. What purpose is served by Lawrence's repeating, with or without variation, his central themes? Trace one theme through the essay (Hawthorne's duplicity, female diablery, the white psyche, blood-consciousness) and discuss the effectiveness of its presentation. Or discuss repetition in a section of the essay; for example, seduction in pars. 62, 67, 72, 75 (Consider the context of each passage).

20. Why is the biological process of metamorphosis an effective symbol both of growth and of destruction (par. 10)? How does *the growing of a dragon-fly inside a chrysalis or cocoon* destroy *the larva grub* (par. 10)? Why does Lawrence symbolize growth as destruction (pars. 10 and 12)? What is *the secret chrysalis* in *The Scarlet Letter* (par. 12)? Why is Hawthorne described as a *blue-eyed darling* in par. 5 and a *blue-eyed Wunderkind* in par. 193? Why does Lawrence end his essay by turning away from Hawthorne's achievement (par. 194–195)?

DICTION AND TONE

Lawrence's diction and tone reflect his complex purposes and high degree of involvement. His diction ranges from the dialectal *smarm* (par. 169), to the technical *ithyphallic* (par. 159), to the coined *blood-consciousness* (par. 31). His tone ranges, with facile rapidity, from the apocalyptic (pars. 31–35) to the personal (pars. 36–40).

1. The expressions *nice as pie, goody-goody, and lovey-dovey* (par. 5) are curiously informal for inclusion in a critical essay, especially an essay which presents a shocking and original view of a respectable classic—one respectable enough to be taught to high school students. Why does Lawrence introduce these phrases, and particularly why so early in the essay? Would the entire essay be more effective—more convincing—if Lawrence presented his argument in more conventional prose? Argue that Lawrence's sometimes shocking diction and tone are necessary (or unnecessary) to the achievement of his purposes.

2. Why use the rare word *momentaneously* (par. 20)? What does the word connote? Can a word new to the reader carry connotations? How? See *Webster's Unabridged*, third edition, for a definition (D.H. Lawrence is cited). Does "momentary" in the sense of "lasting a very short time" contain the full contextual meaning of the word in par. 20? In the same sentence is the coined word *blood-knowledge*. Is it defined in context? Can you think of a more conventional word which means the same thing? What purpose is served by coined words? (See White's *The Door* for other examples.) Why are they so seldom effective?

3. Are Adam's words too trivial in par. 22? What purpose is served by the sudden change in tone?

4. In par. 24 Lawrence uses—as he does in several other paragraphs—two kinds of typographic intensives: italics and uppercase. Usually emphasis (see Glossary) is better achieved by other devices. Try rewording *Not doing it, but KNOWING about it.* Recast the entire paragraph, trying to achieve emphasis without the use of special typography. Write in acceptable college prose.

5. Why *self-cannibalizing* in this religious context (par. 55)? What is the tone of *God knows what a lot you'll know* (par. 55)?

6. What does the warning mean in par. 56? What is the tone?

7. Compare the diction and tone of par. 122 with pars. 119–120. Argue for or against the effectiveness of Lawrence's shocking comment. What does the word *law* mean in the two contexts?

8. Why does Lawrence use the phrase *spiritual fornicator* (par. 141) in this context?

9. Why use the curious word *smarm* (par. 169)?

10. What is the purpose of the joke (par. 5) *which doesn't mean she saw him too late?*

11. Lawrence's diction and tone are startlingly different from Hawthorne's. What is the purpose of Lawrence's following or preceding his quotations from Hawthorne with paraphrases or comments, some of them invidious? See pars. 90, 92, 122, 144, 145, 149, 151, 153, 155, etc.

12. Why does Lawrence follow *pure in spirit* with the word *Hi-tiddly-i-ty* (par. 99)?

13. Par. 101 is a single word—*Flop*. Argue for or against its appropriateness to its context.

APPLICATIONS TO WRITING

1. Swift (*A Modest Proposal*) shocks the reader into sensibility through the medium of controlled eighteenth-century prose. The incongruity between his subject—an argument for eating the children of the poor— and his conventional diction and tone is the main source of his power. Lawrence shocks the reader with his hornet-like twentieth-century prose (the first version of his essay was published in 1919). And one of the sources of his powerful effect is his incongruous subject, the ultra-respectable classic, *The Scarlet Letter*.

Write a composition on any of the following subjects, using diction and tone different from your subject's. Do not imitate Lawrence's style. (See Katherine Anne Porter for another example.) You may use your ordinary composition style for some of these subjects, if you wish: a radio commercial on a teen-age station; a political platform in a student body election; a speech by Winston Churchill; an outmoded entry from H. W. Fowler's *A Dictionary of Modern English Usage*, first edition; a single article from Tom Wolfe's *The Kandy-Kolored Tangerine-Flake Streamline Baby* (published 1965); the Lawrence essay above.

2. Lawrence presents his theories about Americans through his interpretation of *The Scarlet Letter*. What *gives the show away* (par. 59) for your generation? Present your theories through the interpretation of a single book, phrase, article of dress, sport, attitude, gesture, car, or experience.

THE WOODEN UMBRELLA

KATHERINE ANNE PORTER

> . . . I want to say that just today I met Miss Hennessy and she was
> carrying, she did not have it with her, but she usually carried a wooden
> umbrella. This wooden umbrella is carved out of wood and looks like a
> real one even to the little button and the rubber string that holds it to-
> gether. It is all right except when it rains. When it rains it does not open
> and Miss Hennessy looks a little foolish but she does not mind because it
> is after all the only wooden umbrella in Paris. And even if there were
> lots of others it would not make any difference.
>
> Gertrude Stein: Everybody's Autobiography

When Kahnweiler the picture dealer told Miss Stein that Picasso
had stopped painting and had taken to writing poetry, she confessed
that she had "a funny feeling" because "things belonged to you and
writing belonged to me. I know writing belongs to me, I am quite
certain," but still it was a blow. ". . . No matter how certain you
are about anything belonging to you if you hear that somebody says
it belongs to them it gives you a funny feeling." [1]

Later she buttonholed Picasso at Kahnweiler's gallery, shook him,
kissed him, lectured him, told him that his poetry was worse than bad,
it was offensive as a Cocteau drawing and in much the same way, it
was unbecoming. He defended himself by reminding her that she
had said he was an extraordinary person, and he believed an extraor-

547

dinary person should be able to do anything. She said that to her it was a repellent sight when a person who could do one thing well dropped it for something else he could not do at all. Convinced, or defeated, he promised to give back writing to its natural owner. [2]

Writing was no doubt the dearest of Miss Stein's possessions, but it was not the only one. The pavilion atelier in rue de Fleurus was a catch-all of beings and created objects, and everything she looked upon was hers in more than the usual sense. Her weighty numerous divans and armchairs covered with dark, new-looking horsehair; her dogs, Basket and Pépé, conspicuous, special, afflicted as neurotic children; her clutter of small tables each with its own clutter of perhaps valuable but certainly treasured objects; her Alice B. Toklas; her visitors; and finally, ranging the walls from floor to ceiling, giving the impression that they were hung three deep, elbowing each other, canceling each other's best effects in the jealous way of pictures, was her celebrated collection of paintings by her collection of celebrated painters. These were everybody of her time whom Miss Stein elected for her own, from her idol Picasso (kidnapped bodily from brother Leo, who saw him first) to miniscule Sir Francis Rose, who seems to have appealed to the pixy in her. [3]

Yet the vaguely lighted room where things accumulated, where they appeared to have moved in under a compulsion to be possessed once for all by someone who knew how to take hold firmly, gave no impression of disorder. On the contrary, an air of solid comfort, of inordinate sobriety and permanence, of unadventurous middle-class domesticity—respectability is the word, at last—settled around the shoulders of the guest like a Paisley shawl, a borrowed shawl of course, something to be worn and admired for a moment and handed back to the owner. Miss Stein herself sat there in full possession of herself, the scene, the spectators, wearing thick no-colored shapeless woolen clothes and honest woolen stockings knitted for her by Miss Toklas, looking extremely like a handsome old Jewish patriarch who had backslid and shaved off his beard. [4]

Surrounded by her listeners, she talked in a slow circle in her fine deep voice, the word "perception" occurring again and again and yet again like the brass ring the children snatch for as their hobby horses whirl by. She was in fact at one period surrounded by snatching children, the literary young, a good many of them American, between two wars in a falling world. Roughly they were divided into two parties: those who were full of an active, pragmatic unbelief, and those who searched their own vitals and fished up strange horrors in the style of *transition*. The first had discovered that honor is only a word, and an embarrassing one, because it was supposed to mean something wonderful and was now exposed as meaning nothing at all. For them, nothing worked except sex and alcohol and pulling apart their lamentable midwestern upbringings and scattering the pieces. Some of these announced that they wished their writings to be as free from literature as if they had never read a book, as indeed too many of them had not up to the time. The *transition* tone was even more sinister, for though it was supposed to be the vanguard of international experimental thought, its real voice was hoarse, anxious, corrupted mysticism speaking in a thick German accent. The editor, Eugene Jolas, had been born in the eternally disputed land of Alsace, bilingual in irreconcilable tongues, French and German, and he spoke both and English besides with a foreign accent. He had no mother tongue, nor even a country, and so he fought the idea of both, but his deepest self was German: he issued frantic manifestoes demanding that language be reduced to something he could master, crying aloud in "defense of the hallucinative forces," the exploding of the verb, the "occult hypnosis of language," "chthonian grammar"; reason he hated, and defended the voice of the blood, the disintegration of syntax—with a special grudge against English—preaching like an American Methodist evangelist in the wilderness for "the use of a language which is a mantic instrument, and which does not hesitate to adopt a revolutionary attitude toward word syntax, going even so far as to invent a hermetic language, if necessary." The final aim was "the illumination of a collective reality and a totalistic universe." Meanwhile Joyce, a man with a mother-tongue if ever there was one, and a master of languages, was mixing them in strange new forms to the delight and enrichment of language for good and all. [5]

Miss Stein had no problems: she simply exploded a verb as if it were a soap bubble, used chthonian grammar long before she heard it named (and she would have scorned to name it), was a born adept in occult hypnosis of language without even trying. Serious young men who were having a hard time learning to write realized with relief that there was nothing at all to it if you just relaxed and put down the first thing that came into your head. She gave them a romantic name, the Lost Generation, and a remarkable number of them tried earnestly if unsuccessfully to live up to it. A few of them were really lost, and disappeared, but others had just painted themselves into a very crowded corner. She laid a cooling hand upon their agitated brows and asked with variations, What did it matter? There were only a few geniuses, after all, among which she was one, only the things a genius said made any difference, the rest was "just there," and so she disposed of all the dark questions of life, art, human relations, and death, even eternity, even God, with perfect Stein logic, bringing the scene again into its proper focus, upon herself. [6]

Some of the young men went away, read a book, began thinking things over, and became the best writers of their time. Humanly, shame-facedly, they then jeered at their former admiration, and a few even made the tactical error of quarreling with her. She enjoyed their discipleship while it lasted, and dismissed them from existence when it ended. It is easy to see what tremendous vitality and direction there was in the arts all over the world; for not everything was happening only in France, for life was generated in many a noisy seething confusion in many countries. Little by little the legitimate line of succession appeared, the survivors emerged each with his own shape and meaning, the young vanguard became the Old Masters and even old hat. [7]

In the meantime our heroine went on talking, vocally or on paper, and in that slow swarm of words, out of the long drone and mutter and stammer of her lifetime monologue, often there emerged a phrase of ancient native independent wisdom, for she had a shrewd deep knowledge of the commoner human motives. Her judgments

were neither moral nor intellectual, and least of all aesthetic, indeed
they were not even judgments, but simply her description from observation of acts, words, appearances giving her view; limited, personal in the extreme, prejudiced without qualification, based on assumptions founded in the void of pure unreason. For example,
French notaries' sons have always something strange about them—
look at Jean Cocteau. The Spaniard has a natural center of ignorance,
all except Juan Gris. On the other hand, Dali had not only the
natural Spanish center of ignorance, but still another variety, quite
malignant, of his own. Preachers' sons do not turn out like other
people—E. E. Cummings, just for one. Painters are always little short
round men—Picasso and a crowd of them. And then she puts her
finger lightly on an American peculiarity of our time: ". . . so perhaps they are right the Americans in being more interested in you
than in the work you have done, although they would not be interested in you if you had not done the work you had done." And she
remarked once to her publisher that she was famous in America not
for her work that people understood but for that which they did not
understand. That was the kind of thing she could see through at a
glance. [8]

It was not that she was opposed to ideas, but that she was not
interested in anybody's ideas but her own, except as material to put
down on her endless flood of pages. Like writing, opinion also
belonged to Miss Stein, and nothing annoyed her more—she was
easily angered about all sorts of things—than for anyone not a genius
or who had no reputation that she respected, to appear to be thinking in her presence. Of all those GI's who swarmed about her in her
last days, if any one showed any fight at all, any tendency to question
her pronouncements, she smacked him down like a careful grandmother, for his own good. Her GI heroes Brewsie and Willie are
surely as near to talking zombies as anything ever seen in a book, and
she loved, not them, but their essential zombiness. [9]

Like all talkers, she thought other people talked too much, and
there is recorded only one instance of someone getting the drop on
her—who else but Alfred Stieglitz? She sat through a whole session at

their first meeting without uttering one word, a feat which she mentioned with surprised approval. If we knew nothing more of Stieglitz than this we would know he was a great talker. She thought that the most distressing sound was that of the human voice, other peoples' voices, "as the hoot owl is almost the best sound," but in spite of this she listened quite a lot. When she was out walking the dogs, if workmen were tearing up the streets she would ask them what they were doing and what they would be doing next. She only stopped to break the monotony of walking, but she remembered their answers. When a man passed making up a bitter little song against her dog and his conduct vis-à-vis lamp posts and house walls, she put it all down, and it is wonderfully good reporting. Wise or silly or nothing at all, down everything goes on the page with the air of everything being equal, unimportant in itself, important because it happened to her and she was writing about it. [10]

II

She had not always been exactly there, exactly that. There had been many phases, all in consistent character, each giving way in turn for the next, of her portentous being. Ford Madox Ford described her, in earlier Paris days, as trundling through the streets in her high-wheeled American car, being a spectacle and being herself at the same time. And this may have been near the time of Man Ray's photograph of her, wearing a kind of monk's robe, her poll clipped, her granite front and fine eyes displayed at their best period. [11]

Before that, she was a youngish stout woman, not ever really young, with a heavy shrewd face between a hard round pompadour and a round lace collar, looking more or less like Picasso's earliest portrait of her. What saved her then from a good honest husband, probably a stockbroker, and a houseful of children? The answer must be that her envelope was a tricky disguise of Nature, that she was of the company of Amazons which nineteenth-century America produced among its many prodigies: not-men, not-women, answerable to no function in either sex, whose careers were carried on, and how successfully, in whatever field they chose: they were educators, writers, editors, politicians, artists, world travelers, and international hostesses, who lived in public and by the public and played out their self-assumed, self-created rôles in such masterly freedom as only a few early medieval queens had equaled. Freedom to them meant precisely freedom from men and their stuffy rules for women. They usurped with a high hand the traditional masculine privileges of movement, choice, and the use of direct, personal power. They were few in number and they were not only to be found in America, and Miss Stein belonged with them, no doubt of it, in spite of a certain temperamental passivity which was Oriental, not feminine. With the top of her brain she was a modern girl, a New Woman, interested in scientific experiment, historical research, the rational view; for a time she was even a medical student, but she could not deceive herself for long. Even during her four years at Radcliffe, where the crisp theories of higher education battled with the womb-shaped female mind (and they always afterward seemed foolish to her at Radcliffe) she worried and worried, for worrying and thinking were synonyms to her, about the meaning of the universe, the riddle of human life, about time and its terrible habit of passing, God, death, eternity, and she felt very lonely in the awful singularity of her confusions. Added to this, history taught her that whole civilizations die and disappear utterly, "and now it happens again," and it gave her a great fright. She was sometimes frightened afterward, "but now well being frightened is something less frightening than it was," but her ambiguous mind faced away from speculation. Having discovered with relief that all knowledge was not her province, she accepted rightly, she said, every superstition. To be in the hands of fate, of magic, of the daemonic forces, what freedom it gave her not to decide, not to act, not to accept any responsibility for anything—one held the pen and let the mind wander. One sat down and somebody did everything for one. [12]

Still earlier she was a plump solemn little girl abundantly uphol-stered in good clothes, who spent her allowance on the work of Shelley, Thackeray, and George Eliot in fancy bindings, for she loved reading and *Clarissa Harlowe* was once her favorite novel. These early passions exhausted her; in later life she swam in the relaxing bath of detective and murder mysteries, because she liked somebody being dead in a story, and of them all Dashiell Hammett killed them off most to her taste. Her first experience of the real death of somebody had taught her that it could be pleasant for her too. "One morning we could not wake our father." This was in East Oakland, California. "Leo climbed in by the window and called out that he was dead in his bed and he was." It seems to have been the first thing he ever did of which his children, all five of them, approved. Miss Stein declared plainly they none of them liked him at all: "As I say, fathers are depressing but our family had one," she confessed, and conveys the notion that he was a bore of the nagging, petty sort, the kind that worries himself and others into the grave. [13]

Considering her tepid, sluggish nature, really sluggish like something eating its way through a leaf, Miss Stein could grow quite animated on the subject of her early family life, and some of her stories are as pretty and innocent as lizards running over tombstones on a hot day in Maryland. It was a solid, getting-on sort of middle-class Jewish family of Austrian origin, Keyser on one side, Stein on the other: and the Keysers came to Baltimore about 1820. All branches of the family produced their individual eccentrics—there was even an uncle who believed in the Single Tax—but they were united in their solid understanding of the value of money as the basis of a firm stance in this world. There were incomes, governesses, spending money, guardians appointed when parents died, and Miss Stein was fascinated from childhood with stories about how people earned their first dollar. When, rather late, she actually earned some dollars herself by writing, it changed her entire viewpoint about the value of her work and of her own personality. It came to her as revelation that the only difference between men and four-footed animals is that men can count, and when they count, they like best to count money. In her first satisfaction at finding she had a commercial value, she went on a brief binge of spending money just for the fun of it. But she really knew better. Among the five or six of the seven deadly sins which she practiced with increasing facility and advocated as virtues, avarice became her favorite. Americans in general she found to be rather childish about money: they spent it or gave it away and enjoyed it wastefully with no sense of its fierce latent power. "It is hard to be a miser, a real miser, they are as rare as geniuses it takes the same kind of thing to make one, that is time must not exist for them. . . . There must be a reality that has nothing to do with the passing of time. I have it and so had Hetty Green . . ." and she found only one of the younger generation in America, a young man named Jay Laughlin, who had, she wrote, praising him, avarice to that point of genius which makes the true miser. She made a very true distinction between avarice, the love of getting and keeping, and love of money, the love of making and spending. There is a third love, the love of turning a penny by ruse, and this was illustrated by brother Michael, who once grew a beard to make himself look old enough to pass for a G.A.R. veteran, and so disguised he got a cut-rate railway fare for a visit home during a G.A.R. rally, though all the men of his family fought on the Confederate side. [14]

The question of money and of genius rose simultaneously with the cheerful state of complete orphanhood. Her mother disappeared early after a long illness, leaving her little nest of vipers probably without regret, for vipers Miss Stein shows them to have been in the most Biblical sense. They missed their mother chiefly because she had acted as a buffer between them and their father, and also served to keep them out of each other's hair. Sister Bertha and Brother Simon were simple-minded by family standards, whatever they were, Brother Leo had already started being a genius without any regard for the true situation, and after the death of their father, Brother Michael was quite simply elected to be the Goat. He had inherited the family hatred of responsibility—from their mother, Miss Stein believed, but not quite enough to save him. He became guardian, caretaker, business manager, handy-man, who finally wangled incomes for all of them, and set them free from money and from each other. It is pleasant to know he was a very thorny martyr who did a great deal of resentful lecturing about economy, stamping and shouting around the house with threats to throw the whole business over and let them fend for themselves if they could not treat him with more consideration. With flattery and persuasion they would cluster around and get him back on the rails, for his destiny was to be useful to genius, that is, to Miss Stein. [15]

She had been much attached to her brother Leo, in childhood they were twin souls. He was two years older and a boy, and she had learned from Clarissa Harlowe's uncle's letter that older brothers are superior to younger sisters, or any boy to any girl in fact. Though she bowed to this doctrine as long as it was convenient, she never allowed it to get in her way. She followed her brother's advice more or less, and in turn he waited on her and humored and defended her when she was a selfish lazy little girl. Later he made a charming traveling companion who naturally, being older and a man, looked after all the boring details of life and smoothed his sister's path everywhere. Still, she could not remember his face when he was absent, and once was very nervous when she went to meet him on a journey, for fear she might not recognize him. The one thing wrong all this time was their recurring quarrel about who was the genius of the two, for each had assumed the title and neither believed for a moment there was room for more than one in the family. By way of proving himself, brother Leo took the pavilion and atelier in the rue de Fleurus, installed himself well, and began trying hard to paint. Miss Stein, seeing all so cozy, moved in on him and sat down and began to write—no question of trying. "To try is to die," became one of her several hundred rhyming aphorisms designed to settle all conceivable arguments; after a time, no doubt overwhelmed by the solid negative force of that massive will and presence, her brother moved out and took the atelier next door, and went on being useful to his sister, and trying to paint. [16]

But he also went on insisting tactlessly that he, and not she, was the born genius; and this was one of the real differences between them, that he attacked on the subject and was uneasy, and could not rest, while his sister reasoned with him patiently at first defending her title, regretting she could not share it. Insist, argue, upset himself and her as much as he liked, she simply, quietly knew with a Messianic revelation that she was not only a genius, but *the* genius, and sometimes, she was certain, one of not more than half a dozen real ones in the world. During all her life, whenever Miss Stein got low in her mind about anything, she could always find consolation in this beautiful knowledge of being a born genius, and her brother's contentiousness finally began to look like treason to her. She could not forgive him for disputing her indivisible right to her natural property, genius, on which all her other rights of possession were founded. It shook her—she worried about her work. She had begun her long career of describing "how every one who ever lived eats and drinks and loves and sleeps and talks and walks and wakes and forgets and quarrels and likes and dislikes and works and sits,"—everybody's autobiography, in fact, for she had taken upon herself the immense task of explaining everybody to himself, of telling him all he needed to know about life, and she simply could not have brother Leo hanging around the edges of this grandiose scheme pinching off bits and holding them up to the light. By and by, too, she had Alice B. Toklas to do everything for her. So she and her brother drifted apart, but gradually, like one of Miss Stein's paragraphs. The separation became so complete that once, on meeting her brother unexpectedly, she was so taken by surprise she bowed to him, and afterward wrote a long poem about it in which her total confusion of mind and feeling were expressed with total incoherence: for once, form, matter and style stuttering and stammering and wallowing along together with the agitated harmony of roiling entrails. [17]

III

There are the tones of sloth, of that boredom which is a low-pressure despair, of monotony, of obsession, in this portrait; she went walking out of boredom, she could drive a car, talk, write, but anything else made her nervous. People who were doing anything annoyed her: to be doing nothing, she thought, was more interesting than to be doing something. The air of deathly solitude surrounding her; yet the parade of names in her book would easily fill several printed pages, all with faces attached which she could see were quite different from each other, all talking, each taking his own name and person for granted—a thing she could never understand. Yet she could see what they were doing and could remember what they said. She only listened attentively to Picasso—for whose sake she would crack almost any head in sight—so she half-agreed when he said Picabia was the worst painter of all; but still, found herself drawn to Picabia because his name was Francis. She had discovered that men named Francis were always elegant, and though they might not know anything else, they always knew about themselves. This would remind her that she had never found out who she was. Again and again she would doubt her own identity, and that of everyone else. When she worried about this aloud to Alice B. Toklas, saying she believed it impossible for anyone ever to be certain who he was, Alice B. Toklas made, in context, the most inspired remark in the whole book. "It depends on who you are," she said, and you might think that would have ended the business. Not at all. [18]

These deep-set, chronic fears led her to a good deal of quarreling, for when she quarreled she seems to have felt more real. She mentions quarrels with Max Jacobs, Francis Rose, with Dali, with Picabia, with Picasso, with Virgil Thomson, with Braque, with Breton, and how many others, though she rarely says just why they quarreled or how they made it up. Almost nobody went away and stayed, and the awful inertia of habit in friendships oppressed her. She was sometimes discouraged at the prospect of having to go on seeing certain persons to the end, merely because she had once seen them. The world seemed smaller every day, swarming with people perpetually in movement, full of restless notions which, once examined by her, were inevitably proved to be fallacious, or at least entirely useless. She found that she could best get rid of them by putting them in a book. "That is very funny if you write about any one they do not exist any more, for you, so why see them again. Anyway, that is the way I am." [19]

But as she wrote a book and disposed of one horde, another came on, and worried her afresh, discussing their ludicrous solemn topics, trying to understand things, and being unhappy about it. When Picasso was fretful because she argued with Dali and not with him, she explained that "one discusses things with stupid people but not with sensible ones." Her true grudge against intelligent people was that they talked "as if they were getting ready to change something." Change belonged to Miss Stein, and the duty of the world was to stand still so that she could move about in it comfortably. Her top flight of reasoning on the subject of intelligence ran as follows: "The most actively war-like nations could always convince the pacifists to become pro-German. That is because pacifists were such intelligent beings they could follow what any one is saying. If you follow what any one is saying then you are a pacifist you are a pro-German . . . therefore understanding is a very dull occupation." [20]

Intellectuals, she said, always wanted to change things because they had an unhappy childhood. "Well, I never had an unhappy childhood, what is the use of having an unhappy anything?" Léon Blum, then Premier of France, had had an unhappy childhood, and she inclined to the theory that the political uneasiness of France could be traced to this fact. [21]

There was not, of course, going to be another war (this was in 1937!) but if there was, there *would* be, naturally; and she never tired of repeating that dancing and war are the same thing "because both are forward and back," while revolution, on the contrary, is up and down, which is why it gets nowhere. Sovietism was even then going rapidly out of fashion in her circles, because they had discovered that it is very conservative, even if the Communists do not think so. Anarchists, being rarities, did not go out of fashion so easily. The most interesting thing that ever happened to America was the Civil War; but General Lee was severely to be blamed for leading his country into that war, just the same, because he must have known they could not win; and to her, it was absurd that any one should join battle in defense of a principle in face of certain defeat. For practical purposes, honor was not even a word. Still it was an exciting war and gave an interest to America which that country would never have had without it. "If you win you do not lose and if you lose you do not

win." Even as she was writing these winged words, the Spanish Civil
War, the Republicans against the Franco-Fascists, kept obtruding
itself. And why? "Not because it is a revolution, but because I know
so well the places they are mentioning and the things there they are
destroying." When she was little in Oakland, California, she loved
the big, nice American fires that had "so many horses and firemen to
attend them," and when she was older, she found that floods, for one
thing, always read worse in the papers than they really are; besides
how can you care much about what is going on if you don't see it or
know the people? For this reason she had Santa Teresa being indifferent to faraway Chinese while she was founding convents in Spain.
William Seabrook came to see her to find out if she was as interesting
as her books. She told him she was, and he discovered black magic in
the paintings of Sir Francis Rose. And when she asked Dashiell
Hammett why so many young men authors were writing novels about
tender young male heroines instead of the traditional female ones, he
explained that it was because as women grew more and more self-
confident, men lost confidence in themselves, and turned to each
other, or became their own subjects for fiction. This, or something
else, reminded her several times that she could not write a novel,
therefore no one could any more, and no one should waste time trying. [22]

Somehow by such roundabouts we arrive at the important, the
critical event in all this eventful history. Success. Success in this
world, here and now, was what Miss Stein wanted. She knew just
what it was, how it should look and feel, how much it should weigh
and what it was worth over the counter. It was not enough to be a
genius if you had to go on supporting your art on a private income.
To be the center of a recondite literary cult, to be surrounded by
listeners and imitators and seekers, to be mentioned in the same
breath with James Joyce, and to have turned out bales of titles by
merely writing a half-hour each day: she had all that, and what did it
amount to? There was a great deal more and she must have it. As to
her history of the human race, she confessed: "I have always been
bothered . . . but mostly . . . because after all I do as simply as it

can, as commonplacely as it can say, what everybody can and does
do; I never know what they can do, I really do not know what they
are, I do not think that any one can think because if they do, then
who is who?" [23]

It was high time for a change, and yet it occurred at hazard. If
there had not been a beautiful season in October and part of Novem-
ber 1932, permitting Miss Stein to spend that season quietly in her
country house, the *Autobiography of Alice B. Toklas* might never
have been written. But it was written, and Miss Stein became a best
seller in America; she made real money. With Miss Toklas, she had
a thrilling tour of the United States and found crowds of people
eager to see her and listen to her. And at last she got what she had
really wanted all along: to be published in the *Atlantic Monthly* and
the *Saturday Evening Post*. [24]

Now she had everything, or nearly. For a while she was afraid to
write any more, for fear her latest efforts would not please her public.
She had never learned who she was, and yet suddenly she had
become somebody else. "You are you because your little dog knows
you, but when your public knows you and does not want to pay you,
and when your public knows you and does want to pay you, you are
not the same you." [25]

This would be of course the proper moment to take leave, as our
heroine adds at last a golden flick of light to her self-portrait. "Anyway, I was a celebrity." The practical result was that she could no
longer live on her income. But she and Alice B. Toklas moved into an
apartment once occupied by Queen Christina of Sweden, and they
began going out more, and seeing even more people, and talking, and
Miss Stein settled every question as it came up, more and more. But
who wants to read about success? It is the early struggle which makes
a good story. [26]

IV

She and Alice B. Toklas enjoyed both the wars. The first one
especially being a lark with almost no one getting killed where you
could see, and it ended so nicely too, without changing anything. The

second was rather more serious. She lived safely enough in Bilignin throughout the German occupation, and there is a pretty story that the whole village conspired to keep her presence secret. She had been a citizen of the world in the best European tradition; for though America was her native land, she had to live in Europe because she felt at home there. In the old days people paid little attention to wars, fought as they were out of sight by professional soldiers. She had always liked the notion, too, of the gradual Orientalization of the West, the peaceful penetration of the East into European culture. It had been going on a great while, and all Western geniuses worth mentioning were Orientals: look at Picasso, look at Einstein. Russians are Tartars, Spaniards are Saracens—had not all great twentieth-century painting been Spanish? And her cheerful conclusion was, that "Einstein was the creative philosophic mind of the century, and I have been the creative literary mind of the century also, with the Oriental mixing with the European." She added, as a casual after-thought, "Perhaps Europe is finished." [27]

That was in 1938, and she could not be expected to know that war was near. They had only been sounding practice *alertes* in Paris against expected German bombers since 1935. She spoke out of her natural frivolity and did not mean it. She liked to prophesy, but warned her hearers that her prophecies never came out right, usually the very opposite, and no matter what happened, she was always surprised. She was surprised again: as the nations of Europe fell, and the Germans came again over the frontiers of France for the third time in three generations, the earth shook under her own feet, and not somebody else's. It made an astonishing difference. Something mysterious touched her in her old age. She got a fright, and this time not for ancient vanished civilizations, but for this civilization, this moment; and she was quite thrilled with relief and gay when the American Army finally came in, and the Germans were gone. She did not in the least know why the Germans had come, but they were gone, and so far as she could see, the American Army had chased them out. She remembered with positive spread-eagle patriotism that America was her native land. At last America itself belonged to Miss

Stein, and she claimed it, in a formal published address to other Americans. Anxiously she urged them to stay rich, to be powerful and learn how to use power, not to waste themselves; for the first time she used the word "spiritual." Ours was a spiritual as well as a material fight; Lincoln's great lucid words about government of the people by the people for the people suddenly sounded like a trumpet through her stammering confession of faith, she wanted nothing now to stand between her and her newly discovered country. By great good luck she was born on the winning side and she was going to stay there. And we were not to forget about money as the source of power; "Remember the depression, don't be afraid to look it in the face and find out the reason why, if you don't find out the reason why you'll go poor and my God, how I would hate to have my native land go poor." [28]

The mind so long shapeless and undisciplined could not now express any knowledge out of its long willful ignorance. But the heart spoke its crude urgent language. She had liked the doughboys in the other war well enough, but this time she fell in love with the whole American Army below the rank of lieutenant. She "breathed, ate, drank, lived GI's," she told them, and inscribed numberless photographs for them, and asked them all to come back again. After her flight over Germany in an American bomber, she wrote about how, so often, she would stand staring into the sky watching American war planes going over, longing to be up there again with her new loves, in the safe, solid air. She murmured, "Bless them, bless them." She had been impatient with many of them who had still been naïve enough to believe they were fighting against an evil idea that threatened everybody; some of them actually were simple enough to say they had been—or believed they had been—fighting for democratic government. "What difference does it make what kind of government you have?" she would ask. "All governments are alike. Just remember you won the war." But still, at the end, she warned them to have courage and not be just yes or no men. And she said, "Bless them, bless them." [29]

It was the strangest thing, as if the wooden umbrella feeling the rain had tried to forsake its substance and take on the nature of its form; and was struggling slowly, slowly, much too late, to unfold. [30]

PURPOSE AND STRUCTURE

1. Miss Porter originally called this essay *Gertrude Stein: A Self Portrait.* Note the passages drawing upon Stein's own writings as a source for her portrait.

2. Miss Porter alluded to Gertrude Stein in a letter to her editor as "one of the blights and symptoms of her very sick times." With what details does she reflect this feeling about Gertrude Stein? about the times?

3. Mark the passages in which the author reveals herself as fully as she does Stein. By what means do you become aware of Miss Porter's biases, interests, convictions, resentments, prejudices, personality, values? For example, throughout the essay she criticizes Stein's writing practices. By implication you learn Miss Porter's conception of the craft of writing.

4. How does the author convey to the reader a visual image of Stein and her surroundings? Underline specific passages.

5. With what concrete details and images are the personalities of the following developed for the reader: Picasso, Stieglitz, Brewsie and Willie, Brother Leo, Brother Michael?

6. What is the relevance to the author's purpose of Stein's early response to fires and floods? How does the author trace the evolution of Stein's views in Section IV, culminating in the repetition of the umbrella metaphor? How does she reflect her own viewpoint?

7. What specific details support the author's statement that Stein's judgments were *prejudiced without qualification, based on assumptions founded in the void of pure unreason?*

8. Analyze the complicated chronology of the essay. What purpose is served by shifts from the later years to the early years in successive stages and then forward to the first and second war? How does the order in time contribute to unity, coherence, and emphasis? What would be lost or gained if she followed a chronological approach and opened with Stein as a small girl?

9. Demonstrate how selected patterns of speech, diction, images, and allusions contribute to coherence. How does the author achieve a cumulative effect?

DICTION AND TONE

1. Why is the wooden umbrella an effective image for the portrait of Gertrude Stein? Clues appear in the opening quotation about Miss Hennessy's wooden umbrella and in the final paragraph.

2. In a letter to her editor the author admitted that Gertrude Stein has had "A horrid fascination for me, really horrid, for I have a horror of her kind of mind and being. . . ." How does the portrait reveal Miss Porter's horror?

3. Identify the changes in tone or the several voices with which Miss Porter speaks. How is compassion expressed in the conclusion?

4. Mark the passages that might be labeled sarcasm or parody. Distinguish between them.

5. The word *belonged* is used recurrently with reference to what Stein felt belonged to her. What is its meaning in the several contexts? What effect is created by the recurrent use? How does its use help to develop a picture of Gertrude Stein?

6. How are narrative and expository elements merged? Cite examples.

7. Comment on the irony in the following quotations: *he* [Picasso] *promised to give back writing to its natural owner* [2]; *everything she looked upon was hers in more than the usual sense* [3]; *and so she disposed of all the dark questions of life, art, human relations, and death, even eternity, even God, with perfect Stein logic, bringing the scene again into its proper focus, upon herself* [6]; *how can you care much about what is going on if you don't see it or know the people* [22]; *she knew just what it* [success] *was, how it should look and feel, how much it should weigh and what it was worth over the counter* [23].

8. How is irony employed in par. 5?

9. Miss Porter is a master of metaphoric language. Select a number of the most vivid figures of speech and comment on their function in context.

10. Analyze the author's multidimensional approach to her subject in par. 8. Cite other examples in which a single sentence bears the weight of a dual judgment.

11. Underline the images used in par. 14.

12. When is Miss Porter the apparently detached observer? What is the effect of the seeming detachment? When is she directly judgmental? When is she obliquely suggestive? How does she achieve consistency of tone when she employs these various approaches to her subject?

13. The allusion to honor carries overtones of both Shakespeare and Hemingway. Look up the quotation from *Henry IV, Part I* (Act V, Sc. 1), in which Falstaff asks, "What is honor?" In *A Farewell to Arms*, Hemingway writes, "There were many words that you could not stand to hear and finally only the names of places had dignity. . . . Abstract words like glory, honor, courage, and hallow were obscene beside the concrete names of villages." What do these overtones contribute to the essay [5]?

APPLICATIONS TO WRITING

T. S. Eliot used the phrase "objective correlative" to describe the artist's faculty of achieving emotional impact: "The only way of expressing emotion in the form of art is by finding an 'objective correlative'; in other words, a set of objects, a situation, a chain of events which shall be the formula of that *particular* emotion; such that when the external facts, which must terminate in sensory experience, are given, the emotion is immediately evoked." Miss Porter's use of the wooden umbrella is a dramatic example.

1. Write a portrait of someone you know in which you stand aside as a seemingly detached observer but nonetheless convey unmistakably your feelings about your subject by using an appropriate objective correlative.

2. Analyze in detail the elements of irony in *The Wooden Umbrella*.

3. Write a composition in which you develop a carefully documented analysis of one of the questions in the exercises above.

THE DOOR

E . B . W H I T E

Everything (he kept saying) is something it isn't. And everybody is always somewhere else. Maybe it was the city, being in the
city, that made him feel how queer everything was and that it was
something else. Maybe (he kept thinking) it was the names of the
things. The names were tex and frequently koid. Or they were flex
and oid or they were duroid (sani) or flexsan (duro), but everything
was glass (but not quite glass) and the thing that you touched (the
surface, washable, crease-resistant) was rubber, only it wasn't quite
rubber and you didn't quite touch it but almost. The wall, which was
glass but thrutex, turned out on being approached not to be a wall, it
was something else, it was an opening or doorway—and the doorway
(through which he saw himself approaching) turned out to be something else, it was a wall. And what he had eaten not having agreed
with him. [1]

He was in a washable house, but he wasn't sure. Now about those
rats, he kept saying to himself. He meant the rats that the Professor
had driven crazy by forcing them to deal with problems which were
beyond the scope of rats, the insoluble problems. He meant the rats
that had been trained to jump at the square card with the circle in the

middle, and the card (because it was something it wasn't) would give way and let the rat into a place where the food was, but then one day it would be a trick played on the rat, and the card would be changed, and the rat would jump but the card wouldn't give way, and it was an impossible situation (for a rat) and the rat would go insane and into its eyes would come the unspeakably bright imploring look of the frustrated, and after the convulsions were over and the frantic racing around, then the passive stage would set in and the willingness to let anything be done to it, even if it was something else. [2]

He didn't know which door (or wall) or opening in the house to jump at, to get through, because one was an opening that wasn't a door (it was a void, or koid) and the other was a wall that wasn't an opening, it was a sanitary cupboard of the same color. He caught a glimpse of his eyes staring into his eyes, in the thrutex, and in them was the expression he had seen in the picture of the rats—weary after convulsions and the frantic racing around, when they were willing and did not mind having anything done to them. More and more (he kept saying) I am confronted by a problem which is incapable of solution (for this time even if he chose the right door, there would be no food behind it) and that is what madness is, and things seeming different from what they are. He heard, in the house where he was, in the city to which he had gone (as toward a door which might, or might not, give way), a noise—not a loud noise but more of a low prefabricated humming. It came from a place in the base of the wall (or stat) where the flue carrying the filterable air was, and not far from the Minipiano, which was made of the same material nail-brushes are made of, and which was under the stairs. "This, too, has been tested," she said, pointing, but not at it, "and found viable." It wasn't a loud noise, he kept thinking, sorry that he had seen his eyes, even though it was through his own eyes that he had seen them. [3]

First will come the convulsions (he said), then the exhaustion, then the willingness to let anything be done. "And you better believe it *will* be." [4]

All his life he had been confronted by situations which were in-

capable of being solved, and there was a deliberateness behind all
this, behind this changing of the card (or door), because they would
always wait until you had learned to jump at the certain card (or
door)—the one with the circle—and then they would change it on
you. There have been so many doors changed on me, he said, in the
last twenty years, but it is now becoming clear that it is an impossible
situation, and the question is whether to jump again, even though
they ruffle you in the rump with a blast of air—to make you jump.
He wished he wasn't standing by the Minipiano. First they would
teach you the prayers and the Psalms, and that would be the right
door (the one with the circle) and the long sweet words with the
holy sound, and that would be the one to jump at to get where the
food was. Then one day you jumped and it didn't give way, so that
all you got was the bump on the nose, and the first bewilderment, the
first young bewilderment. [5]

I don't know whether to tell her about the door they substituted
or not, he said, the one with the equation on it and the picture of the
amoeba reproducing itself by division. Or the one with the photostatic copy of the check for thirty-two dollars and fifty cents. But the
jumping was so long ago, although the bump is . . . how those old
wounds hurt! Being crazy this way wouldn't be so bad if only, if only.
If only when you put your foot forward to take a step, the ground
wouldn't come up to meet your foot the way it does. And the same
way in the street (only I may never get back to the street unless I
jump at the right door), the curb coming up to meet your foot,
anticipating ever so delicately the weight of the body, which is somewhere else. "We could take your name," she said, "and send it to
you." And it wouldn't be so bad if only you could read a sentence all
the way through without jumping (your eye) to something else on
the same page; and then (he kept thinking) there was that man
out in Jersey, the one who started to chop his trees down, one by one,
the man who began talking about how he would take his house to
pieces, brick by brick, because he faced a problem incapable of solution, probably, so he began to hack at the trees in the yard, began to

pluck with trembling fingers at the bricks in the house. Even if a house is not washable, it is worth taking down. It is not till later that the exhaustion sets in. [6]

But it is inevitable that they will keep changing the doors on you, he said, because that is what they are for; and the thing is to get used to it and not let it unsettle the mind. But that would mean not jumping, and you can't. Nobody can not jump. There will be no not-jumping. Among rats, perhaps, but among people never. Everybody has to keep jumping at a door (the one with the circle on it) because that is the way everybody is, especially some people. You wouldn't want me, standing here, to tell you, would you, about my friend the poet (deceased) who said, "My heart has followed all my days something I cannot name"? (It had the circle on it.) And like many poets, although few so beloved, he is gone. It killed him, the jumping. First, of course, there were the preliminary bouts, the convulsions, and the calm and the willingness. [7]

I remember the door with the picture of the girl on it (only it was spring), her arms outstretched in loveliness, her dress (it was the one with the circle on it) uncaught, beginning the slow, clear, blinding cascade—and I guess we would all like to try that door again, for it seemed like the way and for a while it was the way, the door would open and you would go through winged and exalted (like any rat) and the food would be there, the way the Professor had it arranged, everything O.K., and you had chosen the right door for the world was young. The time they changed that door on me, my nose bled for a hundred hours—how do you like that, Madam? Or would you prefer to show me further through this so strange house, or you could take my name and send it to me, for although my heart has followed all my days something I cannot name, I am tired of the jumping and I do not know which way to go, Madam, and I am not even sure that I am not tired beyond the endurance of man (rat, if you will) and have taken leave of sanity. What are you following these days, old friend, after your recovery from the last bump? What is the name, or is it something you cannot name? The rats have a name for it by this time, perhaps, but I don't know what they call it.

I call it plexikoid and it comes in sheets, something like insulating board, unattainable and ugli-proof. [8]

And there was the man out in Jersey, because I keep thinking about his terrible necessity and the passion and trouble he had gone to all those years in the indescribable abundance of a householder's detail, building the estate and the planting of the trees and in spring the lawn-dressing and in fall the bulbs for the spring burgeoning, and the watering of the grass on the long light evenings in summer and the gravel for the driveway (all had to be thought out, planned) and the decorative borders, probably, the perennials and the bug spray, and the building of the house from plans of the architect, first the sills, then the studs, then the full corn in the ear, the floors laid on the floor timbers, smoothed, and then the carpets upon the smooth floors and the curtains and the rods therefor. And then, almost without warning, he would be jumping at the same old door and it wouldn't give: they had changed it on him, making life no longer supportable under the elms in the elm shade, under the maples in the maple shade. [9]

"Here you have the maximum of openness in a small room." [10]

It was impossible to say (maybe it was the city) what made him feel the way he did, and I am not the only one either, he kept thinking—ask any doctor if I am. The doctors, they know how many there are, they even know where the trouble is only they don't like to tell you about the prefrontal lobe because that means making a hole in your skull and removing the work of centuries. It took so long coming, this lobe, so many, many years. (Is it something you read in the paper, perhaps?) And now, the strain being so great, the door having been changed by the Professor once too often . . . but it only means a whiff of ether, a few deft strokes, and the higher animal becomes a little easier in his mind and more like the lower one. From now on, you see, that's the way it will be, the ones with the small prefrontal lobes will win because the other ones are hurt too much by this incessant bumping. They can stand just so much, eh, Doctor? (And what is that, pray, that you have in your hand?) Still, you never can tell, eh, Madam? [11]

He crossed (carefully) the room, the thick carpet under him softly, and went toward the door carefully, which was glass and he could see himself in it, and which, at his approach, opened to allow him to pass through; and beyond he half expected to find one of the old doors that he had known, perhaps the one with the circle, the one with the girl her arms outstretched in loveliness and beauty before him. But he saw instead a moving stairway, and descended in light (he kept thinking) to the street below and to the other people. As he stepped off, the ground came up slightly, to meet his foot. [12]

PURPOSE AND STRUCTURE

1. In the oblique portrayal of the speaker, what do you learn of his external situation? of his internal life—his despair, fears, dreams, values?

2. In what sense is he an individual? a symbol of twentieth-century man? How is fantasy interlocked with reality? What is achieved by this fusion?

3. What human qualities are magnified and stretched?

4. How does the analogy of the rat experiment permit the writer to ridicule what is fraudulent, absurd, stupid, or evil? How does he point up its absurdity or wrongness? Mark the recurrent passages in which the rat frustration analogy appears.

DICTION AND TONE

1. Document the fact that the speaker is both participant and observer. How does this device permit White to achieve both immediacy and detachment? How does the use of the third person speaker bear upon this question?

2. What clues in allusion, symbol, diction, rhythm, and syntax acquaint you with the implicit meaning of *The Door*?

3. How does the author modulate the seriousness of his subject matter?

How does he use understatement to convey seriousness? How does the speaker avoid self pity?

4. How does the author view the human situation: with Olympian smiling detachment at man's comedy of errors; with compassion for the tragedy inherent in the human condition? Which of these adjectives are appropriate in describing the precise nature of the author's humor: *bitter, shocking, sarcastic, delicate, detached, dry, restrained, biting, bantering, whimsical, fey, compassionate?*

5. How do the syntax and diction corroborate White's statement (in *The Elements of Style*) that style is not a separate entity but non-detachable, unfilterable? What elements of style in *The Door* are symptomatic of the disordered or troubled mind? How are the diction and sentence patterns in the speaker's interior monologue accommodated to his predicament? With these questions in mind, study the sentences in the first paragraph. Find other examples in which the breaks in continuity and rhythm are consonant with the breaks in rhythm in a human life. How do you reconcile these discontinuities with the total effect of careful ordering of experience?

6. What words and phrases evoke visual images? How does the diction produce striking auditory effects?

7. How is the door used as a metaphor? How is it sustained throughout the piece? Write a paragraph elaborating on the symbolic meaning of each of the four doors. Is the house used as a symbol? Discuss its multiple connotations.

8. Demonstrate how the diction draws on the language of advertising and technology, medicine, poetry, and psychology. What role does each of these vocabularies play in relation to purpose and tone?

9. Pronouns have an important structural role in addition to illuminating the situation. Identify the antecedents for *he* [1]; *she* [3]; *they* [5]; *her* [6]; *it* (last three lines of par. 8). Analyze the author's use of verbs, adjectives, and adverbs.

10. How do the following allusions illuminate both purpose and tone: *the washable house* [1]; *the Minipiano* [3]; *the man out in Jersey* [6]; *the poet (deceased)* [7]; *the doctors* [11]?

11. How do the diction and syntax in par. 11 add to its biting irony? What is the nature of the irony in par. 12? What is the literal and

symbolic meaning of the last sentence? Why is it an effective consummation of the basic theme of alienation?

12. Analyze the way in which abstract concepts are developed by concrete detail. For example, note how the author moves from the abstraction of the door to the door with the photostatic copy of the check for thirty-two dollars and fifty cents. How does the use of the photostat rather than a real check or thirty-two paper bills or thirty-two silver dollars illuminate the basic theme? Cite other examples.

APPLICATIONS TO WRITING

1. How are fantasy and reality fused in *The Door* and to what purpose?

2. Develop a thesis, from one of the quotations from *The Door*, using a narrative approach and drawing upon an appropriate analogy as a means of achieving consistency of tone and clarity of perspective: *Everything . . . is something it isn't; This, too, has been tested . . . and found viable; the willingness to let anything be done; There have been so many doors changed on me; one day you jumped and it didn't give way; the first young bewilderment; A problem incapable of solution; The world was young; What are you following these days, old friend? The thing is to get used to it; My heart has followed all my days something I cannot name.*

3. By what means does *The Door* recapitulate western man's attempt to solve the problem of existence and describe his alienation from himself and his culture.

4. Write an "interior monologue" in which you comment on some aspect of your culture.

GLOSSARY

ABSTRACTION, LEVELS OF—distinguished in two ways: in the range between the general and the specific and in the range between the abstract and the concrete.

A general word refers to a class, genus, or group; a specific word refers to a member of that group. *Ship* is a general word, but *ketch, schooner, liner,* and *tugboat* are specific. It must be remembered, however, that the terms *general* and *specific* are relative, not absolute. *Ketch,* for example, is more specific than *ship,* for a ketch is a kind of ship. But *ketch,* on the other hand, is more general than *Tahiti ketch,* for a Tahiti ketch is a kind of ketch.

The distinction between the abstract and the concrete also is relative. Ideas and qualities which are usually embodied in physical things or dramatized by them, but which may be thought of separately (redness, honor), are called abstract; physical things such as *house, shoes,* and *horse* are concrete. Notice, however, that concrete words not only can range further into the specific (*bungalow, moccasin,* and *stallion*), but they also can range back toward the general (*domicile, clothing,* and *cattle*). In making these distinctions between the abstract and the concrete and between the general and the specific, there is no implication that good writing should be specific and concrete and that poor writing is general and abstract. Certainly most good writing is concrete and specific, but it is also general and abstract, constantly moving from the general to the specific and from the abstract to the concrete. See Twain; Melville; Krutch; White (*The Door*).

ALLUSION—a reference to a person, place, or thing, whether real or imaginary: Woodrow Wilson or Zeus, Siam or Atlantis, kangaroo or Phoenix. The allusion is an economical way to evoke an atmosphere, a historical era, or an emotion. See Huxley; Jarrell; Porter; Hardwick.

575

ANALOGY—in exposition, usually a comparison of some length in which the unknown is explained in terms of the known, the unfamiliar in terms of the familiar, the remote in terms of the immediate. See Melville; Huxley (*Pascal*); Bettelheim; Porter.

In argument, an analogy consists of a series of likenesses between two or more dissimilar things, demonstrating that they are either similar or identical in other respects also. The use of analogy in argument is open to criticism, for two things alike in many respects are not necessarily alike in all (for example, lampblack and diamonds are both pure carbon; they differ significantly in their crystal structure). Although analogy never *proves* anything, its dramatic quality, its assistance in establishing tone, its vividness make it one of the most valuable techniques of the writer. See Bettelheim; Plato; Russell.

ANALYSIS—a method of exposition by logical division, applicable to anything that can be divided into component parts: an object, such as a novel, essay, or film, as in Huxley's *The Essay* or in Agee's *Monsieur Verdoux*; a complex idea, as in Langer's *Lord of Creation*; or an organic whole, one in which the parts reciprocally modify each other, as in Ciardi's *Robert Frost: The Way to the Poem*. In the analysis of the purposes and activities of the intellectual, Jarrell describes parts in terms of their characteristic function. Analysis may also be concerned with the connection of events (causal analysis): given this condition or series of conditions, what effects will follow? For example, in her essay Mrs. Langer attempts to show the consequences of man's ability to manipulate symbols and to form abstractions.

ARGUMENT AND PERSUASION are reciprocally related. Formal argument often consists of the following parts: the *proposition*, an assertion that leads to the issue; the *issue*, the aspect of the proposition which the writer is attempting to prove and the question on which the whole argument rests; the *evidence*, the facts and opinions which the author offers as testimony. He may order the evidence deductively by proceeding from certain premises to a *conclusion*; or inductively by generalizing from a number of instances and drawing a *conclusion*. Informal arguments frequently make greater use of the methods of exposition than they do of formal logic. Argument is a mode of discourse; *the* argument, a line of reasoning. See Deduction, Induction, Logic, and Analogy.

The purpose of argument is to persuade. The attempt to distinguish between argument and persuasion is sometimes made by reference to means (argument makes appeals to reason; persuasion, to emotions); sometimes to ends (argument causes someone to change his mind; persuasion moves him to action). These distinctions, however, are more academic than functional, for in practice argument and persuasion are not discrete entities. Yet the proof in argument rests largely upon the objectivity of evidence; the proof in persuasion, upon a subtle and controlled use of language. The diction employed, as well as such literary devices as irony, satire, paradox, metaphor, and allusion, will establish the tone, which in turn may affect the reader's judgment of the objectivity of the evidence and the degree to which he is persuaded by it. The argument in *Freedom and the Responsibility of the Press* is public; the tone, ironic and outspoken. The argument in *Civil Disobedience*, based often on unstated assumptions, constitutes a philosophical inquiry into the nature of man, his conscience, and his government. In *The Subjection of Women* Miss Hardwick develops the argument by focusing on the issue of what in women is given and what is acquired; she brings to bear upon it a rigorous logic, an immense vigor, and a devastating wit. In *What I Believe* Forster persuades by a combination of tough-mindedness and skepticism about his own position. Sartre's argument depends on the resolution of a paradox. In *The Allegory of the Cave*, Plato's consummate power to persuade rests upon the brilliant use of metaphor, the structure of the dialogue, and the unspoken flattery of the reader. Finally, the persuasive power of *A Modest Proposal* lies in its sustained irony: Swift simulates an amorality which is cumulatively revealed in an exaggerated rationality and a view of man which reduces him to an object to be used.

ASSUMPTION—that part of an argument which is unstated because it is either taken for granted by the reader and writer or undetected by them. When the reader consciously disagrees with an assumption, the writer has misjudged his audience by assuming what the reader refuses to concede. See Thoreau; Russell.

ATTITUDE—towards subject, see Tone. Toward audience, see Audience.

AUDIENCE—for the writer, his expected readers. When the audience is a general, unknown one, and the subject matter is closely related to the writer's opinions, preferences, attitudes, and tastes, then the writer's relationship to his audience is in a very real sense his relationship to himself. The writer who distrusts the intelligence of his audience or who adapts his material to what he assumes are the tastes and interests of his readers compromises his integrity.

On the other hand, if the audience is generally known (a college class, for example), and the subject matter is factual information, then the beginning writer may well consider the education, interests, and tastes of his audience. Unless he keeps a definite audience in mind, the beginner is apt to shift levels of usage, use inappropriate diction, and lose the reader by appealing to none of his interests.

"It is now necessary to warn the writer that his concern for the reader must be pure; he must sympathize with the reader's plight (most readers are in trouble about half the time) but never seek to know his wants. The whole duty of a writer is to please and satisfy himself, and the true writer always plays to an audience of one. Let him start sniffing the air, or glancing at the Trend Machine, and he is as good as dead, although he may make a nice living." (Strunk and White, *The Elements of Style*, used with permission of The Macmillan Company.)

CAUSE AND EFFECT—a seemingly simple method of development in which either the cause of a particular effect or the effects of a particular cause are investigated. However, because of the philosophical difficulties surrounding causality, the writer should be cautious in ascribing causes. For the explanation of most processes, it is probably safer to proceed in a sequential order, using transitional words to indicate the order of the process. See Bettelheim; Jarrell; Sartre; Langer.

CLASSIFICATION—an arbitrary systematic arrangement of categories (classes) so that the larger categories include the smaller. By definition, all members of a class have at least one characteristic in common. This characteristic varies with the needs and purposes of the person doing the classifying. Bacon's elaborate classification scheme serves the purpose of logically revealing error; Woolf's fluid classification serves her purpose of revealing the reciprocal relationship between reader and writer; Bigelow's classification is little more than a device for organizing and clarifying a vast and complex area of thought. On the basis of freshly recognized characteristics, Cowley removes Hemingway from the class to which earlier critics had assigned him and reclassifies him.

COHERENCE—literally, a sticking together; therefore, the joining or linking of one point to another. It is the writer's obligation to make clear to the reader the relationship of sentence to sentence and paragraph to paragraph. Sometimes coherence is simply a matter of putting the parts in a sequence which is meaningful and relevant—logical sequence, chronological order, order of importance. Other times it is helpful to underscore the relationship. An elementary but highly useful method of underscoring relationships is the use of transitional words; *but, however, yet* inform the reader that what is to follow contrasts with what went before; *furthermore, moreover, in addition to* continue or expand what went before.

Another elementary way of achieving coherence is the enumeration of ideas—"first," "second," "third"—so as to remind the reader of the development. A more subtle transition can be gained by repeating at the beginning of a paragraph a key word or idea from the end of the preceding paragraph. Such a transition reminds the reader of what has gone before and simultaneously prepares him for what is to come. See Woolf; Baldwin; Cowley.

COMPARISON AND CONTRAST—the presentation of a subject by indicating similarities between two or more things (comparison); by indicating differences (contrast). The basic elements in a comparative process, then, are (1) the various entities compared, and (2) the points of likeness or difference between them. To be comparable, they should be members of the same class (see Classification). For example, life worshipers and death worshipers, both members of· the same class, are comparable. Democracy and communism are not comparable, since the former is a subdivision of a political system and the latter, an economic one. The range of effects that may be achieved in comparison and contrast is reflected in Macaulay's straightforward development of the two aspects of the *persona* of the Puritans; in Mencken's preposterous and paradoxical development of the distinctions between men and women; in Trilling's allusive and fast-paced exploration of the points of contact between literature and psychoanalysis; in Craft's concrete and intimate confrontation of talent and genius; in Huxley's subtle and complex counterpointing of life and death worshipers.

CONCRETENESS—See Abstraction, Levels of.

CONNOTATION—all that the word suggests or implies in addition to its literal meaning. However, this definition is arbitrary and, from the standpoint of the writer, artificial, because the meaning of a word includes *all* that it suggests and implies. For connotative language see Twain; Mencken; Woolf; Camus.

CONTRAST—See Comparison.

COORDINATION—elements of like importance in like grammatical construction. Less important elements should be placed in grammatically subordinate positions. See Parallelism and Subordination. See Krutch; Morgenthau.

DEDUCTIVE REASONING—in logic, deriving a conclusion about a particular example by recognizing that a predetermined generalization is applicable to it; by analogy, in rhetoric, that development which moves from the general to the specific. See Krutch.

DEFINITION—in logic, the placing of the word to be defined in a general class and then demonstrating how it differs from other members of the class; in rhetoric, the meaningful extension (usually enriched by the use of detail, concrete illustrations, anecdote, metaphor) of a logical definition in order to answer fully—though often implicitly—the question, "What is . . .?" Wilder begins his essay with the traditional method of placing his subject in a class (*genus*) and stating what qualities (*differentiae*) distinguish it from other members of the class. Forster limits his subject by explicitly excluding peripheral questions and particularizing his general question by personal example. Morgenthau develops his definition of the components of tragedy and greatness by comparing and contrasting Lincoln and Stevenson. When the subject to be defined is abstract and complex, as in Krutch's *Tragic Fallacy*, it usually requires an extended definition based upon an inquiry that extends beyond the subject of the definition. As a means of defining existential freedom, Dostoyevsky transforms the elementary technique of question and answer into an internal dialectic.

DENOTATION—the literal meaning of a word. See Connotation.

DESCRIPTION—that form of discourse whose primary purpose is to present factual information about an object or experience (objective description); or to report the impression or evaluation of an object or experience (subjective description). Most description combines the two purposes. *It was a frightening night* (an evaluation with which others might disagree). *The wind blew the shingles off the north side of the house and drove the rain under the door* (two facts about which there can be little disagreement). See Twain; Melville; Orwell; Agee (*Knoxville*); Broyard.

DICTION—style as determined by choice of words. Good diction is characterized by precision and appropriateness to subject matter; weak diction, by the use of inappropriate, vague, or trite words. The relationship between the kinds of words a writer selects and his subject matter in large part determines tone. Baldwin's diction—a striking combination of formal public language and informal private language—reflects his subject matter. Hersey's diction does not; his language is deliberately flat and reportorial. Orwell's has a cinematic immediacy; on the other hand, Camus' is abstract yet personal. Russell's diction is formal and poetic, while Lawrence's is by turns colloquial and apocalyptic. Miss Porter is a master of metaphoric language and parody. And White (*The Door*), in the most supple and necessary fashion, creates part of his own language —*tex, koid, sani,* and *duro.* (See Tone.) The deliberate use of inappropriate diction is a frequent device of satire (for satire see Swift).

DISCOURSE, FORMS OF—traditionally, exposition, argument, description, and narration (see entries under each). These four kinds of traditional discourse are rarely found in a pure form. Argument and exposition may be interfused in the most complex fashion. Exposition often employs narration and description for purposes of illustration. It is important to remember, however, that in an effective piece of writing the use of more than one form of discourse is never accidental. It always serves the author's central purpose. For a combination of forms see selections under Identification.

EMPHASIS—the arrangement of the elements of a composition so that the important meanings occur in structurally important parts of the composition. Repetition, order of increasing importance, exclamation points, rhetorical questions, and figures of speech are all devices to achieve emphasis. See Jarrell; Baldwin; White (*The Door*); Sartre; Russell; Wilder.

EVIDENCE—that part of argument or persuasion that involves proof. It usually takes the form of facts, particulars deduced from general principles, or opinions of authorities. See Hardwick.

EXPOSITION—that form of discourse which explains or informs. Most papers required of college students are expository. The *methods* of exposition presented in this text are identification, definition, classification, illustration, comparison and contrast, and analysis (see separate entries in glossary).

FIGURES OF SPEECH—a form of expression in which the meanings of words are extended beyond the literal. The common figures of speech are metaphor, simile, analogy. See Woolf; White (*The Door*); Agee (*Monsieur Verdoux*); Russell.

GENERALIZATION—a general conception or principle derived from particulars. Often, simply a general statement. See Abstraction.

GRAMMAR—a systematic description of a language.

IDENTIFICATION—a process preliminary to definition of a subject. As a method of exposition, it brings the subject into focus by describing it. It attempts to answer the question, "What is X?", not so much by focusing on X as by describing the physical context in which X appears or the situation which evokes it. In Twain, memories are tied to sensory experiences; in Proust, they are the result of successfully wrestling with inchoate glimmerings; in Melville, philosophical abstractions grow out of the concrete objects of everyday life; in Mencken, the "libido" for the ugly is identified by the objects it creates; in Agee, a description of a summer evening evokes a fragile mood; and in Broyard, ambivalent feelings are brought into focus by the account of a Sunday dinner in Brooklyn.

ILLUSTRATION—at its simplest, a particular member of a class used to explain or dramatize the class. The individual member selected must be a fair representative of the distinctive qualities of the class. At its most complex, an illustration provides the particulars on which a generalization is based; the generalization—a type of person or thing, an idea or abstraction—may or may not be explicitly stated. Eiseley makes the witches in *Macbeth* illustrate "projections from our own psyche." Bettelheim transforms what might have been a mere case history into an illustration of a predicament of contemporary man. Fiction may be regarded as an illustration of an implied generalization. In *Some Thoughts on Playwriting*, Thornton Wilder says, "Modern taste shrinks from emphasizing the central idea that hides behind the fiction, but exists there nevertheless. . . ." However, to say that the dialogue in *What Cocktail Party?* illustrates the synthetic personality does injustice to Thurber's humor and wisdom. And to label "the second tree from the corner" as a metaphor for what all men want does not take account of the resonance of White's ironic understatement. Finally, Hemingway's *Big Two-Hearted River* might be called pure narration; to speak of it as illustration is to reduce it to another form of discourse. Obviously the central idea behind a piece of fiction cannot be stated in expository language without loss of precision and power.

IMAGE—a word or statement which makes an appeal to the senses. Thus, there are visual images, auditory images, and so on. As the most direct experience of the world is through the senses, writing which makes use of sense impressions (images) can be unusually effective. See Twain; Eiseley; Agee (*Knoxville*); Camus; Orwell.

INDUCTIVE REASONING—in logic, the formulation of a generalization after the observation of an adequate number of particular instances; by analogy, in rhetoric, that development which moves from the particular to the general. See Proust; Forster (*My Wood*); Hardwick.

INTENTION—for the particular purpose or function of a single piece of writing, see Purpose. Intention determines the four forms of discourse. See Exposition, Argument, Description, Narration. These intentions may be explicitly or implicitly set forth by the writer.

IRONY—at its simplest, involves a discrepancy between literal and intended meaning; at its most complex, it involves an utterance more meaningful (and usually meaningful in a different way) to the listener than to the speaker (dramatic irony). For example, Oedipus' remarks about discovering the murderer of the king are understood by the audience in a way Oedipus himself cannot understand them. The inability to grasp the full implications of his own remark is frequently feigned by the satirist. See Swift; White; Porter; Thurber; Morgenthau.

ISSUE—the limitation of a general proposition to the precise point on which the argument rests. Defeating the issue defeats the argument. Typically the main proposition of an argument will raise at least one issue for discussion and controversy. See Hardwick.

LIMITATION OF SUBJECT—restriction of the subject to one that can be adequately developed with reference to audience and purpose. See Agee (*Monsieur Verdoux*); Forster (*My Wood*); Wilder; Hersey.

METAPHOR—an implied comparison between two things that are seemingly different; a compressed analogy. Effectively used, metaphors increase clarity, interest, vividness, and concreteness. See Woolf; White (*The Door*); Dostoyevsky.

NARRATION—a form of discourse the purpose of which is to tell a story. If a story is significant in itself, the particulars appealing to the imagination, it is *narration*. If a story illustrates a point in exposition or argument, it may be called *illustrative narration*. If a story outlines a process step by step, the particulars appealing to the understanding, it is designated as *expository narration*. See discussion following Hemingway. See also White (*The Second Tree from the Corner*); Broyard.

ORGANIZATION, METHODS OF—vary with the form of discourse. Exposition uses in part, in whole, or in combination identification, definition, classification, illustration, comparison and contrast, and analysis. Argument and persuasion often use the method of organization of inductive or deductive reasoning, or analogy. Description is often organized either around a dominant impression or by means of a spatial arrangement. Narration, to give two examples, may be organized chronologically or in terms of point of view.

PARADOX—an assertion or sentiment seemingly self-contradictory, or opposed to common sense, which may yet be true. See Krutch (*The Tragic Fallacy*); Mencken (*The Feminine Mind*).

PARAGRAPH—serves to discuss one topic or one aspect of a topic. The central thought is either implied or expressed in a topic sentence. Paragraphs have such a great variety of organization and function that it is almost impossible to generalize about them. See the various kinds of paragraph development referred to in the exercises.

PARALLELISM—elements of similar rhetorical importance in similar grammatical patterns. See Coordination. See Krutch; Mencken (*The Feminine Mind*); Thurber; Hardwick.

PARODY—mimicking the language and style of another. See Thurber; Hardwick.

PERSPECTIVE—the vantage point chosen by the writer to achieve his purpose, his strategy. It is reflected in his close scrutiny of, or distance from, his subject; his objective representation or subjective interpretation of it. See Diction; Purpose; Tone. See Broyard; Thurber; Hardwick; Hersey; Lawrence.

PERSUASION—See Argument.

POINT OF VIEW—in description, the vantage point from which the author looks at the described object—see Twain, Mencken (*The Libido for the Ugly*); in narration, the "central intelligence" through whom the author reports the events of the story—see Hemingway, Dostoyevsky; in exposition, the grammatical person (first person, third person, editorial we) through whom the author presents his explanation—see Baldwin, Hersey.

PROPOSITION—See Argument.

PURPOSE—what the writer wants to accomplish with a particular piece of writing.

RHETORIC—the art of using language effectively.

RHETORICAL QUESTION—a question asked in order to induce thought and to provide emphasis rather than to evoke an answer. See Krutch, Morgenthau.

RHYTHM—in poetry and prose, patterned emphasis. Good prose is less regular in its rhythm than poetry. See Krutch; Russell.

SATIRE—the attempt to effect reform by exposing an object to laughter. Satire makes frequent recourse to irony, wit, ridicule, parody. It is usually classified under such categories as the following: social satire, personal satire, literary satire. See Porter; Swift; Thurber.

STYLE—"The essence of a sound style is that it cannot be reduced to rules—that it is a living and breathing thing, with something of the demoniacal in it—that it fits its proprietor tightly and yet ever so loosely, as his skin fits him. It is, in fact, quite as securely an integral part of him as that skin is. . . . In brief, a style is always the outward and visible symbol of a man, and it cannot be anything else." (H. L. Mencken, *On Style*, used with permission of Alfred A. Knopf, Inc.)

"Young writers often suppose that style is a garnish for the meat of prose, a sauce by which a dull dish is made palatable. Style has no such separate entity; it is non-detachable, unfilterable. The beginner should approach style warily, realizing that it is himself he is approaching, no other; and he should begin by turning resolutely away from all devices that are popularly believed to indicate style—all mannerisms, tricks, adornments. The approach to style is by way of plainness, simplicity, orderliness, sincerity." (Strunk and White, *The Elements of Style*, used with permission of The Macmillan Company.)

SUBORDINATION—less important rhetorical elements in grammatically subordinate positions. See Parallelism, Coordination, and Emphasis.

SYLLOGISM—in formal logic, a deductive argument in three steps: a major premise, a minor premise, a conclusion. The major premise states a quality of a class (all men are mortal); the minor premise states that X is a member of the class (Socrates is a man); the conclusion states that the quality of a class is also a quality of a member of the class (Socrates is mortal). In rhetoric, the full syllogism is rarely used; instead, one of the premises is usually omitted. "You can rely on him; he is independent," is an abbreviated syllogism. Major premise: Independent people are reliable; minor premise: He is independent; conclusion: He is reliable. Constructing the full syllogism frequently reveals flaws in reasoning, such as the above, which has an error in the major premise.

SYMBOL—a concrete image which suggests a meaning beyond itself. See White (*The Door*); Porter; Cowley.

TONE—the manner in which the writer communicates his attitude toward the material he is presenting. For his attitude toward his audience, see Audience. Diction is the most obvious means of establishing tone. Baldwin's diction reflects his vision of public race riots and his vision of himself—as an intimate, complex battleground. On the other hand, Hersey's language is only one element in establishing his tone. More important is his selection and arrangement of facts and his refusal to comment freely (as Baldwin comments). Hersey's nearly total absorption by his material results in his tone. Orwell's tone in *Marrakech* is that of a visitor who communicates what he sees, what he feels, and, finally, what he thinks. Camus, writing of another North African city, presents a completely different tone combining a nostalgic mood and an opulent atmosphere. For Camus, Algiers is one of the human situations, the place where man lives the life of the body. Russell's tone rises to his great theme, of first things and of last things. Lawrence, on the other hand, moves back and forth from the personal to revelations from the underworld. Miss Porter reveals her attitude toward her subject—one of "horrid fascination"—through parody, metaphors, and a fluent structure. White's tone (*The Door*) is not so much split as it is shattered; he communicates it through coined fragments of words, incoherent parentheses, and images of induced psychosis. See Diction.

TOPIC SENTENCE—the thesis which the paragraph as a whole develops. Some paragraphs do not have topic sentences.

TRANSITION—the linking together of sentences, paragraphs and larger parts of the composition to achieve coherence. See Coherence.

UNITY—the relevance of selected material to the central theme of an essay. See Coherence. See Sartre.

BIOGRAPHICAL NOTES

JAMES AGEE (1909–1955) was an American poet, novelist, and writer for motion pictures. In 1941 he published a superb description of the life of three white tenant farmer families, *Let Us Now Praise Famous Men*. Both his last novel, *A Death in the Family* (1957), and the play adapted from it, *All the Way Home*, won Pulitzer Prizes. His book, *Agee on Film*, has been widely acclaimed. He wrote the commentary for the documentary film, *The Quiet One*, and the scenario for the popular picture, *The African Queen*.

FRANCIS BACON (1561–1626) was a rare combination of scientist, philosopher, man of letters, and politician. Although his essays are his most popular works, the lesser known *The Advancement of Learning* (1605), *Instauratio Magna*, and *Novum Organum* (1620) greatly influenced subsequent developments in science.

JAMES BALDWIN (1924–   ), born in Harlem, has lived much of his life in New York City. His first novel, *Go Tell It on the Mountain*, was published in 1954. A collection of essays, *Notes of a Native Son*, was published in 1955; his second novel, *Giovanni's Room*, in 1956. *Nobody Knows My Name* (1961), *Another Country* (1962), *The Fire Next Time* (1963), and a play, *Blues for Mr. Charlie* (1964), are his recent works.

BRUNO BETTELHEIM (1903–   ) was born in Austria and received his Ph.D. from the University of Vienna. He came to America in the late thirties and is now a professor of educational psychology at the University of Chicago. He has published *Love is Not Enough—The Treatment of Emotionally Disturbed Children* (1950) and *Truants from Life* (1955).

GORDON E. BIGELOW (1919–   ), an associate professor at the

University of Florida, is mainly interested in American literature, the humanities, and English as a second language.

ANATOLE BROYARD (–) has spent most of his life in Brooklyn and Greenwich Village. He teaches and lectures on popular culture at the New School for Social Research and has published stories and articles in *Partisan Review, Discovery,* and *Commentary.*

ALBERT CAMUS (1913–1960) was a French writer born in Algiers. His first novel, *The Stranger* (1942), was followed by *The Plague* and *The Fall.* Philosophical-political essays were published in *The Rebel* and *The Myth of Sisyphus.* His plays, *Caligula* and *Cross Purpose,* were published in English in 1948. In 1957 he received the Nobel Prize for literature.

JOHN CIARDI (1916–) is Professor of English at Rutgers, poetry editor of the *Saturday Review of Literature,* and director of the Bread Loaf (Vermont) Writers' Conference. He has published several volumes of poetry: *Homeward to America* (1940), *As If* (1955), *I Marry You* (1958).

MALCOLM COWLEY (1898–), American critic, poet, and editor, was one of the many expatriates who lived in Paris in the 1920's. His most famous works include *Exile's Return* (1934), an account of the expatriate generation; *Blue Juniata* (1929) and *A Dry Season* (1941), collections of poetry; *The Literary Situation* (1954), a book of criticism. He has edited works of Hawthorne, Whitman, Fitzgerald, and Hemingway and has served as President of the National Institute of Arts and Letters.

ROBERT CRAFT (1923–), American musician and writer, graduated from the Juilliard School of Music in 1946 and has since directed major orchestras in Europe and the United States. A specialist in the modern repertoire, in recent years Mr. Craft has conducted the music of Arnold Schoenberg, Alban Berg, Anton Webern, and Edgard Varese; but he is most closely associated with Igor Stravinsky, whose music he has frequently conducted and with whom he wrote the four-volume *Conversations with Stravinsky* (1959–63).

FEODOR DOSTOYEVSKY (1821–1881) was educated at a military engineering school in St. Petersburg, but by the time of his graduation had decided upon literature as a career. His work emphasizes the internal life of man. He served a sentence at hard labor in Siberia for participating in liberal activities. Among his distinguished works are *The Double, The House of the Dead, Crime and Punishment, The Idiot, The Possessed,* and *The Brothers Karamazov.*

LOREN EISELEY (1907–   ), one of the more famous American anthropologists, is University Professor of Anthropology and History of Science and head of the Department of History and Philosophy of Science, Graduate School of Arts and Sciences, University of Pennsylvania. Author of *The Immense Journey* (1957) and *The Firmament of Time* (1960), he is a frequent contributor to scientific journals and national magazines.

E. M. FORSTER (1879–   ), English short story writer, novelist, and essayist, is best known for his novel of British and Indian relationships, *A Passage to India.* In addition to his collected stories he has written *The Eternal Moment, Two Cheers for Democracy, Howard's End,* and a book of literary criticism, *Aspects of the Novel.*

ELIZABETH HARDWICK (1916–   ) was awarded a Guggenheim fellowship in 1947. She has published two novels, *The Ghostly Lover* and *The Simple Truth;* a collection of essays, *A View of My Own;* and she has edited *The Selected Letters of William James.* She serves as an advisory editor of the *New York Review of Books* and has contributed to the *Partisan Review, The New Yorker,* and *Harper's.*

ERNEST HEMINGWAY (1898–1961) has exerted a great influence on the American short story and novel since the late twenties. His stories have been collected under the title, *The Fifth Column and the First Forty-nine Stories.* Among his best novels are *The Sun Also Rises, A Farewell to Arms,* and *For Whom the Bell Tolls.* In 1954 he was awarded the Nobel Prize in literature.

JOHN HERSEY (1914–   ) is an American novelist and journalist. His novels include *A Bell for Adano* (1944) and *The Wall* (1950). His famous report, *Hiroshima,* was published in 1946.

ROBERT MAYNARD HUTCHINS (1899–   ), formerly Chancellor of the University of Chicago, is now President of the Fund for the Republic, U.S.A. Among his books are No *Friendly Voice* and *The University of Utopia*.

ALDOUS HUXLEY (1894–1963), son of Leonard Huxley (eldest son and biographer of Thomas Henry Huxley) and Julia Arnold (niece of Matthew Arnold and sister of Mrs. Humphrey Ward), was educated at Eton and Oxford. Among his novels are *Crome Yellow, Antic Hay, Those Barren Leaves, Point Counter Point, Eyeless in Gaza*, and *After Many a Summer Dies the Swan*. He has also written *Brave New World*, and *Brave New World Revisited*, many volumes of essays, including *Do What You Will, Brief Candles, Proper Studies*, and *Ends and Means*.

RANDALL JARRELL (1914–1965) was Professor of English at the Women's College of the University of North Carolina. He is author of *Blood for a Stranger*, his first volume of poems; *Poetry and the Age*, a work of criticism; and *Pictures from an Institution*, a satirical academic novel. As novelist, critic, and poet he was well qualified to defend the role of the intellectual.

JOSEPH WOOD KRUTCH (1893–   ), for several years professor of dramatic literature at Columbia University and drama critic for *The Nation*, now resides in Tucson, Arizona, where he has written several books expressing his philosophy of nature and of man: *The Twelve Seasons, The Desert Year, The Voice of the Desert*, and *The Measure of Man*. He published *The Modern Temper* in 1929.

SUSANNE K. LANGER (1895–   ), a philosopher and critic, wrote about the symbolism of language, myth, and art in *Philosophy in a New Key* (1942), her most famous work. Her other works include *The Practice of Philosophy* (1930), *Introduction to Symbolic Logic* (1937), and *Feeling and Form: A Theory of Art* (1953).

D. H. LAWRENCE (1885–1930) is one of the most important figures of twentieth-century British literature. Remarkably prolific and versatile, in his relatively short life he produced a number of extraordinary novels, including *The White Peacock, Sons and Lovers, The Rainbow, Women in Love, The Plumed Serpent*, and *Lady Chatterley's Lover*; novellas, "The Man Who Died," and "St. Mawr"; a group of short stories; the travel books *Twilight in Italy, Sea and Sardinia, Mornings in Mexico*, and *Etruscan Places; Studies in Classic American Literature*, a brilliant if erratic examination of major American writers of the nineteenth century; two elaborate and eccentric arguments with Freudian psychology, *Psychoanalysis and the Unconscious* and *Fantasia of the Unconscious*; and a large body of poetry.

THOMAS BABINGTON MACAULAY (1800–1859), active in English politics most of his adult life, is best known as historian and critic. His greatest work, *The History of England*, covers approximately seventeen years (1685–1702) in five volumes.

HERMAN MELVILLE (1819–1891) is one of the most distinguished American novelists of the nineteenth century. In addition to *Moby Dick*, his works include *Typee, Pierre,* and *White Jacket.* His story of the ill-fated sailor, *Billy Budd,* has been dramatized and produced on stage and television. It was also made into an opera, *Billy Budd, An Opera in Four Acts,* with E. M. Forster as co-author of libretto.

H. L. MENCKEN (1880–1956) is known as a caustic satirist of the culture of the 1920's; as editor of *Smart Set* and the *American Mercury*; and as author of six volumes of *Prejudices.* His scholarship is reflected in his exhaustive work, *The American Language.*

HANS J. MORGENTHAU (1904–   ) is a regular contributor to *The New Republic.* He has served since 1950 as Director of the Center for the Study of American Foreign Policy at the University of Chicago. Among his published works are *Politics Among Nations* and *The Purpose of American Politics.*

GEORGE ORWELL (1903–1950) was the pseudonym of Eric Blair, an English writer, who at one time served with the Indian Imperial Police in Burma. He fought in the Spanish Civil War, an experience recorded in *Homage to Catalonia.* His books include the satirical fantasy *Animal Farm* and the grim novel *1984.*

PLATO (427?–347 B.C.), Greek philosopher, was author of dialogues in which, through Socrates, his great teacher, he explored truth, art, justice, immortality, love, and the good life. Among the most famous dialogues are *The Republic, Symposium, Apology, Phaedo, Phaedrus,* and *Laws.*

KATHERINE ANNE PORTER (1894–   ) is an American critic and short story writer whose books include *Flowering Judas* (1930), *Noon*

Wine (1937), *Pale Horse, Pale Rider* (1939), *The Days Before* (1952). Her novel *Ship of Fools* won wide recognition.

MARCEL PROUST (1871–1922). His great novel A *la Recherche du Temps Perdu* (1913–27), published in sixteen volumes, was translated and published as *Remembrance of Things Past* (1922–32). His critical essays are collected in a volume entitled *On Art and Literature*.

BERTRAND RUSSELL (1872–   ) was appointed lecturer at Trinity College, Cambridge in 1910. His first important book was *The Principles of Mathematics*. Among his works are *The Problems of Philosophy*, *Mysticism and Logic, Marriage and Morals*, and *The Conquest of Happiness*. He was awarded the Nobel Prize in literature in 1953.

JEAN-PAUL SARTRE (1905–   ), most famous of the French existentialists, is a philosopher and author of numerous works ranging from essays and philosophical-psychological dissertations to plays and novels reflecting his philosophical beliefs. *Existentialism is a Humanism, Being and Nothingness, Anti-Semite and Jew, The Wall, No Exit* are some of his more popular works. He refused to accept the 1964 Nobel Prize for literature.

JONATHAN SWIFT (1667–1745) is generally acknowledged to be the greatest English prose satirist. With savage irony he probes beneath appearances and exposes harsh realities. His hatred of sham and oppression is reflected in *Gulliver's Travels* (1726), a tale delighting children and shocking and challenging adults by its bitter satire of human vices and follies.

HENRY DAVID THOREAU (1817–1862) was a philosopher and poet-naturalist whose independent spirit led him to the famous experiment recorded in *Walden, or Life in the Woods* (1854). Thoreau's passion for freedom and his lifetime resistance to conformity in thought and manners are forcefully present in his famous essay, *On the Duty of Civil Disobedience*.

JAMES THURBER (1894–1961) has recorded his incomparable wit and satire in short stories, essays, and line drawings. *The Thurber Carnival* and *The Thurber Album* represent his own selection of the best of his work; among other books are *My Life and Hard Times, Let Your Mind Alone, My World and Welcome to It,* and *Thurber Country*.

LIONEL TRILLING (1905–   ) is a professor at Columbia University, a novelist, short story writer, and critic. His concern for the moral imagination is expressed in his books of criticism: *The Liberal Imagination*, *The Opposing Self*, and *Beyond Culture*.

MARK TWAIN (1835–1910) is the pen name of Samuel Clemens, American humorist and novelist. His best-loved novels, *The Adventures of Tom Sawyer* and *Huckleberry Finn*, grew out of his own boyhood days in the Mississippi river town of Hannibal, Missouri. His experience for four years as a river pilot is recorded in *Life on the Mississippi*. Other favorites are *Innocents Abroad* and *A Connecticut Yankee at King Arthur's Court*.

E. B. WHITE (1899–   ), perhaps America's best personal essayist, was a contributing editor to *Harper's* magazine (1938–43), and is now a contributing editor of *The New Yorker* magazine. His lightly satirical essays show great depth of feeling. They have been published under the title *Quo Vadimus?*, *The Second Tree from the Corner*, and *One Man's Meat*. Among other books are *The Wild Flag*, *Stuart Little*, *Charlotte's Web*, and his revision, with additions, of Strunk's *The Elements of Style*.

THORNTON WILDER (1897–   ) is an American novelist and playwright. He has taught at the University of Chicago. His novels include *The Cabala* (1926), *The Bridge of San Luis Rey* (1927), *Heaven's My Destination* (1934), and *The Ides of March* (1948). His most famous plays are *Our Town* (1938) and *The Skin of Our Teeth* (1942).

VIRGINIA WOOLF (1882–1941) was an English critic, essayist, and novelist whose fiction is distinguished by the use of the stream of consciousness method. Among her novels are *Mrs. Dalloway*, *To the Lighthouse*, and *The Waves*. Her criticism is contained in *The Common Reader* and *The Second Common Reader*.